Optimality Theory

This is an introduction to Optimality Theory, the central idea of which is that surface forms of language reflect resolutions of conflicts between competing constraints. A surface form is 'optimal' if it incurs the least serious violations of a set of constraints, taking into account their hierarchical ranking. Languages differ in the ranking of constraints; and any violations must be minimal. The book does not limit its empirical scope to phonological phenomena, but also contains chapters on the learnability of OT grammars; OT's implications for syntax; and other issues such as opacity. It also reviews in detail a selection of the considerable research output which OT has already produced. Exercises accompany chapters 1–7, and there are sections on further reading. *Optimality Theory* will be welcomed by any linguist with a basic knowledge of derivational Generative Phonology.

RENÉ KAGER teaches linguistics at Utrecht University, the Netherlands.

CAMBRIDGE TEXTBOOKS IN LINGUISTICS

General editors: S. R. ANDERSON, J. BRESNAN, B. COMRIE, W. DRESSLER, C. EWEN, R. HUDDLESTON, R. LASS, D. LIGHTFOOT, J. LYONS, P. H. MATTHEWS, R. POSNER, S. ROMAINE, N. V. SMITH, N. VINCENT

OPTIMALITY THEORY

In this series

OPTIMALITY THEORY

RENÉ KAGER

CAMBRIDGE
UNIVERSITY PRESS

PUBLISHED BY THE PRESS SYNDICATE OF THE UNIVERSITY OF CAMBRIDGE
The Pitt Building, Trumpington Street, Cambridge CB2 1RP, United Kingdom

CAMBRIDGE UNIVERSITY PRESS
The Edinburgh Building, Cambridge, CB2 2RU, UK http://www.cup.cam.ac.uk
40 West 20th Street, New York, NY 10011–4211, USA http://www.cup.org
10 Stamford Road, Oakleigh, Melbourne 3166, Australia

© Cambridge University Press 1999

First published 1999

Printed in the United Kingdom at the University Press, Cambridge

Typeset in Times $9\frac{1}{2}$/13pt   [GC]

A catalogue record for this book is available from the British Library

Library of Congress cataloguing in publication data

Kager, René.
Optimality theory / René Kager.
  p.   cm. – (Cambridge textbooks in linguistics)
Includes bibliographical references and indexes.
ISBN 0 521 58019 6 (hardback).   ISBN 0 521 58980 0 (paperback)
1. Optimality theory (Linguistics)   I. Title.   II. Series.
P158.42.K35   1999
410′.1 – dc21   98–39103 CIP

ISBN 0 521 58019 6 hardback
ISBN 0 521 58980 0 paperback

CONTENTS

PREFACE

This book presents an introduction to Optimality Theory, a grammatical framework of recent origin (Prince and Smolensky 1993, McCarthy and Prince 1993a, b). The central idea of Optimality Theory (OT) is that surface forms of language reflect resolutions of conflicts between competing demands or *constraints*. A surface form is 'optimal' in the sense that it incurs the least serious violations of a set of violable constraints, ranked in a language-specific hierarchy. Constraints are universal, and directly encode markedness statements and principles enforcing the preservation of contrasts. Languages differ in the ranking of constraints, giving priorities to some constraints over others. Such rankings are based on 'strict' domination: if one constraint outranks another, the higher-ranked constraint has priority, regardless of violations of the lower-ranked one. However, such violation must be minimal, which predicts the *economy* property of grammatical processes. OT's basic assumptions and the architecture of OT grammars will be dealt with in chapters 1 and 2.

Optimality Theory is a development of Generative Grammar, a theory sharing its focus on formal description and quest for universal principles, on the basis of empirical research of linguistic typology and (first) language acquisition. However, OT radically differs from earlier generative models in various ways. To accommodate cross-linguistic variation within a theory of Universal Grammar, OT assumes that universal constraints are violable, while earlier models assumed 'parametric' variation of inviolate principles. Moreover, OT is surface-based in the sense that well-formedness constraints evaluate surface forms only – no structural conditions are placed on lexical forms. Earlier models had assumed Morpheme Structure Constraints, resulting in the duplication of static and dynamic rules in phonotactics. In contrast, OT entirely abandons the notion of rewrite rule, dissociating 'triggers' and 'repairs'. This serves to explain conspiracies: multiple processes triggered by a single output-oriented goal. Finally, OT also eliminates derivations, replacing these by parallelism: all constraints pertaining to some type of structure are evaluated within a single hierarchy. The comparison of OT and its generative ancestors will be the topic of chapter 2, although the issue will reoccur in later chapters (specifically 4, 5, and 9).

Optimality Theory is not a theory of representations, but a theory of interactions of grammatical principles. More accurately, the issue of representations is orthogonal to that of constraint interaction. Therefore the divergence from earlier generative models is less clear-cut in this respect. Most OT literature on phonology, for example, assumes the representational alphabet of non-linear (metrical and autosegmental) phonology. In this book, the emphasis will be on prosodic phenomena, partly reflecting a tendency in the field, and partly the research interests of the author. Some of OT's most striking results have been reached in the domain of prosodically governed phenomena, such as syllable-dependent epenthesis (chapter 3), interactions of syllable weight and metrical structure (chapter 4), and prosodic targets in reduplication (chapter 5). However, our discussion of these phenomena serves to highlight results of OT that are relevant beyond prosody. To support this point, a range of segmental phenomena will be analysed throughout the book. Finally, OT has consequences for representational issues which are more closely connected with grammatical interactions, in particular for featural underspecification, as will be shown in chapters 1, 3, and 9.

Optimality Theory is a general theory of grammar, rather than one of phonology. Therefore this book is not limited in its empirical scope to phonological phenomena, but it also contains chapters on the learnability of OT grammars (chapter 7) and extensions to syntax (chapter 8). Finally, chapter 9 will address a number of important residual issues in OT, focussing on opacity, and discussing current developments in assumptions on lexical representations (versus allomorphy), optionality, absolute ungrammaticality, and various functionally oriented approaches to phonology.

During its brief period of existence, OT has sparked off a large output of articles, PhD dissertations, and volumes. Here we will review a selection of this research output, in a way that maximally highlights the theory's contribution to insights into language. In chapters 2 and 5–8, one particular piece of research will be focussed on, while placing it against a broad theoretical background. Chapter 2 focusses on the analysis of post-nasal-obstruent-voicing effects by Pater (forthcoming), and serves to highlight factorial typology, OT's explanation of conspiracies, and to introduce Correspondence Theory. Chapter 5 is devoted to the Correspondence Theory of reduplication by McCarthy and Prince (1995a, forthcoming), emphasizing 'the emergence of the unmarked' and parallelism of evaluation, and also extending the notion of 'correspondence' to relations between outputs. Chapter 6 discusses Benua's (1995) paper on output-to-output correspondence in truncation, and its extensions to stem-based affixation, while comparing OT and derivational theory for 'cyclic' phenomena. Chapter 7 discusses work by

Tesar and Smolensky (1993, 1998) on the learnability of OT grammars, and its dependence on basic OT notions, such as strict domination, minimal violation, and assumptions on lexical forms. Chapter 8 is devoted to the analysis of Wh-movement and its relation with auxiliary inversion and *do*-support in English by Grimshaw (1997), pointing out the relevance of OT outside phonology.

This book is not a general introduction to phonology, and the reader should come equipped with a basic knowledge of derivational Generative Phonology, including rules and representations, and some knowledge of Minimalist Syntax for chapter 8. Exercises have been added to chapters 1–7 to increase analytic skills and reflection on theoretical issues. Moreover, each chapter contains a list of suggestions for further reading.

The idea for this book arose during a course I taught at the LOT summer school at the University of Amsterdam in 1995. Stephen Anderson, who was present at this course, suggested basing an OT textbook on its contents. For his role in originating this book, I owe him special thanks.

Parts of this book are based on research reported on earlier occasions. Chapter 4 is partly based on Kager (1997a), first presented at the workshop on Derivations and Constraints in Phonology, held at the University of Essex, September 1995. Chapter 6 contains results from Kager (forthcoming), presented at the conference on the Derivational Residue in Phonology, Tilburg University, October 1995. I wish to thank the organizers of these events: Iggy Roca, Ben Hermans, and Marc van Oostendorp. Research for this book was partly sponsored by the Dutch Royal Academy of Sciences (KNAW), whose support is gratefully acknowledged.

For their comments on earlier versions of chapters I wish to thank Peter Ackema, Stephen Anderson, Roger Billerey, Gabriel Drachman, Nine Elenbaas, Bruce Hayes, Claartje Levelt, Ad Neeleman, Joe Pater, Bruce Tesar, Wim Zonneveld, and an anonymous reviewer. These comments have led to a number of substantial improvements. Needless to say, I take the blame for any mistakes in content or my presentation of other researchers' ideas. Thanks to Martin Everaert for supplying the child language data discussed in chapter 7.

Finally, this book would not have been finished without the encouragement and patience of my colleagues, friends, and family. Jacqueline, this book is dedicated to you.

I
Conflicts in grammars

1.1 Introduction: goals of linguistic theory

1.1.1 *Universality*

The central goal of linguistic theory is to shed light on the core of grammatical principles that is common to all languages. Evidence for the assumption that there should be such a core of principles comes from two domains: language typology and language acquisition. Over the past decades our knowledge of linguistic typology has become more and more detailed, due to extensive fieldwork and fine-grained analysis of data from languages of different families. From this large body of research a broad picture emerges of 'unity in variety': core properties of grammars (with respect to the subsystems of sounds, words, phrases, and meaning) instantiate a set of universal properties. Grammars of individual languages draw their basic options from this limited set, which many researchers identify as Universal Grammar (UG). Each language thus reflects, in a specific way, the structure of 'LANGUAGE'. A second source of evidence for universal grammatical principles comes from the universally recurring patterns of first language acquisition. It is well known that children acquiring their first language proceed in remarkably similar ways, going through developmental stages that are (to a large extent) independent of the language being learnt. By hypothesis, the innateness of UG is what makes grammars so much alike in their basic designs, and what causes the observed developmental similarities.

The approach to universality sketched above implies that linguistic theory should narrow down the class of universally possible grammars by imposing restrictions on the notions of 'possible grammatical process' and 'possible interaction of processes'. In early Generative Grammar (Chomsky 1965, Chomsky and Halle 1968), processes took the shape of *rewrite rules*, while the major mode of interaction was *linear ordering*. Rewrite rules take as their input a linguistic representation, part of which is modified in the output. Rules apply one after another, where one rule's output is the next rule's input. It was soon found that this rule-based theory hardly imposes any limits on the notion of 'possible rule', nor on the notion of 'possible rule interaction'. In the late 1970s and early 1980s, considerable efforts were put into constraining both rule typology and interactions. The broad idea was to factor out universal properties of rules in the form of *conditions*.[1] While rules themselves may differ between languages, they must always respect a fixed set of universal principles. Gradually more and more properties were factored out of rules and attributed to universal conditions on rules and representations. Developments came to their logical conclusion in Principles-and-Parameters Theory (Chomsky 1981b, Hayes 1980), which has as its central claim that grammars of individual languages are built on a central core of fixed universal properties (*principles*), plus a specification of a limited number of universal binary choices (*parameters*). Examples of parameters are the side of the 'head' (left or right) in syntactic phrases, or the obligatoriness (yes/no) of an onset in a syllable. At the same time, considerable interest developed in *representations*, as a way of constraining rule application, mainly with respect to *locality* (examples are trace theory in syntax, and underspecification theory in phonology). Much attention was also devoted to constraining rule interactions, resulting in sophisticated theories of the architecture of UG (the 'T'-model) and its components (e.g. Lexical Phonology, Kiparsky 1982b).

1.1.2 *Markedness*

What all these efforts to constrain rules and rule interactions share, either implicitly or explicitly, is the assumption that universal principles can only be universal if they are actually *inviolate* in every language. This interpretation of 'universality' leads to a sharp increase in the abstractness of both linguistic representations and rule interactions. When some universal principle is violated in the output of the grammar, then the characteristic way of explaining this was to set up an intermediate level of representation at which it is actually satisfied. Each grammatical principle thus holds at a specific level of description, and may be switched off at other levels.

This *absolute* interpretation of universality is not the only one possible, however. In structuralist linguistics (Hjelmslev 1935, Trubetzkoy 1939, Jakobson 1941; cf. Anderson 1985), but also in Generative Phonology (Chomsky and Halle 1968, Kean 1975, Kiparsky 1985) and Natural Phonology (Stampe 1972, Hooper 1976), a notion of MARKEDNESS plays a key role, which embodies universality in a 'soft' sense. The idea is that all types of linguistic structure have two values, one of which is 'marked', the other 'unmarked'. Unmarked values are cross-linguistically preferred and basic in all grammars, while marked values are cross-linguistically avoided and used by grammars only to create contrast. For example,

---

[1] For example, SUBJACENCY was proposed as a universal condition on syntactic movement rules and the OBLIGATORY CONTOUR PRINCIPLE as a universal condition on phonological rules.

all languages have unrounded front vowels such as [i] and [e], but only a subset of languages contrast these vowels with rounded front vowels such as [y] and [ø]. Hence, the unmarked value of the distinctive feature [round] is [−round] in front vowels. At a suprasegmental level, markedness affects prosodic categories. For example, the unmarked value for syllable closure is 'open' since all languages have open syllables (CV, V), while only a subset of languages allow closed syllables (CVC, VC).[2] The notion of markedness is not only relevant to sound systems. Markedness principles have been proposed for morphological and syntactic systems as well (Chomsky 1981a).

The markedness approach of linguistic universality is built on two assumptions. First, markedness is inherently a relative concept: that is, a marked linguistic element is not ill-formed *per se*, but only in comparison to other linguistic elements. Second, what is 'marked' and 'unmarked' for some structural distinction is not an arbitrary formal choice, but rooted in the articulatory and perceptual systems. By this combination of two factors, markedness allows an interpretation of universality that is fundamentally different from Principles-and-Parameters Theory, in which markedness has no substantive status in the grammar, but functions as an external system of annotations on parameter values, evaluating a grammar's 'complexity'.[3]

1.2 Basic concepts of OT

OPTIMALITY THEORY (Prince and Smolensky 1993, McCarthy and Prince 1993a,b) turns markedness statements into the actual substance of grammars. Markedness is built into grammars in the form of universal OUTPUT CONSTRAINTS which *directly* state marked or unmarked patterns, for example: 'front vowels are unrounded' or 'syllables are open'. The universal interpretation of markedness constraints is reconciled with the observation that languages, to a certain extent at least, tolerate marked types of structures. Universal markedness constraints can be literally *untrue* for a grammar's output, or to phrase it in optimality-theoretic terms: constraints are VIOLABLE. Violation of a constraint is not a direct cause of ungrammaticality, nor is absolute satisfaction of all constraints essential to the grammar's outputs. Instead what determines the best output of a grammar is the least costly violation of the constraints. Constraints are intrinsically in CONFLICT, hence every logically possible output of any grammar will necessarily violate at least some constraint. Grammars must be able to regulate conflicts between universal constraints, in order to select the 'most harmonic' or 'optimal' output form.

---

[2] Markedness may also involve scales. For example, the higher a consonant's sonority value, the more likely its occurrence in the syllable coda.

[3] For the view of markedness as a criterion external to the grammar, evaluating its complexity, see Chomsky and Halle (1968) and Kean (1975, 1981).

This conflict-regulating mechanism consists of a RANKING of universal constraints. Languages basically differ in their ranking of constraints. Each violation of a constraint is avoided; yet the violation of higher-ranked constraints is avoided 'more forcefully' than the violation of lower-ranked constraints. Accordingly, the notion of 'grammatical well-formedness' becomes a relative one, which is equivalent to the degree of satisfaction of the constraint hierarchy, or HARMONY.

OT's viewpoint of UG is fundamentally different from that of classical rule-based generative theory, where UG is defined as a set of inviolate principles and rule schemata (or 'parameters'). OT defines UG as a set of universal constraints (markedness relations and other types of constraints, as we will see below), and a basic alphabet of linguistic representational categories. In its interactions, it is limited to a single device: constraint ranking. OT still shares with its rule-based generative ancestors the central position taken by UG, as described above. OT *is* a theory of the human language capacity.

The remainder of this chapter is organized as follows. Section 1.2 will introduce basic notions of OT: conflict, constraints, and domination, which will be exemplified in section 1.3. In section 1.4, we will discuss the architecture of an OT grammar. Section 1.5 will deal with interactions of markedness and faithfulness, relating these to the lexicon in section 1.6. A factorial typology of constraint interactions will be developed in section 1.7 and applied to segment inventories in section 1.8. Finally, section 1.9 presents conclusions.

1.2.1 *Language as a system of conflicting universal forces*

At the heart of Optimality Theory lies the idea that language, and in fact every grammar, is a system of conflicting forces. These 'forces' are embodied by CONSTRAINTS, each of which makes a requirement about some aspect of grammatical output forms. Constraints are typically conflicting, in the sense that to satisfy one constraint implies the violation of another. Given the fact that no form can satisfy all constraints simultaneously, there must be some mechanism selecting forms that incur 'lesser' constraint violations from others that incur 'more serious' ones. This selectional mechanism involves hierarchical RANKING of constraints, such that higher-ranked constraints have priority over lower-ranked ones. While constraints are universal, the rankings are not: differences in ranking are the source of cross-linguistic variation.

But before discussing actual constraints and their rankings, let us first find out in a general way about the two major forces embodied by constraints. Two forces are engaged in a fundamental conflict in every grammar. The first is MARKEDNESS, which we use here as a general denominator for the grammatical factors that exert pressure toward *unmarked types of structure*. This force is counterbalanced by

FAITHFULNESS, understood here as the combined grammatical factors *preserving lexical contrasts*. Let us focus on both general forces to find out why they are inherently conflicting.

In sound systems, certain types of structure – segments, segment combinations, or prosodic structures – are universally favoured over others. For example, front unrounded vowels are unmarked as compared to front rounded vowels, open syllables as compared to closed syllables, short vowels as compared to long vowels, and voiceless obstruents compared to voiced obstruents. As was observed above, marked structures are avoided by all languages, while they are completely banned by some languages. Therefore the notion of markedness is inherently *asymmetrical*.

Most phonologists agree that phonological markedness is ultimately GROUNDED in factors outside of the grammatical system proper. In particular, the systems of articulation and perception naturally impose limitations on which sounds (or sound sequences) should be favoured. Yet explaining markedness relations by phonetic factors does not amount to denying the basis of phonology as a grammatical system, for two reasons. The first reason is that phonetic factors are gradient, and add up to numerical patterns, while phonological factors are categorical, producing patterns whose boundaries are clearly cut by categorical distinctions. The symmetry of phonological systems cannot be captured by the interaction of 'raw' phonetic factors. The second reason is that the relative strength of the individual markedness factors varies from language to language, which entails that there must be a language-specific system defining the balance of factors. This is the grammar, a system of ranked constraints, of which phonology is an integral part.

The major force counterbalancing markedness is *faithfulness* to lexical contrasts. A grammar that is maximally 'faithful' to a lexical contrast is one in which output forms are completely congruent with their lexical inputs with respect to some featural opposition. Or to put it differently, the total amount of lexically contrastive variation of some feature is realized in all of the grammar's output forms. For example, a lexical contrast of voicing in obstruents is preserved in output forms regardless of their phonological context (at the end of a word, between vowels, etc.). Thus one may think of faithfulness as the general requirement for linguistic forms to be realized as close as possible to their lexical 'basic forms'. From a functional angle, the importance of faithfulness is clear: to express contrasts of *meaning*, any language needs a minimal amount of formal *contrast*. Formal contrasts should be preserved in realizations of lexical items, and not be 'eroded' (or at least, not too much) by factors reducing markedness. In the realm of sound

5

systems (or 'phonologies'), lexical contrasts are carried by oppositions between sounds, as well as by their combinations. Phonological elements are not the only carriers of lexical contrast. (Although phonology is what we will focus on in this book.) Lexical contrasts are also expressible by word structure (*morphology*) or phrase structure (*syntax*).

Closely related to faithfulness (or preservation of lexical contrasts) is the pressure towards the *shape invariability* of lexically related items in various grammatical contexts. This was known in pre-generative linguistics as 'paradigm uniformity'. Shape invariance of lexical items is understandable as another priority of linguistic communication: there should be a one-to-one relation between lexical items, the 'atoms' of meaning, and the shapes which encode them.

1.2.2 *Conflicts between markedness and faithfulness*

Markedness and faithfulness are inherently *conflicting*. Whenever some lexical contrast is being preserved, there will be some cost associated in terms of markedness *since in every opposition one member is marked*. For example, consider the fact that English limits the possible contrasts in its vowels with respect to the dimensions of backness and rounding: no rounded front vowels stand in contrast to unrounded front vowels. This correlation of rounding and backness in vowels is not idiosyncratic to English, but it reoccurs in a great majority of the world's languages. In fact it is *grounded* in properties of the articulatory and perceptual systems. Yet this restriction is certainly not 'universal' in the sense that all of the world's languages respect it. Many languages do allow a contrast of rounding in front vowels, thus increasing the potential amount of lexical contrast at the expense of an increase in markedness.

Generally we find that the larger the array of means of encoding lexical contrasts, the larger the complexity of the sound system, either in terms of segmental complexity, or in terms of the combinatory possibilities between segments ('phonotactics'). A language can be maximally faithful to meaningful sound contrasts only at the expense of an enormous increase in phonological markedness. Conversely, a language can decrease phonological markedness only at the expense of giving up valuable means to express lexical contrast.

First consider what a hypothetical language would look like at one extreme of the spectrum: a language giving maximal priority to the expression of lexical contrasts, while imposing *no markedness restrictions*. We endow this language with the combined segment inventories of the world's languages, roughly 50 consonants and 30 vowels (Ladefoged and Maddieson 1996). We drop combinatory markedness restrictions, allowing all logically possible segment combinations to form a lexical item. Permutation of these 80 segments into lexical items of two segments already produces some 6,400 items, including [pʰɣ], [ɱʌx], and [ɵɗ], all highly marked. But why stop at two segments per item? By sheer lack of phonotactic limitations, nothing rules out lexical items of 37 or 4,657 segments, or even longer. Now consider the fact that the number of possible lexical items increases exponentially with the number of segments (80^n) so that at segmental length 6 we already approximate an awesome 300 billion potential lexical items. Clearly no human language requires this number of lexical contrasts, hence there is room to impose markedness restrictions on segments and their combinations in lexical items. Since such restrictions make sense from an articulatory and perceptual point of view, we expect to find them.

Let us now turn the tables to find out what a language at the other extreme would look like, a language giving maximal priority to markedness, and minimal priority to the expression of lexical contrasts. Let us assume that this language limits its lexical items to the general shape of CV* (sequences of consonant–vowel), with C $\in$ {p,t,k} and V $\in$ {ɨ,a}.[4] The complete set of potential monosyllables contains 6 items {pɨ, pa; tɨ, ta; kɨ, ka}, the set of disyllables contains 36 (or 6^2) items ({pɨpɨ, papɨ, kɨpɨ...}), trisyllables 216 (or 6^3), etc. But stop! We are overlooking the fact that the unmarked length of lexical item is two syllables (this is the minimum size in many languages and by far the most frequent size in most languages). Since we are assuming that this language is maximally concerned about markedness, we should limit word size to two syllables. The bitter consequence is a mini-lexicon containing at most 36 items. Now consider the fact that the lexicon of an average natural language contains some 100,000 items.[5] It is clear that giving maximal priority to markedness implies an acute shortage of lexical contrasts, which no language can afford.

This comparison of two extremes shows that languages may, in principle at least, go astray in either of two ways: by giving blind priority to expression of lexical contrast, resulting in massive costs in terms of markedness or, at the other end of the spectrum, by giving unlimited priority to markedness reduction, resulting in a fatal lack of contrast.

---

[4] These limitations are actually *grounded* in speech production and perception: every consonant is maximally different from a vowel (hence, all consonants are voiceless stops). Every vowel is maximally different from other vowels (a 2-vowel set, ɨ–a). Every consonant is maximally different from other consonants (place of articulation restricted to labial, alveolar, and velar). Every vowel is preceded by a consonant (no word-initial vowels, no hiatus). Every consonant precedes a vowel for optimal release (hence no consonant clusters nor word-final Cs).

[5] Suppose that our hypothetical language would not respect word size restrictions, having at its disposition all possible CV*-shaped items. Here, with a maximal density of lexical contrast, all potential items up to seven syllables long would not suffice to build the required size of lexicon. This would only reach a moderate total of (46,656 + 7,776 + 1296 + 216 + 36 + 6) = 55,986 lexical items. The average item in this language would be over six syllables long. Without doubt, speaking would become a rather time-consuming activity.

In sum, we have seen that every grammar must reconcile the inherently competing forces of faithfulness to lexical contrasts (the inertness which draws output forms back to their basic lexical shapes) and markedness (minimization of marked forms). However, as we are about to find out, Optimality Theory recognizes no unitary or monolithic forces of faithfulness or markedness: the picture is more fragmented. In the grammars of individual languages, the overall conflict between both 'forces' assumes the form of finer-grained interactions of individual *constraints*. At this level, where individual constraints compete, languages are quite diverse in their resolutions of conflicts between 'markedness' and 'faithfulness'. A language may give priority to faithfulness over markedness with respect to some opposition, but reverse its priorities for another opposition.

Let us now turn to the implementation of these basic ideas in Optimality Theory.

1.2.3 *The OT grammar as an input–output device*

The basic assumption of OT is that each linguistic output form is *optimal*, in the sense that it incurs the least serious violations of a set of conflicting constraints. For a given input, the grammar generates and then evaluates an infinite set of output candidates, from which it selects the optimal candidate, which is the actual output. Evaluation takes place by a set of hierarchically ranked constraints ($C_1 \gg C_2 \gg \ldots C_n$), each of which may eliminate some candidate outputs, until a point is reached at which only one output candidate survives. This elimination process is represented schematically:[6]

(1)   Mapping of input to output in OT grammar

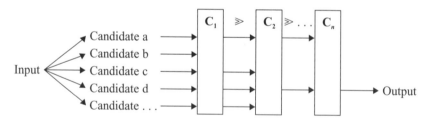

The optimal output candidate is the one that is 'most harmonic' with respect to the set of ranked constraints. 'Harmony' is a kind of relative well-formedness, taking into account the severity of the violations of individual constraints, as determined by their hierarchical ranking. That is, violation of a higher-ranked

---

[6] Elimination of less-harmonic candidates is portrayed in (1) as a serial filtering process, but we will learn to view it as a parallel process, with higher-ranked constraints taking priority over lower-ranked constraints.

constraint incurs a greater cost to harmony than violation of a lower-ranked constraint. Some violations must occur in every output candidate, as constraints impose conflicting requirements. Accordingly, a lower-ranked constraint can be violated to avoid the violation of a higher-ranked one, but violation is always kept to a minimum, given the requirement of maximal harmony.

With the basic assumptions of OT in our minds, let us now turn to a finer-grained discussion of the core notions 'constraints', 'conflict', 'domination', and 'optimality'.

1.2.4 *Constraints: universality and violability*

Our preliminary definition of CONSTRAINT is: a *structural requirement that may be either satisfied or violated by an output form*. A form SATISFIES a constraint if it fully meets the structural requirement, while any form not meeting this requirement is said to VIOLATE it. For the moment we will assume no degrees of violation, so that output forms are simply categorized by a crude binary criterion as either satisfying or violating a constraint. Forms may satisfy constraints *vacuously*, which is the case if a constraint makes a requirement about some structural element that is not present in a particular candidate.

OT recognizes two types of constraints, *faithfulness* constraints and *markedness* constraints. Each individual constraint evaluates one specific aspect of output markedness or faithfulness. Let us now look into the general properties of both types of constraints, and into their functions in the grammar.

Markedness constraints require that output forms meet some criterion of structural well-formedness. As the examples below illustrate, such requirements may take the form of prohibitions of marked phonological structures, including segment types (2a), prosodic structures (2b), or occurrences of segment types in specific positions (2c).

(2)   Examples of markedness constraints
   a. Vowels must not be nasal
   b. Syllables must not have codas
   c. Obstruents must not be voiced in coda position
   d. Sonorants must be voiced
   e. Syllables must have onsets
   f. Obstruents must be voiced after nasals

However, markedness constraints may just as well be stated positively, as in (2d–f). Note that markedness constraints refer to output forms only and are blind to the (lexical) input.

As we have seen in section 1.1, markedness is an inherently asymmetrical notion. Hence, the universal constraint inventory lacks the *antagonist* constraints of (1a–e), which make opposite requirements 'syllables must have codas', 'sonorants must be voiceless', etc.[7]

Faithfulness constraints require that outputs preserve the properties of their basic (lexical) forms, requiring some kind of similarity between the output and its input.

(3)   Examples of faithfulness constraints
    a. The output must preserve all segments present in the input
    b. The output must preserve the linear order of segments in the input
    c. Output segments must have counterparts in the input
    d. Output segments and input segments must share values for [voice]

Faithfulness constraints are, strictly speaking, not pure output constraints, since they take into account elements at two levels: input and output. In contrast, markedness constraints never take into account elements in the input.[8] The important thing is, however, that both kinds of constraints refer to the *output* (exclusively so in markedness, and in relation to the input in faithfulness). OT has no constraints that exclusively refer to the input. (This is a crucial difference from classical generative phonology, as we will see in chapter 2.)

From a functional viewpoint, faithfulness constraints protect the lexical items of a language against the 'eroding' powers of markedness constraints, and thereby serve two major communicative functions. First, they preserve *lexical contrasts*, making it possible for languages to have sets of formally distinct lexical items to express different meanings. Phrasing it slightly differently, with an emphasis on contrast, we may say that faithfulness is what keeps the shapes of different lexical items apart. Second, by limiting the distance between input and output, faithfulness constraints restrict the *shape variability* of lexical items. Faithfulness thus keeps the contextual realizations of a single morpheme (called its *alternants*) from drifting too far apart. This enhances the one-to-one relations of meaning and form. In sum, the overall function of faithfulness is to enforce the phonological shape of lexical forms in the output, as a sort of inertness limiting the distance between outputs and their basic shapes.

Two more assumptions are to be made about constraints in OT: they are *universal* and *violable* requirements on some aspect of linguistic output forms. Let us now focus on each of these properties of constraints. The first property is

---

[7] We will see later that some markedness constraints do have antagonists.
[8] See chapter 9 for OT models which weaken this assumption.

(4)   **Universality**: constraints are universal.

In its strongest interpretation, by which all constraints are part of UG, this implies that all constraints are part of the grammars of all natural languages. This is not to say that every constraint will be equally active in all languages. Due to the language-specific ranking of constraints, a constraint that is never violated in one language may be violated but still be active in a second language, and be totally inactive in yet a third language. This strong interpretation, which leaves no room for language-specific constraints, nor for constraint variability, will be slightly relativized below.

For phonological markedness constraints, 'universality' may be established by a variety of factors, ideally in combination. The first sense of universality is *typological*: a constraint states a preference for certain structures over other types of structures, which reoccurs in a range of unrelated languages. Segmental markedness constraints, for example, may be validated by inspecting the relative markedness of segments in inventories on a cross-linguistic basis. (Such an overview is presented in Maddieson 1984.) However, any exclusively typology-based definition of universality runs the risk of circularity: certain properties are posited as 'unmarked' simply because they occur in sound systems with greater frequency than other 'marked' properties.

Hence, a second (non-circular) criterion of universality should ideally accompany typological criteria: phonological markedness constraints should be *phonetically grounded* in some property of articulation or perception. That is, phonetic evidence from production or perception should support a cross-linguistic preference for a segment (or feature value) to others in certain contexts. For example, there is articulatory evidence (to be reviewed in chapter 2) that voiced obstruents are preferred to voiceless obstruents in a position immediately following a nasal. Indeed many languages avoid or disallow voiceless post-nasal obstruents, neutralizing voicing contrasts in this position.[9] Even though a growing number of constraints has been phonetically grounded (see the suggested readings at the end of this chapter), such grounding is still lacking for others.

It should be clear from this discussion that we should be very careful about positing any constraint lacking both typological motivation and phonetic grounding, even if there is compelling motivation for it from the language data under analysis. Nevertheless, not all constraints that have been proposed in the OT literature satisfy both criteria, indicating that the major issue of universality of constraints has not yet been resolved, since analysts do not share the same criteria. In this book, whenever we employ a constraint that strikes us as 'parochial' or

---

[9] Post-nasal voicing and its typological consequences will be discussed in detail in chapter 2.

language-specific (since it lacks both phonetic grounding and cross-linguistic motivation), this will be indicated.

However, the universality of constraints should directly be relativized somewhat. We will find that in special cases, language-specific elements may occur in constraints of otherwise universal formats. This option is typical for a class of constraints defining the interface of morphology and phonology, so-called 'alignment' constraints, matching up the edges of specific morphemes and prosodic categories. (See chapters 3 and 5.) Such interface constraints define schemata in which individual languages may substitute their specific morphemes.

We now move on to the second major property of OT constraints: their 'softness', or violability. Violability of constraints must be understood in a specific way: the general requirement is that it must be minimal:

(5)   **Violability**: constraints are violable, but violation must be minimal.

No constraint is violated without a compelling reason: avoiding the violation of another higher-ranked constraint. And even if a constraint is violated, violation must be kept to a minimum. Everything else being equal, forms with 'lesser' violations are more harmonic than forms with 'greater' violations. (Exactly how *degree of violation* is determined will be taken up in section 1.4.3.) Violability of constraints is an essential property of OT, representing a radical break away from derivational models, as well as from constraint-based theories, such as *Declarative Phonology* (Bird 1990, Scobbie 1991), which assume that constraints are 'hard' or inviolate. (For a broad comparison with derivational theory, see chapter 2.)

This discussion of violable constraints gives rise to an important new question, to which we now turn: what is the 'optimal' candidate?

1.2.5 *Optimality: domination and conflict*

As mentioned before, optimality is the status of being most harmonic with respect to a set of conflicting constraints. It is now time to take a closer look at the concept of OPTIMAL in OT. The general idea is that the grammar evaluates an infinite set of candidate output forms, all analyses of a given input. From this candidate set it selects the *optimal output*, the one which 'best matches' the set of conflicting constraints. But what precisely does it mean for an output to be 'optimal'? Does it involve some sort of compromise between constraints of different strengths? Or is it perhaps the case that 'weaker' constraints are rendered 'inactive' when they come into conflict with 'stronger' constraints?

In fact optimality involves neither *compromise* nor *suppression* of constraints, but instead it is built on (strict) domination of constraints in a hierarchy.

(6)   **Optimality**: an output is 'optimal' when it incurs the least serious violations of a set of constraints, taking into account their hierarchical ranking.

So we assume that each output form of the grammar is by definition the 'best possible' in terms of the *hierarchy* of constraints, rather than the form which matches all constraints at the same time. 'Perfect' output forms are principally non-existent, as every output form will violate at least some constraints. Therefore the selection of the 'optimal' output form involves setting priorities.

This is where a hierarchy comes into play. Conflicts are resolved by DOMINATION:

(7)   **Domination**: the higher-ranked of a pair of conflicting constraints takes precedence over the lower-ranked one.

This tentative definition will be refined below in section 1.4, on the basis of more complex cases.

The ranking of constraints can be demonstrated by a TABLEAU: this lists two (or any number of) output candidates vertically in random order, and constraints horizontally, in a descending ranking from left to right. The cells contain violation marks '*' incurred by each candidate for the constraint heading the column. Schematically:

(8)   A tableau for simple domination

	C_1	C_2
a. ☞ *candidate a*		*
b. *candidate b*	*!	

The optimal candidate is marked by the index '☞'. This candidate is (8a), which has no violations of the higher-ranked constraint C_1, a constraint violated by its competitor (8b). Note that the optimal candidate (8a) is actually not impeccable itself: it has a violation of C_2, but this flaw is insignificant to the outcome. Although the pattern of violations for C_2 is the reverse of that for C_1, this does not help candidate b. Its violation of C_1 is already fatal, indicated by the accompanying exclamation mark '!' and the shading of cells whose violation content is no longer relevant. In sum, candidate (a) is optimal as *no candidate* is available that fares better, satisfying *both constraints* at the same time. A violation of C_2 is taken for granted, as long as C_1 can be satisfied.

We now turn to exemplification of the ideas that have been introduced thus far.

1.3   Examples of constraint interaction

1.3.1   *Neutralization of voicing contrast in Dutch*

Among the universal and violable constraints is the following:

(9)   ***VOICED-CODA**

Obstruents must not be voiced in coda position.

This is a typical *markedness* constraint, which bans a marked segment type (here: voiced obstruents) from the syllable coda (which is itself a marked position).[10]

Coda obstruents are voiceless in Dutch, as illustrated by the following alternation:

(10)   a. /bɛd/   bɛt   'bed'
               b. /bɛd-ən/ bɛdən 'beds'

Dutch has no voicing contrast in final obstruents, neutralizing it towards voicelessness.

Next consider the evaluation of two candidate outputs for the input /bɛd/, [bɛt], and [bɛd], with respect to *VOICED-CODA:

(11)   Evaluation of two candidates with respect to *VOICED-CODA
               a. [bɛt]   satisfies *VOICED-CODA
                           (since [t] is an obstruent in a syllable coda, and [t] is voiceless)
               b. [bɛd]   violates *VOICED-CODA
                           (since [d] is an obstruent in a syllable coda, and [d] is voiced)

If this constraint were the only one relevant for these forms, then things would be simple. Violators could be dismissed without second thoughts. But in actual grammars things are not that simple since constraints may make conflicting requirements about output forms.

A second constraint of the universal inventory is a typical *faithfulness* constraint, requiring that the input value of the feature [voice] be preserved in the output.

(12)   **IDENT-IO**(voice)

The specification for the feature [voice] of an input segment must be preserved in its output correspondent.

---

[10] Actually *VOICED-CODA can be interpreted as the conjunction of two markedness statements, an idea to which we will return in chapter 9.

This faithfulness constraint mentions a notion 'correspondent', which is tentatively (and very informally) defined as follows:

(13)   **Correspondent**: the output segment that is the 'realization' of an input segment.

This informal definition is precise enough for our present purposes. (We will return to the important notion of 'correspondence', particularly in chapters 2 and 5.)

In a 'correspondence diagram' of the Dutch word [bɛt] 'bed' the input and output segments that are correspondents of one another are connected by vertical lines.

(14)   Correspondence diagram of [bɛt]
        /b ɛ d/ Input
        | | |
        [b ɛ t] Output

This diagram indicates that IDENT-IO(voice) is violated in [bɛt]. Violation arises since [t], a voiceless segment in the output, corresponds with a voiced segment /d/ in the input, and both segments have conflicting values for voice. But at the same time, [bɛt] satisfies the markedness constraint *VOICED-CODA, as [t] is a voiceless obstruent in coda position.

We are, of course, looking at a simple conflict between two constraints, *VOICED-CODA and IDENT-IO(voice). Both constraints make incompatible requirements about the value of voice for any coda obstruent whose input is specified as [+voice]. An evaluation of both candidate outputs, [bɛd] and [bɛt], by the conflicting constraints is shown in (15):

(15)   Evaluation of two candidate outputs for the input /bɛd/
        a. [bɛd] satisfies IDENT-IO(voice), but violates *VOICED-CODA
        b. [bɛt] violates IDENT-IO(voice), but satisfies *VOICED-CODA

Observe the conflict: the evaluation of both output forms is different for each constraint.

This conflict requires resolution, which is the task of the constraint hierarchy. The form [bɛt] emerges as the *optimal* output of the grammar, given the following fragment of the phonology of the language:

(16)   Coda devoicing in Dutch
        *VOICED-CODA ≫ IDENT-IO(voice)

The symbol '≫' connecting both constraints is to be read as 'dominates'. Hence we read (16) as follows: *VOICED-CODA dominates IDENT-IO(voice). Domination ensures that the candidate outputs, [bɛd] and [bɛt], differ in their relative well-formedness with respect to the ranking in (16). Or stated differently, [bɛt] is 'more harmonic' than [bɛd] with respect to the ranking in (16).

(17)   Harmonic ranking of two output candidates for the input /bɛd/ in Dutch

             [bɛt] > [bɛd]

Since we are only considering two candidates here, the harmonic ranking directly gives us the optimal output: [bɛt].

The correctness of this constraint ranking can be represented in a tableau-format:

(18)   Tableau for the input /bɛd/, assuming the Dutch ranking

Candidates:	*Voiced-Coda	Ident-IO(voice)
a. ☞ [bɛt]		*
b. [bɛd]	*!	

The *optimal* candidate in the top row, [bɛt], incurs a violation of Ident-IO(voice) while it satisfies *Voiced-Coda. *Suboptimal* [bɛd] has exactly the reverse pattern of violations: it has a violation mark for *Voiced-Coda, but none for Ident-IO(voice).

Being presented with these two output candidates, the grammar (whose only goal is selecting an optimal output) must settle for a candidate that has a violation of a lower-ranked constraint, simply because no perfect output candidate is available, satisfying both constraints. This point can be made more general: constraints are intrinsically conflicting, hence perfect output candidates will never occur in any tableau:

(19)   **Fallacy of perfection**: no output form is possible that satisfies all constraints.

An output is 'optimal' since there is no such thing as a 'perfect' output: all that grammars may accomplish is to select the most harmonic output, the one which incurs the minimal violation of constraints, taking into account their ranking. Nothing better is available.

Observe that the result of the constraint interaction in Dutch is a neutralization of the voicing contrast in a specific context: the syllable coda. That neutralization indeed takes place can be easily shown by the following set of examples:

(20)   a.i   /bɛd/   bɛt   'bed'

              a.ii   /bɛd-ən/   bɛ.dən 'beds'

              b.i   /bɛt/   bɛt   '(I) dab'

              b.ii   /bɛt-ən/   bɛ.tən '(we) dab'

Neutralization of the sound shapes of two lexical items is the ultimate consequence of the domination of markedness over faithfulness. The lexical contrast between /bɛd/ and /bɛt/, residing in the value of voicing of their final stem consonants, might (in principle at least) have been preserved in all morphological contexts in which they occur. But this is not the case, and a complete neutralization occurs, into [bɛt].

1.3.2 *Preservation of voicing contrast in English*

In English, as opposed to Dutch, an analogous input /bɛd/ is mapped to an output [bɛd], preserving the voicing in the final consonant. Accordingly, English contrasts words such as *bed* and *bet*. This is due to the following fragment of the phonology of this language:

(21)   Preservation of voicing contrast in English
          IDENT-IO(voice) ≫ *VOICED-CODA

In English, IDENT-IO(voice) dominates *VOICED-CODA, which is the reverse ranking of the one we established for Dutch. Accordingly, the 'harmonic ranking' of the output candidates under discussion is reversed, as compared to the one of Dutch:

(22)   Harmonic ranking of two output candidates for the input /bɛd/ in
          English
          [bɛd] > [bɛt]

That is, assuming an input /bɛd/, '[bɛd] is *more harmonic* than [bɛt]' with respect to the ranking in (21).

Again, we illustrate this ranking with the help of a tableau, evaluating the same candidates as we used in tableau (18) for Dutch. Observe that IDENT-IO(voice) and *VOICED-CODA have changed places:

(23)   Tableau for the input /bɛd/, assuming the English ranking

Candidates:	IDENT-IO(voice)	*VOICED-CODA
a. [bɛt]	*!	
b. ☞ [bɛd]		*

The net result of this ranking is that the 'index' pointing at the optimal output has shifted downwards (as compared to tableau 18) to the second candidate under consideration, that is, [bɛd]. Note that by this ranking, English preserves the phonological contrast between distinct lexical items, as in *bed* [bɛd] versus *bet* [bɛt]. (This contrast is actually reinforced by a subsidiary vowel length difference between both words: [beˑd] versus [bɛt].)

1.3.3 *The relation between universal and language-specific*

What we have just witnessed in the examples from Dutch and English is the universal 'pan-grammatical' conflict of markedness and faithfulness taking place on a micro-scale. In both languages, the same conflict arises with respect to preservation of a contrastive property (the feature [voice]), and its neutralization in a specific context (syllable coda). However, the outcome of this conflict is different for both languages. Dutch resolves it in the favour of markedness whereas English favours faithfulness. This shows that universal constraints are ranked in language-specific ways. OT clearly marks off the universal from the language-specific. Both constraints and the general principles of their interaction are universal, while constraint hierarchies are language-specific.

Speaking of *forces* of faithfulness and markedness is somewhat misleading, since this suggests that conflicts between these 'forces' are resolved on a superordinate level in the grammar of a single language. This is clearly not the case. For example, the fact that Dutch ranks markedness above faithfulness with respect to voice in coda obstruents does not imply that it selects the same ranking ($M \gg F$) with respect to voice in other contexts, nor that it selects this ranking with respect to other features in the syllable coda. In Dutch, voice is contrastive in obstruents in onsets (even though voiced obstruents are universally marked). Also, place features are contrastive in obstruents and nasals in codas (in spite of the markedness of labials and velars). This shows that there are no monolithic 'forces' of faithfulness and markedness, but that instead finer-grained interactions occur between the context- and feature-specific versions of these classes of constraints. Still, for expository purposes, the classification of constraints into 'faithfulness' and 'markedness' constraints remains useful, as are shorthand notations such as '$M \gg F$'.

These remarks bring us back to our starting point in this section: the conception of universal grammar in OT. But what exactly do we mean by 'grammar' in the first place? The OT grammar, and its architecture, will be the topic of the next section.

1.4 The architecture of an OT grammar

The OT grammar is an *input–output mechanism* that pairs an output form to an input form (such that each input has precisely one output). To accomplish this function, the grammar contains a division of labour between a component which maps the input onto an infinite set of candidate output forms, and another component that is burdened with *evaluating* the candidate output forms by a set of ranked constraints, and selecting the *optimal* output among these. These two components are known under the names of GENERATOR (or *Gen*) and EVALUATOR (or *Eval*). This grammatical organization is schematically represented in a function notation as follows:

(24) The grammar as an input–output mechanism
    Gen (**input**) $\Rightarrow$ {cand$_1$, cand$_2$ ... cand$_n$}
    Eval {cand$_1$, cand$_2$ ... cand$_n$} $\Rightarrow$ **output**

That is, *Gen* is a function that, when applied to some input, produces a set of candidates, all of which are logically possible analyses of this input. Similarly, *Eval* is a function that, when applied to a set of output candidates, produces an output, the optimal analysis of the input. In addition to *Gen* and *Eval*, the grammar contains a LEXICON storing all lexical forms that are input to *Gen*. Recapitulating, we find the following model of the grammar:

(25) Components of the OT grammar
    LEXICON: contains lexical representations (or underlying forms) of morphemes, which form the input to:
    GENERATOR: generates output candidates for some input, and submits these to:
    EVALUATOR: the set of ranked constraints, which evaluates output candidates as to their harmonic values, and selects the optimal candidate.

Let us now focus on some properties of the different components.

1.4.1 *The LEXICON, and Richness of the Base*
The LEXICON contains all contrastive properties of morphemes (roots, stems, and affixes) of a language, including phonological, morphological, syntactic, and semantic properties. The Lexicon provides the input specifications which are to be submitted to the Generator. In this connection, perhaps the most striking property of the Lexicon, as conceived of in OT, is that no specific property can be stated at the level of underlying representations:

(26) **Richness of the Base**: no constraints hold at the level of underlying forms.

In OT grammatical generalizations are expressed as interactions of constraints *at the level of the output*, never at the input level. Markedness constraints always state requirements of output forms. Faithfulness constraints also evaluate output forms, although they refer to the input level in stating their requirements. The notion of contrast, which derivational theory locates at the level of the lexical representation, is attributed to interactions at the output level in OT. Whether or not a feature is contrastive in some language depends on interactions of output-oriented markedness and faithfulness constraints, either preserving or overruling input specifications (see section 1.5).

OT thus abandons *Morpheme Structure Constraints* (MSCs), which in classical generative phonology (Chomsky and Halle 1968) account for prohibitions against specific types of structure at the level of the morpheme, in specific languages. MSCs were used, for example, to express prohibitions against front rounded vowels, or sequences of three or more consonants, or two labial consonants occurring within a morpheme. In the early 1970s MSCs were argued to be theoretically problematic in the sense that they duplicate information which is, independently, expressed by phonological rewrite rules, or that they globally guide the application of rules, a property called 'structure-preservingness'.[11] By locating the burden of explanation of the lack of specific kinds of structure at the level of the output, OT, in principle at least, circumvents this *Duplication Problem*.

1.4.2 *The GENERATOR, and Freedom of Analysis*

The essential property of the GENERATOR is that it is free to generate any conceivable output candidate for some input. This property is called *Freedom of Analysis*.

(27)   **Freedom of Analysis**: Any amount of structure may be posited.

The only true restriction imposed on all output candidates generated by *Gen* is that these are made up of licit elements from the universal vocabularies of linguistic representation, such as segmental structure (features and their grouping below the level of the segment), prosodic structure (mora, syllable, foot, prosodic word, etc.), morphology (root, stem, word, affix, etc.), and syntax (X-bar structure, heads/complements/specifiers, etc.). Within these limits, 'anything goes'.

Since *Gen* generates all logically possible candidate analyses of a given input, the OT grammar needs no rewrite rules to map inputs onto outputs. All structural changes are applied in one step, in parallel. The evaluation of these candidate analyses is the function of the *Evaluator*, the component of ranked constraints, discussed in section 1.4.3. There we will also discuss the issue of whether or not *Eval* is able to deal with an infinite candidate space.

1.4.3 *The EVALUATOR: economy, strict domination, and parallelism*

The EVALUATOR (henceforth *Eval*) is undoubtedly the central component of the grammar since it is burdened with the responsibility of accounting for all

---

[11] For example, rewrite rules may be blocked if their output would violate a MSC, or may be triggered to repair a violation of a MSC.

observable regularities of surface forms. Although any candidate output can be posited by *Gen*, the crucial role of *Eval* is to assess the 'harmony' of outputs with respect to a given ranking of constraints.

Eval is structured as a (language-specific) hierarchy of universal constraints, plus devices for evaluation. The latter include the means to assess *violation marks* on candidate outputs for every constraint, and the means to *rank* an infinite set of candidate outputs for *harmony* with respect to the hierarchy of constraints, and select the most harmonic one of these as *optimal* – the actual output of the grammar. Let us now take a closer look at each of these devices: the constraint hierarchy, marking of violations, and harmony evaluation.

First, the constraint hierarchy contains all universal constraints (a set called *Con*), which are ranked in a language-specific way. We (tentatively) assume that all constraints are ranked with respect to each other, so as to exclude variable and undetermined rankings. (For cases in which two constraints cannot be ranked with respect to each other, due to a trivial lack of interaction, we nevertheless assume some ranking, arbitrarily one or the other.)

Moreover, within the hierarchy, dominance relations are transitive:

(28)   **Transitivity of ranking**:   *If* $C_1 \gg C_2$ *and* $C_2 \gg C_3$ *then* $C_1 \gg C_3$

This property of ranking will allow us to construct *ranking arguments*, as we will see below.

Second, with respect to *violation marks*, we assume that each output candidate is provided with as many marks as it has violations for a constraint. This number of marks potentially ranges from zero until *infinite*. However, for purposes of determining optimal outputs, an infinite number of marks is never practically relevant. The essence of minimal violation of constraints is that every violation of a constraint serves a purpose: to avoid a violation of some higher-ranked constraint. This is a property which is stated by Prince and Smolensky (1993: 27):

(29)   **Economy**: banned options are available only to avoid violations of higher-ranked constraints and can only be banned *minimally*.

For example, the *Generator* component is free to submit any kind of analysis of (English) /bɛd/ that is couched within the universal alphabet of representational options, including excessively unfaithful candidates such as [pɪlow] and [mætrəs]. But these candidates will be (hopefully!) ruled out regardless of constraint ranking, since they violate faithfulness constraints without compensation from reductions in markedness. This economy property of OT will be discussed in more detail in section 1.7.5.

Third, we have not yet precisely formulated in which way the evaluation of output candidates by ranked constraints proceeds. *Eval* determines the harmonic status of output candidates, and eventually the most harmonic or optimal candidate. To this end, it uses a process by which the set of candidates is reduced until the point is reached at which one output remains. This is a multi-step process, schematically repeated below from (1):

(30)

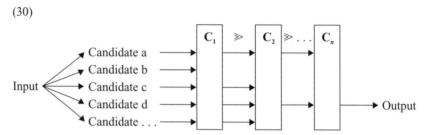

The major property of this evaluation process is that it applies from one state to another without looking ahead to following steps. That is, the elimination of candidate outputs by a constraint C_n is never affected by a lower-ranked constraint C_{n+m}. Stated in a non-serial manner, this implies:

(31)   **Strict domination**: violation of higher-ranked constraints cannot be compensated for by satisfaction of lower-ranked constraints.

Optimality does not involve any kind of compromise between constraints of different ranks.

To illustrate strict domination, let us return to tableau (8) – the cases of simple domination – and ask what would have happened if the first candidate had had not one but two violations of C_2. The following tableau shows that even here, the first candidate would still be optimal, even though its total number of violations is greater:

(32)   Strict domination: multiple violations of a lower-ranked constraint

	C_1	C_2
a. ☞ *candidate a*		**
b. *candidate b*	*!	

No smaller amount of violations can compensate for ranking of constraints. Domination is *strict*: any candidate that incurs a violation of some higher-ranked constraint (on which another candidate incurs no violations) is mercilessly excluded, regardless of its relative well-formedness with respect to any lower-ranked constraints.

There is yet another sense in which domination is strict, which is not illustrated by (32) – constraint violations are never added for different constraints. The added violations of two lower-ranked constraints (C_2 and C_3) are not able to 'cancel' out a single violation of a higher-ranked constraint (C_1):

(33)   Strict domination: violations of multiple lower-ranked constraints

		C_1	C_2	C_3
a. ☞	*candidate a*		*	*
b.	*candidate b*	*!		

That is, lower-ranked constraints cannot 'team up' against a higher-ranked constraint.

We see that there is no element of compromise in the notion 'optimal': evaluation of candidates by the set of constraints is based on strict domination, and accordingly, satisfaction of higher-ranked constraints has uncompromised priority over satisfaction of lower-ranked ones. Uncompromised, since no possible degree of satisfaction of lower-ranked constraints can compensate for the violation of a single high-ranked constraint.

Not all interactions of constraints are of this relatively simple kind, where an optimal candidate satisfies a high-ranked constraint that is violated by all competitors. Actually most interactions involve some degree of violation in the optimal candidate. How can this occur? Violation of a constraint is, by itself, an insufficient ground for ungrammaticality. Recall that the goal of evaluation is to single out one unique form as the most harmonic one. Elimination of all candidates in the set under consideration is therefore not allowed. This is shown in diagram below, where C_1 functions as a *no-pass* filter:

(34)

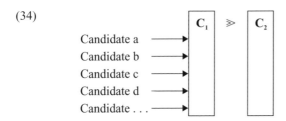

This must be avoided. Hence for a violation of some constraint C_1 to be *fatal* (eliminating from the candidate set any forms which incur it) at least one other form must occur in the candidate set that satisfies C_1 (without being less harmonic on higher-ranked constraints, of course). If no such form can be found, some violation must be taken for granted.

In such a situation, in which all remaining candidate outputs violate a constraint (due to higher-ranked constraints), the *seriousness* of violation must be taken into account for each individual form. That is, forms with *fewer* violation marks of C_1 are preferred to forms with *more* violation marks for C_1. This situation may still produce a ranking argument for C_1 and C_2, as tableau (35) shows:

(35)　　　Amount of violation decisive

	C_1	C_2
a. ☞ *candidate a*	*	*
b. 　　*candidate b*	**!	

Finally, if multiple candidates have the *same* number of violations for C_1 (and this equals the minimal violation in the set), then all survive and are passed on for evaluation by the next constraint down the hierarchy, C_2.[12]

(36)　　　Tie between candidates (with lower-ranking constraint decisive)

	C_1	C_2
a. ☞ *candidate a*	*	*!
b. 　　*candidate b*	*	

This situation can be represented as an *all-pass* filter C_1:

(37)

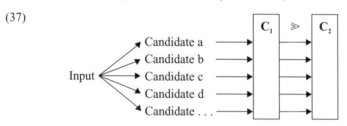

Of course, ties between candidates may also arise between forms that have no violations at all, or between forms that have two, three, or any number of violations.

Finally, we emphasize that lower-ranked constraints are not rendered 'inactive', or switched off by higher-ranked constraints, but that their violation is only avoided with less priority. Lower-ranked constraints may be violated by the

---

[12] Note that in the case of a tie, the ranking of constraints C_1 and C_2 becomes indeterminable from the actual form – however, we assume that this ranking may be established from other forms.

optimal output, but their violation *must be minimal.* Given the chance, any constraint (regardless of its position in the hierarchy) will be active in determining the optimal output.

(38)   Activity of a dominated constraint

	C_1	C_2	C_3
a. ☞ *candidate a*		*	*
b. *candidate b*		**!	
c. *candidate c*	*!		

That C_2 is dominated is apparent from the fact that candidate (38c) is less harmonic than (38a), even though it has no violations of C_2. But C_2 is still active, since it dominates C_3.

The final property of *Eval* to be briefly discussed here is:

(39)   **Parallelism**: all constraints pertaining to some type of structure interact in a single hierarchy.

In a trivial sense, it is parallelism which predicts that faithfulness constraints may interact with markedness constraints in a single hierarchy. But at a higher level of sophistication, parallelism is also the basis of explanation of phenomena involving 'interface' properties. In particular, we will see many examples in this book showing that morphological and phonological properties of an output form are mutually dependent. The most spectacular cases will come from the area of 'prosodic morphology', that is, types of morphology that depend on aspects of syllabification and metrical structure (examples being reduplication, infixation, and truncation). It is parallelism that makes information flow back and forth between 'morphological' and 'prosodic' aspects in such cases. Striking consequences of parallelism will be discussed in later chapters of this book, in particular in chapter 4 (on interactions of quantity and stress) and chapter 5 (on reduplication).

1.4.4 *Fear of infinity*

Freedom of Analysis may seem to pose an overwhelming *computational* problem for the basic function of a grammar, which is to provide a mapping between input and output. Perhaps the most apparent fear is that an infinite candidate space is computationally intractable. Reactions to this point focus on the nature of candidate space, on evaluation strategies which assure a more efficient processing, and on computational results booked so far in modelling OT. For an elaboration of the arguments below, and for some others, see chapter 10 of Prince and Smolensky (1993).

Firstly, it is a well-accepted assumption among linguists that there is a distinction between the grammar (*competence*) and its cognitive implementation (*performance*). This distinction is assumed in most formal theories of grammar, and particularly in generative linguistics (Chomsky 1965). Therefore a model of grammar is adequate to the extent that it explains observed systematicities in natural languages, and the grammatical judgements of speakers. Explaining the actual processing of linguistic knowledge by the human mind is not the goal of the formal theory of grammar, but that of linguistic disciplines (such as psycholinguistics, neurolinguistics, and computional linguistics). The central point is that a grammatical model should not be equated with its computational implementation.

Secondly, turning now to computational plausibility, the fact that candidate space is infinite does not imply that the problem is *logically unsolvable*. You may convince yourself of this by thinking of arithmetic or any kind of numerical problem. For example, there is a unique solution to the equation $3n^2 - 3 = 45$, which you will be able to find after a moment's thought, even though the candidate set (let us say, all integers) is infinite. From a computational viewpoint, the decisive factor is that a guaranteed method (an *algorithm*) exists that will certainly produce a solution for any input. Therefore, no simple argument against OT as being 'computationally intractable' can be based on the observation that candidate space is infinite.[13]

Thirdly, 'smart' computational strategies may eliminate suboptimal candidates by *classes*, rather than on a one-by-one basis. As soon as a candidate has been excluded due to its violation of some constraint C, the evaluation process can immediately eliminate all other candidates that violate this constraint C more severely. This leads us to yet another property of candidate space that might be put to use in computational evaluation models. By far the great majority of candidates proposed by *Gen* can *never* be selected as optimal, under any possible ranking of constraints. Such *intrinsically suboptimal* candidates can be readily identified as follows: they share with another candidate (of the same input) some set of violation marks, but have at least one additional violation of some other constraint (an example will be discussed in section 1.7.5). Sophisticated evaluation strategies may capitalize on this. Since the identification of intrinsically suboptimal candidates involves no ranked constraints, infinite candidate space may be drastically reduced by eliminating the 'worst-of-the-worst' of candidates by preprocessing prior to the evaluation by ranked constraints. Since this preprocessing

---

[13] Conversely, a finite set of candidates does not guarantee that a problem is logically solvable. This argument is due to Alan Prince (presentation at Utrecht University, January 1994).

would eliminate the great majority of candidates, the ultimately relevant remaining part of candidate space may well have quite manageable proportions, and perhaps even reduce to a finite set (Hammond 1997).

Whether or not a computational method can be established for the evaluation of an infinite candidate space in OT grammars is still largely an open issue, but encouraging results are available. For example, Karttunen (1998) demonstrates that 'the computation of the most optimal surface realization of any input string can be carried out entirely within a *finite-state calculus*, subject to the limitation (Frank and Satta (1998)) that the maximal number of violations is bounded'. Karttunen adds that '[i]t is not likely that this limitation is a serious obstacle to practical optimality computations with finite-state systems as the number of constraint violations that need to be taken into account is generally small'.

1.5 **Interactions of markedness and faithfulness**

This section will deal with important types of interactions of markedness and faithfulness constraints, building on key insights of Prince and Smolensky (1993), Kirchner (1995), and Steriade (1995b). In section 1.3.3 we studied final devoicing in Dutch as a case of positional neutralization: the feature [voice] is neutralized in a specific context (the syllable coda), as a result of a markedness constraint dominating a faithfulness constraint. Here we will first extend this simple interaction of markedness and faithfulness to a new phenomenon: allophonic variation. In section 1.6 we will look into the notion of *contrast* as it is defined in OT, and its consequences for *lexical representation*. This will allow us to define more clearly the ranking schemata of faithfulness and markedness constraints that are responsible for the various attested situations ('contrast', 'neutralization', and 'allophonic variation'). In section 1.7 we will summarize these results in the form of a 'factorial typology'. In section 1.8 we will see how *segment inventories* follow from interactions of faithfulness and markedness.

1.5.1 *Allophonic variation*

Consider a language that has no lexical contrast of oral and nasal vowels. In this language oral and nasal vowels are *allophones*, variants of one another which are fully predictable from the phonological contexts. For example, vowels are generally oral except when they directly precede a tautosyllabic nasal stop, in which case they are nasal. This allophonic pattern occurs in many dialects of English; see the examples below:

(40) a.i   cat   [kæt]   b.i   can't   [kæ̃nt]
      a.ii sad   [sæd]   b.ii   sand   [sæ̃nd]
      a.iii met   [mɛt]   b.iii meant   [mɛ̃nt]
      a.iv lick [lɪk]   b.iv   link   [lɪ̃ŋk]

When we say that English lacks a contrast of oral and nasal vowels, we do not imply that English completely lacks either kind of vowels, but only that no word pairs occur that are distinguished by orality/nasality of their vowels. Whatever variation there is between oral and nasal vowels is totally conditioned by the context and does not reflect lexical specification. Vowels are nasal when they precede a tautosyllabic nasal, and are oral in all other contexts. This complementary distribution, and the corresponding lack of word pairs that differ only in the specification of some feature, is what defines an allophonic pattern. How can the allophonic pattern in (40) be stated in terms of violable constraints?

In order to answer this question, we must first identify the set of constraints which are involved. Universally, nasal vowels are 'marked' as compared to oral vowels. Most of the world's languages completely lack nasal vowels, having oral vowels only (Maddieson 1984). Languages may have both oral and nasal vowels, but no languages have only nasal vowels. In sum, when a language has nasal vowels, it must also have oral vowels. The marked status of nasal vowels is expressed by the *context-free* markedness constraint in (41), which militates against nasal vowels:

(41) $*V_{NASAL}$
         Vowels must not be nasal.

When this constraint is undominated in some language, then all of its vowels will be oral, regardless of their lexical specification, or their position in the syllable (before an oral or nasal).

Moreover, many languages tend to nasalize vowels in precisely the position where they are nasal in English: before a tautosyllabic nasal stop. The vowel thus anticipates the nasality of the following stop, a preferred state of affairs from the viewpoint of perception and articulation (Cohn 1993a).[14] Again, a markedness constraint expresses the universal markedness, ruling out oral vowels that precede a tautosyllabic nasal:

(42) $*V_{ORAL}N$
         Before a tautosyllabic nasal, vowels must not be oral.

Observe that this constraint is *context-sensitive*, since it states a connection between the nasality of a vowel and a nasal stop in its context. More precisely, it is violated by an oral vowel that stands directly before a tautosyllabic nasal:

---

[14] Cohn (1993a) argues that nasalization in English vowels is gradient, and has no phonological status, as in French. For the sake of the argument, we will assume here that English nasalization is in fact categorical, although it is crucially non-contrastive.

(43)   a. *$V_{ORAL}N$ satisfied   b. *$V_{ORAL}N$ violated
       i. æn]$_\sigma$ æn]$_\sigma$
       ii. æd]$_\sigma$

If this constraint is undominated, underlying contrasts between oral and nasal vowels (if any) will be neutralized in positions before a tautosyllabic nasal.

1.5.2 *Neutralization and contrast as constraint rankings*

Now consider the consequences of the OT assumption of the *Richness of the Base*, which was stated in section 1.4.1. This says that no constraints restrict the input, or to put it differently, that lexical representations in any language are free to contain any kind of phonological contrast. Whether some surface phonetic contrast (such as that between oral and nasal vowels) is allophonic or lexically distinctive in a language depends on interactions of two basic kinds of constraints: markedness constraints, which express markedness statements, and faithfulness constraints, which penalize deviations of the surface form (output) from its lexical form (input). When markedness dominates faithfulness, the language achieves outputs that are minimally marked, at the expense of a neutralization of lexical contrasts. But when faithfulness dominates markedness, the language makes the reverse choice, realizing its input contrasts at the expense of output markedness:

(44)   a. Markedness ≫ Faithfulness lexical contrasts are neutralized
       b. Faithfulness ≫ Markedness lexical contrasts are expressed

Richness of the Base implies that English (as any other language) is allowed the option of setting up a contrast of oral and nasal vowels in its underlying representations. However, this hypothetical contrast is never realized at the surface, because with respect to nasality/orality in vowels, English happens to be a language of the type (44a), which gives priority to markedness over faithfulness. Whatever lexical contrast of nasality there might be in vowels will be *obscured* by effects of markedness. The input faithfulness constraint that is crucially dominated in English requires that surface values of nasality in vowels are identical to their underlying values:

(45)   **IDENT-IO**(nasal)
       Correspondent segments in input and output have identical values for [nasal].

In a language in which IDENT-IO(nasal) is undominated, any lexical contrast of nasality in vowels will be allowed to surface, uninhibited by the markedness constraints (41–2). Such a language is free to set up and preserve any lexical contrast between oral and nasal vowels *anywhere*, that is, without any neutralization. This situation corresponds to the interaction (44b). But in a language in which IDENT-IO(nasal) is dominated by both of the markedness constraints (41) and (42), any (potential) contrast of orality/nasality in vowels will be fully neutralized, as is the case in allophonic variation. This is the situation (44a), found in English.

Let us now return to the allophonic pattern (40) and find out how this results from the interaction of the three constraints that were introduced earlier. In terms of constraint interaction, faithfulness to the lexical specification of a vowel is completely dominated by markedness constraints reflecting markedness of orality/nasality in vowels. In terms of ranking, IDENT-IO(nasal) is dominated by both markedness constraints:

(46)   Neutralization of lexical contrast
         Markedness $\gg$ Faithfulness
         $*V_{NASAL}$, $*V_{ORAL}N \gg$ IDENT-IO(nasal)

This is an instantiation of the schema in (44a), where markedness constraints completely dominate faithfulness.

The question which arises next is how both markedness constraints, $*V_{ORAL}N$ and $*V_{NASAL}$, are ranked with respect to each other. As we observed earlier in connection with the context-free constraint $*V_{NASAL}$, any language in which this is undominated will totally lack nasal vowels in its surface patterns. This is not the case in English, however, where nasal vowels do occur (as allophones of oral vowels) in specific positions, that is, before tautosyllabic nasal stops. We must therefore refine the ranking in (46) to that in (47):

(47)   Allophonic variation
         Contextual markedness $\gg$ Context-free markedness $\gg$ Faithfulness
         $*V_{ORAL}N$ $\gg$ $*V_{NASAL}$ $\gg$ IDENT-
                                                                 IO(nasal)

This ranking states that nasal realization of vowels before tautosyllabic nasal consonants takes priority over a total lack of nasality in vowels. In sum, both nasal and oral vowels occur at the surface, but their distribution is fixed, rather than free.

This ranking is illustrated in the tableaux (48–51). First consider the case of an oral vowel in the actual output, for example *sad* [sæd]. When we assume that this has an oral vowel in its lexical representation, e.g. /sæd/, matching its surface status, we arrive at the first tableau (48). Candidate (48a) is optimal as it violates none of the constraints in the tableau, regardless of ranking. It satisfies $*V_{ORAL}N$ since this constraint has nothing to say about vowels that stand before oral stops. It also satisfies $*V_{NASAL}$ since it has no nasal vowel. Finally it satisfies IDENT-IO(nasal) because the input and output agree in nasality.

(48)

Input: /sæd/	$*V_{ORAL}N$	$*V_{NASAL}$	IDENT-IO(nasal)
a. ☞ [sæd]			
b. [sæ̃d]		*!	*

The losing candidate [sæ̃d] (48b) is less harmonic than (48a) in two respects. It contains a nasal vowel, fatally violating the markedness constraint $*V_{NASAL}$. It violates IDENT-IO(nasal) as well, as the nasal vowel in the output fails to match its oral correspondent in the input.

Because of Richness of the Base, we must guarantee that this correct result is not negatively affected when we make different assumptions about the nasality of vowels in the input. Indeed, the same candidate [sæd] is selected when the input would contain a nasal vowel, e.g. /sæ̃d/, here in defiance of its surface form. This is shown in tableau (49). Again markedness uniquely determines the outcome, without interference on the part of the faithfulness constraint IDENT-IO(nasal).

(49)

Input: /sæ̃d/	$*V_{ORAL}N$	$*V_{NASAL}$	IDENT-IO(nasal)
a. ☞ [sæd]			*
b. [sæ̃d]		*!	

Note that in this case IDENT-IO(nasal) is violated in the optimal candidate. This motivates the ranking $*V_{NASAL} \gg$ IDENT-IO(nasal), a markedness constraint dominating faithfulness. That is, even if the input of *sad* were to contain a nasal vowel, its nasality would be wiped out in the surface form by markedness constraints. This is of course the central result that we need to account for allophonic variation, in a theory which assumes Richness of the Base.

We can only rightfully claim to have captured the 'complementary distribution' of oral and nasal vowels if we can prove the total 'irrelevance of the input' for words which surface with nasal vowels, for example *sand* [sæ̃nd]. Again we consider two underlying forms, one with an oral vowel and the other with a nasal vowel. Tableau (50) shows that an underlying form with an oral vowel /sænd/ results in an optimal output with a nasal vowel, [sæ̃nd]. This is due to the un-dominated context-sensitive markedness constraint $*V_{ORAL}N$, which requires that vowels are nasal before a tautosyllabic nasal stop:

(50)

Input: /sænd/	$*V_{ORAL}N$	$*V_{NASAL}$	IDENT-IO(nasal)
a.　　[sænd]	*!		
b. ☞ [sæ̃nd]		*	*

Observe that two markedness constraints, $*V_{ORAL}N$ and $*V_{NASAL}$, are in conflict here. The former requires a nasal vowel in the output whereas the latter militates against it. The fact that the actual output [sæ̃nd] has a nasal vowel shows that $*V_{ORAL}N$ dominates $*V_{NASAL}$. (If the ranking had been reverse, the result would have been in favour of candidate 50a, which has an oral vowel.) Observe also that the underlying orality of the vowel in *sand* does not affect the outcome. IDENT-IO(nasal) is violated in the optimal output, since it contains a nasal vowel whereas the input contains an oral vowel. This conclusion is essential to the argument that faithfulness is dominated by *both* markedness constraints. We have already reached this conclusion for $*V_{NASAL}$ in tableau (49), and now we confirm it for $*V_{ORAL}N$.

The argument for the irrelevance of inputs in allophonic patterns is completed by an inspection of tableau (51), which has an underlying form with a nasal vowel, /sæ̃nd/. In this tableau, the same optimal candidate is selected as in the previous one, simply because markedness uniquely determines the outcome.

(51)

Input: /sæ̃nd/	$*V_{ORAL}N$	$*V_{NASAL}$	IDENT-IO(nasal)
a.　　[sænd]	*!		*
b. ☞ [sæ̃nd]		*	

A comparison of tableaux (50) and (51) reveals the complete inactivity of the faithfulness constraint IDENT-IO(nasal). We conclude that the orality/nasality of the underlying vowel is completely irrelevant to the surface distribution of oral and nasal vowels.

1.6 Lexicon Optimization

The main result of the preceding section is that lexical specifications for [nasal] in vowels in English are totally irrelevant to their surface realization. Should we then conclude that the English lexicon is completely unstructured for nasality in vowels, in the sense that the vowels in lexical items *sad* and *sand* are randomly specified for this feature? Or should we still insist that the lexicon be kept 'clean' from featural noise, and contain only feature values that are actually related to output values? An answer to this question is potentially relevant to language acquisition. In order to build a lexicon, the learner must somehow be able to determine *underlying* forms, for example to infer the underlying form of *sad* on the basis of its surface form [sæd]. When we concentrate on possible values for nasality in the vowel, there is a choice of two lexical representations, /sæd/ and /sæ̃d/. We have seen that, given the ranking of *V$_{\text{NASAL}}$ over IDENT-IO(nasal), both lexical representations result in identical outputs. This ranking completely *masks* the input, obscuring empirical evidence that the learner might use to base his/her choice of an underlying form on.

It has been proposed that in the absence of empirical evidence for one input form over another, the input should be selected that is closest to the output, in this case /sæd/. That is, wherever the learner has no evidence (from surface forms) to postulate a specific diverging lexical form, (s)he will assume that the input is identical to the surface form. In terms of constraint violations, this strategy has the advantage of minimizing the violation of faithfulness, *as compared to any other hypothetical inputs producing the same output*. This strategy is called *Lexicon Optimization* in Prince and Smolensky (1993: 192):

(52)   **Lexicon Optimization**: suppose that several different inputs I$_1$, I$_2$..., I$_n$ when parsed by a grammar G lead to corresponding outputs O$_1$, O$_2$..., O$_n$, all of which are realized as the same phonetic form Φ – these inputs are *phonetically equivalent* with respect to G. Now one of these outputs must be the most harmonic, by virtue of incurring the least significant violation marks: suppose this optimal one is labelled O$_k$. Then the learner should choose, as the underlying form for Φ, the input I$_k$.

This principle is, in its turn, an elaboration of an idea of Stampe (1972), who suggested that underlying forms should always match surface forms in the absence of evidence to the contrary. (The 'masking' effect of one underlying form, /sæ̃d/, by another, /sæd/, is called 'Stampean occultation' in Prince and Smolensky 1993.)

An alternative to Lexicon Optimization is to assume that certain inputs contain no specification with respect to a feature (Kiparsky 1985, Steriade 1987, Archangeli 1988). This *underspecification* analysis of nasality in vowels is based on the idea that the burden of explanation for contrastive versus allophonic patterns is in the underlying form, rather than in the relationship between underlying form and surface form, as is the case in OT.[15]

---

[15] See Smolensky (1993), Inkelas (1995) and Itô, Mester, and Padgett (1995) for comments on underspecification in OT.

Importantly, Lexicon Optimization does not contradict the assumption of Richness of the Base, even though it may give rise to lexicons that are 'impoverished' in terms of featural 'noise'. The burden of explanation still remains on the interaction of markedness and faithfulness. More specifically, the ranking markedness ≫ faithfulness implies that it is not an accidental observation that nasality is never distinctive in vowels in English – on the contrary, this is a solid effect of constraint interactions in the English grammar.

1.7   A factorial typology of markedness and faithfulness

In the remainder of this chapter we will consider the consequences of reranking the three constraint types which we have assumed in the analysis of allophonic variation, that is: context-*free* markedness, context-*sensitive* markedness, and faithfulness. We will see that by reranking these three constraint types into different hierarchies, a 'factorial typology' arises which exactly matches the attested cross-linguistic variation in terms of allophonic variation, positional neutralization, and free contrast. This will provide further support for the 'markedness' approach of allophonic variation which we have used so far, as well as for the assumption of Richness of the Base.

1.7.1   *Typological goals of OT*

The important notion of *factorial typology* requires some explanation, before we actually construct one. The key assumption of OT is that grammars are means to resolve conflicts between universal constraints. More specifically, the grammar of an individual language is a specific way, out of many possible, to rank a set of universal and violable constraints. Differences between languages must therefore be due to different rankings of a single set of universal constraints. To state it differently, we can build one grammar out of another by a rearrangement of its basic universal material, that is, by 'reranking' the constraints.

The relative success of any theory of grammar should be measured by its ability to characterize the notion of 'possible grammar' (see again the remarks in the introduction of this chapter). Constructing grammars ('constraint hierarchies') of individual languages may tell us much about the ways in which linguistic properties are interconnected within a single linguistic system. But what we are eventually interested in are *typological* results of the theory, that is, the predictions it makes about clusterings of linguistic properties, on a broad cross-linguistic basis. For example, the theory should explain why no languages occur that have a contrast of oral and nasal vowels, but contextually restrict this contrast to vowels immediately preceding nasal stops (neutralizing it everywhere else). Languages of this kind are logically possible, yet unattested. Can this situation be described by a reranking of the constraints governing nasality in vowels? Conversely, we should ask what language types would arise by reranking a number of constraints that are motivated in the analysis of an individual language. Does reranking of these constraints produce attested languages as well?

Taken quite literally, the reranking approach would predict that any new grammar that arises from a reranking of any pair of constraints will precisely correlate with one of the world's languages. This prediction is based on the deeply naive assumption that every possible ranking should be instantiated by some attested language. This is naive, just as it is deeply naive to expect that all logically possible permutations of genetic material in the human genome are actually attested in individual humans. Therefore, in order to test the typological predictions of the theory of contrast and contextual neutralization presented in this section, we will rerank *types* of constraints (rather than individual constraints) of the general types 'faithfulness', 'contextual markedness', and 'context-free markedness'. The resulting factorial typology will be matched with broad *typological* diversity between languages, along the dimensions that these constraint types represent. (Of course, this is not to deny that cases can occur in which it is more useful to compute factorial typologies of individual constraints.)

1.7.2 *Constructing a factorial typology*

To construct a factorial typology of a set of constraints, we sum up all logically possible rankings of this set of constraints, and compute the different outcomes. With large sets of constraints the number of possible rankings rises steeply, as with a constraint set of size n, we must consider all $n!$ rankings. (This equals 2 rankings for 2 constraints, 6 rankings for 3, 24 for 4, 120 for 5, 720 for 6, etc.) Fortunately, many of the individual rankings in a factorial typology produce identical surface patterns. Therefore the number of predicted patterns is much smaller than the total number of logically possible rankings. Keeping these remarks in mind, we now turn to a real case.

Our goal is to construct a factorial typology of the constraint types introduced so far (faithfulness constraints, context-free and context-sensitive markedness constraints). One proviso has to be made: actual grammars rank individual constraints, not 'constraint types'. (For example, no grammar ranks all faithfulness constraints above all markedness constraints, for reasons discussed in section 1.2.2.) Nevertheless, we will *generalize* the factorial typology by a reranking of constraint types. Accordingly, the emerging factorial typology should be taken as a catalogue of general effects, which may be instantiated in an individual grammar with respect to specific features.

A factorial typology of markedness and faithfulness is presented below, resulting from a reranking of both markedness constraint types with faithfulness. We will abbreviate these types of markedness constraints as *MC-free* (for context-free markedness constraint) and *MC-sensitive* (for context-sensitive markedness constraint).

(53)   A factorial typology of markedness and faithfulness
         a. MC-free ≫ MC-sensitive, Faithfulness   Lack of variation
                                                     (unmarked)
         b. MC-sensitive ≫ MC-free ≫ Faithfulness   Allophonic variation
         c. MC-sensitive ≫ Faithfulness ≫ MC-free   Positional neutralization
         d. Faithfulness ≫ MC-sensitive, MC-free   Full contrast

The attentive reader may have noted that we have only four rankings here, rather than the predicted six (or 3!). This reduction is due to the fact that in rankings (53a) and (53d), the mutual ranking of the bottom two constraints is of no importance to the outcome.

The following subsections discuss how these situations arise from these rankings, and also illustrate each ranking by tableaux for contrastive nasality in vowels.

1.7.3 *Neutralization: lack of variation versus allophonic variation*

Both (53a) and (53b) are situations of complete neutralization, since in both cases there is a total lack of activity of the faithfulness constraint, which is at the very bottom of the hierarchy. The difference between the rankings resides in whether or not the neutralized feature is 'contextually coloured', that is, subject to allophonic variation.

First consider the situation of total lack of variation, which is produced by ranking (53a), due to an undominated context-free markedness constraint for some feature [αF]. Accordingly the unmarked value of this feature (for segments of a given type), [uF], will always appear at the surface, regardless of its underlying specification, and regardless of the context. This results in the complete neutralization of this feature in the direction of the unmarked value. Such total *lack of variation* for a given feature (in all segments of some type) is widely attested for different features among the world's languages.

For example, if the constraint $*V_{NASAL}$ is undominated, then all surface vowels are oral, even those vowels which are underlyingly nasal, and even those vowels which are adjacent to a nasal consonant. This is illustrated in the set of four tableaux below. Each of these tableaux takes as its input one of the four possible combinations of input nasality in vowels (nasal versus oral) and output context of the vowel (preceding a nasal [n] or an oral [l]). All four possible inputs {/pan/ ~ /pãn/ ~ /pal/ ~ /pãl/} map onto oral output vowels:

(54)   Lack of variation of nasality in vowels (total orality)

$*V_{NASAL} \gg *V_{ORAL}N$, IDENT-IO(nasal)

(i) Input: /pan/	$*V_{NASAL}$	$*V_{ORAL}N$	IDENT-IO(nasal)
a. pãn	*!		
b. ☞ pan		*	

(ii) Input: /pãn/	$*V_{NASAL}$	$*V_{ORAL}N$	IDENT-IO(nasal)
a. pãn	*!		
b. ☞ pan		*	*

(iii) Input: /pal/	$*V_{NASAL}$	$*V_{ORAL}N$	IDENT-IO(nasal)
a. pãl	*!		
b. ☞ pal			

(iv) Input: /pãl/	$*V_{NASAL}$	$*V_{ORAL}N$	IDENT-IO(nasal)
a. pãl	*!		
b. ☞ pal			*

Observe that the ranking of $*V_{ORAL}N$ and IDENT-IO(nasal) with respect to one another is totally irrelevant to the outcome, since the orality of the vowel is uniquely determined by $*V_{NASAL}$.

Ranking (53b) produces the typologically common case of *allophonic variation*, of which we have already encountered an example in the form of vowel nasalization before tautosyllabic nasals in English. As compared to the previous ranking, (53a), this ranking maintains complete neutralization, yet it allows for some variation in output values for the relevant feature. For example, both values of nasality in vowels do occur in surface forms, although their distribution is totally determined by the context. Vowels are nasal before nasal consonants (regardless of their input specification), and they are oral in all other contexts (regardless of their input specification). Although tableaux of English examples have already been presented in section 1.5.2, we include new tableaux here for maximal clarity:

(55)   Allophonic variation of nasality in vowels
          $*V_{ORAL}N \gg *V_{NASAL} \gg \text{IDENT-IO(nasal)}$

(i) Input: /pan/	$*V_{ORAL}N$	$*V_{NASAL}$	IDENT-IO(nasal)
a. ☞ pãn		*	*
b. pan	*!		

(ii) Input: /pãn/	$*V_{ORAL}N$	$*V_{NASAL}$	IDENT-IO(nasal)
a. ☞ pãn		*	
b. pan	*!		*

(iii) Input: /pal/	$*V_{ORAL}N$	$*V_{NASAL}$	IDENT-IO(nasal)
a. pãl		*!	*
b. ☞ pal			

(iv) Input: /pãl/	$*V_{ORAL}N$	$*V_{NASAL}$	IDENT-IO(nasal)
a. pãl		*!	
b. ☞ pal			*

The two remaining rankings in the factorial typology, (53c) and (53d), produce varying degrees of contrastiveness, as we will see below.

1.7.4 *Contrast: positional neutralization versus full contrast*

Ranking (53c) produces a *positional neutralization* of underlying feature values. This is a situation in which an underlying contrast is freely realized in most contexts, but where it is neutralized in a specific context. For example, nasality is contrastive in vowels, except in the context before a nasal consonant, where all vowels are nasal:

(56)   Positional neutralization of nasality in vowels before nasal consonants
          $*V_{ORAL}N \gg \text{IDENT-IO(nasal)} \gg *V_{NASAL}$

(i) Input: /pan/	$*V_{ORAL}N$	IDENT-IO(nasal)	$*V_{NASAL}$
a. ☞ pãn		*	*
b. pan	*!		

(ii) Input: /pãn/	$*V_{ORAL}N$	IDENT-IO(nasal)	$*V_{NASAL}$
a. ☞ pãn			*
b. pan	*!	*	

(iii) Input: /pal/	$*V_{ORAL}N$	IDENT-IO(nasal)	$*V_{NASAL}$
a. pãl		*!	*
b. ☞ pal			

(iv) Input: /pãl/	$*V_{ORAL}N$	IDENT-IO(nasal)	$*V_{NASAL}$
a. ☞ pãl			*
b. pal		*!	

Finally, the logically opposite situation of (53a) is that produced by ranking (53d), where a faithfulness constraint governing a feature dominates all markedness constraints (governing this feature). This produces a pattern in which input feature specifications are freely realized, that is, a situation of *full contrast* for the relevant feature.

For nasality, this ranking produces a situation in which underlying specifications in vowels are realized at the surface, regardless of their adjacency to nasal consonants:

(57)   Full contrast of nasality in vowels
IDENT-IO(nasal) ≫ $*V_{NASAL}$, $*V_{ORAL}N$

(i) Input: /pan/	IDENT-IO(nasal)	$*V_{NASAL}$	$*V_{ORAL}N$
a. pãn	*!	*	
b. ☞ pan			*

(ii) Input: /pãn/	IDENT-IO(nasal)	$*V_{NASAL}$	$*V_{ORAL}N$
a. ☞ pãn		*	
b. pan	*!		*

(iii) Input: /pal/	IDENT-IO(nasal)	$*V_{NASAL}$	$*V_{ORAL}N$
a. pãl	*!	*	
b. ☞ pal			

(iv) Input: /pãl/	IDENT-IO(nasal)	*V$_{NASAL}$	*V$_{ORAL}$N
a. ☞ pãl		*	
b. pal	*!		

Again, this *free contrast* is a cross-linguistically common type of situation.

1.7.5 *Positional neutralization of voice in Dutch*

It will now be clear that Dutch final devoicing is an example of positional neutralization: it produces a neutralization of the feature [voice] in obstruents in the
specific context of a syllable coda, while leaving unaffected the lexical distribution of [voice] in obstruents in other contexts. To fit the Dutch case into the
ranking schemata of the previous section, we must first determine which context-
free markedness constraint is involved in the ranking.

The unmarked value for the feature [voice] in obstruents is [−voice], as stated
in VOICED OBSTRUENT PROHIBITION (58c, henceforth VOP, after Itô and Mester
1998), which is accompanied by the other two constraints relevant to the Dutch
devoicing pattern:

(58)   a. ***VOICED-CODA**   (*context-sensitive markedness constraint*)
           Coda obstruents are voiceless.
        b. **IDENT-IO**(voice)   (*faithfulness constraint*)
           The value of the feature [voice] of an input segment must be
           preserved in its output correspondent.
        c. **VOP**   (*context-free markedness constraint*)
           *[+voi, −son]
           No obstruent must be voiced.

These three constraints are ranked in the following way in Dutch, instantiating the
pattern of positional neutralization (53c) with respect to the feature [voice]:

(59)   Ranking producing positional neutralization of voice in Dutch
        MC-sensitive ≫ Faithfulness   ≫ MC-free
        *VOICED-CODA ≫ IDENT-IO(voice) ≫ VOP

This ranking states that a voiceless realization of obstruents in coda position takes
priority over preservation of [voice] in coda obstruents. However, preservation of
input values of [voice] takes priority over the complete devoicing of obstruents.
In sum, the contrast of voiced and voiceless obstruents is positionally neutralized
in the syllable coda. Elsewhere, a contrast is possible – input values of [voice] are
preserved in the output.

In terms of concrete examples, this ranking correctly predicts that the output of /bɛd/ is [bɛt], which is unfaithful to input values for [voice] *only in its coda consonant*. But the voiced onset consonant /b/ is protected from the complete devoicing of obstruents required by the context-free markedness constraint VOP (hence, *[pɛt]). This interaction is shown by tableau (60), containing all four logically possible combinations of [voice] in the onset and coda consonants:

(60)

Input: /bɛd/	*VOICED-CODA	IDENT-IO(voice)	VOP
a. ☞ [bɛt]		*	*
b. [pɛt]		**!	
c. [bɛd]	*!		**
d. [pɛd]	*!	*	*

Two candidates (60c–d) are eliminated by undominated *VOICED-CODA, as each contains a voiced obstruent in coda position. Both remaining candidates (60a–b) satisfy *VOICED-CODA, hence both are passed on for evaluation by the next-lower-ranked constraint in the hierarchy, IDENT-IO(voice). Although both (60a) and (60b) violate IDENT-IO(voice), the former is selected since it violates IDENT-IO(voice) *minimally*. It has only one violation, while its contestant (60b) incurs two violations, one more than is strictly necessary. This result reflects an important property of the architecture of OT: a constraint can be 'active' even when it is dominated by one or more other constraints. *Constraints may be violated, but violation must be minimal*. This property of constraint interactions will reoccur many times in this book.

Another major property of constraint interaction is also illustrated by tableau (60). This is that *some candidates can never emerge as optimal, regardless of the ranking of constraints*. To see this, consider output candidate (60d), [pɛd], which preserves the input value for [voice] in its coda consonant, but is unfaithful to [voice] in its onset consonant. This incurs violations for each of the three constraints in the tableau: it violates *VOICED-CODA as it has a voiced coda obstruent [d], it violates IDENT-IO(voice) as it is unfaithful to the input value of [voice] in one of its consonants (the onset [p]), and finally it violates VOP because it contains a voiced obstruent [d]. Under what constraint ranking might this candidate be selected as optimal? The surprising answer is: 'under no ranking', since all logically possible rankings of the three constraints evaluate (60d) as *suboptimal to some other candidate*. To prove this point, we need not go through all tableaux of all possible rankings, although this method will certainly lead to the same conclusion. A more general proof is available. To mark a candidate *cand₁* as 'intrinsically suboptimal', it suffices to identify a rivalling candidate $cand_2$ which shares with $cand_1$ the violation marks for every constraint, except for at least one constraint C, on which $cand_2$ is more harmonic. If such a constraint C exists, then $cand_2$ must be a better candidate than $cand_1$ regardless of the ranking of C, since the minimal difference in violation marks always works in its favour, even if C were to dwell at the very bottom of the hierarchy.

There happens to be such a candidate $cand_2$ in tableau (60): candidate (60a), [bɛt], shares with candidate [pɛd] (60d) one violation mark for IDENT-IO(voice), and one for VOP, yet it minimally improves over (60d) with respect to *VOICED-CODA. Hence:

(61)   [bɛt] > [pɛd] For input /bɛd/, *irrespective* of ranking.

This does *not* imply that [bɛt] is the optimal candidate under *any ranking*: it clearly is not (only consider rankings in which either *VOICED-CODA or VOP is undominated). It does imply, however, that [pɛd] is 'intrinsically suboptimal' – which means that it will never be selected as optimal under any logically possible ranking of the three constraints under consideration.

This result, although apparently limited to the interaction of the three constraints in tableau (60), in fact has broader typological implications. A prediction follows from it, which is stated in general terms as follows. Assume a context-free markedness constraint banning one value of a feature [αF], and another context-sensitive markedness constraint banning the same value [αF] in a specific context. The prediction is that no language can have a contrast of [±F] *exclusively* in the context where a context-sensitive markedness constraint bans [αF]. This seems to be correct, although further testing may be required.

One particular language type excluded is one that has a lexical contrast of voicing exclusively in syllable codas. See the following hypothetical pattern of contrast:

(62)   A hypothetical language that is predicted not to occur
            a. a contrast of voice in syllable codas
                    lap ~ lab, pot ~ pod, muuk ~ muug
            b. but no contrast of voice elsewhere
                    paa (*baa), ma.tol (*ma.dol), tol.ku (*tol.gu)

Such a language would preserve a contrast of voice in the coda, but neutralize it elsewhere. That is, it would map an input /bɛd/ onto an optimal output [pɛd]. But we have just seen that such a mapping is ruled out on principled grounds, since it involves the selection of an intrinsically suboptimal candidate. The asymmetry between onsets and codas is due to a context-sensitive markedness constraint

*VOICED-CODA which rules out [+voice] in the syllable coda, while there is no analogous context-free markedness constraint which rules out any feature of voice *specifically* in the onset.

Alternative theories which do not assume markedness to be the actual substance of the grammar fail to derive this general prediction. For example, a rule-based theory in which the notion of 'markedness' is an external criterion fails to predict that hypothetical languages such as (62) should not exist. This is because phonological rules that neutralize a contrast of voice are 'natural' in *any context*, regardless of whether they apply in onset or in coda position. A rule neutralizing voicing in onsets is 'natural' in this general sense, and no language that has this rule is committed to having a second rule neutralizing voicing in codas as well. Therefore a grammar which neutralizes a voicing contrast in all contexts except in codas should be possible, even though it would be 'complex' (in the sense that different rules would be employed, instead of a single general one).

1.7.6 *Typology: some preliminary conclusions*
To wind up this section let us now summarize the results. At the heart of OT is the notion that grammars of individual languages instantiate general ranking schemata of constraints of different types. The basic method of checking the typological predictions made by the theory is that of constructing a factorial typology by the reranking of constraints of different types. In this section we have constructed a basic factorial typology of faithfulness and markedness, and found that all predicted types of input–output relationships are attested. By varying the ranking of faithfulness with respect to (context-free and context-sensitive) markedness constraints, we found a factorial typology which ranged from a situation of total neutralization on the one hand, to that of total freedom of contrast on the other hand. In between these extremes, we identified two intermediate situations: allophonic variation (a specific kind of neutralization which allows two values of some feature in the output), and positional neutralization (a situation in which a feature is contrastive, except in a specific context, in which it is neutralized). We elaborated on positional neutralization of voice in Dutch to demonstrate two typical properties of constraint interaction in OT. In the first place, we found that dominated constraints may still be active, in the sense that a constraint, even when it is violated, must be minimally violated. Secondly, we found that some output candidates are intrinsically suboptimal to others, regardless of ranking. This captures certain typological observations with respect to positional neutralization.

1.8 On defining segment inventories
This section will show how segment inventories result from interactions of faithfulness constraints and markedness constraints. The discussion is related to the

notion of Lexicon Optimization (section 1.6). As before, we will draw heavily on Prince and Smolensky (1993).

Recall that the main type of conflict in OT is that between markedness constraints and faithfulness constraints. Faithfulness constraints militate against any loss of contrast, enforcing identity between the input and the output. Markedness constraints are natural antagonists of faithfulness constraints, militating against marked structures in the output. They may produce the effect of a loss of a feature value present in the input, if that value is a 'marked' value.

1.8.1 *Markedness constraints on scales*

Markedness is intrinsically a relative notion. That is, which types of elements are 'marked' and which are 'unmarked' can be established only in comparison to other elements. For example, we cannot say that nasalized vowels are intrinsically marked; they are marked in relation to oral vowels only. Moreover, markedness often involves a hierarchy of segment types, each member of which is more marked than successive members of the hierarchy. For example, it has been argued in the literature on segmental markedness that *coronals* are universally less marked than *labials* (Paradis and Prunet 1991).

To capture this relative markedness of segment types, Prince and Smolensky (1993) introduce the idea that markedness relations can be organized in a scalar fashion, as in the 'harmony scale' Cor > Lab. Moreover, the ranking of constraints that govern markedness relations along a single dimension (such as place of articulation) is universally fixed. In the case in hand the constraints governing the relative markedness of labials and coronals are intrinsically ranked as below:

(63)   Universal ranking for markedness constraints governing place of articulation

         *[lab] $\gg$ *[cor]

Presumably this ranking is universal, hence respected by every constraint hierarchy. Note that, by itself, this partial ranking makes no predictions about which segments are actually attested in a segment inventory of a particular language, and which are not. Inventories emerge from interactions of markedness constraint hierarchies (as in 63) with faithfulness constraints, which serve to preserve input segmental contrasts in the output. Generally speaking, the higher faithfulness constraints are ranked, the larger the segment inventory will be. And vice versa, the lower faithfulness is ranked, the smaller the inventory.

1.8.2 *Interaction of markedness scales and faithfulness*

Now consider the faithfulness constraint militating against differences of place features in the input and output:

(64)   **IDENT-IO**(Place)
         The specification for place of articulation of an input segment must
         be preserved in its output correspondent.

This correspondence constraint is satisfied by (65a); but it is violated by (65b):

(65)   a. /p/ Input   b. /p/ Input
              | |
            [p] Output   [t] Output

Let us now consider two grammars differing only in the ranking of IDENT-
IO(Place) with respect to the markedness constraints of (63). One grammar that
we will consider ranks IDENT-IO(Place) above both markedness constraints:

(66)   A grammar that is maximally faithful to place of articulation
         IDENT-IO(Place) ≫ *[lab] ≫ *[cor]

This grammar is maximally faithful to its input place of articulation, due to high-
ranked IDENT-IO(Place). It is more important to be faithful to the input place of
articulation of a segment than to its output markedness. The tableaux (67.i–ii),
one for each input segment /p/ and /t/, illustrate this:

(67.i)

/...p.../	IDENT-IO(Place)	*[lab]	*[cor]
a. ☞ [...p...]		*	
b. [...t...]	*!		*

(67.ii)

/...t.../	IDENT-IO(Place)	*[lab]	*[cor]
a. [...p...]	*!	*	
b. ☞ [...t...]			*

These tableaux can be summarized as follows: whatever place of articulation is
specified at the lexical level will reach the surface level. Accordingly, the segment inventory of this language will contain two places of articulation: {labial,
coronal}.

Next consider a second grammar, which ranks IDENT-IO(Place) more modestly:

(68)   A grammar that is less faithful to place of articulation
         *[lab] ≫ IDENT-IO(Place) ≫ *[cor]

This grammar is less faithful (than the one in 66) to its input place features. It
blocks the surfacing of *any labial in the input* since the markedness constraint

militating against this segment type outranks the faithfulness constraint IDENT-IO(Place). Accordingly, any input labial surfaces as a coronal, if it surfaces at all:[16]

(69.i)

/...p.../	*[lab]	IDENT-IO(Place)	*[cor]
a. [...p...]	*!		
b. ☞ [...t...]		*	*

(69.ii)

/...t.../	*[lab]	IDENT-IO(Place)	*[cor]
a. [...p...]	*!	*	
b. ☞ [...t...]			*

This amounts to a *neutralization* (loss of contrast) of place-of-articulation features, in the favour of coronals. In fact the surface level of such a language would present no evidence whatsoever for input labials. For the learner, it would be senseless to set up a lexical contrast among labials and coronals, since such a contrast would be entirely overruled by markedness effects. Prince and Smolensky (1993) refer to the obscuring of input contrasts as 'Stampean occultation', stating it as a principle of *Lexicon Optimization* (see section 1.6).

1.8.3 *Conclusions and predictions*

In sum, we have found that the resulting consonant inventories depend on the ranking of faithfulness constraints with respect to the markedness constraints. With respect to place of articulation, we have found the following relation between ranking and inventory:

(70)   Ranking   Inventory
        a. IDENT-IO(Place) ≫ *[lab] ≫ *[cor]   {p, t}
        b. *[lab] ≫ IDENT-IO(Place) ≫ *[cor]   {t}

The interesting consequence of this approach is that segment inventories need no longer be stipulated at the level of lexical forms, as in derivational theory. Instead, the ranking of faithfulness constraints amongst markedness constraints is part of the grammar, hence it is automatically respected at the level of the output.

---

[16] Of course one might also consider the logical possibility that input labials are simply deleted – there is no way of telling the difference between both possibilities since it is impossible to establish the presence of input labials.

Derivational theory arrives at the same result by stipulating that the output of (lexical) rules must contain no segments that are not part of the input inventory: this is referred to as the 'structure-preserving' property of phonological rules (Kiparsky 1985).

Another interesting consequence of this theory of segmental markedness is that it predicts that 'unmarked' segments will emerge wherever faithfulness constraints are put 'out of control'. Some segment types in every inventory (for example, coronals) are less marked than other segments, even though the grammar allows both more and less marked segments at the surface level, due to high-ranked faithfulness constraints. However, given the chance, the grammar will still favour unmarked segments over marked segments. This occurs in special situations in which, for some reason, input faithfulness requirements no longer hold. This prediction has been confirmed robustly for a wide range of situations in a wide range of languages.

Consider, for example, *epenthesis*: a segment appears in the output exclusively for phonotactic reasons, as in the case of a vowel inserted to break up a consonant cluster. By its very nature, the inserted vowel lacks a counterpart in the input. It cannot be subject to input faithfulness, so that its featural content is fully determined by markedness factors. The prediction is that epenthetic segments are segmentally unmarked or easily influenced by segments in their contexts. This, and other related observations, is presented in (71).

(71)   a. *Epenthetic segments* are less marked than *'lexically sponsored' segments*.
         (Explanation: epenthetic segments have no input counterparts, hence they are 'free' of faithfulness constraints. See chapter 3.)
      b. *Segments in reduplicants* are less marked than *segments in their bases*.
         (Explanation: 'copied' segments have no input counterparts, hence they are 'free' of faithfulness constraints. See chapter 5.)
      c. *Segments in affixes* are less marked than *segments in roots*.
         (Explanation: 'affix faithfulness' is intrinsically lower-ranked than 'root faithfulness'. See chapters 5 and 9.)

The observations in (71a–c) will all be confirmed in later chapters, in the light of insights into faithfulness–markedness interactions.

1.9 Conclusion

In this chapter we have laid out the foundations on which OT is built, and pointed out the most important linguistic phenomena that fall in its scope. In the discussions throughout this chapter, one aspect of OT stood out: the interaction of faithfulness and markedness. We have seen that all general phonological phenomena discussed here are variations on this theme: the notion of contrast, and, related to this, allophonic variation, neutralization, and lexical representations, and finally, the notion of segment inventory. In every case, a phonological pattern resulted from (more or less complex) interactions of constraints that preserve lexical input properties (faithfulness), and others that reduce output markedness. In later chapters of this book, we will maintain this perspective, and generalize it to a range of other linguistic phenomena.

The following eight chapters of this book will each be devoted to a research topic in which OT has left its marks. Chapter 2 addresses functional relations among processes, comparing OT with rule-based theory from this perspective. Chapter 3 discusses syllable structure and related phenomena, such as syllabically governed epenthesis and deletion. Chapter 4 deals with metrical phenomena, particularly word stress and quantity effects. Chapter 5 addresses the morphology–phonology interface, focussing on reduplication, and also extends the notion of 'correspondence' beyond relations of input and output. Chapter 6 further extends correspondence to relations between morphologically related output forms, covering paradigm regularity. Chapter 7 is devoted to the issues of learnability and acquisition. Chapter 8 contains applications of OT outside phonology in syntax. Finally, chapter 9 discusses residual issues, focussing on issues that deserve further research (in particular, opacity) as well as on current theoretical developments.

SUGGESTIONS FOR FURTHER READING

General introductions to phonology

Goldsmith, John (1990) *Autosegmental and metrical phonology.* Oxford: Basil Blackwell.

Kaye, Jonathan (1990) *Phonology: a cognitive view.* Hillsdale: LEA.

Kenstowicz, Michael (1994a) *Phonology in generative grammar.* Oxford: Basil Blackwell.

Kenstowicz, Michael and Charles Kisseberth (1979) *Generative phonology: description and theory.* San Diego: Academic Press.

Roca, Iggy (1994) *Generative phonology.* London and New York: Routledge.

Constraints in phonology

Hayes, Bruce (1986) Inalterability in CV Phonology. *Language* **62**. 321–51.

McCarthy, John (1986) OCP effects: gemination and antigemination. *Linguistic Inquiry* **17**. 207–63.

Odden, David (1986) On the role of the Obligatory Contour Principle in phonological theory. *Language* **62**. 353–83.

Paradis, Carole (1988) On constraints and repair strategies. *The Linguistic Review* **6**. 71–97.

Yip, Moira (1988) The Obligatory Contour Principle and phonological rules: a loss of identity. *Linguistic Inquiry* **19**. 65–100.

General introductions to OT

Archangeli, Diana (1997) Optimality Theory: an introduction to linguistics in the 1990s. In D. Archangeli and D. T. Langendoen (eds.), *Optimality Theory: an introduction*. Oxford: Blackwell. 1–32.

Burzio, Luigi (1995) The rise of Optimality Theory. *Glot International* **1:6**. 3–7.

Prince, Alan and Paul Smolensky (1997) Optimality: from neural networks to universal grammar. *Science* **275**. 1604–10.

Sherrard, Nicholas (1997) Questions of priorities: an introductory overview of Optimality Theory in phonology. In Roca. 43–89.

Founding papers of OT

McCarthy, John (1993) A case of surface constraint violation. In C. Paradis and D. LaCharite (eds.), *Constraint-based theories in multilinear phonology*, special issue of *Canadian Journal of Linguistics* **38**. 169–95.

Prince, Alan and Paul Smolensky (1993) Optimality Theory: constraint interaction in generative grammar. Ms., Rutgers University, New Brunswick, and University of Colorado, Boulder. RuCCS-TR-2. [To appear, Cambridge, Mass.: MIT Press.]

Phonetic grounding of constraints

Archangeli, Diana and Douglas Pulleyblank (1994) *Grounded phonology*. Cambridge, Mass.: MIT Press.

Hayes, Bruce (1996a) Phonetically driven phonology: the role of Optimality Theory and inductive grounding. Ms., UCLA. [ROA-158, http://ruccs.rutgers.edu/roa.html]

Myers, Scott (1997b) Expressing phonetic naturalness in phonology. In Roca. 125–52.

Steriade, Donca. (1995b) *Positional neutralization*. Ms., University of California, Los Angeles.

Markedness and underspecification

Archangeli, Diana (1988) Aspects of underspecification theory. *Phonology* **5**.183–207.

Inkelas, Sharon (1995) The consequences of optimization for underspecification. In J. Beckman (ed.), *Proceedings of NELS* **25**. 287–302. [ROA-40, http://ruccs.rutgers.edu/roa.html]

Itô, Junko, R. Armin Mester, and Jaye Padgett (1995) Licensing and underspecification in Optimality Theory. *Linguistic Inquiry* **26**. 571–613.

Steriade, Donca (1995a) Underspecification and markedness. In Goldsmith. 114–74.

OT in computational phonology

Eisner, Jason (1997) Efficient generation in primitive Optimality Theory. *Proceedings of the 35th Annual Meeting of the Association for Computational Linguistics.* [ROA-206, http://ruccs.rutgers.edu/roa.html]

Ellison, Mark T. (1994) Phonological derivation in Optimality Theory. *Proceedings of the fifteenth International Conference on Computational Linguistics*, II. Kyoto, Japan. 1007–13. [ROA-75, http://ruccs.rutgers.edu/roa.html]

Hammond, Michael (1997) Parsing syllables: modeling OT computationally. Ms., University of Arizona. [ROA-222, http://ruccs.rutgers.edu/roa.html, parser code available from author, http://www.u.arizona.edu/~hammond]

Walther, Markus (1996) OT SIMPLE – A construction-kit approach to Optimality Theory implementation. Ms., Heinrich Heine Universität, Düsseldorf. [Software and paper can be downloaded from http://www.phil-fak.uni-duesseldorf.de/~walther/otsimple.html. Also ROA-152, http://ruccs.rutgers.edu/roa.html]

EXERCISES

1 Japanese

Consider the following distribution of [g] and [ŋ] in Japanese (Itô and Mester 1997):

(i)	geta	*ŋeta	'clogs'
	giri	*ŋiri	'duty'
	guchi	*ŋuchi	'complaint'
	go	*ŋo	'(game of) Go'
(ii)	kaŋi	*kagi	'key'
	kaŋo	*kago	'basket'
	kaŋŋae	*kaŋgae	'thought'
	tokaŋe	*tokage	'lizard'

    a.   State the generalization for the distribution of [g] and [ŋ]. Categorize this distribution in terms of the typology discussed in section 1.7.

    b.   Account for this generalization by a set of ranked constraints.

    c.   Support your analysis by tableaux of *geta* and *kaɲi*.

2 English

Consider the following English word pairs, some of which display alternations of voice:

(i)	cat	[kæt]	cats	[kæts]
	dog	[dɔg]	dogs	[dɔgz]
	hen	[hen]	hens	[henz]
(ii)	twelve	[twelv]	twelfth	[twelfθ]
	eight	[eɪt]	eighth	[eɪtθ]
	ten	[ten]	tenth	[tenθ]

    a.   What are the underlying forms of the suffixes in (i) and (ii)?

    b.   To account for these alternations, you need a new constraint. State this constraint (as generally as possible). To what extent is this constraint phonetically grounded?

    c.   Rank the constraints, motivating each individual ranking by at least one form. Support your analysis by tableaux of *cats, dogs, hens, twelfth*, and *eighth*.

2
The typology of structural changes

2.1 Introduction

In this chapter we will learn how a range of phonological processes can be triggered by a single markedness constraint, depending on its interactions with faithfulness constraints. *Unity in diversity* among processes is predicted by OT, due to its surface-oriented nature. To satisfy a markedness constraint in the output, various 'repair strategies' can be applied to the input; whichever is chosen depends on the relative ranking of different faithfulness constraints. The main result of this chapter will be a typological one: functionally related phonological processes arise by reranking universal constraints. This factorial typology of processes is based on *Correspondence Theory* (McCarthy and Prince 1995a, forthcoming), a subtheory of faithfulness constraints allowing a limited set of structural changes, such as deletions, insertions, fusions, and featural changes.

This chapter is organized as follows. Section 2.1 will compare OT and rule-based theory with respect to their core devices: constraints versus rewrite rules. Section 2.2 will discuss the analysis of Pater (forthcoming) of nasal substitution in Indonesian, a process avoiding NÇ̊ (a nasal-and-voiceless-obstruent sequence) and introduce major correspondence constraints. Section 2.3 will develop the factorial typology of NÇ̊ effects, while section 2.4 will focus on 'conspiracies' of related processes within a language. Finally, section 2.5 will present conclusions.

2.1.1 *An initial comparison with rule-based theory*

In classical generative phonology the grammar is an input–output mechanism, just as it is in OT. However, the key mechanism is the *rewrite rule*, rather than the output constraint. An example of a rewrite rule is devoicing of obstruents in the coda (Dutch, chapter 1):

(1)   Coda devoicing as a rewrite rule
         $[-son] \rightarrow [-voice] / \underline{\quad}]_\sigma$

Although rewrite rules are language-specific in the sense that not all grammars share the same set of rules, their format is universal. A, B, X, and Y are natural classes of elements:

(2)   Format of context-sensitive rewrite rule
          A → B / X ___ Y

Element A (the *focus*) is rewritten as element B in the *context* of elements X and Y. Each rule makes precisely one '*structural change*' (A → B) to the input. For a rule to apply to an input, the input must match the rule's '*structural description*' (XAY). The structural change eliminates the configuration XAY, resulting into the output configuration (XBY).

(3)   Application of a rewrite rule
          Input: ... XAY ...
                       ⇓
          Output: ... XBY ...

The repertory of structural changes to be described by rewrite rules includes *permutations* (replacement of 'A' by 'B', both non-null), *insertions* (where 'A' is null), and *deletions* (where 'B' is null).

2.1.1.1   *Triggers and changes*
We may distinguish two aspects in each context-sensitive rewrite rule:

(4)   Two aspects of context-sensitive rewrite rules
          a. a *structural description*, XAY, which defines the rule's input, a
             'trigger'
          b. a *structural change*, A → B, which defines the rule's output
             (XBY)

Each aspect has a counterpart in OT. First, the *trigger* is a negative constraint (*XAY), defining a configuration to be avoided. Second, the *structural change* becomes a context-free rewrite operation (A → B), which is attributed to the *Generator* component, one out of many changes possible under Freedom of Analysis.

Since *Gen* is contextually blind, 'application' of a process fully depends on *Eval*, more specifically on the language-specific interaction of a markedness constraint (*XAY) and a faithfulness constraint militating against this change (*A → B):

(5)   Trigger and anti-change in OT
　　　　a. *XAY   'Avoid the configuration XAY' (markedness)
　　　　b. *A → B 'A must not be realized as B' (faithfulness)

For the structural change to apply, the faithfulness constraint must be dominated by the markedness constraint – the 'trigger'. In the reverse ranking, the change will not apply.

(6)   Application and non-application in OT
　　　　a. Ranking for 'application':   Markedness ≫ Faithfulness
　　　　　　　　　　　　　　　　　　　　　*XAY   ≫ *A → B
　　　　b. Ranking for 'non-application': Faithfulness ≫ Markedness
　　　　　　　　　　　　　　　　　　　　　*A → B   ≫ *XAY

For example, IDENT-IO(voice) is dominated by *VOICED-CODA in Dutch, while English has the reverse ranking. We have now distinguished two aspects in rewrite rules, 'trigger' and 'change', and seen how OT decomposes processes into pairs of antagonistic constraints.

2.1.1.2   *The notion of 'structural change'*

Until here the OT and rule-based scenarios match fairly well: both identify element /A/ as a focus of change, triggered by a structural description or a negative constraint *XAY. However, we now arrive at an important point of difference. OT predicts that the output goal of avoiding *XAY is attainable in various ways. That is, whatever structural change A → B may represent, it is only one out of a range of changes generated by *Gen*, none of which is bound to a specific structural description. On Freedom of Analysis, *Gen* is free to propose any kind of change to the input element /A/, including 'no change' at all:

(7)   Some candidate analyses of an input /... XAY .../

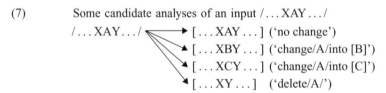

/... XAY .../ ⟶ [... XAY ...] ('no change')
　　　　　　　　[... XBY ...] ('change/A/into [B]')
　　　　　　　　[... XCY ...] ('change/A/into [C]')
　　　　　　　　[... XY ...]　('delete/A/')

For example, *VOICED-CODA in Dutch is satisfied by obstruent devoicing, but potentially it might also have been satisfied by obstruent deletion or coda nasalization.

　　Satisfaction of *XAY is not uniquely achieved by changes in /A/, but may equally well arise as a result of changes in any of its neighbouring segments X or Y, by insertion of an element B, or more generally by any change eliminating [XAY]:

(8)　　　More candidate analyses of an input /...XAY.../, which leave 'A' unaffected

/...XAY.../   → [AY]   ('delete /X/')
              [XAB]   ('change /Y/ into [B]')
              [XABY] ('insert [B] between A and Y')
              [XA]   ('delete /Y/')

All analyses proposed by *Gen* are submitted to *Eval* for parallel evaluation. Crucially, all candidate analyses of (7) which change /A/ are evaluated in a single pool of candidates together with those of (8), which employ different types of changes. Each analysis has a 'price tag' attached, in terms of constraint violations. The single analysis that is perfectly faithful to the input, /XAY/, is the canonical violator of the *markedness* constraint *XAY. All candidate analyses changing the input violate one or the other *faithfulness* constraint, depending on the nature of the change. Hence, the relative success of each candidate fully depends on the interaction of *XAY with other constraints.

If *XAY is undominated, *some change* must be made. The nature of this change (deletion, insertion, feature change, etc.) depends upon the relative ranking of faithfulness constraints. Generally speaking, the *lowest-ranking* faithfulness constraint is the one to be violated in the actual output. For example, any grammar in which 'segment preservation' (MAX-IO) outranks 'featural identity' (IDENT-IO) will prefer a featural change 'A → B' to the deletion of 'A'. Other structural changes arise under different rankings of faithfulness constraints, yielding a factorial typology of structural changes. (See section 2.3.)

2.1.2 *Two differences between OT and rule-based theory*

2.1.2.1 *Conspiracies and the functional unity of processes*

In the preceding discussion, we have learned that rule-based and constraint-based theories differ in the following way. In rule-based theory, the structural condition and structural change are *linked* in the rule; a rule uniquely determines the structural change in response to the structural condition. In OT, structural condition and structural changes must always be evaluated among other possible resolutions of constraint violations. Therefore OT predicts that a markedness constraint may trigger various types of structural changes, depending on its interaction with faithfulness constraints. Different languages should therefore pursue different 'repair strategies' in attaining identical output goals. (In section 2.4 we will see that different repair strategies may even occur within a single language as a result of a single constraint ranking.)

In contrast, rule-based theory fails to make this prediction of the functional unity of processes because it has no formal means of expressing the notion of 'output goal' of a phonological rule. The functional unity among rules attaining the same goal, either within a single language or across languages, remains unexplained. This problem was signalled as early as Kisseberth (1970) in a paper carrying the meaningful title 'On the functional unity of phonological rules'. As an example, consider the set of rules in (9). All function to avoid the configuration *XAY, yet these rules cannot be formally related:

(9)   A set of functionally coherent rules
        a. A → B / X ___ Y   d. Y → Z / XA ___
        b. A → C / X ___ Y   e. Ø → B / XA ___Y
        c. A → Ø / X ___ Y   f. X → Ø / ___ AY

This reoccurrence of a common output factor which guides different rules, without being explicitly stated in the rules, is called a *conspiracy* (Kisseberth 1970). As we will see in section 2.2, functionally related processes are straightforwardly dealt with by OT.

Another observation difficult to explain by rule-based theory is that the 'dynamic' phonology of a language (structural changes brought about by the collective rewrite rules) is closely related to the 'static' phonology (the structural conditions holding for all lexical items: *Morpheme Structure Constraints*). For example, a rule of vowel epenthesis breaking up a consonant cluster arising by morpheme concatenation satisfies a goal generally respected by all morphemes of the language. Output goals of rules are mirrored by the structure of morphemes, without any formal recognition of this similarity in the grammar. This defect is known as the *Duplication Problem* (Kenstowicz and Kisseberth 1977).

Before OT, phonologists had already realized that output constraints are necessary ingredients of grammatical theory. As a response to rule conspiracies and the Duplication Problem, they introduced output constraints to block or trigger the application of rules. Among the first output constraints were the OCP in autosegmental theory ('no identical adjacent autosegments', Goldsmith 1976), and the No-Clash constraint in metrical theory (Liberman 1975). Such additions resulted in mixed models, containing both rules and output constraints. Various proposals were made for interactions of rules and constraints, such as the *Theory of Constraints and Repair Strategies* (Paradis 1988), and *Persistent Rule Theory* (Myers 1991).

Mixed models naturally lead to overlapping functions of rules and constraints, as rules preserve specific structural conditions. These state configurations to be 'repaired' by a structural change, hence they are interpretable as 'rule-specific negative constraints'. Output targets are stated both in the rules and in the constraints, producing an overlap in theoretical machinery.

But problems of mixed models do not end with a certain amount of conceptual overlap. Such models involve an extremely complicated interaction of rules and constraints. A rule may apply in violation of a constraint, which violation is later 'repaired' by some subsequent rule. Therefore a mixed model must not only stipulate structural conditions of the rules and the linear ordering of the rules, but also interactions of rules and output constraints, defining the conditions under which output constraints can be 'temporarily' violated. OT avoids such interactional complexity by limiting grammatical interactions to constraints. This *unification of interaction* makes OT, both conceptually and computationally, a much simpler theory than any mixed model.

The next question, to be addressed below, is: are rule-based grammars and OT grammars equivalent in the sense that they may perform the same kinds of input–output mappings?

2.1.2.2 *Intermediate levels in derivations*
The second major difference from rule-based theory resides in the notion of 'derivation'. In rule-based theory, application of rules follows the principle of *linear* (*serial*) *ordering*, rather than a parallel mapping according to a hierarchy of 'importance', as in OT. Linearly ordered rewrite rules map inputs into outputs by a derivation:

(10)   A derivational grammar as an input–output mechanism

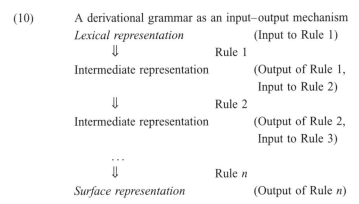

Lexical representation	(Input to Rule 1)
⇓　　　　　Rule 1	
Intermediate representation	(Output of Rule 1, Input to Rule 2)
⇓　　　　　Rule 2	
Intermediate representation	(Output of Rule 2, Input to Rule 3)
. . .	
⇓　　　　　Rule *n*	
Surface representation	(Output of Rule *n*)

What is essential about a derivation is that *each step* is a miniature input–output mapping. That is, a rewrite rule takes as its input a state of affairs left by the previous rule, makes a change, and passes its output on to the next rewrite rule. In a derivation the application of a rule solely depends on whether the structural description is met by the output of the immediately preceding rule. Rules are

57

blind to their own outputs, which they produce mechanically. Moreover, each rule is blind to the output of the derivation as a whole, which arises only after the last rule has applied. It is thus predicted that the application of a rule can never depend on its eventual consequences at the surface.

To appreciate the unlimited potential of intermediate representations in rule-based theory, consider the following hypothetical derivation.

(11)   Lexical form: /XAY/
          Rule 1 A → B / X ___   XBY
          Rule 2 Y → Z / B ___   XBZ
          Rule 3 B → C / X ___ Z   XCZ
          Surface form: [XCZ]

Segment B is first introduced by Rule 1, then triggers a change in a neighbouring segment Y due to Rule 2, and is finally deleted by Rule 3. Segment B, which plays an active role in the derivation, is not present in the input nor in the output. It is *abstract*, being present only at an intermediate stage of the representation between the application of Rules 1 and 3. Rule-based theory predicts that such situations should occur in natural languages, since they arise as a natural consequence of rule interaction.

In contrast, OT attributes major importance to the surface level in the interaction of constraints, disallowing access to intermediary levels between the input and output. Constraints refer to either the *output alone* (in markedness constraints), or the *input and output in combination* (in faithfulness constraints of the 'correspondence' format). This predicts that no property of phonological forms depends on information that is not present in the output – either in the output alone, or in the relation between the input and output.

It is, of course, an empirical matter to decide on the correctness of this prediction. Do phonologies of natural languages ever show the degree of abstractness predicted by rule-based theory, as illustrated in derivation (11)? It has been argued, on the basis of evidence from well-studied cases, that phonological rules may refer to elements at a level of representation that does not coincide with the output (see Kisseberth 1969 on Yokuts). In most of such cases this level was identified as the input, which is not an intermediate level. But in other cases the abstract element was indeed argued to be introduced by rule (see Brame 1974 on Palestinian Arabic). Both types of 'opacity' are potential problems for surface-oriented OT – we will return to this issue in chapter 9. Meanwhile, however, it seems fair to conclude that the radical abstractness of the type (11) that rule-based theory predicts to be possible in natural languages is rarely – if ever – attested. Overwhelmingly, phonological generalizations refer to the *output*, possibly in relation to the input.

2.2 Nasal substitution and related effects

In this section we will look into evidence from segmental phonology which supports both predictions made in section 2.1. First we will find that a single markedness constraint can trigger an array of structural changes, even within a single language. Discussion will be based on the analysis of nasal substitution and related effects by Pater (forthcoming). This analysis is couched in the framework of Correspondence Theory, a subtheory of OT which allows a limited set of structural changes (McCarthy and Prince 1995a). Second, we will find that the surface level is essential in capturing phonological generalizations.

2.2.1 *Nasal substitution in Indonesian*

The well-known pattern of nasal substitution in Indonesian (e.g., Halle and Clements 1983) appears in verbs prefixed by /məN-/ (where '/N/' indicates a nasal that is not specified for place of articulation):

(12)   Nasal substitution in Indonesian
          a.i   /məN-pilih/   məmilih   'to choose, to vote'
          a.ii   /məN-tulis/   mənulis   'to write'
          a.iii /məN-kasih/   məŋasih   'to give'
          b.i   /məN-bəlih/   məmbəlih   'to buy'
          b.ii   /məN-dapat/   məndapat   'to get, to receive'
          b.iii /məN-ganti/   məŋganti   'to change'

The generalization can be stated as follows: when the input contains a sequence of a nasal followed by a *voiceless obstruent*, the latter is deleted, leaving its place of articulation on the nasal. This is arguably a case of *coalescence* (segment fusion), since the consonant in the output has the characteristics of both input counterparts: the nasality of the lefthand consonant, and the place of articulation of the righthand consonant. Turning to (12b), we see that a voiced obstruent is retained in the output form, as part of a nasal-plus-voiced-obstruent cluster. At the lexical level, the forms in (12a) differ from those in (12b) only in their voicing of the first stem consonant.

To reinforce the arguments for the coalescence analysis, let us first try to sidestep it by breaking the substitution pattern into two ordered rules. Such an analysis is actually possible, but we will soon find that it is inadequate. It runs as follows. Nasal assimilation copies the place of articulation of the obstruent onto the nasal; then a second rule deletes a voiceless consonant which follows a nasal:[1]

---

[1] This is a so-called 'counterbleeding' rule order: deletion might have eliminated the context of application for assimilation by applying first, but failed to do so. The reverse 'bleeding' rule order is discussed below. See chapter 9 for further discussion of counterbleeding in OT.

(13)   Nasal substitution as a sequence of rules
         Lexical form: /məN-pilih/ /məN-bəlih/
         Nasal assimilation   məmpilih   məmbəlih
         Post-nasal voiceless consonant deletion məmilih   ---
         Surface form: [məmilih]   [məmbəlih]

Pater (following Stahlke 1976) points out that an ordered rule analysis predicts
that both rules should occur independently. While nasal assimilation is a cross-
linguistically highly common process, no typological evidence seems to exist for
the second rule in isolation. That is, 'post-nasal voiceless consonant deletion'
seems always to apply in combination with nasal assimilation. By splitting the
process of nasal substitution into two parts, the incorrect prediction is made that
assimilation and deletion may apply in the reverse order in different languages,
as in the derivation below:

(14)   Nasal substitution: the 'dumb' rule order
         Lexical form: /məN-pilih/ /məN-bəlih/
         Post-nasal voiceless consonant deletion məNilih   ---
         Nasal assimilation   ---   məmbəlih
         Surface form: [məɲilih]   [məmbəlih]

In sum, the fact that the two changes cannot be typologically disentangled, and
the fact that the nasal always preserves the place of articulation of the deleted
consonant, both point to a *coalescence*: the input nasal and voiceless stop merge
into a single nasal of the place of articulation of the input stop. An ordered rule
analysis entirely misses this point. (See de Haas 1988 for similar arguments about
vowel coalescence.)

There is independent evidence for the coalescence analysis within the phonology of Indonesian. Consider the reduplication pattern of prefixed roots (Lapoliwa
1981):

(15)   a. /məN-kata-RED-i/   məɲata-ɲata -i 'to speak ill of someone'
         b. /məN-gərak-RED/   məŋgərak-gərak 'to move something
                                                              repeatedly'
         c. /məN-əlu-RED-kan/ məɲəlu-əlu-kan 'to praise'

Examples (15b–c) show that the nasal of a prefix is not normally copied by
reduplication, and that reduplication is limited to segments of the root. The prefix-
final nasal in (15c) is [ŋ], a nasal with the default place of articulation. But
example (15a) shows that a prefixal nasal that is the result of 'nasal substitution'
is copied along. The criterion for the copying of a nasal cannot be that it is

assimilated to the place of articulation of a root consonant. This is because both (15a) and (15b) involve assimilation, while only the nasal in (15a) is copied. Therefore the criterion for copying must be stronger: a nasal is copied only if it results from fusion with the root consonant. In copying the material of the root, the nasal must be copied along, simply because it is (partly) made up of a root segment.

Assuming the correctness of the coalescence analysis, the first question which we must ask is this: why are voiced obstruents preserved, but voiceless obstruents coalesced? Pater argues that the coalescence is triggered by a prohibition against sequences of a nasal and a voiceless obstruent, stated as a contextual markedness constraint:

(16)   ***NC̥**
            No nasal plus voiceless obstruent sequences.

This markedness constraint *NC̥ is *grounded* in articulatory mechanisms as follows (see, among others, Huffman 1993, Hayes and Stivers 1995).[2] Nasal consonants involve airflow through the nose, which is achieved by lowering the velum, the valve separating the oral and nasal cavities. Going from a nasal consonant into an obstruent involves a raising of the velum, cutting off the air from passing through the nose. However, the raising of the velum takes some time and is not yet completed at the point where the obstruent begins. At that point (which is actually perceptually determined), there is still a bit of air flowing out of the nose, so-called 'nasal leak'. As long as air is flowing, this will facilitate voicing. There is a second factor facilitating voicing throughout the nasal-plus-obstruent cluster. Once the velum is raised high enough to cut off nasal leak, it continues to rise toward the high position characteristic of obstruents. Consequently the volume of the oral cavity expands, rarefying the air column sitting above the glottis. This causes a small leak of air through the glottis, again facilitating prolonged voicing. Both mechanisms, nasal leak and velum raising, cooperate to facilitate continuous voicing throughout a nasal-obstruent cluster. In sum, a nasal-plus-voiced obstruent cluster is more phonetically natural than a nasal-plus-voiceless-obstruent cluster.

The post-nasal voicing effect is wide-spread in the world's languages. Moreover, it occurs in child language (Drachman and Malikouti-Drachman 1973, Smith 1973, Vogel 1976, cited in Pater forthcoming). The markedness constraint *NC̥ (15) directly encodes the phonetic basis of the effect. Pater (forthcoming) shows that *NC̥ produces a range of effects in various languages, of which nasal

---

[2] There is a complementary perceptual explanation due to Ohala and Ohala (1993).

substitution is only one. Moreover, the full range of effects is due to interactions of *NÇ with other (mostly faithfulness) constraints.

We first consider the analysis of *nasal substitution.* In Indonesian, *NÇ is ranked sufficiently high so as to disallow outputs containing a nasal plus voiceless obstruent.[3] Indonesian uses nasal substitution (or fusion) as a strategy to resolve violations of *NÇ. Clearly fusion involves some divergence from the input form, hence a violation of some faithfulness constraint. To find out which faithfulness constraint is violated under fusion, let us consider the correspondence diagram of the fusion of the input sequence /N–p/:

(17)   Correspondence diagram for fusion
        Input: $N_1 \, p_2$
                  \\/
        Output: $m_{1,2}$

Fusion is a 'split' correspondence between a pair of input segments and a single output segment. This involves violation of some faithfulness constraint(s), as the input segments /N, p/ do not stand in a perfect one-to-one relation with two output segments. The broken one-to-one relation between the input and output has two aspects: *feature identity* and *segment correspondence.*

With respect to *feature identity* it will be clear that the fusion of two non-identical segments typically involves the violation of some IDENT-IO constraints. This is because a single output segment cannot preserve the feature specifications of *both* input segments if these are conflicting. In a fusion of /N–p/ into [m], for example, featural specifications of both input segments /N, p/ are preserved, except for the manner features of input /p/. For /p/, the features specifying sonority class, nasality, and voicing fail to reoccur in output [m], leading to violation of various IDENT-IO constraints. On the other hand, some feature specifications of the input segments are preserved. Place of articulation of input /p/ is preserved in output [m], as well as manner of input /N/. Nor is there any loss of identity for place of articulation for input /N/, which is arguably unspecified for place features. On the whole, we find that violations of featural identity are minimal: they are limited to manner of the input obstruent.

As Pater points out, OT predicts that segment fusion should be more likely when the input segments are more similar: that is, when the violation of faithfulness constraints involved is relatively small. We will return to the role of featural

---

[3] Below we will find that NÇ-sequences do occur root-internally in Indonesian. Then we will address the issue of what makes nasal substitution apply only across morpheme boundaries.

faithfulness in fusion in more detail in section 2.2.2. There we will also address the question of what causes the obstruent (rather than the nasal) to give up its manner specifications.

The second aspect of fusion is pure *segment correspondence*, disregarding feature content. Consider again the correspondence diagram of fusion in (17), in which two input segments correspond to a single output segment. Observe that no input segment is deleted since both input segments have output correspondents. Nor is any segment inserted in the output (that is not present in the input). However, some information is lost in the output that was still present in the input: the *linear ordering* of the input segments.

Accordingly Pater adopts the following correspondence constraint:[4]

(18)   **LINEARITY-IO**
        The output reflects the precedence structure of the input, and vice versa.

This constraint is violated by diagram (17) in the following way. In the input the segment /N/ precedes the segment /p/. Both segments share a correspondent [m] in the output. But no precedence relation is defined on the output segment [m], since it is not a sequence of segments but a single segment. (Of course, the subscripts on input and output segments have nothing to do with linear ordering.) The output has lost information that was present in the input (its precedence structure) – a clear violation of faithfulness.

Pater argues that LINEARITY-IO is independently needed in correspondence theory as the constraint militating against *metathesis*. Metathesis is the phenomenon of two segments reversing their linear order:

(19)   Correspondence diagram for metathesis

        Input: C_1 C_2

        Output: C_2 C_1

---

[4] McCarthy and Prince (1995a) argue for a separate anti-coalescence constraint: UNIFORMITY:

(i)   UNIFORMITY-IO
        No element of the output has multiple correspondents in the input.

Contrary to LINEARITY, this makes no demands on the linear ordering of morphemes in the input. This is a genuine advantage, as the assumption that morphemes are linearly ordered in the input is problematic, as we will see in chapter 5 on reduplication. (For linear ordering of morphemes may well depend on phonological information that is not present in the input.) See also Lamontagne and Rice (1995) for analysis of coalescence in Correspondence Theory.

Again, no segments are deleted or inserted, but the precedence structure is not preserved in the output.

We now return to the analysis of nasal substitution in Indonesian and consider the ranking of the constraints introduced so far. The very fact that LINEARITY-IO is violated in nasal substitution (i.e. coalescence) gives evidence that *NÇ ranks above LINEARITY-IO. The ranking argument has the following logical form:

(20)   Faithful   < Coalesced   Markedness ≫ Faithfulness
         candidate   candidate
         məm₁p₂ilih < məm₁,₂ilih *therefore* *NÇ   ≫ LINEARITY-IO

That is, the faithful candidate [məm₁p₂ilih] is less harmonic than the coalesced candidate [məm₁,₂ilih]. From this it follows that *NÇ (the constraint that is violated in the 'losing' candidate [məm₁p₂ilih]) dominates LINEARITY-IO (the constraint that is violated in the 'winning' candidate [məm₁,₂ilih]).

This ranking argument is proved by the following tableau:

(21)

Input: /məN₁-p₂ilih/	*NÇ	LINEARITY-IO
a. məm₁p₂ilih	*!	
b. ☞ məm₁,₂ilih		*

This is the basis of the analysis of nasal substitution: a contextual markedness constraint (*NÇ) dominates a faithfulness constraint (LINEARITY-IO).

2.2.2 *Alternative strategies to satisfy *NÇ*

Next we consider the question of what logically possible strategies other than nasal substitution might have satisfied *NÇ. The alternative strategies are: *deletion, epenthesis, post-nasal voicing*, and *denasalization*. We will find that all of these processes, except epenthesis, are attested in some language other than Indonesian. In a rule format, these processes are given below:

(22)   a. Deletion   [+nas] → Ø   /   ___ [−voice]
         b. Epenthesis   Ø → ə   / [+nas] ___ [−voice]
         c. Post-nasal voicing [−son] → [+voice] / [+nas] ___
         d. Denasalization   [+nas] → [−nas]   /   ___ [−voice]

Written in the standard rule format, these four processes seem to have little in common. But a generalization lurks beneath the surface: all four processes apply in the context of a nasal plus voiceless consonant. To put it even more strongly: all four processes have the effect of 'undoing' this context: they avoid the violation of *NÇ. However, this functional unity is left unexpressed in the rule format. Consider the following hypothetical rule, applying in the same context of nasal plus voiceless consonant:

(23)   Post-nasal spirantization [−voice] → [+continuant] / [+nas] ___

Judging by its context of application, this hypothetical rule falls into the same 'class' of rules as those in (22). Yet it has a completely different status, since it fails to avoid a violation of *NÇ. In order to express the typologically favoured status of these rules over other rules that apply in the same context, such as (23), the markedness criterion of rule-based theory must have the power to detect the output goals of rules. However, the 'goal' of a rule can be detected only by taking into consideration both its structural context (here: NÇ) and its structural change (here: *undoing* NÇ). To detect a rule's goal is, by itself, in contradiction to the fundamental assumption of rule-based theory that rules apply blindly, ignorant of their eventual effects at the surface. Building surface-sensitivity into rules would move rule-based theory closer to surface-oriented OT – see again section 2.1.2.1.

The fact that all four processes in (22) except vowel epenthesis are typologic-ally attested is by itself sufficient reason to favour a theory which expresses their functional unity. But an even stronger case is made by Pater on the basis of the observation that some of these processes cooccur within a single language. While the occurrence of functionally related rules in different languages might still be taken as coincidental, their cooccurrence in the same language is an even stronger argument for OT. These cases will be discussed in section 2.3.

The actual response to *NÇ in a particular language follows from the interac-tion of *NÇ with the set of faithfulness constraints. The logic of this interaction can be stated as follows. Assume some high-ranked markedness constraint, such as *NÇ. To satisfy it, a change is necessary, which will inevitably violate *some* faithfulness constraint. By itself the fact that some change is to be made does not predict *which* change will be made. But we know beforehand that the grammar will militate against any change regardless of what it may be, simply because any change will violate at least some faithfulness constraint. It may seem as if every grammar makes the following contradictory requirement:

(24)   Repair the configuration *NÇ, but
         • do not change a segment (nasal or obstruent) into another segment;
         • do not fuse two segments (nasal and obstruent) into a single segment;
         • do not delete a segment (nasal or obstruent);
         • do not insert a segment.

This is like making the impossible requirement: 'remove the stain from the carpet, but do not use water, or foam, or acid, or scissors, or...' How to break the spell?

However, the requirement in (24) is contradictory only when each of the logically possible changes is equally 'expensive' in terms of violations of faithfulness. Of course, in OT structural changes are never equally expensive, due to strict domination. Therefore, the relative ranking of the faithfulness constraints determines the change which serves as 'repair' of *NÇ. This is the central insight which lies at the heart of OT's ability to deal with functionally related processes – that is, with process typology.

Now let us assume a schematic hierarchy as in (25). The top-ranking markedness constraint *NÇ is, potentially at least, satisfiable by the violation of any constraint of the set {Faith-IO$_1$ ... Faith-IO$_n$}:

(25)   *NÇ, Faith-IO$_1$ ≫ Faith-IO$_2$ ... ≫ Faith-IO$_n$

Violation must be minimal, hence the grammar will select output forms which satisfy the higher-ranking constraints, at the expense of violations of lower-ranking constraints. This means that the *lowest-ranking* faithfulness constraint will be violated. In sum, the specific method which a language selects to satisfy some high-ranking markedness constraint only depends on the lowest-ranking faithfulness constraint. (In terms of the stained carpet analogue used above, one might say that using scissors or acid to remove the stain would ruin the carpet, outweighing the gains, so that the least expensive option is using foam, at least if water does not do the job.)

Next observe that the relative ranking of the faithfulness constraints that dominate Faith-IO$_n$ is immaterial to the outcome. The violation of Faith-IO$_n$ alone suffices to avoid violation of all other constraints; this is to say that no further violations of higher-ranking faithfulness constraints are necessary. Since unnecessary violations are *always* avoided, none of the faithfulness constraints dominating Faith-IO$_n$ will in fact be violated. This, in its turn, means that we will typically find no positive evidence for the mutual ranking of the set of higher-ranking faithfulness constraints. Positive evidence for ranking is always contingent upon the violation of a constraint in the actual form. Therefore all we know is that Faith-IO$_n$ is ranked below *all* the other faithfulness constraints. The ranking of the set of remaining faithfulness constraints cannot be established.

For Indonesian we already know that the dominated constraint Faith-IO$_n$ must be Linearity-IO. We now substitute Linearity-IO in (25), and also replace the abstract set of faithfulness constraints {Faith-IO$_1$, Faith-IO$_2$...} by the set of informal faithfulness constraints of (24). After doing this, we arrive at:

(26)   *NC̥, *No-deletion, No-epenthesis, No-denasalization, No-voicing* ≫
            LINEARITY-IO

But this is, of course, not the end of the story. We must now formalize the
constraints that are loosely referred to as 'No-deletion', 'No-epenthesis', etc. in
(26) as *correspondence constraints*, which militate against divergences of input
and output along one dimension. Informally, the general format of this type of
constraint is as follows:

(27)   *Correspondence constraint*: the output equals the input for some
            property *P*.

We already know two correspondence constraints from chapter 1: IDENT-
IO(voice) and IDENT-IO(nasal), both members of the IDENTITY family of constraints. In both of these constraints the relevant 'property P' was *featural identity*
of corresponding segments. We now see that LINEARITY-IO is another example
of a correspondence constraint, matching *linear order* of corresponding segments.
The anti-deletion and anti-epenthesis statements of (24) require new types of
correspondence constraints. Let us now see what these are.

2.2.2.1 *Deletion and MAX-IO*

The first strategy that Indonesian might have employed to satisfy *NC̥ is to simply
delete one of the input segments (nasal or voiceless obstruent). For example,
the deletion of the nasal in /məN₁-p₂ilih/ would produce an unattested output
*[məp₂ilih], where *NC̥ would be (trivially) satisfied since the nasal is no longer
present. However, such deletion would violate the correspondence constraint
MAX-IO.

(28)   **MAX-IO**
            Input segments must have output correspondents.
            ('No deletion')

The violation of MAX-IO in the suboptimal output [məp₂ilih] is illustrated by the
diagram below. Note that input /N₁/ lacks an output correspondent:

(29)   Correspondence diagram for nasal deletion
            Input: N₁ p₂
                        |
            Output: p₂

The very fact that this strategy is left unemployed in Indonesian points to the
conclusion that MAX-IO dominates LINEARITY-IO:

(30)   Max-IO ≫ Linearity-IO

məp$_2$ilih < məm$_{1,2}$ilih

That is, the preservation of input segments in the output has a higher priority than the preservation of precedence relations of the input. This ranking argument is proved correct by tableau (31):[5]

(31)

Input: /məN$_1$-p$_2$ilih/	Max-IO	*NÇ̥	Linearity-IO
a. məp$_2$ilih	*!		
b. ☞ məm$_{1,2}$ilih			*

We simply add Max-IO to the set of undominated constraints, since there is no evidence for its ranking with respect to *NÇ̥. (Since we focus here on the candidates relevant to the ranking of Max-IO and Linearity-IO, we omit the 'fully faithful' analysis [məm$_1$p$_2$ilih] from this tableau and those that follow. This is of course ruled out by undominated *NÇ̥.) Later we will see that some languages actually select nasal deletion as a strategy to satisfy *NÇ̥. The difference between Indonesian and these 'deleting' languages will be construed as a difference in constraint ranking.

2.2.2.2 *Epenthesis and Dep-IO*

A second strategy to satisfy *NÇ̥, one which simultaneously satisfies Linearity-IO, is epenthesis of a segment between the nasal and obstruent, undoing their adjacency. With schwa as epenthetic vowel, this would produce an incorrect output *[məŋ$_1$əp$_2$ilih]. Epenthesis violates another important segment correspondence constraint, Dep-IO. This militates against segments in the output that have no correspondents in the input.

(32)   **Dep-IO**

Output segments must have input correspondents.

('No epenthesis')

A diagram illustrates the violation of Dep-IO in [məŋ$_1$əp$_2$ilih]:

---

[5] To complete formally the argument that Max-IO dominates Linearity-IO, we must show that a third candidate [məp$_2$ilih], which deletes input /N/, does not violate Linearity-IO. (If both 31a and 31b were to violate Linearity-IO, then Max-IO would be decisive regardless of its ranking.) On a more formal interpretation of Linearity-IO, this constraint cannot be violated under deletion. That is, precedence relations can only be distinct if both input segments have correspondents in the output.

(33)   Correspondence diagram for schwa epenthesis

    Input: N_1 p_2
             | |
    Output: η_1 ə p_2

The output segment [ə] lacks an input correspondent, in violation of DEP-IO.

The observation that the epenthetic output *[məŋ₁əp₂ilih] is ill-formed again leads to a ranking argument of a type that is now familiar:

(34)   DEP-IO ≫ LINEARITY-IO
        məŋ₁əp₂ilih < məm₁,₂ilih

Tableau (35) confirms the correctness of this ranking:

(35)

Input: /məN₁-p₂ilih/	DEP-IO	*NC̥	LINEARITY-IO
a. məŋ₁əp₂ilih	*!		
b. ☞ məm₁,₂ilih			*

We therefore add yet another correspondence constraint (DEP-IO) to the set of undominated constraints.

2.2.2.3 Post-nasal voicing and IDENT-IO(voice)

Both alternatives to coalescence that we have discussed above, deletion and epenthesis, involved 'pure' segment correspondence, and no featural identity. However, considering the full range of possible 'repairs' of *NC̥ leads us to segmental changes, that is, into issues of featural identity. The third alternative strategy to satisfy *NC̥ involves such a featural change of input segments. This strategy is *post-nasal voicing*. The output *[məm₁b₂ilih], which results from post-nasal voicing, violates identity with respect to the feature [voice], since this is the single difference between input /p/ and its output correspondent [b].

(36)   Correspondence diagram for post-nasal voicing

    Input: N_1p_2 [−voice]
             | |
    Output: m_1b_2 [+voice]

However, we cannot identify the relevant constraint as IDENT-IO(voice), for the following reason. If it were indeed IDENT-IO(voice) that ruled out a candidate *[məm₁b₂ilih], then this constraint would incorrectly rule out the (actual) coalesced form [məm₁,₂ilih] as well. Here voiceless /p/ in the input corresponds with voiced [m] in the output, which produces a (phonetic) voicing contrast between both correspondents:

(37)   Correspondence diagram for fusion

Input: N_1p_2 [−voice]

\\/

Output: $m_{1,2}$ [+voice]

Pater proposes that the relevant identity constraint is more specific than IDENT-IO(voice), in the sense that it is restricted to voicing in obstruents. This more specific constraint is IDENT-IO(ObstruentVoice):

(38)   **IDENT-IO**(ObsVce)

Correspondent obstruents are identical in their specification for voice.

('No changes in the voicing of obstruents')

Note that IDENT-IO(ObsVce) applies equally well in the analysis of devoicing that was proposed in section 2.1.4, where IDENT-IO(voice) functioned to militate against alternations of voice in obstruents.[6]

In Indonesian IDENT-IO(ObsVce) clearly dominates LINEARITY-IO:

(39)   IDENT-IO(ObsVce) ≫ LINEARITY-IO

$məm_1b_2ilih$ < $məm_{1,2}ilih$

The relevant candidates are evaluated by the following tableau:

(40)

Input: /məN₁-p₂ilih/	IDENT-IO (ObsVce)	*NÇ̥	LINEARITY-IO
a. $məm_1b_2ilih$	*!		
b. ☞ $məm_{1,2}ilih$			*

2.2.2.4 *Denasalization and IDENT-IO(nasal)*

The final alternative (to nasal substitution) that we will consider is *denasalization*. By changing the input nasal of /Np/ into an oral consonant, producing [pp], the violation of *NÇ̥ is equally well avoided. This strategy, as applied to our example, would produce an unattested output [məp₁p₂ilih]. This would violate a featural identity constraint IDENT-IO(nasal) requiring that corresponding segments have the same specification for [nasal]. See the diagram below:

---

[6] It may seem that we can dispense with reference to obstruents by IDENT-IO(ObsVce) if we adopt contrastive underspecification (Steriade 1987), a theory in which features are only specified in segment types in which they are contrastive, for example, [voice] in obstruents. However, we would still need some constraint militating against the neutralization of voicing contrasts in sonorants, since languages exist that have contrastive voicing in nasals, such as Burmese (Ladefoged and Maddieson 1996).

(41)   Correspondence diagram for denasalization
         Input: [+nasal] N_1 p_2
                          | |
         Output: [−nasal] p_1 p_2

Again a subtle technical problem arises that must be solved to make the analysis work. If denasalization is to be effectively excluded by IDENT-IO(nasal), then this constraint must not be violated by the optimal coalescence candidate [məm$_{1,2}$ilih]. We repeat the diagram for coalescence with the relevant feature specifications for [nasal] added:

(42)   Correspondence diagram for fusion
         Input: [+nasal] N_1p_2 [−nasal]
                          \/
         Output: [+nasal] $m_{1,2}$

Apparently coalescence violates IDENT-IO(nasal) with respect to the input obstruent /p/, whose specification [−nasal] fails to reoccur in the output.

Pater argues, though, that there is a major difference between denasalization (41) and fusion (42). It is known from many processes involving [nasal] that only the positive specification of this feature is ever 'phonologically active'. This observation has led several researchers (Cohn 1993b, Piggott 1993, Rice 1993, Steriade 1993, Trigo 1993) to assume that [nasal] is a *monovalent* feature, one that has only one (positive) value. Under denasalization, [nasal] is lost from input /N/ (see 43a). But under nasal substitution there is no such loss of [nasal] from input /N/, nor from the input obstruent (see 43b).

(43)   Correspondence diagrams for denasalization and fusion, with mono-
         valent [nasal]
         a. Input: [nasal] N_1 p_2 b. Input: [nasal] N_1p_2
                             | | \/
            Output: p_1 p_2 Output: [nasal] $m_{1,2}$

At worst, nasal substitution involves an 'insertion' (rather than loss) of [nasal]: input /p$_2$/ lacks [nasal], while its output correspondent [m$_2$] is specified as [nasal]. (Arguably this is not a faithfulness violation at all because the feature [nasal] in output [m] is not 'inserted' in any sense: it simply corresponds to the nasality of one of [m]'s input correspondents.)

    Pater proposes to capture the distinction between the 'deletion' and 'insertion' of a feature in the format of featural identity constraints. This will now include a

'direction'. For example, if the input specification of some feature must be preserved in the output, then the direction is 'from I to O', as in (44):

(44)   **IDENT-I→O**(nasal)
         Any correspondent of an input segment specified as F must be F.
         ('No denasalization')

This constraint militates against denasalization. Since denasalization is not
employed as a strategy to avoid violations of *NÇ in Indonesian, IDENT-
I→O(nasal) must dominate the constraint that is violated under pressure of *NÇ.
This is LINEARITY-IO. Again, we arrive at a ranking argument similar to the one
we encountered on various earlier occasions:

(45)   IDENT-I→O(nasal) ≫ LINEARITY-IO
         məp$_1$p$_2$ilih < məm$_{1,2}$ilih

The correctness of this ranking appears from the following tableau:

(46)

Input: /məN$_1$-p$_2$ilih/	IDENT-I→O (nasal)	*NÇ	LINEARITY-IO
a. məp$_1$p$_2$ilih	*!		
b. ☞ məm$_{1,2}$ilih			*

As we will see in section 2.3.4, denasalization is employed as a strategy to satisfy
*NÇ in a number of languages.

2.2.2.5 *A summary of *NÇ effects*

We have now discussed four alternative strategies to satisfy *NÇ (or *NÇ effects)
which, logically speaking, Indonesian might have employed instead of nasal substitution. Results so far are summarized in the following table:

(47)

	Candidate	Strategy employed	Ranking
a.	məm$_{1,2}$ilih	Nasal substitution	*NÇ ≫ LINEARITY-IO
b.	*məm$_1$b$_2$ilih	Post-nasal voicing	IDENT-IO(ObsVce) ≫ LINEARITY-IO
c.	*məp$_1$p$_2$ilih	Denasalization	IDENT-I→O(nasal) ≫ LINEARITY-IO
d.	*məp$_2$ilih	Nasal deletion	MAX-IO ≫ LINEARITY-IO
e.	*məŋ$_1$əp$_2$ilih	Vowel epenthesis	DEP-IO ≫ LINEARITY-IO

This produces the following ranking for Indonesian nasal substitution:

(48)   Indonesian nasal substitution
         *NÇ, DEP-IO, MAX-IO, IDENT-I→O(nasal), IDENT-IO(ObsVce) ≫
         LINEARITY-IO

Tableau (49) evaluates all candidates discussed thus far:[7]

(49)

Input: /məN₁-p₂ilih/	*NÇ	DEP -IO	MAX- IO	IDENT-I→O (nasal)	IDENT-IO (ObsVce)	LINEARITY- IO
a. ☞ məm₁,₂ilih						*
b. məm₁b₂ilih					*!	
c. məp₁p₂ilih				*!		
d. məp₂ilih			*!			
e. məŋ₁əp₂ilih		*!				
f. məm₁p₂ilih	*!					

Of course, the fact that each candidate violates precisely one constraint is not a logical necessity, but a restriction on the candidate set made for presentational reasons only. *Gen* is free to propose any candidate analyses violating more than a single constraint of the set in tableau (49). These candidates would, of course, be suboptimal to those in (49).

For example, in addition to the candidate set evaluated in (49) we may consider a candidate having violations of both LINEARITY-IO and IDENT-I→O(nasal). This candidate would have both coalescence and loss of [nasal] from the input, as in *[məp₁,₂ilih] (50c). We might even consider another candidate having, on top of violations of LINEARITY-IO and IDENT-I→O(nasal), an additional violation of IDENT-IO(ObsVce), as in *[məb₁,₂ilih] (50d). These 'overly-unfaithful' candidates are simply excluded by the current hierarchy:

---

[7] Yet another candidate, discussed by Pater at the end of his paper, involves nasalization of the post-nasal obstruent, as in *[məm₁m₂ilih] with a *geminate nasal*. Given the current constraint ranking this candidate is actually optimal, as it has no violations of any constraints in tableau (49). (According to Pater this pattern is attested in Konjo, where it is partially conditioned by the type of prefix.) Note that this 'gemination candidate' [məm₁m₂ilih] minimally differs from the 'fusion candidate' [məm₁,₂ilih] in the following way. In the former, the output segment [m₂] is specified as [nasal], contrary to its input correspondent /p/. In the fusion candidate, the specification [nasal] of the output segment [m₁,₂] reoccurs in one of its input correspondents, /N₁/. We therefore assume that the gemination candidate is ruled out by a constraint militating against [nasal] in an output segment whose input correspondent is not specified as [nasal]. A constraint that has this effect is IDENT-O→I(nasal), that is, the reverse of IDENT-I→O(nasal).

(50)

Input: /$\text{məN}_1\text{-p}_2\text{ilih}$/	*NÇ	DEP-IO	MAX-IO	IDENT-I→O (nasal)	IDENT-IO (ObsVce)	LINEARITY-IO
a. ☞ $\text{məm}_{1,2}\text{ilih}$						*
b. $\text{məp}_1\text{p}_2\text{ilih}$				*!		
c. $\text{məp}_{1,2}\text{ilih}$				*!		*
d. $\text{məb}_{1,2}\text{ilih}$				*!	*	*

Why even pay attention to these candidates? Is it not merely logical that 'the worst of the worst' is excluded? But actually we have arrived at an important result here: OT predicts that the 'simplest' change should be made to avoid the violation of some markedness constraint. Although two, or in fact any possible number of changes could be made in order to avoid violation of *NÇ, *only one change suffices*: nasal substitution (or coalescence). No more changes occur than are strictly necessary. Prince and Smolensky (1993) have stated this as the 'Economy principle of OT', repeated below from chapter 1 (29):

(51)   **Economy**: banned options are available only to avoid violations of higher-ranked constraints and can only be banned *minimally*.

In chapter 1 we have already arrived at a similar result in the discussion of devoicing in Dutch, but then we did not take into account any alternative strategies of avoiding violation of obstruent voicing in codas. Here we have found evidence for the economy property from a case that involves a consideration of various possible changes, rather than just one.

Let us now find out if rule-based theory makes the same prediction of 'economy'. The notion of *faithfulness* is absent from rule-based theory altogether, so it is difficult to see how application of a rule might be blocked in a case where an earlier rule has already 'accomplished' a surface target. However, rule-based theory happens to arrive at the same prediction of economy for rules sharing the same structural description. This prediction follows from rule ordering. Consider, for example, the functionally related rules of Post-nasal voicing and Denasalization (before voiceless obstruents). Whichever applies first will destroy the context of application for the other rule:

(52)   Mutual blocking of functionally related rules by ordering

	a. Input:	/mp/	b. Input:	/mp/
	Post-nasal voicing	mb	Denasalization	pp
	Denasalization	---	Post-nasal voicing	---
	Output:	[mb]	Output:	[pp]

Both cases exemplify 'bleeding' rule orders: one rule destroys the context of application for another rule. Rule-ordering is indeed crucial to economical outputs, as simultaneous application of both rules would produce *[bb], a non-economical output. The equivalence of rule-ordering theory and OT with respect to the mutual blocking of functionally related processes is not generally extendable to all cases of economy, however. In later chapters (for example, chapter 8 on syntax), we will find that OT offers a more principled account of economy phenomena than rule-based theory. But also see chapter 9 for a discussion of opacity, a phenomenon which apparently falsifies economy.

The next subsection will refine the analysis of nasal substitution in Indonesian by showing the relevance of morphological context. This discussion will be based on data of nasal plus obstruent sequences which we have not looked into so far.

2.2.3 *Morphological effects*

2.2.3.1 *Root-internal blocking*

All cases thus far involved a nasal in a prefix before a root-initial obstruent. Pater points out, however, that Indonesian does not ban sequences of nasal plus voiceless consonant across the board. Consider the following root-internal occurrences of this sequence:

(53)   Root-internal occurrences of NC̥ in Indonesian
     a. əmpat   'four'
     b. untuk   'for'
     c. muŋkin   'possible'

The same sequence that is excluded across a prefix–root boundary[8] is apparently allowed root-internally. Pater observes that the root-internal prohibition against nasal substitution exemplifies a cross-linguistic tendency for root-internal segments to be more resistant to phonological processes than segments in other positions. There is a well-known class of processes that apply only across morpheme boundaries, but fail to apply inside a morpheme, displaying the *derived environment* effect (Mascaró 1976, Kiparsky 1982b, 1993a).

To account for this cross-linguistic tendency in OT, it has been recently proposed that faithfulness requirements are enforced more strictly within the root than in non-root morphemes, such as affixes (McCarthy and Prince 1995a). This

---

[8] Nasal substitution does not apply across all prefix–root junctures. Certain prefix boundaries are 'opaque' to nasal substitution, for example /məN-pər-besar/ [məmpərbesar] 'to enlarge'.

is captured by root-specific versions of faithfulness constraints, ranked above general versions of these constraints.[9]

(54)   Root-Faithfulness ≫ Faithfulness

Application of a phonological process across a morpheme boundary shows that 'general' faithfulness is ranked below some markedness constraint. And non-application in a root-internal context shows that 'root-faithfulness' dominates this markedness constraint. We thus find 'sandwiching' of a markedness constraint between a root-particular faithfulness constraint and the general faithfulness constraint:

(55)   Non-application within the root, application elsewhere in the word
             Root-Faithfulness ≫ Markedness ≫ Faithfulness

This is the general ranking schema for non-application of a process within a root. (When the markedness constraint would dominate both others, no 'root-effect' would occur.)

Pater goes on to propose a root-particular version of LINEARITY-IO:

(56)   **ROOTLIN-IO**
             The output reflects the precedence structure of the input segments of the root, and vice versa.

Sandwiching of the phonotactic constraint *NÇ in between ROOTLIN-IO and LINEARITY-IO produces the following (partial) ranking:

(57)   Blocking of root-internal fusion
             ROOTLIN-IO ≫ *NÇ ≫ LINEARITY-IO

This ranking correctly accounts for the blocking of root-internal fusion, as shown in the following tableau:

(58)

Input: /$\text{əm}_1\text{p}_2\text{at}$/	ROOTLIN-IO	*NÇ	LINEARITY-IO
a. ☞ $\text{əm}_1\text{p}_2\text{at}$		*	
b. $\text{əm}_{1,2}\text{at}$	*!		*

[9] This ranking has been argued to be universal, but this is difficult to establish. It is only when root-faithfulness (the more specific constraint) dominates the general constraint that any root-faithfulness effects become apparent. Under the reverse ranking, with the general constraint taking priority, root-faithfulness is simply suppressed.

Finally we need to integrate this partial ranking with the other correspondence constraints argued for in the previous section. This in fact is quite simple. Within roots no alternative strategies (neither deletion, epenthesis, post-nasal voicing, nor denasalization) are ever employed to avoid violation of *NC̥. Hence, all correspondence constraints militating against these strategies dominate *NC̥. The complete ranking is given in (59).

(59)   Indonesian nasal substitution, final ranking
        DEP-IO, MAX-IO, IDENT-I→O(nasal), IDENT-IO(ObsVce),
        ROOTLIN-IO ≫ *NC̥ ≫ LINEARITY-IO

2.2.3.2 *An alternative analysis*

It may be worth exploring an alternative to this analysis that is not based on root-specific faithfulness constraints, but rather on the notion that morphemes are not linearly ordered in the input. (See also note 4.) On this account, there is no input linear ordering between the prefix and the root, hence no linear ordering is present in the input between the prefix nasal and root obstruent. In contrast, all root-internal occurrences of nasal and obstruent do have an input linear ordering. What blocks nasal substitution in root-internal contexts is LINEARITY-IO, which must therefore be ranked above *NC̥.

(60)

Input: /əm₁p₂at/	LINEARITY-IO	*NC̥
a. ☞ əm₁p₂at		*
b. əm₁,₂at	*!	

Nasal substitution across a prefix–root boundary cannot involve violation of LINEARITY, but it does violate the correspondence constraint UNIFORMITY-IO (McCarthy and Prince 1995a).

(61)   **UNIFORMITY-IO**
        No element of the output has multiple correspondents in the input.
        ('No coalescence')

This 'anti-coalescence' constraint must be dominated by *NC̥, as tableau (62) shows:

(62)

Input: /məN₁, p₂ilih/	LINEARITY-IO	*NC̥	UNIFORMITY-IO
a. məm₁p₂ilih		*!	
b. ☞ məm₁,₂ilih			*

Let us now balance the pros and cons of this analysis. On the positive side, it avoids root-specific faithfulness constraints, thereby restricting the machinery of OT. Root-particular faithfulness constraints may eventually turn out to be independently required but the null-hypothesis is that faithfulness constraints are 'blind' to morphological structure. Another advantage is avoidance of the assumption that morphemes must be linearly ordered in the input. (In chapter 5 we will see that this assumption is problematic because of affixations whose linear position with respect to the stem depends on output phonological structure, such as infixation and reduplication.) On the negative side, it sets up a correspondence constraint for coalescence, losing the unified account of coalescence and metathesis.

2.3   The typology of *NC̥ effects

This section will deal with the cross-linguistic status of *NC̥ and strategies that languages may employ to resolve its violation. Recall from section 2.2 that the type of change (in response to some phonotactic constraint) depends on the ranking of correspondence constraints militating against specific changes. Specifically, the observed effect involves violation of the *lowest*-ranking correspondence constraint in the hierarchy. This constraint is crucially dominated by the markedness constraint (the 'trigger'), as well as by other faithfulness constraints, whose violation is 'more expensive'. For example, nasal substitution emerges if LINEARITY-IO is lowest-ranking, nasal deletion if MAX-IO is lowest-ranking, etc. Abstracting away from interactions with other faithfulness constraints in the hierarchy, we arrive at the following typology of *NC̥ effects:

(63)   A typology of *NC̥ effects
          a. Nasal substitution   *NC̥ ≫ LINEARITY-IO   'No coalescence'
          b. Nasal deletion   *NC̥ ≫ MAX-IO   'No deletion'
          c. Vowel epenthesis   *NC̥ ≫ DEP-IO   'No epenthesis'
          d. Post-nasal voicing   *NC̥ ≫ IDENT-IO(ObsVce)   'No obstruent
                                                              voicing'
          e. Denasalization   *NC̥ ≫ IDENT-I→O(nasal)   'No
                                                              denasalization'

The theory of correspondence constraints is, in a certain sense, the *theory of phonological changes*. It predicts the possible effects that may occur cross-linguistically in response to phonotactic constraints. What we are specifically interested in in this section is whether the full range of *NC̥ effects predicted by this typology is indeed attested cross-linguistically. As we will see, the empirical coverage is quite high: all *NC̥ effects occur except (vowel) epenthesis.

2.3.1 *Nasal deletion in Kelantan Malay*

The first *NÇ effect to be discussed is *nasal deletion*, the deletion of a nasal before a voiceless consonant. This avoids violation of *NÇ by simply removing the segment that induces voicing in the following obstruent.

Among the languages which Pater mentions as examples of nasal deletion are the Kelantan dialect of Malay, and the African languages Venda, Swahili, and Maore. Nasal deletion has also been reported for child language, in English, Greek, and Spanish. All in all, this is an impressive list of cases, which gives additional force to the observation that it is always the *nasal* that is deleted, rather than the obstruent.[10] This is an issue about which Pater makes no conclusive statements, but only some interesting suggestions.[11]

Pater gives no examples of nasal deletion in Kelantan-like languages, and hence we will follow his schematic account. An input sequence of a nasal (N_1) plus a voiceless consonant (T_2) maps onto a single output segment that is identical to T_2. That is, an input segment N_1 has no output correspondent:

(64)   Correspondence diagram for nasal deletion

Input: $N_1 T_2$

Output: T_2

This involves the violation of MAX-IO. Hence we may infer that MAX-IO is the lowest-ranking faithfulness constraint in the hierarchy:

(65)   Ranking for nasal deletion in Kelantan-like languages
         *NÇ, DEP-IO, IDENT-I→O(nasal), IDENT-IO(ObsVce), LINEARITY-IO ≫ MAX-IO

This ranking predicts nasal deletion, as illustrated below for the candidate set previously evaluated in the Indonesian tableau (49). Participating segments are indicated by symbols ('N' = nasal, 'T' = voiceless obstruent, 'D' = voiced obstruent').

---

[10] Recall that the Indonesian case is analysed as a fusion rather than the deletion of the obstruent on the basis of various kinds of evidence: the stability of the obstruent's place of articulation, as well as the behaviour of substitutions under reduplication.

[11] Pater suggests that nasals are 'weaker' than obstruents in various respects. First, nasals tend to assimilate the place of articulation of the obstruent, rather than the reverse. Second, the deletion of nasals in NÇ (rather than obstruents) suggests a similar weakness. Apparently, faithfulness requirements for obstruents are stricter than those for nasals. To implement this idea, Pater proposes to relativize faithfulness constraints with respect to major class, branching out MAX-IO into OBSMAX ('No deletion of obstruents') and NASMAX ('No deletion of nasals'), with the former universally outranking the former.

(66)

Input: /N₁ T₂/	*NC̥	Dep -IO	Ident-I→O (nasal)	Ident-IO (ObsVce)	Linearity-IO	Max-IO
a. N₁,₂					*!	
b. N₁ D₂				*!		
c. T₁ T₂			*!			
d. ☞ T₂						*
e. N₁əT₂		*!				
f. N₁ T₂	*!					

2.3.2 *Vowel epenthesis*

The second predicted *NC̥ effect is *vowel epenthesis*, the insertion of a segment between the nasal and voiceless consonant to undo their adjacency. Pater reports that this *NC̥ effect is not attested in any natural language, as far is currently known. He makes various suggestions towards an explanation of this potential gap in the typology, for which we refer the reader to the paper.

2.3.3 *Post-nasal voicing in Puyu Pungo Quechua*

The third predicted *NC̥ effect is *post-nasal voicing*, the neutralization of the voicing contrast in obstruents following nasals. According to Pater, post-nasal voicing is by far the most common of all *NC̥ effects. It occurs in various languages ranging from Zoque to the Puyu Pungo dialect of Quechua. The pattern of post-nasal voicing in Puyu Pungo Quechua (Orr 1962, Rice 1993, as cited in Pater forthcoming) is exemplified below.

(67)   Post-nasal voicing in Puyu Pungo Quechua
             a.i sinik-pa 'porcupine's'   a.ii kam-ba   'yours'
             b.i wasi-ta 'in the jungle'   b.ii wakin-da 'the others'

Post-nasal voicing amounts to the following correspondence diagram:

(68)   Correspondence diagram for post-nasal voicing
             Input: m_1p_2 [−voice]
                     | |
             Output: m_1b_2 [+voice]

Different values of the feature [voice] in the input obstruent and its output correspondent incur a violation of the featural identity constraint Ident-IO(ObsVce). Accordingly, this must be the lowest-ranking faithfulness constraint in the hierarchy:

(69)   Ranking for post-nasal voicing in Puyu Pungo-like languages
         *NÇ, Dep-IO, Max-IO, Ident-I→O (nasal), Linearity-IO ≫
         Ident-IO(ObsVce)

Tableau (70) evaluates various candidates that match the alternative *NÇ effects.

(70)

Input: /kam$_1$-p$_2$a/	*NÇ	Dep -IO	Max- IO	Ident- I→O(nasal)	Linearity- IO	Ident-IO (ObsVce)
a. kam$_{1,2}$a					*!	
b. ☞ kam$_1$b$_2$a						*
c. kap$_2$p$_2$a				*!		
d. kap$_2$a			*!			
e. kam$_1$əp$_2$a		*!				
f. kam$_1$p$_2$a	*!					

Puyo Pungo Quechua shares with Indonesian the phenomenon that the ban on NÇ sequences is relaxed root-internally. (An example presented by Pater is [šiŋki] 'soot'.) Of course this points to the undominated position of RootLin-IO, similarly to Indonesian.

2.3.4 *Denasalization in Mandar*
The fourth and final *NÇ effect to be discussed is *denasalization* of the nasal preceding the voiceless obstruent. Pater reports that denasalization is attested in at least three languages: Toba Batak, Kaingang, and Mandar. The Mandar pattern (Mills 1975, as cited in Pater forthcoming) is exemplified below:

(71)   Denasalization in Mandar
         a. /maN-dundu/ mandundu 'to drink'
         b. /maN-tunu/   mattunu 'to burn'

Denasalization involves a loss of the feature [+nasal], which is present on the input nasal, in its output correspondent, an obstruent.

(72)   Correspondence diagram for post-nasal voicing
         Input: [+nasal] N$_1$ t$_2$
                          | |
         Output: [−nasal] t$_1$ t$_2$

This amounts to violation of IDENT-I→O(nasal). Hence this must be the lowest-ranking faithfulness constraint in the hierarchy:

(73) Ranking for denasalization in Mandar-like languages
*NÇ, DEP-IO, MAX-IO, IDENT-IO(ObsVce), LINEARITY-IO ≫ IDENT-I→O(nasal)

That denasalization is indeed the correct outcome of constraint evaluation is shown in the following tableau:

(74)

Input: /maN-tunu/	*NÇ	DEP-IO	MAX-IO	IDENT-IO (ObsVce)	LINEARITY-IO	IDENT-I→O(nasal)
a. man$_{1,2}$unu					*!	
b. man$_1$d$_2$unu				*!		
c. ☞ mat$_1$t$_2$unu						*
d. mat$_2$unu			*!			
e. man$_1$ət$_2$unu		*!				
f. man$_1$t$_2$unu	*!					

Mandar, unlike Indonesian and Puyo Pungo Quechua, completely disallows NÇ sequences, extending the ban to root-internal contexts (where post-nasal obstruents are always voiced, resulting in a lack of alternations). In Pater's approach to root-specific faithfulness, this property of Mandar can be accounted for by a reranking of *NÇ, so that it comes to dominate ROOTLIN-IO.

2.3.5 *The typology of *NÇ effects: conclusions*

The conclusion of this typology section is that theoretical predictions about *NÇ effects are (mostly) correct. All predicted effects, with the exception of vowel epenthesis, are attested in some language. The architecture of OT brings out the functional unity of these effects: all are resolutions of a potential violation of a phonotactic constraint, *NÇ, militating against sequences of nasal plus voiceless obstruent. Correspondence Theory has the ability of predicting typologies, factoring out universally possible 'responses' to some phonotactic constraint. Whether or not a language employs a specific effect as a response to *NÇ depends on a language-specific ranking of universal correspondence constraints. The nature of the *NÇ effect shows which correspondence constraint is violated; this in its turn pinpoints the correspondence constraint which is violated as the lowest ranking in the hierarchy. Finally, we repeat the conclusion from section 2.2.2 that OT predicts that languages make economical use of the available 'repair strategies'. This prediction follows from the minimization of violation of constraints, one of the corner stones of OT.

In the next section we will strengthen these conclusions by a discussion of the co-occurrence of multiple *NÇ effects within a single language.

2.4 Conspiracies of nasal substitution and other processes

So far we have discussed cases in which *NÇ is satisfied by a single process per language (with the option of blocking this process root-internally). The argument made on the basis of these cases is that OT captures the functional unity of these processes by separating the trigger (*NÇ) and the effect (the relative ranking of faithfulness constraints). Here we will consider various strategies to satisfy *NÇ within a single language, OshiKwanyama, a western Bantu language (Steinbergs 1985, as cited in Pater forthcoming).

The first *NÇ effect is a phonotactic pattern which holds as a *static* generalization for all roots of the language: post-nasal voicing is a morpheme-structure constraint. But a *dynamic* view of post-nasal voicing is warranted by patterns of loan words from English:[12]

(75)   Post-nasal voicing in OshiKwanyama loan words
        a. sitamba 'stamp'
        b. pelanda 'print'
        c. oinga   'ink'

OshiKwanyama loan words display no voicing alternations in stops to directly support the process interpretation, as the nasal-plus-stop cluster occurs internal to the root, rather than across a morpheme boundary. Nevertheless a 'dynamic' view is supported by the fact that post-nasal voicing is productive: it affects loan words having a nasal-plus-voiceless-stop cluster in their source language, amounting to a positional neutralization.

The other *NÇ effect found in OshiKwanyama is nasal substitution. This occurs in root-initial position, following a prefix ending in a nasal (precisely as in Indonesian):

(76)   Root-initial nasal substitution in OshiKwanyama
        a. /eːN-pati/ eːmati 'ribs'
        b. /oN-pote/ omote 'good-for-nothing'
        c. /oN-tana/ onana 'calf'

---

[12] For approaches to loan word phonology in OT, see Yip (1993) and Itô and Mester (1995).

This process is supported by alternations, naturally, because it applies across a morpheme boundary.

There is, of course, a clear functional unity between post-nasal voicing and nasal substitution. Both serve to resolve violations of *NÇ. Such functional unity of processes within a language is known as a *conspiracy* (Kisseberth 1970) and, as we learned in section 2.1.2, rule-based theory cannot formally capture this situation. Observe that even under a static (rather than 'dynamic') interpretation of post-nasal voicing, its functional unity with nasal substitution still remains to be accounted for. (In that case, OshiKwanyama can be argued to exemplify the 'duplication problem'.)

Pater gives a straightforward analysis of the OshiKwanyama *NÇ conspiracy, one which uses no other constraints than those independently motivated by previous cases. In a nutshell, the analytic problem that must be resolved is the following. So far we have assumed that the nature of the effect was tantamount to pinpointing the dominated correspondence constraint in the hierarchy. But here we have *two* *NÇ effects, and we naturally wonder if both can be related to a violation of some correspondence constraint without running into a constraint ranking paradox. Post-nasal voicing violates IDENT-IO(ObsVce), while nasal substitution violates LINEARITY-IO. But how could both (at the same time) be the lowest-ranking correspondence constraint in the hierarchy?

Pater answers this question quite simply. Both processes differ in their *domains*. Post-nasal voicing applies root-internally, that is, in a context where resolutions of *NÇ violations are hampered by root-specific faithfulness (ROOT-LIN-IO). In contrast, fusion (or nasal substitution) applies across the prefix–root boundary, escaping from any (possibly) detrimental effects of ROOTLIN-IO. This opens up the possibility of designating fusion as the 'primary' *NÇ effect, while blocking it root-internally by undominated ROOTLIN-IO, where it is supplanted by the 'secondary' *NÇ effect: post-nasal voicing. Once we see the outlines of the analysis, it is fairly easy to state it in a constraint interaction. We will build the ranking piece by piece, making full use of analytic insights inherited from discussions of fusion and post-nasal voicing in Indonesian and Puyu Pungo Quechua.

The first building block is the ranking that accounts for nasal substitution, as well as its root-internal blocking. This is copied straight away from the analysis of Indonesian:

(77)   Nasal substitution, and its root-internal blocking
         ROOTLIN-IO ≫ *NÇ ≫ LINEARITY-IO

That is, LINEARITY-IO can be violated under pressure of *NC̥, while ROOTLIN-IO cannot.

The second building block is post-nasal voicing, which we copy from the analysis of Puyo Pungo Quechua:

(78) Post-nasal voicing
      *NC̥ ≫ IDENT-IO(ObsVce)

That is, featural identity of voice in obstruents can be violated under pressure of *NC̥.

One question remains: what is the relative ranking of LINEARITY-IO and IDENT-IO(ObsVce)? This is in fact a specific form of a general analytic problem stated above: how could both LINEARITY-IO and IDENT-IO(ObsVce) be the lowest-ranking correspondence constraint in the hierarchy? Now we see the relevance of the idea of designating fusion as the 'primary' *NC̥ effect, and post-nasal voicing as the 'secondary' *NC̥ effect. This has a direct implication for the relative ranking of both correspondence constraints involved. This is stated below:

(79) Fusion preferred to post-nasal voicing
      *NC̥ ≫ IDENT-IO(ObsVce) ≫ LINEARITY-IO

Both correspondence constraints are dominated by *NC̥. Therefore, in principle, both are violable to resolve *NC̥ violations. Yet the language will select a violation of the lowest-ranking constraint (LINEARITY-IO) *wherever this is possible*. This is equivalent to saying that fusion is the primary *NC̥ effect. It will only resort to the secondary *NC̥ effect of post-nasal voicing in contexts *where fusion fails*, due to some higher-ranking constraint.

All we need to do now is put the rankings together:

(80) The OshiKwanyama *NC̥ conspiracy
      ROOTLIN-IO, *NC̥ ≫ IDENT-IO(ObsVce) ≫ LINEARITY-IO

It remains to illustrate the correctness of this analysis by two tableaux, one of a case of fusion, and the other of a case of post-nasal voicing.

The fusion tableau (81) serves to illustrate the status of fusion as the 'primary' effect on post-nasal voicing. The correspondence constraint which is violated by fusion (LINEARITY-IO) is ranked at the bottom of the hierarchy. Therefore its violation (that is, a fusion) is preferred to the violation of IDENT-IO(ObsVce), that is, post-nasal voicing:

(81)

Input: /eːN₁-p₂ati/	RootLin- IO	*NÇ	Ident- IO(ObsVce)	Linearity- IO
a. ☞ eːm₁,₂ati				*
b. eːm₁b₂ati			*!	
c. eːm₁p₂ati		*!		

Even though fusion disrupts the input's linear ordering of segments, no fatal violation of RootLin-IO follows from this. This is because the violation involves segments belonging to different morphemes. The violation of Linearity-IO in the optimal form [eːm₁,₂ati] is taken for granted since this is the least expensive violation of a correspondence constraint in the hierarchy.[13]

Turning to the post-nasal voicing tableau, we see that RootLin-IO precludes the option of fusion, which is otherwise the primary *NÇ effect. With fusion ruled out, the grammar is thrown back onto its secondary resources in dealing with NÇ sequences, post-nasal voicing:

(82)

Input: /sitam₁p₂a/	RootLin- IO	*NÇ	Ident- IO(ObsVce)	Linearity- IO
a. sitam₁,₂a	*!			*
b. ☞ sitam₁b₂a			*	
c. sitam₁p₂a		*!		

The fusion candidate, which was still a 'winner' in the previous tableau, is now taken out of the race by RootLin-IO. Of the remaining candidates, the one with post-nasal voicing incurs the least expensive violation.

2.5 Conclusion: a comparison with rule-based theory

Let us now turn to a final comparison with rule-based theory. Consider the following set of rules, all of which (except epenthesis) state processes which have figured prominently in the preceding discussions:

---

[13] The difference with tableau (58) for Indonesian is that Ident-IO(ObsVce) is now included, in a position below *NÇ.

(83)

Language	Strategy employed	Rule
a. Indonesian	Nasal substitution	[−son, −voice] → Ø / [+nasal] ___
b. Kelantan	Nasal deletion	[+nasal] → Ø / ___ [−son, −voice]
c. (unattested)	Vowel epenthesis	Ø → V / [+nasal] ___ [−son, −voice]
d. Puyo Pungo	Post-nasal voicing	[−son] → [+voice] / [+nasal] ___
e. Mandar	Denasalization	[+nasal] → [−nasal] / ___[−son, −voice]

As we have observed earlier, the rules of this set are functionally related, but the nature of the relationship is very difficult to capture in rule-based theory. The diagram below portrays four of these rules as changes from an initial state [+nasal][−voice]. The four output states are placed next to the diagram.

(84)

a. [+nasal] Ø   (nasal substitution)
b.   Ø   [−voice] (nasal deletion)

d. [+nasal] [+voice] (post-nasal voicing)
e. [−nasal] [−voice] (denasalization)

It is clear that this set of output states share no positive characteristics: they do not form a natural class. All that unites them is the fact that they are *not* [+nasal][−voice]. However, this is a negative characteristic, which also includes many more states than those of (84a–e). Aiming at a positive common definition, one might note that all are derivationally related to a common single input state [+nasal][−voice]. Again, this definition is not sufficiently precise, as it includes many more output states than the above set. The single definition to capture accurately the relevant set of output states combines both criteria: it defines the set as (i) being derivationally related to the input state [+nasal][−voice], as well as (ii) not matching the output state [+nasal][−voice]. Or to put it in plain prose, these are precisely the rules that *repair* the ill-formed input configuration *NÇ. Rule-based theory is able to capture the functional unity of rules only at the expense of becoming *teleological* – that is, by acknowledging the insight that structural changes function to 'undo' their structural descriptions.

The same point can be made with even more force on the basis of the functionally related rules of post-nasal voicing and nasal substitution in OshiKwan-yama. The shared goal of both rules is precisely to avoid the sequence [+nasal][−voice]. Again, this goal is not one that can be simply inferred from the statements of both rules. Their structural changes may differ, but both function to avoid *NÇ. Conspiracies cannot be explained by rule-based theory, but they are within the scope of explanation of OT. This success is due to two factors. First, OT defines structural well-formedness on surface representations, rather than on input (or intermediate) representations. Second, OT separates the 'triggers' of changes from the actual changes.

SUGGESTIONS FOR FURTHER READING

Rule-ordering theory

Bromberger, Sylvain and Morris Halle (1989) Why phonology is different. *Linguistic Inquiry* **20**. 51–70.

Kenstowicz, Michael and Charles Kisseberth (1979) *Generative phonology: description and theory.* New York: Academic Press. [chapter 2, Phonological rules and representations, and chapter 8, Rule interaction]

Rules versus constraints

Blevins, Juliette (1997) Rules in Optimality Theory: two case studies. In Roca. 227–60.

Noyer, Rolf (1997) Attic Greek accentuation and intermediate derivational representations. In Roca. 501–26.

Segmental versus featural identity

Lombardi, Linda (1995a) Laryngeal neutralization and alignment. In Beckman, Walsh Dickey, and Urbanczyk. 225–48.

Zoll, Cheryl (1996) Parsing below the segment in a constraint based framework. PhD dissertation, University of California, Berkeley. [ROA-143, http://ruccs.rutgers.edu/roa.html]

Factorial typology

Myers, Scott (1997a) OCP effects in Optimality Theory. *Natural Language and Linguistic Theory* **15**. 847–92.

EXERCISES

1 A *NÇ̥ conspiracy in Modern Greek

Pater (1996) discusses a conspiracy of *NÇ̥ effects in Modern Greek (Newton 1972). The effects are twofold: *post-nasal voicing* occurs in (i), while *nasal deletion before a cluster of voiceless obstruents* occurs in (ii):

(i.a)   /pemp-o/   pembo   'I send'
(i.b)   /ton#topo/   tondopo 'the place'
(ii.a) /e-pemp-sa/   epepsa   'I send – aorist'
(ii.b) /ton#psefti/   topsefti 'the liar' (Cypriot dialect)[14]

   a. Propose an analysis of this conspiracy, extending the analysis of *NÇ̥ effects given in section 2.2. You will need at least one new constraint. Motivate this constraint, and rank it.

   b. Is your current analysis capable of excluding the suboptimal form *epembza*? If not, can you repair this defect by an additional constraint? Motivate and rank it.

   c. Present tableaux of *pembo* and *epepsa*.

2 Kikuyu verbs

Kikuyu (Clements 1985b) has alternations due to interacting processes which affect *place of articulation, continuancy,* and *voicing,* as illustrated by the following verb forms:

Imperative	1 sg. imperfect	
βur-a	m-bur-eetɛ	'lop off'
tɛm-a	n-dɛm-ɛɛtɛ	'cut'
reh-a	n-deh-eetɛ	'pay'
cin-a	ɲ-jin-eetɛ	'burn'
kom-a	ŋ-gom-ɛɛtɛ	'sleep'
ɣor-a	ŋ-gor-eetɛ	'buy'

   a. For each of these three alternations, decide which pairs of markedness and faithfulness constraints are relevant. Rank each pair of constraints.

   b. Try to explain the fact that only prefix consonants alternate in place of articulation, while initial root consonants remain stable. What assumptions do you make about the input form of the prefix? Discuss any consequences for Lexicon Optimization.

   c. Integrate the three rankings found under (a–b) into a total ranking. Are any of the pairs of constraints found in (a) dependent upon other pairs? Motivate each subranking by a form.

   d. Present tableaux of *βur-a* and *m-bur-eetɛ*.

---

[14] Pater, based on Newton (1972), reports that '[i]n all dialects, the nasal is deleted within the word [ii.a], and in most dialects, including Cypriot, it is deleted in an article preceding a noun, except in "slow, deliberate speech" [ii.b]'.

3 Voicing assimilation in Dutch

Consider the pattern of voicing assimilation in Dutch (Trommelen and Zonneveld 1979):

(i)	/p+d/	bd	stropdas	'tie'
	/t+b/	db	witboek	'white book'
	/k+d/	gd	zakdoek	'handkerchief'
(ii)	/d+k/	tk	bloedkoraal	'red coral'
	/d+p/	tp	huidplooi	'skin crease'
	/b+k/	pk	slobkous	'gaiter'
(iii)	/s+b/	zb	kasboek	'cash book'
	/x+b/	ɣb	lachbui	'fit of laughter'
	/f+b/	vb	lafbek	'coward'
(iv)	/ɣ+t/	xt	hoogtij	'heyday'
	/z+p/	sp	kaaspers	'cheese press'
	/v+k/	fk	lijfknecht	'serf'
(v)	/k+v/	kf	boekvorm	'book form'
	/p+z/	ps	diepzee	'deep-sea'
	/t+z/	ts	hartzeer	'heartache'
(vi)	/s+v/	sf	bosveen	'peat'
	/f+z/	fs	strafzaak	'trial'
	/x+v/	xf	pechvogel	'unlucky person'
(vii)	/d+v/	tf	handvat	'handle'
	/d+z/	ts	Noordzee	'North Sea'
	/b+z/	ps	krabzeer	'scratching sore'
(viii)	/z+v/	sf	kaasvorm	'cheese mould'
	/v+z/	fs	drijfzand	'quicksand'
	/ɣ+v/	xf	hoogvlakte	'plateau'

Two types of voicing assimilation interact in this pattern.

a. Which are these? State the generalization(s) concerning voicing assimilation.

b. To account for the contrast between (i) and (ii), you need a new constraint. State this constraint. Does it fit in with the format of constraints that has been assumed so far? Hint: is this a faithfulness constraint or a contextual markedness constraint, or neither?

c. To account for the forms in (vii–viii) you need yet another constraint. State this constraint and rank it with respect to the other constraints.

d. Support your final analysis by tableaux of *kasboek* and *handvat*.

3
Syllable structure and economy

3.1 Introduction

The syllable is a major ingredient of phonological generalizations. It is crucial in defining phonotactic patterns: well-formed sequences of segments, in particular of consonants and vowels. The syllable also governs patterns of epenthesis and deletion, as discussed below. It supplies a level of prosodic organization between segments and higher-level prosodic units: the 'foot' and the 'prosodic word' (chapter 4). Finally, the syllable functions in the demarcation of morpheme edges, as we will see below, and in defining the position and shape of affixes (particularly infixes, discussed here, and reduplication, to be discussed in chapter 5).

The syllable is defined as a prosodic category organizing segments in sequences according to their sonority values. Each syllable has a sonority peak (*nucleus*), usually a vowel, possibly surrounded on both sides by margin segments of lower sonority, usually consonants (*onset, coda*). We make the slightly simplifying assumption that syllables are organized into constituents in the following way:

(1)

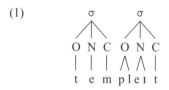

This flat structure defines the syllable as a constituent that has a tripartite organization, consisting of an onset, a nucleus, and a coda, of which only the nucleus is universally obligatory. We assume that consonants must be syllabified into margins, that is onset or coda, while vowels must be syllabified as nuclei. Yet this simple flat syllabic model can be used to explain important cross-linguistic observations. Languages differ with respect to syllable structure along various dimensions related to the tripartite structure of (1), the onset, nucleus, and coda, as we will see shortly in section 3.2.[1] The model will serve as the basis of the analysis of epenthesis and deletion in section 3.3–5.

Syllabic well-formedness will turn out to be yet another instantiation of the basic conflict between *faithfulness* and *markedness* (or structural well-formedness). The range of syllable types allowed by individual languages arise by interactions of syllabic well-formedness constraints and segmental faithfulness constraints. The precise nature of these interactions will be the primary concern of this chapter. Again we will pay much attention to the issue of *language typology*, as we did in both earlier chapters. Finally, by defining syllable well-formedness in terms of constraint interactions, this chapter also presents the point of departure for further applications of the syllable in stress systems and in prosodic morphology in later chapters.

In this chapter we will review results of research on syllable structure, and place these in the overall perspectives of the goals and issues in OT. First, in section 3.2 we will look into basic typological observations on syllable structure, and see how OT captures these by well-formedness constraints. Section 3.2 will place syllable-governed epenthesis and deletion in the perspective of conflicts between well-formedness and faithfulness. Our discussion will draw heavily on the typological results of Prince and Smolensky (1993), transposed into a correspondence format. After studying epenthesis patterns in various languages, we will develop a factorial typology of syllabic well-formedness and faithfulness constraints in section 3.3. This will explain some major cross-linguistic properties of epenthesis, in particular its 'economy'. Next section 3.4 will deal with the cross-linguistically common case of blocking of epenthesis and deletion at word edges. This will lead us to the introduction of the concept of *alignment* (McCarthy and Prince 1993a), the matching of (morphological and prosodic) edges, enforced by constraints. Section 3.5 addresses the quality of epenthetic segments, focussing on their minimal markedness and contextual colouring, relating these properties to the discussion of segment inventories of chapter 1. Phonotactic functions of the syllable, in particular coda conditions, will be the topic of section 3.6. Finally, section 3.7 will summarize the results.

3.2 The basic syllable typology

3.2.1 *Onsets and codas*

Typological studies of syllable structure (for example, Jakobson 1962, Greenberg 1978, Kaye and Lowenstamm 1981, Itô 1986; see for an overview Blevins 1995)

---

[1] In chapter 4 we will find evidence for a more sophisticated view of syllable structure, one that accommodates the notion of 'syllable weight'.

have revealed solid cross-linguistic preferences for certain syllable types over other types. In this section we will focus on a well-known cross-linguistic asymmetry of onsets and codas: syllables prefer to begin with a *consonant*, whereas they prefer to end in a *vowel*.

Following standard terminology, we will refer to syllable-initial consonants as the 'onset' of the syllable. The important typological finding with respect to onsets is that all languages allow them, and none exclude them. That is:

(2)   Implicational universal for syllable onsets
         If a language has syllables that lack an onset, then it also has syllables that have an onset.

Accordingly languages fall into two large classes: those allowing onset-less syllables, such as Japanese, Diola-Fogny, Ponapean, and English, and those that do not allow onset-less syllables, such as Temiar, Axininca Campa, and Arabic (Itô 1989). The crucial point is that no languages are known that *disallow* onsets.

Some languages actually 'supply' an onset when no consonant is available in the input. Such *epenthesis* of a consonant in onset position occurs in Axininca Campa (Payne 1981, Itô 1989, McCarthy and Prince 1993b), see the examples in (3).

(3)   Consonant epenthesis in Axininca Campa
         a. /no-N-koma-i/ noŋkomati   'he will paddle'
         b. /no-N-č^{h}ik-i/ noɲč^{h}iki (*noɲč^{h}ikti) 'he will cut'

Note that [t]-epenthesis applies only in (3a), where two vowels are adjacent in the input, while there is no need for epenthesis in (3b), where the input supplies a consonant as an onset to the final syllable. We will return to this pattern of consonant epenthesis in section 3.3.2, where we will analyse it as an interaction of syllabic well-formedness and faithfulness constraints. Here we will focus on the syllabic well-formedness aspect, the avoidance of onset-less syllables, to which we now turn.

We conclude from the typological results and epenthesis data that the presence of an onset is an *unmarked* situation as compared to its absence. This is expressed in the structural well-formedness constraint ONSET (Itô 1989, Prince and Smolensky 1993):

(4)   **ONSET**
         *[$_\sigma$ V ('Syllables must have onsets.')

This constraint requires that syllables must not begin with vowels; it is satisfied only by syllables that have an initial consonant, or *onset*. Therefore languages in which ONSET is undominated have obligatory onsets. Finally, ONSET is 'grounded' in the articulatory and perceptual systems: the best starting point for a vowel is a preceding consonant (rather than another vowel).

At the right margin of the syllable, the unmarked situation is the reverse, because here the *lack* of a consonant is universally preferred to the presence of one:

(5)   Implicational universal for syllable-final segments
            If a language has closed syllables, then it also has open syllables.

Again, languages fall into two large classes, according to whether they allow or disallow codas. For example, Arabic, Tunica, and English allow codas, while Fijian, Mazateco, and Cayuvava disallow codas (Blevins 1995). Crucially, *no languages* are known in which syllables *must have codas*.

As before, languages may employ strategies to 'repair' imperfect syllables, such as the epenthesis of a vowel in order to avoid a coda. Such epenthesis occurs in Boumaa Fijian (Dixon 1988), a language in which syllables strictly conform to the shapes CV or V. Consider the following words, all realizations of English loans ending in consonants:

(6)   Vowel epenthesis in Boumaa Fijian
            a. kaloko 'clock'
            b. aapolo 'apple'
            c. tʃone   'John'

Again faithfulness is violated because vowel epenthesis causes a divergence between the input and the output.

Both language typology and the wide-spread occurrence of processes which avoid codas suggest that the 'unmarked' situation is for syllables to lack codas. This unmarked situation is encoded in the following well-formedness constraint.

(7)   **No-Coda**
            *C]$_\sigma$ ('Syllables are open.')

This constraint requires that syllables must not end in a consonant, or *coda*. Languages in which No-Coda is undominated have open syllables only. Like Onset, this constraint is 'grounded' in the perceptual system: coda consonants, particularly those standing before another consonant, tend to be unreleased, and hence lack perceptual cues that are present in prevocalic consonants, which are released (Ohala 1990, Steriade 1995b).

In sum, the two syllable form constraints Onset and No-Coda evaluate the four logically possible syllable types as below:

(8)   Syllable type   Onset   No-Coda
    a. CV   ✓   ✓
    b. CVC   ✓   *
    c. V   *   ✓
    d. VC   *   *

This is not a tableau: observe that the constraints are not in a conflicting relationship, but merely cross-classify the four logical possibilities. The conclusion to be drawn from this table is that CV is the 'perfect' syllable shape, while all remaining shapes {CVC, V, VC} are 'less perfect', by having a coda, or lacking an onset, or having both defects.

We are already able to account for an important cross-linguistic observation: single intervocalic consonants are universally syllabified as *onsets*, rather than codas.[2]

(9)   Universal syllabification of single intervocalic consonants
    CV.CV > CVC.V

This follows from the fact that both well-formedness constraints, Onset and No-Coda, favour an onset syllabification of (10a) over the alternative coda syllabification of (10b):

(10)

Input: /baba/	Onset	No-Coda
a. ☞ ba.ba		
b. bab.a	*!	*!

Regardless of the ranking of both constraints, a single intervocalic consonant is always optimally syllabified as an onset to the second syllable, rather than as a coda to the first. This reflects the 'asymmetrical' nature of both syllabic well-formedness constraints.

3.2.2 *Complex onsets and codas*

So far our syllable typology has only considered the mere presence or absence of onsets and codas. But languages also differ along the dimension of *complexity* of syllable margins. For example, a language may allow codas, but still disallow

---

[2] In the literature two languages have been reported to be exceptional to this generalization, by syllabifying a single intervocalic consonant 'backward' as the coda of the preceding syllable. Both cases, Oykangand (Sommer 1981) and Barra Gaelic (Borgstrøm 1937), are doubtful, however. See for discussion Clements (1986), McCarthy and Prince (1993b), Blevins (1995).

'complex' codas, that is, codas consisting of two or more consonants. In such a language, codas must be 'simple', that is, consist of one consonant.

Observe that the use of the terminology 'complex' and 'simple' already suggests a markedness relation in this respect: indeed many languages restrict the complexity of syllable margins – complex onsets are universally marked as compared to simple onsets; complex codas are marked as compared to simple codas. The unmarked status of simple onsets and codas is supported by various kinds of evidence.

First consider the implicational universals below:

(11)   Implicational universal for onset complexity
         If a language allows complex onsets, then it also allows simple onsets.

(12)   Implicational universal for coda complexity
         If a language allows complex codas, then it also allows simple codas.

Crucially, no languages have syllables with complex margins, while disallowing syllables with simple margins.

Another type of evidence for the marked status of complex margins is the fact that many languages actively avoid complex onsets and codas. Typical avoidance strategies are vowel epenthesis and consonant deletion. Some languages, such as Lenakel (Lynch 1974, Blevins 1995), avoid both types of complex margins (onsets and codas) by a single strategy, that of vowel epenthesis:[3]

(13)   Avoidance of complex margins by vowel epenthesis in Lenakel
         a. /t-n-ak-ol/   tɨ.na.gɔl   'you (sg.) will do it'
         b. /t-r-kən/   tɨr.gən   'he will eat it'
         c. /ark-ark/   ar.ga.rɨkʰ   'to growl'
         d. /kam-n-m̄an-n/   kam.nɨ.m̄a.nɨn   'for her brother'[4]

An epenthetic vowel [ɨ] breaks up clusters of two consonants at the beginning (13a–b) or end (13c–d) of a word, as well as clusters of three consonants in medial position (13d). A medial cluster of two consonants (such as /rk/ in 13c) is not broken up by epenthesis, as this can be split between two syllables without need for a complex margin: the first consonant syllabifies as a simple coda, and the second as a simple onset.[5]

---

[3] Lynch (1974: 87) reports that word-initial consonant-glide-clusters are permitted.

[4] The actual form is [kam.nɨ.m̄ɒ.nɨn]. Here /a/ has undergone a process of rounding into [ɒ] applying when /a/ is adjacent to a velarized labial (Lynch 1974: 97).

[5] We focus on obligatory epenthetic vowels, abstracting away from *optional* epenthetic vowels that may be inserted in clusters of two consonants before unstressed vowels (Lynch 1974: 84).

In spite of the appearance that may be given by the Lenakel examples, no intrinsic typological connection has been established between complexity of onsets and codas. The following table shows that all combinations of onset and coda complexity occur in the world's languages (Itô 1986, Blevins 1995):

(14) A typology of margin complexity

	Simple codas only	*Complex codas allowed*
Simple onsets only	CV, CVC (Japanese, Yokuts)	CV, CVC, CV**CC** (Finnish, Tunica)
Complex onsets allowed	CV, CVC, **CC**V, **CC**VC (Spanish,[6] Sedang)	CV, CVC, CV**CC**, **CC**V, **CC**VC, **CC**V**CC** (English, Totonac)

This shows that two structural well-formedness constraints are needed to capture margin complexity: one for onsets, and another for codas. These constraints are stated below:

(15) ***Complex^{Ons}**
*$[_\sigma$ CC ('Onsets are simple')

(16) ***Complex^{Cod}**
*CC $]_\sigma$ ('Codas are simple')

Any language in which *Complex^{Ons} is undominated has simple onsets only (this is the case in languages such as Japanese, Yokuts, Finnish, and Tunica). And any language in which *Complex^{Cod} is undominated allows no complex codas, if it allows codas at all (as is the case in Japanese, Yokuts, Spanish, and Sedang).[7]

We have seen that syllables are subject to structural well-formedness constraints. Syllable inventories of languages behave *symmetrically* with respect to these constraints. At this point the following question naturally arises: why do 'imperfect' syllable types such as CVC, V, VC, or VCC, occur at all in the world's languages? Why do languages not radically eliminate any syllabic imperfection, to become perfect CV-languages? That is, why are not all languages like Boumaa Fijian? The answer to this question, to be given in the next section, is characteristic of OT: input *faithfulness* may prevent the segmental changes necessary to create perfect syllables. That is, languages may tolerate imperfect syllables, but only under

[6] Spanish rarely allows complex codas word-finally, e.g. *biceps* (Harris 1983). Another language of this type is Canela-Krahô (Popjes and Popjes 1986).

[7] Whether or not a language has codas depends on the ranking of No-Coda, the constraint ruling out codas regardless of their complexity.

duress of faithfulness. In the next section we will take a detailed look at the interaction of faithfulness and syllabic well-formedness.

3.3 Epenthesis and the conflict of well-formedness and faithfulness

Stated in optimality-theoretic terms, epenthesis involves a violation of faithfulness: the epenthetic segment has no counterpart in the input. This violation of faithfulness is due to dominant syllable well-formedness constraints, such as ONSET and NO-CODA, discussed in the previous section. Reconsider consonant epenthesis in the onset in Axininca Campa, an example of which is repeated below from (3):

(17)   /no-N-koma-i/ noŋ.ko.ma.ti > noŋ.ko.ma.i

The epenthetic output [noŋ.ko.ma.ti] contains a segment that has no input counterpart, a violation of faithfulness. Still, this is preferred to the 'faithful' candidate *[noŋ.ko.ma.i], which has a syllable without an onset, thus violating ONSET. We recognize a now-familiar theme, the conflict of well-formedness (here, 'avoidance of marked syllable structure') and faithfulness (here 'avoidance of lexically unsponsored segments'). In sum, epenthesis involves a resolution of this conflict at the expense of faithfulness: *the costs of inserting a (non-underlying) segment are less than those of imperfect syllable structure*. This section will develop an optimality model of epenthesis capturing this insight, which has a range of typological consequences. Before looking into the model, we need to discuss briefly its theoretical origins.

3.3.1 *A brief history of epenthesis*

The key insight that epenthesis and syllabification are inextricably connected already appeared in derivational phonology (Selkirk 1981, Itô 1986, 1989). According to Selkirk and Itô an epenthetic segment is an empty structural position whose presence is required by a language-specific 'syllable template'. This template defines whether or not an onset is obligatory, whether or not a coda is allowed, etc. In this model, epenthesis is driven by an imperfect match between input segments and the syllable template. An imperfect match may arise, for example, when the input contains a sequence of two vowels, without an intervening consonant, whereas the syllable template requires an obligatory onset. Syllabification then enforces the template by providing an empty onset position: one that is not filled by an input consonant. Empty syllabic positions must receive some phonetic interpretation ('spelling out' their features) at the end of the derivation. For example, the empty onset of the final syllable in the Axininca example [noŋkomati] is spelled out as [t].

(18)

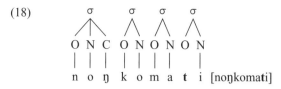

n o ŋ k o m a t i [noŋkomati]

In this model epenthesis is a fully automatic consequence of syllabification, a spell-out of an empty templatic position. Accordingly there are no 'rules' of epenthesis, but only rules of syllabification enforcing the syllable template. Whether or not epenthesis applies in a language only depends on the template: this may require specific positions to be obligatory. Anticipating OT constraint ranking, Itô (1989) argues that templates enforce universal syllabification principles with different 'strengths'. For example, languages such as Axininca Campa (which enforce onsets by consonant epenthesis) use a strengthened version of the *Onset Principle* ('avoid onset-less syllables'). This version Itô dubs the *Strict Onset Principle*: 'onset-less syllables are impossible'. Thus, cross-linguistic variation in onset epenthesis is due to a single binary parameter: languages select either the 'weak' Onset Principle or the 'strong' Strict Onset Principle.

Prince and Smolensky (1993) take these ideas to their logical conclusion, deriving 'relative strength' of templatic principles from constraint ranking. In their Optimality model, output constraints assume the function of defining syllabification and epenthesis. The grammar is an evaluation device selecting the most harmonic output from an infinite candidate set, according to a language-specific ranking of universal constraints. OT does away with language-specific templates: cross-linguistic variation in epenthesis patterns is explained by variation in constraint ranking. For example, Prince and Smolensky argue that in languages enforcing syllable onsets by consonant epenthesis, ONSET takes precedence over the faithfulness constraint FILL, requiring that 'syllable positions must be filled with underlying segments'. Note that FILL is indeed violated in the output (18). This output is 'unfaithful' to its underlying segments as it contains a syllabic position that is left unfilled by an underlying segment.

Prince and Smolensky's model is known as *Containment Theory*, after its central assumption that no element may be literally removed from the input form. The input is thus contained in every candidate output, including those candidate outputs in which it is left unpronounced. In Containment Theory, the deletion of a segment does not involve its removal from the output (this is ruled out by containment). Instead the input segment is *left unparsed by a syllable*, hence phonetically uninterpreted (compare 'Stray Erasure' in McCarthy 1979, Steriade 1982, Itô 1986). Analogously to FILL, deletion is penalized by a faithfulness constraint PARSE 'underlying segments must be parsed into syllable structure'. See the hypothetical example of a deletion of a consonant /p/ in (19):

(19)   Deletion and epenthesis in Containment Theory (O = onset, N = nucleus, C = coda)

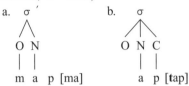

In (19a), a segment /p/ is left phonetically uninterpreted as it is not syllabified. Epenthesis of [t] (19b) is the exact opposite situation: a syllabic position is phonetically interpreted even though it is not filled by a segment. Prince and Smolensky's OT model of epenthesis thus preserves the central assumption of the earlier (Selkirk–Itô) derivational theory, that epenthetic segments are empty syllable positions.

Correspondence Theory (McCarthy and Prince 1995a) drops Prince and Smolensky's notion of containment. That is, it is no longer required that the input be contained in each output candidate. Consequently epenthetic segments are no longer viewed as the phonetic interpretations of empty positions, but rather as (full-fledged) output segments that have no counterparts in the input. This correctly predicts that the feature contents of epenthetic segments may participate in phonological processes (Davis 1995). The faithfulness role of containment, restricting divergence between input and output (penalizing 'overparsing' and 'underparsing'), is transferred to correspondence. Correspondence, as we learned in chapter 1, is a relation between pairs of segments in the input and output. It is subject to constraints requiring various kinds of congruence between segments in input and output (such as identity, linearity, etc.). In spite of the differences between Containment Theory and Correspondence Theory, the latter preserves the insight that epenthesis and deletion both reflect the dominance of syllabic well-formedness over faithfulness. In the following subsections we will develop a correspondence model of epenthesis capturing this insight.

3.3.2   *Introducing two correspondence constraints*

3.3.2.1   *The 'anti-epenthesis' constraint DEP-IO*
Epenthesis involves a violation of faithfulness: the output diverges from the input by the presence of an epenthetic segment, one that is not 'sponsored' by lexical

representation. The faithfulness constraint militating against epenthesis is DEPENDENCY-IO (or DEP-IO), after McCarthy and Prince (1995a):[8]

(20)   **DEP-IO**
       Output segments must have input correspondents. ('No epenthesis')

This constraint is violated by any output segment that lacks a correspondent in the input. Such a violation is incurred by epenthetic [**t**] in the example [noŋkomati] from Axininca Campa, introduced in the preceding section. This violation is shown in a diagram below that indicates corresponding segments through vertical lines. Note that the input contains no segment corresponding to output [**t**]:

(21)   Violation of DEP-IO in [noŋ.ko.ma.ti]

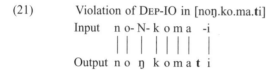

       Input   n o- N- k o m a   -i
       Output n o ŋ k o m a t i

Other examples of Axininca Campa show that epenthetic [**t**] occurs between every pair of vowels that are in adjacent morphemes in the input:

(22)   a.i   /no-N-koma-i/   noŋkomati   'he will paddle'
       a.ii   /no-N-koma-aa-i/   noŋkomataati   'he will paddle
                                                        again'
       a.iii /no-N-koma-ako-i/   noŋkomatakoti   'he will paddle
                                                        for'
       a.iv   /no-N-koma-ako-aa-i-ro/ noŋkomatakotaatiro 'he will paddle
                                                        for it again'
       b.i   /no-N-čʰik-i/   noɲčʰiki   'he will cut'
       b.ii   /no-N-čʰik-aa-i/   noɲčʰikaati   'he will cut
                                                        again'
       b.iii /no-N-čʰik-ako-i/   noɲčʰikakoti   'he will cut for'
       b.iv   /no-N-čʰik-ako-aa-i-ro/ noɲčʰikakotaatiro 'he will cut for
                                                        it again'

Epenthesis in onsets shows that Axininca ranks DEP-IO below ONSET, the structural well-formedness constraint whose violation epenthesis avoids. Onset epenthesis involves the following ranking:

(23)   Epenthesis in onset
       ONSET ≫ DEP-IO

---

[8] DEP-IO was introduced in chapter 1, but left unillustrated.

This ranking is demonstrated by the following tableau. It contains two candidates, which differ only in the presence versus absence of an epenthetic consonant.

(24)

Input: /no-N-koma-i/	ONSET	DEP-IO
a. ☞ noŋ.ko.ma.ti		*
b. noŋ.ko.ma.i	*!	

In sum, epenthesis is the assertion of syllabic well-formedness at the expense of input faithfulness.

3.3.2.2 The 'anti-deletion' constraint MAX-IO

Next consider the possibility of a second strategy that might have been employed to avoid onset-less syllables in Axininca Campa: the deletion of a vowel. This might have resulted in *[noŋ.ko.ma], by deletion of the suffix vowel /i/ following the root vowel /a/.[9] Vowel deletion is a cross-linguistically common reaction to hiatus; however, not so in Axininca Campa, which prefers consonant epenthesis:

(25)   Consonant epenthesis preferred to vowel deletion
         [noŋ.ko.ma.ti] > *[noŋ.ko.ma]

Segment deletion is a violation of faithfulness, just as epenthesis is. It is the mirror-image case: *an input segment has no counterpart in the output.* The constraint that enforces the preservation of input segments in the output is MAXIMALITY-IO (or MAX-IO):

(26)   **MAX-IO**
         Input segments must have output correspondents. ('No deletion')

Importantly, MAX-IO does *not* require that an input segment and its corresponding output segment have identical feature content. (This requirement is made by another faithfulness constraint introduced in chapter 1: IDENT-IO.) All that is required by MAX-IO is that for every output segment there is *some* input segment corresponding to it. This is tantamount to a ban on the deletion of input segments – hence MAX-IO is the *anti-deletion* constraint.

Consider the following diagram, which shows that MAX-IO is actually violated in the output candidate *[noŋ.ko.ma], as the input segment /i/ has no output counterpart:

---

[9] Rather arbitrarily, we consider the deletion of a suffix vowel, rather than a root vowel – both options are equivalent with respect to the violation of faithfulness involved. But see chapter 2 for McCarthy and Prince's proposal that root faithfulness outranks affix faithfulness.

(27)   Violation of MAX-IO in *[noŋ.ko.ma]

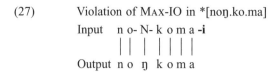

Compare this diagram with the one in (21), to see that epenthesis and deletion are mirror-image cases from the viewpoint of input correspondence.

The fact that Axininca Campa prefers consonant epenthesis to vowel deletion tells us that MAX-IO dominates DEP-IO. The former is not violable under duress of ONSET, whereas the latter is. Combining our conclusions, we arrive at the following total ranking:

(28)   Consonant epenthesis preferred to vowel deletion in hiatus resolution
         ONSET, MAX-IO ≫ DEP-IO

This ranking is illustrated by the following tableau, which contains both candidates of the preceding tableau, plus the 'deletion' candidate (29b):

(29)

Input: /no-N-koma-i/	ONSET	MAX-IO	DEP-IO
a. ☞ noŋ.ko.ma.ti			*
b. noŋ.ko.ma		*!	
c. noŋ.ko.ma.i	*!		

Note that each candidate incurs a violation of one constraint. As we may predict from the discussion in chapter 2, the optimal output (29a) violates the *lowest-ranking* faithfulness constraint, here DEP-IO. The lowest-ranking faithfulness constraint is, by definition, the one whose violation is 'least expensive'. It is violated in order to avoid violation of both higher-ranking constraints, ONSET and MAX-IO, whose mutual ranking is irrelevant here.

The insight that the lowest-ranking constraint determines the outcome allows us to construct a factorial typology of these three constraints. Only three rankings need to be considered, one for each constraint in lowest-ranking position:

(30)   A factorial typology of onset-driven epenthesis and deletion
         a. ONSET, MAX-IO ≫ **DEP-IO** Consonant epenthesis to create onset.
         b. ONSET, DEP-IO ≫ **MAX-IO** Vowel deletion to avoid onset-less syllable.
         c. MAX-IO, DEP-IO ≫ **ONSET** No deletion, nor epenthesis to create onset.

Ranking (30a) produces the case of onset epenthesis, where DEP-IO is violated, of which Axininca Campa is an example. Ranking (30b) is the case of vowel deletion in hiatus, to avoid an onset-less syllable, violating MAX-IO. This is also a cross-linguistically common strategy occurring in languages such as Modern Greek and Yokuts. Finally, ranking (30c) represents languages that disallow deletion and epenthesis as strategies to avoid onset-less syllables: when all strategies to attain unmarked structures are blocked, marked structures are necessarily allowed. This happens at the expense of syllabic well-formedness (ONSET). This is also a cross-linguistically common case, occurring in English and other languages.

In sum, we have found that the range of syllable structures of a language depends on the interaction between syllabic well-formedness and faithfulness. In the next section we will extend the factorial typology to all four constraints that were used so far: ONSET, NO-CODA, DEP-IO, and MAX-IO. This extended typology will explain some major cross-linguistic properties of epenthesis and deletion.

3.3.3 *Economy, or against excessive epenthesis*

A general consequence of minimal violation is that changes of the input take place *only under duress*. Without proper incentive, *no change will take place*. The logic of economy is shown in tableau (31). Two realizations of an input /A/ are compared as to their relative harmony. The first realization of /A/, the output candidate, [A], incurs no violation of the well-formedness constraint, and is also faithful to its input. The second realization of /A/, the output candidate, [B], is also structurally well-formed, but incurs a minimal violation of faithfulness. Faithfulness will always decide in favour of the most faithful candidate, [A], at the expense of less faithful candidate [B], regardless of the ranking of constraints.

(31)

/A/	Well-formedness	Faithfulness
a. ☞ [A]		
b.　　[B]		*!

It is only when a structural well-formedness constraint militates against output [A] (e.g. a constraint *[A]) that the output may be forced to diverge from the input, given the ranking Well-formedness ≫ Faithfulness.

This principle of 'inertness-by-default', or 'economy', is a direct consequence of minimal violation. Or stated differently (Prince and Smolensky 1993),

(32)　　　*do only when necessary.*

Now consider what '*do only when necessary*' predicts for epenthesis. As we saw earlier, epenthesis incurs a violation of faithfulness, as adding a segment entails some divergence between output and input. Given the presence of the 'anti-epenthesis' constraint DEP-IO in all grammars, no excess epenthesis will take place, regardless of its ranking. Pressure to violate DEP-IO may *only* reside in dominant well-formedness constraints, specifically ONSET and NO-CODA.

It has been argued by Prince and Smolensky (1993) that regardless of the ranking of DEP-IO, ONSET, and NO-CODA, specific kinds of epenthesis are generally disfavoured. For example, the epenthesis of a consonant as a syllable coda cannot be modelled under any logically possible ranking of syllabic well-formedness and faithfulness constraints, as we will see below. Such typological results are essential since they show that OT, a theory of violable constraints, is still capable of ruling out logically possible but cross-linguistically unattested situations. Or to state it differently, an empirically restrictive linguistic theory requires no inviolable constraints.

3.3.3.1 *Predictions about epenthesis*

Here we will consider the following three predictions:

(33)   Three predictions derived from minimal violation
 a. Epenthesis never results in an increase of structural markedness.
 b. Epenthesis always results in a decrease of structural markedness.
 c. Epenthesis always applies *minimally*, that is, precisely to the extent that is necessary to improve structural markedness.

Let us now see how these typological predictions follow from constraint interaction.

The first prediction is that epenthesis never results in an *increase* of markedness, as compared to a non-epenthetic output. For example, epenthesis never creates a marked structural position, such as a coda. By definition, marked positions cannot be required by structural constraints. Hence, epenthesis of a coda consonant is inherently anti-harmonic, regardless of the mutual ranking of syllabic well-formedness (NO-CODA) and faithfulness (DEP-IO). We consider a hypothetical example /baba/, with an epenthetic consonant [ʔ]:

(34)   No consonant epenthesis ([ʔ]) in coda position:

Input: /baba/	ONSET	NO-CODA	DEP-IO
a. ☞ ba.ba			
b. baʔ.ba		*	*

The epenthetic candidate (34b) is less harmonic than its non-epenthetic competitor (34a) in two respects, as it violates both NO-CODA and DEP-IO. Conversely
no well-formedness constraints are satisfied by (34b) which (34a) violates. This
means that (34b) will always be less harmonic than (34a), in any grammar,
regardless of the ranking of the constraints. (Since any violation will be fatal to
34b, no exclamation marks have been added.)

By the same reasoning, no vowel will be epenthesized adjacent to another
vowel, since that produces unnecessary violations of both ONSET and DEP-IO:

(35)   No vowel epenthesis ([i]) next to another vowel:

Input: /baba/	ONSET	NO-CODA	DEP-IO
a. ☞ ba.ba			
b. ba.i.ba	*		*

Again the ranking of the constraints involved is irrelevant to the outcome.

The second prediction is that epenthesis is *excluded whenever it yields no gains*
in terms of structural well-formedness. For example, the epenthesis of an entire
CV syllable, even though this violates no well-formedness constraints, is intrinsically non-harmonic, since nothing is gained by it.[10] Assuming an epenthetic
onset [ʔ] plus a nuclear [i], this would produce (36b):

(36)   No epenthesis of an entire syllable ([ʔi]):

Input: /baba/	ONSET	NO-CODA	DEP-IO
a. ☞ ba.ba			
b. ba.ʔi.ba			*!*

Considering the shape of the epenthetic syllable, we find that this is structurally
perfect, since CV has an onset and lacks a coda. Then why is epenthesis of such
a perfect syllable nevertheless excluded? This reflects a fundamental property of
constraint evaluation. The criterion for evaluation is *minimization of ill-formed
structures*, rather than maximization of well-formed structures. Nothing is gained
by adding any 'structurally perfect' elements without an accompanying reduction
of ill-formedness. When no structural improvements are attained by adding an

---

[10] In fact, languages are known in which the epenthesis of an entire syllable is forced by
superordinate prosodic well-formedness constraints. For example, syllable epenthesis may
augment a monosyllabic form in order to satisfy a high-ranking 'minimal word' constraint to
the effect that every word be disyllabic; cf. McCarthy and Prince (1993b). See chapter 4.

element, its addition is ruled out by faithfulness constraints. This is what occurs in tableau (36). There is no 'bonus' for addition of the structurally perfect epenthetic syllable in the columns below the well-formedness constraints ONSET and NO-CODA, but simply a lack of marks, indicating an absence of violation of these constraints. In this respect, the epenthetic candidate (36b) fares *no better* than the 'faithful' candidate (36a). In the end, it is faithfulness that swings the balance in favour of (36a).

The third prediction is that epenthesis always applies *minimally*. That is, no more segments are epenthesized than are strictly required to minimize the violation of syllabic well-formedness. This prediction is actually a corollary of both predictions made above. Epenthesis serves to minimize the violation of well-formedness constraints. Any additional epenthesis on top of this minimum, which yields no further gains in well-formedness, is unnecessary – hence it is blocked by faithfulness, as we will illustrate in the next section.

3.3.3.2 *Minimal epenthesis in Lenakel*

Consider the epenthetic examples from Lenakel (Lynch 1974, Blevins 1995), presented earlier in (13). Epenthesis of [ɨ] breaks up any consonant clusters that would otherwise surface as complex syllable margins:

(37)   a. /t-n-ak-ol/   ti.na.gɔl   'you (sg.) will do it'
                                          *tna.gɔl
            b. /ark-ark/   ar.ga.rɨk^h 'to growl'
                                          *ar.gark^h
            c. /kam-n-m̃an-n/ kam.nɨ.m̃a.nɨn   'for her brother'
                                          *kam.nm̃ann, *kamn.m̃ann

No complex margins occur in Lenakel, hence *COMPLEX^{ONS} and *COMPLEX^{COD} are both undominated. We combine both into a 'cover' constraint *COMPLEX 'no complex syllable margins'. Since epenthesis applies to avoid violations of *COMPLEX, the latter constraint must dominate DEP-IO:

(38)   Vowel epenthesis triggered to avoid complex margins
            *COMPLEX ≫ DEP-IO

The relevant observation is that no more vowels are inserted than are necessary to avoid violations of *COMPLEX:

(39)   Vowel epenthesis as a minimal adjustment in Lenakel
            ar.ga.rɨk^h > a.rɨ.ga.ri.gɨ
            ti.na.gɔl > ti.na.gɔ.lɨ
            kam.nɨ.m̃a.nɨn > *ka.mɨ.nɨ.m̃a.nɨ.nɨ

Note that all *suboptimal* righthand forms are perfectly structured strings of CV syllables. All syllables have (simple) onsets, while none have codas. But in spite of their structural perfection, these candidates fall short of being selected. Apparently, vowel epenthesis is not available in Lenakel as a general strategy to avoid codas, but only as a more restricted strategy to avoid complex codas and onsets. To put it differently, input faithfulness takes priority over avoidance of codas:

(40)   Vowel epenthesis unavailable to avoid codas
          DEP-IO ≫ NO-CODA

In sum, the faithfulness constraint DEP-IO is sandwiched between two syllabic structural well-formedness constraints, *COMPLEX and NO-CODA:

(41)   Preliminary ranking for Lenakel vowel epenthesis
          *COMPLEX ≫ DEP-IO ≫ NO-CODA

Tableau (42) considers five candidates differing only in the number of epenthetic vowels. At the top we find the most faithful candidate (42a), which has no violations of DEP-IO; at the bottom is the structurally perfect candidate (42e), which has no violations of well-formedness constraints *COMPLEX and NO-CODA. The winner, (42c), stands in between both extremes. Still there is no 'trade-off' between faithfulness and well-formedness, as everything follows from strict domination.

(42)

Input: /kam-n-m̄an-n/	*COMPLEX	DEP-IO	NO-CODA
a. kamn.m̄ann	*!*		**
b. kam.nɨ.m̄ann	*!	*	**
c. ☞ kam.nɨ.m̄a.nɨn		**	**
d. ka.mɨ.nɨ.m̄a.nɨn		***!	*
e. ka.mɨ.nɨ.m̄a.nɨ.nɨ		***!*	

Candidate (42c) is optimal since it has the *minimal* number of violations of DEP-IO that are necessary to avoid violations of *COMPLEX. This minimum number of violations is two: fewer would not do to avoid complex margins (42a–b), while more violations are ruled out by faithfulness (42d–e).[11] In conclusion, epenthesis is *economical* – no more vowels are inserted than are strictly necessary to avoid violations of syllable well-formedness.

---

[11] Of course, the prediction that epenthesis applies 'minimally' is *relativized* to the grammar. In Lenakel 'minimal' has a different meaning than in a language which completely avoids codas (due to undominated NO-CODA).

That No-Coda is still active despite the fact that it is dominated is shown by the tableau of [ti.na.gɔl]:

(43)

Input: /t-n-ak-ol/	*Complex	Dep-IO	No-Coda
a. tna.gɔl	*!		*
b. ☞ ti.na.gɔl		*	*
c. it.na.gɔl		*	**!
d. ti.na.gɔ.li		**!	

The faithful non-epenthetic candidate (43a) is eliminated by undominated *Complex. Initial epenthesis, as in (43c), successfully avoids a complex onset, at the expense of only one violation of Dep-IO. But there is an even more successful competitor, which has both of these virtues, plus the additional advantage of having one fewer violation of No-Coda. This is (43b), where 'smart' epenthesis breaks up consonant clusters in such a way that both consonants form onsets in the ouput.[12]

The attentive reader may have noticed that avoidance of complex margins may be achieved in more than one way, even for two epenthetic vowels. Three output candidates that were left unconsidered in tableau (42) are presented in (44). All are suboptimal as compared to [kam.ni.m̃a.nin]:

(44)   Positional preferences in epenthesis, unaccounted for by present analysis:

        kam.ni.m̃a.nin > *ka.min.m̃a.nin, *kam.ni.m̃an.ni, *ka.min.m̃an.ni

The model of epenthesis that we have developed so far has no means to make structural distinctions among these candidates. Observe that all four incur identical violations of syllabic well-formedness constraints (in particular, of No-Coda). Positional preferences for epenthetic elements will be discussed in the next section.

3.3.4 *Alignment and epenthesis*

The simple model of epenthesis that we have developed so far does not account for any *morphological* influence over epenthesis. Such influence has been pointed out for various languages by Kenstowicz (1994b), Spencer (1994), and Blevins (1995). Cross-linguistic evidence shows that epenthesis applies in such a way that morphological constituents are maximally respected. For example, epenthesis

---

[12] In section 3.3.4 we will find that there is yet another constraint favouring non-initial epenthesis, one requiring the coincidence of morphological and prosodic edges.

tends to respect the *contiguity* of segments by applying between morphemes, rather than inside morphemes. Epenthesis also tends to highlight the *edges* of morphemes, for example by making the beginning of a morpheme coincide with the beginning of a syllable. Such morphological factors in epenthesis make sense from the viewpoint of the processing system: the processing of lexical elements is improved when their realizations are constant and signalled by prosodic edges.

3.3.4.1 *Alignment and epenthesis in Axininca Campa*

As an example of the relevance of word edges to epenthesis, reconsider the pattern of [t]-epenthesis in Axininca Campa, a pattern analysed earlier in section 3.3.2. There we concluded that epenthesis serves to avoid onset-less syllables. McCarthy and Prince (1993a, b) draw attention to the fact that epenthesis fails to apply in *word-initial* position:

(45)   Lack of initial epenthesis in Axininca Campa
         a. /osampi/   osampi   *tosampi   'ask'
         b. /i-N-koma-i/ iŋkomati *tiŋkomati 'he will paddle'

What blocks epenthesis initially? Naively, one might be tempted to relax the constraint ONSET in word-initial syllables. This would lead to a specific version of this constraint:

(46)   **ONSET** (naive version, to be rejected)
         Syllables must have onsets, *except word-initially.*

However, (46) is not a very illuminating way to approach this pattern. The first problem is its relation to the general constraint ONSET, which has no such 'exception' clause. If this is replaced by (46), then we can no longer explain the fact that in some languages all syllables must have onsets, regardless of their position in the word. Alternatively, if (46) is interpreted as independent of the general constraint, then a redundancy problem arises: the same requirement ('syllables must have onsets') is stated by two separate constraints in the universal inventory. Such a redundancy should be avoided, as it amounts to the loss of generalization. A second problem is that (46) fails to explain why the exception clause for onsets holds for *word-initial* syllables, that is, for word-initial position. There is much evidence (from a range of phenomena other than epenthesis) that the left edge of the word is 'respected' by phonological changes. This inertness of the left word edge is expressed by the constraint ALIGN-L (after McCarthy and Prince 1993a):[13]

---

[13] McCarthy and Prince (1993a) state ALIGN-L on the Stem, rather than on the Grammatical Word.

(47) **ALIGN-L**

The left edge of the Grammatical Word coincides with the left edge of the PrWd.

Alignment is a much more general phenomenon than may be suggested by this constraint, which is only one member of a constraint type of which we will see many more examples in this book. In section 3.4 we will generalize the format of alignment constraints.[14]

The *misaligned* nature of the suboptimal candidate [tosampi] is shown in diagram (48), representing both its prosodic and morphological structure:

(48)

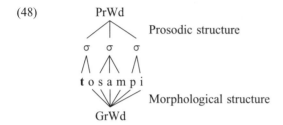

Note that the left edge of the Grammatical Word is defined by the initial segment of the stem [o], whereas the left edge of the Prosodic Word is defined by the epenthetic segment [t]. Hence both edges do not coincide, in violation of ALIGN-L.

The relation between [t]-epenthesis and its blocking in word-initial position now becomes clear. It is just another interaction of conflicting, violable constraints: alignment takes priority over avoidance of onset-less syllables. This is stated in the ranking in (49), which includes the subranking ONSET ≫ DEP-IO from (23) above:

(49) Onset epenthesis respecting left word edge

ALIGN-L ≫ ONSET ≫ DEP-IO

Having factored out the 'left-edge' effect, we may now dispense with the 'odd' exception clause in the ONSET constraint (46), restoring this constraint to its original generality.

A translation of (49) into a prose statement would read as follows:

(50) Avoid epenthesis,

except when this provides an onset to an otherwise onset-less syllable,

except when this syllable stands in initial position.

---

[14] McCarthy and Prince (1995a) restate alignment as a correspondence constraint ANCHORING, requiring that corresponding segments in the input and output both stand at an edge. See section 3.6.3.

As Prince and Smolensky (1993) point out, such exception clauses are highly common in generalizations about linguistic patterns. OT is ideally suited to capture such situations. Constraints are the substance of the theory, expressing linguistic generalizations without qualification about 'exception clauses'. The latter function, encoding the relative scopes of generalizations, is attributed to the constraint hierarchy. Therefore, constraints can be highly general, as long as they are violable as well.

A full account of the Axininca epenthetic pattern should also address the ranking of MAX-IO. Earlier we found that MAX-IO and ONSET were both undominated, but that was before the initial blocking data in (45) had entered the picture, telling us that ONSET is dominated. However, we still have no reason to 'demote' MAX-IO, and we will keep it at the top of the hierarchy, where it sits together with ALIGN-L:

(51)

Input: /osampi/	ALIGN-L	MAX-IO	ONSET	DEP-IO
a. ☞ o.sam.pi			*	
b.　　to.sam.pi	*!			*
c.　　sam.pi		*!		

The ranking MAX-IO ≫ ONSET has no negative consequences for the analysis presented in section 3.3.2. This ranking correctly predicts that vowel deletion is not allowed as a strategy to avoid onset-less syllables in Axininca Campa.

3.3.4.2 *Alignment and epenthesis in Lenakel*

We now return to the cases of Lenakel epenthesis that we left slightly unresolved in section 3.3.3.2. All forms in (52a–b) have the minimal number of epenthetic vowels to avoid violations of *COMPLEX. And all have the same number of violations of NO-CODA. Then what causes the ill-formedness of the starred forms?

(52)   a. /ark-ark/   ar.ga.rɨkʰ   'to growl'
                    *ar.gar.gɨ
     b. /kam-n-m̄an-n/   kam.nɨ.m̄a.nɨn   'for her brother'
                    *kam.nɨ.m̄an.nɨ

This question is now answered as follows: both starred output forms violate *alignment* at their right edges. A word-final epenthetic vowel is misaligning since it breaks PrWd's coincidence with the right edge of the Grammatical Word. This is shown once more in the form of hierarchical representations in (53) which compare the optimal forms (which satisfy right-edge alignment) and suboptimal forms (violating right-edge alignment):

(53)   Coincidence of morphological edges and prosodic edges in Lenakel
         a. /ark-ark/   b. /kam-n-m̃an-n/

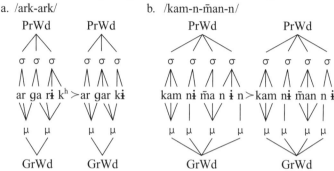

The righthand candidate of each pair is misaligned, because the epenthetic vowel stands at the right edge of the PrWd, thus obstructing the coincidence of morphological and prosodic edges.

In addition to the left-edge aligning constraint motivated for Axininca Campa we also need a right-edge aligning constraint. It is stated in (54), after McCarthy and Prince (1993a):

(54)   **ALIGN-R**
         The right edge of a Grammatical Word coincides with the right edge of a syllable.

Observe that both alignment constraints introduced thus far, ALIGN-L and ALIGN-R, share a common format, in the sense that two categories (a morphological and a phonological) are related by one of their edges (left or right). We will return to this generalized format of alignment constraints in section 3.4.

ALIGN-R may be considered undominated in Lenakel because it is never violated by epenthesis. We turn to the tableau of [ar.ga.rikʰ] to illustrate its role.

(55)

Input: /ark-ark/		ALIGN-R	*COMPLEX	DEP-IO	NO-CODA
a.	ar.garkʰ		*!		**
b. ☞	ar.ga.rikʰ			*	**
c.	ar.gar.gɨ	*!		*	**
d.	a.rɨ.ga.rikʰ			**!	*
e.	a.rɨ.ga.rɨ.gɨ	*!		***	

The non-epenthetic (fully faithful) candidate (55a) is naturally ruled out by *COMPLEX. Of the remaining candidates, two (55c, e) violate ALIGN-R. The choice among the remaining two candidates (55b, d) is made on the basis of economy of epenthesis. Only one vowel suffices to avoid complex syllable margins, as in (55b).

Is there any evidence for left-alignment in Lenakel on the basis of epenthesis? In fact ALIGN-L is never violated, as epenthesis never applies word-initially. With ALIGN-L undominated, the effects attributed earlier to No-CODA (see tableau 43) may now be reattributed to ALIGN-L. See the diagram in (56):

(56)   /t-n-ak-ol/

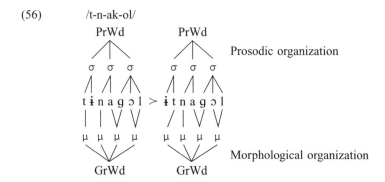

A tableau showing the activity of ALIGN-L is given below:

(57)

Input: /t-n-ak-ol/	ALIGN-L	ALIGN-R	*COMPLEX	DEP-IO	No-CODA
a.　　tna.gɔl			*!		*
b. ☞ tɨ.na.gɔl				*	*
c.　　ɨt.na.gɔl	*!				**
d.　　tɨ.na.gɔ.lɨ		*!		**	

(This does not affect the ranking argument given earlier for DEP-IO ≫ No-CODA, because epenthesis *never* applies to avoid codas, regardless of position.)

Having ruled out epenthesis at both edges of the word, we now turn to yet another potential output form for (52b), *[ka.mɨn.m̃a.nɨn], which differs from the optimal output [kam.nɨ.m̃a.nɨn] only in the position of the leftmost epenthetic vowel. The diagram below shows both candidates:

(58)   /kam-n-m̃an-n/

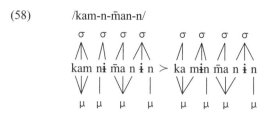

What we see is that epenthesis harmonizes with the morphological structure of the word in the following way: ideally each morpheme begins a new syllable; epenthesis helps to attain this goal by inserting a vowel directly after a morpheme-initial consonant, rather than before it.[15] This is yet another form of 'morpho-prosodic' alignment, now between the edges of morphemes and those of syllables. More precisely, we may state this as:

(59)   **ALIGN-MORPH-L**
         The left edge of a morpheme coincides with the left edge of a syllable.

If this were undominated, then no syllable would contain segmental material belonging to different morphemes. (For maximally one morpheme can be left-aligned with a syllable.) Considering the syllabification of the optimal output [kam.nɨ.m̃a.nɨn], we see that ALIGN-MORPH-L cannot be undominated. Here the final morpheme /-n/ is not left-aligned with a syllable, but instead shares a syllable with the final consonant of the preceding morpheme /-m̃an-/.

To find out by which constraint ALIGN-MORPH-L is dominated, we must imagine what the 'ideal' syllabification of this word would be, *if it were undominated*. Whatever rules out this form must be the dominant constraint that we are looking for. It is easy to see that this is *[kam-nɨ-m̃an-nɨ], a form in which all morphemes are left-aligned with a syllable. This output crucially differs from the optimal (attested) output in the position of the second epenthetic vowel. This stands in final position of the word, violating ALIGN-R. The ranking argument immediately emerges:

---

[15] Lynch (1974: 89) states the generalization about medial vowel epenthesis as follows: 'Clusters of three non-syllabics are not permitted in Lenakel surface representations. When they do arise, generally at morpheme boundaries, schwa is obligatorily inserted between the second and third member of the cluster of non-syllabics . . . Now when the morphemes with an initial two-consonant cluster are immediately preceded by a consonant-final morpheme, schwa is inserted between the second and third consonants of the resultant cluster.' All examples of medial epenthesis in triconsonantal clusters which Lynch presents indeed have a morphological structure of the following kind: the first consonant belongs to a different morpheme from the other consonants, for example /kam-n-m̃an-n/ 'for her brother', /əs-ət-pn-aan/ 'don't go up there!', or /k-ar-pkom/ 'they're heavy'. These three forms surface as [kam.nɨ.m̃a.nɨn], [əs.ɨd.bə̰.nan], and [kar.bə̰.gɔm], respectively.

(60)   ALIGN-R ≫ ALIGN-MORPH-L
         kam.nɨ.m̃a.nɨn > kam.nɨ.m̃an.nɨ

In the competition among morphemes for prosodic alignment, the grammatical word is stronger than the morpheme.

Next, ALIGN-MORPH-L can also be ranked with respect to DEP-IO. The argument is based on the forms [ar.ga.rɨkʰ] and [tɨ.na.gɔl]. Both forms violate ALIGN-MORPH-L to some extent. To 'repair' the misalignment of morphemes and syllable edges, one might attempt to add epenthetic syllables, resulting in [a.rɨkʰ-a.rɨkʰ] and [tɨ-nɨ-akʰ-ɔl]. But this leads to fatal additional violations of DEP-IO:

(61)   DEP-IO ≫ ALIGN-MORPH-L
         /ark-ark/   ar.ga.rɨkʰ > a.rɨg.a.rɨkʰ
         /t-n-ak-ol/ tɨ.na.gɔl > tɨ.nɨ.ag.ɔl

That is, economy of epenthesis has higher priority than morpho-syllabic alignment.

It is not possible to rank ALIGN-MORPH-L with respect to NO-CODA. Therefore we rank both constraints at the bottom of the hierarchy, which now takes its final form:

(62)   Final ranking for Lenakel epenthesis
         ALIGN-L, ALIGN-R, *COMPLEX ≫ DEP-IO ≫ ALIGN-MORPH-L, NO-CODA

In sum, three constraint types interact in the Lenakel pattern of epenthesis: (i) alignment constraints, (ii) syllable well-formedness constraints, and (iii) faithfulness constraints.

The correctness of this ranking is demonstrated by the tableaux (63–5). The first tableau evaluates candidates for the input /kam-n-m̃an-n/. The non-epenthetic candidate (63a) fatally violates *COMPLEX. Its competitors all violate DEP-IO to the same extent in having two epenthetic vowels, but their evaluation is drastically different.

(63)

Input: /kam-n-m̃an-n/	ALIGN-L	ALIGN-R	*COMPLEX	DEP-IO	ALIGN-MORPH-L	NO-CODA
a. kamn.m̃ann			*!*		**	**
b. ☞ kam.nɨ.m̃a.nɨn				**	*	**
c. ka.mɨn.m̃a.nɨn				**	**!	**
d. kam.nɨ.m̃an.nɨ		*!		**		**

The single candidate that has no violations of ALIGN-MORPH-L is eliminated by ALIGN-R (63d). Among the remaining candidates (63b–c), the former is selected as it has one fewer violation of ALIGN-MORPH-L than its competitor.

Both following tableaux demonstrate the ranking of DEP-IO over ALIGN-MORPH-L. The topmost pairs of candidates of both tableaux are eliminated by *COMPLEX. Of the remaining set of candidates, the most 'economical' ones in terms of DEP-IO, (64c) and (65c), are selected at the expense of candidates (64d) and (65d), which are perfectly aligned.

(64)

Input: /ark-ark/	ALIGN-L	ALIGN-R	*COMPLEX	DEP-IO	ALIGN-MORPH-L	NO-CODA
a. ar.gark^h			*!		*	**
b. arg.ark^h			**!			**
c. ☞ ar.ga.rik^h				*	*	**
d. a.rig.a.rik^h				**!		**

(65)

Input: /t-n-ak-ol/	ALIGN-L	ALIGN-R	*COMPLEX	DEP-IO	ALIGN-MORPH-L	NO-CODA
a. tna.gɔl			*!		***	*
b. tnag.ɔl			*!		**	**
c. ☞ ti.na.gɔl				*	**	*
d. ti.ni.ag.ɔl				**!		**

This concludes the analysis of epenthesis in Lenakel. We have seen how the interaction of three types of constraints (syllabic well-formedness, faithfulness, and morpho-prosodic alignment) produces a complex pattern of epenthesis. Our most important findings are 'economy' (epenthesis only when necessary) and 'alignment' (the edges of morphological constituents and prosodic constituents must coincide). The next subsection elaborates on the second finding, extending the notion of 'alignment' to new applications.

3.4 Generalized Alignment

The notion of 'alignment' originates in phrasal phonology, where it was developed in the analysis of relations between syntactic constituents and prosodic phrases

(Selkirk 1986, Selkirk and Shen 1990). This 'edge-based' theory of the syntax–phonology interface was adopted into OT by McCarthy and Prince (1993a), who claim that the prosody–morphology interface should be defined exclusively in terms of alignment constraints. Yet, alignment not only serves to match edges of morphological and prosodic categories, but also edges of phonological constituents (syllable, foot, PrWd). In recent OT the notion of alignment has assumed a range of applications that goes far beyond the types of cases seen above.

In all alignment constraints seen so far, ALIGN-L, ALIGN-R, and ALIGN-MORPH-L, the edge of a grammatical category (grammatical word or morpheme) is paired with the edge of a prosodic category (prosodic word or syllable). See (66):

(66)

		GramCat	ProsCat	Edge
a.	ALIGN-L	GrWd	PrWd	Left
b.	ALIGN-R	GrWd	Syllable	Right
c.	ALIGN-MORPH-L	Morpheme	Syllable	Left

In principle, alignment requirements may be stated on other morphological constituents (for example, stem, root, or affix) and/or prosodic constituents (for example, foot or mora). This generalized theory states that alignment constraints come in different types, differing with respect to the type of categories and edge to which they refer.

3.4.1 *The format of alignment constraints*

In order to fulfil all these diverse functions, alignment must have a very general format, which McCarthy and Prince (1993a) name 'Generalized Alignment'. This is stated below:

(67) **Generalized Alignment**

Align (Cat_1, $Edge_1$, Cat_2, $Edge_2$) $=_{def}$

$\forall$ Cat_1 $\exists$ Cat_2 such that $Edge_1$ of Cat_1 and $Edge_2$ of Cat_2 coincide.

Where Cat_1, Cat_2 $\in$ ProsCat $\cup$ GramCat

$Edge_1$, $Edge_2$ $\in$ {Right, Left}

Four aspects of this constraint format merit discussion: (i) categories that may appear in alignment constraints, (ii) the choice of the edges, (iii) the order in which the categories appear in the constraint, and (iv) how to evaluate violations of alignment constraints.

First, the categories 'Cat_1' and 'Cat_2' range over the alphabets of grammatical and phonological categories, for example:

(68)   GramCat: {Word, Stem, Root, Affix...}
         ProsCat: {PrWd, Foot, Syllable, Mora...}

These categories can also be filled by *specific morphemes* in the grammars of individual languages. This involves a weakening of the assumption that constraints are universal, at least on its strictest interpretation. However, such weakening seems to be tolerable for the following reasons. First, the *format* of alignment constraints is universal, which imposes strong limitations on what elements affix-specific constraints can refer to (that is, edges of morphological or prosodic categories). Second, relativization to specific morphemes is limited to alignment constraints, prohibiting morpheme-specific markedness and faithfulness constraints. Third, alignment constraints may assume the function of designating an affix as either a prefix or a suffix, depending on the edge of the word (left/right) with which it aligns. Such a view is strongly supported by infixation, as we will see in section 3.4.2.

The second aspect of Generalized Alignment concerns the pairing of edges. In (67), 'Edge$_1$' and 'Edge$_2$' range over two values: Left and Right. Although it is not logically necessary that alignment constraints relate pairs of *identical* edges (that is, both left, or both right) for both categories, such matching is implicitly assumed by most researchers. Nevertheless, alignment constraints have been proposed which pair opposite edges.[16]

A third aspect of the format of Generalized Alignment which deserves attention is the *asymmetrical* relation between both categories involved. By 'asymmetrical' we mean that the order in which both categories occur in the constraint statement is not random. The first category mentioned is connected with a universal quantifier '∀', and the second category with an existential quantifier '∃'. Accordingly there exists a difference in logical interpretation between the following alignment types:

(69)   a. **ALIGN** (Stem, R, σ, R)
            For every stem there must be some syllable such that the right edge of the stem matches the right edge of the syllable.
         b. **ALIGN** (σ, R, Stem, R)
            For every syllable there must be some stem such that the right edge of the syllable matches the right edge of the stem.

---

[16] An example is ALIGN-AFX (McCarthy and Prince 1993b) which aligns the left edge of a suffix with the right edge of a PrWd.

The scope difference will turn out to have considerable empirical effects which, however, we will not be able to illustrate until chapter 4 on metrical theory. However, here we may already fathom the potential relevance of the asymmetry by spelling out the conditions under which the different constraints in (69a–b) are satisfied or violated.

Consider the schematic examples in (70). The first constraint, ALIGN (Stem, R, σ, R), is violated by any stem whose right edge fails to coincide with the right edge of some syllable. This is the case in (70c), where the rightmost syllable is separated from the right edge of the stem by one or more extrasyllabic segments. In (70d) no syllable is present, in which case violation is self-explanatory. The constraint is satisfied in (70a) and (70b).

(70)		ALIGN (Stem, R, σ, R)	ALIGN (σ, R, Stem, R)
	a. $[\sigma]_{Stem}$	satisfied	satisfied
	b. $[\sigma_1\sigma_2]_{Stem}$	satisfied	violated (by σ_1)
	c. $[\sigma\ldots]_{Stem}$	violated	violated
	d. $[\ldots]_{Stem}$	violated	satisfied (vacuously)

In contrast, the constraint ALIGN (σ, R, Stem, R) is violated by any syllable whose right edge fails to coincide with the right edge of some stem. This is violated when a syllable is separated from the right edge of a stem by any elements, either a syllable (70b) or a segment (70c). This constraint may be satisfied in one of two ways: a stem is either monosyllabic (70a), or has no syllables. We find that all four possible combinations of satisfaction and violation are instantiated.

The fourth issue is that of *how to evaluate violations* of alignment constraints. In the literature a number of subissues have been identified, and discussion is ongoing. In McCarthy and Prince (1993a) it is suggested that evaluation of alignment constraints has two dimensions, which may be specified for each individual constraint.

One dimension, which also applies outside alignment constraints proper, is that of absolute versus gradient evaluation. *Absolute* constraints are either satisfied or violated, and fail to take into account degree of violation. These either incur one violation mark, or none. (Nevertheless, there may be multiple independent violations of an absolute constraint in a single candidate, which are added up in the relevant cell.) *Gradient* constraints are different in that they take into account degree of violation. Their evaluation is always scalar, ranking all candidates by their relative (dis)satisfaction of a goal. (For example, a constraint may pick out the candidate in which stress falls on the 'heaviest' syllable, comparing this with the heaviness of stressed syllables in other candidates.) Thus far in this book, we have not come across any examples of gradient constraints. When a cell in some tableau contained multiple violation marks, this was always due to multiple independent violations of an absolute constraint in a single candidate, rather than to gradient evaluation. Alignment constraints are typically evaluated gradiently, measuring the distance between both edges referred to in the constraint.

Gradient evaluation implies that some *unit* must be specified by which violations are measured. If an alignment constraint requires two edges to match, then are violations of the constraint measured in segments, syllables, or perhaps features? No general answer to this question has been given in the literature, and it has been proposed that the element type is established on a constraint-by-constraint basis. However, the *segment* is by far the most common element measured by alignment constraints, and it seems to be a 'default'. Apparently distances are measured in *syllables* only by alignment constraints which refer to feet, locating stresses with respect to edges, which will be discussed in chapter 4.[17]

Alignment constraints form a family of constraints. A *constraint family* is a set of constraints sharing a general format. Another example of a family of constraints is the featural identity constraint IDENTITY-IO[F], requiring identity of the values of some feature (for example, [voice]), between correspondents in input and output. Yet another example is the set of context-free markedness constraints that ban different places of articulation, such as *[lab], *[cor], introduced in chapter 1. Other examples of constraint families will be introduced later in this book.

The next subsection will illustrate the use of alignment as a gradient constraint in accounting for infixation in Tagalog. This analysis directly connects to the main topic of this chapter, syllable well-formedness.

3.4.2 *Alignment and infixation in Tagalog*

Consider the pattern of -*um*-infixation in Tagalog (French 1988), which serves as a further illustration of the role of alignment constraints, as well as their gradient evaluation. The generalization is that -*um*- is infixed immediately after the onset of the word (see 71b–c), if it has one; if the word has no onset, -*um*- becomes a prefix (see 71a):

(71)   Tagalog prefixal infixation
         a. /um + alis/   um-alis   'leave'
         b. /um + tawag/   t-um-awag 'call, pf., actor trigger'
         c. /um + gradwet/ gr-um-adwet 'graduate'

---

[17] It has been suggested that alignment constraints which refer to units of a prosodic category C_n are evaluated by units of the next-lower category in the prosodic hierarchy, C_{n-1}. Syllable and foot indeed stand in such a relation. See chapter 4 for the analysis of word edge effects in metrical systems, and its relation with extrametricality.

The prefix skips over the initial onset, settling itself between a consonant and vowel in the base, with which it integrates into a well-formed sequence of syllables. (Tagalog is a language allowing for complex onsets and for codas.) What infixation apparently avoids is an output in which the vowel of *-um-* lacks an onset, while its consonant syllabifies as a coda, as in *um-tawag. Avoidance of ill-formed syllables is what drives *-um-*infixation.

Apparently the morphology (*um*-affixation) depends on the prosody of the output. This is an important insight and we will see that it can be easily expressed in OT, because of its 'parallelism'. Constraints of morphological well-formedness are ranked in a single hierarchy together with constraints of syllabic well-formedness. Both types of constraint evaluate the same candidate set, of which a single candidate is selected as 'optimal' with respect to the total, integrated hierarchy. Here we can discern a morphological constraint making requirements on the position of *-um-* in the word, which conflicts with constraints of syllabic well-formedness. As always, conflicts are resolved in conformity with the core principles of strict domination and minimal violation.

The analysis by Prince and Smolensky (1993) of this pattern is strikingly simple, and directly encodes the dominance of prosody over morphological requirements. The prosodic constraint that comes into play here is NO-CODA, repeated below from (7):

(72)   **NO-CODA**
         *C]$_\sigma$ ('Syllables are open.')

This interacts with a morphological alignment constraint expressing the status of *-um-* as an affix that must be as close as possible to the left edge of the word:[18]

(73)   **ALIGN-*um*-L**
         Align the left edge of *-um-* with the left edge of the PrWd.

In fact, this is nothing but the requirement that '*-um-* is a prefix'. This requirement is stated in the form of an alignment of *-um-* with the Prosodic Word. Like other constraints, this morphological constraint is in principle violable. As we will see, the violability of ALIGN-*um*-L is the key to its distribution. All we need to assume is that this is a *gradient* constraint, that evaluates candidates as to their relative success in placing *-um-* at the left edge.

The following ranking of NO-CODA and ALIGN-*um*-L produces the mixed effect of 'infixation' in some contexts, and of 'prefixation' in other contexts:

---

[18] ALIGN-*um*-L renames Prince and Smolensky's EDGEMOST(*um*, L).

(74)   **P-constraint ≫ M-constraint**

No-Coda   ≫ Align-*um*-L

The ranking states that Tagalog assigns greater importance to the avoidance of codas than to the prefixal status of the affix -*um*-. However, -*um*- asserts itself maximally as a prefix, in the sense that it stands *as close as possible* to the left edge of the word, respecting the superordinate requirements of prosody. This is illustrated by the tableau of *gr-um-adwet*.

(75)

Input: {um, gradwet}	No-Coda	Align-*um*-L
a. **um**.grad.wet	***!	
b. **gum**.rad.wet	***!	g
c. ☞ gru.**ma**d.wet	**	g r
d. gra.**um**.dwet	**	g r a!
e. gra.**dum**.wet	**	g r a! d
f. grad.**wu**.met	**	g r a! d w
g. grad.we.**umt**	**	g r a! d w e
h. grad.we.**tum**	**	g r a! d w e t

Candidate (75a), where -*um*- is a genuine prefix, has three violations of No-Coda, one more than necessary. (The present tableau does not evaluate any candidates having fewer than two violations of No-Coda, since these would violate other top-ranking faithfulness constraints, such as Max-IO and Dep-IO.) No improvement with respect to No-Coda is reached in candidate (75b), which infixes -*um*- between the first and second consonants of the base. Each of the remaining candidates (75c–h) incurs two violations of No-Coda. Among these, the one is selected that minimally violates the next constraint down the hierarchy, Align-*um*-L. This is a gradient constraint, violations of which are measured by segments lying between the left word edge and the affix -*um*-. The optimal output, (75c), minimally violates Align-*um*-L, hence maximally respects the prefixal status of -*um*-. All remaining candidates (75d–h) violate Align-*um*-L to a larger degree than is strictly necessary.

As mentioned earlier, this analysis is based on *parallel* evaluation of prosodic and morphological constraints. Any theory that separates out the evaluation of morphological and prosodic well-formedness to different levels cannot capture the same generalization. For example, compare the way in which rule theory might deal with the Tagalog pattern. This analysis would involve 'extraprosodicity' of the word onset, rendering it 'invisible' to affixation. Next, *-um-* is prefixed to the residue (here the word minus the word onset), which begins with a vowel. Finally, the word onset is rendered visible again, producing the effect of '*um*-infixation'.

(76)   a. extraprosodicity   gradwet → ⟨gr⟩adwet
         b. prefixation to residue: ⟨gr⟩adwet → ⟨gr⟩-**um**-adwet
         c. undoing extraprosodicity: ⟨gr⟩-um-adwet → gr-um-adwet

This analysis leaves unexpressed the relation between the prosodic shape of the affix, *-um-* (VC), and its surface distribution, immediately after the word onset. Extraprosodicity is unable to make this connection, since it is formally separated from the affixation that it serves to potentiate. Under this analysis the fact that the infix has the skeletal shape VC is an arbitrary property. For example, an extraprosodicity analysis handles with equal ease an imaginary pattern for a hypothetical infix with the shape CV, say *-mu-*, for example in *mu-abot, t-mu-awag, gr-mu-adwet*.

(77)   a. extraprosodicity   gradwet → ⟨gr⟩adwet
         b. prefixation to residue: ⟨gr⟩adwet → ⟨gr⟩-**mu**-adwet
         c. undoing extraprosodicity: ⟨gr⟩-mu-adwet → gr-mu-adwet

One might argue that such infixations never arise because they would seriously violate the phonotactic principles of the language (more specifically, the requirements that onsets be maximally binary, and that hiatus is ill-formed). However, this is precisely the point to be made against the extraprosodicity analysis: it fails to express the overall contribution of prosodic well-formedness to the distribution of the infix *-um-*.

3.5 The quality of epenthetic segments

Thus far in this chapter we have only considered the distribution of epenthetic segments, not their phonetic content. But from the viewpoint of Correspondence Theory, the quality of epenthetic segments is just as interesting as their distribution. Epenthetic segments are special in that they lack input counterparts. Hence we expect that their featural realization is due to *output* factors only. This is precisely what we find in most languages: epenthetic segments tend to be realized as the 'minimally marked' segment, and tend to be subject to contextual colouring (Selkirk 1981, Itô 1986, Lowenstamm and Kaye 1986):

(78)   a. Epenthetic segments tend to be 'minimally marked' qua feature
             composition.
         b. Epenthetic segments tend to be contextually coloured.

There is a close connection between both properties: an epenthetic segment is featurally dependent. Given the fact that an epenthetic segment has no input features to be faithful to, their feature content is delegated to markedness constraints. Among these are two sets of constraints that come into play.

3.5.1 *Minimal markedness and contextual colouring*

The first type of constraints determining segment quality are those expressing 'pure' featural markedness. The very essence of an epenthetic segment is that it does not occur in the input, hence it has no lexical feature specification to be faithful to. With input faithfulness constraints (especially, IDENT-IO) irrelevant, the feature content of epenthetic segments depends on the *context-free markedness* constraints. This correctly predicts that cross-linguistically, featurally unmarked vowels such as [i], [ɨ], and [ə] are often selected as epenthetic vowels. In consonants, one finds a similar preference for featural unmarkedness. Many languages select [ʔ], a stop that lacks supralaryngeal specifications. Other languages select the semivowel [j], the consonantal counterpart of [i], or alveolar [t], which has the least marked place of articulation [cor].

The second type of constraints that can influence the choice of epenthetic segments are *contextual markedness constraints*. Featural values of segments, either epenthetic or non-epenthetic, may depend on neighbouring segments by assimilation. Assimilation in a non-epenthetic segment occurs at the expense of faithfulness to its input specification. Here assimilatory forces are intrinsically in conflict with contrast-preserving forces: the result depends on interactions between contextual constraints (striving for assimilated outputs), and faithfulness constraints (striving for maximally faithful outputs). In contrast, when an epenthetic segment assimilates to a neighbouring segment, input faithfulness never comes into play, as the epenthetic segment lacks an input. With faithfulness constraints excluded as anti-assimilatory factors, it is predicted that the quality of epenthetic segments strongly depends on contextual markedness constraints. In many languages, epenthetic segments indeed undergo considerable 'colouring' by their contexts.

Is there a contradiction? Both predictions cannot be true at the same time. That is, assimilation of an epenthetic segment to its context produces a segment that is no longer 'minimally marked' due to its assimilated marked features. As always, we expect that the outcome is determined by the interaction of both types of constraints, context-free and contextual markedness. When the former outrank the latter, as in (79a), the epenthetic segment displays no contextual variation and is minimally marked. But under the reverse ranking, in (79b), minimal markedness is violated in the interest of contextual colouring.

(79)   Factorial typology of quality of epenthetic segments

    a. Context-free markedness $\gg$ Contextual markedness
        Epenthetic segment is minimally marked.

    b. Contextual markedness $\gg$ Context-free markedness
        Epenthetic segment is contextually coloured.

Of course, this is only a schematic typology. In reality the factors in this typology are not unary, but composite. 'Context-free markedness' comprises the set of individual featural markedness constraints, grouped in hierarchies that are to some extent universal. And the factor 'context-sensitive markedness' denotes a set of constraints whose ranking is, again, partly universal. The interaction will usually not result in a complete victory of one factor over the other, but a more fragmented picture will be presented, with contributions made by both context-free and contextual factors. Once again we turn to Lenakel for exemplification.

3.5.2 *The epenthetic vowels of Lenakel*

Lenakel, the language analysed in some detail above, actually has two epenthetic vowels: [ə] and its allophone [ɨ]. Both vowels are contextually predictable, and occur in complementary distribution. So far we have only considered examples containing epenthetic [ɨ], a high central unrounded vowel. This occurs after *coronal* consonants, defined by the set {t, s, n, r, l}.[19]

(80)   Epenthetic [ɨ] appears after coronals

    a. /t-n-ak-ol/   tɨ.na.gɔl   'you (sg.) will do it'
    b. /ark-ark/   ar.ga.rɨkʰ   'to growl'
    c. /kam-n-m̄an-n/ kam.nɨ.m̄a.nɨn 'for her brother'
    d. /r-n-ol/   rɨ.nɔl   'he has done it'

Cross-linguistically, high central [ɨ] is a fairly frequent choice for an epenthetic vowel. A contextual relation between coronals and high vowels is cross-linguistically less common than between coronals and front vowels (Hume 1992). However, the Lenakel data clearly support such a relation.

    Its counterpart is a mid central unrounded vowel [ə], differing from [ɨ] only in its vowel height. This epenthetic vowel occurs after non-coronal consonants.

(81)   Epenthetic [ə] appears after non-coronals (from Lynch 1974)

    a. /to-rm-n/   tɔr.mən   'to his father' (p. 87)
    b. /apn-apn/ ab.na.bən 'free' (p. 88)

---

[19] As well as after /v/. This surprising fact becomes more natural upon considering the phonetics of /v/: 'a high central glide with varying, though weak, amounts of bilabial articulation' (Lynch 1974: 21). That is, /v/ shares both its centrality and height with [ɨ].

    c. /k-ar-pkom/ kar.bə.gɔm 'they're heavy' (p. 90)

    d. /r-əm-əŋn/ rɨ.mə.ŋən 'he was afraid of him/it' (p. 88)

Again, Lenakel is far from unique in having [ə] as an epenthetic vowel. (Other languages, such as Dutch, have [ə] as their only epenthetic vowel.) In Lenakel, epenthetic [ə] appears after non-coronals, that is, in the *elsewhere* context, complementary to the context of [ɨ]. This accords with schwa's status as minimally marked: a mid central unrounded vowel.

The position of epenthetic vowels in the Lenakel vowel inventory is stated below:

(82)   Lenakel vowel inventory (with epenthetic vowels circled)

	front	central	back		i	ɨ	u	e	ə	o	a
high	i	(ɨ)	u	high	+	+	+	−	−	−	−
mid	e	(ə)	o	low	−	−	−	−	−	−	+
low		a		back	−	+	+	−	+	+	+
				round	−	−	+	−	−	+	−

First note that both epenthetic vowels are [−low, +back, −round], all featurally unmarked values. More formally, epenthetic vowels never violate any of the following context-free markedness constraints:

(83)   ***[+low], *[+round], *[−back]**

To pinpoint the difference between epenthetic and lexical vowels, let us address the issue of what licenses lexical vowels such as low [a], round [o]–[u], or front [e]–[i] in Lenakel. The answer resides in featural *faithfulness* to the input. What makes an epenthetic vowel different from a lexical vowel is that only the latter has input specifications, among which are values such as [+low], [+round], or [−back]. Lexical vowels are faithful to their input as IDENT-IO constraints for different features outrank context-free markedness constraints:

(84)   Non-reduction of input vowels in Lenakel

          IDENT-IO(low), IDENT-IO(round), IDENT-IO(back) ≫ *[+low], *[+round], *[−back]

IDENT-IO constraints are irrelevant to epenthetic vowels (because these have no lexical inputs), and therefore epenthetic vowels must fully comply with context-free markedness.[20]

---

[20] Unmarkedness of epenthetic vowels arises in underspecification theory (Archangeli 1988) by 'featural emptiness'. That is, an epenthetic segment is maximally underspecified.

Next, what causes the contextual variation in vowel height among the epenthetic vowels? This variation reflects interaction of a context-free markedness constraint with a contextual markedness constraint. This interaction, which was schematically presented in (79b) as the ranking of 'contextual colouring', involves a pair of markedness constraints. In Lenakel, the dominated member of the pair is a context-free markedness constraint, violated in contexts where [i] appears. This is a constraint militating against high vowels:

(85)   *[+high]

This is in competition with the 'dominant' member of the pair, a contextual markedness constraint requiring that coronals be followed by high vowels:

(86)   **Cor-high**
         Coronals are followed by high vowels.

Cor-high sets up the pressure under which *[+high] may be violated. Accordingly, it must dominate *[+high]:

(87)   Cor-high ≫ *[+high]

Integrating this interaction with the current ranking, we arrive at the complete hierarchy:

(88)   Contextual variation between epenthetic [ə] and [i] in Lenakel
         Ident-IO(low/round/back) ≫ *[+low], *[+round], *[−back] ≫ Cor-high ≫ *[+high]

Strictly speaking, we have no evidence to rank Cor-high below context-free markedness constraints. This ranking was chosen only because of gains in perspicuity in the tableaux.

Tableau (89) evaluates candidates for an input /t-n-ak-ol/. Five candidates (89a–e) vary in the choice of epenthetic vowel, ranging from [ə] to [a]. All five are faithful to the input vowels, /a/ and /o/. In the columns of context-free markedness constraints, each cell holds the combined violation marks for non-epenthetic and epenthetic vowels. Therefore each of the candidates (89a–e) has at least one mark for *[+low], due to [a], and another for *[+round], due to [ɔ]. Additional marks for *[+low] and *[+round], which are *fatal*, are due to epenthetic vowels ([a] in 89e, [u] in 89d). Candidate (89c), with epenthetic [i], fatally violates *[−back]. The remaining candidates (89a) and (89b) have epenthetic [ə] and [i], respectively. The former fatally violates context-sensitive Cor-high, incurring two violations, for *tə* and *na*, even though it satisfies context-free *[+high]. The optimal candidate (89b) has the reverse pattern, violating *[+high] while violating Cor-high only once (for *na*):

(89)

Input: /t-n-ak-ol/	IDENT-IO	*[+low]	*[+round]	*[−back]	COR-high	*[+high]
a. tə.na.gɔl		*	*		**!	
b. ☞ ti.na.gɔl		*	*		*	*
c. ti.na.gɔl		*	*	*!	*	*
d. tu.na.gɔl		*	**!		*	*
e. ta.na.gɔl		**!	*		**	
f. ti.nɨ.gəl	*!*					**

The bottom candidate (89f) represents the reduction of the input vowels /a/ and /o/ to [ɨ] and [ə], respectively. These are the least marked vowels, taking into account contextual factors for this form. Such a reduction is excluded by IDENT-IO, a shorthand notation for three IDENT-IO constraints with respect to individual features [low]–[round]–[back].

Next consider tableau (90) of the form [tɔr.mən]. Again a subset of candidates (90c–e), containing either front, rounded, or low epenthetic vowels, are excluded by the context-free constraints. The bottom candidate (90f) fatally violates featural faithfulness. The remaining pair (90a–b) are evaluated vacuously by COR-high since only the lexical vowel violates it, while the epenthetic vowel is not in the relevant context (following a coronal). These candidates are submitted to the next-lower constraint, *[+high], which selects the former (90a) because its epenthetic vowel [ə] is non-high:

(90)

Input: /to-rm-n/	IDENT-IO	*[+low]	*[+round]	*[−back]	COR-high	*[+high]
a. ☞ tɔr.mən			*		*	
b. tɔr.mɨn			*		*	*!
c. tɔr.min			*	*!	*	*
d. tɔr.mun			**!		*	*
e. tɔr.man		*!	*		*	
f. tɨr.mən	*!					*

This tableau shows that schwa [ə] is the minimally unmarked vowel with respect to the context-free markedness constraints. Hence, it appears as the epenthetic vowel wherever possible: wherever contextual constraints do not stand in its way.

Our discussion of the factors governing the quality of epenthetic segments leads to the following conclusions. The quality of epenthetic segments is 'minimized', to avoid unnecessary violations of featural markedness constraints. This follows straightforwardly from the natural assumption that epenthetic segments are not represented in the input, and from the principle of minimal violation, a cornerstone of OT. The choice of epenthetic segments depends on interactions of contextual and context-free markedness constraints.

The second conclusion is that markedness constraints jump into activity in special situations where faithfulness constraints are irrelevant. This situation arises for a segment lacking an input counterpart, that is, an epenthetic segment. The minimized markedness of epenthetic segments is due to the activity of featural markedness constraints, which are normally 'dormant' due to dominating featural faithfulness constraints. Such a situation has been referred to by McCarthy and Prince (1994a) as 'the emergence of the unmarked'. (See chapter 5 for extensive discussion of this effect.)

3.5.3 *Epenthetic morphemes*

Languages occur in which the choice of epenthetic segments is not completely a matter of 'the emergence of the unmarked', but is to some extent morphologically governed.[21] For example, Mohawk (Piggott 1995) has three epenthetic vowels [e], [a], [i], which have a partly morphological, and partly phonological distribution. We may call such elements *epenthetic morphemes* (or *augments*) since they have minimal or zero semantic content. Lexical input specification of augments renders faithfulness constraints relevant to their realization, for which reason augments behave like lexical vowels. The other interesting issue is the factors governing the distribution of the contextual variants of augments, their *allomorphs*. We assume an allomorph to be a lexically listed shape of a morpheme, which cannot be derived by the 'productive' phonology of the language. We then predict that the different allomorphs, being semantically non-distinct from one another, have a distribution that is uniquely governed by phonological markedness. Such *phonologically-driven allomorphy* is attested in many languages (McCarthy and Prince 1993b, Mester 1994, Kager 1996). See chapter 9 for further discussion.

3.6 Coda conditions

To wind up this chapter, we consider in more detail the *phonotactic* role of the syllable. Many languages restrict the type of consonant that may occur in the syllable coda (Prince 1984, Itô 1986, 1989, Clements 1990, Goldsmith 1990). In

---

[21] Steriade (1995a) mentions Hindi, Hungarian, Basque, Maltese Arabic, and Tiberian Hebrew as languages in which epenthetic vowels have lexical properties.

chapter 1 we encountered a case of coda neutralization in Dutch, a language disallowing voiced obstruents in codas. But such 'coda conditions' are much more general: in this section we will look into cases from other languages. Our goal will be to strengthen a conclusion reached in chapter 2: that phonological processes may be functionally related, which is captured straightforwardly in OT. We will discuss three strategies which languages employ to resolve violations of a 'coda-condition', a constraint militating against place features in the syllable coda.

3.6.1 *Homorganic clusters in Japanese*

A fairly common type of restriction on coda consonants is that these must share the place of articulation with the immediately following onset consonant. This coda condition is in force in Japanese (Itô 1989). In intervocalic clusters, the coda consonant is either the first half of a geminate, or a nasal preceding a homorganic stop:

(91)   Homorganic clusters in Japanese
        a. Geminates   b. Homorganic Nasal +
                                                  Obstruent

        kap.pa   'a legendary being'   tom.bo   'dragonfly'
        kit.te   'stamp'   non.do   'tranquil'
        gak.koo 'school'   kaŋ.gae 'thought'
        c. Excluded hypothetical cases: *kap.ta, *tog.ba, *pa.kap, etc.

The constraint militating against codas having independent place of articulation is stated below, after Itô (1989):

(92)   **CODA-COND**
        *Place]$_\sigma$

The intended interpretation of this constraint is: 'a coda cannot license place features'.[22] That is, a coda can contain place features only when these are simultaneously associated with a syllable position outside the coda, such as the second syllable's onset in (93a):

(93)

---

[22] This slightly simplifies the discussion, abstracting away from the 'Linking Constraint', which in Itô (1989) accounts for the distinction between (93a) and (93b). Prince (1984), Goldsmith (1990), and Itô and Mester (forthcoming) propose various technical explanations of homorganicity. See chapter 9 for a radically different approach, known as 'positional faithfulness'.

Shared place of articulation between the coda and the following onset is therefore not in violation of the CODA-COND. In contrast, the /k/ in the coda of structure (93b) violates it.

Although no alternations are present, we must allow the possibility of consonant clusters in the input whose members have different places of articulation, e.g. /kakpa/. This follows from the assumption of Richness of the Base: OT has no constraints on inputs. Any (hypothetical) heterorganic inputs should be overruled by CODA-COND. This implies that one consonant in the cluster must lose its place features, thereby violating:

(94)   **IDENT-IO**(Place)
        Correspondents in input and output have identical place features.

This constraint is dominated by CODA-COND:

(95)   Place assimilation to resolve violations of the coda condition
        CODA-COND ≫ IDENT-IO(Place)

Now assume a hypothetical input /kakpa/. A strictly faithful analysis of this input would be [kak.pa], with the first syllable's coda violating CODA-COND. The optimal analysis eliminates the place features of one of the consonants in the cluster /kp/. See tableau (96).

(96)

Input: /kakpa/	CODA-COND	IDENT-IO(Place)
a. ☞ kap.pa		*
b. kak.pa	*!	

Observe that a morpheme-internal input cluster such as /kp/ would be completely obscured by this ranking. Since there would be no evidence for the input quality of the consonant cluster, there is no more suitable input for the output form [kap.pa] than /kappa/ itself, which is identical to the output. *Lexicon Optimization* would select /kappa/ since its mapping relation to the output [kap.pa] involves no violation of IDENT-IO(Place).

This observation actually points to a hidden weakness in this analysis: it is unable to predict which of the two input consonants is 'charged' for violation of the coda condition. (That is, [kak.ka] would be an equally harmonic outcome.) However, typological evidence suggests that the choice is not random. Cases from other languages involving *alternations* display a strong preference for the *first* consonant in the cluster (the coda) to lose its place features, rather than the second one. (In section 3.6.3 we will look into a case involving deletion.)

3.6.2 *Vowel epenthesis in Ponapean*

We have now seen a 'static' coda condition, one unaccompanied by alternations. Let us now look into a case which involves alternations, as well as a second strategy to resolve violations of the coda condition. Ponapean (Rehg and Sohl 1981, Itô 1989) epenthesizes a vowel ([e] or [i]) into heterorganic consonant clusters which arise by the morphology, to avoid violation of the coda condition. Like Japanese, Ponapean enforces coda consonants which are homorganic with the following onset consonant.

(97)　　　Vowel insertion in Ponapean

　　　　　a. /a**k**-dei/　　a.ke.dei　　*ak.dei　　'a throwing contest'
　　　　　b. /kiti**k**-men/　ki.ti.ki.men　*ki.tik.men 'rat indef.'

The epenthetic vowel makes the lefthand consonant in the cluster to syllabify as an onset, rather than as a coda. As an onset, this consonant can maintain its place features without violating CODA-COND, while at the same time satisfying IDENT-IO(Place). But of course, these benefits come at a cost: a violation of the anti-epenthesis constraint DEP-IO. This scenario is expressed by the following ranking:

(98)　　　Vowel epenthesis to resolve violations of the coda condition
　　　　　CODA-COND, IDENT-IO(Place) ≫ DEP-IO

The violation of DEP-IO, the lower-ranked of both faithfulness constraints, is the least expensive way to satisfy the coda condition. (Japanese has reversed priorities.)

　Consider three output candidates for the input /ak-dei/ in tableau (99). The fully faithful candidate (99a), which preserves place of articulation while avoiding epenthesis, fatally violates CODA-COND. To avoid such a violation, two strategies are considered, as represented by candidates (99b–c). Both violate some faithfulness constraint. The former, (99b), with a homorganic cluster, violates IDENT-IO(Place). Its competitor (99c), with an epenthetic vowel, violates DEP-IO. Because of strict domination, the lower-ranking of the two faithfulness constraints gives in:

(99)

Input: /ak-dei/	CODA-COND	IDENT-IO(Place)	DEP-IO
a.　　ak.dei	*!		
b.　　ad.dei		*!	
c. ☞ a.ke.dei			*

Observe that although vowel epenthesis leads an output syllabification that has no coda, it is not triggered by No-Coda. (Ponapean allows for homorganic coda–onset sequences.)

Finally we must address the fact that the coda condition is violable in Ponapean in a specific context: the final consonant of the word, a coda itself. What blocks epenthesis in word-final position? Arguably, this blocking effect is due to ALIGN-R, as in Lenakel (see section 3.3.4.2). This implies the subranking ALIGN-R ≫ CODA-COND, which is integrated in the final ranking below:

(100)　　　Final ranking for Ponapean

　　　　　ALIGN-R, IDENT-IO(Place) ≫ CODA-COND ≫ DEP-IO

A tableau shows the interaction of these four constraints for [naŋ.kep] 'inlet':

(101)

Input: /naŋkep/	ALIGN-R	IDENT-IO(Place)	CODA-COND	DEP-IO
a.　　naŋ.ke.pi	*!			*
b.　　naŋ.ke?		*!		
c. ☞ naŋ.kep			*	

Candidate (101a) fatally violates ALIGN-R. Another strategy to satisfy the coda condition, seen in candidate (101b), is the deletion of place features from the coda consonant, which yields a glottal stop [?]. This runs into a fatal violation of IDENT-IO(Place), however.[23]

3.6.3　*Consonant deletion in Diola-Fogny*

A third logically possible strategy to avoid violation of the coda condition is the deletion of a consonant in a heterorganic cluster. This strategy is employed by Diola-Fogny (Sapir 1965, Steriade 1982, Itô 1986):

(102)　　　Consonant deletion in Diola-Fogny

　　　　　a. /let-ku-jaw/　le.ku.jaw　*let.ku.jaw　'they won't go'

　　　　　b. /jaw-bu-ŋar/　ja.bu.ŋar　*jaw.bu.ŋar　'voyager'

It readily appears that the core of the analysis must be a domination of CODA-COND over the anti-deletion constraint MAX-IO:

---

[23] Ponapean allows homorganic final clusters, for example, *mand* 'tame', *emp* 'coconut crab'. Here alignment blocks final epenthesis (*[em.pi]), while economy rules out medial epenthesis (*[em.ip]), which fails to cancel the violation of the coda condition. Note that homorganicity of final clusters is not predicted under an extrametricality analysis (Itô 1989).

(103)   Consonant deletion to resolve violations of the coda condition
          CODA-COND ≫ MAX-IO
          le.ku.jaw > let.ku.jaw

We cannot present the complete analysis before having addressed two interesting issues, each of which merits detailed discussion: the choice of the deleted consonant in a cluster, and the immunity of the word-final consonant. Both issues have consequences for the view of the morphology–phonology interface.

The first issue is the choice of the deleted consonant in the cluster. Observe that the lefthand consonant is deleted, while the righthand consonant is preserved. A possible interpretation of this is that a coda consonant, rather than an onset consonant, is deleted. But how can a coda-onset asymmetry on deletion be accounted for in a theory based on output constraints? Should we first syllabify the input to identify the deleted consonant as a coda, before we can delete it?

(104)   σ σ σ   σ σ σ
                             ΛΛΛ   ΛΛΛ
          /let-ku-jaw/ → let.ku.jaw → le.ku.jaw

This would reintroduce a derivation, thereby giving up the idea that constraints evaluate surface forms only.

But another interpretation of the deletion asymmetry is possible, one requiring no intermediate level of representation.[24] Observe that the deleted consonant is final in its morpheme, while the preserved consonant is morpheme-initial. This deletion pattern may serve to keep *syllable structure maximally isomorphic to morphological structure*. To see this, we must consider the two output forms which arise by deletion of either the lefthand consonant (105a) or the righthand consonant (105b). The syllable structure is represented on top of the segments, while morphological structure is represented below:

(105)   a. σ σ σ   b. σ σ σ
             ΛΛΛ   ΛΛΛ
             le ku jaw (*perfectly aligned*)   le tu jaw (*mis-aligned*)
             VVV   VIV
             μ μ μ   μ μ μ

The preference for the lefthand candidate is another case of morpho-prosodic alignment, of which we have seen earlier cases in this chapter. (See again the discussion of Lenakel.) The constraint enforcing alignment of morphological edges and syllable edges is ALIGN-MORPH-L (repeated below from 59):

---

[24] This analysis misses the generalization that a coda consonant is deleted, rather than an onset one. Chapter 9 will sketch an alternative analysis based on 'positional faithfulness'.

(106)   **ALIGN-MORPH-L**

The left edge of every morpheme coincides with the left edge of a syllable.

The ranking of this constraint with respect to CODA-COND ≫ MAX-IO cannot be exactly established. This is due to the fact that ALIGN-MORPH-L is not in conflict with either of the two constraints: it only serves as a tie-breaker between two deletion candidates (107a) and (107b) which equally satisfy (or violate) CODA-COND and MAX-IO.

(107)

Input: /let-ku-jaw/	ALIGN-MORPH-L	CODA-COND	MAX-IO
a. let.ku.jaw		**!	
b. ☞ le.ku.jaw		*	*
c. le.tu.jaw	*!	*	*

Since ALIGN-MORPH-L is not violated in any example presented earlier, we will assume it to be undominated.

The second issue is the preservation of the word-final consonant. Apparently the grammar of Diola-Fogny exerts pressure to leave the right edge of the grammatical word unaffected. This actually overrides the coda condition. What constraint is responsible for the preservation of the rightmost segment in the word?

In earlier sections (section 3.3.4.2 on Lenakel and section 3.6.2 on Ponapean) we encountered an alignment constraint that might, in principle at least, do the job. This constraint is ALIGN-R, requiring that the right edge of every grammatical word coincide with the right edge of a PrWd. See the diagrams below:

(108)   a. PrWd   b. PrWd

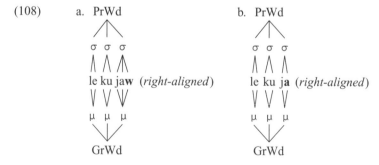

But now observe that both structures are *perfectly aligned* since the rightmost segment of each GrWd matches the rightmost segment of PrWd. In (108a) this rightmost segment is [w], and in (105b) it is [a]. Both are the rightmost remaining segments of the grammatical word, which are rightmost in the PrWd. Therefore 'standard' alignment does not work.

What we are looking for is a novel type of alignment, which actually inspects the correspondence relation between the rightmost segments in the *input* and *output*. Input–output diagrams of the two major candidates clarify the kind of correspondence relation which is relevant. This relation is intact in (109a), while it is broken in (109b):

(109)   a. Input: l e t k u j a w   b. Input: l e t k u j a w
            | | | | | | | | | | | | |
         Output: l e   k u j a w   Output: l e   k u j a

The relevant correspondence constraint focusses on the rightmost segments in the input and output. It identifies the rightmost segment of the output grammatical word, and then it identifies the rightmost segment of the input grammatical word. When the segments are correspondents, as in (109a), then the constraint is satisfied. But when the segments are not correspondents, as in (109b), then the constraint is violated.

This correspondence constraint is ANCHORING-IO (McCarthy and Prince 1995a):

(110)   **ANCHORING-IO**(GrWd, R)
            Any segment at the right periphery of the output GrWd has a correspondent at the right periphery of the input GrWd.
            ('No deletion/epenthesis at the edge.')

This adds another correspondence constraint to the current inventory, which already has four: DEP-IO, MAX-IO, IDENT-IO, and LINEARITY-IO.[25] The function of ANCHORING-IO is to block *deletion at the edge* of a grammatical word.

Interestingly, ANCHORING-IO militates against *epenthesis* at word edges as well. Any non-correspondence of segments in the input and output at the right edge will violate ANCHORING-IO, regardless of whether it is caused by deletion or insertion of a segment. To block epenthesis at word edges in Axininca Campa, Lenakel, and Ponapean, we have thus far assumed Generalized Alignment constraints, ALIGN-L and ALIGN-R. It now seems that our theoretical machinery is becoming redundant, as the two tools may do the same job. McCarthy and Prince (1995a, forthcoming) propose to merge both into a single constraint format, arguing that ANCHORING subsumes Generalized Alignment.[26] We will not pursue this issue here, but return to the analysis of Diola-Fogny.

---

[25] Not counting UNIFORMITY-IO, which was briefly discussed at the end of chapter 2.
[26] See chapter 5 (section 5.7), for more on this unification.

Having defined the constraint which blocks deletion of word-final segments, we must now rank it. The ranking of ANCHORING-IO with respect to the core inter-action of CODA-COND ≫ MAX-IO is readily established. As we observed above, its function is to block consonant deletion at the right word edge, resisting the pressure from CODA-COND. Hence we find the following interaction:

(111)   Blocking of coda deletion at the word end
          ANCHORING-IO(GrWd, R) ≫ CODA-COND
          le.ku.jaw > le.ku.ja

This result is now integrated into the previously assumed ranking:

(112)   Final ranking for Diola-Fogny
          ANCHORING-IO(GrWd, R) ≫ CODA-COND ≫ MAX-IO

The tableau of [le.ku.jaw] shows its two main competitors, [let.ku.jaw] and [le.ku.ja], as well as their evaluation under the hierarchy.

(113)

Input: /let-ku-jaw/	ANCHORING-IO (GrWd, R)	CODA-COND	MAX-IO
a. let.ku.jaw		**!	
b. ☞ le.ku.jaw		*	*
c. le.ku.ja	*!		**

Note that this exemplifies a perfect twofold domination: each lower ranking con-straint is violated to avoid violation of a higher-ranking constraint. The 'nested' logical structure of the generalization is stated below:

(114)   'Input consonants are preserved,
              except when these have place features and are syllabifiable as codas,
              except when these stand at the right edge of a grammatical word.'

This finishes the analysis of Diola-Fogny consonant deletion. In the discussion section below we will return to the relation of this pattern to the other two patterns (assimilation and epenthesis) discussed earlier in this section.

3.6.4   *Coda conditions: a comparison with rule-based theory*
In this section we will address the functional relation among the three processes which were discussed in this section, that is: place assimilation in Japanese, vowel epenthesis in Ponapean, and consonant deletion in Diola-Fogny. All three pro-cesses are depicted below in rule format, using the notational means of auto-segmental phonology:

(115)   a. *Place assimilation*:

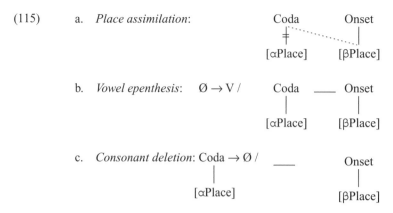

   b. *Vowel epenthesis*:   Ø → V /   Coda ____ Onset

   c. *Consonant deletion*: Coda → Ø /   ____   Onset

All three rules share a common structural description: all are triggered by a coda that fails to share its place of articulation with the following onset. All function to eliminate this configuration, by different structural changes. The first rule assimilates the onset's place features back to the preceding coda, making it share its features. The second rule inserts a vowel between the onset and the coda, turning the offending coda consonant into an onset. And the third rule flatly deletes the coda consonant.

However, there is no formal recognition of this functional unity among the rules. The argument is analogous to the one made in chapter 2 for the processes applying in the *NC̥ (nasal-plus-voiceless-consonant) context. To capture the functional unity of a set of rules, it does not suffice for these rules to share a structural description. Nor does it suffice for their outputs to lack codas with place features. The proper generalization combines both aspects: all rules function so as to eliminate the configuration that forms their structural description. Any theory that fails to recognize the output as a level at which phonological generalizations hold fails to capture the functional unity of these phonological processes. In contrast, OT captures this functional unity straightforwardly, thereby creating unity in typological diversity.

3.7 Conclusion

Syllables are key factors in stating phonological generalizations. In this chapter we have focussed on two types of phenomena in which syllables play a major role: epenthesis and the phonotactics of 'coda' consonants. Throughout this chapter we have kept an eye on a set of more general issues in OT:

Process format. We have learned that syllable-dependent processes, like any other phonological processes, involve interactions of 'markedness' constraints and faithfulness constraints. A 'change' (deletion, insertion, or featural change) is made at the cost of some faithfulness constraint, but only to avoid the violation of higher-ranking well-formedness constraints. Correspondence Theory defines a set of constraint families that militate against changes of various kinds – deletions, insertions, featural changes, etc. The way in which the grammar reacts in order to avoid a violation of some well-formedness constraint depends on the relative ranking of the correspondence constraints.

Process economy. Changes are always 'economical' – faithfulness rules out any change on top of those which are strictly necessary. We have seen this economy property in two aspects of epenthesis: its distribution and the quality of the epenthetic segment.

Language typology. Languages differ in terms of constraint rankings. Therefore to evaluate a set of constraints on a cross-linguistic scale, constructing factorial typologies is essential. We have found valuable typological results with respect to syllable structure. In a nutshell, languages all strive toward the ideal CV syllable format; more complex types of syllable structure involve a cost in markedness constraints which is only enforceable through faithfulness constraints.

The following chapter will generalize this approach one level up in the prosodic hierarchy.

SUGGESTIONS FOR FURTHER READING

The syllable in phonological theory

Blevins, Juliette (1995) The syllable in phonological theory. In Goldsmith. 206–44.

Clements, George N. and Samuel J. Keyser (1983) *CV phonology: a generative theory of the syllable.* Cambridge, Mass.: MIT Press.

Hayes, Bruce (1989) Compensatory lengthening in moraic phonology. *Linguistic Inquiry* **20**. 253–306.

Syllables in OT

Broselow, Ellen, Su-I Chen, and Marie Huffman (1997) Syllable weight: convergence of phonology and phonetics. *Phonology* **14**. 47–82.

Rosenthall, Sam (1997) The distribution of prevocalic vowels. *Natural Language and Linguistic Theory* **15**. 139–80.

Alignment and syllabification

Kenstowicz, Michael (1994b) Syllabification in Chukchee: a constraints-based analysis. In A. Davison, N. Maier, G. Silva, and W. S. Yan (eds.), *Proceedings of the Formal Linguistics Society of the Midwest* **4**. Iowa City: University of Iowa. 160–81.

McCarthy, John and Alan Prince (1993a) Generalized Alignment. In G. Booij and J. van Marle (eds.), *Yearbook of Morphology 1993*. Dordrecht: Kluwer. 79–153.

Merchant, Jason (1996) Alignment and fricative assimilation in German. *Linguistic Inquiry* **27**. 709–19.

EXERCISES

1 -*um*-infixation in Ilokano

Ilokano (Hayes and Abad 1989) has a pattern of *um*-infixation that is almost identical to that of Tagalog, discussed in section 3.4.2. For Ilokano it is reported that speakers have the free variant *g-um-radwet* next to *gr-um-adwet*.

    a.   What ranking of constraints would produce the output *g-um-radwet*? Are No-CODA and ALIGN-*um*-L sufficient, or do we need any additional constraint(s)?

    b.   Compute a factorial typology of the constraints that you have used in your analysis.

2 Epenthesis in Harari

Consider the following two paradigms of the root /sbr/ 'break' in Harari (Leslau 1958, Kenstowicz and Kisseberth 1979):

	Imperfect		*Negative imperfect*	
2 masc.	tisäbri	/t-säbr/	zätsibär	/zä-t-sbär/
2 fem.	tisäbri	/t-säbr-i/	zätsibäri	/zä-t-sbär-i/
3 masc.	yisäbri	/y-säbr/	zäysibär	/zä-y-sbär/
3 fem.	tisäbri	/t-säbr/	zätsibär	/zä-t-sbär/
1 pl.	nisäbri	/n-säbr/	zänsibär	/zä-n-sbär/
2 pl.	tisäbru	/t-säbr-u/	zätsibäru	/zä-t-sbär-u/
3 pl.	yisäbru	/y-säbr-u/	zäysibäru	/zä-y-sbär-u/

For the purposes of the problem, you are free to ignore the variation in the stem shapes (/säbr/ versus /sbär/), which is under morphological control.

    a.   What is the ranking of constraints underlying this pattern of epenthesis? Do you need any new constraints? (Hint: why not **tisäbir* instead of *tisäbri*?)

    b.   Support your analysis by tableaux of *tisäbri* and *zätsibär*.

4
Metrical structure and parallelism

4.1 Introduction

This chapter deals with word stress patterns in the framework of OT. Within phonology, word stress patterns stand out as being typically governed by conflicting forces, as was recognized in studies in pre-OT metrical phonology. Before we can actually point out the interactions of conflicting metrical constraints, we must first become familiar with some results of the metrical theory of word stress.

Our representational basis is *metrical phonology*, a theory developed in the 1970s, the central assumption of which is that stress is a rhythmic phenomenon, encoded by strong–weak relations between syllables (Liberman and Prince 1977, Hayes 1980, 1995, Halle and Vergnaud 1987). Consider the stress pattern of the word *Alabama*, which contains two pairs of syllables standing in such a strong–weak relationship – [æ̀.lə.bǽ.mə]. We analyse this word rhythmically into two *metrical feet* of two syllables each – [æ.lə] and [bæ.mə]:

(1)　　　　(.　　*　)　PrWd-level
　　　　　(* .)(*　.)　Foot-level
　　　　　æ.lə.bæ.mə　Syllable-level

The rhythmically strong syllables are initial in the foot: such feet are called *trochees*. Each foot is represented by a pair of parentheses, and an asterisk on top of the strong syllable, while the weak syllable has a dot. We will refer to the strong syllable of a foot as its *head*, and to the weak syllable as its *non-head*. Note that the strong syllable of the final foot is more prominent than that of the initial foot. This weak–strong relationship between feet is represented by yet another metrical constituent, on the next-higher prosodic level – that of the PrWd. Again, relative prominence is marked by a dot and an asterisk, now sitting on top of heads of feet.

Extensive research in the typology of word stress (e.g. Hayes 1995) has shown that stress patterns are a domain of potentially conflicting forces, among which are *rhythm* (the pressure toward regularly alternating distributions of strong and weak syllables), *quantity-sensitivity* (the pressure to match syllable weight and prominence), and *edge-marking* (the pressure to mark the edges of morphological domains by strong syllables). OT is naturally equipped to capture interactions of conflicting forces, and to establish interactions between prosodic levels, by its *parallelism*. Finally, OT's reranking approach to typology makes it a highly suitable basis to capture cross-linguistic variation between metrical systems. This chapter will develop the analytical tools by which OT achieves these ends.

We will proceed as follows. In section 4.2, we will become familiar with the major cross-linguistic 'forces' in word stress, among which are rhythm, quantity-sensitivity, and edge-marking. This section will also introduce the representational tools of metrical theory, the universal alphabet of prosodic categories, including the syllable, the foot, and the PrWd. In section 4.3 we will present a case-study of Hixkaryana, and see how this language accommodates the conflicts between metrical forces. In the course of this case-study, metrical 'forces' will be translated one by one into a small set of metrical constraints. These constraints will be placed in a broader typological perspective in section 4.4, where a number of basic interaction schemata will be introduced. Section 4.4 also develops a factorial typology by reranking a subset of metrical constraints, matching it against what is known about cross-linguistic variation in stress systems. A case-study of another language, Southeastern Tepehuan, will serve to highlight a comparison with rule-based parametric metrical theory in section 4.5. Finally, section 4.6 will deal with the interactions between metrical constraints and faithfulness constraints, which point to 'parallellism' and a typical OT perspective.

4.2 Word stress: general background

4.2.1 *Four cross-linguistic preferences*

Before developing an OT theory of word stress, we must first familiarize ourselves with a number of important cross-linguistically common properties of stress languages. The best known of these properties are the following four.

The culminative property. It is typical for stress languages that morphological or syntactic constituents (stem, word, phrase, etc.) have a single prosodic peak. This is known as the *culminative* property of stress. Many languages impose this 'stressability requirement' on content words (nouns, verbs, adjectives, adverbs) only; function words (articles, pronouns, prepositions, etc.) need not be stressed, and are prosodically dependent on content words.

Closely related to stressability, languages may require content words to have some minimum size, for example two syllables, or a single heavy syllable. This 'minimal word' typically equals a single *foot*, a rhythmic unit consisting of two syllables or two moras (length units). Languages may actively reinforce a binary word minimum by prosodically expanding any word that would otherwise fall below the minimum, by adding an augment of a mora or vowel to a subminimal word. This is illustrated by examples from Levantine Arabic (lengthening, 2a) and Iraqi Arabic (epenthesis, 2b), both from Broselow (1995):

(2)   Epenthesis driven by the minimal word
            a. /sʔal/ sʔaal 'ask, masc. sing.'
            b. /drus/ idrus 'study'

The binary foot size is related to the rhythmic property, which will be discussed below.

The demarcative property. Stress tends to be placed near edges of constituents (phrases, words, stems, etc.). This is the *demarcative* property, which has been argued to facilitate the processing of grammatical units in perception. Cross-linguistically favoured positions for primary word stress are the *initial* syllable (3a: Pintupi, Australian; Hansen and Hansen 1969), the *prefinal* (or penultimate) syllable (3b: Warao, South American; Osborn 1966), and the *final* syllable (3c: Weri, New Guinea; Boxwell and Boxwell 1966).

(3)   Three cross-linguistically favoured positions of primary stress
            a. initial   **púli**ŋkalatʲu   'we (sat) on the hill'
            b. prefinal yapurukitane**há**se 'verily to climb'
            c. final   akʊnete**pál**   'times'

These positions are ranked in decreasing order of popularity among the world's languages. The low ranking of pattern (3c) illustrates a dispreference against final stress, evidence for which will be adduced in section 4.3. (Secondary stresses are left unmarked in 3.)

Some languages mark both edges of a word, while other languages mark edges of morphemes contained within a word (root, stem, affix). Both strategies are exemplified by Sibutu Sama, a language of the southern Philippines (Allison 1979). The *word* is marked on its prefinal syllable, and the *stem* and every *prefix* on their initial syllables:

(4)   Demarcative stress highlighting edges of morphemes
            a. pìna-bìssaláhan   'to be persuaded'
            b. màka-pàgba-bìssaláhan 'able to cause persuasion'

This example illustrates how word stress may serve to highlight morphological structure.

The rhythmic property. Stress languages have a clear tendency towards rhythmic patterns, with strong and weak syllables spaced apart at regular intervals. Rhythmic alternation is manifested in a number of ways: by avoidance of adjacent stressed syllables ('clashes') or long strings of unstressed syllables ('lapses'). Rhythmic alternation is 'directional', that is, oriented with respect to an edge of the word, beginning or end. For example, Pintupi (5a) stresses the initial syllable plus following alternate non-final syllables, while Warao (5b) stresses the prefinal syllable and alternating preceding syllables.

(5)   Binary alternation of stresses
        a.i   (tʲí.ḷi).(rì.ŋu).(làm.pa).tʲu   'the fire for our benefit flared up'
        a.ii (yú.ma).(ɟìŋ.ka).(mà.ra).(tʲà.ɟa).ka   'because of mother-in-law'
        b.i   (yà.pu).(rù.ki).(tà.ne).(há.se)   'verily to climb'
        b.ii e.(nà.ho).(rò.a).(hà.ku).(tá.i)   'the one who caused him to eat'

Bracketed two-syllable portions are *metrical feet*: the smallest units of linguistic rhythm. All feet in (5) are *trochees*: here the initial syllable is strong and the second weak. As we will see below, languages may also select *iambs* (whose second syllable is strong).

The rhythmic spectrum is occupied at one end by languages that have a maximally dense rhythmic organization, like Pintupi and Warao. Yidiɲ (Dixon 1977) even enforces binary rhythm by apocopating a vowel of words with three or five syllables, to make it fit the binary mould:

(6)   Strict parsing of PrWd by feet in Yidiɲ
        a. /durguu-mu /   (dur.gúum)   'mopoke owl-ABL'
        b. /galambaraa-mu/ (ga.lám).(ba.ráam) 'march fly-ABL'

At the opposite end of the rhythmic spectrum we find 'unbounded' languages, which have no alternating rhythm, allowing long strings of unstressed syllables with a single stress per word. (Examples are Khalka Mongolian, Classical Arabic, and Eastern Cheremis.) In this chapter we will focus on 'bounded', rhythmically alternating, stress systems.

Quantity-sensitivity. Stress naturally prefers to fall on elements which have some intrinsic prominence. For example, stress tends to be attracted by long vowels (rather than by short vowels), by diphthongs (rather than monophthongs), and by closed syllables (rather than open syllables). Attraction of stress by heavy syllables is known as 'quantity-sensitivity'. This phenomenon is exemplified by the

Australian language Nunggubuyu (Hore 1981; 7a) and the South American language Hixkaryana (Derbyshire 1979; 7b):

(7)   Heavy syllables attracting stresses
            a. (l̀àa).(ĺáag)   'almost'
            b. (nák).(ɲóh).(yát͡ʃ).(ke.náː).no 'they were burning it'

While heavy syllables attract stress, we also find a reverse phenomenon of quantity being adapted to prominence. Stressed vowels tend to lengthen, increasing syllable weight, as in Hixkaryana (8a; see also section 4.3). Conversely, vowels in unstressed syllables tend to shorten or reduce, decreasing syllable weight, as in English *át̠om̠* ~ *at̠ómic* (8b):

(8)   Stress contrasts supported by lengthening and reduction
            a. (ne.mɔ́ː).(ko.tɔ́ː).no 'it fell'
            b. (ǽ.təm) ~ ə.(tʰó.mɪk)

Mutually reinforcing relations of prominence and quantity are highly typical for stress systems. (Although stress may be attracted by high-toned vowels, quantitative processes supporting tonal contrasts are rare in tone and pitch accent languages.)

4.2.2 *An alphabet of prosodic categories*

In order to represent stress, metrical theory first assumes a set of universal prosodic categories in a hierarchical relation: the prosodic hierarchy (Selkirk 1980, McCarthy and Prince 1986).

(9)   Prosodic hierarchy

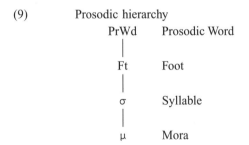

Every prosodic category in the hierarchy has as its *head* an element of the next-lower level category. More precisely, every PrWd contains a (main-stressed) *foot*, every foot contains a (stressed) *syllable*, while every syllable contains a *mora*, a unit of quantity.

Second, to represent distinctions of vowel length and syllable weight, a theory of *quantity* is required. Following Van der Hulst (1984), Hyman (1985), and Hayes

(1989), we will assume *moraic theory*. According to this theory, a syllable's quantity is a function of its number of weight-bearing units, or moras. Universally, short vowels are represented by one mora, while long vowels have two. The mora is symbolized by the Greek letter 'μ':

(10)   a. Light syllables (one mora)   b. Heavy syllables (two moras)

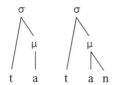   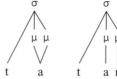

These diagrams represent weight, omitting the division into subsyllabic constituents *onset–nucleus–coda*.[1] CV syllables are universally light (monomoraic), while CVV syllables are universally heavy (bimoraic). The weight of a CVC syllable depends on whether or not its coda consonant is moraic. This varies from language to language, and is determined by the ranking of WEIGHT-BY-POSITION (Hayes 1989, Sherer 1994):

(11)   **WEIGHT-BY-POSITION**
         Coda consonants are moraic.

For languages treating CVC as light, we assume that WEIGHT-BY-POSITION ranks below a constraint militating against bimoraic syllables.[2]

Third, a theory of rhythmic units or *feet* assumes the following universal inventory (McCarthy and Prince 1986, Hayes 1987, 1995, Kager 1993):

(12)   a. *Syllabic trochee* (quantity-insensitive): (σσ)
         b. *Moraic trochee* (quantity-sensitive):   **(LL) (H)**
         c. *Iamb* (quantity-sensitive):   **(LL) (H) (LH)**

In the notation of quantitative foot shapes, we will use 'L' for a light syllable and 'H' for a heavy syllable. The head of the foot (stressed syllable) will be marked by bold-face. It is a topic of debate whether the foot inventory should be enforced by violable constraints, or 'hard-wired' in the universal alphabet of prosodic representations.[3] In section 4.4, we will find out to what extent this seemingly

---

[1] Not taking a position on the issue of whether moraic theory should incorporate a subsyllabic constituent 'rhyme' (see for an overview Steriade 1988b), we will maintain these labels as convenient shorthand notations. For reasons irrelevant here, we assume non-moraic consonants (onsets, and coda consonants in light syllables) to adjoin below moras.
[2] WEIGHT-BY-POSITION was originally conceived of as a 'parameter', since languages differ in analysing CVC syllables as light or heavy.
[3] For example, unheaded feet have been proposed by Crowhurst and Hewitt (1995), double-headed feet by Bye (1996), and non-moraic syllables by Kager (1989) and Kirchner (1991).

arbitrary collection of feet is deducible from the interaction of constraints, such as those governing quantity-sensitivity, foot size, etc.

4.3   Case-study: rhythmic lengthening in Hixkaryana

With this brief survey in mind, we will now delve into a genuine metrical system, that of Hixkaryana, and try to spot 'metrical forces' at work. Not surprisingly, we will find fierce competition between forces, or, stated in OT terminology, conflicting universal constraints. Hixkaryana (Derbyshire 1979) is a language of the Cariban family, and is spoken in the Amazon (northern Brazil). It has no distinctive vowel length – all surface length reflects rhythmic organization, or so-called 'rhythmic lengthening'. To see what is *rhythmic* about lengthening, consider the following examples, in which foot structure has been marked.

(13)   Words consisting of open syllables only
         a. (to.róː).no   'small bird'
         b. (a.tʃóː).wo.wo   'wind'
         c. (ne.móː).(ko.tóː).no 'it fell'

The generalization that governs the lengthening pattern is the following: *in words of three or more syllables, every even-numbered non-final open syllable is stressed, and its vowel is lengthened.* This alternating length pattern can be characterized as 'iambic': it involves a grouping of syllables into weak–strong rhythmic units, of which the strong syllable is lengthened (Hayes 1995). In (13) this rhythmic unit, the 'canonical iamb' (**LH**), occurs once in words of three and four syllables, and twice in five-syllable words.

Surprisingly, in a disyllabic word consisting of two open syllables, the first syllable (rather than the second) is lengthened:

(14)   Initial lengthening in disyllabic word
         (kʷáː).ja 'red and green macaw'

Divergence from iambic rhythm is not a totally idiosyncratic fact, though, as it is related to a more general observation, that final syllables in Hixkaryana never undergo vowel lengthening, and are never stressed. Whatever factor blocks final stress and lengthening may also 'push' the rhythmic peak backward onto the first syllable.

Turning now from open syllables to closed syllables, we find that these are always stressed, but that their vowels never lengthen. Even though closed syllables fail to undergo lengthening themselves, they do affect the lengthening pattern of open syllables, serving as reference points in counting syllables. For example, in words that have a closed syllable in initial position, the lengthening pattern is similar to that of (13), but with the difference that it is 'shifted' one syllable to the right:

(15)   Words beginning with a closed syllable
  a. (ák).(ma.táː).ri   'branch'
  b. (tóh).(ku.rʲéː).ho.na   'to Tohkurye'
  c. (tóh).(ku.rʲéː).(ho.náː).(ha.ʃáː).ha 'finally to Tohkurye'

In such words length occurs on odd-numbered syllables (third, fifth, seventh, etc.), rather than on even-numbered ones (second, fourth, etc.). More generally, the lengthening pattern in a sequence of open syllables starts over again at each closed syllable:

(16)   Words with multiple closed syllables
  a. (nák).(ɲóh).(yátʃ).(ke.náː).no 'they were burning it'
  b. (kʰa.náː).(níh).no   'I taught you'
  c. (mi.háː).(na.níh).no   'you taught him'

In section 4.3.1 we will develop a rule-based analysis, after Hayes (1995). Then we will turn to an OT analysis in section 4.3.2, and point out its descriptive and conceptual advantages.

4.3.1 *A rule-based analysis*
A rule-based analysis of the Hixkaryana pattern would proceed in the following five steps (after Hayes 1995):

(17) Step 1: Syllabify (open syllables are light, closed syllables are heavy).

    Step 2: Mark the final syllable of each word as *extrametrical*.

    Step 3: Assign iambs {(LH), (LL), (H)} iteratively from left to right.

    Step 4: When the entire metrical domain is a single light syllable, assign (L) to it.

    Step 5: Lengthen the vowel of each strong open syllable.

In Step 2, *extrametricality* is the property of being 'invisible' to rules of foot construction. This analysis is illustrated by the derivations in (18):

(18)   /atʃowowo/ /kʷa.ja/ /tohkurʲehona/
  Step 1: a.tʃo.wo.wo kʷa.ja toh.ku.rʲe.ho.na
  Step 2: a.tʃo.wo.<wo> kʷa.<ja> toh.ku.rʲe.ho.<na>
  Step 3: (a.tʃó).wo.<wo> ---   (tóh).(ku.rʲé).ho.<na>
  Step 4: ---   (kʷá).<ja> ---
  Step 5: (a.tʃóː).wo.<wo> (kʷáː).<ja> (tóh).(ku.rʲéː).ho.<na>

Even though this analysis correctly captures the lengthening pattern, it has a number of important conceptual drawbacks.

First, the rule that assigns iambs (Step 3) is not intrinsically connected to the rule that lengthens open syllables in strong positions of feet (Step 5), although both rules aspire toward a single output target: the canonical iamb (**LH**). This generalization is missed.

Second, this analysis relies on an intermediate stage in the derivation of disyllabic words in which a degenerate foot (**L**) is temporarily allowed (Step 4). This foot is repaired at the surface by lengthening its vowel into (**H**). This (**L**) foot is abstract since the output pattern contains only (**H**) and (**LH**). Again, a generalization is missed.

Third, the analysis fails to explain why a degenerate foot is assigned in disyllabic words, whereas the prefinal syllable of the longer words in (18) remains unparsed. That is, Step 4 is just an ad hoc incarnation of 'culminativity' – it only applies in disyllabic words to satisfy the imperative that every word must have a foot.

4.3.2 *An OT analysis*

Instead we will find it more fruitful to look at Hixkarayana length and stress as a system of *conflicting preferences*. We will find out how these conflicts are resolved by comparing the actual outputs with potential outputs, which might have arisen if the priorities between preferences had been different. That is, *logically possible but suboptimal* outputs serve to support ranking arguments. Ranking arguments will turn out to have a general form: for a pair of an actual form and a suboptimal form, a constraint violated by the suboptimal form (but satisfied in the actual form) dominates a constraint of which the violation pattern is the reverse. (A more complete and formal treatment of what constitutes a ranking argument in OT will be presented in chapter 7.)

In each step, we will proceed as follows. First an actual form will be juxtaposed with a potential form, one which might have been, but is not, realized. We will then identify two conflicting preferences, relating these to the cross-linguistically recurrent properties of stress systems of section 4.2. Preferences will then be translated into universal metrical constraints, which will be ranked one by one on the basis of the available empirical evidence. Finally, we will integrate the subranking thus found into the (current) total ranking for the metrical pattern of Hixkaryana.

The metrical constraints to be introduced in the analysis of Hixkaryana will be discussed in more detail in section 4.4. (There proper credit will be given to their inventors, and all constraints will be motivated in more detail, paying attention to their function and format.)

What conflicting preferences hide behind the length pattern of Hixkaryana? A first conflict that we identify is that between a preference for the 'canonical iamb'

(**LH**), versus a preference for 'final syllables to be unstressed'. A disyllabic word of two open syllables can (potentially, at least) be metrified as a canonical iamb, by lengthening the vowel of its second syllable. However, this potential form is not what we actually find. Vowel length is absent from the final syllable, and instead length occurs initially. We can write this as a statement of 'relative metrical harmony' in (19), where the symbol '>' is to be read as 'is a better metrification than':

(19)   (kʷáː).ja > (kʷa.**jáː**)

It is apparently more important *to leave the final syllable unfooted* than it is *for every foot to be a canonical* (**LH**) *iamb*. Both preferences can be translated directly into metrical constraints. The first states that final syllables must not be metrified:

(20)   **NONFINALITY**
        No foot is final in PrWd.

The second constraint defines the 'best' rhythmic shape of the iamb, a foot having weak–strong prominence and a quantitative make-up 'light-heavy' (Hayes 1995). UNEVEN-IAMB says that (**LH**) is a 'better iamb' than (**LL**) or (**H**):[4]

(21)   **UNEVEN-IAMB**
        (**LH**) > (**LL**), (**H**)

The harmony statement in (19) translates into a ranking argument for these constraints:

(22)   NONFINALITY ≫ UNEVEN-IAMB

Tableau (23) supports this ranking. Each candidate violates one constraint while satisfying the other. The optimal candidate is (23a) since it satisfies the highest-ranking constraint of the two, NONFINALITY:

(23)

Input: /kʷaja/	NONFINALITY	UNEVEN-IAMB
a. ☞ (kʷáː).ja		*
b. (kʷa.jáː)	*!	

We will now extend this simple ranking (using the same basic method) until we arrive at a complete characterization of the Hixkaryana lengthening pattern.

---

[4] In section 4.4.5 we will decompose requirements on prominence (iambs vs. trochees) and quantitative structure (LL vs. LH, H vs. LH, etc.) that are combined in UNEVEN-IAMB.

Let us consider another potential way out of the dilemma of conflicting constraints. It seems that both the Scylla of NonFinality and the Charybdis of Uneven-Iamb can be avoided by an output that has *no feet at all*. This 'unparsed' output vacuously satisfies both Uneven-Iamb and NonFinality, simply because it has no foot to be evaluated. Then why would Hixkaryana still prefer the input /kʷaja/ to surface with a foot, even when this foot fails to match the best form?

(24)   (kʷáː).ja > **kʷa.ja**

The unparsed output violates the imperative that grammatical words must have prosody – the 'culminative' property:

(25)   **GrWd=PrWd**
         A grammatical word must be a prosodic word.

From this constraint it indirectly follows that grammatical words must have minimally one foot. Recall from section 4.2.2 that every prosodic category (PrWd, foot, and syllable) takes as its head a category of the next-lower category. Therefore, *every PrWd must have a foot as its head*. Requiring PrWd-status of a grammatical word thus amounts to requiring that it must have at least a foot.

The preference for grammatical words to be PrWds (hence to have feet) is stronger than the dispreference against 'bad' iambs:

(26)   GrWd=PrWd ≫ Uneven-Iamb

A tableau illustrates this ranking:

(27)

Input: /kʷaja/	GrWd=PrWd	Uneven-Iamb
a. ☞ (kʷáː).ja		*
b. kʷajá	*!	

Culminativity of stress outranks foot well-formedness. This is precisely the generalization left uncaptured by the rule-based analysis.

A second piece of evidence showing that final syllables are strongly preferred to remain unfooted is the length pattern of words with four open syllables. Here the second syllable is lengthened, while the fourth syllable remains short. Apparently the left hand parse, with a single canonical (**LH**) iamb, is preferred to the right hand parse, which has two:

(28)   (a.ʧóː).wo.wo > (a.ʧóː).(**wo.wóː**)

This shows that it is more important *to leave the final syllable unfooted* than it is *for all syllables to be parsed by feet.* Or, translating the latter preference into a constraint:

(29)   **PARSE-SYL**
         Feet are parsed by feet.

The resulting ranking of these two constraints is:

(30)   NONFINALITY ≫ PARSE-SYL

(31)

Input: /atʃowowo/	NONFINALITY	PARSE-SYL
a. ☞ (a.tʃóː).wo.wo		**
b. (a.tʃóː).(wo.wóː)	*!	

This ranking is confirmed by disyllabic words – see the harmonic comparison in (19).

We have found that NONFINALITY dominates both UNEVEN-IAMB and PARSE-SYL, but is it also possible to establish a ranking between both dominated constraints? We start by asking under what conditions UNEVEN-IAMB and PARSE-SYL could *possibly conflict.* Relevant contexts are those in which a more complete metrification would produce non-canonical feet.

Three-syllable forms, for example, cannot be exhaustively parsed without violating UNEVEN-IAMB. We therefore compare the pair of forms (32). Does this harmonic ranking tell us that UNEVEN-IAMB dominates PARSE-SYL?

(32)   (to.róː).no > (to.róː).(nóː)

Unfortunately, this pair tells us nothing about the ranking we are interested in, as there is an independent explanation for the suboptimality of the righthand form: it fatally violates NONFINALITY. All we can infer from (32) is a confirmation of the ranking NONFINALITY ≫ PARSE-SYL. Still, we have learnt something from this failure: we must compare forms that do not involve violations of NONFINALITY.

We start looking for other evidence bearing on the ranking of UNEVEN-IAMB and PARSE-SYL. Such evidence may come from a comparison of four-syllable forms.

(33)   (a.tʃóː).wo.wo > (a.tʃóː).(wóː).wo
         > (áː).(tʃo.wóː).wo

A single-foot parse is preferred to a two-foot parse even if this respects NONFINALITY. As indicated, a two-foot parse might have either a (LH) iamb plus a (H) heavy foot (with the second and third syllable long), or (H) plus (LH) (with the first and third syllable long). Both two-foot parses are rejected, though, in favour of a single-foot parse. This shows that it is more important *for every foot to be a canonical* (**LH**) *iamb*, than it is *for all syllables to be parsed by feet*. Or, in terms of constraint ranking:

(34)   UNEVEN-IAMB ≫ PARSE-SYL

This ranking is supported by a tableau:

(35)

Input: /aʧowowo/	UNEVEN-IAMB	PARSE-SYL
a. ☞ (a.ʧóː).wo.wo		**
b. (a.ʧóː).(wóː).wo	*!	*
c. (áː).(ʧo.wóː).wo	*!	*

This is an important result showing that ranking arguments are consistent with *transitivity*. To see this, we must recapitulate some results. Firstly, NONFINALITY dominates UNEVEN-IAMB (see tableau 23). Secondly, UNEVEN-IAMB dominates PARSE-SYL (see tableau 35). Thirdly, NONFINALITY dominates PARSE-SYL (tableau 31), confirming transitivity of strict domination. We now arrive at the following hierarchy:

(36)   GRWD=PRWD, NONFINALITY ≫ UNEVEN-IAMB ≫ PARSE-SYL

Tableau (37) summarizes two results booked so far. It proves UNEVEN-IAMB ≫ PARSE-SYL, as well as NONFINALITY ≫ PARSE-SYL (as already established by tableau 31):

(37)

Input: /aʧowowo/	NONFINALITY	UNEVEN-IAMB	PARSE-SYL
a. ☞ (a.ʧóː).wo.wo			**
b. (a.ʧóː).(wóː).wo		*!	*
c. (a.ʧóː).(wo.wóː)	*!		

The optimal candidate (37a) violates PARSE-SYL more severely than any of its competitors (37b–c). However, these competitors fatally violate either NONFINALITY (37c) or UNEVEN-IAMB (37b), both of which dominate PARSE-SYL.

What other preferences govern the length pattern of Hixkaryana? For example, is there any evidence for quantity-sensitivity apart from a preference for the canonical iamb? Such evidence indeed exists, and it comes from two sources.

The first finding is that it is more important *to stress heavy syllables* than *for every foot to be a* (**LH**) *iamb*. Evidence comes from the pair in (38). The actual form stresses a heavy syllable, but has a non-canonical foot (**H**). The suboptimal form has one canonical foot, but fails to stress the heavy syllable.

(38)   (tóh).(ku.rʲéː).ho.na > **toh**.(ku.rʲéː).ho.na

We conclude that 'foot-form' has less priority than quantity-sensitivity.

The suboptimal status of the righthand form in (38) is due to a constraint enforcing quantity-sensitivity, the close relation between syllable weight and prominence. This is the 'Weight-to-Stress-Principle' (henceforth WSP):

(39)   **WSP**
          Heavy syllables are stressed.

This constraint is violated by any heavy syllable that is not prominent, either within a foot or outside a foot. The harmonic relation in (38) translates into a ranking argument:

(40)   WSP ≫ Uneven-Iamb

A related piece of evidence for quantity-sensitivity comes from a comparison made in (41). Both the actual (lefthand) form and the potential (righthand) form contain one foot in initial position that is not a canonical iamb, (**H**) and (**HH**), respectively. Although the righthand form might seem preferable for its more complete parsing, it is suboptimal. The origin of its failure is its quantity-disrespecting initial foot:

(41)   (tóh).(ku.rʲéː).ho.na > (**toh**.kúː).(rʲe.hóː).na

This evidence tells us that it is more important *to stress heavy syllables* than it is *for all syllables to be parsed by feet*. We now infer the ranking

(42)   WSP ≫ Parse-Syl

WSP is actually undominated in Hixkaryana, for both kinds of heavy syllables, CVC and CVV, are stressed without exception. We thus rank WSP right at the top of the hierarchy, together with GrWd=PrWd and NonFinality:[5]

(43)   GrWd=PrWd, NonFinality, WSP ≫ Uneven-Iamb ≫ Parse-Syl

---

[5] NonFinality and WSP potentially conflict in a PrWd ending in a closed syllable. If the closed syllable is stressed, then WSP ≫ NonFinality; if it is unstressed, then NonFinality ≫ WSP. Unfortunately this ranking cannot be established since Hixkaryana lacks final closed syllables. Speculatively, the lack of final CVC might be construed as support for the undominated status of NonFinality and WSP: violation of both constraints is avoided at the expense of final consonant deletion, violating Max-C. However, no alternations occur.

Tableau (44) lays out the most complex interaction of metrical constraints that we have seen thus far, involving the full hierarchy in (43) except GRWD=PRWD.

(44)

Input: /tohkur^{j}ehona/	NONFINALITY	WSP	UNEVEN-IAMB	PARSE-SYL
a. ☞ (tóh).(ku.r^{j}é:).ho.na			*	**
b. (tóh).(ku.r^{j}é:).(hó:).na			**!	*
c. (tóh).(ku.r^{j}é:).(ho.ná:)	*!		*	
d. (toh.kú:).(r^{j}e.hó:).na		*!	*	*
e. toh.(ku.r^{j}é:).ho.na		*!		***

The tableau contains the quantity-disrespecting candidates (44d–e), presented earlier in (38) and (41), which fatally violate WSP. Candidate (44b), in comparison to optimal (44a), has an additional parsed syllable, causing an additional (and fatal) violation of UNEVEN-IAMB. Such an additional violation of UNEVEN-IAMB is avoided by candidate (44c), but at a high price: a fatal violation of NON-FINALITY. This once again corroborates that NONFINALITY ≫ PARSE-SYL, as we had already established in tableau (31).

Continuing our search for priorities, we find that it is more important *to avoid monomoraic (**L**) feet*, than *to avoid vowel length in underlyingly short vowels* (where the input has none). The evidence consists of the comparison of both forms in (45), where a disyllabic form that has a (**H**) foot with a lengthened vowel is preferred to a potential form involving no lengthening, but a monomoraic (**L**) foot.

(45)   (k^{w}á:).ja > (k^{w}á).ja

This demonstrates that DEP-μ-IO (the 'anti-lengthening' constraint) is relatively weak:

(46)   **DEP-μ-IO**
          Output moras have input correspondents.

What the harmonic comparison (45) directly tells us is that DEP-μ-IO is dominated by FT-BIN, which we will learn to know as the 'anti-degenerate-foot' constraint:

(47)   **FT-BIN**
          Feet are binary under moraic or syllabic analysis.

FT-BIN is undominated in Hixkaryana: no forms contain light stressed syllables, and hence no forms contain (L) feet. Because of this, the ranking FT-BIN ≫ DEP-μ-IO is not particularly informative about the precise position of DEP-μ-IO in the constraint hierarchy.

Fortunately, a second source of evidence bearing on this ranking can be identified. In fact, every word that has a lengthened vowel in a (LH) iamb tells us that the avoidance of vowel length (DEP-μ-IO) is subordinated to the preference for every foot to be a canonical (LH) iamb (UNEVEN-IAMB). So much is shown, for example, by a comparison of an actual trisyllabic form in (48) to a potential form that omits vowel length:

(48)   (to.róː).no > **(to.ró)**.no

This means that we can now add FT-BIN and DEP-μ-IO to the hierarchy, and locate the latter as accurately as possible – in a position directly dominated by UNEVEN-IAMB:

(49)   GRWD=PRWD, NONFINALITY, FT-BIN, WSP ≫ UNEVEN-IAMB ≫ PARSE-SYL, DEP-μ-IO

What remain to be clarified are the factors that determine the position of feet with respect to the edges of the PrWd. We have already seen that words of four open syllables fall into a metrification that has only one canonical iamb (see 33). Still, this single foot can be placed in two different positions, even respecting NONFINALITY in both cases. Comparison of the actual four-syllable form with a potential form shows that the foot is preferrably *initial* in the word. (This is Hixkaryana's form of 'demarcative stress'):

(50)   (a.tʃóː).wo.wo > a.(tʃo.wóː).wo

This preference for 'feet to be initial in the PrWd' is translated into a maximally general constraint:

(51)   **ALL-FT-LEFT**
         Every foot stands at the left edge of the PrWd.

Violations of this constraint will amount to the number of syllables between a foot and the left edge of the word. When a word contains multiple feet, the violations for all feet will be added up. This is an example of a *gradient* constraint.

How is ALL-FT-LEFT ranked with respect to other constraints? To find out we must identify forms in which it is actually violated. There happen to be plenty of forms in which ALL-FT-LEFT is violated: every PrWd having more than one foot constitutes a violation, as only one foot per PrWd can be strictly initial. We thus find that it is more important *for all syllables to be parsed by feet* than it is *for every foot to stand at the left edge*:

(52)   (ne.mó:).(ko.tó:).no > (ne.mó:).**ko.to**.no

Accordingly, we find the important ranking:

(53)   PARSE-SYL ≫ ALL-FT-LEFT

The resulting integrated hierarchy of all constraints for Hixkaryana is in (54):[6]

(54)   GRWD=PRWD, NONFINALITY, FT-BIN, WSP

≫

UNEVEN-IAMB

≫

PARSE-SYL

≫

ALL-FT-LEFT, DEP-μ-IO

Note that we now predict that WSP must dominate ALL-FT-LEFT, by transitivity. This prediction is confirmed by the comparison in (55):

(55)   (kʰa.ná:).(nɨ́h).no > (kʰa.ná:).**nɨh**.no

The following display summarizes all rankings that we have found, and for each ranking, the evidence on which it is based.

(56)

It's more important:		*than it is:*
• to leave the final syllable unfooted		for every foot to be a (LH) iamb
NONFINALITY	≫	UNEVEN-IAMB
(kʷá:).ja	>	(kʷa.**já:**)
• for every word to contain a foot		for every foot to be a (LH) iamb
GRWD=PRWD	≫	UNEVEN-IAMB
(kʷá:).ja	>	**kʷa.ja**
• to avoid (L) feet		to avoid vowel length
FT-BIN	≫	DEP-μ-IO
(kʷá:).ja	>	**(kʷá)**.ja
• for every foot to be a (LH) iamb		to avoid vowel length
UNEVEN-IAMB	≫	DEP-μ-IO
(to.ró:).no	>	**(to.ró)**.no

---

[6] This analysis has been influenced by analyses of iambic patterns in Axininca Campa (McCarthy and Prince 1993b, Hung 1994) and Carib (Van der Hulst and Visch 1992, Kenstowicz 1995).

- to stress heavy syllables
  WSP ≫ UNEVEN-IAMB
  (tóh).(ku.rʲéː).ho.na > toh.(ku.rʲéː).ho.na
- to stress heavy syllables
  WSP ≫ PARSE-SYL
  (tóh).(ku.rʲéː).ho.na > (toh.kúː).(rʲe.hóː).na
- for every foot to be a (LH) iamb
  UNEVEN-IAMB ≫ PARSE-SYL
  (a.tʃóː).wo.wo > (a.tʃóː).(wóː).wo
- to leave the final syllable unfooted
  NONFINALITY ≫ PARSE-SYL
  (a.tʃóː).wo.wo > (a.tʃóː).(wo.wóː)
- to parse all syllables by feet
  PARSE-SYL ≫ ALL-FT-LEFT
  (ne.móː).(ko.tóː).no > (ne.móː).ko.to.no

for every foot to be a (LH) iamb

to parse all syllables by feet

to parse all syllables by feet

to parse all syllables by feet

for every foot to be at the left edge

To wind up the analysis of Hixkaryana, we present extensive tableaux of four key forms (57–60).

(57)

Input: /kʷaja/	NON-FINALITY	GRWD= PRWD	FT-BIN	WSP	UN-EVEN-IAMB	PARSE-SYL	ALL-FT-LEFT	DEP-μ-IO
a. ☞ (kʷáː).ja					*	*		*
b. (kʷá).ja			*!		*	*		
c. kʷa.ja		*!				**		
d. (kʷa.jáː)	*!							*

(58)

Input: /torono/	NON-FINALITY	GRWD= PRWD	FT-BIN	WSP	UN-EVEN-IAMB	PARSE-SYL	ALL-FT-LEFT	DEP-μ-IO
a. ☞ (to.róː).no						*		*
b. (to.ró).no					*!	*		
c. (to.róː).(nóː)	*!				*		**	**

(59)

Input: /atʃowowo/	Non-Finality	GrWd= PrWd	Ft-Bin	WSP	Un-Even-Iamb	Parse-Syl	All-Ft-Left	Dep-μ-IO
a. ☞ (a.tʃóː).wo.wo						**		*
b. a.(tʃo.wóː).wo						**	*!	*
c. (a.tʃóː).(wóː).wo					*!	*	**	**
d. (a.tʃó).wo.wo					*!	**		
e. (a.tʃóː).(wo.wóː)	*!						**	**

(60)

Input: /tohkurʲehona/	Non-Finality	GrWd= PrWd	Ft-Bin	WSP	Un-Even-Iamb	Parse-Syl	All-Ft-Left	Dep-μ-IO
a. ☞ (tóh).(ku.rʲéː).ho.na					*	**	*	*
b. (tóh).ku.(rʲe.hóː).na					*	**	**!	*
c. (toh.kúː).(rʲe.hóː).na				*!	*	*	**	**
d. toh.(ku.rʲéː).ho.na				*!		***	*	*
e. (tóh).(ku.rʲéː).(ho.náː)	*!				*		*, ***	**

4.3.3 *Conclusions*

This analysis of Hixkaryana illustrates important ingredients of the analysis of word stress patterns: basic metrical constraints and their interactions in producing a rhythmic pattern. Note in particular the following four rankings:

(61)   Binary rhythm starting at the left word edge
        Ft-Bin ≫ Parse-Syl ≫ All-Ft-Left

(62)   Metrical inertness of the final syllable
        NonFinality ≫ Parse-Syl

(63)   Subminimal lengthening
        GrWd=PrWd, Ft-Bin ≫ Dep-μ-IO

(64)   Iambic lengthening
        Uneven-Iamb ≫ Dep-μ-IO

These ranking schemata will be placed in broader typological perspective in section 4.4–5.

Returning to a basic theme of this book, the interaction of well-formedness and faithfulness, we have seen another example of this in the analysis of Hixkaryana: rhythmic vowel lengthening (at the expense of DEP-μ-IO, the 'anti-lengthening' constraint) is forced by foot-form constraints (FT-BIN and UNEVEN-IAMB). This interaction is interesting since it is 'parallel', in the following sense: evaluation of foot form takes place in a single hierarchy together with the evaluation of input faithfulness. There is a major difference between the OT analysis and the derivational analysis in this respect. In the derivational analysis vowel lengthening is a way to 'repair' ill-formed feet created by previous metrification rules. This division of labour is due to the strict distinction in rule-based theory between rules of metrical parsing and rules of quantitative adjustment. The former construct feet, while the latter carry out the quantitative changes required to render the feet 'perfect'. In OT no such serial interaction of metrical parsing and quantitative changes is possible, as intermediate levels of derivation are lacking. All aspects of foot well-formedness (their distribution and quantitative make-up) are evaluated at one level: the output. Consequently the OT analysis integrates aspects of foot well-formedness in a more generalizing way.

4.4 A set of metrical constraints

In this section we will present a set of metrical constraints. We will also place the metrical constraints that were introduced in the analysis of Hixkaryana in a broader cross-linguistic perspective, by relating them to our discussion of common preferences in stress systems in section 4.2. In the course of the exposition, additional constraints will be introduced, which are (as the earlier-mentioned constraints) identical in name and effect to constraints in standard OT literature (particularly: Prince and Smolensky 1993: 28–32, 38–66, McCarthy and Prince 1993a, b: 150–6), unless specific mention is made of a deviation.

4.4.1 *Rhythm: FT-BIN, PARSE-SYL, and ALL-FT-X*

As a powerful cross-linguistic preference in stress languages, we have identified *rhythm*, or regular alternation of strong and weak syllables. In metrical phonology, such alternating patterns are interpreted as the grouping of syllables into rhythmic units – or *feet*.

The fundamentally rhythmic requirement that feet be binary is expressed in FT-BIN (Prince 1980, Kager 1989, Prince and Smolensky 1993):

(65)   **FT-BIN**
         Feet are binary under moraic or syllabic analysis.

A foot must contain either two moras, as in (H) or (LL), or two syllables, as in (σσ). A key function of FT-BIN is to exclude *degenerate feet* (L), which contain a single light syllable. Many languages have an absolute ban on degenerate feet, due to undominated FT-BIN. The usual diagnostic of undominated FT-BIN is the absolute enforcement of the minimal word.

Enforcing rhythmic binarity, FT-BIN also plays a key role in rhythmic alternation. Note that FT-BIN by itself does not suffice to guarantee the binary alternation of weak and strong syllables. This requires something more – all syllables must be parsed by feet (Hayes 1980, Halle and Vergnaud 1987, Prince and Smolensky 1993):

(66)   **PARSE-SYL**

        Syllables are parsed by feet.

Syllables violating this constraint (any which are not parsed by a foot) will be assumed to be metrified as immediate daughters of PrWd. This assumption is known as *weak layering* (Itô and Mester 1992). The Hixkaryana example [(to.ró:).no], represented hierarchically, has a weakly-layered final syllable, one that is unparsed by a foot:

(67)   PrWd

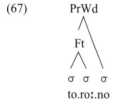

to.ro:.no

Only the final syllable, the one that is unparsed by a foot, violates PARSE-SYL.

In combination, high-ranking FT-BIN and PARSE-SYL have the effect of enforcing binary alternation: a parse of the word into multiple binary feet. When a word can be *fully* parsed by binary feet without any violation of FT-BIN or PARSE-SYL, the foot distribution is uniquely determined by both constraints. Then an exhaustive parsing arises, with all feet packed tight together. This is the case, for example, in words with an even number of light syllables; see (68a). But in words with an odd number of light syllables, one syllable must remain that cannot be parsed by binary feet. Accordingly, there are multiple ways in which a maximally dense distribution of feet can be achieved; see (68b).

(68)   a.   (σσ)(σσ)(σσ)   Exhaustive parsing: feet packed tightly

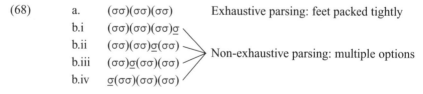

Here the constraint pair FT-BIN or PARSE-SYL fails to uniquely determine foot distribution. To produce a genuine rhythmic distribution of feet, one oriented

toward a specific edge of the word, a foot alignment constraint must pick out one of the parsings in (68b.i–iv). Such a constraint is stated below after McCarthy and Prince (1993a):

(69)   **ALL-FT-LEFT**
         Align (Ft, Left, PrWd, Left)
         Every foot stands at the left edge of the PrWd.

This is an alignment constraint of the general format 'Align (Cat$_1$, Edge$_1$, Cat$_2$, Edge$_2$)' (see chapter 3), requiring that the left edge of every foot coincide with the left edge of a PrWd. This is satisfied only in the case of a single foot standing at the absolute left edge of the word: any additional foot will incur a violation, since two feet cannot both stand at the left edge. If undominated, ALL-FT-LEFT enforces a single foot per PrWd – a 'non-iterative' pattern.

But then how can ALL-FT-LEFT resolve ties among candidates containing multiple feet, such as those in (68)? The answer is simple and straightforward. Each foot that is not in absolute initial position incurs some violation of ALL-FT-LEFT. If we count the distance between a foot and the left word edge in *syllables*, then each foot will incur a violation of ALL-FT-LEFT that equals this number. In words containing multiple feet, we simply add up violations for individual feet to arrive at the total violation of ALL-FT-LEFT. The candidate incurring the smallest total violation wins. This is an example of a *gradient* constraint.

A 'left-oriented' distribution of feet is achieved under the ranking ALL-FT-LEFT ≫ ALL-FT-RIGHT (its mirror image). In tableau (70), commas separate the violations per foot, counting foot by foot from the relevant word edge. Exclamation marks are placed at the point at which the number of violations becomes fatal:

(70)

Left-oriented rhythm	ALL-FT-LEFT	ALL-FT-RIGHT
a. ☞ $(\sigma\sigma)(\sigma\sigma)(\sigma\sigma)\sigma$	**, ****	*, ***, *****
b. $(\sigma\sigma)(\sigma\sigma)\sigma(\sigma\sigma)$	**, *****!	***, *****
c. $(\sigma\sigma)\sigma(\sigma\sigma)(\sigma\sigma)$	***, ****!*	**, *****
d. $\sigma(\sigma\sigma)(\sigma\sigma)(\sigma\sigma)$	*, ***, ***!**	**, ****

Reversing the ranking of both constraints will have the effect of a 'right-oriented' rhythm:

(71)

Right-oriented rhythm	ALL-FT-RIGHT	ALL-FT-LEFT
a. $(\sigma\sigma)(\sigma\sigma)(\sigma\sigma)\sigma$	*, ***, **!***	**, ****
b. $(\sigma\sigma)(\sigma\sigma)\sigma(\sigma\sigma)$	***, ***!**	**, *****
c. $(\sigma\sigma)\sigma(\sigma\sigma)(\sigma\sigma)$	**, ****!*	***, *****
d. ☞ $\sigma(\sigma\sigma)(\sigma\sigma)(\sigma\sigma)$	**, ****	*, ***, *****

The highest-ranked foot alignment constraint determines the directionality of foot parsing. Non-directional candidates such as (70b, c) and (71b, c) can never be optimal, regardless of the ranking of foot alignment constraints.[7] This captures the fact that rhythmic patterns are directional, as a wave starting at one edge and flowing towards the other edge.

Both rhythmic types are attested in a number of languages. Left-oriented rhythm is exemplified by the Australian language Pintupi (Hansen and Hansen 1969, Hayes 1995), which stresses the initial syllable and following odd-numbered syllables, except the final. Right-oriented rhythm is exemplified by the Amazonian language Warao (Osborn 1966, Hayes 1980), which stresses the penult and preceding alternating syllables.

(72) a. Pintupi: Fᴛ-Bɪɴ ≫ Pᴀʀsᴇ-Sʏʟ ≫ Aʟʟ-Fᴛ-Lᴇғᴛ
　　　(tʲú.ṭa).ja　　　　　　　'many'
　　　(má.ḷa).(wà.na)　　　　'through (from) behind'
　　　(pú.ḷiŋ).(kà.la).tʲu　　　'we (sat) on the hill'
　　　(tʲá.mu).(lìm.pa).(tʲùŋ.ku)　'our relation'
　　　(tʲí.ḷi).(rì.ɳu).(làm.pa).tʲu　'the fire for our benefit flared up'
　　b. Warao: Fᴛ-Bɪɴ ≫ Pᴀʀsᴇ-Sʏʟ ≫ Aʟʟ-Fᴛ-Rɪɢʜᴛ
　　　ko.(rá.nu)　　　　　　　'drink it!'
　　　yi.(wà.ra).(ná.e)　　　　'he finished it'
　　　(yà.pu).(rù.ki).(tà.ne).(há.se)　'verily to climb'
　　　e.(nà.ho).(rò.a).(hà.ku).(tá.i) 'the one who causes him to eat'

In both languages, degenerate feet are avoided at the expense of violations of Pᴀʀsᴇ-Sʏʟ. This signals an important interaction between Fᴛ-Bɪɴ and Pᴀʀsᴇ-Sʏʟ which will return in various forms in the remainder of this chapter:

---

[7] In section 4.4.3 we will see that such patterns arise due to interactions with word alignment constraints.

(73)   Maximally binary metrification

FT-BIN ≫ PARSE-SYL ≫ ALL-FT-X

A tableau of the Pintupi example [(pú.ɭiŋ).(kà.la).tʲu] serves to illustrate the activity of all three constraints in this ranking:

(74)

Input: /puɭiŋkalatʲu/	FT-BIN	PARSE-SYL	ALL-FT-LEFT
a. ☞ (pú.ɭiŋ).(kà.la).tʲu		*	**
b. (pú.ɭiŋ).ka.(là.tʲu)		*	***!
c. pu.(ɭíŋ.ka).(là.tʲu)		*	*, **!*
d. (pú.ɭiŋ).ka.la.tʲu		**!*	
e. (pú.ɭiŋ).(kà.la).(tʲù)	*		**, ****

Undominated FT-BIN rules out degenerate feet (as in 74e), at the expense of violations of PARSE-SYL (74a–d). But since PARSE-SYL is *minimally* violated, any metrifications having multiple unparsed syllables (74d) are ruled out. All remaining metrifications have multiple feet (74a–c), at the expense of multiple violations of ALL-FT-LEFT. *Minimal* violation of ALL-FT-LEFT results in an optimal output whose collective feet stand as close as possible to the left word edge – this is (74a).

Related to rhythmic distribution of stresses, two more preferences have been observed to be strong in many languages. First, adjacent stressed syllables (*clashes*) are often avoided:

(75)   ***CLASH**
         No stressed syllables are adjacent.

*CLASH has its roots in pre-OT work (Liberman 1975, Liberman and Prince 1977, Prince 1983, Hammond 1984, Selkirk 1984). See section 4.4.5 for further discussion.

Second, final syllables are 'metrically inert', in a double sense. For Hixkaryana, we have seen that final syllables must be *unfooted* – the PrWd must not end in a foot. But for many other languages, a somewhat weaker requirement holds that the final syllable must be *unstressed* – the PrWd must not end in a stressed syllable. Both requirements are put in a single statement in Prince and Smolensky's version of NONFINALITY:

(76)   **NONFINALITY**
         No prosodic head is final in PrWd.

This is the OT counterpart of 'extrametricality' in rule-based theory. It is not completely clear whether both interpretations of NonFinality ('unparsed'/'unstressed' final syllable) should be merged in a single constraint.[8]

4.4.2 *Culminativity: GrWd=PrWd and word minima*

As was explained in section 4.3, the culminative property is enforced by a constraint requiring that every grammatical word must be a prosodic word as well:

(77)   **GrWd=PrWd**
         A grammatical word must be a PrWd.

The prosodic hierarchy guarantees that every PrWd dominates at least one foot – hence the combined result of GrWd=PrWd and the prosodic hierarchy is that every grammatical word has at least one stressed syllable – the culminative property. (Most languages make a distinction in prominence among multiple feet in a word. The issue of how to capture this distinction by constraints, and how to locate the strongest foot – primary stress – in a word, will be dealt with in section 4.4.3.)

Related to GrWd=PrWd is the notion of *word minimum* – the requirement that a word have minimally two moras or syllables. A word minimum can be enforced in various ways, for example by 'subminimal lengthening', making a monomoraic word bimoraic, or by the epenthesis of a vowel into a monosyllabic word, making it disyllabic. The example below is taken from Mohawk (Piggott 1995):

(78)   /k-tat-s/ ík.tats 'I offer it'

This effect is due to GrWd=PrWd in combination with Ft-Bin. The chain of reasoning is as follows. By GrWd=PrWd, a grammatical word must equal a prosodic word. By the prosodic hierarchy, a PrWd must dominate a foot. Finally, by Ft-Bin, a foot must have two moras or syllables. Epenthesis (or 'augmentation' of the subminimal form) is enforced when the 'anti-epenthesis' constraint Dep-IO is dominated by GrWd=PrWd and Ft-Bin:

(79)   Word minimum enforced by epenthesis
         GrWd=PrWd, Ft-Bin ≫ Dep-IO

This interaction is illustrated for the Mohawk example below:

---

[8] *Clash and NonFinality were collapsed by Hung (1994) into a single constraint Rhythm 'every strong syllable must be followed by a weak syllable'. See Elenbaas (1996, 1999) for empirical arguments against this merging.

(80)

Input: /k-tat-s/	GrWd=PrWd	Ft-Bin	Dep-IO
a. ☞ (ík.tats)			*
b. (ktáts)		*!	
c. ktats	*!		

The next section deals with metrical sensitivity to word edges.

4.4.3 *Demarcative stress: ALIGN-HD and ALIGN-WD*

Another strong cross-linguistic preference (mentioned earlier in section 4.2) is for stresses to fall at edges of the domain: the so-called *demarcative* property of stress. In OT, edge-marking is due to alignment constraints requiring cooccurrence of edges of categories, for example of the prosodic categories PrWd and Ft. We have already seen two constraints to that effect: ALL-FT-LEFT and ALL-FT-RIGHT. Here we will extend the family of metrical alignment constraints with four members, coming in two pairs.

The first pair of metrical alignment constraints, LEFTMOST and RIGHTMOST, align the strongest foot (or 'head' foot) with a specified edge of the word. (These constraints are named after EDGEMOST from Prince and Smolensky 1993):

(81)   a. **LEFTMOST**
           Align (Hd-Ft, Left, PrWd, Left)
           The head foot is leftmost in PrWd.
     b. **RIGHTMOST**
           Align (Hd-Ft, Right, PrWd, Right)
           The head foot is rightmost in PrWd.

The function of 'peak-aligning' constraints is dual. First, they serve to locate the primary stress on a foot standing at the specified edge of the word. Thus far we have had no constraints making prominence distinctions among feet; since most languages make such distinctions, (81a, b) are well-supported.

     The second function of LEFTMOST/RIGHTMOST is perhaps less obvious – it appears in the analysis of so-called *bidirectional* stress systems. Such systems are characterized by a rhythmic pattern that is oriented toward two word edges, rather than toward a single edge. For example, the Australian language Garawa (Furby 1974, Hayes 1980, McCarthy and Prince 1993a) stresses the initial syllable and alternating syllables preceding the penult. Feet are oriented toward the right edge (as is evident from words of seven or more syllables), but the primary stress is always initial. See (82a).

(82) a. Garawa: Ft-Bin, Leftmost ≫ Parse-Syl ≫ All-Ft-Right

(pún.ja).ɭa 'white'

(ká.ma).ɭa.(ɽì.ɲi) 'wrist'

(yá.ka).(là.ka).(làm.pa) 'loose'

(ŋán.ki).ɽi.(kì.rim).(pà.yi) 'fought with boomerangs'

b. Piro: Ft-Bin, Rightmost ≫ Parse-Syl ≫ All-Ft-Left

ru.(tx̱í.tx̱a) 'he observes taboo'

(sà.lwa).ye.(hká.kna) 'they visit each other'

(pè.ʧi).(ʧhì.ma).(tló.na) 'they say they stalk it'

(rù.slu).(nò.ti).ni.(tká.na) 'their voices already changed'

The mirror-image system of Garawa is exemplified by Piro (Matteson 1965, Hayes 1995), which stresses the penult and alternate syllables following the initial syllable. See (82b).

The analysis of bidirectional stress patterns involves domination of peak alignment over foot alignment *at the opposite edge*. Thus, Leftmost dominates All-Ft-Right in the analysis of Garawa, while Rightmost dominates All-Ft-Left in the analysis of Piro. The basis of the rankings is the normal interaction producing binary alternation in the analyses of Pintupi/Warao, that is, Ft-Bin ≫ Parse-Syl ≫ All-Ft-X. This ranking is now extended by inclusion of undominated peak alignment constraints, as in the rankings given in (82). The tableau of a seven-syllable example of Garawa is presented below:

(83)

Input: /ŋankiɽikirimpayi/	Ft-Bin	Leftmost	Parse-Syl	All-Ft-Right
a. ☞ (ŋán.ki).ɽi.(kì.rim).(pà.yi)			*	**, *****
b. (ŋán.ki).(ɽì.ki).rim.(pà.yi)			*	***, *****!
c. (ŋán.ki).(ɽì.ki).(rìm.pa).yi			*	*, ***, ****!*
d. (ŋán.ki).ɽi.ki.rim.(pà.yi)			**!*	*****
e. (ŋán.ki).ɽi.ki.rim.pa.yi			**!***	*****
f. ŋan.(kí.ɽi).(kì.rim).(pà.yi)		*!	*	**, ****
g. (ŋán.ki).(ɽì.ki).(rìm.pa).(yì)	*!			*, ***, *****

By undominated Leftmost, every word has an initial main stress foot (excluding 83f). By Ft-Bin, all feet are binary (excluding 83g). Among the remaining candidates, Parse-Syl picks out candidates that have a single unparsed syllable (excluding 83d–e). The survivors (83a–c) differ only in the distribution of their three feet (of which the initial one is fixed by LEFTMOST). Minimal violation of ALL-FT-RIGHT draws all feet as close as possible to the right edge, selecting (83a). In sum, main stress is placed at the left edge due to LEFTMOST, while all other stresses are distributed directionally due to ALL-FT-RIGHT.

The second pair of demarcative constraints is stated in (84):

(84)   a. **ALIGN-WD-LEFT**
           Align (PrWd, Left, Ft, Left)
           Every PrWd begins with a foot.
        b. **ALIGN-WD-RIGHT**
           Align (PrWd, Right, Ft, Right)
           Every PrWd ends in a foot.

These constraints are functional antagonists of ALL-FT-LEFT and ALL-FT-RIGHT. Instead of making a requirement about feet (in terms of word edges), they make a requirement about word edges (in terms of feet). Accordingly, they are violated when no foot is present at the specified edge of the word. (Recall the discussion of 'asymmetric' alignment in chapter 3, section 3.4.1.)

The analytic function of these constraints resides in *complex bidirectional systems*, of which an example, Indonesian (Cohn 1989), is given below:

(85)   Indonesian: FT-BIN, RIGHTMOST ≫ ALIGN-WD-L ≫ PARSE-SYL ≫
        ALL-FT-R
        a. bi.(cá.ra)   'speak'
        b. (kòn.ti).nu.(á.si)   'continuation'
        c. (è.ro).(dì.na).(mí.ka)   'aerodynamics'
        d. (à.me).ri.(kà.ni).(sá.si) 'Americanization'

In Indonesian primary stress falls on the penultimate syllable, while words of minimally four syllables long have an initial secondary stress. Words of six or more syllables display an alternating stress pattern starting at the right edge. Ignoring the right-aligned position of primary stress, this foot distribution looks much like that of Garawa (82a), with one major difference: three-syllable words have a right-aligned foot, rather than a left-aligned foot. Upon comparing the Indonesian pattern to that of Piro (82b), we find that everything is identical except words of seven syllables long. These have secondary stress on the third syllable in Piro, but on the fourth syllable in Indonesian.

(86)

	3 syllables	5 syllables	7 syllables
Indonesian	bi.(cá.ra)	(kòn.ti).nu.(á.si)	(à.me).ri.(kà.ni).(sá.si)
Garawa	(pún.ja).ḷa	(ká.ma).ḷa.(r̥ì.ɲi)	(ŋán.ki).r̥i.(kì.rim).(pà.yi)
Piro	ru.(t̪x̣í.t̪x̣a)	(sà.lwa).ye.(hká.kna)	(rù.slu).(nò.ti).ni.(tká.na)

In sum, the Indonesian rhythmic pattern is a hybrid of the Garawa and Piro patterns. It has undominated RIGHTMOST, as in Piro, but the active foot-alignment constraint is ALL-FT-RIGHT, as in Garawa. Accordingly, ranked in between undominated RIGHTMOST and ALL-FT-RIGHT in the Indonesian grammar must be ALIGN-WD-LEFT:

(87)   a. RIGHTMOST ≫ ALIGN-WD-LEFT
              bi.(cá.ra) > (bí.ca).ra
      b. ALIGN-WD-LEFT ≫ ALL-FT-RIGHT
              (kòn.ti).nu.(á.si) > kon.(tì.nu).(á.si)
              (à.me).ri.(kà.ni).(sá.si) > (à.me).(rì.ka).ni.(sá.si)

A tableau of a three-syllable word shows why the metrical grammar of Indonesian is distinct from that of Garawa: RIGHTMOST dominates ALIGN-WD-LEFT.

(88)

Input: /bicara/	FT-BIN	RIGHTMOST	ALIGN-WD-LEFT	PARSE-SYL	ALL-FT-RIGHT
a. ☞ bi.(cá.ra)			*	*	
b. (bí.ca).ra		*!		*	*
c. (bì).(cá.ra)	*!				**

The tableau of a seven-syllable word shows that Indonesian and Piro have distinct metrical grammars: alternating stresses run from the right edge in Indonesian, rather than from the left edge, as in Piro.

(89)

Input: /amerikanisasi/	FT-BIN	RIGHT-MOST	ALIGN-WD-LEFT	PARSE-SYL	ALL-FT-RIGHT
a. ☞ (à.me).ri.(kà.ni).(sá.si)				*	**, *****
b. (à.me).(rì.ka).ni.(sá.si)				*	***, *****!
c. (à.me).ri.ka.ni.(sá.si)				**!*	*****
d. a.(mè.ri).(kà.ni).(sá.si)			*!	*	**, ****
e. a.me.ri.ka.ni.(sá.si)			*!****	*****	
f. (à.me).(rì.ka).(ní.sa).si		*!		*	*, ***, *****
g. (à.me).(rì.ka).(nì.sa).(sí)	*!				*, ***, *****

4.4.4 *A factorial typology of rhythmic and demarcative constraints*

We summarize the discussion of rhythmic patterns of section 4.4.1 and section 4.4.3 in a factorial typology. The set of constraints under reranking consists of PARSE-SYL and the metrical alignment constraints ALL-FT-X, X-MOST, and ALIGN-WD-X, with 'X' taking values 'left' or 'right'.

First, when ALL-FT-X is undominated, non-iterative systems arise, since only one foot can stand at the absolute edge of the word. This single-sided non-iterative pattern can be modified into a double-sided non-iterative pattern by ranking ALIGN-WD-**Y** above ALL-FT-**X** (with X, Y referring to opposite edges).

(90)   Non-iterative binary systems
         a. ALL-FT-X ≫ PARSE-SYL   (single-sided non
                                             iterative)
         b. ALIGN-WD-**Y** ≫ ALL-FT-**X** ≫ PARSE-SYL (double-sided non-
                                             iterative)

The second major group of metrical systems is characterized by the presence of alternating rhythm. The distribution of feet is such that all stand maximally close to an edge of the word, either the left or right edge. This maximal rhythmic organization is guaranteed by PARSE-SYL, which dominates ALL-FT-X. This is achieved by the following ranking:

(91)   FT-BIN ≫ PARSE-SYL ≫ ALL-FT-X

A factorial typology of iterative systems with strictly binary rhythm arises on the basis of this ranking schema when we vary the rankings of ALL-FT-X with respect to the PrWd-alignment constraints. (FT-BIN remains undominated throughout the factorial typology.)

(92)   Iterative binary systems
         a. FT-BIN, **X**-MOST ≫ PARSE-SYL ≫ ALL-FT-**X**
            unidirectional   (Pintupi/Warao)
         b. FT-BIN, **X**-MOST ≫ PARSE-SYL ≫ ALL-FT-**Y**
            bidirectional (simple)   (Piro/Garawa)
         c. FT-BIN, **X**-MOST ≫ PARSE-SYL ≫ ALIGN-WD-**Y** ≫ ALL-FT-**X**
            bidirectional (complex)   (Indonesian)

Observe that other rankings of these constraints, or of different values for X and Y, will result in a duplication of patterns that have already been covered.

4.4.5 *Quantity-sensitivity and foot form: WSP and RнTYPE*

The final cross-linguistic preference to be discussed in this section is quantity-sensitivity, the matching of syllable weight and prominence. Perhaps the most important constraint in this respect is the Weight-to-Stress Principle (Prince 1983, Prince and Smolensky 1993):

(93) **WSP**
Heavy syllables are stressed.

WSP relates syllable weight and metrical prominence. Or, as argued by Prince (1983), this amounts to the natural requirement that *intrinsic sonority prominence* of heavy syllables be registered as *stress prominence*. This relation between sonority and prominent positions in prosodic structure can also be seen in syllabification – segments of the highest sonority are the optimal syllable peaks (Prince and Smolensky 1993).[9]

Two additional foot-form constraints determine the rhythmic type of feet (that is, iambic or trochaic):[10]

(94)   a. **RHTYPE=I**
         Feet have final prominence.
     b. **RHTYPE=T**
         Feet have initial prominence.

These constraints simply state the position of the head in a foot, without requiring that this matches its quantitative make-up. Partly this function is carried out by WSP, but this is not the end of the story, as we will now see.

Tabulating the quantitative shapes of iambs and trochees that violate neither FT-BIN nor WSP, we arrive at the following:

(95) | | Satisfy WSP & FT-BIN | Violate WSP | Violate FT-BIN |
|---|---|---|---|
| Iambs: | **(H), (LL), (LH)** | **(HL), (HH)** | **(L), (LLL),** etc. |
| Trochees: | **(H), (LL), (HL)** | **(LH), (HH)** | **(L), (LLL),** etc. |

The combined filtering functions of WSP and FT-BIN still underdetermine the choice of quantitative make-up of iambs and trochees. For example, consider two logically possible iambic and trochaic parses of the following sequences:

(96)   Iambs   ...(LL)(LL)(H)...   or   ...L)(LL)(LH)...
         Trochees ...(H)(LL)(LL)...   or   ...(HL)(LL)(L...

---

[9] Related constraints require that stressed syllables be heavy (SWP, Riad 1992) or that within a domain the heaviest syllable be stressed (PK-PROM, Prince and Smolensky 1993).

[10] For arguments that RHTYPE=I should be eliminated as a constraint, see van de Vijver (1998).

Extensive cross-linguistic research into stress systems (Hayes 1995) reveals that the 'best' quantitative shapes of disyllabic iambs and trochees are **(LH)** and **(LL)**, respectively.

(97)   Quantitative asymmetry between iambs and trochees (Hayes 1995):
         Iambs: **(LH)** > **(LL)** 'Uneven' iambs are preferred to 'even'
                    iambs.
         Trochees: **(LL)** > **(HL)** 'Even' trochees are preferred to 'uneven'
                    trochees.

We have already observed a preference for uneven iambs **(LH)** to even iambs **(LL)** in the length pattern of Hixkaryana. Hayes (1995) supports the uneven iamb with cases of iambic lengthening from many languages. There is ample cross-linguistic evidence for the reverse preference for quantitative evenness in trochaic systems. For example, English and Fijian shorten a long vowel precisely in those contexts where the resulting light syllable is footed with a following light syllable in an even ('balanced') trochee **(LL)**. The example below is from English (Myers 1987, Prince 1990):

(98)   a. *cone*   [(kóːn)]   **(H)**
         b. *con-ic* [(kó.nɪk)] **(LL)** > [(kóː).nɪk] **(H)L**

Ideally, a single explanation would exist for the markedness of both uneven **(HL)** trochees and even **(LL)** iambs. Various attempts at rhythmic explanations have been made in the pre-OT literature, which will not be reviewed here (Hayes 1985, 1995, Prince 1990). Let us instead consider an approach developed in Kager (1993, 1995), based on the idea that a heavy syllable is rhythmically composed of two microbeats, one on each composing mora (Prince 1983). In (99) the microbeats of a heavy syllable are represented in a grid-notation (where '*' represents a strong beat, and '.' a weak beat):

(99)   * .   micro-level strong–weak rhythmic contour of a heavy syllable
         [μμ]
          \|/
          σ

This micro-level strong–weak contour on heavy syllables is grounded in sonority factors: in a CVC syllable, for example, the vocalic peak is intrinsically of higher sonority, and hence of greater prominence, than the consonantal coda. (More generally, the sonority peak of the syllable is situated as early as possible in the nucleus.)

We can now represent iambs and trochees of different quantitative compositions in the following way, to bring out their rhythmic contours at the (moraic) micro-level:

(100)   a. ending in strong–weak   b. not ending in strong–weak

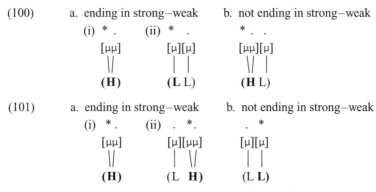

(101)   a. ending in strong–weak   b. not ending in strong–weak

Note that at this micro-rhythmic level, the cross-linguistically preferred feet {(**H**), (**LL**), (**LH**)} end in a strong–weak contour, while 'dispreferred' {(**HL**), (**LL**)} do not end in such a contour. The preference for feet of the first type is stated in the following constraint:

(102)   **RH-CONTOUR**
        A foot must end in a strong–weak contour at the moraic level.

We will assume that this constraint underlies the quantitative asymmetry in the foot inventory. Languages having this constraint in a high-ranked position of the grammar employ strategies to avoid (**HL**) trochees or (**LL**) iambs, depending on interactions with specific faithfulness constraints. Languages having it in a low-ranked position, specifically below faithfulness constraints preserving input quantity, will allow these anti-rhythmical feet, which gives the impression of 'quantity-insensitive' stress.

Let us now turn to some other issues in the theory of quantity-sensitivity. The first relates to the often made assumption that quantity-sensitivity is a property of languages as a whole (and of prosodic systems in particular), which can be switched 'on' or 'off'. In the pre-OT literature, this was encoded as a parameter of foot construction (Hayes 1980), or a choice of foot type from the universal inventory (moraic trochee versus syllabic trochee, Hayes 1995). If the OT approach is generally correct, then this 'holistic' view cannot be correct, for the following reasons.

First, it is held that grammars are rankings of all universal constraints, rather than rankings of specific sets of constraints selected on a language-specific basis. This has an important consequence: all constraints are potentially active in every grammar. The presence of a quantity contrast[11] in a language leaves open the

---

[11] For example, a vowel length contrast reflects the domination of faithfulness (MAX-μ-IO) over markedness (NO-LONG-V, Rosenthall 1994).

ranking of metrical constraints which refer to this quantity contrast (such as WSP or RH-CONTOUR). It is then predicted that constraint re-rankings produce various *degrees of quantity-sensitivity.* Typological studies of trochaic languages with quantity contrasts (Kager 1992a, b) confirm this scattered picture: there is a range from fully quantity-sensitive systems, in which every heavy syllable is stressed, to systems which assign more importance to other factors, such as binary rhythm, at the expense of stress on heavy syllables. (But no language completely disrespects its quantity-contrast in its metrical system, and there is always some aspect to which quantity does matter. For example, most languages have bimoraic word minima.)

The second reason for which quantity-(in)sensitivity cannot be a global property of languages is that the pre-OT foot inventory is decomposed into rhythmic and quantitative constraints, such as FTBIN, WSP, RH-CONTOUR, and RHTYPE. Under this approach, no direct counterpart of quantity-insensitive feet remains, and quantity-disrespecting effects which were previously attributed to the 'syllabic trochee' must now be reattributed to rhythmic constraints. As pointed out by Kager (1992a, 1995), one of the strongest rhythmic factors to produce quantity-disrespecting stress patterns is *clash avoidance.* When NO-CLASH takes precedence over WSP, some heavy syllables must give up their prominence in order to avoid a clash with a neighbouring stressed syllable. This is the case in Estonian, Finnish, and other trochaic languages. (See Alber 1997 for an analysis along these lines.)

Another important issue in quantity-sensitivity is its relationship with processes of epenthesis (or lengthening) and deletion (or shortening). It has been argued in the metrical literature that such processes may achieve metrical targets, for example ideally shaped feet (Dresher and Lahiri 1991, Hayes 1995). This observation has led to the hypothesis that phonologies are 'metrically coherent': foot well-formedness is initially asserted in metrical parsing, and is reasserted by the quantitative changes operating on the output of parsing. Such metrical coherence is entirely expected under OT, since this theory no longer makes a distinction of labour between 'initial metrical parsing' and 'quantitative processes': both are evaluated at a single level, that of the output. Accordingly cases that are put forward as examples of 'metrical coherence' are straightforwardly analysed under OT.

Very interesting examples showing the relevance of foot shape and foot position to quantitative changes come from two Polynesian languages, Boumaa Fijian and Tongan. Both languages avoid a quantitative sequence of a heavy plus light syllable at the end of a word (HL#) and both strive toward a situation in which a bimoraic trochee is right-aligned in the word. To achieve this goal, Boumaa Fijian (Dixon 1988, Prince 1990, Hayes 1995) employs trochaic shortening, while Tongan

(Churchward 1953, Mester 1991, Prince and Smolensky 1993, Hayes 1995) breaks the long vowel:

(103) Two reactions to a sequence ... HL#
    a. Fijian: trochaic shortening
        /siiβi/   sí.βi   'to exceed'
        /siiβi-ta/ sii.βí.ta 'to exceed-TRANS'
    b. Tongan: vowel breaking
        /huu/   húu   'to go in'
        /huu-fi/   hu.úfi 'to open officially'

The grammars of both languages have undominated foot shape constraints FT-BIN and RH-CONTOUR, as well as undominated RIGHTMOST. But they differ minimally in the reranking of ONSET and MAX-μ-IO. Fijian gives up input quantity to attain the perfect bimoraic foot at the right edge (violating MAX-μ-IO):

(104)

Input: /siiβi/	FT-BIN	RIGHTMOST	RH-CONTOUR	ONSET	MAX-μ-IO
a. ☞ (sí.βi)					*
b. si.(í.βi)				*!	
c. (síi.βi)			*!		
d. (síi).βi		*!			
e. (sìi).(βí)	*!				

Tongan selects another strategy to accomplish the same configuration: it breaks the long vowel into two short vowels, respecting input quantity, but violating ONSET:

(105)

Input: /huu-fi/	FT-BIN	RIGHTMOST	RH-CONTOUR	MAX-μ-IO	ONSET
a. (hú.fi)				*!	
b. ☞ hu.(ú.fi)					*
c. (húu.fi)			*!		
d. (húu).fi		*!			
e. (hùu).(fí)	*!				

We find another example of functionally related processes (see chapters 2 and 3). Both vowel shortening (Fijian) and vowel breaking (Tongan) serve to achieve a single output goal: the perfect bimoraic foot at the right word edge.

The next section supports these results by a case-study of Southeastern Tepehuan, a language that exhibits an interesting interaction of foot shape and quantitative processes.

4.5 Case-study: rhythmic syncope in Southeastern Tepehuan

This section deals with interactions between well-formedness constraints and faithfulness constraints, focussing on rhythmically induced vowel deletion in Southeastern Tepehuan.

4.5.1 *Accent and syncope: the patterns*

Southeastern Tepehuan (E. Willett 1982, T. Willett 1991, Rice 1992, Kager 1997a) is an Uto-Aztecan language spoken southeast of Durango in Mexico. It has an interesting process of vowel deletion (*syncope*) in prosodically defined contexts: vowel deletion is 'rhythmic', in the sense that alternating vowels are affected. Surprisingly, there is no phonetic evidence for a corresponding rhythmic pattern that might condition syncope. Lacking this pattern, we must answer two questions: (i) what prosodic factors trigger syncope? (ii) what blocks the application of syncope to adjacent syllables? As we will see, an interaction of prosodic well-formedness constraints with segmental faithfulness constraints captures the syncope pattern, without reference to an abstract layer of syncope feet or an intermediary level of derivation.

Before we can look into the contexts of syncope, we must discuss the place of the accent. Accent falls on the initial stem syllable when it is heavy (long-vowelled or closed), see (106a–c). It falls on the second stem syllable if this is heavy while the first syllable is light; see (106d–f). (No stem begins with a sequence of two light syllables: this output gap is due to syncope.) The accent pattern points to a single iamb (**H**) or (**LH**) at the left edge:

(106)   #(**H**)   #(**LH**)

     a. (vóo).hi 'bear'   d. (ta.káa).ruiʔ 'chicken'

     b. (kár).vaʃ 'goat'   e. (sa.pók) 'story'

     c. (táat).pɨʃ 'fleas'   f. (ta.pɨ̍ʃ) 'flea'

As mentioned, Southeastern Tepehuan has a vowel alternation[12] that is due to *syncope* of vowels in even-numbered open syllables (107c), including long vowels

---

[12] Two other vowel alternations will not be discussed here: vowel shortening and apocope. See Kager (1997a) for an integrated analysis of syncope, apocope, and shortening.

(107d). Syncope applies in the domain of the stem, which may include a reduplicant prefix (107b–d).

(107)   a. /tɨroviɲ/   (tɨ́r).viɲ   'rope'
          b. /tɨ̈-tɨroviɲ/   (tɨ̈t).ro.piɲ   'ropes'
          c. /maa-matuʃidʲaʔ/ (máam).tuʃ.dʲaʔ 'will teach'
          d. /gaa-gaagaʔ/   (gáaʔŋ).gaʔ   'he will look around for it'

Examples in (108) illustrate the blocking of syncope in heavy syllables following
a *light* first syllable. In (108a–b) this is shown for the context #CVCVV, and in
(108c–d) for the context #CVCV(V)C.

(108)   a. /takaaruiʔ/   (ta.káa).ruiʔ 'chicken'
          b. /va-vaiɲum/   (va.pái).ɲum 'metals'
          c. /ka-karvaʃ/   (ka.kár).vaʃ   'goats'
          d. /ha-haannuʈ/   (ha.háan).nuʈ 'clothes'

The central question is: what is the relation between metrical structure and syncope? The alternating nature of syncope suggests a foot-based analysis. Yet there
is no secondary stress pattern supporting this hypothesis.

4.5.2 *An OT analysis*

Our analysis of syncope in Southeastern Tepehuan starts from the following
observation. Syncope obviously occurs at the expense of input vowels, hence
there must be some output target that is achieved at the expense of faithfulness. Below we will argue that this target is *exhaustive parsing* of syllables
by feet. By deleting vowels, the number of syllables will be reduced as well,
and thereby the number of violators of PARSE-SYL. To those who have carefully
read through the previous sections, syncope may sound a rather absurd strategy
to achieve an exhaustive metrical parsing. Did we not conclude from analyses of
Hixkaryana, Pintupi, Warao, Garawa, and other languages, that exhaustivity is
attained by multiple (iterative) footing, hence rhythmic alternation due to a ranking PARSE-SYL ≫ ALL-FT-L? Why would languages which opt for this ranking
need vowel deletion to achieve exhaustivity? This question is equal to asking
under what conditions vowel deletion is triggered in Southeastern Tepehuan.

    What is the difference between the strategies, iterative footing and syncope, in
terms of constraint rankings? It resides in the priorities of three factors: 'faithfulness to input vowels' (MAX-V-IO), 'proximity of feet to edges', and 'exhaustivity'.
Core rankings are below:

(109)   Two strategies toward exhaustive metrification
         a. Iterative footing (Pintupi):   PARSE-SYL, MAX-V-IO ≫
                                                ALL-FT-L
         b. Syncope (Southeastern Tepehuan): ALL-FT-L ≫ PARSE-SYL ≫
                                                MAX-V-IO

A preliminary answer to the question 'What causes syncope in Southeastern Tehe-
huan?' is this: the language gives *more priority to its metrification than to its
input vowels*. It allows only one foot per word, strictly at the left edge. This foot
should parse as many syllables as possible – but it must not grow larger than the
disyllabic iamb. Any syllables that are not contained by it violate PARSE-SYL. A
most effective way of reducing the number of such syllables is deleting their
vowels, without which they must perish. Yet there is a powerful constraint oppos-
ing 'across-the-board' vowel deletion: all outputs must be syllabified in keeping
with rigid phonotactics which rule out complex onsets and codas. In sum, while
syncope is set in motion by prosodic well-formedness constraints at the *metrical*
level, it is simultaneously checked by prosodic well-formedness constraints at the
syllabic level.

But what is the role of segmental faithfulness in this all-prosodic conflict? As
we will see, it plays a key role: while *vowels* are easily deleted, *consonants* are
not. But since consonants need to be parsed into well-formed syllables, a necessary minimum of vowels must remain. Paradoxically, faithfulness to consonants
is the key factor in the preservation of vowels by an indirect link – the canonical
syllable.

This scenario is deeply *parallel* in the following sense. Interaction occurs
between well-formedness constraints whose targets are at different levels of the
prosodic hierarchy – the foot and the syllable. Metrical structure mounts pressure
to minimize syllable number, yet syllable well-formedness militates against this.
At the level of the syllable, consonants (immune to deletion due to high-ranking
faithfulness) require vowels to be able to surface in well-formed syllables. Therefore segmental faithfulness to consonants, indirectly, saves a certain number of
vowels from deletion.

Let us now consider how this syncope scenario is encoded in constraint interaction. We start by observing that ranking (109b) has two subrankings, ALL-FT-L
≫ PARSE-SYL and PARSE-SYL ≫ MAX-V-IO. Both will be motivated below.

First, Southeastern Tepehuan has non-iterative footing. This implies that it
has the reverse ranking (at least, as compared to Pintupi) of ALL-FT-L and
PARSE-SYL:

(110) ALL-FT-L ≫ PARSE-SYL

    a. /CVVCVCVCVC/   (CVVC).CV.CVC   > (CVV).CV.CV.CVC

       /tɨ-tɨroviɲ/   (tɨ́ɨt).ro.piɲ   (tɨ́ɨ).(tɨ.rò).(pìɲ)

    b. /CVVCVCVCVCVC/ (CVVC).CVC.CVC > (CVV).CV.CV.CV.CVC

       /maa-matuʃidʲaʔ/ (máam).tuʃ.dʲaʔ   (máa).(ma.tù).(ʃi.dʲàʔ)

This key ranking is illustrated in a tableau:

(111)

Input: /tɨ-tɨroviɲ/	ALL-FT-L	PARSE-SYL
a. ☞ (tɨ́ɨt).ro.piɲ		**
b. (tɨ́ɨ).(tɨ.rò).(pìɲ)	*!, ***	

Second, the subranking PARSE-SYL ≫ MAX-V-IO expresses that syncope serves to improve exhaustive footing. This is demonstrated schematically in CV-skeletal forms, as well as in genuine forms, in (112). Observe that the optimal outputs are closer to exhaustive parsing than their competitors, since they contain a smaller number of unparsed syllables.

(112) PARSE-SYL ≫ MAX-V-IO

    a. /CVVCVCVCVC/   (CVVC).CV.CVC   > (CVV).CV.CV.CVC

       /tɨ-tɨroviɲ/   (tɨ́ɨt).ro.piɲ   (tɨ́ɨ).tɨ.ro.piɲ

    b. /CVVCVCVCVCVC/ (CVVC).CVC.CVC > (CVV).CV.CV.CV.CVC

       /maa-matuʃidʲaʔ/ (máam).tuʃ.dʲaʔ   (máa).ma.tu.ʃi.dʲaʔ

(113)

Input: /tɨ-tɨroviɲ/	PARSE-SYL	MAX-V-IO
a. ☞ (tɨ́ɨt).ro.piɲ	**	*
b. (tɨ́ɨ).tɨ.ro.pìɲ	***!	

Observe also that the optimal forms of (112) have not yet *completely* achieved the target, as they still contain two unparsed syllables each. How can exhaustivity form the pressure behind syncope if it cannot be achieved completely? The answer is typical of OT: there is yet another factor which precludes the full achievement of the target, and this has priority. To find out what this factor is, all we have to do is take 'exhaustive parsing' to its ultimate logical conclusion, and see what happens.

Note that optimal forms of (112) cannot be compressed any further by the deletion of additional vowels without fatally violating rigid syllable phonotactics of Southeastern Tepehuan, requiring syllables to have non-branching margins. This is due to undominated *COMPLEX.

(114)   *COMPLEX ≫ PARSE-SYL
   a. /CVVCVCVCVC/   (CVVC).CV.CVC   > (CVVC).CCVC
      /tɨ-tɨroviɲ/   (tɨ́ɨt).ro.piɲ   (tɨ́ɨt).rpiɲ
   b. /CVVCVCVCVCVC/   (CVVC).CVC.CVC > (CVVC).CCVCC
      /maa-matuʃidʲaʔ/   (máam).tuʃ.dʲaʔ   (máam).ʧadʲʔ

Righthand forms in (114) fatally violate undominated *COMPLEX, even though they have one fewer unparsed syllable than the optimal forms. A tableau shows this for (114a):

(115)

Input: /tɨ-tɨroviɲ/	*COMPLEX	PARSE-SYL
a. ☞ (tɨ́ɨt).ro.piɲ		**
b. (tɨ́ɨt).rpiɲ	*!	*
c. (tɨ́ɨt).ropɲ	*!	*

Next observe that, unlike vowels, consonants are never deleted under pressure of exhaustivity. For example, the stem /karvaʃ/ might, in principle, surface as a single (**LH**) iamb without violation of PARSE-SYL, if only one of its medial consonants were deleted: e.g. *(ka.váʃ) or *(ka.ráʃ), rather than (kár).vaʃ. This never occurs – outputs must preserve the consonants of their inputs. Therefore MAX-C-IO must dominate PARSE-SYL:

(116)

Input: /karvaʃ/	MAX-C-IO	PARSE-SYL
a. ☞ (kár).vaʃ		*
b. (ka.váʃ)	*!	
c. (ka.ráʃ)	*!	

Summing up results of the discussion so far, we arrive at the preliminary ranking in (117):

(117)   *COMPLEX, ALL-FT-L, MAX-C-IO ≫ PARSE-SYL ≫ MAX-V-IO

This is the basic analysis: modifications will later be added, in a more detailed discussion. But it is not too early to claim an important result. This is that we have an explanation for the alternating or *rhythmic* character of syncope. Syncope of vowels in adjacent syllables would necessarily lead to consonant clusters that cannot be parsed by canonical syllables, while any deletion of consonants is blocked (see again 115–16 for evidence).

Another immediate result, again typical of OT, is this: if the 'target' of syncope is exhaustive parsing of syllables into feet, then we predict that no deletion takes place when nothing can be gained by it – when it would yield no progress in terms of syllable parsing. This is exactly what we find. In (118) syncope fails to apply, simply because it would not move the output any closer to the target, exhaustivity. Everything else being equal, it is always better to be faithful to input segments:

(118)   /takaarui?/   (ta.káa).rui? > *(ták).rui?

Thus MAX-V-IO may be dominated, but that does not mean that its role is neglectable:

(119)

Input: /takaarui?/	*COMPLEX	ALL-FT-L	PARSE-SYL	MAX-V-IO
a. ☞ (ta.káa).rui?			*	
b. (ták).rui?			*	*!
c. (ta.káa).(rùi?)		*!		

Thus far we have developed the idea that exhaustivity of metrical parsing and left foot alignment have priority over realizing underlying vowels in the output. Forces that drive vowel deletion are effectively counterbalanced by phonotactics: syllables must not have branching margins. Having completed the core of the analysis, we now move on to some residual matters.

First consider the fact that there is another potential method by which outputs may improve their completeness of metrification. By shortening the initial long vowel in /tʉ-tɨroviɲ/, a canonical (LH) iamb would be created in the proper place, producing *[(tʉ.tɨr).piɲ]. This output would fare better in terms of exhaustivity than the actual output [(tʉ̈t).ro.piɲ]. What blocks initial shortening here is the templatic requirement that the reduplicative prefix must equal a heavy syllable (McCarthy and Prince 1986, 1993b):[13]

(120)   **RED**=σ$_{\mu\mu}$
          The reduplicant equals a heavy syllable.

---

[13] The prosodic size of the reduplicative prefix (a heavy syllable or a light syllable) is based on a stem-specific choice: compare the examples in (107b–d) with those in (108b–d). 'Reduplicative allomorphy' is apparently not governed by phonological or morphological factors. See Kager (1997a) for details.

The relevant ranking is that in (121), and illustration of it is offered in tableau (122):

(121)   RED=$\sigma_{\mu\mu}$ ≫ PARSE-SYL
          /CVVCVCVCVC/   (CVVC).CV.CVC > (CV.CVC).CVC
          /tɨ-tɨroviɲ/   (tíɨt).ro.piɲ   (tɨ.tír).piɲ

(122)

Input: /tɨ-tɨroviɲ/	RED=$\sigma_{\mu\mu}$	PARSE-SYL
a. ☞ (tíɨ-t).ro.piɲ		**
b. (tɨ-tír).piɲ	*!	*

Second, we must pay attention to yet another aspect of prosodic well-formedness: foot shape. Southeastern Tepehuan iambs are (H) and (LH), but never (LL). Avoidance of (LL) is attributed to RH-CONTOUR (102), requiring iambs to end in falling sonority contours (or heavy syllables (CVC, CVV, or CVVC) in the case of Southeastern Tepehuan). This is the second force (besides PARSE-SYL) driving syncope. It explains why syncope affects all inputs beginning with #CVCV:

(123)   /tɨroviɲ/   (tír).viɲ > (tɨ.ró).viɲ

RH-CONTOUR is undominated, here at the expense of the 'anti-vowel-deletion' constraint MAX-V-IO. Interestingly, the 'royal way' to satisfy RH-CONTOUR, by lengthening a vowel to create the canonical (LH) iamb, is blocked:

(124)   /tɨroviɲ/   (tír).viɲ > (tɨ.róː).viɲ

This signals that the constraint militating against vowel lengthening, DEP-µ-IO, dominates the 'anti-deletion' constraint MAX-V-IO. In sum, we have the following ranking:

(125)   Weight increase of stressed syllables at the expense of input vowels
          RH-CONTOUR, DEP-µ-IO ≫ MAX-V-IO

This ranking is illustrated by the forms of (123–4) in tableau (126):

(126)

Input: /tɨroviɲ/	RH-CONTOUR	DEP-µ-IO	MAX-V-IO
a. ☞ (tír).viɲ			*
b. (tɨ.ró).viɲ	*!		
c. (tɨ.róː).viɲ		*!	

Finally we must consider in more detail the quantitative shape of the foot, and try to integrate foot shape constraints into the current ranking. So far we have assumed that the single foot standing initial in the stem is a binary iamb with its strong syllable heavy, (**H**) or (**LH**). This selection of iambs is due to a set of four undominated constraints stated in (127), which will be united here into a cover constraint FT-FORM (for expository reasons).

(127) **FT-FORM** (cover constraint)
 a. FT-BIN   Feet are binary under moraic or syllabic analysis.
 b. RHTYPE=I   Feet are right-headed.
 c. RH-CONTOUR Feet must end in a strong–weak contour at the moraic level.
 d. WSP-FT   Heavy syllables within the foot are prominent.

Note that WSP-FT serves to exclude the 'anti-rhythmic' iamb (**HH**) (see Kager 1997a).

Adding up all the subrankings motivated so far, we arrive at:

(128) Rhythmic vowel deletion in Southeastern Tepehuan
 *COMPLEX, FT-FORM, ALL-FT-LEFT, RED=$\sigma_{\mu\mu}$, MAX-C-IO ≫ DEP-μ-IO ≫ PARSE-SYL ≫ MAX-V-IO

The 'rhythmicity' of the syncope pattern follows from this ranking – there is no need to set up an intermediate representation of iterative trochees, as in the rule-based analysis (see section 4.5.3).

Tableaux (129–30) illustrate the full constraint ranking in action.

(129)

Input: /takaarui?/	*COMPLEX	FT-FORM	ALL-FT-L	RED=$\sigma_{\mu\mu}$	MAX-C-IO	DEP-μ-IO	PARSE-SYL	MAX-V-IO
a. ☞ (ta.káa).rui?							*	
b. (ták).rui?							*	*!
c. (ta.káar)					*!			*
d. (ta.káa).(rùi?)			*!*					
e. (ta.kaa.rúi?)		*!						
f. (tak.rúi?)		*!						*
g. (ta.káar?)	*!							*

(130)

Input: /tɨ-tɨroviɲ/	*COMPLEX	FT-FORM	ALL-FT-L	RED =σ_μμ	MAX-C-IO	DEP-μ-IO	PARSE-SYL	MAX-V-IO
a. ☞ (tɨ́t).ro.piɲ							**	*
b. (tɨ́ɨ).tɨ.ro.piɲ							***!	
c. (tɨ́ɨt).piɲ					*!		*	**
d. (tɨ.tɨ́r).piɲ				*!			*	*
e. (tɨ́ɨt).(ro.pìɲ)			*!					*
f. (tɨ.tɨ́r).piɲ		*!					*	*
g. (tɨ́ɨt).ropɲ	*!						*	**

4.5.3 *Alternative: a rule-based analysis*

Analysing the Southeastern Tepehuan syncope pattern, derivational theory has one option available that is lacking from OT: setting up an intermediate level of the derivation that contains an exhaustive parsing into binary feet, from which syncope may be predicted. In such an analysis, syncope would become a 'natural' reduction rule: weakening unstressed syllables all the way up to the point of deletion. For principled reasons, such an analysis is unavailable in OT: well-formedness constraints refer to the surface level only, and cannot have access to any other derivational 'level'.

A derivational analysis based on intermediate levels is given below (after Rice 1992):

(131)   a. *Syllabify*:   Assign syllable structure.
        b. *Assign feet*:   Build left-headed quantity-sensitive feet from left
                            to right.
        c. *End Rule Left*: Promote the leftmost foot to main stress.
        d. *Syncopate*:   Delete vowels in non-head syllables (and
                            resyllabify).

This analysis is illustrated in (132) by the derivation of [(máam).tuʃ.dʲaʔ]:

(132)   UR   /maa-matuʃidʲaʔ/
        Syllabify   maa.ma.tu.ʃi.dʲaʔ
        Assign feet   (máa.ma).(tú.ʃi).(dʲáʔ)
        End Rule Left (máa.ma).(tù.ʃi).(dʲàʔ)
        Syncopate   (máam).(tùʃ).(dʲàʔ)
        PR   [(máam).tuʃ.dʲaʔ]

Although the analysis derives most forms correctly, it runs into conceptual and empirical problems that cannot be solved without additional machinery, including extra rules and even output constraints.

First, the complete lack of surface secondary stress must be accounted for by a rule of *stress conflation* (Halle and Vergnaud 1987), eliminating secondary stress feet. This rule obscures the conditioning environment on which syncope is based, rendering the process 'opaque'. From the viewpoint of the language learner, the abstractness of this analysis, as well as the extrinsic rule ordering on which it is based, is problematic. (See chapter 9 for discussion of opacity in OT.)

Second, iterative uneven trochees do not suffice to predict the syncope and accent pattern. Problematic are words beginning with a sequence #CVVCVV. Recall that syncope deletes the long vowel in the second syllable, as in /gaa-gaaga?/ → [gáa?ŋ.ga?]. Quantity-sensitive footing produces a monosyllabic foot on the heavy second syllable, which must be first deleted in clash, before syncope applies, see (133b). Now compare these #CVVCVV cases with those beginning with a sequence #CVCVV, as in [ta.káa.rui?] (133a). These surface with accent on the second syllable. The quantity-sensitive trochaic parsing results in the intermediary stage [(tá).(káa).(rúi?)], in which the first foot, rather than the second, is deleted. The foot deletion rule should be quantity-sensitive in order to make the proper distinction: if both syllables are equally heavy (#HH, as in 133b), it deletes the righthand foot, but if the lefthand syllable is lighter (#LH, as in 133a), it deletes the lefthand foot:

(133)	UR	a. /takaarui?/	b. /gaa-gaaga?/
	Syllabify	ta.kaa.rui?	gaa.gaa.ga?
	Assign feet	(tá).(káa).(rúi?)	(gáa).(gáa).(gá?)
	Delete foot	**ta**.(káa).(rúi?)	(gáa).**gaa**.(gá?)
	End Rule L	ta.(káa).(rùi?)	(gáa).gaa.(gà?)
	Syncopate	---	(gáag).(gà?)
	Conflate	(ta.káa).rui?	(gáag).ga?
	PR	[(ta.káa).rui?]	[(gáa?ŋ).ga?]

The quantity-sensitive destressing rule that compares the relative weight of the first two syllables is a powerful device. Still worse, this analysis misses the generalization that destressing and syncope conspire toward outputs that begin with iambs: (**H**) or (**LH**).

Third, of the four trochees that the analysis sets up to define the context of syncope {(**LL**), (**HL**), (**H**), (**L**)}, three never surface (only (**H**) does). This greatly contributes to the abstractness of the analysis. (Moreover, two of these abstract trochees, degenerate (**L**) and uneven (**HL**), are cross-linguistically marginal; see Hayes 1995.) In spite of the used trochees, surface stress contours in the stem,

#H and #LH, are easily interpreted as *iambic*, given the fact that foot constituency is inaudible.

Fourth, the rule-based analysis must be extended by phonotactic output conditions on syncope that block it when it would create a sequence that cannot be syllabified. For example, the initial light syllable in a word beginning with #CVCVV (cf. [ta̲.káa.ruiʔ]) must not undergo syncope, even though destressing places it in a metrically weak position. Another context in which the rule-based analysis cannot do without an output constraint is that of an initial closed syllable that is followed by a light syllable, again metrically weak (cf. [vát.vi̲.rak]):

(134)

		a. /takaaruiʔ/	b. /vatvirak/
UR		/takaaruiʔ/	/vatvirak/
Syllabify		ta.kaa.ruiʔ	vat.vi.rak
Assign feet		(tá).(káa).(rúiʔ)	(vát.vi).(rák)
End Rule L		ta.(káa).(rùiʔ)	(vát.vi).(ràk)
Syncopate		***blocked***	***blocked***
Conflate		(ta.káa).ruiʔ	(vát.vi).rak
PR		[(ta.káa).ruiʔ]	[(vát.vi).rak]

Clearly this blocking reflects an *output constraint* on syncope: it must not create syllables with branching onsets or codas (cf. *COMPLEX). Output constraints on syncope defeat the derivational nature of rule-based theory. But a mixed theory that has both rules and output constraints might still be acceptable if the rules were motivated independently of the constraints so as to satisfy output targets, which is not the case here, as the previous three objections have shown. Without such independent evidence for separate rules and constraints, the OT analysis remains conceptually superior.

Let us summarize the results, and make a final comparison between the rule-based analysis and the OT analysis. Below I have summed up five contexts in which syncope in Southeastern Tepehuan is blocked, and the explanations for blocking by both analyses:

(135)   **Rhythmicity**: no syncope of both vowels in adjacent syllables.
         Rule-based analysis: There is an abstract intermediate level in the derivation at which words are parsed exhaustively by binary feet. Targets of syncope are syllables in weak positions of binary feet.
         OT analysis: Deletion of vowels in adjacent syllables would inevitably create clusters of three or more consonants. These long clusters cannot be syllabified without fatally violating undominated syllable well-formedness constraints, in particular *COMPLEX. (There is no remedy in further simplifying clusters by deletion of consonants: this escape route is effectively shut off by undominated MAX-C-IO.)

(136)   **Initial blocking**: no syncope of a vowel in an initial syllable.
          Rule-based analysis: Syncope feet are trochaic, hence the initial syl-
          lable is rhythmically strong. But when the initial syllable is rhythm-
          ically weak (as in #CVCVV...) syncope must be blocked by an
          output constraint against complex onsets.
          OT analysis: Vowels in initial syllables are immune from syncope
          since their deletion (in #CVCV or #CVCVV) would produce an out-
          put #CCV(V), again in violation of *COMPLEX.

(137)   **Quantity-sensitivity I**: no syncope of a vowel in a closed syllable.
          Rule-based analysis: Syncope feet are quantity-sensitive, and closed
          syllables are heavy. Hence closed syllables are heads of feet.
          OT analysis: Again, the deletion of a vowel in a closed syllable would
          result in a fatal violation of *COMPLEX.

(138)   **Quantity-sensitivity II**: no syncope of a light syllable following a
          closed syllable.
          Rule-based analysis: Blocked by an output constraint against com-
          plex margins.
          OT analysis: Again, the deletion of a vowel in a closed syllable would
          result in a fatal violation of *COMPLEX.

(139)   **Quantity-sensitivity III**: no syncope of long vowel following initial
          light syllable.
          Rule-based analysis: Quantity-sensitive destressing repairs the (inter-
          mediary) trochaic parse #(L)(H) into #L(H).
          OT analysis: Nothing is gained by syncope in terms of exhaustivity.
          Since there is no trigger, there will be no effect – faithfulness forbids.

In sum, we find that a rule-based analysis uses excessive machinery to achieve
effects that an OT analysis attributes to a single interaction. Let me hasten to add
that the rule-based analysis reviewed here (essentially Rice 1992) might perhaps
be improved in ways which reduce the machinery. The reason to dedicate so much
discussion to this analysis was not pointed against this specific analysis, but rather
to point out various general problems that are inherent to derivational theory.

4.5.4 *Parallel interactions between prosodic levels*
The analysis of Southeastern Tepehuan is based on 'parallel' interaction of
metrical well-formedness and faithfulness. In earlier sections we have observed
PARSE-SYL active in its most obvious role, of enforcing exhaustive parsing in languages such as Pintupi. However, as the analysis of Southeastern Tepehuan shows,
vowel deletion is yet another strategy to achieve the same goal of exhaustivity:

when a vowel is deleted, its syllable goes, and with it a potential violator of PARSE-SYL. In evaluating this deletion strategy towards exhaustivity, it is helpful to make explicit the truth conditions of PARSE-SYL:

(140)   Dual interpretation of PARSE-SYL
          a. IF X forms a syllable, THEN X must be parsed by a foot.
             ('bottom-up')
          b. IF X is not parsed by a foot, THEN X must not form a syllable.
             ('top-down')

It is not too difficult to imagine under which conditions the deletion strategy may become 'optimal'. Even though vowel deletion involves the violation of a segmental faithfulness constraint (MAX-V-IO), there may be 'special' reasons favouring it over the standard way of achieving exhaustivity (the creation of multiple feet). Of course, these 'special' reasons have to do with the *costs* of multiple feet in terms of metrical well-formedness violations. A major candidate for a constraint resisting the assignment of multiple feet is ALL-FT-X.

Perhaps the clearest contribution of OT to the field of prosody resides in capturing parallel interactions of prosodic well-formedness constraints and faithfulness constraints, allowing for a highly generalizing theory of quantitative phenomena (vowel shortening, vowel lengthening, gemination, syncope, word minima, etc.). Parallelism establishes complete communication between all levels of the prosodic hierarchy. Consequently, changes at lower prosodic levels have effects at higher levels, and vice versa. In rule-based theory it is not a priori impossible to describe such chains of effects between prosodic levels. In fact, quantitative rules may refer to foot structure, while foot assignment rules may refer to quantity. But such descriptive means leave totally unexpressed the organicity of metrical systems. The achievement of OT is its elegance of expression: no direction of processes (upward or downward through the prosodic hierarchy) needs to be stipulated, as effects of changes at different levels are weighed against each other. If some action 'downstairs' happens to be too 'costly' in terms of the constraint hierarchy, then an alternative action in the 'upstairs' region will automatically occur.

4.6 Conclusions

The typology of metrical systems has been a highly fruitful branch of pre-OT phonology. Theoretical attractiveness of this field resides mainly in two factors: on the one hand, the relative autonomy of metrical principles from segmental phonology; on the other hand, a great deal of cross-linguistic variation in stress systems. In rule-based theory, this invited an approach based on metrical principles and parameters, resulting in a typology that had the dual qualities of compactness and symmetry (though perhaps it was overly symmetric, as Hayes 1995 emphasized). In comparison, OT offers a number of additional advantages over rule-based theory in the field of metrical phonology.

Meanwhile we have also learned a bit more about the architecture of OT itself. We have seen new episodes in the ongoing battle between *faithfulness* and *well-formedness*. This conflict was at the heart of the success in handling parallel interactions of rhythm and syncope in Southeastern Tepehuan: input vowels are sacrificed to achieve better parsing. The key observation was that input vowels are never given up for free: there must be some pressure (due to a well-formedness constraint) to syncopate, and when vowels are deleted, their number always (precisely) suffices to restore the balance. This is the economy principle '*do-only-when-necessary*', a true hallmark of OT.

SUGGESTIONS FOR FURTHER READING

Metrical phonology

Halle, Morris and Jean-Roger Vergnaud (1987) *An essay on stress*. Cambridge, Mass.: MIT Press.

Hayes, Bruce (1995) *Metrical stress theory: principles and case studies*. University of Chicago Press.

(1980) A metrical theory of stress rules. PhD dissertation, MIT, Cambridge, Mass. (Published 1985, New York: Garland Press.)

Prince, Alan (1983) Relating to the grid. *Linguistic Inquiry* **14**. 19–100.

Selkirk, Elisabeth O. (1984) *Phonology and syntax: the relation between sound and structure*. Cambridge, Mass.: MIT Press.

Metrical studies in OT

Cohn, Abigail and John McCarthy (1994) *Alignment and parallelism in Indonesian phonology*. Ms., Cornell University and University of Massachusetts, Amherst. [ROA-25, http://ruccs.rutgers.edu/roa.html.]

Inkelas, Sharon (forthcoming) *Exceptional stress-attracting suffixes in Turkish: representations vs. the grammar*. To appear in Kager, Van der Hulst, and Zonneveld. [ROA-39, http://ruccs.rutgers.edu/roa.html]

Kager, René (1994) Ternary rhythm in alignment theory. Ms., Utrecht University. [ROA-35, http://ruccs.rutgers.edu/roa.html]

Kenstowicz, Michael (1995a) Cyclic vs. non-cyclic constraint evaluation. *Phonology* **12**. 397–436.

Pater, Joe (1995) On the nonuniformity of weight-to-stress and stress preservation effects in English. Ms., McGill University. [ROA-107, http://ruccs.rutgers.edu/roa.html]

EXERCISES

1 Wargamay

Consider the stress pattern of the Australian language Wargamay (Dixon 1981):

(i)	báda	'dog'
(ii)	gaɡara	'dilly bag'
(iii)	gíɖawùlu	'freshwater jewfish'
(iv)	ɖurágaymìri	'Niagara Vale-FROM'

    a. State the generalizations governing the position of primary and secondary stress.

    b. What ranking of metrical constraints accounts for this pattern? Support your analysis by a tableau of *ɖurágay-mìri*.

2 Manam

Manam stress (Lichtenberk 1983) is exemplified by the set of syllabified words below:

(i)	pá.tu	'stone'
(ii)	si.ŋá.ba	'bush'
(iii)	ta.nép.wa	'chief'
(iv)	mà.la.bóŋ	'flying fox'
(v)	ém.be.ʔi	'sacred flute'
(vi)	ta.nèp.wa.tí.na	'real chief'

    a. State the generalizations governing the position of primary and secondary stress.

    b. What ranking of metrical constraints accounts for this pattern? Support your analysis by tableaux of *si.ŋá.ba*, *mà.la.bóŋ*, *ém.be.ʔi*, and *ta.nèp.wa.tí.na*.

3 Murinbata

The stress pattern of Murinbata (Street and Mollinjin 1981) is exemplified below:

(i)	bá	'march fly'
(ii)	mámŋe	'I/he/she/ said/did to her'
(iii)	lámalà	'shoulder'
(iv)	wálʊmʊ́ma	'blue-tongue lizard'
(v)	pʰɛ́rɛwɛ́rɛʈɛ̀n	(season just before the 'dry' when grass dries, seeds fall, etc.)

Street and Mollinjin claim that all non-final stresses are primary, whereas final stresses are secondary. For the purposes of this problem, you can ignore distinctions among stresses.

    a. State the generalizations governing the positions of stresses.

    b. What ranking of metrical constraints accounts for this pattern? Support your analysis by a tableau of *pʰɛ́rɛ́wɛ́rɛʈɛ̀n*.

    c. Discuss the consequences of this analysis for the interpretation of FT-BIN. Hint: is the degenerate foot the only type of non-binary foot?

    d. Discuss any differences in foot-alignment between Murinbata and Pintupi (section 4.4.1), taking into account the similarities between the stress patterns of these languages.

4 Warlpiri

In bare stems, Warlpiri (Nash 1980) has a stress pattern typical of Australian languages:

(i)	wáti	'man'
(ii)	wátiya	'tree'
(iii)	mánaŋkàḷa	'spinifex plain'

The special interest of the pattern resides in its sensitivity to morphological structure.

(iv)	wáti-ŋka	'man-LOC'
(v)	wáti-ŋkà-ḷu	'man-LOC-ERG'
(vi)	yápa-ḷàŋu-ḷu	'person-for example-ERG'
(vii)	wátiyà-ḷa	'tree-LOC'
(viii)	wátiya-ḷà-ḷu	'tree-LOC-ERG'
(ix)	yápaḷa-ŋùḷu	'father's mother-ELAT'
(x)	mánaŋkàḷa-ḷa	'spinifex-LOC'
(xi)	mánaŋkàḷa-ḷà-ḷu	'spinifex-LOC-ERG'

    a. State the generalizations governing the stress pattern of bare stems and suffixed words.

    b. What constraint ranking accounts for the pattern of bare stems? Support your analysis by tableaux of *wátiya* and *mánaŋkàḷa*.

    c. Now consider suffixed stems, which require an extension of the basic analysis. State a constraint aligning morphemes with feet. Integrate this in the current ranking.

    d. Support your analysis by tableaux of *wátiyà-ḷa, wátiya-ḷà-ḷu,* and *yápa-ḷàŋu-ḷu*.

    e. Nash (1980) provides no examples of the type 'trisyllabic stem plus trisyllabic affix'. What would your analysis predict for such examples? How does this issue bear on the ranking of the alignment constraint?

5 A factorial typology of stress systems

a. Construct a factorial typology of the following five metrical constraints: PARSE-SYL, LEFTMOST, RIGHTMOST, ALL-FT-L, ALL-FT-R. Assume that FT-BIN and RHTYPE=T are undominated in all rankings. Base the typology on four-syllable and five-syllable words composed of light syllables. Identify any rankings that produce identical stress systems.

b. How many different stress systems does your typology predict? Characterize each of the predicted systems in prose, making sure that your description is sufficiently general, as well as precise enough to capture all distinctions.

c. Instantiate the factorial typology with actual stress systems (discussed in this chapter, or introduced in preceding exercises). Do you find any gaps in the typology? Try to fill these by consulting metrical literature referred to in 'Suggestions for further reading'.

5
Correspondence in reduplication

5.1 Introduction

A central idea of OT is that the optimal output form arises from competition of markedness constraints and faithfulness constraints. Markedness constraints require that output forms match certain segmental or prosodic targets. Faithfulness constraints require that outputs be identical to their lexical inputs, each militating against some type of change – segment deletion, segment insertion, or featural changes. Both constraint types are inherently in conflict: markedness constraints trigger changes, while faithfulness constraints, by their very nature, oppose changes. Moreover, faithfulness constraints state their requirements about input–output relations in terms of *correspondence*.

This central idea will be extended in this chapter to a phenomenon that has been a hotly debated topic in pre-OT phonology (e.g. Wilbur 1973, Marantz 1982, Broselow and McCarthy 1983, McCarthy and Prince 1986, Shaw 1987, Uhrbach 1987, Steriade 1988a), and continues to be a focus of OT research: *reduplication*. From a purely morphological point of view, reduplication is 'simply' a kind of affixation, both in its morpho-syntactic contribution (it forms morphological categories, such as plural), and in its linear position with respect to the stem (preceding it, as a prefix, or following it, as a suffix). But from a phonological viewpoint, the special property of reduplication is that the reduplicative affix is not fully specified for segmental content. Its segmental content is *copied* from the stem that undergoes reduplication. Reduplication is therefore by its very nature a phenomenon involving phonological *identity* between the 'reduplicant' and the 'base' to which it adjoins. (Both terms are used informally here, and will be defined in section 5.2.)

Segmental and prosodic identity of the reduplicant and the base is obvious in the case of *total reduplication*, which involves copying of a complete word. The following examples of total reduplication in Indonesian (Cohn 1989) show that it is impossible to tell apart the reduplicant from the base:

(1)   Indonesian plural reduplication (total reduplication, copies entire
        word)
        a. wanita   wanita-wanita   'women'
        b. mašarakat mašarakat-mašarakat 'societies'

But other languages have reduplication processes that copy only part of the
segments of the base. This phenomenon is known as *partial* reduplication. For
example, reduplication in the Wakashan language Nootka (Stonham 1990) copies
the first sequence of consonant plus vowel (CV or CVV) of the base, and prefixes
this material to the base:

(2)   Nootka reduplication (copies initial CV(V) sequence, equalling open
        syllable)
        a. čims-'iːħ či-čims-'iːħ 'hunting bear'
        b. waːs-čił waː-waːs-čił 'naming where...'

Observe that the reduplicant prefixes [či-] in (2a) and [waː-] in (2b), both open
syllables, do not match similar open syllables in the base, but copy segments that
stand in closed syllables: [čim] and [waːs] in the base.

The size of the reduplicant in partial reduplication varies between languages.
This is clear from a comparison of the Nootka pattern (2) with reduplication in
the Australian language Diyari (Austin 1981, Poser 1989, McCarthy and Prince
1994a):

(3)   Diyari reduplication (copies initial foot, minus coda of second syllable)
        a. wi.ḷa   wi.ḷa -wi.ḷa   'woman'
        b. kuḷ.ku.ŋa kuḷ.ku -kuḷ.ku.ŋa 'to jump'
        c. tʲil.par.ku tʲil.pa -tʲil.par.ku 'bird species'

Here the reduplicant is a disyllabic unit, specifically a *binary foot*, although surprisingly it is not simply a copy of the first two syllables of the base. The restriction holds that the second syllable of the reduplicant is *open*, regardless of
whether the second syllable in the base is open or closed. This is shown in (3c),
where the reduplicant [tʲil.pa -] fails to match the first two syllables of the base,
[tʲil.par], the second of which is closed.

5.1.1 *Shape invariance*

The reduplication patterns that we have seen thus far illustrate two observations that will become of central importance in this chapter. The first observation
is that the reduplicant tends to have an *invariant prosodic shape* that has no one-
to-one relation with a prosodic unit in the base. In both Nootka and Diyari, the

reduplicants can be described in terms of prosodic units (syllable and foot). However, in neither case does the reduplicant exactly match an analogous prosodic unit in the base.[1]

(4)   Reduplication does *not* copy a prosodic constituent

     a. Nootka (σ): <u>waː</u>-waːs-čił   (*not* *<u>waːs</u>-waːs-čił)

     b. Diyari (Ft): <u>tʲil.pa</u> -tʲil.par.ku(*not* *<u>tʲil.pa</u> -tʲil.par.ku)

For this reason reduplication cannot be simply 'constituent copying', but it involves a prosodic shape invariant in the reduplicant, also known as a reduplicative *template*. This observation of shape invariance was first stated by Moravcsik (1978), and it has become the basis of the 'template-and-association' theory of reduplication (e.g. Marantz 1982, Clements 1985a, McCarthy and Prince 1986). The OT approach to reduplication is, to a certain extent, a continuation of templatic theory in the sense that constraints may govern the prosodic size of a reduplicant. But it diverges from templatic theory by decomposing templatic requirements into independent prosodic constraints and alignment constraints, as we will see in section 5.3.

5.1.2 *Unmarkedness of the reduplicant*

The first observation naturally leads us to a second one, which can also be illustrated by reduplications in Nootka and Diyari. Reduplicants tend to have *unmarked phonological structures*, as compared to the phonotactic options generally allowed in the language. In Nootka, unmarked prosodic structure emerges in the reduplicant prefix, an *open syllable* (2). This is interesting since Nootka does not generally ban codas. Nevertheless we know that open syllables are universally less marked than closed syllables, from various kinds of evidence discussed in chapter 3, in particular cross-linguistic patterns of epenthesis. (The unmarked status of open syllables is captured in OT by the constraint No-Coda.) The reduplicant prefix in Diyari (3) matches a *disyllabic foot*, another unmarked prosodic unit, as we know from stress patterns and word minima, as discussed in chapter 4. (The constraint Ft-Bin captures the unmarked status.) Incidentally, the

---

[1] One reduplication pattern is known which involves copying of an entire prosodic unit. In the Australian language Yidiɲ (Dixon 1977, McCarthy and Prince 1986) plurals arise by prefixing an exact copy of the *first foot* of the base, that is, including its syllabification:

   (i)   Yidiɲ plural reduplication (copies initial two syllables, or foot)

          a. mulari   <u>mula</u>-mula.ri   'initiated men'

          b. gindalba <u>gindal</u>-gindal.ba 'lizard species' (plural)

Note that the reduplicant in (a) ends in /a/, matching this segment's position at the end of a foot in the base. And in (b), the reduplicant ends in /l/, matching this segment's position in a closed syllable in the base.

Diyari reduplicant ends in an open syllable, again an unmarked prosodic unit, even though closed syllables occur in Diyari stems.[2]

The observation that reduplicants tend to have unmarked phonological structures (that is, as compared to the general phonotactic possibilities of the language) was stated explicitly by Steriade (1988a: 80):

> Prosodic templates frequently eliminate certain unmarked options from their syllabic structures. Although the language may in general allow complex onsets or consonantal nuclei, the template might specifically revoke these options.
>
> We observe the following range of syllabic simplification in prosodic templates: onset simplification (Tagalog *ta-trabaho*, *bo-bloaut* from McCarthy and Prince 1986: 16); coda simplification (Sanskrit intensive *kan-i-krand* [...]); coda drop (cf. the French hypocoristics *zabe*, *mini* from (*i*)*zabel*, (*do*)*minik*); elimination of consonantal nuclei (Sanskrit perfect *va-vṛma* [...]).

This observation will become a focal point of attention in this chapter. The question is, what explains it? Steriade, working in a derivational framework, proposed that marked syllable properties are literally *cancelled* from the reduplicant. This proposal assumes that a reduplicant, in a specific stage of its derivation, is a full copy of its base, including its syllable structure. For example, a derivation of the Nootka examples (left undiscussed by Steriade) would involve the following two steps:

(5) a. Copying of the base
(total copy, including
syllabification)

b. Elimination of marked
structure disallowed by
the template (=syllable,
with codas disallowed)

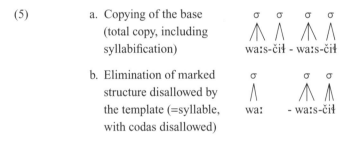

Steriade's proposal maintained the formal distinction between a morphological operation (affixation, copying) and its construction-specific phonology: the *cancellation of marked properties*. This strict division of labour between morphology and phonology was indeed assumed by most generative linguists in the 1970s and 1980s (although there were some exceptions; see for example Anderson 1975). But a fundamental question remains unanswered by Steriade's full-copy-plus-cancellation theory: why is it that cancellations of prosodically marked structure

---

[2] The interesting question of what causes the asymmetry between the first and second syllable in the reduplicant in (4b) (in terms of markedness) will be addressed in section 5.4.

fail to affect the base? We might state the unmarkedness as a template-specific fact, but that only raises another question: what makes reduplication templates so 'vulnerable' to simplification? A priori, the universal markedness principles treat 'template' and 'base' alike, since both are built of the same stuff.

As McCarthy and Prince note, the key to the problem resides in the very fact that reduplication is, by nature, a phenomenon which is *dependent in its identity upon another morpheme*. Since the reduplicant is not burdened with lexical contrasts, its phonological form naturally drifts towards the unmarked. There is a straightforward expression of this idea in OT, which involves ranking of markedness constraints between input faithfulness constraints and copying constraints ('reduplicative identity' constraints). In the base, the effects of markedness remain hidden behind other factors, in particular the preservation of contrast (faithfulness). But unmarked structures (open syllables) manifest themselves in contexts where input faithfulness has no 'grip', such as the reduplicant, which has no specification of input segments. Any language, given the chance, will develop unmarked structures in contexts where the influence of faithfulness is absent. This *emergence of the unmarked* (McCarthy and Prince 1994a) provides a major argument for the OT assumption that languages are subject to universal markedness constraints (see section 5.3).

5.1.3 *Identity of reduplicant and base*

A third important observation on reduplication should be added to those discussed in the preceding sections: reduplicants tend to preserve *phonological identity with the base*. The pressure towards identity may even happen at the cost of transparency in the application of the phonology, giving rise to so-called *overapplications* or *underapplications* of phonology. Overapplication refers to a situation in which the reduplicant 'undergoes' some change, even though it fails to satisfy the structural condition of this change. Underapplication is the reverse situation, in which a reduplicant fails to undergo some change, even though it meets the context in which this change normally takes place. Both effects simultaneously occur in Javanese, as the examples show (Dudas 1976, Kiparsky 1986, Steriade 1988a):

(6)

	underlying	surface	reduplicated	
a.i	/donga/	do.ngɔ	do.ngɔ-do.ngɔ	'prayer'
a.ii	/donga-ne/	do.nga.ne	do.nga-do.nga.ne	(*do.ngɔ-do.nga.ne)
b.i	/abur/	a.bʊr	a.bʊ.r-a.bʊr	(*a.bu.r-a.bʊr)
b.ii	/abur-e/	a.bu.re	a.bu.r-a.bu.re	'flight'

In (6a.ii), a process of word-final 'a-*rounding*' /a/ → [ɔ] underapplies in the reduplicant, even though its final vowel matches the context of application. In (6b.i), another process of *closed syllable laxing* /u/ → [ʊ] overapplies to the reduplicant, even though it fails to meet the structural requirement of a closed syllable. In both cases, the reduplicant maintains segmental identity with the base.

The 'underapplication' and 'overapplication' of phonology in reduplication was first observed by Wilbur (1973: 58), and stated in the form of the 'Identity Constraint':

(7)   **The Identity Constraint**
        There is a tendency to preserve the identity of R_o [*reduplicant*] and R_r [*base*] in reduplicated forms.

This is not a constraint in the sense of OT: observe the phrasing 'tendency'. However, it provides the basis of a constraint-based theory of overapplication and underapplication effects in reduplication, which we will learn about in section 5.4 of this chapter. The basic idea has already been hinted at in the preceding discussion: maximal identity of reduplicant and base increases the transparency of morphological reduplication, but at the cost of a loss of transparency in the phonology (Anderson 1975). Grammars define language-specific ways to reconcil both conflicting forces.

We may summarize the discussion so far by the following three observations:

(8)   Three cross-linguistic tendencies in reduplication
        a. **Shape invariance**
           Reduplication tends to be defined in prosodic units independent of the base. (That is, reduplicants do not copy prosodic constituency from the base.)
        b. **Unmarkedness**
           Reduplicants tend to have phonologically unmarked structures *vis-à-vis* the phonotactics of the language. (That is, reduplicants display a subset of the phonotactic options generally allowed in the language.)
        c. **Identity**
           Reduplication tends to preserve full phonological identity with the base. (That is, reduplication may involve overapplication and underapplication of phonology to preserve such identity.)[3]

Is there an inconsistency between 'shape invariance' and 'prosodic unmarkedness'? If a reduplicant template equals a marked prosodic unit (for example, a heavy syllable), could this not lead to *increased* markedness in the reduplicant, as compared to the base? There is no inconsistency since, as (8b) states, the

---

[3] As far as is currently known, the effects of overapplication and underapplication are limited to 'segmental' phonology, with a remarkable lack of 'copying' of aspects of syllable structure or foot structure.

proper basis for comparison is not the actual base, but rather the overall prosodic possibilities of the language.

For example, reduplication in Agta (Healey 1960, Marantz 1982) copies enough segments from the initial portion of the base to form a heavy syllable:

(9)   Agta reduplication (copies enough material to form a heavy syllable)
        a. ba.ri 'body'   bar-ba.ri-k kid-in 'my whole body'
        b. tak.ki 'leg'   tak-tak.ki   'legs'

Form (9a) may be said to involve literally an *increase* of markedness in the reduplicant, as compared to the base. While the base [ba.ri] has only open syllables, the reduplicant is a closed syllable [bar-], combining in it segments that are copied from the base's initial open syllable, plus the onset of its second syllable. However, Agta is a language which happens to allow for closed syllables. (In terms of ranking, it has MAX-IO ≫ NO-CODA.) Therefore, even if the reduplicant is prosodically marked as compared to the *particular* base with which it combines, this markedness still falls within the margins of the *overall* phonology of the language.

In reduplicative morphology, as in other kinds of morphology, conflicting forces are at work; naturally, different languages select different types of reconciliations of these conflicts. The very goal of optimality-based approaches to reduplication is to factor out the complex patterns of reduplication into interactions of general principles of structural well-formedness and correspondence, that is, to constraint interactions.

5.1.4 *The Basic Model*

In this chapter we will use the three observations in (8) as our point of departure in a discussion of the 'Correspondence Theory of reduplication' (McCarthy and Prince 1994a, b, 1995a, forthcoming). This theory claims that reduplication patterns arise by interactions of three constraint types: (a) *well-formedness* constraints, encoding markedness principles; (b) *faithfulness* constraints, requiring lexical forms and surface forms to be identical; and (c) *base–reduplicant-identity* constraints, requiring identity between the reduplicant and its base. By reranking these three types of constraints, Correspondence Theory aims to explain the broad typological differences and similarities among patterns of reduplication in the world's languages, as well as the specific patterns of individual languages. The following issue will be raised time and again in our discussion of reduplication patterns throughout this chapter:

> What interaction of well-formedness, faithfulness, and base–reduplicant identity underlies the pattern of reduplication in some language *L*?

We will address this issue in the context of what McCarthy and Prince (1995a, forthcoming) call the 'Basic Model'. This model, as depicted in (10), has an input and an output level. The input of reduplication consists of a segmentally empty reduplicative affix, which is abbreviated as Af_{RED} or RED, plus the stem to which the affix adjoins. Input faithfulness constraints require that the stem's input specifications be preserved in the output – the 'base' of the base–reduplicant combination. Base–reduplicant identity constraints require that both parts of this output base–reduplicant combination be identical in some respect.

(10)   **Basic Model**
          Input: /Af_{RED} + **Stem**/
                            ⇕   *IO-Faithfulness*
          Output: **R** ⇔ **B**
                   BR-Identity

Not shown in this model are the two remaining constraint types which come into play in reduplication. *Well-formedness* constraints require that the output (base reduplicant) meet certain unmarked structures. *Alignment* constraints require that base and reduplicant be 'glued' together along the edges of specific prosodic constituents.

5.1.5 *Organization of this chapter*

This chapter is organized as follows. In section 5.2, we will introduce the notions and constraints which are central in the Correspondence Theory of reduplication. Each constraint will be presented in the context of a simple analysis of some reduplication pattern. We will also try to explain the observation that reduplicants tend to be unmarked (as compared to the phonotactic options in the language): the *emergence of the unmarked* in the reduplicant. Section 5.3 will develop the notion of 'template' in OT, explaining unmarked prosodic shapes by constraint interactions. Section 5.4 discusses alignment in infixing reduplication, building the first argument for parallelism in the prosody–morphology interface. Results of sections 5.3–4 will be summarized in section 5.5. Section 5.6 addresses *over-application* and *underapplication* in reduplicative morphology, focussing on typology and developing yet another argument for parallelism. Finally, section 5.7 contains an overview of Correspondence Theory as developed in this chapter.

5.2   Reduplicative identity: the constraints

5.2.1 *The notions 'reduplicant', 'base', and 'correspondence'*

Before we actually discuss the constraints of reduplicative identity, we must first define the notions of 'reduplicant' and 'base' in a more precise way than we have done so far. First and foremost, both notions refer to *strings of output segments*, rather than to input strings. (In fact, it will be essential that there is *no* such thing as the phonological *input* representation of a reduplicative affix.) Reference to the output shapes of reduplicant and base is at the heart of the Correspondence Theory of reduplication.

The definitions of 'reduplicant' and 'base' that are given by McCarthy and Prince (1994b) are paraphrased in (11):

(11)   The '**reduplicant**' is the string of segments that is the phonological realization of some reduplicative morpheme RED, which is phonologically empty.

The '**base**' is the output string of segments to which the reduplicant is attached, more specifically:
- for reduplicative *prefixes*, it is the *following* string of segments
- for reduplicative *suffixes*, the *preceding* string of segments

Note that the reduplicant need not be identical to a unique morpheme, for example a root. That reduplication may copy more than just a single morpheme is shown by examples from the Bantu language Kinande (Mutaka and Hyman 1990, McCarthy and Prince 1995b):

(12)   Kinande noun reduplication (copies final two syllables of base)
    a. ku-gulu-<u>gulu</u>   'real leg'
    b. mú-twe-<u>mú-twe</u>   'real head'
    c. mw-ána-<u>mw-ána</u>   'real child'

This is a case of *suffixing* reduplication, with a disyllabic reduplicant, which has been underlined. Following the definition in (11), the base contains all material preceding the reduplicant. Observe that in all examples in (12) the base contains both prefixal and root material. More specifically, prefixes are *ku-* and *mu-/mw-*, roots *gulu-*, *twe-*, and *ana-*. Observe that the disyllabic reduplicant may consist entirely of segments copied from the root, as in (12a). This occurs when the root provides enough segments to fill the disyllabic reduplicant. But examples (12b–c) show that the reduplicant copies additional segments from the prefix, if the root's segmental material does not by itself suffice to 'fill out' both syllables of the reduplicant. In sum, we find that the base may span a string of segments that exceeds a single morpheme.

The one-to-one relationship between morphemes and reduplicants may also be broken in the opposite direction, when a part of the stem serves as the reduplicant's base. In some languages the reduplicant affixes to a base-string that is smaller than the stem. This phenomenon is known as 'internal reduplication'. In the examples below, note that the reduplicant adjoins as a prefix to the bimoraic stress foot in the Polynesian language Samoan (Marsack 1962, Broselow and McCarthy 1983).

(13)   Samoan plural reduplication (copies initial CV of stress foot before the foot)
      a.i nófo   no-nófo 'sit'
      a.ii táa   ta-táa 'strike'
      b.i a.lófa a-lo-lófa 'love'
      b.ii fa.náu fa-na-náu 'be born, give birth'

In examples (13a), reduplication may easily give the appearance of a prefixation to the stem, since the stem happens to be the size of a bimoraic foot. But examples (13b) show that this naive hypothesis is incorrect, since here the reduplicant shows up in the middle of a stem. According to the definition in (11), the *base* of an internal reduplication is the string of segments following the reduplicative prefix. (The analysis of the interesting phenomenon of 'internal' reduplication will be deferred to section 5.4.)

With the preliminary definitions of 'reduplicant' and 'base', we can now move on to another notion that requires definition: '*correspondence*' in reduplication. In previous chapters we have seen correspondence relationships between input and output elements, to which we attributed the term 'faithfulness'. In fact, this notion of correspondence is all we need to capture the identity relation between the base and the reduplicant, if only we generalize it a bit. We will see that faithfulness (or *input-to-output* correspondence) and reduplicative identity (or *base-to-reduplicant* correspondence) are just two aspects of a general relation defined between elements in two representations. Pairs of representations can be either an *output* form and an *input* form, or a *reduplicant* and its *base*.

    McCarthy and Prince (1995a: 262) define this generalized notion of 'correspondence' as follows:[4]

(14)   **Correspondence.** Given two strings S_1 and S_2, *correspondence* is a relation $\mathcal{R}$ from the elements of S_1 to those of S_2.
      Correspondents. Elements $\alpha \in S_1$ and $\beta \in S_2$ are referred to as *correspondents* of one another when $\alpha \, \mathcal{R} \, \beta$.

From here on, we must be somewhat more specific about what it means for two elements to be *correspondents*. Following McCarthy and Prince (1995a) we make the simplifying assumption that elements standing in correspondence are

---

[4] A precursor of the notion 'correspondence' is proposed in Bybee (1988).

segments, although it would be a straightforward matter to generalize the notion to other elements, such as moras, syllables, or even distinctive features. Moreover, we will assume that correspondence relations are supplied by *Gen*; accordingly, any pair of segments (when a member of the pairs of strings defined above) can be correspondents. Like all other aspects of representations, correspondence relations are evaluated by *Eval* using ranked constraints. Crucially we do not make the assumption that corresponding segments must be segmentally identical. This will allow us to account for featural changes between input and output separately from insertion and deletion.

Taking the Samoan example /RED + nofo/, we assume that *Gen* produces output can-didates supplied with all logically possible correspondence relations. Consider a subset of output candidates, in which subscript indexes indicate correspondence relations:

(15)   /RED + nofo/   Comments

    a. $n_1\, o_2$ $- n_1\, ó_2\, f\, o$ (**f, o** in base lack correspondents, others identical)

    b. $n_1\, o_2$ $- n\, ó_2\, f_1\, o$ (**n, o** in base lack correspondents, $\mathbf{n_1}$, $\mathbf{f_1}$ distinct)

    c. $n_1\, o_2\, f_3\, o_4 - n_1\, ó_2\, f_3\, o_4$ (all segments have identical correspondents in the same linear order: 'perfect correspondence')

    d. $f_1\, o_2\, f_3\, o_4 - n_1\, ó_2\, f_3\, o_4$ (all segments have correspondents in the same linear order, although $\mathbf{f_1}$, $\mathbf{n_1}$ are distinct)

    e. $o_4\, f_3\, o_2\, n_1 - n_1\, ó_2\, f_3\, o_4$ (all segments have identical correspondents but in the reverse linear order)

    f. $n_1\, o_2\, f\, o - n_1\, ó_2\, f\, o$ (**f, o** -twice- lack correspondents, others identical)

These candidates (and many others) are then submitted to *Eval* for evaluation by violable correspondence constraints, interacting with faithfulness constraints and well-formedness constraints. The forms and functions of base–reduplicant correspondence constraints are a topic to which we now turn.

We will extend the set of faithfulness constraints known from previous chapters: MAX-IO, DEP-IO, IDENT-IO, LINEARITY-IO, and ANCHORING-IO, to the base–reduplicant relation. The first step is a generalization of the IO-faithfulness constraints to other kinds of strings, including base and reduplicant. According to definition (14), correspondence is a relation between elements in two strings: S_1

and S_2. Applying this generalization to the first three IO-faithfulness constraints mentioned above, we arrive at the following set:

(16)   Generalized correspondence constraints

      a. **MAXIMALITY**

         Every element of S_1 has a correspondent in S_2.

      b. **DEPENDENCE**

         Every element of S_2 has a correspondent in S_1.

      c. **IDENTITY[F]**

         Let α be a segment in S_1 and β be a correspondent of α in S_2.

         If α is [γF], then β is [γF].

To arrive at actual base–reduplicant identity constraints, we must substitute S_1 and S_2 by the specific strings relevant to reduplication, reduplicant (R) and base (B). This step will be taken in the next section for MAXIMALITY, DEPENDENCE, and IDENTITY.

5.2.2   *MAX, DEP, and IDENT*

5.2.2.1   *Violation of MAX-BR in Nootka*

In input faithfulness, MAX-IO is the 'anti-deletion' constraint. In reduplication the notion of deletion is not accurate, since no segment in a reduplicant has an input correspondent. The reduplicative instantiation of MAXIMALITY, MAX-BR, requires that every element of the base must reoccur in the reduplicant. This is the 'total reduplication' constraint:

(17)   **MAX-BR**

      Every element of B has a correspondent in R.

      ('No partial reduplication')

If MAX-BR is undominated, total reduplication will indeed result, as in Indonesian (1). But if it is dominated by a well-formedness constraint militating against any kind of elements that might result from total reduplication, then partial reduplica-tion will be the outcome, as in Nootka (2), Diyari (3), and Samoan (13).

    Let us take a closer look at the Nootka example (2a), discussed earlier as a case of unmarked syllable structure in the reduplicant. Recall that the reduplicant in [či-čims'iːħ] is an open syllable, omitting the coda consonant *m* (and remaining segments of the base). If *m* were copied, it would syllabify as a coda in the reduplicant, *[čim.čims'iːħ]. Clearly, Nootka avoids this marked syllable structure in the reduplicant. But then why does it allow the same marked structures in the base? McCarthy and Prince (1994a) show that the answer is surprisingly simple. The first step in the argument is that the total avoidance of codas in the reduplicant must be due to the well-formedness constraint No-Coda, which out-ranks the reduplicative identity constraint Max-BR:

(18)   Partial reduplication due to avoidance of codas
        No-Coda ≫ Max-BR

This ranking is illustrated by tableau (19). The total reduplication candidate (19d) is ruled out by No-Coda, since a better candidate (19a) is available which has fewer violations of this constraint:

(19)

Input: /Red-čims-'iːħ/	No-Coda	Max-BR
a. ☞ či-čim.s'iːħ	**	****
b. čim-čim.s'iːħ	** *!	***
c. čim.s'iː-čim.s'iːħ	** *!	*
d. čim.s'iːħ-čim.s'iːħ	** *!*	

Violations of No-Coda are marked independently for every coda in every candidate, that is, regardless of whether it stands in the reduplicant or the base. Observe that the base has two closed syllables, hence incurs two violations of No-Coda by itself. (We will find out shortly why these violations are unavoidable.) But No-Coda disallows further violations in the reduplicant, sharply limiting its size to an open syllable at the expense of violations of Max-BR. In the optimal candidate (19a) Max-BR is violated four times, once for each base segment missing from the reduplicant.

Of course, this cannot be the complete story, because the consonants [m] and [ħ] that are banned from the reduplicant freely occur as codas in the base. Base segments are different from reduplicant segments in being subject to *input faithfulness*. Their deletion is penalized by Max-IO. Hence, No-Coda must, in its turn, be dominated by Max-IO:

(20)   Emergence of the unmarked in Nootka reduplication
        Schema   Faithfulness ≫ Well-formedness ≫ Reduplicative
                                                         identity
        Instantiation Max-IO   ≫ No-Coda   ≫ Max-BR

The 'sandwiching' of well-formedness between both kinds of correspondence constraints is what makes the base more faithful to input segments than the reduplicant.

To prove our point, let us inspect tableau (21). This includes all four candidates of the previous tableau, plus one critical new candidate (21e), representing a

reduction of the base back to a monosyllabic format, matching the prosodic shape
of the reduplicant:

(21)

Input: /RED-čims-'iːħ/	MAX-IO	NO-CODA	MAX-BR
a. ☞ či-čim.s'iːħ		**	****
b. čim-čim.s'iːħ		** *!	***
c. čim.s'iː-čim.s'iːħ		** *!	*
d. čim.s'iːħ-čim.s'iːħ		** *!*	
e. či-či	*!***		

Candidate (21e) seems to have much in its favour. It is composed of two open
syllables (satisfying NO-CODA). Both of its base segments have correspondents in
the reduplicant (satisfying MAX-BR). However, it fatally violates faithfulness by
omitting four segments in the base which are present in the *input* – incurring four
marks for MAX-IO. Crucially, MAX-IO does not militate against the omission of
input segments in the reduplicant. This is because *the reduplicant has no input
segments* of its own, to which it might potentially be faithful. This is the essence
of reduplication: a reduplicative affix has no input segments, hence escapes from
the 'gravity forces' of faithfulness.

This argument shows that unmarked syllable structure (open syllables) suddenly and unexpectedly come to the surface in contexts where input-to-output
faithfulness has no 'grip'. This *emergence of the unmarked* is a major argument
for OT's assumption that languages are all subject to the same set of universal
markedness constraints. Effects of markedness may remain hidden behind other
factors, in particular preservation of contrast (faithfulness). But any language,
given the chance, will develop unmarked structures in contexts where influence
of contrast-preserving factors is absent. In reduplication, such cases are easily
dismissed as '*imperfect* copying'. This qualification is correct from the viewpoint
that what counts towards 'perfection' is faithfulness. But it seems equally correct
to say that reduplication of the Nootka type involves a kind of unmarked *perfection* that is otherwise lacking from the surface phonology of the language.

This analysis exemplifies the general line of reasoning to be pursued in the rest
of this chapter. For every pattern of reduplication, we will attempt to reduce it to
interacting constraints of well-formedness, faithfulness, and reduplicative identity.

5.2.2.2 *Violation of DEP-BR in Makassarese*
Next we turn to the logical counterpart of MAX-BR, the constraint DEP-BR.
Recall from chapter 2 that DEP-IO is the 'anti-epenthesis' constraint, militating

against any segments in the output which have no correspondents in the input. Analogously, DEP-BR requires that segments in the reduplicant must have correspondents in the base:

(22)   **DEP-BR**
         Every element of R has a correspondent in B.

If undominated, the reduplicant is composed solely of segments that occur in the base. In fact DEP-BR was satisfied in every example of reduplication that we have seen thus far. What could a violation look like?

An example of a violation of DEP-BR occurs in Makassarese (Aronoff et al. 1987, McCarthy and Prince 1994a). Reduplication copies the first two syllables of a (trisyllabic or longer) base, but also adds an epenthetic consonant /ʔ/ at the end of the reduplicant:

(23)   Makassarese reduplication (copies first two syllables, adding epen-
         thetic /ʔ/)
         a. <u>kaluʔ</u>-kalu.arak 'ant'
         b. <u>manaʔ</u>-mana.ra 'sort of tower'
         c. <u>balaʔ</u>-bala.o   'toy rat'
         d. <u>baiʔ</u>-bai.ne   'many women'

Observe that epenthesis is blocked at the end of the base, pointing to a strict enforcement of DEP-IO. We will not present the complete analysis by McCarthy and Prince, since it is fairly complex, and we refer the interested reader to the original work.

5.2.2.3   *Violation of IDENT-BR in Akan*

Finally, the reduplicative instantiation of IDENTITY is IDENT-BR. This constraint requires featural identity between correspondents in base and reduplicant.

(24)   **IDENT-BR[F]**
         Let α be a segment in B, and β be a correspondent of α in R.
         If α is [γF], then β is [γF].

Thus far we have only seen cases where this constraint was actually satisfied. However, it would not be a true OT constraint if it were unviolable. Violations of IDENT-BR are due to differences in feature values of corresponding segments in reduplicant and base. As we expect, featural deviations in the reduplicant (as compared to the base) tend to reduce the *segmental markedness* in the reduplicant. For example, a feature contrast occurring in the base may be disallowed in the reduplicant. This gives the appearance of *neutralization* of segmental contrasts in the reduplicant, as compared to the base.

An example of a reduction of featural markedness in the reduplicant, discussed by McCarthy and Prince (1995a), is reduplication in Akan (Schachter and Fromkin 1968):

(25)   Reduced segmental markedness in Akan reduplication

     a. si-siʔ 'stand'   f. bu-bu(ʔ) 'bend'

     b. fɪ-fɪʔ 'vomit'   g. sʊ-sʊ(ʔ) 'carry on the head'

     c. si-seʔ 'say'   h. su-soʔ 'seize'

     d. sɪ-sɛʔ 'resemble'   i. sʊ-sɔʔ 'light'

     e. sɪ-saʔ 'cure'

The vowel in the reduplicative CV-prefix is a copy of the base vowel in every respect, except that it is always *high*. Raising of mid vowels has a striking parallel in the cross-linguistically common phenomenon of *vowel reduction* occurring in unstressed syllables. Reduction amounts to the loss of featural contrasts in metrically weak positions, hence a replacement of marked segments by unmarked segments.[5]

McCarthy and Prince (1995a) analyse the loss of vowel height contrasts in the Akan reduplicant as another *emergence of the unmarked*. Crucially vowels in the base are exempt from the neutralization of height contrasts taking place in reduplicants. Hence the IDENT-IO constraint for [high] must dominate the context-free markedness constraint *[−high], which bans [−high] vowels:

(26)   Faithfulness   ≫ Well-formedness

     IDENT-IO(high) ≫ *[−high]

This is a straightforward example of a preservation of contrast due to the domination of a faithfulness constraint over a markedness (well-formedness) constraint, of a kind that we have studied in detail in chapter 1. The ranking is illustrated in the following tableau:

(27)

Input: /soʔ/	IDENT-IO(high)	*[−high]
a. ☞ soʔ		*
b. suʔ	*!	

Next observe that a reduction of the vowel height contrast *does* occur in the reduplicant. This is another *emergence of the unmarked*: the reduplicant contains

---

[5] An analysis by Marantz (1982) was based on a prespecification of the feature [+high] in the reduplicant, overriding the copied melody. McCarthy and Prince (1995a) criticize this analysis for prespecifying an *unmarked* feature value, [+high]. Underspecification Theory (Kiparsky 1985, Archangeli 1988) predicts that only marked values can be lexically specified.

Correspondence in reduplication

segments of lesser markedness than the corresponding base segments. This effect arises due to the lack of an input correspondent for a vowel in a reduplicant, which is thus exempt from faithfulness requirements. For unmarked vowels to arise in the reduplicant, the markedness constraint *[−high] must actually dominate the reduplicative identity constraint IDENT-BR(high), requiring identity between the base and reduplicant for the feature [high]. This analysis involves the type of ranking that we saw earlier for Nootka.

(28)   Emergence of the unmarked in Akan reduplication
        Schema   Faithfulness   ≫ Well-formedness ≫ Reduplicative
                                                           identity
        Instantiation IDENT-IO(high) ≫ *[−high]   ≫ IDENT-
                                                           BR(high)

We have now arrived at the first part of an explanation for the different behaviours of the reduplicant and base with respect to marked segments.

The second part is to prove that no reduction of markedness can apply to the base without also applying to the reduplicant. For this purpose, let us turn to tableau (29):

(29)

Input: /RED-soʔ/	IDENT-IO(high)	*[−high]	IDENT-BR(high)
a. ☞ su-soʔ		*	*
b. so-soʔ		**!	
c. su-suʔ	*!		
d. so-suʔ	*!	*	*

Optimal (29a) preserves the input value [−high] in the stem vowel, due to undominated IDENT-IO(high), thus violating *[−high]. Minimal violation of *[−high] blocks a second occurrence of [−high] in the reduplicant, even though this would yield complete identity between the reduplicant and the base (29b).

Next consider candidate (29d), whose reduplicant vowel copies the input's value for [−high], while its base vowel is unfaithful to this value. This pattern of vowel height is precisely the reverse of that in the optimal candidate, where the unmarked value emerges in the reduplicant. Could this reversed pattern of reduction in base and reduplicant arise in any language? The correct prediction is that it cannot, since no constraint ranking can derive it. Candidate (29c) is identical in its pattern of violation marks to candidate (29d), except for *[−high] and IDENT-BR(high), which evaluate (29d) as worse than (29c). Therefore (29d) cannot be optimal *under any possible ranking* of these constraints, since in the end it will always fall victim to *[−high] or IDENT-BR(high), regardless of where these are ranked, rendering it suboptimal to (29c). No reduction of markedness is possible in the base without an accompanying reduction of markedness in the reduplicant, which is a significant result.

5.2.3 *Why input faithfulness and reduplicative identity cannot be unified*

So far we have seen 'reduplicative' counterparts of the constraint triplet MAX-IO, DEP-IO, and IDENT-IO. We have learned why the reduplicant can have a reduction of markedness as compared to the base, and why things could not have been reversed.

One major question has not yet been answered: if input-to-output faithfulness and base-to-reduplicant identity are *both* due to correspondence constraints, then would it not be possible to unify both types of constraints into a single generalized set? One glance at any reduplication example discussed above tells us that this conclusion cannot hold.

Consider the case of Nootka discussed earlier. If No-CODA were to dominate *both* MAX-BR *and* MAX-IO, then all words in the language, reduplicated and non-reduplicated words alike, would be strictly open-syllabled. Of course we know that such languages are attested ('CV-languages', as have been discussed in chapter 3). But Nootka happens not to be among these languages since it allows codas, for example in bases of the reduplicative examples that we saw. It follows that Nootka maintains dominance of faithfulness (MAX-IO) over the well-formedness constraint No-CODA. Suppose that we were to take the bold step of collapsing both MAX constraints into a single constraint, then the inevitable result for Nootka would be disastrous. We would end up with either total reduplication (30b), or a simplification of the base into an open syllable (31c), depending on ranking:

(30)

Input: /RED-čims-'iːħ/		MAX-IO/BR	No-CODA
a.	či-čim.s'iːħ	*!***	**
b. ☞	čim.s'iːħ-čim.s'iːħ		****
c.	či-či	*!***	

(31)

Input: /RED-čims-'iːħ/		No-CODA	MAX-IO/BR
a.	či-čim.s'iːħ	*!*	****
b.	čim.s'iːħ-čim.s'iːħ	*!***	
c. ☞	či-či		****

In sum, we must distinguish input-to-output faithfulness and base-to-reduplicant identity for empirical reasons: base and reduplicant may differ in their phonotactic options, which implies that both types of constraints are ranked in different positions in the hierarchy.[6]

In the next section we will introduce two more BR-correspondence constraints.

5.2.4 *ANCHORING and CONTIGUITY*

So far all reduplicative examples have been of the following general type: *starting at an edge of the base* (the left edge in the case of a reduplicative prefix, the right edge in the case of a reduplicative suffix), a *contiguous* substring of base segments is copied to the reduplicant:

(32)   Anchoring and contiguity satisfied by various reduplications
        a. prefixing Diyari: tʲilpa -tʲilparku
        b. suffixing Kinande: ku-gulu- gulu
        c. infixing   Samoan: a-lo-lófa

Anchoring and *contiguous* copying are highlighted in correspondence diagrams in (33). In each diagram, reduplicant and base are represented parallelly, as in IO-correspondence:

(33)   a. tʲi l pa -   R   b. -gulu R   c. l o-   R
         | | | | | | | | | | |
        tʲi l parku B   kugulu B   l ofa B

In (33a), the leftmost segment in the reduplicative prefix [tʲilpa] corresponds with the leftmost segment in the base [tʲilparku]. The corresponding segments [tʲilpa] form a contiguous string of both the base and the reduplicant. In (33b), the rightmost segment in the reduplicant [-gulu] corresponds with the rightmost base segment, [kugulu]. The corresponding segments [gulu] form a contiguous string of both the base and the reduplicant. In (33c), the leftmost segment in the reduplicant [lo-] corresponds with the leftmost segment of the base. (Recall that the 'base' is defined as the segment string to which the reduplicant is adjoined. For reduplicative prefixes, it is the *following string* of segments: here the foot [lofa] to which the reduplicant is prefixed.) The corresponding segments [lo] are a contiguous string of both base and reduplicant.

In all three cases, correspondence holds between contiguous strings of segments which are 'anchored' at an edge. However, this is not a logical necessity in reduplication. As we will see, partial reduplication need not respect 'contiguity'

---

[6] A more comprehensive exploration of the interactions between both types of correspondence constraints and well-formedness constraints will take place in section 5.6.

and 'anchoring', which we will state as violable constraints in the following two
subsections.

5.2.4.1 *Violation of* ANCHORING *in Sanskrit*

The first constraint, ANCHORING, requires correspondence between two major
landmarks in the base and reduplicant: segments standing at edges. Depending on
whether the reduplicant is a prefix or a suffix, this requirement must hold at the
left or right edge. (A prefix-initial segment must correspond with the initial segment of the base, while a suffix-final segment must correspond with the final
segment of the base.) This requirement is stated in a general way in (34):[7]

(34)   **ANCHORING-BR**
          Correspondence preserves alignment in the following sense: the left
          (right) peripheral element of R corresponds to the left (right) periph-
          eral element of B, if R is to the left (right) of B.

Convince yourself that all reduplications that we have seen so far satisfy this
constraint: see again the diagrams in (33).

But ANCHORING-BR is actually a violable constraint, as can be illustrated by
the perfective prefixing reduplication pattern of Sanskrit (Whitney 1889, Steriade
1988a). In all examples below the reduplicant 'simplifies' the complex onset of
the base, 'dropping' the initial consonant of a cluster [sk] or [st]:

(35)   Sanskrit perfective reduplication, full grade (copies first CV, drop-
          ping /sC/)
          a. <u>ka</u>-skand-a 'leap'
          b. <u>ta</u>-stamb^{h}-a 'prop'

Onset simplification is yet another illustration of reduction of syllabic markedness
in the reduplicant (Steriade 1988a). This goes at the expense of MAX-BR; also,
what is more, of ANCHORING-BR. The violation of ANCHORING-BR in [ka-skand-
a] is shown in (36). The leftmost segment of the base, the [s], fails to correspond
to the leftmost segment of the reduplicant, the [k]:

(36)   Correspondence diagram for violation of ANCHORING-BR

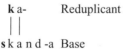

---

[7] Recall that in chapter 3 we saw its input-faithfulness version, ANCHORING-IO, active in the
   blocking of consonant deletion at the edge of a stem in Diola-Fogny.

As Steriade observes, there is a change towards *less marked* structure in the reduplicant. A *complex onset* in the base ([sk]) is 'simplified' into a simple onset ([k]) in the reduplicant. Lack of complex onsets in Sanskrit reduplicants is due to *COMPLEX, a syllabic well-formedness constraint introduced in chapter 3.

This 'emergence of the unmarked' is due to a ranking of *COMPLEX above both MAX-BR and ANCHORING-BR. But *COMPLEX must itself be dominated by MAX-IO, for complex onsets freely surface in the base. The preliminary ranking is:

(37)　　　　Emergence of the unmarked in Sanskrit reduplication
　　　　　　Schema　　　Faithfulness ≫ Well-formedness ≫ Reduplicative
　　　　　　　　　　　　　　　　　　　　　　　　　　　　　　　　　　identity
　　　　　　Instantiation MAX-IO　　　≫ *COMPLEX　　　≫ MAX-BR,
　　　　　　　　　　　　　　　　　　　　　　　　　　　　　　　　　ANCHORING-BR

5.2.4.2　*Violation of CONTIGUITY in Sanskrit*

The Sanskrit perfect reduplication pattern also serves to clarify the notion of *contiguity*. Although ANCHORING-BR is violated in the examples in (35), these examples still preserve the 'contiguity' of corresponding elements in the base and the reduplicant. As shown in (36), the two segments that stand in correspondence, [ka], form a contiguous substring of *both* base and reduplicant. This property is stated in constraint format in (38):

(38)　　**CONTIGUITY-BR**
　　　　　The portion of the base standing in correspondence forms a contiguous string, as does the correspondent portion of the reduplicant.

CONTIGUITY-BR requires the reduplicant to be a contiguous substring of the base, leaving no medial gap. In Diyari prefixing reduplication (33a), this protects reduplicant-medial coda consonants, though not reduplicant-final ones: tʲil.pa -tʲil.par.ku, *tʲi.pa -tʲil.par.ku.

Like previous base–reduplicant identity constraints, CONTIGUITY-BR is violable. To see this we must consider another set of examples of Sanskrit perfective reduplication (Whitney 1889, as cited in Steriade 1988a: 120):

(39)　　Sanskrit perfective reduplication, full grade (copies first CV, dropping C_2)
　　　　a. pa-prat^h-a　　'spread'
　　　　b. ma-mnaː-u　　'note'
　　　　c. sa-swar　　　 'sound'
　　　　d. da-d^{h}wans-a 'scatter'

Violation of CONTIGUITY-BR is illustrated in (40). The corresponding string of elements in reduplicant and base, [pa], is not a contiguous substring of the base, since in the base [r] interferes. The segment /r/ in the base is *skipped*:

(40)   Correspondence diagram for violation of CONTIGUITY-BR

p a-   Reduplicant
| |
p r a tʰ -a Base

As in the previous example of Sanskrit of section 5.2.4.1, we find that the reduplicant is of lesser markedness than its base, since it contains no complex onset. Again onset simplification is due to *COMPLEX. This points to an interaction of faithfulness, well-formedness, and reduplicative identity constraints that is very similar to what we saw earlier in (37):

(41)   Emergence of the unmarked in Sanskrit reduplication
          Schema   Faithfulness ≫ Well-formedness ≫ Reduplicative
                                               identity
          Instantiation MAX-IO   ≫ *COMPLEX   ≫ MAX-BR,
                                                    CONTIGUITY-BR

A final aspect of the Sanskrit pattern merits consideration. Reduplication copies the second consonant in a base beginning with /s/ + plosive ([ka̲-skand-a], 35a), whereas it copies the initial C in all other /CC/-initial bases ([pa̲-pratʰ-a], 39a). Gnanadesikan (1995) observes that the choice depends on sonority. The consonant of *lowest sonority* is the one to surface in the reduplicant. Plosives rank lower on the sonority scale than fricatives:

(42)   **Sonority scale**
          plosives–fricatives–nasals–liquids–vocoids

The preference for low-sonority onset segments coincides with the preference for abrupt rises of sonority at the beginning of the syllable (Clements 1990).[8] We will not present an analysis of sonority-governed onset simplification, and refer the reader to Gnanadesikan (1995).

5.2.5 *The emergence of the unmarked*
An observation that has been made time and again in previous sections is that reduplicants eliminate segmental or prosodic markedness, whereas the same

---

[8] We also observe the logically complementary requirement of that made by HNUC (Prince and Smolensky 1993), that syllable nuclei are maximally sonorous.

markedness is tolerated in any non-reduplicant in the language. The interaction of faithfulness, well-formedness, and reduplicative identity constraints that produces an unmarked reduplicant is referred to by McCarthy and Prince (1994a) as an 'emergence of the unmarked'. It is stated in (43):

(43)   Ranking schema for emergence of the unmarked
         IO-faithfulness ≫ Well-formedness ≫ BR-identity

We have already seen three examples of this ranking schema. The first was reduplication in Nootka (20), which produces an *open syllable*, even though the language allows closed syllables in other morphemes than reduplicants. The second was Akan reduplication (28), which produces high reduplicant vowels, even where the base contains non-high vowels. Finally, Sanskrit reduplication (37–41) produces *single onsets* where the base contains a complex onset. All three rankings (repeated below) are instantiations of the schema (43):

(44)   a. Nootka: Max-IO   ≫ No-Coda ≫ Max-BR
         b. Akan: Ident-IO(high) ≫ *[−high] ≫ Ident-BR(high)
         c. Sanskrit: Max-IO   ≫ *Complex ≫ Max-BR

This completes our discussion of reduplicative identity constraints. In the next section we will look into another core ingredient of analyses of reduplication: the constraints that determine the prosodic shape invariant.

5.3 From classical templates to generalized templates

5.3.1 *The 'classical template' in Agta*

We will now address the first observation made in the introduction of this chapter. That is, reduplicants tend to have prosodic shape invariants which are not necessarily related to a prosodic unit in the base. To learn about the contributions of OT in this respect, we must first focus on aspects of the ancestor theory of templates, and then compare these aspects with the OT viewpoint. We will outline the 'classical' template as it played a role in pre-OT prosodic morphology, discussing the major conceptual changes with respect to templates that took place as a result of OT.

A CVC shape invariant occurs in the following examples of reduplication in Agta (Healey 1960, Marantz 1982, McCarthy and Prince 1986), partly repeated from (9):

(45)   Agta reduplication (copies enough material to form a heavy syllable)
         a. ba.ri 'body' → <u>bar</u>-ba.ri-k kid-in 'my whole body'
         b. tak.ki 'leg' → <u>tak</u>-tak.ki   'legs'

The generalization is that the reduplicant has the size of a heavy syllable, regardless of whether the segments which fill it are taken from open or closed syllables in the base. To account for such shape invariance, Marantz (1982) assumed a notion of 'template', a morpheme having the defining property of being *melodically empty*. In his template-and-association theory, all prosodic properties defining shape-invariance of reduplicants are stated in the template. The Marantzian template is a sequence of '*skeletal*' segments, for example CVC- in the case of Agta, to which the melodic content of the base is associated from a fully copied string. Unassociated melodic elements are deleted:

(46) $C V C + C V C V$ *copy* $C V C + C V C V$ *assoc.* $C V C + C V C V$

           b a r i   b a r i b a r i   b a r (i) b a r i

CV-templates were replaced by prosodic templates by McCarthy and Prince (1986, 1990), whose *Prosodic Morphology Hypothesis* says that 'templates are defined in terms of authentic units of prosody: mora (μ), syllable (σ), foot (F), prosodic word (W), and so on' (1990: 209). In Agta, the reduplicative template is a *heavy syllable* $\sigma_{\mu\mu}$. McCarthy and Prince argued that all other aspects of the reduplicant's make-up (the presence of an onset, obligatory coda to satisfy syllable weight, etc.) follow from universal principles as well as language-specific principles of well-formedness. For example, since coda consonants make weight in Agta, the second mora in the template is satisfied by associating a consonant to it:

(47) $\sigma_{\mu\mu} + \sigma_\mu \sigma_\mu$ *copy* $\sigma_{\mu\mu} + \sigma_\mu \sigma_\mu$ *associate* $\sigma_{\mu\mu} + \sigma_\mu \sigma_\mu$

           b a r i   b a r i b a r i   b a r (i) b a r i

This 'classical' theory of reduplicative templates includes other prosodic categories, such as the 'core syllable' σ_μ (Sanskrit), the disyllabic foot (Diyari), and PrWd (Indonesian).

It is a straightforward matter to translate this derivational analysis of Agta into ranked OT constraints; all it takes is defining a templatic constraint:

(48)   **RED**=$\sigma_{\mu\mu}$
          The reduplicant is a heavy syllable.

and ranking this above the competing constraints NO-CODA and MAX-BR (the OT analogue of full-copying-and-association). A simple tableau illustrates this ranking:

(49)

Input: /RED + bari/	RED=$\sigma_{\mu\mu}$	No-Coda	Max-BR
a. ☞ bar-ba.ri		*	*
b. ba-ba.ri	*!		**
c. ba.ri-ba.ri	*!		

In early OT, McCarthy and Prince (1993b: 82) construed 'templates' as constraints on the prosody–morphology interface, *alignment constraints* asserting the coincidence of edges of morphological and prosodic constituents:

> The place to look for generalization of the notion of template, we propose, is in the family of constraints on the prosody/morphology interface, such as ALIGN. The idea is that the Reduplicant must be in a particular alignment with prosodic structure. The strictest such alignments will amount to classical templates.

The 'classical template' is thus translated into a constraint schema (McCarthy and Prince 1993b):

(50)   Constraint schema for classical templates
         MCAT=PCAT
              where **Mcat** ≡ Morphological Category ≡ Prefix, Suffix, RED,
              Root, Stem, LexWd, etc.
              and **Pcat** ≡ Prosodic Category ≡ Mora, Syllable (type), Foot
              (type), PrWd (type), etc.

However, recent developments in OT have surpassed this simple translation of 'classical templates' into constraints. This new approach to templates in OT will now be illustrated by an analysis of Diyari reduplication, which involves a sharp reduction of the role of templates, and a correspondingly increased role for general prosodic constraints.

5.3.2 *The Generalized Template in Diyari*

McCarthy and Prince (1986) assumed a *monolithic* notion of the template, as a single unit combining in it all invariant shape properties of the reduplicant, ranging from its status as a prefix or suffix to its prosodic size. McCarthy and Prince (1994a, 1994b) argued against this view of templates, and proposed to eliminate it by interactions among independently motivated constraints. This approach is known as 'Generalized Template' theory. Its key idea is that templatic specification is minimal, consisting only of a statement to the effect that the reduplicant equals an 'affix' or 'stem'. Any shape characteristics of reduplicants are derived from interactions of prosodic well-formedness constraints and constraints on

reduplicative identity.[9] Such a 'decomposition' of the classical template into interactions of constraints is a highly natural result in OT.

We will illustrate this approach by an analysis of reduplication in Diyari, after
McCarthy and Prince (1994a, forthcoming). The Diyari pattern was introduced in
section 5.1, where we already observed the disyllabicity of the reduplicant, a
shape invariance which we linked with the category *foot*. Feet are primarily units
of stress, and quite appropriately, properties of the Diyari stress system will
explain the disyllabicity of the reduplicant. We must therefore begin by studying
Diyari stress in some detail.

Diyari lacks a distinction of syllable weight: all its syllables count as light.
Hence, feet are binary under syllabic analysis, or in metrical terms, feet are
disyllabic trochees. The stress pattern of (unreduplicated) stems is illustrated in
(51). Primary stress is initial, and a secondary stress falls on the third syllable of
a four-syllable stem:

(51)   a. kána   'man'
         b. tʲílparku 'bird species'
         c. wílapìna 'old woman'

From chapter 4, we know that this iterative stress pattern is due to the constraint
ranking in (52). This in fact equals the ranking for Pintupi (see again tableau 74
in chapter 4):

(52)   FT-BIN ≫ PARSE-SYL ≫ ALL-FT-LEFT

A second observation directly relevant to the disyllabic size of the reduplicant is
that this equals the minimal prosodic word of Diyari: all stems are minimally
disyllabic.[10]

Our hypothesis that the reduplicant is a PrWd, which was based on its disyllabic size, is confirmed by stress patterns. The examples below show that a primary stress falls on both the base and the reduplicant:

(53)   a. wíla   → wíla -wíla   'woman'
         b. tʲílparku → tʲílpa -tʲílparku 'bird species'
         c. wílapìna → wíla -wílapìna   'old woman'

Since each primary stress heads one PrWd, we must conclude that the reduplicant
equals a PrWd itself.

---

[9] This step was anticipated by Steriade (1988a), and more explicitly by Shaw (1991), who
claims that 'Template = sum of constraints on prosodic weight and constraints on markedness
on its σ structure' (pp. vii–1).

[10] Poser (1989) observes that the only exception is the monosyllabic function word *ya* 'and'.

In 'classical template' theory (McCarthy and Prince 1986) this pattern involves a reduplicative template that directly encodes the prosodic size of the reduplicant as a foot, which equals a 'minimal PrWd'. In OT, setting up a templatic constraint analogous to the classical template is certainly possible, for example 'RED=Ft'. But a far more interesting approach is possible, which makes the metrical phonology of the language do most of the work, and also eliminates the template in its classical sense of a prosodic shape invariant associated with a morphological category. This new approach is known as Generalized Template theory (McCarthy and Prince 1994b). As stated earlier, its key idea is that the shape invariance of reduplicative templates is the net result of interaction between prosodic well-formedness constraints and constraints of reduplicative identity, an approach which radically simplifies the specification of the reduplicative morpheme as either 'stem' or 'affix'. Recall the important observation made in section 5.1.2, that reduplicants tend to have unmarked prosodic structures. This is explained by making well-formedness constraints directly responsible for determining shapes of reduplicants. Accordingly, we must strip templates of any template-specific prosodic requirements, reducing them to a bare minimum and specifying them maximally as the morphological categories 'affix' or 'stem', differing from their non-reduplicative counterparts only in having no segmental input specification. Their prosodic shapes will then emerge from constraint interaction.

In the case of Diyari, all we need to state specifically for the reduplicant is that it equals a stem:

(54)   **RED=STEM**
         The reduplicant is a stem.

This is the only requirement specific to reduplication. It sets in motion a chain of effects, defining the prosodic shape of the reduplicant by interactions of prosodic constraints that are not specific to reduplication, but independently motivated in the Diyari stress system.

The reduplicant's stem status implies its PrWd status, mediated by undominated STEM=PRWD, a constraint requiring that a stem must equal a PrWd:

(55)   **STEM=PRWD**
         A stem equals a PrWd.

This is nothing but the minimal stem requirement of Diyari, independently motivated for non-reduplicative categories. Naturally the *reduplicant-as-a-stem* is automatically subject to any prosodic limitation that may hold for PrWd. Crucially, PrWd must be minimally a foot in size, due to the prosodic hierarchy, in which every PrWd is headed by a foot. This single-foot minimum translates as a *disyllabic minimum*, due to undominated FT-BIN. (Diyari has no contrast of syllable weight, hence feet are strictly disyllabic.)

We have now tracked the chain of effects which follow from a single requirement that the reduplicant is a stem, resulting in the prediction that the reduplicant is minimally disyllabic. However, the Diyari reduplicant is not only minimally disyllabic, but rather *exactly disyllabic*. Earlier theories of reduplication took this exact size to be an indication of its templatic nature, assuming a morphological template of the exact size of a metrical category, here a foot (Poser 1989). However, a more interesting approach is possible, as McCarthy and Prince (1994a, 1995a) demonstrate. The exact limitation of the reduplicant to a single foot follows from interactions of metrical constraints which are independently motivated for Diyari.

Observe that the single-foot reduplicant is in most ways *metrically perfect* since its single foot is aligned at both edges, while it has no unparsed syllables. Consider three candidate reduplicants for 'old woman' (53c), of two, three, and four syllables:

(56)   a. [(wí.la)]-
        b. [(wí.la).pi.]-
        c. [(wí.la).(pì.na)]-

The trisyllabic reduplicant (56b) is less harmonic than a disyllabic one (56a) in terms of PARSE-SYL. In a trisyllabic reduplicant, one syllable must remain unparsed since feet are strictly binary, while a disyllabic reduplicant can be exhaustively parsed by a single foot. Moreover, a four-syllable reduplicant (56c) is less harmonic than a disyllabic one. This is because to parse four syllables it takes two feet, one of which is necessarily misaligned at the left edge, violating ALL-FT-LEFT. We find that a disyllabic reduplicant approximates the metrically ideal PrWd, one exhaustively parsed by a single, perfectly aligned foot:

(57)   a. The reduplicant's foot is disyllabic (by FT-BIN)
        b. The reduplicant's syllables are exhaustively parsed (by PARSE-SYL)
        c. The reduplicant's foot is left-aligned, hence single-footed (by ALL-FT-L)

This is an *emergence of the unmarked* in the Diyari reduplicant. Its ideal disyllabic size, favoured by the sum of metrical constraints, is not attested in 'normal' non-reduplicative stems, which exceed disyllabicity in the case of trisyllabic or quadrisyllabic stems.

Correspondence in reduplication

Next we turn to the issue of what constraint interaction limits perfect disyllabicity to reduplicants, while leaving other stems free to surpass it. Non-reduplicant stems fail to undergo segment deletion in order to attain a perfect disyllabic size: IO-faithfulness takes precedence over metrical well-formedness. But for the reduplicant, priorities are reversed. Metrical well-formedness takes precedence over reduplicative identity, and as a result reduplication is partial, approaching the ideal metrical size. The schematic interaction is:

(58)   Emergence of the unmarked in Diyari reduplication
         Schema   Faithfulness ≫ Well-formedness   ≫ Reduplicative
                                                               identity
         Instantiation Max-IO   ≫ Metrical constraints ≫ Max-BR

The full hierarchy involves a ranking of all metrical well-formedness constraints. Some of these are in fact undominated (STEM=PRWD, FT-BIN), while others (PARSE-SYL, ALL-FT-LEFT) are dominated by segmental faithfulness (MAX-IO). At the bottom of the hierarchy we find MAX-BR, enforcing reduplicative identity.

(59)   Diyari disyllabic reduplication
         MAX-IO, RED=STEM, STEM=PRWD, FT-BIN ≫ PARSE-SYL ≫ ALL-FT-LEFT ≫ MAX-BR

This analysis is illustrated by the tableaux (60–1). We leave out any candidates violating undominated RED=STEM, focussing on the effects of the genuinely prosodic constraints. Tableau (60) shows reduplication of a trisyllabic stem.

(60)

Input: /RED + tʲilparku/	MAX-IO	STEM=PRWD	FT-BIN	PARSE-SYL	ALL-FT-LEFT	MAX-BR
a. ☞ [(tʲíl.pa)]-[(tʲíl.par).ku]				*		r, k, u
b. [(tʲíl.par).ku]-[(tʲíl.par).ku]				**!		
c. [(tʲí)]-[(tʲíl.par).ku]			*!	*		l,p,a,r,k,u
d. [(tʲí -tʲil).(pàr.ku)]		*!			σσ	l,p,a,r,k,u
e. [(tʲíl.pa)]-[(tʲíl.pa)]	r!,k,u					

Candidate (60e) deletes input segments, fatally violating MAX-IO. Next, candidate (60d) represents an attempt at prosodically integrating a monosyllabic reduplicant with the base at the expense of STEM=PRWD. Remaining candidates differ in the number of syllables in the reduplicant. A monosyllabic reduplicant (60c) fails on undominated FT-BIN, while a trisyllabic total reduplicant (60b) excessively violates PARSE-SYL. Therefore disyllabic reduplication (60a) is optimal even though it has three violations of MAX-BR.[11]

Tableau (61) is yet another illustration of the same point with a subtle difference: an attempt at total reduplication (candidate 61b) now falls victim to ALL-FT-LEFT, instead of PARSE-SYL (as in the previous tableau).

(61)

Input: /RED + wilapina/	MAX-IO	STEM=PRWD	FT-BIN	PARSE-SYL	ALL-FT-LEFT	MAX-BR
a. ☞ [(wí.la)]-[(wí.la).(pì.na)]					σσ	p, i, n, a
b. [(wí.la).(pì.na)]-[(wí.la).(pì.na)]					σσσ!σ	
c. [(wí.la).pì .]-[(wí.la).(pì.na)]				*!	σσ	n, a
d. [(wí)]-[(wí.la).(pì.na)]			*!		σσ	l,a,p,i,n,a
e. [(wí.la)]-[(wí.la)]	p!i,n,a					

This analysis of Diyari has shown that 'unmarked' prosody in the shape and size of the reduplicant is indeed due to universal prosodic markedness constraints. But it takes *violable* constraints to reach this conclusion: the same universal markedness constraints which govern the reduplicant are massively violated in the non-reduplicative forms of the language. This is not an inconsistency, but simply reflects the differences in strength and scope of two sets of correspondence constraints: input–output and base–reduplicant.

In the next section, we will add a final ingredient to the analysis of reduplication: the constraints determining the position of the reduplicant.

5.4 From circumscription to alignment

5.4.1 *Infixing reduplication and prosodic circumscription*

The template-and-association theory of reduplication (Marantz 1982, McCarthy and Prince 1986) involves a strict separation between the morphological operation (the affixation of a prosodic template) and the phonological operation (the association of the segments of the base, subject to language-specific and universal principles). However, this separation of morphology and phonology causes a number of descriptive problems that turn out to undermine the very fundamentals of the theory.

---

[11] Observe that yet another candidate, [(tʲíl.par)]-[(tʲíl.par).ku], with the reduplicant ending in a closed syllable, is not given in (60). As we have shown in section 5.2.2.1 for Nootka, this candidate will be excluded by the ranking NO-CODA ≫ MAX-BR.

One problem involves 'internal' reduplication: in many languages the reduplicant is an affix to a 'prosodically circumscribed' part of the stem. For example, Samoan (Marsack 1962) prefixes the reduplicant to the *stress foot*:

(62)   Samoan (reduplicant is prefixed to the stress foot)
        a. fa.náu → fa-<u>na</u>-náu 'be born, give birth'
        b. a.lófa → a-<u>lo</u>-lófa 'love'

Timugon Murut (Prentice 1971) prefixes the reduplicant to a part of the stem that is *the residue of 'subtracting' its initial vowel* (or initial onsetless syllable):

(63)   Timugon Murut infixing reduplication: prefixation skips over stem-initial onsetless syllable
        a.i   bulud   → <u>bu</u>-bulud   'hill/ridge'
        a.ii tuluʔ   → <u>tu</u>-tuluʔ   'point at'
        a.iii dondoʔ → <u>do</u>-dondoʔ 'one'
        b.i   ulampoy → u-<u>la</u>-lampoy (no gloss)
        b.ii indimo → in-<u>di</u>-dimo 'fives times'
        b.iii ompod → om-<u>po</u> -pod 'flatter'

The fundamental analytic problem is this: in order to apply the 'morphological operation' (the prefixation of a template), some prosodic operation must first take place, establishing the 'base' of prefixation – its precise position internal to the stem. Development of the theory led to a skipping mechanism termed 'prosodic circumscription' (McCarthy and Prince 1990, 1995b). Circumscription places a cut in the stem at a prosodically defined position, either before or after a prosodic unit (or a segment, as in Timugon Murut), thus splitting the domain into two parts. Reduplication takes as its base one part ('positively' circumscribing the foot in Samoan, while 'negatively' circumscribing the initial vowel in Timugon Murut), and subsequently both parts are reunited, producing the 'infixation':

(64)   Circumscription analyses of Samoan and Timugon Murut infixing reduplication

Stem	fanáu	ulampoy
Circumscribe	{fa} {**náu**}$_{Ft}$	{**u**}$_V$ {lampoy}
Reduplicate (σ)	{fa} {<u>na</u>-náu}$_{Ft}$	{u}$_V$ {<u>la</u>-lampoy}
Reunite	fa-na-náu	u-la-lampoy

Technically speaking, prosodic circumscription saves the day. It produces a generalizing and ingenious analysis of internal reduplication, but that is where it ends. The analysis still fails to answer the fundamental question of *why a morphological operation should apply to the output of a prosodic operation*. Prosodic circumscription has no purpose but to serve the morphology with a base of reduplication.[12] Moreover, circumscription leaves the relation between the position of the infix and its status as a reduplicant unexplained. Consider, for example, the fact that in Timugon Murut infixation it is an initial *vowel* which is skipped rather than a consonant, a fact which should be related to the *perfect CV shape* of the reduplicant (it has an onset and lacks a coda). What we do not find, and will probably not find in any language, is the reverse pattern in which an initial consonant, but not an initial vowel, is skipped (*b-u-ulud*, *u-ulampoy*). The point is clear: circumscription helps to fulfil the requirements of prosody – yet this is totally unclear from the analysis: circumscription is principally unable to look ahead to the output of reduplication in order to locate the position of the cut.

McCarthy and Prince (1993a) observe another major defect of the circumscription analysis: it leaves unexpressed the cross-linguistic generalization that it is a *reduplicative* infix that skips over the initial vowel. The reduplicant is totally dependent on its base for its segmental content. Therefore an onset consonant must be copied from the base, which is exactly what circumscription accomplishes: it makes the reduplicant sit before a CV sequence in the base. But, in principle, the same circumscription analysis might have been employed for the infixation of a (hypothetical) *non-reduplicative* affix, for example, **-ka-**:

(65)   Hypothetical infixation
           a. bulud   → **ka**-bulud
           b. ulampoy → u-**ka**-lampoy

However, such patterns are remarkably absent from the world's languages. This can only be due to the fact that a fully specified affix is not segmentally dependent on its stem, and hence need not immediately precede a consonant in the stem. But circumscription theory is unable to make this connection, since it totally separates the circumscription operation from the morphological operation that it 'potentiates'.

> A circumscriptional analysis cannot explain why, in all known cases, it is always a *reduplicative* infix that skips over the initial onsetless syllable.
>
> (McCarthy and Prince 1993a: 126)

These problems turn out to be serious enough to warrant a new approach, one in which morphology and prosody apply 'in parallel' and in which *alignment* plays a central role. Such an approach is highly compatible with the organization of the grammar in OT, where prosodic constraints and morphological constraints are part of the same hierarchy. This approach will now be illustrated for infixing reduplication in Timugon Murut.

---

[12] Actually, circumscription saw various other ingenious applications in prosodic morphology (see McCarthy and Prince 1990, 1995b), which also are subject to the same general criticisms.

5.4.2 *Infixing reduplication and alignment*

Let us now consider the analysis of Timugon Murut infixing reduplication in OT. As we noted earlier, the interest of this pattern is that it is partly prefixing, and partly infixing. The reduplicant is a light syllable prefix located strictly at the beginning of the word if the base begins with a consonant (66a). But if the word begins with a vowel, the prefix becomes an infix, skipping over an initial onsetless syllable (66b):

(66)   Timugon Murut (repeated from 63)

        a. bulud   → <u>bu</u>-bulud   'hill/ridge'

        b. u.lampoy → u-<u>la</u>-lampoy (no gloss)

This initial-vowel-skipping reduplication pattern is fairly common cross-linguistically.

    McCarthy and Prince's analysis captures the following idea. The reduplicative infix sits initially in the word, except when prefixation would produce an onsetless reduplicant syllable, as in the case of a vowel-initial stem (67):

(67)   u-<u>la</u>-lampoy > *<u>u</u>-ulampoy (rejected due to extra violation of ONSET)

The basic constraint interaction is analogous to that of Tagalog -*um*-infixation, discussed in chapter 3, section 3.4.2. It involves domination of ONSET[13] over an 'edgemost' constraint requiring that the reduplicant be left-aligned in the word:

(68)   **ALIGN-RED-L**

        Align the left edge of the reduplicant with the left edge of the PrWd.

This interaction is illustrated by tableau (69), which also presents a third candidate (69c), showing the activity of ALIGN-RED-L in keeping the infix 'leftmost' in the word:

(69)

Input: /RED, ulampoy/	ONSET	ALIGN-RED-L
a. ☞ u-<u>la</u>-lampoy	*	u
b. <u>u</u>-ulampoy	**!	
c. ulam-<u>po</u>-poy	*	ul!am

The reduplicative *prefix* becomes an *infix* because of a high-ranking prosodic constraint. Even if the prefix cannot be a genuine prefix, it still locates itself as

---

[13] Undominated input faithfulness constraints, DEP-IO and MAX-IO, block consonant epenthesis and vowel deletion as strategies to avoid onset-less syllables.

close as possible to the left edge, which is what makes (69a) more harmonic than (69c).

This finishes the core of the analysis. Its success (as compared to circumscription) is due to two factors. First, the fact that 'prosody' and 'morphology' operate *in parallel*, rather than serially. The position of the infix ('morphology') depends on the relative prosodic well-formedness of the output. The second key feature of this analysis is the violability of constraints. The requirement that the 'reduplicant is a prefix' (ALIGN-RED-L) is violable precisely to the extent necessary to avoid violation of prosodic well-formedness (ONSET).

There are some residual issues, to which we now turn. Consider another logically possible strategy to avoid excessive violation of ONSET, while keeping the reduplicative affix strictly initial in the word. This strategy is to copy yet another segment of the base, producing the candidate **ul-ulampoy*. It may appear that this is a genuine improvement over *u-la-lampoy*: both have one onset-less syllable, but the former is a perfect prefix, while the latter is a near miss. Then what excludes **ul-ulampoy*? Observe that the single 'improvement' of **ul-ulampoy* over **u-ulampoy* resides in its lesser violation of ONSET, due to its additional onset consonant [l]. But in order to make this [l] a genuine onset, it must syllabify 'into' the base, thereby blurring the edge between reduplicant and base.

(70)   u-la-lampoy > *u.l-u.lampoy (rejected due to violation of RED=σ)

This violates the undominated templatic alignment constraint RED=σ:

(71)   **RED=σ**
         Align both edges of the reduplicant with the edges of a syllable.

This is an example of a templatic alignment constraint.[14] It actually fulfils two functions. It enforces the alignment of the reduplicant with a syllable, and it also restricts the size of the reduplicant to a single syllable. We assume gradient evaluation for RED=σ, with one violation for each segment exceeding the strict syllable-size of the reduplicant.

The interaction is shown in tableau (72), where violations of both constraints are marked by the offending segments:

(72)

Input: /RED, ulampoy/	RED=σ	ALIGN-RED-L
a. ☞ u-la-lampoy		u
b. u.l-u.lampoy	l!	

---

[14] We leave open the consequences of adopting this constraint for Generalized Template theory.

As noted above, apart from its alignment function, RED=σ is also responsible for the size limitation of the reduplicant to one syllable. Therefore it must dominate MAX-BR, ruling out output forms such as *u-*lam.poy-lam.poy*.

Let us now turn to the interaction between IO-faithfulness constraints and syllabic well-formedness constraints. Timugon Murut disallows consonant epenthesis and vowel deletion as strategies to 'repair' onset-less or closed syllables. From this we conclude that faithfulness (DEP-IO, MAX-IO) dominates prosodic well-formedness (ONSET, NO-CODA):

(73)

Input: /ulampoy/	DEP-IO	MAX-IO	ONSET	NO-CODA
a. ☞ u.lam.poy			*	**
b. lam.poy		*!		**
c. u.la.po		*!*	*	
d. Tu.lam.poy	*!			**
e. u.la.mA.po.yA	*!*		*	

It thus appears that reduplicative infixation in Timugon Murut is yet another *emergence of the unmarked*: markedness constraints that are 'normally' invisible in the phonology of the language suddenly jump into full activity in situations where input faithfulness is not at stake.[15]

There is independent evidence from reduplication for the activity of NO-CODA, a constraint whose effects are 'normally' suppressed by faithfulness. The infix is always of the shape CV, even though a closed syllable would no doubt be preferable on MAX-BR:

(74)   u-<u>la</u>-lampoy $>$ *u-<u>lam</u>-lampoy (rejected due to violation of NO-CODA)

Therefore NO-CODA must dominate MAX-BR.

Let us now put all pieces together, and consider the complete analysis. We have evidence for three undominated constraints: RED=σ, DEP-IO, MAX-IO. These dominate a pair of syllable well-formedness constraints: ONSET and NO-CODA, which in their turn dominate two reduplicative constraints: ALIGN-RED-L and MAX-BR:

---

[15] In fact, one input faithfulness constraint is violated under infixation: CONTIGUITY-IO.

(75)   RED=σ, DEP-IO, MAX-IO ≫ ONSET, NO-CODA ≫ ALIGN-RED-L,
         MAX-BR

This total ranking is illustrated by the tableau of [u-la-lam.poy]:

(76)

Input: /RED, ulampoy/	RED=σ	DEP-IO	MAX-IO	ONSET	NO-CODA	ALIGN-RED-L	MAX-BR
a. ☞ u-la-lam.poy				*	**	u	mpoy
b. u-lam-lam.poy				*	***!	u	poy
c. u-u.lam.poy				**!	**		lampoy
d. ul.-u.lam.poy				**!	***		ampoy
e. la-lam.poy			*!		**		mpoy
f. Tu-Tu.lam.poy		*!			**		lampoy
g. u.l-u.lam.poy	l!			*	**		ampoy
h. u-lam.poy-lam.poy	p!oy			*	****	u	

Finally, reconsider the serial analysis of this pattern presented in section 5.4.1, which was based on the circumscription of the initial vowel and prefixation of the reduplicant to the residue of the base. We ended section 5.4.1 by reflecting on the observation, due to McCarthy and Prince (1993a), that a circumscriptional analysis is principally unable to explain why it is always a *reduplicative* infix that skips over the initial onset-less syllable.

Now observe that an OT analyis *does* make this prediction, for nothing would be gained (over simple prefixation) by the infixation of a segmentally specified prefix /ka-/. Both of the output candidates forms below have one violation of the constraint ONSET:

(77)   **ka**-u.lam.poy > u-**ka**-lam.poy

Hence the choice is automatically made in favour of the optimally aligned prefixation candidate. (We leave it to the reader to work out the details in a tableau.)

5.5 'Classical' versus OT-based prosodic morphology: conclusions
The following overview sums up the major differences, discussed in the preceding sections, between 'classical' and OT-based prosodic morphology:

(78)　　　　　Classical prosodic morphology　　OT-based prosodic
　　　　　　　　　　　　　　　　　　　　　　　　　　morphology

　　　　　a. Templates have fixed prosodic shapes. Templates emerge from
　　　　　　　　　　　　　　　　　　　　　　　　　　interactions.
　　　　　b. Prosodic circumscription of domains. Violable alignment
　　　　　　　　　　　　　　　　　　　　　　　　　　constraints.
　　　　　c. Serialism: morphology $\rightarrow$ prosody.　Parallelism: prosody $\gg$
　　　　　　　　　　　　　　　　　　　　　　　　　　morphology.

The modifications of the classical theory of prosodic morphology are integrated
into the revised version of the principles of prosodic morphology:

(79)　　　　New prosodic morphology (McCarthy and Prince 1993b: 138)
　　　　　a. **Prosodic Morphology Hypothesis**
　　　　　　　Templates are constraints on the prosody/morphology inter-
　　　　　　　face, asserting the coincidence of morphological and prosodic
　　　　　　　constituents.
　　　　　b. **Template Satisfaction Condition**
　　　　　　　Templatic constraints may be undominated, in which case they
　　　　　　　are satisfied fully, or they may be dominated, in which case they
　　　　　　　are violated minimally, in accordance with general principles of
　　　　　　　Optimality Theory.
　　　　　c. **Ranking Schema**
　　　　　　　P $\gg$ M

In the following sections, we will discuss further evidence that lends support to
the OT-based theory of reduplication. We will first turn to another central theme
of research in reduplication theory, 'overapplication' and 'underapplication'.

5.6　Overapplication and underapplication in reduplication

5.6.1　*Introduction*

As we saw in previous sections, the basic idea behind the OT model of reduplication is that reduplicative identity constraints compete with well-formedness
constraints; within the same form, well-formedness constraints compete with
input-faithfulness constraints. Both two-way interactions are summed up below:

(80)　　　a. Well-formedness $\Leftrightarrow$ Base–Reduplicant Identity
　　　　　b. Well-formedness $\Leftrightarrow$ Input–Output Faithfulness

The most complex interaction combining all these ingredients that we have seen thus far is the 'emergence of the unmarked':

(81)   IO-Faithfulness ≫ Well-formedness ≫ BR-Identity

But this interaction does not exhaust the possibilities of the Correspondence Theory of reduplication. Simple reranking predicts that reduplicative identity may be *promoted* to a position in the hierarchy where it produces a more complete identity between the base and reduplicant than we have seen until here. Particularly, high-ranked base–reduplicant identity may cause the transfer of context-sensitive phonological properties of the base to the reduplicant. Such effects are known as 'overapplication' and 'underapplication', and in this section we will discuss their analysis by McCarthy and Prince (1995a, forthcoming).

The basis of the OT model of overapplication and underapplication resides in an observation by Wilbur (1973: 58):

(82)   **The Identity Constraint**
         There is a tendency to preserve the identity of R_o and R_r in reduplicated forms.

The function of overapplication and underapplication is to make the relation between the base and the reduplicant more 'transparent' (see Anderson 1975 for an earlier statement of this idea). Before we turn to actual cases of overapplication and underapplication, we first consider a case of 'normal' application.

5.6.2   *Normal application in Washo*

An example of 'normal' application of phonology to the base and reduplicant comes from reduplication in Washo (Jacobsen 1964), which is discussed in Wilbur (1973):

(83)   Normal application of coda devoicing in Washo
         a.   /RED + wis-i/   wi̱s̱-wi.si   'it's squeaking'
         b.i   /RED + wed-i/   we̱ṯ-we.di   'it's quacking'
         b.ii /RED + bag-i/   ba̱ḵ-ba.gi   'he's smoking'
         b.iii /RED + šub-i/   šu̱p̱ -šu.bi   'he's crying gently'

The reduplicant prefix, a heavy syllable, copies the first CVC string from the base. Note that if the base contains a voiced obstruent, this appears as voiceless in the reduplicant. This is due to the familiar process of coda devoicing, which applies generally in Washo. In contrast, the intervocalic obstruent in the base reflects its input status, unhampered by coda devoicing. The result is featural non-identity for [voice] between the corresponding segments in the reduplicant and the base.

The Washo pattern of 'normal' application follows naturally from the interaction of the following three constraints:

(84)   ***Voiced-Coda**
No voiced coda.

(85)   **Ident-IO**(voice)
Let α be a segment in I, and β be a correspondent of α in O.
If α is [γvoice], then β is [γvoice].

(86)   **Ident-BR**(voice)
Let α be a segment in B, and β be a correspondent of α in R.
If α is [γvoice], then β is [γvoice].

Because Washo has 'normal' coda devoicing outside reduplication, *Voiced-Coda must dominate Ident-IO(voice). But in its turn, Ident-IO(voice) must dominate Ident-BR(voice). Loss of identity between the reduplicant's coda consonant and its correspondent, the intervocalic base consonant, is less important than the preservation of the input value of [voice]. This can be inferred from the following harmonic relation:

(87)   <u>wet</u>-we.di > <u>wet</u>-we.ti Hence Ident-IO(voice) ≫ Ident-BR(voice)

Base–reduplicant identity is sacrificed for the preservation of input voice. In principle, the outcome might have been different (with devoicing 'overapplying' to the consonant in the base, to render it identical to the coda consonant in the reduplicant). (Actually, we will come across such 'reduplicant-to-base backcopying' cases later in this chapter.)

Adding these rankings up, we find:

(88)   Normal application of coda devoicing in Washo reduplication
*Voiced-Coda ≫ Ident-IO(voice) ≫ Ident-BR(voice)

The following tableau illustrates 'normal' application of coda devoicing in Washo:

(89)

Input: /RED + wed-i/	*Voiced-Coda	Ident-IO (voice)	Ident-BR (voice)
a. ☞ <u>wet</u>-we.di			*
b. <u>wet</u>-we.ti		*!	
c. <u>wed</u>-we.di	*!		

In sum, the 'normal' application of phonology in the reduplicant is due to the dominated position of a base–reduplicant identity constraint below both input-faithfulness and well-formedness.

(90)   Ranking schema for normal application

Well-formedness $\gg$ IO-Faithfulness $\gg$ BR-Identity

Let us now turn to overapplication and find out about the ranking schema underlying this phenomenon.

5.6.3 *Overapplication in Malay*

Wilbur defines overapplication as follows: the reduplicant undergoes some phonological process even though it fails to meet the structural condition. That is, 'a rule applies in the "wrong" environment'.

A spectacular example of overapplication of phonology in reduplication comes from Malay (Onn 1976, Kenstowicz 1981, McCarthy and Prince 1995a, forthcoming). Malay has a complementary ('allophonic') distribution of oral and nasal vocoids (vowels and semivowels). When a word contains a nasal consonant, all vocoids that follow this nasal are also nasalized. Vocoids that are not in post-nasal position are always oral, with one exception: in reduplications nasal harmony overapplies, as shown in the vocoids that are underlined in (91).

(91)   Overapplication in Malay nasal harmony[16]

	Stem		Reduplicated	
a.i	hamɔ̃	'germ'	a.ii	hãmɔ̃-hãmɔ̃	'germs'
b.i	waɲĩ	'fragrant'	b.ii	w̃ãɲĩ-w̃ãɲĩ	(intensified)
c.i	aŋãn	'reverie'	c.ii	ãŋãn-ãŋãn	'ambition'
d.i	aŋẽn	'wind'	d.ii	ãŋẽn-ãŋẽn	'unconfirmed news'

Nasality in the underlined vocoids cannot have 'normal' spreading as its source, as nasal harmony applies exclusively rightwards. This a clear example of a phonological process overapplying to establish complete featural identity between the reduplicant and the base. Observe that reduplicant and base are featurally identical; for this reason it is impossible to identify the initial or final elements as either the 'reduplicant' or 'base'. However, the identification of the reduplicant is irrelevant to the argument: all that matters is that these are reduplicated forms, while nasal harmony overapplies exclusively in this context.

---

[16] Nasality is transcribed in glides by McCarthy and Prince (1995a), but not by Onn (1976), the source.

Which constraints are involved? Let us first take a look at the mechanism that is responsible for the complementary (allophonic) distribution of oral and nasal vocoids: nasal vocoids occur in post-nasal position, and oral vocoids elsewhere. This we recognize as a typical case of complete dominance of markedness constraints with respect to [nasal] over IO-faithfulness: see chapter 1, section 1.5.2. Two markedness constraints govern the distribution of [nasal]. The first is context-sensitive, and it excludes a sequence of a nasal and an oral vocoid, see (92).

(92) $*NV_{ORAL}$
         *[nas]⌢[−nas, vocalic]

This is undominated in Malay: no oral vocoids ever follow a nasal in the same word.

The second constraint active here is a context-free markedness constraint that excludes nasal vocoids:

(93) $*V_{NASAL}$
         No nasal vocoids.

Obviously, $*V_{NASAL}$ is dominated by $*NV_{ORAL}$ in Malay, since nasal vocoids *do occur* – but *only in post-nasal contexts*, precisely where they are required by $*NV_{ORAL}$.

Recall from chapter 1 that a complementary distribution points to the dominance of markedness constraints over IO-faithfulness constraints. Here the relevant faithfulness constraint is:

(94)   **IDENT-IO**(nasal)
         Let α be a segment in I, and β be a correspondent of α in O.
         If α is [γnasal], then β is [γnasal].

When this is dominated by both markedness constraints governing nasality, the outcome will be that input values of [nasal] in vocoids are totally irrelevant to their output values. That is, whatever the lexical specification of [nasal] in a vocoid may be, its surface value only reflects markedness constraints. (Naturally the language learner is never tempted to posit lexical values of [nasal] that are irrecoverable from the surface evidence; this is 'Lexicon Optimization' or 'Stampean occultation'; see again chapter 1.)

These remarks lead us to the following ranking:

(95)   Nasal harmony in Malay
         $*NV_{ORAL} \gg *V_{NASAL} \gg$ IDENT-IO(nasal)

Two tableaux of the same non-reduplicated form [waɲĩ] (differing in input specification for the feature [nasal] in vocoids) serve to demonstrate the irrelevance of the input. First consider tableau (96), which takes as its input a form /waɲĩ/ that is actually identical to the surface form:

(96)

Input: /waŋĩ/	*NV$_{\text{ORAL}}$	*V$_{\text{NASAL}}$	IDENT-IO(nasal)
a. ☞ waŋĩ		*	
b. w̃ãŋĩ		**!*	**
c. waŋɪ	*!		*

The outcome would have been precisely the same if one or both vocoids had had different input values for [nasal], for example the reverse pattern /w̃ãŋɪ/:

(97)

Input: /w̃ãŋɪ/	*NV$_{\text{ORAL}}$	*V$_{\text{NASAL}}$	IDENT-IO(nasal)
a. ☞ waŋĩ		*	***
b. w̃ãŋĩ		**!*	*
c. waŋɪ	*!		**

This analysis of the nasal harmony pattern serves as a necessary preparation for the analysis of overapplication in reduplication, which is our genuine interest in Malay. Recall that reduplicant and base are *always* featurally identical, even though the context of nasalization is not met by the reduplicant. All we need to do to capture this identity of base and reduplicant is rank IDENT-BR(nasal) at the top of the hierarchy, next to *NV$_{\text{ORAL}}$:

(98)   Overapplication of nasal harmony in Malay
        IDENT-BR(nasal), *NV$_{\text{ORAL}}$ ≫ *V$_{\text{NASAL}}$ ≫ IDENT-IO(nasal)

This ranking captures the basic nature of overapplication: a well-formedness constraint at the top of the hierarchy, *NV$_{\text{ORAL}}$, is 'amplified' by a reduplicative identity constraint, IDENT-BR(nasal), which carries its effects over to the reduplicant. The overapplication of nasal harmony occurs at the expense of additional violations of *V$_{\text{NASAL}}$:

(99)   w̃ãŋĩ$_{\text{R}}$-w̃ãŋĩ$_{\text{B}}$ > waŋĩ$_{\text{R}}$-w̃ãŋĩ$_{\text{B}}$

The nasalization of the initial vocoids [w̃ã] in the *base* is due to their post-nasal position (with the triggering nasal as part of the reduplicant), that is, to 'normal' nasal harmony. The same holds for the last vowel in the reduplicant. But things are different for the initial vocoids [w̃ã] of the *reduplicant*: being in word-initial position, these vocoids are *outside the scope of 'normal' nasal harmony*. They do 'undergo' nasalization, however, in order to retain featural identity with their nasalized correspondents [w̃ã] in the base.

Let us now turn to the constraint-based evaluation of some output candidates for the reduplicated form of /waŋĭ/. The primary contestors of the optimal candidate (100a) are [waŋĭ -waŋĭ] (100b), which preserves reduplicative identity by 'underapplying' nasal harmony, and [waŋĭ-w̃ãŋĭ] (100c), which would be the output of 'normal' application:

(100)

Input: /RED + waŋĭ/	IDENT-BR (nasal)	*NV$_{ORAL}$	*V$_{NASAL}$	IDENT-IO (nasal)
a. ☞ w̃ãŋĭ -w̃ãŋĭ			******	**
b. waŋĭ -waŋĭ		*!*	**	
c. waŋĭ -w̃ãŋĭ	*!*		****	**

First, candidate (100b) preserves reduplicative identity at the expense of *NV$_{ORAL}$, which is directly fatal. This is the 'underapplication' candidate: an attempt to establish identity by overriding the application of nasal harmony where it should have applied. However, the undominated position of the constraint enforcing nasal harmony (*NV$_{ORAL}$) precludes this attempt. (It may seem that underapplication effects can be simply derived from the promotion of IO-faithfulness over a phonological constraint; however, matters are not so simple, as we will see below.)

Second, the *normal application* candidate (100c) is doomed because it establishes 'normalcy' at the expense of base–reduplicant identity. This is fatal, due to undominated IDENT-BR(nasal).

Recall that due to the complete featural identity of the reduplicant and base, it is actually impossible to tell the reduplicant and base apart. So far we have been assuming that reduplication is prefixation, but in fact it might just as well be *suffixation*. In what respect would the analysis become different if the reduplicant were suffixed to the base? The answer is: surprisingly little. This is due not so much to the markedness constraints, whose evaluation is blind to notions such as base and reduplicant (and registers violations to both equally alike), but to the correspondence constraints.

First, observe that evaluations by IDENT-BR(nasal) are unaffected by the different analysis into reduplicant + base: its violations remain the same, regardless of what strings are taken as reduplicant and base. Second, in principle at least, the identification of the base is relevant to IDENT-IO(nasal), since only base segments are subject to faithfulness. But we have just seen that this constraint is ranked low enough never to be of relevance to the nasal harmony pattern. Hence the 'suffixation' tableau in (101) is identical to the 'prefixation' tableau (100) in all relevant aspects. The single (irrelevant) difference is the evaluation by IDENT-IO(nasal).

(101)

Input: /waŋĩ + RED/	IDENT-BR (nasal)	*NV$_{ORAL}$	*V$_{NASAL}$	IDENT-IO (nasal)
a. ☞ w̃ãŋĩ-w̃ãŋĩ			******	**
b. waŋĩ-waŋĩ		*!*	**	
c. waŋĩ-w̃ãŋĩ	*!*		****	

Note that if prefixation were actually suffixation, then Malay nasal harmony would be an *overapplication of phonology to the **base***, rather than to the reduplicant. The fact that this effect easily falls out of constraint interaction initially seems a liability of the parallel OT model, rather than a strength. Does not this parallel model predict languages in which a phonological property is 'back-copied' from the reduplicant onto the base? The answer is simple: this is an empirical issue. There is no a priori reason to assume that back-copying does not occur in the languages of the world. (It is actually attested, as we will see below for Southern Paiute.)[17]

Let us now draw conclusions from the discussion of Malay. First, we have found strong evidence for the role of base–reduplicant identity, hence for the notion of 'output-to-output correspondence', which is deeply parallel. Perhaps this argument gains in depth if we compare the analysis with a serial analysis. McCarthy and Prince (1995a, forthcoming) point out that the Malay pattern poses severe problems for a serial theory, in which the surface identity of reduplicant and base is due to a 'copy' rule. This copies the segmental content of the base onto the reduplicant. Now consider an analysis of [w̃ãŋĩ-w̃ãŋĩ] in which the reduplicant is a prefix.[18] The nasalization of the initial segments [w̃ã] in the reduplicant can only be understood as being due to the copy rule, as these segments are not in the proper context for nasalization. (They do not follow a nasal consonant.) The string [w̃ã] must therefore be copied from the nasalized base segments [w̃ã], which, at that point in the derivation, must already have been nasalized. From this it follows that *the copy rule must apply after the rule of nasalization*. This is what it means for a rule to 'overapply' in serial theory: the effects of a phonological rule in the base are copied onto the reduplicant. But there is a snag: nasalization of base segments [w̃ã] is itself triggered by a preceding nasal – but the base itself

---

[17] A precursor of the correspondence analysis of back-copying effects can be found in Russell (1993).

[18] The problems posed to serial theory by a *suffixing* analysis of Malay reduplication are even more severe, as this involves 'back-copying' onto the base. However, since there is no way of knowing which analysis (prefixing or suffixing) is correct, it is only fair to base an argument on the prefix analysis. In section 5.6.5 we will look into a clear case of 'back-copying'.

contains none! The trigger of nasalization in the base can only be the preceding nasal segment [ŋ], which is part of the reduplicant. There is a paradox: by its very nature, a reduplicant segment is a result of the copy rule. Hence *the copy rule must also precede nasalization*. This mutual dependence of reduplicant and base is shown by arrows in the diagram in (102):

(102)　　　- - - - - - - -> [ŋ] in reduplicant induces nasalization of initial base
　　　　　　　　　　　　segments

　　　　　w̃ãŋĩ + w̃ãŋĩ

　　　　　<- - - - - - - - nasalized portion [w̃ã] of base copied to reduplicant

This two-sided information flow requires a complex rule ordering in which the 'copy' rule applies twice in the derivation: once before nasalization, and once after it:

(103)　　　Underlying form　　/RED　+ waŋɪ/
　　　　　　　Copy　　　　　　waŋɪ + waŋɪ
　　　　　　　Nasalization　　waŋɪ̃ + w̃ãŋĩ
　　　　　　　Copy　　　　　　w̃ãŋĩ + w̃ãŋĩ
　　　　　　　Surface form　　[w̃ãŋĩ + w̃ãŋĩ]

The basic claim of derivational theory is that rules apply in a strict linear order. Hence, a reapplication of a rule in a single derivation (within a single domain) should be allowed under extremely limited circumstances only. More specifically, it has been proposed (see Myers 1991) that some rules reapply whenever their structural description is met.[19] If the Malay *copy* rule belongs to this class of *persistent rules*, then what exactly does it mean for it to apply 'whenever its structural description is met'? McCarthy and Prince argue that the only reasonable interpretation is: 'whenever base and reduplicant are non-identical', which is, of course, a condition on the *surface identity* of the base and reduplicant, or an 'output-to-output' correspondence constraint in disguise.

The second result of the preceding section is a (preliminary) ranking schema for overapplication. The core property of overapplication, as compared to normal application (90), is this: a reduplicative identity constraint is promoted to an undominated position:

(104)　　　Ranking schema for overapplication
　　　　　　　BR-Identity, Well-formedness ≫ IO-Faithfulness

---

[19] The standard example of a persistent rule is 'resyllabification', which reapplies after every rule that affects syllable structure.

Let us now evaluate this schema in a broader typological context. As has been emphasized at various points in this book, a highly suitable way to assess overall typological predictions of the theory is to construct a factorial typology by permutation of constraint rankings. The central claim of the Basic Model of Correspondence Theory is that reduplication patterns depend on interactions of three constraint types: well-formedness, BR-identity, and IO-faithfulness. We have now seen the following three ranking schemata (repeated from 43, 90, and 104 above):

(105)   a. Ranking schema for emergence of the unmarked
            IO-Faithfulness ≫ Well-formedness ≫ BR-Identity
         b. Ranking schema for normal application
            Well-formedness ≫ IO-Faithfulness ≫ BR-Identity
         c. Ranking schema for overapplication
            BR-Identity, Well-formedness ≫ IO-Faithfulness

What we see is a progressively lowered position of IO-faithfulness in the hierarchy from (105a) to (105c). To complete this factorial typology, we will now add the case of total domination of well-formedness by IO-faithfulness and BR-identity, which is stated in (105d) as 'total non-application':

(105)   d. Ranking schema for total non-application
            IO-Faithfulness, BR-Identity ≫ Well-formedness

This ranking prohibits any changes potentially 'triggered' by well-formedness in either the base or reduplicant. The base must be faithful to its input due to IO-faithfulness ≫ well-formedness, while the reduplicant copies this unmodified input shape due to BR-identity ≫ well-formedness. This case is hardly interesting, as it involves no phonology 'at work' at all, hence we did not discuss it previously. Yet, it is instantiated in every case in which lexical contrasts are preserved in the base, as well as copied to the reduplicant.

Let us now return to the issue of underapplication. So far, McCarthy and Prince's Basic Model has been able to accommodate normal application and overapplication. It may seem that the factorial typology has exhausted all logical possibilities, among which we did not identify underapplication. This conclusion comes as a mild shock: how does the Basic Model deal with underapplication? This issue will occupy us in the next section.

5.6.4 *Underapplication in Japanese*

Wilbur (1973) defines underapplication as the non-application of a phonological process in the reduplicant even though this meets the structural condition. That is, 'a rule fails to apply in the "right" environment'.

Before looking into an actual case of underapplication, let us see if we can define its general properties in terms of the Basic Model. First, some process must be blocked in a context *in which it normally applies*. The fact that the process normally applies in non-reduplication contexts implies that well-formedness outranks IO-faithfulness. (Under the reverse ranking IO-faithfulness would simply *always* block the process.) Second, the fact that underapplication is reduplication-specific makes it an identity effect: its analysis will therefore involve high-ranked base–reduplicant identity. To our surprise, we find that the combined rankings result, once again, in the ranking schema of *overapplication*, stated in (104). To distinguish overapplication from underapplication, we need something extra. This 'something extra' is another constraint that has the effect of *blocking* the change, and must be an antagonist of the well-formedness constraint that *triggers* the change:

(106)   Ranking schema for underapplication
          BR-Identity, **B**locker-constraint ≫ **T**rigger-constraint ≫
          IO-Faithfulness

Are we on the right track? In fact, this general argument seems to produce nothing but a fatal inconsistency: since how can a change *ever* apply, if the constraint that triggers it is itself dominated by a constraint blocking the change?

The answer takes into account the fact that the relevant segments appear *twice* in a base–reduplicant combination: once in the base, and once in the reduplicant. Moreover, the phonological contexts in which these correspondents occur are typically different. For example, let us assume that one segment (of a pair of correspondents) is in a 'blocking' context, while its counterpart is in a 'triggering' context. By top-ranking BR-identity, the correspondents in reduplicant and base must be identical. In such a situation, whichever segment wins can only depend on the 'push–pull' of the blocker- and trigger-constraints. Therefore, in underapplication there is an undominated constraint blocking the change in *either the base, or the reduplicant*. If this argument sounds too abstract, we will now make it more concrete step by step in the analysis of an actual underapplication case.

An example of underapplication due to an undominated blocker-constraint is the pattern of 'reduplicated mimetics' in Japanese (Mester and Itô 1989, McCarthy and Prince 1995a, forthcoming). Japanese has a general phonological process by which [g] alternates with [ŋ], depending on position in the word. In fact these segments are allophones, since they are in complementary distribution. What is relevant here is that [g] occurs word-initially, while [ŋ] occurs medially:

(107)   Complementary distribution of [g], [ŋ] in Japanese

	#g			VŋV	
a.i	geta	'clogs'	b.i	kaɲi	'key'
a.ii	giri	'duty'	b.ii	oyuɲu	'to swim'
a.iii	gai-koku	'foreign country'	b.iii	koku-ɲai	'abroad'

McCarthy and Prince (1995a, forthcoming) argue that the alternations are triggered by two phonotactic well-formedness constraints. The first rules out a voiced velar oral stop:

(108)   **PostVcls**
         No voiced velar oral stops.

This registers as a markedness constraint the effects of a property of articulation: voicing is difficult to maintain in an oral velar stop, due to the limited size of the oral cavity (Ohala 1983, Vance 1987). In order to maintain voicing, air will be let out of the nasal cavity, with as a result a velar nasal. Indeed languages occur that have voiced oral stops [b] and [d], but not [g] (an example is Dutch). This is the 'trigger-constraint', producing the impetus for nasalization of [g] into [ŋ] to occur. PostVcls is essentially a *context-free* markedness constraint (in spite of its name, suggesting some post-vocalic context).

The second markedness constraint involved in the allophonic pattern rules out word-initial velar nasals:

(109)   *[ŋ
         No word-initial velar nasals.

The fact that [g] occurs word-initially in Japanese, shows that *[ŋ dominates PostVcls. Moreover, IO-faithfulness with respect to the feature [nasal] is totally dominated by these phonotactic constraints, since the pattern is totally predictable (allophonic).

(110)   Allophonic variation of [g] and [ŋ] in Japanese
         Blocker-constraint ≫ Trigger-constraint ≫ IO-Faithfulness
         *[ŋ   ≫ PostVcls   ≫ Ident-IO(nasal)

This is just another instantiation of the allophonic ranking schema of chapter 1. But it also instantiates a part of the ranking schema (106), containing the configuration of a blocker-constraint, a trigger-constraint, and IO-faithfulness. (We will turn to identity effects in reduplication shortly.) This interaction is illustrated by two tableaux:

(111)

Input: /gara/	*[ŋ	POSTVCLS	IDENT-IO(nasal)
a. ☞ gara		*	
b. ŋara	*!		*

(112)

Input: /kagi/	*[ŋ	POSTVCLS	IDENT-IO(nasal)
a. kagi		*!	
b. ☞ kaŋi			*

In these tableaux, both velars are attributed to an input oral stop [g]. But in fact, there is no evidence for this, and the presence of [g] or [ŋ] in the input is totally irrelevant. (The tableaux would remain essentially the same if the inputs had been /ŋara/ and /kaŋi/, with only some irrelevant changes of violation marks in the IO-faithfulness column.)

Let us now turn to reduplication. Voiced velar stop nasalization underapplies in reduplicated mimetics, where both the base and the reduplicant have the voiced stop [g], rather than the nasal [ŋ]. Consider the examples in (113):

(113)   Underapplication of voiced velar stop nasalization in reduplicated mimetics
a. gara-gara 'rattle'   (*gara-ŋara, *ŋara-ŋara)
b. geji-geji 'centipede'   (*geji-ŋeji, *ŋeji-ŋeji)
c. gera-gera 'laughing'   (*gera-ŋera, *ŋera-ŋera)

With 'normal' application of voiced velar stop nasalization, we would have expected *[gara-ŋara]. With 'overapplication', we would have expected *[ŋara-ŋara]. Since there is no evidence for oral or nasal stops in the input, pattern (113) may equally well be considered an overapplication of initial velar stop denasalization, or an underapplication of velar stop nasalization. This does not affect the argument, though, because the pattern involves all ingredients that are characteristic of the underapplication schema (106). In sum, we have an interaction of the following four constraint types:

(114)   a. BR-Identity: IDENT-BR(nasal)
b. Blocker-constraint: *[ŋ
c. Trigger-constraint: POSTVCLS
d. IO-faithfulness: IDENT-IO(nasal)

We have just seen a partial ranking in (110) of all constraints except BR-identity. Arguably it is BR-identity that makes voiced velar stop nasalization underapply in medial position in reduplicated mimetics. In (115), the sources of both occurrences of [g] in [gara-gara] are attributed to their respective sources.

(115)   [g] due to IDENT-BR(nasal) ≫ PostVcLs
              |
        gara-gara
              |
        [g] due to *[ŋ ≫ PostVcLs

Accordingly we add the factor of BR-identity to the analysis, in the form of undominated IDENT-BR(nasal). The four constraints in (114) are then ranked according to the schema of underapplication (106):

(116)   Ranking for underapplication of voiced velar stop nasalization in Japanese

         BR-Identity,   Blocker- ≫ Trigger- ≫ IO-Faithfulness
                         constraint   constraint

         IDENT-BR(nasal), *[ŋ   ≫ PostVcLs ≫ IDENT-IO(nasal)

This ranking is illustrated by the following tableau:

(117)

Input: /gara + RED/	IDENT-BR (nasal)	*[ŋ	PostVcLs	IDENT-IO (nasal)
a. ☞ gara-gara			**	
b. ŋara-ŋara		*!		*
c. gara-ŋara	*!		*	

The 'normal application' candidate (117c) fatally violates IDENT-BR(nasal), while the 'overapplication' candidate (117b) suffers from a word-initial [ŋ], fatally violating *[ŋ. Satisfaction of both high-ranked constraints happens at the expense of a double violation of PostVcLs in the optimal candidate (117a), hence this is an 'underapplication'.

Now that we have identified pairs of well-formedness constraints to be relevant to underapplication, we must return to overapplication, and see how this finding relates to this case. In fact, the situation is completely symmetrical. The difference between an overapplication and an underapplication resides in the relative position of the blocker-constraint and the trigger-constraint. The resulting ranking schemata are given in (118):

(118)   a. Ranking schema for underapplication

BR-Identity, Blocker-constraint ≫ Trigger-constraint ≫
IO-Faithfulness

          b. Ranking schema for overapplication

BR-Identity, Trigger-constraint ≫ Blocker-constraint ≫
IO-Faithfulness

To show how the expanded overapplication schema (118b) subsumes the case of Malay, we repeat it below (from 98):

(119)   Overapplication of Malay nasalization in the expanded schema

BR-Identity,	Trigger-	≫	Blocker-	≫	IO-Faithfulness
	constraint		constraint		
IDENT-BR(nasal),	$*NV_{ORAL}$	≫	$*V_{NASAL}$	≫	IDENT-IO(nasal)

The ranking schemata (118) summarize the results of our discussion of overapplication and underapplication. As we have seen in the case of Japanese, it is sometimes not clear whether the 'special' behaviour of reduplicants with respect to phonological processes is to be referred to as 'overapplication' or 'underapplication'. Whenever the phonology involved has an allophonic character, both terms seem to fit equally well. However, it is not so much the terminology that matters, but the insights expressed by the analysis: the 'special' behaviour of reduplication is a kind of identity effect, and the correspondence model takes this identity effect to be the heart of the matter.

But the ultimate (and most dramatic) consequence of the output correspondence approach to reduplication is yet to be discussed: the case of back-copying of reduplicant phonology into the base. To this we will now turn.

5.6.5 *The case for parallelism: base copies reduplicant in Southern Paiute*

In all cases of reduplicative identity that were discussed until here, the overapplication or underapplication occurred in the reduplicant. However, nothing in the model predicts that this should be the case. If phonology may 'overapply' or 'underapply' because of BR-identity, then why not in the base? The clearest evidence for the parallel OT model of reduplication is that of BR-identity inducing an overapplication or underapplication in the *base*. This is what we will call 'reduplicative back-copying':

(120)   **Reduplicative back-copying**: the overapplication or underapplication of some process in the base, under pressure to preserve identity with the reduplicant.

The logic of the situation is identical to that of overapplication and underapplication in the reduplicant, which we have discussed until here: it is the preservation of identity of base and reduplicant that overrules a 'normal' application of some process. What makes a process 'overapply' or 'underapply' to the base, rather than the reduplicant, depends on the relative ranking of the 'blocker' and 'trigger' well-formedness constraints governing each of the correspondent's segments in the base and the reduplicant.

Back-copying effects from reduplicant to base seem to occur (upon preliminary analysis, at least) in several languages, as McCarthy and Prince (1995a, forthcoming) show. We focus on a case from Southern Paiute (Sapir 1930). This language has an allophonic distribution of the labio-velar glide [w] and the labialized nasal [ŋ^w], which is contextually conditioned essentially like the alternation of [g] and [ŋ] in Japanese. That is, the glide [w] occurs in the onset of a word, but it alternates with the nasal [ŋ^w] in medial positions.

(121)   Alternations of [w], [ŋ^w] in Southern Paiute

   #w   **Vŋ^{w}V**

a.i wa'aŋi 'to shout'   a.ii tïꞏ'-ŋ^{w}a'aŋi   'to give a good shout'

b.i waix̱a- 'to have a council'   b.ii nɪaꞏ'vɪ-ŋ^{W}aix̱apꞏɪ 'council (of chiefs)'

The analysis of the allophonic pattern resembles that of Japanese: again two phonotactic constraints dominate an IO-faithfulness constraint. One phonotactic constraint blocks the nasalization of /w/ in word-initial positions, and is stated as:

(122)   *[ŋ^w

        No word-initial labio-velar nasals.

Presumably this constraint can be simplified to the anti-initial-velar-nasal constraint *[ŋ that is undominated in Japanese and English. Then the shared labiality of both alternants, [w] and [ŋ^w], must be due to undominated IDENT-IO(labial), preserving input labiality.[20]

The second phonotactic constraint required in this pattern is:[21]

(123)   *VwV

        No intervocalic labio-velar glides.

This constraint plays the role of 'trigger-constraint' for intervocalic nasalization of /w/. It must therefore dominate IDENT-IO(nasal).

---

[20] The fact that input /w/ alternates with [ŋ^w], rather than another labial consonant such as [b] or [m], may be attributed to faithfulness constraints as well.

[21] *VwV may be reducible to a more general ban on post-vocalic glides, a kind of 'minimal sonority distance' effect. See Rosenthall (1994) for discussion of a similar effect in Lenakel.

Next, observe that reduplication deviates from the alternation pattern of (121), in the sense that roots beginning with [w] *unexpectedly* retain this glide in an intervocalic position after a reduplicant.

(124)   Underapplication of medial nasalization in the base in Southern
          Paiute
          a.i wïyï- 'vulva'   a.ii wï-wïxïA-   'vulvas (obj.)'
          b.i wayi- 'several enter'   b.ii wa-wa'xɪpiɣa 'all entered'

This is a case of underapplication: a phonological process is blocked in a context where it would 'normally' apply, due to the inhibiting effect of BR-identity. The analysis is not too difficult, and essentially mirrors the analysis of Japanese (116):

(125)   Underapplication of medial nasalization in the base in Southern
          Paiute
          BR-Identity,   Blocker- ≫ Trigger- ≫ IO-Faithfulness
                            constraint   constraint
          IDENT-BR(nasal) *[ŋ^w ≫ *VwV   ≫ IDENT-IO(nasal)

With undominated BR-identity, the initial consonants of reduplicant and base must both be glides [w], or both be nasal [ŋ^w]. The initial consonants of reduplicant and base are in different phonological contexts, each of which falls in the scope of different phonotactic constraints, *[ŋ^w and *VwV. Hence, the outcome (double [w] or double [ŋ^w]) depends on the relative ranking of these constraints. Obviously *[ŋ^w must take precedence over *VwV since the double [w] pattern is what surfaces.

Tableau (125) illustrates this ranking:

(126)

Input: /RED + wïyï-A/	IDENT-BR (nasal)	*[ŋ^w	*VwV	IDENT-IO (nasal)
a. ☞ wï-wïxïA-			*	
b. ŋ^{w}ï-ŋ^{w}ïxïA-		*!		
c. wï-ŋ^{w}ïxïA-	*!			

This tableau is almost identical to that of underapplication in Japanese reduplicative mimetics (117). The single difference is that in Southern Paiute effects of reduplicative identity unambiguously appear *on the base*, whereas in Japanese the identification of the reduplicant and base was unclear – reduplication being total.

Underapplication of a phonological process to the base is an important finding, and we should rule out any alternative analyses. Crucially, underapplication of medial nasalization depends on identity, rather than on some obscure morphological property of reduplication. The additional data below show that intervocalic nasalization is perfectly productive in reduplication, as long as both the reduplicant and base are in intervocalic position. Such a double intervocalic context is easily created: when a vowel-final prefix precedes the reduplicant, labio-velar nasals *do* occur in both reduplicant and base:

(127)   Normal application of medial nasalization in the base in Southern Paiute
        a.i wïnɪ-   'to stand'
        a.ii ya-ŋʷɪ-ŋʷïnɪxɑ'- 'while standing and holding'

Note that this is precisely the result that is expected under the analysis given above: since none of the corresponding consonants in reduplicant and base are in word-initial position, the constraint *[ŋʷ is never active, so that the next-lower ('trigger'-)constraint *VwV determines the outcome.

If this argument is indeed valid, then these data constitute a severe problem for a derivational theory, which is based on *copying*. The copy rule always copies a string of segments of the base, upon the reduplicant. Copying of segments of the reduplicant into the base is a complete mystery under this theory.

To wind up this section, let us now generalize the findings for Southern Paiute to general ranking schemata for 'back-copying'. For the case of underapplication to the base, the schema is (128):

(128)   Ranking schema for 'back-copying' underapplication
        BR-Identity, **B**locker-constraint ≫ Trigger-constraint ≫
        IO-Faithfulness
        where the 'triggering' context is met by the **base** (rather than the reduplicant).

The overapplication case arises by reversing the ranking of the 'trigger' and 'blocker':

(129)   Ranking schema for 'back-copying' overapplication
        BR-Identity, Trigger-constraint ≫ **B**locker-constraint ≫
        IO-Faithfulness
        where the 'blocking' context is met by the **base** (rather than the reduplicant).

This concludes the section on overapplication and underapplication. The final section of this chapter provides an overview of Correspondence Theory, to the point where we have seen it now.

5.7 Summary of Correspondence Theory

Input–output faithfulness and base–reduplicant identity are notions of a general theory of *correspondence* which includes constraints requiring identity between elements in pairs of representations. Thus far in this book we have applied Correspondence Theory to the pairs of representations in (130):

(130)   Scope of Correspondence Theory (so far in this book)
           a. Input and output   -IO 'faithfulness'
           b. Base and reduplicant -BR 'reduplicative identity'

The notion of *correspondence* is defined such that it covers both situations (McCarthy and Prince 1995a, forthcoming):

(131)   **Correspondence**
           Given two strings S_1 and S_2, related to one another as input–output, base–reduplicant, etc., *correspondence* is a relation $\Re$ from the elements of S_1 to those of S_2. Elements $\alpha \in S_1$ and $\beta \in S_2$ are referred to as *correspondents* of one another when $\alpha\Re\beta$.

Given this general definition of correspondence, the correspondence constraints (MAX, DEP, etc.) must be *relativized* for different values of S_1 and S_2. For example, we saw in section 5.2.3 that it is necessary for empirical reasons to distinguish MAX-IO from MAX-BR. In fact, MAXIMALITY now becomes a 'family' of constraints, whose members are distinguished by their values of S_1 and S_2 (*Input–Output, Base–Reduplicant*, etc.). Before discussing the actual members of these constraint families, we have to repeat some basic assumptions of Correspondence Theory.

The output-generating component *Gen* supplies pairs of strings S_1 and S_2, as well as any correspondence relationships holding between the elements of these strings. That is, correspondence is not a relationship that is 'established' by constraints, but rather one that is *evaluated* by constraints. Constraints evaluating the *Gen*-supplied correspondence relationships are crucially violable, giving rise to optimal candidates displaying imperfect correspondence relations. These imperfections appear as 'deletion', 'epenthesis', 'feature change', 'metathesis', 'partial reduplication', 'skipping', etc.

Following McCarthy and Prince (1994b, forthcoming), I will introduce the notions of 'domain of $\Re$' and 'range of $\Re$'. Defined formally, these are stated as in (132):

(132)   **Domain**($\Re$): for a relation $\Re \subset A \times B$, $x \in \text{Domain}(\Re)$ iff $x \in A$ and $\exists y \in B$ such that $x\Re y$
           Range($\Re$): $y \in \text{Range}(\Re)$ iff $y \in B$ and $\exists x \in A$ such that $x\Re y$

In these definitions, a structure S_i is encoded as a set of elements. The relation $\mathfrak{R}$ on elements of structures (S_1, S_2) is defined as a subset, or any subset, of $S_1 \times S_2$. Paraphrasing the definitions, we say that x (an element of A) is in the *domain* of $\mathfrak{R}$ if and only if there is some y (an element of B), such that x and y are related by $\mathfrak{R}$. Accordingly, y (an element of B) is in the *range* of $\mathfrak{R}$ if and only if there is some x (an element of A), such that x and y are related by $\mathfrak{R}$.

For example, the first correspondence constraint family, MAXIMALITY, has as its *domain* the set of elements in S_1 (either the input or the base), and as its *range* the set of elements standing in correspondence, which is a subset of S_2 (either the output or the reduplicant):

(133)   **MAXIMALITY**
        'Every element of S_1 has a correspondent in S_2.'
            Domain($\mathfrak{R}$) = S_1
        Members: S_1 S_2 Effect:
        MAX-IO   Input   Output   'No deletion of segments'
        MAX-BR   Base   Reduplicant 'Total reduplication'

MAX-IO was introduced in chapter 1 as the 'anti-deletion' constraint. In this chapter we have seen another important member of the MAXIMALITY family, MAX-BR, the constraint enforcing total reduplication. (Chapter 6 will extend the MAXIMALITY family to still other S_1–S_2 pairs, such as 'Base' and 'Truncated form'.)

The second family of constraints, DEPENDENCE, we have come to know by its most prominent member DEP-IO, the 'anti-epenthesis' constraint.

(134)   **DEPENDENCE**
        'Every element in S_2 has a correspondent in S_1.'
            Range($\mathfrak{R}$) = S_2
        Members: S_1 S_2 Effect:
        DEP-IO   Input   Output   'No epenthesis of segments'
        DEP-BR   Base   Reduplicant 'No base-alien segments in the
                                       reduplicant'

DEP-IO is the 'anti-epenthesis' constraint (which was motivated at length in chapter 3). Its counterpart in base–reduplicant identity is DEP-BR, the constraint militating against 'base-alien' segments in the reduplicant.

Third, the presence or absence of a corresponding element must be distinguished from its *featural* identity, which is evaluated by yet another constraint family:

(135)   IDENTITY[F]

'Correspondent segments have identical values for feature [F].'

If $\alpha \mathcal{R} \beta$ and α is $[\gamma F]$, then β is $[\gamma F]$

Members:	S_1	S_2	Effect:
IDENT-IO[F]	Input	Output	'No featural changes'
IDENT-BR[F]	Base	Reduplicant	'No featural discrepancy between R and B'

By varying features for [F], different members of the IDENTITY family arise. Research in progress presents evidence for certain extensions of IDENTITY. In its current formulation, IDENTITY is 'symmetrical' for S_1 and S_2. For a pair of corresponding segments, values of [F] are simply compared, without checking whether discrepancies are due to 'deletion' or 'insertion' of [F]. Pater (forthcoming), as reviewed in chapter 2, argues for an *asymmetrical* format of IDENTITY on the basis of segmental fusions, distinguishing IDENT-I→O[F] from IDENT-O→I[F]. Another extension of IDENTITY distinguishes positive and negative values of the same feature, IDENT[+F] and IDENT[−F] (McCarthy and Prince forthcoming). Finally, IDENTITY is *segment-based* in the following sense: featural identity is evaluated indirectly through corresponding segments, instead of directly through corresponding features. A strictly segmental view of IDENTITY may have to be abandoned in favour of a featural view, to account for autosegmental phenomena, such as 'floating features' and 'featural stability'. This would involve a distinction between MAX[F] and DEP[F] (see Zoll 1996).

Fourth, the constraint militating against medial epenthesis and/or deletion:

(136)   **(I-, O-) CONTIGUITY**

'The portion of S_1 standing in correspondence forms a contiguous string, as does the correspondent portion of S_1.'

I-CONTIG ('No Skipping')   Domain($\mathcal{R}$) is a single contiguous string in S_1

O-CONTIG ('No Intrusion')   Range($\mathcal{R}$) is a single contiguous string in S_2

Members:	S_1	S_2	Effect:
CONTIG-IO	Input	Output	'No medial epenthesis or deletion of segments'
CONTIG-BR	Base	Reduplicant	'No medial intrusion or skipping in reduplicant'

McCarthy and Prince (forthcoming) distinguish two forms of this constraint, I-CONTIG and O-CONTIG, differing as to which string (S_1 or S_2) is taken as basic with respect to the other. Accordingly violations of CONTIG are of two types, called *skipping* and *intrusion*. In the base–reduplicant domain, CONTIG-BR is respected if the reduplicant copies a contiguous substring of the base, for example in the reduplication patterns (32). It is violated if the reduplicant contains a medial gap as compared to the base (*skipping*, cf. Sanskrit, section 5.2.4.2), while in the case of *intrusion*, the reduplicant contains a medial segment not present in the base. Likewise, CONTIG-IO demands that input–output mappings involve contiguous substrings. It is violated by medial deletion (*skipping*) and medial epenthesis (*intrusion*). CONTIG-IO is motivated by languages which prohibit morpheme-internal epenthesis (e.g. Chukchee; Kenstowicz 1994b, Spencer 1994) and by languages which restrict deletion to segments in morpheme-peripheral positions (Diyari; McCarthy and Prince 1994a).

Fifth, LINEARITY, the 'anti-metathesis' constraint:

(137)   **LINEARITY**
          'S_1 is consistent with the precedence structure of S_2, and vice versa.'
              Let $\alpha, \beta \in S_1$ and $\alpha', \beta' \in S_2$
              If $\alpha \mathcal{R} \alpha'$ and $\beta \mathcal{R} \beta'$, then
                    $\alpha < \beta$ iff $\neg\, (\beta' < \alpha')$
          Members: S_1 S_2 Effect:
          LINEAR-IO   Input   Output   'No metathesis'
          LINEAR-BR   Base   Reduplicant   'No segment reversal in
                                        reduplicant–base'

We have seen the faithfulness version of this constraint LINEAR-IO active in chapter 2 in Pater's analysis of coalescence in Indonesian. However, McCarthy and Prince attribute the 'no coalescence' function of LINEARITY to a separate faithfulness constraint, UNIFORMITY ('no element of S_2 has multiple correspondents in S_1). See also McCarthy (1995a) and Hume (1995).

Sixth, ANCHORING, the constraint which is responsible for 'edge-in' mapping:

(138)   **{RIGHT, LEFT}ANCHORING**
          'Any element at the designated periphery of S_1 has a correspondent at the designated periphery of S_2.'
              Let *Edge*(X, {L, R}) = the element standing at the *Edge* = L, R of X.
              RIGHT-ANCHOR. If α = Edge(S_1, R) and β = Edge(S_2, R) then $\alpha \mathcal{R} \beta$.
              LEFT-ANCHOR. Likewise, *mutatis mutandis*.
          Members: S_1 S_2 Effect:
          ANCHOR-IO   Input   Output   'No epenthesis or deletion at edges'
          ANCHOR-BR   Base   Reduplicant   'Edge-in association'

Correspondence in reduplication

In chapter 3, we saw evidence for Anchor-IO, blocking epenthesis at morpheme edges in Lenakel. Its counterpart in reduplication, Anchor-BR, enforces *edge-in* association. It requires that the initial (or final) segment of the reduplicant stand in correspondence with the initial (or final) segment in the base. A specification of the edge (L/R) in Anchoring serves to distinguish prefixing and suffixing reduplication. (The former ranks L-Anchor ≫ R-Anchor, the latter has the reverse ranking.) McCarthy and Prince (forthcoming) argue that Anchoring should subsume *Generalized Alignment*. Their unification builds on the idea that edges of constituents can also be matched by the correspondence of *segments standing at edges*, using the Anchoring format. Correspondence of peripheral segments in constituents (for example, Stem and PrWd) within a single output form implies that correspondence becomes a *reflexive relation*. McCarthy and Prince give a hypothetical case (*bí.ta*) where 'the left edge of the foot and the head syllable align because *b* and its correspondent (which is, reflexively, *b*) are initial in both'.

SUGGESTIONS FOR FURTHER READING

Pre-OT studies of prosodic morphology

Broselow, Ellen and John McCarthy (1983) A theory of internal reduplication. *The Linguistic Review* **3**. 25–89.

Clements, George N. (1985a) The problem of transfer in nonlinear morphology. *Cornell Working Papers in Linguistics* **7**. 38–73.

Marantz, Alec (1982) Re reduplication. *Linguistic Inquiry* **13**. 435–83.

McCarthy, John (1981) A prosodic theory of non-concatenative morphology. *Linguistic Inquiry* **12**. 373–418.

McCarthy, John and Alan Prince (1986) Prosodic morphology. Ms., University of Massachusetts, Amherst and Brandeis University.

Steriade, Donca (1988a) Reduplication and syllable transfer in Sanskrit and elsewhere. *Phonology* **5**. 73–155.

Correspondence Theory

Reduplication

Blevins, Juliette (1996) Mokilese reduplication. *Linguistic Inquiry* **27**. 523–30.

Downing, Laura J. (forthcoming) Verbal reduplication in three Bantu languages. To appear in Kager, van der Hulst, and Zonneveld.

Klein, Thomas B. (1997) Output constraints and prosodic correspondence in Chamorro reduplication. *Linguistic Inquiry* **28**. 707–15.

McCarthy, John and Alan Prince (1994a) The emergence of the unmarked: Optimality in Prosodic Morphology. In M. González (ed.), *Proceedings of the North-East Linguistics Society* **24**. 333–79.

(forthcoming) Faithfulness and identity in prosodic morphology. To appear in Kager, van der Hulst, and Zonneveld.

Myers, Scott and Troi Carleton (1996) Tonal transfer in Chichewa. *Phonology* **13**. 39–72.

Urbanczyk, Suzanne (1996) Morphological templates in reduplication. In K. Kusumoto (ed.), *Proceedings of the North-East Linguistics Society* **26**. 425–40.

(forthcoming) Double reduplications in parallel. To appear in Kager, van der Hulst, and Zonneveld. [ROA-73, http://ruccs.rutgers.edu/roa.html]

Coalescence

Lamontagne, Greg and Keren Rice (1995) A correspondence account of coalescence. In Beckman, Walsh Dickey, and Urbanczyk. 211–23.

Pater, Joe (forthcoming) Austronesian nasal substitution and other NC̥ effects. To appear in Kager, van der Hulst, and Zonneveld. [ROA-92, http://ruccs.rutgers.edu/roa.html]

Metathesis

Hume, Elizabeth (1995) Beyond linear order: prosodic constraints and C/V metathesis. *Proceedings of the Formal Linguistics Society of the Midwest* **6**. Bloomington: Indiana University Linguistics Club.

McCarthy, John (1995a) Extensions of faithfulness: Rotuman revisited. Ms., University of Massachusetts, Amherst. [ROA-110, http://ruccs.rutgers.edu/roa.html]

Featural identity

Alderete, John, Jill Beckman, Laura Benua, Amalia Gnanadesikan, John McCarthy, and Suzanne Urbanczyk (1997) Reduplication with fixed segmentism. Ms., University of Massachusetts, Amherst. [ROA-226, http://ruccs.rutgers.edu/roa.html]

Gnanadesikan, Amalia (1995) Markedness and faithfulness constraints in child phonology. Ms., University of Massachusetts, Amherst. [ROA-67, http://ruccs.rutgers.edu/roa.html]

Lombardi, Linda (1995b) Why Place and Voice are different: constraint interactions and feature faithfulness in Optimality Theory. Ms., University of Maryland, College Park. [ROA-105, http://ruccs.rutgers.edu/roa.html]

McCarthy, John (1997) Process specific constraints in Optimality Theory. *Linguistic Inquiry* **28**. 231–51.

Myers, Scott (1997a) OCP effects in Optimality Theory. *Natural Language and Linguistic Theory* **15**. 847–92.

Miscellaneous

Bat-El, Outi (1996) Selecting the best of the worst: the grammar of Hebrew blends. *Phonology* **13**. 283–328.

Itô, Junko, Yoshihisa Kitagawa, and R. Armin Mester (1996) Prosodic faithfulness and correspondence: evidence from a Japanese argot. *Journal of East Asian Linguistics* **5**. 217–94.

EXERCISES

1 Reduplication in Axininca Campa

Consider a sample of reduplicated forms of Axininca Campa (Payne 1981, Spring 1990, McCarthy and Prince 1995b) below.

Suffixing reduplication in Axininca Campa

(i.a)	.	kawosi	→	kawosi-<u>kawosi</u>	'bathe'
(i.b)		koma	→	koma-<u>koma</u>	'paddle'
(ii.a)		osampi	→	osampi-<u>sampi</u>	'ask'
(ii.b)		osaŋkina	→	osaŋkina-<u>saŋkina</u>	'write'

Observe that the reduplicant suffix copies all segments of consonant-initial roots (i). But roots beginning with a vowel (ii) are not copied entirely – here the reduplicant omits the initial vowel. The question then is, what constraint interaction accounts for this pattern.

a. Identify the well-formedness and BR-identity constraints that are actively involved in shaping the reduplicant, and rank them.

b. Consult chapter 3 (section 3.3.4.1) for an analysis of consonant epenthesis in Axininca Campa, involving MAX-IO and DEP-IO. Then integrate the analysis of epenthesis with the reduplication analysis.

c. Explain how your ranking correctly excludes *_sampi-sampi_ and *_tosampi-tosampi_ (with epenthetic **t**).

d. Next, consider another ill-formed candidate, *_osampi-tosampi_, with epenthesis in the reduplicant, but not in the base. Integrate the responsible constraint in your ranking.

e. What excludes the 'infixational' candidate *osamp-osamp-i*? Integrate the responsible constraint in your ranking.

f. Present all results in a tableau of *osampi-sampi*.

2 Reduplication in Oykangand

The prefixing reduplication pattern of Oykangand (Sommer 1981, McCarthy and Prince 1986) is exemplified below:

Oykangand prefixing reduplication

(i.a)	eder	→ ed-eder	'rain'
(i.b)	igun	→ ig-igun	'go'
(ii)	algal	→ alg-algal	'straight'

Assume that the reduplicant's final consonant syllabifies as the onset for the base-initial vowel (*e.d-e.der*, *i.g-i.gun*, *al.g-al.gal*). This syllabification poses the analytic challenge.

a. Identify the constraints determining the reduplicant's size and syllabification, and rank them.

b. Explain how your ranking excludes **al.gal-al.gal* and **a.l-al.gal.*

c. What excludes the 'infixational' candidates **e-der-der* and **i-gun-gun*? Integrate the responsible constraint in your ranking.

d. Present all results in a tableau.

3 Infixing reduplication in Pangasinan

Pangasinan has various reduplication patterns (Benton 1971, McCarthy and Prince 1986), among which are the following:

Pangasinan infixing reduplication

(i.a)	sakey	→ saksakey	'one'
(i.b)	talo	→ taltalora	'three'
(ii.a)	apat	→ apatpatira	'four'
(ii.b)	anem	→ anemnemira	'five'

This is infixing reduplication, very similar to the pattern of Timugon Murut (discussed in section 5.4.2). The patterns of Pangasinan and Timugon Murut differ minimally, though.

a. Accurately describe this difference in prose.

b. Starting from the constraint ranking of Timugon Murut (section 5.4.2), can you change this minimally so that the Pangasinan pattern is obtained?

    c.   Explain how your analysis excludes *a-<u>pa</u> -pa.ti.ra, *<u>ap</u> -a.pa.ti.ra, and *<u>a.p</u> -a.pa.ti.ra.

    d.   Present all results in a tableau.

4 Infixing reduplication in Mangarayi

Mangarayi has infixing reduplication in plurals (Merlan 1982, McCarthy and Prince 1986, 1993a), as exemplified below:

Mangarayi infixing reduplication

(i.a)	gabuji	→	gababuji	'old person'
(i.b)	yirag	→	yirirag	'father'
(ii.a)	jimgan	→	jimgimgan	'knowledgeable person'
(ii.b)	waŋgij	→	waŋgaŋgij	'child'

The special feature of this infixing pattern is the first consonant of the root, which always immediately precedes the reduplicant.

    a.   Which constraint interaction accounts for the *position* of the reduplicant immediately after the first consonant of the root?

    b.   Rank the constraints determining the reduplicant's *size*, and integrate this ranking with your earlier results. Hint: reconsider your analysis of Oykangand (see exercise 2).

    c.   Explain how your analysis excludes *<u>jim</u> -jim.gan, *j-<u>im</u>-im.gan, and *j-<u>i.m</u>-im.gan.

    d.   Present all results in a tableau.

5 A factorial typology of reduplicative systems

    a.   Construct a factorial typology of the five constraints Align-Red-L, Max-BR, No-Coda, Onset, and red=σ. Identify any rankings that produce identical reduplicative systems.

    b.   How many reduplicative systems does your typology predict? Characterize each of the predicted systems in prose, making sure that your description is sufficiently general as well as precise enough to capture all distinctions.

    c.   Instantiate the factorial typology with reduplication systems (discussed in this chapter or introduced in preceding exercises). Do you find any gaps in the typology?

6
Output-to-output correspondence

6.1 Introduction

In this chapter we will consider similarities in the shapes of morphologically related words which are not due to common inputs. We will pursue the idea that such similarities involve the notion of 'output-to-output correspondence', the maximization of phonological identity between morphologically related output forms.

A theoretical precursor of OO-correspondence, the notion of 'paradigm uniformity', enjoyed a long tradition in pre-generative linguistics (see for example Kuryłowicz 1949). This notion played a modest role in generative phonology (but see Kiparsky 1982a), where similarities between morphologically related forms were attributed to derivational means, in particular the *phonological cycle*. Recently, paradigm uniformity has been revived in OT by Benua (1995), Flemming (1995), McCarthy (1995a), Burzio (1996), Kenstowicz (1996), Steriade (1996), and others. Disregarding the technical differences between these proposals (referred to as either 'paradigm uniformity', 'uniform exponence', 'base-identity', or 'OO-correspondence'), we will subsume all under the general notion of OO-correspondence.

OO-correspondence elaborates on the notion of 'reduplicative identity', discussed in chapter 5. The reduplicant, part of a surface form, is subject to correspondence constraints requiring *idèntity* with its base, which is part of the same surface form. Interactions between reduplicant–base-identity constraints and markedness constraints turned out to be a variation on the major type of constraint interaction in OT: that between faithfulness and markedness.

For example, we discovered a deep similarity between constraints militating against the deletion of input segments, and those enforcing 'total reduplication'. Both constraints require that elements in one string (input or reduplicant's base) match elements in another string (output or reduplicant). These (and other) similarities were captured by a small set of generalized correspondence constraints: MAXIMALITY, DEPENDENCE, IDENTITY, LINEARITY, CONTIGUITY, and ANCHORING. We also learned that correspondence offers an explanation of underapplication and overapplication in reduplicative morphology, based on interactions of markedness constraints and correspondence constraints: IO-faithfulness and BR-identity. This analysis produced new evidence for *parallelism*, based on the observation that identity effects may 'back-copy' to the base, as in the case of Malay vowel nasalization.

In this chapter, Correspondence Theory will be extended to fresh empirical domains, again involving correspondence between outputs, in particular to *morphological truncation* (Benua 1995, McCarthy 1995a) and *stem-based affixation* (Burzio 1994, 1996, Benua 1995, Kenstowicz 1996, Steriade 1996). A new and highly interesting aspect of these phenomena, as compared to reduplication, is that they involve correspondence between *separate output forms*: words. In reduplication, BR-correspondence is defined as a relation between pairs of representations that are *co-present* in a single output form. But co-presence no longer holds for truncation, nor for stem-based affixation, where each of the representations involved is a stem, a free-standing element of a morphological paradigm. Pairs of forms to be related by OO-correspondence can be either a truncated form and the stem on which it is based, or an affixed form and the non-affixed stem on which it is based.

(1)   Extending the scope of Correspondence Theory
        a. Lexical–surface   (IO) Chapters 1–2
        b. Base–reduplicant   (BR) Chapter 5
        c. Base–truncated stem (BT) This chapter, section 6.2
        d. Stem–affixed stem   (BA) This chapter, sections 6.3–4

The generalization that covers truncation and stem-based affixation is that in both cases the derived form (the truncated form, or the affixed form) copies a phonological property of its 'base' (the non-truncated output form, or the stem in a stem-based affixation). In both cases, the base is a free-standing form – an output. This extension of Correspondence Theory to relations between free-standing output forms is the topic of this chapter. We will learn that OO-identity effects involve both the *underapplication* and *overapplication* of phonology to a morphologically derived (truncated or affixed) form. As we concluded earlier for reduplication, these effects result from a small number of ranking schemata: interactions of IO-faithfulness, OO-identity, and markedness constraints.

This chapter is organized as follows. First, in section 6.2, we will look into identity effects in truncation, on the basis of case-studies of English nicknames and Icelandic truncation. Section 6.3 will extend Correspondence Theory to relations between an affixed word and the stem on which it is based, considering English data. Finally, section 6.4 will show how OO-correspondence serves to reanalyse data that were analysed by the phonological cycle in derivational theory. Here we will focus on examples from Palestinian Arabic, keeping an eye on the advantages of the correspondence model over a serial ('cyclic') analysis.

6.2 Identity effects in truncation

6.2.1 *Introduction*

Truncation is a general term for any morphological category that is derived by a systematic phonological shortening of a basic form. A cross-linguistically common type of truncation is the formation of 'hypocoristics' by shortening a name (*nicknames*). It has been observed for various languages that truncations preserve phonological properties of their base, even though these properties need not be contextually motivated in the truncated form (Anderson 1975, Benua 1995, McCarthy 1995a). We will discuss Benua's idea that maximization of phonological identity between a truncated form and its base involves OO-correspondence, a notion that is modelled after base-reduplicant identity.

This section is organized as follows. Section 6.2.2 will outline the analysis of morphological truncation in Correspondence Theory. Discussion will focus on examples from American English, analysed by Benua (1995). In section 6.2.3 this analysis will be generalized into a proposal of a *Basic Model*, analogous to that for reduplication in chapter 5. Finally, section 6.2.4 will discuss truncation in Icelandic, again following the analysis by Benua (1995).

6.2.2 *Truncation in American English*

A set of examples motivating OO-correspondence in truncation is given in (2). All examples in the bottom row are truncations of names (into nicknames) in American English:

(2)   a.i Larry [læ.ri]   b.i Harry [hæ.ri]   c.i Sarah [sæ.rə]
       a.ii Lar   [lær]   b.ii Har   [hær]   c.ii Sar   [sær]

Kahn (1976) and others have observed that the vowels in the truncated forms are 'exempt' from certain phonological regularities that govern underived words. In particular, American English lacks the low front vowel [æ] in syllables closed by /r/, realizing this vowel by its low back allophone [ɑ], as in *car* (3a). In contrast, [æ] freely occurs in syllables closed by other consonants than /r/ (3b), as well as syllables in which /r/ is not tautosyllabic (3c).

(3)   _r]σ   _C]σ   _]σ rV
        a.i   car [kɑr]   b.i   kat [kæt]   c.i   carry [kæ.ri]
        a.ii   mar [mɑr]   b.ii   map [mæp]   c.ii   marry [mæ.ri]
        a.iii lark [lɑrk]   b.iii last [læst]   c.ii   Larry [læ.ri]

259

Non-truncated words in American English never contain [æ] in a /r/-closed syllable: *[ær]. Nevertheless, all truncated forms in (2) have precisely this sequence, for example *Lar* [lær]. Apparently truncated forms 'copy' the vowel of their base, in spite of the allophonic pattern (which would predict the truncated form *[lɑr]).

6.2.2.1 *An OO-correspondence analysis*

Benua (1995) argues that the vowel in the truncated form *Lar* [lær] is related to the vowel in its base *Larry* [læ.ri] by a correspondence relation. This relation is marked in (4) by a line connecting the vowels in the truncated form and the base:

(4)　　　　　Larry [læ.ri] **Base**

　　　　　　　　　│

　　　　　Lar　　[lær]　**Truncated form**

The requirement that the corresponding vowels in the base and truncated form are *identical* in their feature content produces a kind of 'underapplication' of the allophonic distribution in the truncated form. The realization of the low vowel as [ɑ] before tautosyllabic /r/ fails to occur, as that would obliterate the identity between the truncated form and its 'base'. This is fully analogous to the underapplication effects in reduplication in chapter 5. This analogy is strikingly supported by the constraint interaction underlying the pattern, as we will see.

First, the allophonic distribution of front [æ] and back [ɑ] instantiates a schema for allophonic variation seen in chapter 1:

(5)　　　　　Schema for allophonic variation
　　　　　　　Contextual markedness ≫ Context-free markedness ≫ Faithfulness

This ranking schema is instantiated by the following three constraints:[1]

(6)　　　　a. ***ær]**$_\sigma$
　　　　　　　No /æ/ before tautosyllabic /r/.

　　　　　　b. ***BACK-low**
　　　　　　　Low vowels are front.

　　　　　　c. **IDENT-IO**(back)
　　　　　　　Let α be a segment in the input, and β be a correspondent of α
　　　　　　　in the output. If α is [γback], then β is [γback].

---

[1] Constraints (6a–b), in spite of their idiosyncratic appearances, are in fact phonetically grounded. First, *ær]$_\sigma$ captures the well-known centralization of vowels before [r], here relativized to the domain of the syllable. Second, *BACK-low is not mentioned by Benua (1995), who gives only a partial analysis of the allophonic pattern. *BACK-low functions to support the lexical contrast in low vowels along the front–back dimension, which is otherwise based on length (/æ/~/ɑː/). This makes sense as a language-specific instantiation of a 'no-perceptual-confusion' principle.

The irrelevance of the input is shown in the following tableaux of [kɑr] and [læ.ri]:

(7)

Input: /kær/	*ær]$_\sigma$	*BACK-low	IDENT-IO(back)
a.　　[kær]	*!		
b. ☞ [kɑr]		*	*

(8)

Input: /lɑri/	*ær]$_\sigma$	*BACK-low	IDENT-IO(back)
a. ☞ [læ.ri]			*
b.　　[lɑ.ri]		*!	

To state underapplication as a constraint interaction, we need a constraint IDENT-BT(back), requiring featural identity of backness between the base and its truncated form:

(9)　　**IDENT-BT**(back)

Let α be a segment in the base, and β be a correspondent of α in the truncated form. If α is [γback], then β is [γback].

The truncated form [lær] shows that IDENT-BT(back) dominates *ær]$_\sigma$, and by transitivity, all constraints dominated by it:

(10)　　Underapplication of backness adjustment in truncated forms

IDENT-BT(back) ≫ *ær]$_\sigma$ ≫ *BACK-low ≫ IDENT-IO(back)

This interaction is illustrated by the tableau of the truncated form [lær]:

(11)

Input: /lɑri/ Base: [læ.ri]	IDENT-BT(back)	*ær]$_\sigma$	*BACK-low	IDENT-IO(back)
a.　　[lɑr]	*!		*	
b. ☞ [lær]		*		

In sum, an allophonic process which adjusts the backness of vowels in /r/-closed syllables is blocked in the truncated form, thereby maximizing phonological identity with its base. This blocking is highly similar to 'underapplication' effects in reduplication. Both increase the shape identity between surface forms, either reduplicant–base or truncated form and base.

This resemblance between reduplication and truncation has been stated in terms of interactions between identity and markedness in (12):

(12)   Underapplication in reduplication and truncation
        a. In reduplication: BR-Identity ≫ Markedness ≫ IO-Faithfulness
        b. In truncation: BT-Identity ≫ Markedness ≫ IO-Faithfulness

Overapplication, the opposite situation of underapplication, is also attested in the truncation patterns of the world's languages. We will consider an example of overapplication in a different type of phenomenon, that of stem-based affixation, in section 6.3.

6.2.2.2 *A derivational analysis*

A derivational analysis of the underapplication effect in truncation faces severe problems. To derive truncated forms, a problematic kind of ordering has to be called on. Rule ordering must be such that a morphological rule (truncation) follows an allophonic rule (specifying backness in low vowels, with reference to tautosyllabic /r/).

(13)   /læri/ Lexical form
          læ.ri Syllabification, Backness Adjustment æ → ɑ / __ r]$_\sigma$
          lær   Truncation
          [lær] Surface form

If the ordering were reverse (i.e. 'feeding'), then Backness Adjustment would have a chance to apply to the output of truncation, which is a closed syllable, incorrectly predicting *[lɑr]. This ordering of allophonic rules before morphological rules is problematic to the standard version of derivational theory according to which all morphological rules are in the lexicon, and all allophonic rules in the post-lexical component (Lexical Phonology, Kiparsky 1982b). But even if it were assumed that Backness Adjustment is a lexical rule (that is, in spite of its allophonic character), the derivational analysis would still face a second problem. That is, it cannot explain why Backness Adjustment fails to reapply to the output of truncation. Note that truncation is followed by the automatic resyllabification of /r/ into the preceding syllable. At that point in the derivation, an *automatic reapplication* of Backness Adjustment must be blocked. However, this blocking must be stipulated by brute-force means.

6.2.3 *Truncation: the Basic Model*

In this subsection we will extract the general properties of Benua's analysis of truncation in American English into a Basic Model of OO-correspondence, which is similar to that of reduplication. The correspondence model of truncation is presented below:

(14)   **Basic Model of morphological truncation**

BT-Identity
Base ⇔ Truncated form
IO-Faithfulness   ⇕
Input

The *truncated form* (T) is a stem, a free-standing form, hence an output. This is related to a non-truncated form, itself a stem and free-standing form, which Benua (1995) refers to as the *base* (B). This base, like any output form, has its own *input* (I). Correspondence between elements in the input *I* and base *B* (an output) is evaluated by *IO-faithfulness* constraints, in a standard way. Correspondence between the truncated form *T* and its base *B* is evaluated by *BT-identity* constraints, militating against any dissimilarities between both.

This Basic Model, when applied to the truncated form [lær], which we discussed in the previous section, indicates the following correspondence relations holding between the base, its input, and the truncated form.

(15)   Correspondence relations in truncated form [lær]

BT-Identity
B [læri] ⇔ **T** [lær]
IO-Faithfulness   ⇕
I /lAri/

BT-identity constraints comparing the identity of morphologically related forms presuppose the notion of *correspondence*, a relation holding between pairs of segments in two strings, whose definition (McCarthy and Prince 1995a) is repeated below from chapter 5:

(16)   **Correspondence**
           Given two strings S_1 and S_2, *correspondence* is a relation $\mathcal{R}$ from the elements of S_1 to those of S_2. Segments α (an element of S_1) and β (an element of S_2) are referred to as *correspondents* of one another when $\alpha\mathcal{R}\beta$.

This notion of correspondence is general enough to include relations between two separate output forms. The strings S_1 and S_2 are instantiated by two free-standing, morphologically related outputs. This is OO-correspondence (Benua 1995, McCarthy 1995a, Burzio 1996). Here we consider the case of morphological truncation, where OO-correspondence takes the form of a relation between segments in a 'truncated form' and its 'base'.[2]

The constraints enforcing BT-identity are highly similar to BR-identity constraints (relating base and reduplicant) introduced in chapter 5. MAX-BT requires, for example, that every element in the base must have a correspondent in the truncated form.

(17)   **MAX-BT**
         Every element in B has a correspondent in T.

DEP-BT requires that every element in the truncated form have a correspondent in the base.

(18)   **DEP-BT**
         Every element in T has a correspondent in B.

IDENT-BT[F] requires that correspondents in the base and the truncated form have identical values for feature [F].

(19)   **IDENT-BT[F]**
         Let α be a segment in the base, and β be a correspondent of α in the truncated form. If α is [γF], then β is [γF].

Other correspondence constraints (ANCHORING-BT, LINEARITY-BT, CONTIGUITY-BT) may eventually be necessary, but the above set of three suffices for the cases discussed here.

Finally, we need to address the constraints that trigger the truncation as such. These constraints are counterparts of the 'templatic' constraints in reduplication. Benua (1995) has little to say about this issue, but we may assume an analysis along the lines of Itô (1990). The basic idea is that truncated forms are morphological *stems*, and accordingly must fulfil all relevant prosodic requirements for stems. Perhaps the most important requirement is that a stem must equal a PrWd:

(20)   **STEM=PRWD**
         A stem equals a PrWd.

From this requirement the *minimum* size of the truncated form follows, typically a binary (bimoraic or bisyllabic) foot. PrWd-status entails foot-status by the prosodic hierarchy, as we saw in chapter 5, section 5.3.2.

The *maximum* size of the truncated form can then be modelled by morphoprosodic alignment constraints. For example, a cross-linguistically common size

---

[2] The term 'base' was chosen so as to reflect the strong similarities with other types of OO-correspondence, for example reduplication and truncation.

of truncated forms is a *heavy syllable* (Mester 1990). This equals the smallest possible foot, hence the minimal PrWd. Analogously to the constraint RED=σ from chapter 5, this can be stated as follows:

(21)   TRUNC=σ
         A truncated form equals a syllable.

An alternative, potentially more interesting, analysis would be analogous to 'the emergence of the unmarked' template shape (McCarthy and Prince 1994a; see the analysis of disyllabic reduplication in Diyari in chapter 5). If we assume that truncation involves a segmentally empty morpheme 'TRUNC' (analogous to 'RED' in reduplication), the prosodically unmarked single-foot size of the truncated form will follow from the ranking: Markedness ≫ MAX-BT.

With these remarks in our minds, we now turn to the analysis of Icelandic truncation.

6.2.4 *Truncation in Icelandic*

6.2.4.1 *Introducing the pattern*
Icelandic deverbal action nouns are truncations of the infinitive, which arise by the deletion of its final vowel (Árnason 1980: 52, Anderson 1982: 6, Kiparsky 1984: 156). Examples are given below:

(22)   Infinitive   Deverbal action noun
     a.i   klifra   'climb'   klifr   'climbing'
     a.ii   kumra   'bleat'   kumr   'bleating'
     a.iii   grenja   'cry'   grenj   'crying'
     b.i   söötra   'sip'   söötr   'sipping'
     b.ii   puukra   'conceal'   puukr   'concealment'
     b.iii   kjöökra   'wail'   kjöökr   'wailing'
     b.iv   siifra   'lament'   siifr   'lamentation'

It can be argued that deverbal action nouns are derived from infinitives by the truncation of *-a* (rather than the other way around, deriving infinitives by the suffixation of *-a*). Deverbal action nouns have two idiosyncratic phonological properties that set them apart from other forms. First, they may end in a cluster of consonants that has a *rising sonority*, such as [tr], [kr], [fr], [mr], or [nj], whereas word-final clusters in Icelandic are generally of falling sonority, for example *björn* 'bear', *folald* 'young foal'. The second idiosyncratic property of deverbal action nouns is that they may contain a long vowel standing before a consonant cluster, whereas final consonant clusters are generally preceded by short vowels; see again *björn*.

The generalization is that both idiosyncratic properties of deverbal action nouns (that is, final clusters of rising sonority and long vowels before clusters) preserve phonological identity between the truncated form and the infinitive (Anderson 1975, Benua 1995). In the infinitival base, consonant clusters of rising sonority incur no violation of phonotactics, as they stand before a vowel, forming a licit onset. And long vowels in infinitives are syllable-final, a position in which length is phonotactically allowed. (Stressed open syllables always contain long vowels.)

(23)   Identity of length and consonant cluster in base and truncated form
        söö.tra   Infinitive: 'to sip'
        söötr   Deverbal action noun: '(the act of) sipping'

Vowel length and consonant cluster originate in the infinitive, and both are preserved in the related deverbal action noun. Deverbal action nouns thus preserve the phonological shape of the related infinitive, although they fail to provide the prosodic context which 'normally' licenses these shape characteristics. Or to state it differently, deverbal action nouns 'copy' infinitival phonology, but thereby violate otherwise generally respected constraints on the word-level phonology of Icelandic.

Benua (1995) argues that identity effects are due to OO-correspondence constraints which require complete phonological identity between a truncated form and its base. These identity constraints dominate markedness constraints (which are responsible for ruling out final clusters of rising sonority, and long vowels before consonant clusters). Before we can discuss the precise interactions of identity constraints and markedness constraints, we must first find out how Icelandic 'normally' avoids violations of markedness constraints. That is, what produces the stringent phonotactic restrictions on non-truncated forms?

6.2.4.2 *Sonority restrictions*

Let us first discuss the restriction that words should not end in a sequence of consonants of rising sonority. Inputs ending in consonant clusters of rising sonority can be repaired in two ways, of which we will discuss one, epenthesis.[3] Final clusters of the form consonant-plus-/r/ (in shorthand notation /Cr/), are broken up by epenthesis of [u] (Anderson 1974, 1975):

(24)   Epenthesis: normal application
        a. /tek-r/   te.**kur** 'take (pres.ind.)'
        b. /hest-r/ hes.**tur** 'horse (nom.sg.)'

---

[3] A second repair strategy is the deletion of a word-final glide /j/ after a consonant, for example /bylj/ [byl] 'snowstorm (nom.sg.)'. See for details Benua (1995).

Avoidance of final clusters of rising sonority is cross-linguistically common. It is known as the SONORITY SEQUENCING PRINCIPLE (Clements 1990). This generalization can be stated as a markedness constraint:[4]

(25)   SON-SEQ

Complex onsets rise in sonority, and complex codas fall in sonority.

SON-SEQ dominates the 'anti-epenthesis' constraint DEP-IO. For if the ranking were reverse, no epenthesis would take place. Epenthesis is selected as a repair strategy for /Cr/ clusters, over another logically possible strategy, the deletion of a consonant in the final cluster. The choice of (vowel) epenthesis over (consonant) deletion shows that MAX-IO dominates DEP-IO. This is a familiar interaction of which we have seen examples in chapter 3. In tableau (26) this interaction is shown by evaluations of three candidates for the input /tek-r/:

(26)

/tek-r/	SON-SEQ	MAX-IO	DEP-IO
a. ☞ te.kur			*
b. tek		*!	
c. tekr	*!		

We assume that the position of the epenthetic vowel inside the stem is due to high-ranking ANCHORING-IO, which rules out the candidate [te.kru].

6.2.4.3 *Quantitative restrictions*

The second phonotactic restriction that appears to be disrespected by deverbal action nouns is the ban against long vowels in words of the type CVCC. Let us take a closer look at the distribution of quantity in Icelandic. Stressed vowels are always long in open syllables, and short in non-final closed syllables:

(27)   Stressed long vowel in open   Stressed short vowel in closed
              syllable   syllable
         a.i   höö.fuð 'head'   b.i   har.ður 'hard'
         a.ii aa.kur 'field'   b.ii el.ska 'love'
         a.iii faa.ra 'ride'   b.iii kal.la 'call'

In monosyllables, stressed vowels are always long before single consonants (28b), but they are short before consonant clusters (28c).

---

[4] The situation is somewhat more complex, since consonant clusters of rising sonority occur: *vopn* 'weapon', *kukl* 'witchcraft', *vatn* 'water' (all examples cited from Booij 1986). These examples suggest that the prohibition against codas of rising sonority falls apart into several constraints, with *Cr] dominating other *CC] constraints in which the second consonant is not /r/.

(28)   Length in Icelandic monosyllables

long in CVV	long in CVVC	short in CVCC
a.i skoo 'shoe'	b.i haas 'hoarse'	c.i björn 'bear'
a.ii buu 'homestead'	b.ii ljoos 'light'	c.ii haft 'have'
a.iii /tɛɛ/ 'tea'	b.iii skiip 'ship'	c.iii skips 'ship's'

This pattern can be understood as an interaction of two constraints. (The analysis developed from here on is the author's.) The first is STRESS-TO-WEIGHT (Myers 1987, Riad 1992):

(29)   **STRESS-TO-WEIGHT**
        If stressed, then heavy.

The second constraint trims syllabic 'overweight' by militating against trimoraic syllables:

(30)   ***3μ**
        No trimoraic syllables.

In combination, high-ranking STRESS-TO-WEIGHT and *3μ have the effect that all stressed syllables are bimoraic. In principle, there are two ways in which a syllable can be bimoraic. The first is by *vowel lengthening*. This occurs in open syllables (where no coda consonant is available), and in syllables closed by a single consonant. The second way in which weight may arise is by rendering a *coda consonant moraic*. This is what we will assume for syllables closed by two consonants (CVCC). The analytic problem is this: why do syllables closed by a single consonant (CVVC) behave like open syllables (CVV) for vowel lengthening?

The fact that vowels are long before a single word coda shows that final consonants are non-moraic. (If the final consonant in [haas] 'hoarse' were moraic, then there would be no need for vowel length.) Non-moraicity of final consonants is due to the constraint in (31) (Lorentz 1996, Borowsky and Harvey 1997):[5]

(31)   ***FINAL-C-μ**
        The final consonant is weightless.

This is a kind of NONFINALITY constraint (see chapter 4) at the level of the mora. For words ending in a consonant cluster, it only affects the final consonant.

---

[5] Actually Icelandic has word-final geminate consonants, e.g. [visː] 'certain', but these are never preceded by long vowels (behaving like consonant clusters in this respect). Therefore *FINAL-C-μ is dominated by a faithfulness constraint preserving input quantity in consonants. See Spaelti (1994) and Lorentz (1996) for analyses of similar phenomena in Norwegian and Swiss German.

Next consider the question of how to block *CVVCC syllables, that is, a long vowel before a final cluster. We explain this blocking by the ban on trimoraic syllables, on the assumption that the first consonant in the cluster is moraic. This mora renders vowel length impossible (for trimoraic syllables are ruled out by *3μ). Moraic status of coda consonants is due to the following constraint (Hayes 1989):

(32)   **WEIGHT-BY-POSITION**
         Coda consonants are moraic.

Evidently WEIGHT-BY-POSITION must be dominated by *FINAL-C-μ, since the vowel length in CVVC-monosyllables shows that the final consonant is weightless.

(33)   *FINAL-C-μ ≫ WEIGHT-BY-POSITION
         [haas] > [has]

In contrast, the final consonant in CVCC-monosyllables remains weightless due to *FINAL-C-μ, while the prefinal one is obligatorily moraic. Consider the following two possibilities for satisfying syllable bimoraicity in a monosyllable ending in a cluster:

(34)   Syllable weight satisfied by moraic coda rather than long vowel
         [björn] > [jöörn]

The actual form [björn] has a short vowel, from which we infer that the initial consonant in the cluster is moraic. The suboptimal form [jöörn] has a long vowel, but none of the coda consonants is moraic. We thus find a preference for a moraic coda (WEIGHT-BY-POSITION) to a long vowel.

Since vowel length is an input property, the neutralization of length before a cluster in CVCC syllables must happen at the expense of a violation of a faithfulness constraint militating against changes in input length. This faithfulness constraint is WT-IDENT-IO, stated below in the correspondence format (McCarthy 1995a):

(35)   **WT-IDENT-IO**
         If $\alpha \in$ Domain(f),
         if α is monomoraic, then $f(\alpha)$ is monomoraic. ('no lengthening')
         if α is bimoraic, then $f(\alpha)$ is bimoraic.   ('no shortening')

WT-IDENT-IO requires identical quantity of output segments and their input correspondents. This requirement is made in both directions, so that the constraint militates against both the addition of quantity ('lengthening') and loss of quantity ('shortening').

Since surface vowel length entirely depends on stress and syllable structure in Icelandic, WT-IDENT-IO must be dominated by the length-inducing constraint

(Stress-to-Weight), as well as by the length-inhibiting constraints (*3μ, Weight-by-Position). Since we already know that *Final-C-μ ≫ Weight-by-Position, we arrive at:

(36)   Stress-to-Weight, *Final-C-μ, *3μ ≫ Weight-by-Position ≫ Wt-Ident-IO

This ranking correctly predicts that underlying vowel length is irrelevant to the outcome. Regardless of whether an input vowel is long or short, it will be long if and only if it stands in a stressed open syllable. The tableaux (37–9) demonstrate the irrelevance of input length by reversing it (as compared to the output).

The first tableau is simple: the requirement that the stressed syllable be heavy means that the vowel of /sko/ is lengthened, regardless of the violation of faithfulness to length.

(37)

Input: /sko/	Stress-to-Weight	*Final-C-μ	*3μ	Weight-by-Position	Wt-Ident-IO
a. ☞ skoo					*
b. sko	*!				

The second tableau, of [haas], is slightly more complicated. It shows that the vowel of a CVC input lengthens to satisfy Stress-to-Weight. Strategies to retain input shortness of the vowel fail, specifically that of making the coda moraic, which fails on *Final-C-μ:

(38)

Input: /has/	Stress-to-Weight	*Final-C-μ	*3μ	Weight-by-Position	Wt-Ident-IO
a. ☞ haas				*	*
b. has		*!			
c. has	*!			*	

Weight-by-Position is violated in the optimal candidate to avoid violation of *Final-C-μ.

The third tableau, of [björn], adds the factor of a final consonant cluster. Strategies to preserve the hypothetically long input vowel all fail. First, preserving vowel length in a syllable with a moraic coda (39c) simply fails on *3μ. Second, preserving length by keeping both coda consonants weightless (39b) fails on non-minimal violation of WEIGHT-BY-POSITION:

(39)

Input: /bjöörn/	STRESS-TO-WEIGHT	*FINAL-C-μ	*3μ	WEIGHT-BY-POSITION	WT-IDENT-IO
a. ☞ bj**ö**rn				*	*
b. bj**öö**rn				**!	
c. bj**öö**rn			*!	*	

This tableau thus demonstrates the ranking WEIGHT-BY-POSITION ≫ WT-IDENT-IO.

In sum, input vowel length is completely overruled by quantitative well-formedness of the syllable. The latter requirements can now be written as a cover constraint:

(40) **QUANT-FORM** (cover term for constraint interaction)
STRESS-TO-WEIGHT, *FINAL-C-μ, *3μ ≫ WEIGHT-BY-POSITION

With SON-SEQ (from section 6.2.4.2) and QUANT-FORM available as the constraints spelling out the 'phonotactic laws' in the phonology of Icelandic, we can now return to the original problem of accounting for the violations of these phonotactics in truncated forms.

6.2.4.4   OO-correspondence in truncation

The analysis of truncation requires three constraints which are specific to truncation. First, a 'templatic' constraint requiring that truncated forms be monosyllabic:

(41) **TRUNC=σ**
A truncated form equals a syllable.

This constraint is undominated, as far as the examples can tell us. (As mentioned above, the effect may also be due to an 'emergence of the unmarked', but we will not pursue this idea.)

Second, a constraint requiring identical quantity between correspondents in the base and the truncated form:

(42) **WT-IDENT-BT**
If $\alpha \in$ Domain(f),
if α is monomoraic, then $f(\alpha)$ is monomoraic.   ('no lengthening')
if α is bimoraic, then $f(\alpha)$ is bimoraic.   ('no shortening')

This is of course the output-to-output variant of WT-IDENT-IO, introduced in (35). However, as we will soon find out, this identity constraint is crucially ranked higher in the grammar than the faithfulness constraint.

Third, a constraint militating against the 'loss' of base segments in the truncated form. This 'anti-truncation' constraint is stated as a member of the MAX-family:

(43)   **MAX-BT**
         Every element of B has a correspondent in T.
         ('No truncation')

The crucial interactions of these constraints have been spelled out below. Monosyllabicity of truncation has priority over preserving segments of the base in the truncated form (44a). In its turn, segmental base identity has priority over phonotactic requirements (with respect to sonority and quantity), giving the over/underapplication effects (44b). Finally, identity of vowel length (in base and truncated form) has priority over quantitative requirements (44c):

(44)   a. TRUNC=σ ≫ MAX-BT
            söötr > söö.tra
         b. MAX-BT ≫ SON-FORM, QUANT-FORM
            söötr > sööt
         c. WT-IDENT-BT ≫ QUANT-FORM
            söötr > sötr

Integrating all this into a total hierarchy, we arrive at:

(45)   Icelandic truncation
         TRUNC=σ, WT-IDENT-BT ≫ MAX-BT ≫ SON-SEQ, QUANT-FORM ≫
         WT-IDENT-IO

The tableau of [söötr] is straightforward now.

(46)

Input: /sötr-a/ Base: [söö.tra]	TRUNC=σ	WT-IDENT-BT	MAX-BT	SON-SEQ	QUANT-FORM	WT-IDENT-IO
a. ☞ söötr			*	*	*	*
b. sööt			**!			*
c. sötr		*!	*	*		
d. söö.tra	*!					*
e. söö.tur	*!		*			*

With any disyllabic candidates (46d–e) eliminated by TRUNC=σ, the choice is among three candidates: [sötr] (46c), [sööt] (46b), and [söötr] (46a). The first of these has a short vowel, fatally violating undominated WT-IDENT-BT. Among the remaining candidates (46a–b), the optimal one is (46a), since this minimally violates MAX-BT. This happens at the expense of the violation of both phonotactic constraints (SON-SEQ, QUANT-FORM).

6.2.4.5 *A derivational analysis*

Kiparsky (1984: 156) proposes that truncation is due to a late phonological rule of /a/-deletion, rather than to a (subtractive) morphological process. As shown in the derivation below, this /a/-deletion rule applies after syllabification and vowel lengthening:

(47)   UR   /sötr-a/
          Syllabification   sö.tra
          Vowel lengthening   söö.tra
          /a/-deletion   söötr
          PR   [söötr]

By stating truncation as a phonological rule, the generalization is saved that all morphology is additive – not subtractive. But another generalization is missed: only truncation produces output forms which violate the (otherwise completely respected) phonotactics of Icelandic, including sonority-based and quantitative restrictions. As Anderson (1975) observes, such violations serve to preserve maximal phonological identity between the truncated form and infinitive. The OT analysis captures this insight, while the derivational analysis ignores it.

6.3 Identity effects in stem-based affixation

This section will discuss a second source of evidence for OO-correspondence: the phonology of stem-based affixations. Empirically, we will focus on identity phenomena in stems and affixed forms in American English.

6.3.1 *Identity and stem-based affixation in English*

A second argument for OO-correspondence presented by Benua (1995) again involves a set of vowel alternations in American English. Here we consider dialects spoken in the Philadelphia–New York region. These dialects have a tense allophone [E] of the low front vowel [æ] in closed syllables before certain consonants, among which /s/, for example *pass* [pEs], but *passive* [pæ.sɪv] (48a).[6] Note that æ-tensing does not apply in open syllables before /s/; see (48b–c):

---

[6] The sets of tautosyllabic consonants that trigger æ-tensing vary slightly between the dialects, but this is irrelevant for the following argument. See Ferguson (1975), Dunlop (1987).

(48)   æ-tensing: normal application

a.i	pass	[pEs]	b.i	passive	[pæ.sɪv]	c.i	acid	[æ.sɪd]

a.i   pass [pEs]   b.i   passive   [pæ.sɪv]   c.i   acid [æ.sɪd]
a.ii mass [mEs]   b.ii massive   [mæ.sɪv]   c.ii tacit [tæ.sɪt]
a.iii class [klEs]   b.iii classic   [klæ.sɪk]   c.iii lasso [læ.so]

The words in (48b) are morphologically related to those of (48a) by affixation of adjectival /-ɪv/ and /-ɪk/, both so-called Class 1 affixes. The words in (48c) are simplex stems.

Next observe that in the same dialects, words which are suffixed by Class 2 suffixes (*-ing*, *-able*, and *-y*) display special behaviour with respect to æ-tensing (Dunlop 1987). The stems of (48a) preserve their tense allophone [E] under Class 2 suffixation:

(49)   æ-tensing: overapplication in Class 2 affixed forms

a.i pass   [pEs]   b.i class   [klEs]   c.i mass   [mEs]
a.ii passing [pE.sɪŋ] b.ii classy [klE.si] c.ii massable [mE.sə.bl̩]

Preservation of [E] in the affixed form can be considered an 'overapplication' of æ-tensing. æ-tensing overapplies in the sense that the vowels in open syllables of *passing*, *classy*, and *massable* surface as tense, even though they fail to meet the context of tensing. The affixed form 'copies' the vowel quality of its stem, in which tensing applies normally.

The key difference between Class 1 and Class 2 affixes is that only the latter require a *stem*, a free-standing lexical item, as their base (Kiparsky 1985, Inkelas 1989, Borowsky 1993). It has often been observed (starting with Siegel 1974) that Class 1 affixations behave in many phonological aspects as morphologically underived words. For example, compare the identical vocalisms of *pass-ive* (48b.i) and *acid* (48c.i). The base of a Class 1 affix need not be a free-standing stem, but it can be a morpheme which does not occur independently: a *root*. (For example, the root *aggress-* occurs in *aggress-ive* and *aggress-ion*; the root *pacif-* in *pacif-ic* and *pacif-y*.) This difference between Class 1 and Class 2 affixation is crucial to the observed differences in allophonic distribution between both types of word formation.

6.3.2 *Stem-based affixation: the Basic Model*

Benua (1995) argues that phonological identity effects in Class 2 affixation are due to OO-correspondence. Overapplication in *passing* is due to its relatedness to its base, *pass* [pEs]. In a diagram, this is portrayed as follows ('B' abbreviates base, and 'A' 'affixed form'):

(50)　　　**Basic Model of stem-based affixation**

$$BA\text{-}Identity$$

$$[pEs] \Leftrightarrow [pE.sɪŋ]$$

IO-Faithfulness　　⇕

$$/pæs/(cf.\ passive)$$

Benua (1995: 51) argues more generally that 'Class 2 affixation is derived through an O/O correspondence with the unaffixed word.' This OO-correspondence relation is analogous to that seen in truncated forms in the previous subsection.[7]

Two constraint interactions are relevant. First, the allophonic distribution of tense and lax low vowels, once more, points to the allophonic ranking schema of chapter 1:

(51)　　　Schema for allophonic variation

　　　　　Contextual markedness ≫ Context-free markedness ≫ Faithfulness

The contextual markedness constraint is æ-TENSING, militating against [æ] in closed syllables. It outranks a context-free markedness constraint *TENSE-low, requiring low vowels to be lax.

(52)　　　a. **æ-TENSING**

　　　　　*æC]$_\sigma$

　　　　　'No [æ] in closed syllables'[8]

　　　　　b. ***TENSE-low**

　　　　　Low vowels are lax.

　　　　　c. **IDENT-IO**(tense)

　　　　　Let α be a segment in the input, and β be a correspondent of α in the output.

　　　　　If α is [γtense], then β is [γtense].

This ranking is supported by the following tableaux of [pEs] and [æ.sɪd], which show that input values of [tense] are overruled:

(53)

Input: /pæs/	æ-TENSING	*TENSE-low	IDENT-IO(tense)
a.　　[pæs]	*!		
b. ☞ [pEs]		*	*

---

[7] Benua (1997) argues that Class 1 affixation is subject to its own set of OO-identity constraints. These constraints are ranked below those for Class 2 affixation: *OO$_2$-Identity* ≫ *OO$_1$-Identity*.

[8] Benua refers to æ-TENSING as a 'descriptive' constraint, since 'it must be specific to the [æ]~[E] alternation, and not force tensing of other vowels'. In contrast, *TENSE-low is *grounded* to the extent that it reflects the cross-linguistically common tendency to avoid tensing in low vowels.

(54)

Input: /ɛsɪd/	æ-TENSING	*TENSE-low	IDENT-IO(tense)
a. ☞ [æ.sɪd]			*
b.　　[ɛ.sɪd]		*!	

The second interaction relevant to the affixed form [pɛ.sɪŋ] relates to BA-identity. The relevant BA-identity constraint requires that the tenseness of a vowel in the base and its correspondent in the affixed form should be identical.

(55) **IDENT-BA(tense)**

Let α be a segment in the base, and β be a correspondent of α in the affixed form. If α is [γ tense], then β is [γ tense].

This constraint outranks *TENSE-low, as is supported by the selection of [pɛ.sɪŋ] rather than [pæ.sɪŋ].

(56) IDENT-BA(tense) ≫ *TENSE-low

[pɛ.sɪŋ] > [pæ.sɪŋ]

In sum, the overapplication follows from the ranking in (57).

(57) Overapplication of allophonic phonology in Class 2 affixed forms

IDENT-BA(tense), æ-TENSING ≫ *TENSE-low ≫ IDENT-IO(tense)

The interaction of these constraints is shown in a tableau of the affixed form [pɛ.sɪŋ]:

(58)

Input: /pæs/ Base: [pɛs]	IDENT-BA(tense)	æ-TENSING	*TENSE-low	IDENT-IO(tense)
a.　　[pæ.sɪŋ]	*!			
b. ☞ [pɛ.sɪŋ]			*	*

Upon comparing this tableau with that of truncation [lær] in (11), it will be clear that, once more, we witness a domination of a markedness constraint over an OO-identity constraint. The analysis of stem-based affixation is fully analogous to that of truncation, and both show that Correspondence Theory elegantly captures relations between output forms.

Again, a derivational analysis of the pattern is possible, but it encounters problems that are analogous to those pointed out in section 6.2.4.5 with respect to truncation. The general idea of a derivational analysis is ordering the allophonic rule which adjusts tenseness in closed syllables before the morphological rule of Class 2 affixation.

(59) /pæs/ Lexical form
pEs Tenseness Adjustment
pE.sɪŋ Class 2 affixation, resyllabification
[pE.sɪŋ] Surface form

This analysis is subject to the same criticisms as the derivational analysis of truncation that was discussed earlier. By ordering an allophonic rule (of Tenseness Adjustment in closed syllables) before a morphological rule (of /-ɪŋ/ affixation), it violates standard assumptions of Lexical Phonology (Kiparsky 1985). That is, allophonic rules should not apply in the lexical component, since they are not structure-preserving.[9]

6.4 The cycle versus base-identity

6.4.1 *Introduction*

Proponents of serial theory have argued for derivational levels which do not coincide with the input, nor with the output. An important argument for intermediate derivational levels was based on phonological properties carried over from morphologically simplex forms to complex forms. Such transderivational transfer was modelled as the *transformational cycle* (Chomsky and Halle 1968), a mode of rule application in morphologically complex words in which rules apply in an 'inside-out' fashion, from smaller to larger morphological domains. Cyclic rule application is intrinsically derivational, as it implies intermediate levels between the input and output at which phonological generalizations are captured.

Like derivational theory, OT searches for explanation in maximizing generalizations at some level of the grammar. The output is the privileged level at which significant linguistic generalizations are captured. OT grammars map underlying representations (lexical inputs) into surface forms (outputs) without intermediate levels, drastically reducing derivations to *one-step* mappings. The crucial difference between both theories resides in how interactions between generalizations

---

[9] Most dialects of English offer other examples of underapplication and overapplication in words derived by Class 2 affixes. Among these are the following two processes (Borowsky 1993):

Simplification of final /mn/		Syllabicity of /r/	
hymn	/hɪmn/	hinder	/hɪndr/
hymn-al	[hɪmnəl]	hinder-ance	[hɪndrəns]
hymn#	[hɪm]	hinder#	[hɪndr̩]
hymn#ing	[hɪmɪŋ]	hinder#ing	[hɪndr̩ɪŋ]

Final nasal cluster simplification 'overapplies' in [hɪmɪŋ], and /r/-syllabification in [hɪndr̩ɪŋ].

take place: either by linear precedence of rules (derivational theory) or by hierarchical ranking of constraints (OT).

Here we will compare two theoretical means of capturing transderivational identity: the *cycle* and *base-identity*. To evaluate predictions made by derivational theory and OT, we will analyse interactions of stress and vowel deletion in Palestinian Arabic. This language has a set of suffixes which, like Class 2 suffixes in English, exhibit 'special' phonological behaviour. Words derived by these suffixes display an underapplication of a vowel deletion process that 'normally' applies to words of analogous segmental make-up and stress pattern. A cyclic analysis of these underapplication effects (Brame 1974) will be compared with an analysis using base-identity (Kenstowicz 1996, Steriade 1996, Kager forthcoming).

Discussion is organized as follows. In section 6.4.2, we will compare derivational theory and OT with respect to 'transderivational' relations, on the basis of data from Palestinian Arabic involving underapplication of vowel deletion with respect to the surface stress pattern. An analysis will be proposed featuring a new kind of base-identity constraint, requiring identity between vowels in the affixed form and *stressed* correspondents in the base. We will argue for a notion of 'paradigmatic relatedness', predicting the morphological relations under which two forms display phonological identity effects. Section 6.4.3 will compare this base-identity analysis with a cyclic analysis in derivational theory. Section 6.4.4 discusses similar identity effects in epenthesis in Palestinian Arabic. Here we will focus on the possibility, predicted by OT, that an output form reflects the effects of both IO-faithfulness constraints and BA-identity constraints. This will support parallel evaluation of output forms, in the sense that both the base and lexical input are accessible simultaneously. Section 6.4.5 will contain conclusions.

6.4.2 *Underapplication of syncope in Palestinian Arabic*

6.4.2.1 *The cyclic analysis*

A famous example of cyclic rule application comes from the interaction of stress and vowel deletion in Palestinian Arabic, as analysed by Brame (1974). The stress rule interacts with a rule of *i-Syncope*, deleting unstressed /i/ in open non-final syllables. This is stated below:

(60) **i-Syncope**

$$\begin{bmatrix} i \\ -\text{stress} \end{bmatrix} \rightarrow \emptyset \, / \, \_\_ \, CV$$

Verbal forms inflected for subject (person, number, and gender) illustrate the application of i-Syncope:

(61)   Normal application of i-Syncope in verbal forms with subject suffixes

    a.   /fihim/   'to understand' (verb stem)

    b.i   /fihim/   fíhim   'he understood'

    b.ii /fihim-na/   fhím-na 'we understood'

    b.iii /fihim-u/   fíhm-u   'they understood'

Observe that i-Syncope preserves stressed vowels, hence it must be ordered after stress. The stress rule of Palestinian Arabic (which we will not state here in rule notation) places stress on a heavy penultimate syllable, otherwise on the antepenult. Derivations of these forms are presented in (62):

(62)

	/fihim/	/fihim-na/	/fihim-u/
Stress	fíhim	fihím-na	fíhim-u
i-Syncope	---	fhím-na	fíhm-u
	[fíhim]	[fhím-na]	[fíhm-u]

So far, we have not seen any cases of cyclic rule application. The actual examples on which Brame (1974) rested his case for transderivational preservation of stress are verbal forms containing accusative suffixes. Accusative suffixes express morphological features of the *object*. More precisely, verbal forms may be inflected for person, number, and gender of the object by a suffix that is added to a verb form inflected for subject. Observe that bold-face [i] in the forms in (63c) fails to delete, even though it stands in the context of i-Syncope, an open unstressed non-final syllable.

(63)   Normal application and underapplication of i-Syncope in accusatives

    a.   /fihim/   fíhim   'he understood'

    b.i   /fihim-ak/   fíhm-ak   'he understood you m.'

    b.ii /fihim-ik/   fíhm-ik   'he understood you f.'

    b.iii /fihim-u/   fíhm-u   'he understood him'

    c.i   /fihim-ni/   fihím-ni *fhím-ni 'he understood me'

    c.ii /fihim-ha/   fihím-ha *fhím-ha 'he understood her'

    c.iii /fihim-na/   fihím-na *fhím-na 'he understood us'

Brame observes that the accusative forms in which [i] fails to delete are all based on a free form [fíhim] (63a) in which this [i] is *stressed*. The generalization is that i-Syncope 'underapplies' in any affixed form that has a morphological base form in which [i] is stressed. Or to state it differently, any [i] having a stressed *correspondent* in the base is protected from deletion.

The correctness of this generalization is shown by *possessives*, nouns which contain a suffix indicating person and number of the possessor. Observe that i-Syncope is blocked in the bold-face vowels of these forms. Like accusatives, possessives have morphologically related nouns in which the corresponding [i] is stressed (Kenstowicz and Abdul-Karim 1980):

(64)   Underapplication of i-Syncope in possessives
        a. /birak/   bírak   'pools'
        b. /birak-u/ bírak-u   'his pools'
        c. /birak-na/ birák-na *brák-na 'our pools'

Again, underapplication of i-Syncope correlates with the presence of a stressed [i] in a base form. Unstressed [i] in [birák-na] is left unaffected by syncope when this vowel is stressed in the base [bírak]. And precisely as we saw before for the accusative forms, the possessive forms are formed by the addition of a (possessive) suffix to a free form (or 'base'), which is inflected itself.

Underapplication of i-Syncope cannot be due to an actual (secondary) stress on the initial syllable of accusatives and possessives, e.g. [fìhím-na] and [bìrák-na]. Kenstowicz and Abdul-Karim (1980) found that for speakers of Palestinian Arabic the analogous form that is based on a CaCaC verb, e.g. [ḍaráb-na], is *ambiguous* between 'we hit' and 'he hit us'. If there is no phonetic difference between the two forms, then certainly there cannot be a secondary stress on the [i] that is protected from syncope in the accusatives and possessives. This then makes the property which is responsible for the blocking of i-Syncope in accusatives and possessives 'abstract' to a certain degree. Of course, the abstractness of the property which blocks i-Syncope was precisely what raised Brame's interest. Stress is not present in lexical representations, nor is it present at the surface on the vowel which is mysteriously protected from i-Syncope. Hence it must be the case that i-Syncope applies to a level of representation *intermediate* between the lexical representation and the surface representation. This, in turn, implies that phonological theory should allow such intermediate levels of representation. Thus, what Brame argued for is that *derivations* are an essential part of phonological theory.

In derivational theory the notion of 'relatedness' between forms is characteristically modelled in derivational terms, that is, *cyclically*. Under cyclic application, an ordered set of phonological rules (R_1–R_n) first apply to the minimal morphological domain, and then to successively larger domains. Brame (1974) assumes that accusatives and possessives have an additional internal layer of morphological structure, which triggers a cyclic application of the stress rule.

The cyclically assigned stress on the first syllable of [fíhim] is carried over to the second cycle [[fihím]-na], even though it becomes subordinated to the new main stress. The secondary stress protects the initial syllable's vowel against post-cyclic i-Syncope. Finally, initial secondary stress is erased by a post-cyclic rule of *Destressing*:

(65)

	Input	[fihim-na]$_{Subj}$	[fihim-u]$_{Subj}$	[[fihim]na]$_{Acc}$	[[fihim]u]$_{Acc}$
	Cycle1				
	Stress	fihím-na	fíhim-u	fíhim	fíhim
	Cycle2				
	Stress	---	---	fihím-na	(*vacuous*)
	Post-cyclic				
	i-Syncope	fhím-na	fíhm-u	*blocked*	fíhm-u
	Destressing	*n.a.*	*n.a.*	fihím-na	*n.a.*
	Output	fhímna	fíhmu	fihímna	fíhmu

This analysis was regarded as strong evidence for extrinsic rule ordering, in the sense that a phonological property (stress) that is acquired in the course of the derivation blocks a rule that is sensitive to its presence (i-Syncope), even though it is absent from the surface form due to a subsequent rule that deletes it (Destressing). This is achieved by linearly ordered rules that are 'blind' to underlying representations ('no globality'), and have access only to the representation that arises at the point in the derivation at which they apply.

6.4.2.2 *The base-identity analysis*

How can underapplication of i-Syncope be analysed in OT, a theory which (in its strictest form) avoids derivations, hence lacks the intermediary level of representation which Brame argued for? An OT analysis based on base-identity was proposed by Kenstowicz (1996), Steriade (1996), and Kager (forthcoming). We will discuss it below.

Let us return to the initial generalization made by Brame: the unstressed vowel [i] in an accusative or possessive is protected from deletion *if its counterpart in the base word is stressed*. Blocking of i-Syncope is a kind of base-identity, keeping morphologically related forms maximally similar in their phonological form. Accordingly the central idea of the OT analysis is that underapplication of i-Syncope is due to OO-correspondence. Let us now develop such an analysis.[10]

From here on, we will use the notion of 'base' in a specific sense, making explicit two criteria. First, the base is a free-standing output form of the language, that is, a *word*. Second, the base is *compositionally related* to its derived counterpart (the affixed form or truncated form). That is, the base contains a proper subset of the grammatical (semantic, morphological) features of the derived form.

---

[10] The analysis presented below draws on Kager (forthcoming).

(66)   **Definition of 'base'**

a. The base is a free-standing output form – a *word*.

b. The base contains a *subset of the grammatical features* of the derived form.

Note that the morphological relation between a truncated form and its base is included in this definition. Both occur as free-standing independent words. Truncation also matches the second criterion. Consider, for example, the morpho-semantic status of a truncated form in Icelandic, the deverbal action noun. This properly contains the morpho-semantic features of the infinitive, which is its base. In fact, the only thing that is 'subtractive' about truncation is phonological: the truncated form is a segmental reduction of the base. From a morpho-semantic viewpoint, truncation is an *addition*, precisely as overt affixation. (Note that the very terminology 'truncation' correctly suggests that the truncated form results from a morphological operation on the base.)

This definition of 'base' is precise enough to capture the distinction among subject and accusative forms in Palestinian Arabic which is relevant for the (under)application of i-Syncope.

Subject forms such as [fhím-na] 'we understood' (61b.ii) have *no base* since no form occurs which matches both criteria for 'base-hood'. In particular, the verb stem /fihim/ 'to understand', which would be appropriate in a compositional sense, lacks inflection features. Hence the verb stem is no word, thereby failing the first criterion. Nor can the word [fíhim] 'he understood' serve as the base for [fhím-na] 'we understood'. These words are not compositionally related to one another, because of a conflict of inflectional features (1sg. versus 2pl.), thereby failing the second criterion.

Accusative forms, in contrast, have bases by both criteria. For example, the form [fihím-na] 'he understood us' has as its base a free-standing form [fíhim] 'he understood', of which it contains all morpho-semantic features. More generally, every accusative form has precisely one subject form which is its base.

(67)   Form   Gloss   Base   Gloss

a.i   [fhím-na]   'we understood'   (none)

a.ii [fíh.mu]   'they understood'   (none)

b.i   [fihím-na] 'he understood us'   [fíhim] 'he understood'

b.ii [fíhm-u]   'he understood him'   [fíhim] 'he understood'

By the same criteria, *possessive* forms have bases, for example [birák-na] 'our pools' has as its base the word [bírak] 'pools', which contains a subset of its morpho-semantic features.

Keeping these remarks on the notion of base in our minds, we can now return to the original problem, of how to characterize underapplication of i-Syncope in object forms and possessives. As we have seen, the generalization is that i-Syncope 'underapplies' to vowels which are *stressed* in the *base*:

(68)   a. [fíhim] 'he understood' ↔ [fihím-na] 'he understood him'
        b. [bírak] 'pools'   ↔ [birák-na] 'our pools'

From here on, graphic means will serve to indicate the correspondence relations between an affixed form and (on the one hand) its input and (on the other hand) its base. These relations will be marked by vertical lines between correspondents at three levels (input, output, and base). In (69a), bold-face [**i**] indicates the underapplication of i-Syncope in the output:

(69)   a. 'he understood us'   b. 'we understood'

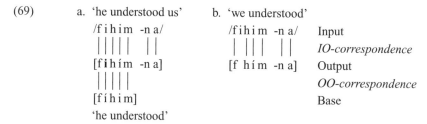

The correspondence-based perspective of this pattern is that syncope 'underapplies' in the accusative and possessive because the relevant vowels have *stressed correspondents* in the base. More precisely, syncope is blocked by an OO-correspondence constraint requiring that vowels which are stressed in the base must have correspondents in the affixed form:

(70)   **HEADMAX-BA**

        Every segment in the base's *prosodic head* has a correspondent in the affixed form.

This is a *head-identity* constraint, which involves an extension of correspondence to stress properties of segments. Such an extension was proposed by McCarthy (1995a) and Alderete (1995).

Vowel deletion ('i-Syncope') is triggered by a markedness constraint disallowing [i] in open syllables.[11]

---

[11] This constraint is modelled after an analogous constraint No [a] in Orgun (1995). An interesting question is whether No [i] can be decomposed into general constraints which, taken together, produce its effects. Presumably this is possible, if we assume a constraint against monomoraic syllables (argued for by Broselow 1992: 32), and rank this in between faithfulness constraints for specific vowels, for example IDENT-IO[a] ≫ *σ$_\mu$ ≫ IDENT-IO[i]. We will not pursue this issue here, but maintain the formulation of No [i] as it is.

(71)   **No [i]**
         /i/ is not allowed in light syllables.

Note that no reference is made to stress, an aspect that will be confirmed in section 6.4.4, where we discuss the interaction of syncope, stress, and epenthesis.

No [i] clearly outranks the faithfulness constraint requiring that input segments have correspondents in the output (McCarthy and Prince 1995a):

(72)   **Max-IO**
         Every segment in the input has a correspondent in the output.

This ranking is motivated by the fact that deletion occurs in forms such as [fhímna] 'we understood', which satisfy No [i] at the expense of Max-IO.

The underapplication of i-Syncope requires HeadMax-BA ≫ No [i] since deletion is blocked wherever base-identity is active. The constraint ranking that now arises is (73):

(73)   Underapplication of i-Syncope
         HeadMax-BA ≫ No [i] ≫ Max-IO

The analysis is illustrated by tableaux (74–5). Only candidates that satisfy the canonical stress patterns of Palestinian Arabic are considered; the issue of how stress interacts with the processes of syncope and epenthesis will be taken up in section 6.4.4 below.

Tableau (74) illustrates the underapplication of i-Syncope, while tableau (75) shows how syncope occurs in a form that lacks a base:

(74)

Input: /fihim-na/ Base: [fí.him]	HeadMax-BA	No [i]	Max-IO
a. ☞ [fi.hím.na]		*	
b. [fhím.na]	*!		*

(75)

Input: /fihim-na/ Base: *none*	HeadMax-BA	No [i]	Max-IO
a. [fi.hím.na]		*!	
b. ☞ [fhím.na]			*

This shows that we are on the right track: the basic observation that i-Syncope underapplies in accusatives with consonant-initial suffixes has now been accounted for.

Next let us consider forms that have vowel-initial suffixes, the accusative [fíh.mu] 'he understood him' (with its base [fí.him] 'he understood'), and the subject form [fíh.mu] 'they understood' (lacking a base). The constraint ranking correctly predicts that i-Syncope applies in both forms, resulting in a pair of homophonous outputs. In the accusative form, the second occurrence of [i] in the stem is freely deleted since its counterpart in the base is not stressed. Therefore HEADMAX-BA is not violated in candidate (76b), and the outcome is left to the markedness constraint No [i]:

(76)

Input: /fihim-u/ Base: [fí.him]	HEADMAX-BA	No [i]	MAX-IO
a. [fí.hi.mu]		*!*	
b. ☞ [fíh.mu]			*
c. [fhí.mu]	*!	*	*

In the subject form, HEADMAX-BA is simply irrelevant, since there is no base in this case:

(77)

Input: /fihim-u/ Base: *none*	HEADMAX-BA	No [i]	MAX-IO
a. [fí.hi.mu]		*!*	
b. ☞ [fíh.mu]			*
c. [fhí.mu]		*!	*

In sum, syncope is not blocked by the presence of a counterpart vowel in the base, but only by the presence of a *stressed* counterpart vowel in the base.

6.4.3 *The cycle versus base-identity*

From the above discussion a number of general conclusions can be drawn. First, the notion 'base' in OO-correspondence is firmly linked to compositionality. Second, the assumption that the base is a free-standing output form correctly predicts that transderivational relations involve output forms. This prediction does not follow from derivational theory, since what counts as a *cycle* is inherently unconstrained by the criterion of 'free-standing form'. Any layer of morphological structure, regardless of its relation with free-standing words, is predicted potentially to display cyclicity. In order to distinguish between subject morphology and object morphology in Palestinian Arabic verbs, Brame had to make the (arbitrary) assumption that only the latter type invokes cyclicity. However, if matters had been reverse (with subject morphology invoking cyclicity), this would have been equally easy to express on the cyclic theory.[12]

Let us make a more detailed comparison between the base-identity analysis and the cyclic derivational analysis, based on the subject form [fihmu] 'they understood'. The cyclic analysis (in derivation 65) imposes a condition on i-Syncope restricting its application to unstressed vowels. This stress condition crucially protects the vowel in the initial syllable of /fihim-u/ against i-Syncope, in order to rule out the incorrect form *[fhimu].

In the base-identity analysis, no need arises for such a stress condition, and actually it would be impossible to state anything like it. It is impossible to refer to lack of stress in the target vowel of syncope, as this vowel does not appear in the output. Nor could blocking of initial syncope be attributed to base-identity, since subject forms generally lack a base. Instead, the base-identity analysis blocks candidate (77c) *[fhi.mu] by the *same constraint* that triggers i-syncope in the first place: No [i]. If the goal of i-Syncope is the avoidance of light syllables containing [i], then some progress toward this goal must be made in the output, due to *minimal violation*. (Compare optimal [fih.mu] in 77b, which has no open syllables with [i], with suboptimal *[fhi.mu] in 77c, where one open syllable with [i] is still present.)

Nevertheless, the base-identity analysis does still require *some* reference to stress to account for underapplication effects, as in the accusative form [fihimna] (74a). As we have seen, reference to stress is made by HEADMAX-BA, a base-identity constraint requiring that stressed vowels be preserved in morphologically related forms. The difference in approach between the analyses can be stated as follows: the OT analysis rationalizes the reference to stress as a case of paradigm uniformity, involving OO-correspondence. The derivational analysis instead takes the paradigmatic dimension in blocking to be coincidental, and views blocking as due to the presence of an *abstract stress* at an intermediate level of derivation. Which view is more appropriate?

Arguably, the abstractness of the cyclic analysis, in spite of its striking appearance, constitutes a drawback in terms of learnability. In general, the language learner is presented with extra difficulties in learning a rule whose effects are obscured at the surface level. The stress that is present at the intermediate level of representation (where it blocks i-Syncope) is no longer present at the surface level, and hence has to be 'inferred' or 'reconstructed' by a morphological

---

[12] This objection does not hold for the prosodic theory of Lexical Phonology that was developed by Inkelas (1989), which links the notion of 'cyclic category' to its prosodic independence.

analysis of the relevant word. That is, the abstract stress in [fihímna] must be related to the fact that it *actually* appears in [fíhim]. Now observe that assuming this morphological reconstruction process is tantamount to establishing a 'paradigmatic link' between a derived form and its base, precisely as in the OT analysis. The only difference is that an OT analysis turns this reference to morphologically related forms into a *principle of grammar*, taking the form of OO-correspondence. But this step pays off, since it eliminates abstractness. As a general strategy, eliminating abstractness is attractive in terms of learnability.

However, it is fair to point out a liability of the OT analysis, one which derivational theory avoids. The derivational analysis assumes that phonological surface specifications of every output form are derived on the basis of information present in lexical representations, plus its internal morphological structure. In a way, every complex form is 'self-sufficient', which gives a restrictive *local* theory of trans-derivational relations. This localism no longer holds under OO-correspondence, where surface specification of a morphologically complex word becomes dependent upon surface properties of *other* words. The important question is: to what extent is Correspondence Theory able to impose *restrictions* on *logically possible* paradigmatic relations?[13] Does the elimination of abstractness compensate for this increase in globality? At present, it is very difficult to answer this question. However, whatever loss of restrictiveness may occur as a result of the increase in globality must be compensated for by constraining the notion of 'paradigmatic relation'. The definition of 'base', as presented here, is an attempt at constraining the notion of OO-correspondence.

6.4.4 *Epenthesis and opacity of metrical structure*

We now turn to opacity of metrical structure. We will first discuss the process of epenthesis as a source of metrical opacity, and its interactions with base-identity and faithfulness. Then we will discuss the metrical constraints proper, ranking them with respect to the constraints responsible for epenthesis and syncope.

Palestinian Arabic has a process of i-*Epenthesis*, which inserts [i] between the first and second consonant in a sequence of three consonants, or between two consonants at the end of the word:

(78)   i-Epenthesis
$$\emptyset \rightarrow i \; / \; C \underline{\quad} C \left\{ \begin{matrix} C \\ \# \end{matrix} \right\}$$

---

[13] Various answers to this question were given by Benua (1995), Buckley (1995), Flemming (1995), Orgun (1994, 1995, 1996), Kenstowicz (1996), Steriade (1996), Kager (forthcoming), and others.

This process is the source of opaque stress in possessive examples such as those in (79a.iii, 79b.iii) below. Epenthetic vowels appear in bold-face:

(79)   Epenthesis and opaque stress in Palestinian Arabic
        a.i   /fihm/   fí.him   'understanding'
        a.ii   /fihm-u/   fíh.mu   'his understanding'
        a.iii /fihm-na/   fí.him.na *fi.hím.na   'our understanding'
        b.i   /ʔakl/   ʔá.kil   'food'
        b.ii   /ʔakl-u/   ʔák.lu   'his food'
        b.iii /ʔakl-ha/   ʔá.kil.ha *ʔa.kíl.ha   'her food'

Stress is 'opaque' in the sense that it fails to accord with surface syllabification. Palestinian generally stresses the penultimate syllable if it is heavy, and otherwise the antepenult. (Here we disregard final stress on 'superheavy' syllables.) Nevertheless, forms (79a.iii–b.iii) are stressed on their antepenults, in spite of their closed (heavy) penults.

In a derivational analysis, this interaction involves ordering i-Epenthesis *after* stress. The derivation in (80) shows how i-Epenthesis comes 'too late' to determine surface stress:

(80)   /fihm/   /fihm-u/   /fihm-na/
        Stress Cycle 1 fíhm   fíhm   fíhm
               Cycle 2 fíhm   fíhm-u   fíhm-na
        i-Epenthesis   fíhim   ---   fíhim-na
                        [fíhim]   [fíhmu]   [fíhimna]

Again the question arises as to how OT captures the opacity. Let us first see what constraint interaction produces i-Epenthesis.

Epenthesis is triggered by a combination of two high-ranked constraints on syllable well-formedness (81a–b), which we will combine into a cover constraint SYLL-FORM:

(81)   **SYLL-FORM**
        a. *COMPLEX (cf. Prince and Smolensky 1993)
           No complex syllable margins.
        b. SON-SEQ   (cf. Clements 1990)
           Complex onsets rise in sonority, and complex codas fall in sonority.

Avoidance of syllabic ill-formedness takes priority over avoidance of epenthetic vowels. Or, to state it in terms of constraint ranking: *COMPLEX ≫ DEP-IO.[14]

---

[14] Perhaps more appropriately, *CCC, since at the word beginning complex onsets are allowed, and actually created by the deletion of input vowels (cf. [fhím-na]).

Violations of *COMPLEX can be avoided in two different ways, that is, by epenthesis between the first and the second consonant, or after the second consonant.

(82)   a. C_CC   fí.him.na
         b. CC_C   *fíh.mi.na

In a derivational analysis, the locus of epenthesis is stated in the rule. More sophisticated derivational analyses would predict the locus from directional syllabification (see Itô 1989). Neither of these options is available in an OT analysis. There are no rules in OT, let alone directional rules.

Once again, base-identity is involved. If we consider the optimal output form [fí.him.na], we find that this maximally resembles its base, in the sense that both vowels appearing in the base [fí.him] are preserved in the affixed form. The fact that one of the vowels (underlined in 83a) is 'epenthetic' with respect to the *input* is simply irrelevant for base-identity:

(83)   a. /f i h m -n a/   b. /f i h m -n a/ Input
            ||| | || ||| | ||
            [f í h i m -n a]   [f í h m i -n a] Output
            ||||| |||| |
            [f í h i m]   [f í h i m]   Base

Correspondence between base and output is broken in (83b), where the epenthetic vowel **[i]** lacks a correspondent in the base. This points to a base-identity constraint of the MAX type, requiring that base segments have correspondents in the output (the affixed form):

(84)   **MAX-BA**
         Every segment in the base has a correspondent in the affixed form.

MAX-BA is more general than HEADMAX-BA as it does not refer to stress in the base vowel. Both constraints also differ in their positions in the ranking, crucially with respect to No [i]. MAX-BA outranks No [i], whereas HEADMAX-BA ranks below it, as the following syncope data show:

(85)   a. HEADMAX-BA ≫ No [i]   /fihim-na/ 'he understood us'
                                   [fihím-na] > [fhím-na]
         b. No [i] ≫ MAX-BA   /fihim-u/ 'he understood him'
                                   [fíhm-u] > [fíhim-u]

The next question is: if the (bold-face) vowel in [fí.him.na] 'our understanding' copies the epenthetic vowel in its base [fí.him] 'understanding', then what predicts the epenthesis site in the base? We must consider two candidates, one with stem-internal epenthesis, [fí.him], the other with stem-external epenthesis, [fíh.mi]. The former is selected by a Generalized Alignment constraint (chapter 3, after McCarthy and Prince 1993a):

(86)   ALIGN-R

$]_{GrWd} =]_\sigma$

This constraint is apparently undominated in Palestinian Arabic.

Let us briefly consider the featural content of the epenthetic vowel, which depends on featural markedness (chapter 3). Epenthetic [i] is apparently less marked than any other vowel. This result follows from the context-free markedness constraint *[−high]:

(87)   *[−high]

In the tableaux below we will not include this constraint, and tactitly assume it by including only [i] as an epenthetic vowel.[15]

After this preliminary analysis, let us now localize the source of metrical opacity. As we have seen, opacity resides in the lack of accordance between stress and syllabification in surface forms. Palestinian Arabic generally assigns stress to any heavy penultimate syllable. Then why is epenthetic [i] in [fi.him.na] and [ʔá.kil.ha] *unstressed* even though it stands in a closed penult, a syllable that normally attracts stress? The rejection of stress by epenthetic vowels is in fact a cross-linguistically common phenomenon (Piggott 1995, Alderete 1995). To capture it, Alderete (1995) proposes a *head dependence* constraint requiring that stressed vowels must have input correspondents:

(88)   HEADDEP-IO

Every vowel in the output's prosodic head has a correspondent in the input.

Epenthetic [i] in [fí.him.na] lacks a correspondent in the input, as illustrated by the diagram in (89a). Therefore stressing it would violate HEADDEP-IO. In contrast, the stressed vowel in [ba.kár.na] 'our cattle' (89b), with a base [bá.kar] 'cattle', has an input correspondent and hence stressing it does not violate HEADDEP-IO.

---

[15] See Abu-Salim (1980) for data showing that [u] patterns much like [i] in syncope and epenthesis.

(89)   a. /f i h m -n a/   b. /b a k a r -n a/ Input

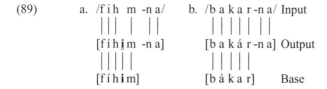

[f í h i̱ m -n a]   [b a k á r -n a] Output

[f í h i m]   [b á k a r] Base

Indirectly, form (89b) rules out an alternative hypothesis about opaque stress in [fi.hím.na], according to which a vowel that is stressed in the output must have a *stressed* correspondent in the base. This hypothesis is ruled out since the stressed output vowel of form (89b) has no stressed correspondent in the base.

'Metrical opacity' can now be modelled as the domination of an identity constraint over a metrical well-formedness constraint. More precisely, HEADDEP-IO dominates the well-formedness constraint which is responsible for stress on heavy (penultimate) syllables (the Weight-to-Stress Principle, or WSP, Prince and Smolensky 1993):

(90)   Metrical opacity in Palestinian Arabic
        HEADDEP-IO ≫ WSP

The reverse ranking would produce penultimate stress, e.g. *[fihím-na], rather than [fíhim-na].

The analysis of vowel–zero alternations in Palestinian is illustrated by three tableaux of minimally contrasting output forms: [fihím-na] 'he understood us' in (91), [fhím-na] 'we understood' in (92), and [fíhim-na] 'our understanding' in (93).

(91)

Input: /fihim-na/ Base: [fí.him]	SYLL-FORM	HEADMAX-BA	No [i]	HEADDEP-IO	MAX-BA	WSP
a. ☞ [fi.hím.na]			*			
b. [fí.him.na]			*			*!
c. [fíh.mi.na]			*		*!	
d. [fhím.na]		*!			*	
e. [fíhm.na]	*!				*	

(92)

Input: /fihim-na/ Base: *none*	SYLL-FORM	HEADMAX-BA	No [i]	HEADDEP-IO	MAX-BA	WSP
a. [fi.hím.na]			*!			
b. [fí.him.na]			*!			*
c. [fíh.mi.na]			*!			
d. ☞ [fhím.na]						
e. [fíhm.na]	*!					

The final tableau is the crucial one: it shows the opacity effect with respect to epenthetic [i]:

(93)

Input: /fihim-na/ Base: [fí.him]	SYLL-FORM	HEADMAX-BA	No [i]	HEADDEP-IO	MAX-BA	WSP
a. [fi.hím.na]			*	*!		
b. ☞ [fí.him.na]			*			*
c. [fíh.mi.na]			*		*!	
d. [fhím.na]		*!			*	
e. [fíhm.na]	*!				*	

Finally we are in a position to substantiate the claim that the interaction of epenthesis and stress in Palestinian Arabic involves the parallel evaluation of IO-faithfulness and OO-identity. Such parallelism is demonstrated by the activity, within the same hierarchy, of both constraint types. Note that within a single output form [fi.him.na] (93b) the bold-face vowel is treated as *epenthetic* with respect to the input (which is why it cannot surface as stressed – due to HEADDEP-IO), while it is, paradoxically, treated as *non-epenthetic* with respect to the base (which is why it must be retained – due to MAX-BA).

6.4.5 *Conclusions*

The OT analysis of Palestinian Arabic stress and vowel–zero alternations leads to a number of conclusions with respect to the morphology–phonology interface. On first inspection, the opacities in these patterns seem to be problematic to OT, and to support intermediate levels of representation and the derivational mechanism of the cycle. However, as we now see, an analysis which is based on OO-correspondence is equally adequate in descriptive terms, and it has the additional conceptual advantage of eliminating abstractness. A definition of '*base*' was proposed, as a free-standing form compositionally related to the complex word. Finally, the evaluation of OO-correspondence and IO-correspondence in output forms turns out to be a parallel process.

6.5 Output-to-output correspondence: conclusions

The goal of this chapter was to discuss extensions of Correspondence Theory to two novel empirical domains, morphological truncation and stem-based affixation. It may be too early for an evaluation of the overall merits of the base-identity approach, but certainly the first results are encouraging.

Brame's famous cyclic analysis of vowel–zero alternations and stress in Palestinian Arabic has stood as a major example of intermediate levels in phonology for a long period. The correspondence analysis maintains its essential insight – that morphologically complex forms depend on less complex forms in their phonological shape, but it eliminates the serial (or transderivational) nature of the dependence relation. At the same time it eliminates the abstractness involved in the serial analysis. Brame's analysis was abstract in the sense that a blocking of syncope was attributed to a pre-surface stress pattern in the complex form rather than to the stress pattern in the base form, where it is overt.

The consequences of this base-identity approach for other empirical domains remain to be determined by careful analysis. For example, to what extent can the notion of possible paradigmatic relation be constrained in Correspondence Theory? Another focus of attention of future OT research will be on phenomena that have been argued to require intermediate levels of derivation in serial theory. Among these are a set of phenomena that were analysed by so-called 'counterfeeding' and 'counterbleeding' rules orders in serial theory. That is, OT must develop a theory of *opacity*. We will return to this important issue in chapter 9.

SUGGESTIONS FOR FURTHER READING

Identity in truncation

Benua, Laura (1995) Identity effects in morphological truncation. In Beckman, Walsh Dickey, and Urbanczyk. 77–136. [ROA-74, http://ruccs.rutgers.edu/roa.html]

Colina, Sonia (1996) Spanish truncation processes: the emergence of the unmarked. *Linguistics* **34**. 1199–218.

Identity in affixation

Burzio, Luigi (forthcoming) Cycles, regularization, and correspondence. To appear in J. Dekkers, F. van der Leeuw, and J. van de Weijer (eds.), *Optimality Theory: syntax, phonology, and acquisition*. Oxford University Press.

Itô, Junko and R. Armin Mester (1997) Correspondence and compositionality: the *Ga-gyo* variation in Japanese phonology. In Roca. 419–62.

Kager, René (forthcoming) Surface opacity of metrical structure in Optimality Theory. To appear in Hermans and van Oostendorp.

Kenstowicz, Michael (1996) Base-identity and uniform exponence: alternatives to cyclicity. In J. Durand and B. Laks (eds.), *Current trends in phonology: models and methods*. CNRS, Paris X, and University of Salford: University of Salford Publications. 363–93. [ROA 103, http://ruccs.rutgers.edu/roa.html]

The phonology–morphology interface

Inkelas, Sharon (1996) Dominant affixes and the phonology–morphology interface. In U. Kleinhenz (ed.), *Interfaces in phonology*. Studia Grammatica 41. Berlin: Akademie Verlag. 128–54.

EXERCISES

1 Spanish

Spanish (Harris 1983) neutralizes place of articulation (to alveolars) in coda consonants. Neutralization is illustrated by the following alternations, where input palatals /ʎ, ɲ/ in coda position surface as alveolars [l, n], respectively:

/donθeʎ-a/	donθeʎa	'lass'	/desdeɲ-ar/	desdeɲar	'to disdain'
/donθeʎ-a-s/	donθeʎas	'lass, pl.'	/desdeɲ-os-o/	desdeɲoso	'disdainful'
/donθeʎ/	donθel	'lad, sg.'	/desdeɲ/	desden	'disdain, sg.'

Neutralization of place of articulation 'overapplies' in the following plurals:

/donθeʎ-es/	donθeles	'lad, pl.'	/desdeɲ-es/	desdenes	'disdain, pl.'

    a. Rank the constraints pertaining to coda neutralization of place features.

    b. Next analyse the overapplication effect, proposing an OO-correspondence constraint and ranking it with respect to the constraints you found in (a).

    c. Discuss any assumptions that you have found necessary with respect to the notion 'base', then explain the contrasts [donθeʎa] ~ [donθeles] and [desdeɲoso] ~ [desdenes].

    d. Present tableaux of [donθeʎa], [donθel], and [donθeles].

2 Belfast English

In Belfast English (Harris 1990, Borowsky 1993) alveolar non-continuants [t, d, n, l] are dentalized to [t̪, d̪, n̪, l̪], respectively, before rhotics [ər], [r]:

fat	[fæt]	late	[leɪt]	train	[t̪reɪn]	matter	[mæt̪ər]
wide	[waɪd]	dine	[daɪn]	drain	[d̪reɪn]	spider	[spaɪd̪ər]
fill	[fɪl]	kill	[kɪl]	ladder	[læd̪ər]	pillar	[pɪl̪ər]

However, dentalization fails to apply before the comparative and agentive suffixes /-r/, even though these are phonetically indistinguishable from the endings in *spider* etc.:

[t]	matter	[t]	fatter
[d]	spider	[d]	wider
[l]	pillar	[l]	filler

    a.   Propose an analysis of the allophonic variation between alveolars and dentals, setting up a contextual markedness constraint. (Assume that dentals are [+distrib], while alveolars are [−distrib].) To show the allophonic nature of the distribution, present two tableaux of *train*, one for each possible input value of [distrib] (/treɪn/ and /t̪reɪn/).

    b.   Next analyse the underapplication of dentalization, introducing a new OO-correspondence constraint pertaining to [distrib], and ranking it with respect to the constraints of (a).

    c.   Present tableaux of *fat, matter*, and *fatter*, for both possible input values of [distrib].

3 Factorial typology of OO-correspondence

    a.   Compute the factorial typology of IO-correspondence, OO-correspondence, context-free, and contextual markedness constraints. Make sure that you cover 'normal application', 'overapplication', and 'underapplication'. (Follow the methodology of chapter 5, section 5.6.)

    b.   Compare your factorial typology with the one presented in chapter 5 on reduplication. Do you find any significant differences? In particular, does the factorial typology of OO-correspondence contain the analogue of 'reduplicative back-copying'? (Chapter 5, section 5.6.5.)

    c.   Construct an imaginary case of back-copying to the base in stem-based affixation, and try to instantiate it by an actual case in a real language. Comment on your findings addressing any consequences for the notion 'base', addressing any consequences for the notion 'base'.

7
Learning OT grammars

7.1 Introduction

Generative theory assumes that the grammars of individual languages are all variations on a single theme, that of Universal Grammar. By hypothesis, UG is innate rather than acquired, and hence it defines the range of possibilities within which natural languages fall. From this viewpoint the study of first language acquisition becomes of crucial relevance to the study of natural language, as it may offer a window onto properties of UG, hence into the human language faculty. The central issue in first language acquisition is this: how do principles of UG determine the acquisition process?

In previous studies, this issue of language acquisition has been approached from a variety of viewpoints and methods. Some researchers study data from children's language, while others consider the preconditions that are necessary to make a grammar learnable.

One field of investigation is based on the collection of data from children's speech, in the form of corpora of spontaneous speech, or elicited through experimental methods. Researchers study these data in close connection with assumptions about UG, and attempt to establish the relevant properties of UG which guide the child during her acquisition of the target grammar (Nouveau 1994, Demuth 1995, Gnanadesikan 1995, Goad 1997).

The second field of investigation, which we will actually focus on in this chapter, is *learnability*. Here the central issue is what formal and substantive properties of universal grammar make it possible that grammars of individual languages can actually be learned. OT makes a number of assumptions about UG which are very different from other models, particularly *Principles-and-Parameters Theory* (Wexler and Culicover 1980, Hyams 1986, Dresher and Kaye 1990), which defines the learner's task as determining values of a set of universally available binary choices, each corresponding to an inviolate property of the target grammar. In contrast, OT assumes that UG defines a set of universal and violable constraints, as well as principles by which constraints interact. Individual languages differ along the dimension of constraint ranking (as well as in their lexicons). If grammars are essentially rankings of universal constraints, then acquiring a language must involve the acquisition of a language-specific hierarchy of universal constraints. The language learner has exclusive access to the output forms of the target language, and is faced with the task of extracting the information from these outputs that is necessary to rank all constraints in a way predicting the outputs. What strategies might the language learner use to bring this task to a successful end? What guarantee is there that the child will eventually arrive at the target grammar by a process of ranking and reranking constraints? These and other questions will be central in this chapter.

This chapter is organized as follows. In section 7.2 we focus on the issue of the learnability of OT grammars. Assuming that languages differ mainly by their constraint rankings, can it be proved that it is actually possible for the language learner to infer the correct ranking on the basis of output data? We will discuss results of a learning algorithm developed by Tesar and Smolensky (1993), which lead to a positive answer to the above question. The algorithm will be seen in action in section 7.3. In section 7.4 we will discuss aspects of language acquisition which are currently not included in this model, and we will review some attempts to include these. Finally, section 7.5 will sketch an approach to adapt the algorithm to the complications involved in learning phonological 'alternations'.

7.2   Learning constraint rankings

7.2.1   *Defining the problem*

The specific question which we will address in this section is this: given the availability of a set of surface forms of the target language, and a set of universal constraints, is it possible for the language learner to discover the correct constraint ranking of the target language? If so, what strategies does the learner use to discover the proper ranking? We will discuss an approach to the issue of learnability of OT grammars which was developed by Tesar and Smolensky (1993). The learning algorithm serves as a model of the language learner, and it is faced with the task of constructing a hierarchy of constraints for a language on the basis of *output* forms of this language. Results of the algorithm are positive, in the sense that it is indeed possible to deduce constraint rankings on the basis of a given input plus an output. This result is of key importance to the assumption that grammars are essentially language-specific hierarchies of constraints.

7.2.2 *The constraint demotion algorithm: basic ideas*

An algorithm developed by Tesar and Smolensky demonstrates that it is possible to deduce rankings of constraints on the basis of output forms plus a set of universal constraints. The algorithm assumes that the *input* (the form from which the attested output derives) is *given*. Moreover it assumes that the *output* is a *linguistically structured* representation, rather than a raw phonetic form. Both assumptions represent idealizations of a real-life learning situation (in which inputs have to be inferred by the learner, and outputs are raw acoustic forms). In a more sophisticated learning algorithm, these idealizations will have to be abandoned. We will address various possibilities of how this might be achieved in sections 7.4–7.5.

The Tesar and Smolensky algorithm is based on an idea which we have, implicitly, made use of several times before in this book. That is, information about constraint ranking can be extracted from the *violation* (rather than satisfaction) of constraints in the optimal candidate. The key idea is that *constraints which are violated in the optimal output must be dominated by some other constraint*. To identify the relevant dominating constraint(s), the algorithm compares the attested output to various other (suboptimal) candidates. For each pair consisting of the attested output and a suboptimal candidate, it lists constraints which are violated by one member of the pair, but not by the other, and vice versa. From this 'crossed' comparison, the algorithm then deduces the constraint hierarchy which pairs the attested form as the optimal output to a given input. In this way, maximal use is made of information provided by the single source of positive evidence: output forms.

The central principle by which the algorithm applies is 'constraint demotion'. The initial state of the algorithm is one in which all constraints are unranked with respect to one another. That is, all constraints are undominated. See (1):

(1)   **Initial state of the constraint hierarchy**
        $\{C_1, C_2, C_3 \ldots C_n\}$

Starting from this initial unranked state, the algorithm gradually develops a hierarchy by reranking constraints. Reranking is only allowed if there is *positive evidence* in the form of a constraint violation in the optimal output. Reranking always involves the *demotion* (rather than promotion) of a constraint below another constraint. Demotion is *minimal* in the sense that a constraint is demoted to a position immediately below the highest-ranking constraint that induces its violation in the optimal output. See (2), in which constraints are indicated by the symbol C plus a subscript:

(2) **Demote C_2 below C_4** **Demote C_3 below C_4** **Demote C_1 below C_3**
$\{C_1 \ldots C_3, C_4 \ldots C_n\}$ $\{C_1 \ldots C_4 \ldots C_n\}$ $\{C_4 \ldots C_n\}$
$\gg$ $\gg$ $\gg$
$\{\mathbf{C_2}\}$ $\{C_2, \mathbf{C_3}\}$ $\{C_2, C_3\}$
$\gg$
$\{\mathbf{C_1}\}$

Sets of constraints included in pairs of curly brackets '{ ... }' are unranked with respect to one another. Such a set of constraints is called a *stratum*. A stratum may also consist of a single constraint, as illustrated by stratum $\{C_2\}$ in the hierarchy which arises after the demotion of this constraint. A hierarchy containing (one or more) strata is called a *stratified hierarchy*.

(3) **A stratified hierarchy**
$\{C_1 \ldots C_n\}$
$\gg$
$\{C_{n+1} \ldots C_p\}$
$\gg$
$\ldots$
$\{C_{q+1} \ldots C_r\}$

It is important to bear in mind that the stratified hierarchies which arise in the course of progress of the algorithm are *hypothetical*. At each moment during the learning process, stratified hierarchies represent the *current* knowledge which the learner at that moment has accumulated about constraint interactions underlying a given output form. This knowledge is dynamic, as it continuously changes while the learning algorithm processes information from output forms. After all information has been 'absorbed' from some output form in the form of rankings, the 'current' hierarchy may already fully match the hierarchy of the target grammar. But it is equally possible that the hierarchy is still incomplete, meaning that one or more constraints have not yet been assigned to their proper positions. Crucial evidence required to complete the hierarchy may reside in 'new' output forms, which the algorithm has not yet considered. In this sense, the learner can never be sure that the acquisition process has terminated after any output form. However, any new output form the learner encounters may only serve to *refine* the current hierarchy, rather than totally redefine it. This is because (by hypothesis) all output forms of the target language *consistently* reflect a single constraint hierarchy.

We now turn to a demonstration of Tesar and Smolensky's algorithm in action.

7.3 Learning the Pintupi grammar of stress

7.3.1 *The target grammar*

The learning problem to be solved is this: to deduce the ranking of constraints correctly predicting the stress pattern of the Australian language Pintupi (Hansen and Hansen 1969; Hayes 1995). Recall from chapter 4 (section 4.4.1) that Pintupi words have initial primary stress, and secondary stresses on alternating odd-numbered syllables. Final syllables are always unstressed. An example of a five-syllable word, together with its metrical parsing, is given in (4):

(4)   (pú.ʎiŋ).(kà.lɑ).tʲu 'we (sat) on the hill'

The Pintupi pattern is due to an interaction of universal and violable metrical constraints, among which are the following six (from chapter 4, section 4.4.1 and section 4.4.3):

(5)   a. **FT-BIN**
                 Feet are binary under moraic or syllabic analysis.
             b. **PARSE-SYL**
                 Syllables are parsed by feet.
             c. **LEFTMOST**
                 Align (Hd-Ft, L, PrWd, L) 'The head foot is initial in PrWd.'
             d. **RIGHTMOST**
                 Align (Hd-Ft, R, PrWd, R) 'The head foot is final in PrWd.'
             e. **ALL-FT-LEFT**
                 Align (Ft, L, PrWd, L)   'Feet are initial in PrWd.'
             f. **ALL-FT-RIGHT**
                 Align (Ft, R, PrWd, R)   'Feet are final in PrWd.'

The grammar of Pintupi ranks these constraints in the following way (the notation identifies four strata in the hierarchy):

(6)   A fragment of the grammar of Pintupi
             {FT-BIN, LEFTMOST}
                 ≫
             {PARSE-SYL, RIGHTMOST}
                 ≫
             {ALL-FT-LEFT}
                 ≫
             {ALL-FT-RIGHT}

For completeness this ranking is illustrated by a tableau for the input /puʎiŋkalatʲu/ in (7):

(7)

Input: /puɭiŋkalatʲu/	FT- ¦ LEFT- BIN ¦ MOST	PARSE- ¦ RIGHT- SYL ¦ MOST	ALL-FT-L	ALL-FT-R
a. ☞ (pú.ɭiŋ).(kà.la).tʲu		* ¦ ***	**	*, ***
b. (pú.ɭiŋ).ka.(là.tʲu)		* ¦ ***	***!	***
c. (pú.ɭiŋ).ka.la.tʲu		**!* ¦ ***		***
d. pu.ɭiŋ.ka.(lá.tʲu)	*!**	*** ¦	***	
e. (pú.ɭiŋ).(kà.la).(tʲù)	*! ¦	¦ ***	**, ****	*, ***

As always, violations of foot alignment constraints are marked in syllables.

7.3.2 *Defining the task of the learning algorithm*

Thus far we have tacitly assumed that the hierarchy in (6), as any hierarchy which we have posited so far, is deducible from output forms. But is this implicit assumption correct? May we indeed assume that output forms suffice to characterize uniquely the grammar which generates them? If this turns out not to be the case, then the grammar of Pintupi, or of any other language, would not be learnable. This would pose an unsurmountable problem for the linguistic theory at stake, since any theory which posits unlearnable grammars cannot be a correct theory of the human language capacity.

Therefore what we must do is put the theory under discussion, Optimality Theory, to the test, and find out whether an OT grammar is actually learnable. To this end, we will use a *model* of the language learner. This model will reflect certain assumptions about the organization of the grammar, specifically the assumption that the grammar of any natural language consists of a strict hierarchy of universal and violable constraints (among other aspects, such as a lexicon).

The model takes the shape of a *learning algorithm*, which is nothing but a series of instructions which, if blindly followed, will lead to a certain goal. What we want from the learning algorithm is stated in general terms in (8):

(8)   **Task of the learning algorithm**
       To deduce the constraint hierarchy under which the given surface
       form emerges as the optimal output of the given input form.

The specific task of the algorithm in the Pintupi learning situation is to deduce the ranking of constraints in (5) which correctly predicts the given output form [(pú.ɭiŋ).(kà.la).tʲu] on the basis of a given input /puɭiŋkalatʲu/. To this end, the learning algorithm is provided with precisely this information:

(9)   a. UG, including the six universal constraints in (5)

b. An output form [(pú.ʃiŋ).(kà.la).tʲu]

c. An input form /puʃiŋkalatʲu/

7.3.3   *The initial state, and Mark-Data Pairs*

What the algorithm does first is *initializing* the hierarchy. Recall that the algorithm initially expects that all constraints are unranked. This is equal to the assumption that all constraints are undominated, sharing a single 'stratum' in the hierarchy:

(10)   Initial state of the constraint hierarchy

{ALL-FT-L, ALL-FT-R, FT-BIN, LEFTMOST, PARSE-SYL, RIGHTMOST}

Out of this initial single 'mother' stratum, the learning algorithm will develop a complete hierarchy by a consecutive demotion of constraints into new lower strata. Demotion will take place on the basis of information which is deduced from a comparison of constraint violations in the optimal form and those in suboptimal candidates. Such comparison of candidates requires some crucial pre-processing of information, to which we now turn.

As stated earlier, we assume that the learning algorithm is fed with the surface form [(pú.ʃiŋ).(kà.la).tʲu], including its metrical structure, and together with the information that its input is the form /puʃiŋkalatʲu/ 'we (sat) on the hill'.

(11)   Input: /puʃiŋkalatʲu/   'we (sat) on the hill'

Output: [(pú.ʃiŋ).(kà.la).tʲu]

The task for the learner (in its model form, the algorithm) is to deduce the grammar which leads to this particular pairing of input and output. Deducing the grammar means: ranking universal constraints into a hierarchy under which [(pú.ʃiŋ).(kà.la).tʲu] is the *most harmonic* output form of /puʃiŋkalatʲu/, out of all possible output forms. This implies that all possible output forms of /puʃiŋkalatʲu/ are somehow available to the learner, together with violation marks for specific constraints which render them suboptimal. But are suboptimal forms available? It has been observed by generative linguists time and again that a child learning her native language has access to *positive evidence* only. That is, the ungrammaticality of forms is never directly offered as data to the learner.[1]

In OT terminology, the child has direct access to *optimal* outputs of the grammar, while suboptimal output forms ('negative evidence') are not part of the child's linguistic environment. For the sake of the argument, let us reduce the data available to the learner of Pintupi (who is faced with the task of constructing the

---

[1] Except in cases where the child is explicitly corrected.

metrical grammar in 6) to only a single piece of positive evidence, that is, the output form (11). Consequently the learner is deprived of any suboptimal outputs of /puɭiŋkalatʲu/, such as candidates (7b–e) in the above tableau. Thus far in this book, we have built arguments for constraint rankings on the comparison of 'suboptimal' candidate outputs with the actual 'optimal' output. This is the only method that produces valid ranking arguments. But if (as we now assume) the learner has no access to suboptimal forms, then how could the relevant rankings ever be inferred? It seems that the learner has got stuck before she has even started. How to break the spell?

The learner's strategy is to make maximal use of information which is *implicit* in the surface form, but which is nevertheless reconstructable. If [(pú.ɭiŋ).(kà.la).tʲu] is the optimal output of the input /puɭiŋkalatʲu/, then *any output candidate must be suboptimal*, by definition. The learner may freely posit literally any output candidate as a competitor of [(pú.ɭiŋ).(kà.la).tʲu], and still be sure that this hypothetical competitor is less harmonic. The algorithm capitalizes on this, and generates a set of suboptimal candidates,[2] which are the competitors for [(pú.ɭiŋ).(kà.la).tʲu], for example the following set:

(12)   [(pú.ɭiŋ).ka.(là.tʲu)], [(pú.ɭiŋ).ka.la.tʲu], [pu.ɭiŋ.ka.(lá.tʲu)],
         [(pú.ɭiŋ).(ká.la).(tʲù)]

She is then automatically served with information packages of the following kind:

(13)   ***subopt***   <   ***opt***
     b* < *a   [(pú.ɭiŋ).ka.(là.tʲu)]   <   [(pú.ɭiŋ).(kà.la).tʲu]
     c* < *a   [(pú.ɭiŋ).ka.la.tʲu]   <   [(pú.ɭiŋ).(kà.la).tʲu]
     d* < *a   [pu.ɭiŋ.ka.(là.tʲu)]   <   [(pú.ɭiŋ).(kà.la).tʲu]
     e* < *a   [(pú.ɭiŋ).(kà.la).(tʲù)]   <   [(pú.ɭiŋ).(kà.la).tʲu]

Each chunk of information consists of a harmonic ranking of two candidates, one of which is a suboptimal output form (*subopt*), and the other the optimal output form (*opt*).[3]

---

[2] There is a procedure for automatically selecting informative suboptimal candidates, which is called *Error-Driven Constraint Demotion* (Tesar 1995). See also note 7.

[3] Given Freedom of Analysis, *Gen* will supply the learner with an infinite number of such pairs. Clearly not all such pairs are informative to the learner, due to the presence of a large number of 'intrinsically suboptimal' candidates (see again chapter 1, section 1.7.5). The issue of how to deal with such 'noise' in the data will not be discussed here; in any event, no negative effects arise for the learner by considering 'intrinsically suboptimal' candidates. Moreover, the algorithm does not know beforehand how many 'mark-data pairs' must be considered in order to arrive at the target grammar, nor is it necessary to know this. The 'ideal' learner will consider all available information, after which she will positively have acquired the target grammar, as will be shown below.

This is the point at which constraint evaluation comes into play. OT is based on the central claim that the observed surface form is the most 'harmonic' output (of all possible output candidates), given some specific ranking of violable constraints. The optimal output may violate constraints – and in fact it always will. However, the very fact that the observed output is *optimal* implies that no other output is possible which is more harmonic, at least not under the same constraint ranking. The learner can simply be certain that any constraint violation in the observed output is forced. That is, if the optimal output violates a constraint C_1, then any suboptimal output which respects C_1 must itself violate some higher-ranking constraint C_2 which is unviolated in the optimal output. (For if C_1 were not violated in the optimal form, then this form would have been suboptimal itself.) The key to the problem of establishing the unknown constraint ranking is precisely this property of OT grammars. The learner must identify the constraint violations in the observed output (which is optimal by definition), matching these against violations of other constraints in suboptimal outputs. From this information, she deduces the 'target' constraint hierarchy.

The learning algorithm starts by constructing an overview of constraint violations for each pair in the list (13). The result is tabulated in (14). Each row represents the marks of one pair in (13). For each candidate pair, a cell in the column *loser-marks* lists all violation marks of the suboptimal candidate, while a cell in the column *winner-marks* lists all violation marks of the optimal candidate. Violations are indicated by an asterisk before the name of the violated constraint. Candidates inducing multiple violations of the same constraint are doubly marked for this constraint. (As in tableau 7 of [(pú.[iŋ).(kà.lɑ).tʲu].)

(14)   Mark-data Pairs

subopt < *opt*		*loser-marks*	*winner-marks*
b < a	[(pú.[iŋ).kɑ.(là.tʲu)] < [(pú.[iŋ).(kà.lɑ).tʲu]	{*ALL-FT-L, *ALL-FT-L, *ALL-FT-L, *ALL-FT-R, *ALL-FT-R, *ALL-FT-R, *PARSE-SYL, *R-MOST, *R-MOST, *R-MOST}	{*ALL-FT-L, *ALL-FT-L, *ALL-FT-R, *ALL-FT-R, *ALL-FT-R, *ALL-FT-R, *PARSE-SYL, *R-MOST, *R-MOST, *R-MOST}
c < a	[(pú.[iŋ).kɑ.lɑ.tʲu] < [(pú.[iŋ).(kà.lɑ).tʲu]	{*ALL-FT-R, *ALL-FT-R, *ALL-FT-R, *PARSE-SYL, *PARSE-SYL, *PARSE-SYL, *R-MOST, *R-MOST, *R-MOST}	{*ALL-FT-L, *ALL-FT-L, *ALL-FT-R, *ALL-FT-R, *ALL-FT-R, *ALL-FT-R, *PARSE-SYL, *R-MOST, *R-MOST, *R-MOST}

subopt < opt	loser-marks	winner-marks
d < a [pu.ʅiŋ.kɑ.(lá.tʲu)] < [(pú.ʅiŋ).(kɑ̀.lɑ).tʲu]	{*ALL-FT-L, *ALL-FT-L, *ALL-FT-L, *L-MOST, *L-MOST, *L-MOST, *PARSE-SYL, *PARSE-SYL, *PARSE-SYL}	{*ALL-FT-L, *ALL-FT-L, *ALL-FT-R, *All-FT-R, *ALL-FT-R, *All-FT-R, *PARSE-SYL, *R-MOST, *R-MOST, *R-MOST}
e < a [(pú.ʅiŋ).(kɑ̀.lɑ).(tʲù)] < [(pú.ʅiŋ).(kɑ̀.lɑ).tʲu]	{*ALL-FT-L, *ALL-FT-L, *ALL-FT-L, *ALL-FT-L, *ALL-FT-R, *ALL-FT-R, *ALL-FT-R, *ALL-FT-R, *FT-BIN, *R-MOST, *R-MOST, *R-MOST}	{*ALL-FT-L, *ALL-FT-L, *ALL-FT-R, *ALL-FT-R, *ALL-FT-R, *ALL-FT-R, *PARSE-SYL, *R-MOST, *R-MOST, *R-MOST}

Observe that every pair of (13) contains the optimal output [(pú.ʅiŋ).(kɑ̀.lɑ).tʲu].
This is a logical necessity, since the optimal candidate is the single one which is
presented to the learner. Since every harmonic comparison involves the optimal
output, every cell *winner-marks* will contain identical sets of violation marks. In
contrast, the contents of *loser-marks* differ from row to row.

7.3.4 *Mark Cancellation*
The table of 'mark-data pairs' in (14) provides the 'raw' information that the
algorithm processes in order to arrive at the target grammar. However, from this
table to the target is still a long way to go. It will be clear that in its present form,
the table cannot provide the basis for ranking constraints, since for each mark-
data pair, identical violation marks occur in both the cells 'loser-marks' and
'winner-marks'. The algorithm must first 'purify' this information by cancelling
out marks from the table which have no information value.

The first step to take is eliminating from this table any marks which are *shared*
by winner and loser. Given the logic of OT, shared violations can never result in
harmony differences between two candidates, hence cannot provide information
about constraint ranking. As we already mentioned, the raw information in table
(14) is 'purified' by the cancellation of violation marks which have no information value. Before we discuss how the algorithm performs this function, let us
take a look at the new mark-data pairs table (15), where cancelled marks have
been struck out.

(15)　　　Mark-data Pairs after Cancellation

subopt < opt	loser-marks	winner-marks
b < a　[(pú.ʃiŋ).kɑ.(là.tʲu)] < [(pú.ʃiŋ).(kà.lɑ).tʲu]	{*~~ALL-FT-L~~, *~~ALL-FT-L~~, *ALL-FT-L, *~~ALL-FT-R~~, *~~ALL-FT-R~~, *~~ALL-FT-R~~, *~~PARSE-SYL~~, *~~R-MOST~~, *~~R-MOST~~, *~~R-MOST~~}	{*~~ALL-FT-L~~, *~~ALL-FT-L~~, *ALL-FT-R, *~~ALL-FT-R~~, *~~ALL-FT-R~~, *~~ALL-FT-R~~, *~~PARSE-SYL~~, *~~R-MOST~~, *~~R-MOST~~, *~~R-MOST~~}
c < a　[(pú.ʃiŋ).kɑ.lɑ.tʲu] < [(pú.ʃiŋ).(kà.lɑ).tʲu]	{*~~ALL-FT-R~~, *~~ALL-FT-R~~, *~~ALL-FT-R~~, *~~PARSE-SYL~~, *PARSE-SYL, *PARSE-SYL, *~~R-MOST~~, *~~R-MOST~~, *~~R-MOST~~}	{*ALL-FT-L, *ALL-FT-L, *~~ALL-FT-R~~, *~~ALL-FT-R~~, *~~ALL-FT-R~~, *ALL-FT-R, *~~PARSE-SYL~~, *~~R-MOST~~, *~~R-MOST~~}
d < a　[pu.ʃiŋ.kɑ.(là.tʲu)] < [(pú.ʃiŋ).(kà.lɑ).tʲu]	{*~~ALL-FT-L~~, *~~ALL-FT-L~~, *ALL-FT-L, *L-MOST, *L-MOST, *L-MOST, *~~PARSE-SYL~~, *PARSE-SYL, *PARSE-SYL}	{*~~ALL-FT-L~~, *~~ALL-FT-L~~, *ALL-FT-R, *ALL-FT-R, *ALL-FT-R, *ALL-FT-R, *~~PARSE-SYL~~, *R-MOST, *R-MOST, *R-MOST}
e < a　[(pú.ʃiŋ).(kà.lɑ).(tʲù)] < [(pú.ʃiŋ).(kà.lɑ).tʲu]	{*~~ALL-FT-L~~, *~~ALL-FT-L~~, *ALL-FT-L, *ALL-FT-L, *ALL-FT-L, *ALL-FT-L, *~~ALL-FT-R~~, *~~ALL-FT-R~~, *~~ALL-FT-R~~, *~~ALL-FT-R~~, *FT-BIN, *~~R-MOST~~, *~~R-MOST~~, *~~R-MOST~~}	{*~~ALL-FT-L~~, *~~ALL-FT-L~~, *~~ALL-FT-R~~, *~~ALL-FT-R~~, *~~ALL-FT-R~~, *~~ALL-FT-R~~, *PARSE-SYL, *~~R-MOST~~, *~~R-MOST~~, *~~R-MOST~~}

How does this cancellation take place? First we should realize that the *absolute* number of violations of some constraint is never relevant to a candidate's well-formedness. Instead, what is relevant is the difference in violations of a constraint with other candidates. For constraints which can have multiple violations per candidate, what really matters is which of the candidates violates the constraint worst (rather than absolute numbers of marks). In order to establish a difference in violations of a single constraint between two candidates, mark cancellation is done on an *item-by-item* basis. See, for example, the first pair in table (15), in which two marks *ALL-FT-L are cancelled, so that one mark remains in the cell *loser-marks*.

This insight is captured by the first two steps of the algorithm *Mark Cancellation*:

(16)　　**Mark Cancellation**

　　　　For each pair (*loser-marks*, *winner-marks*) in *mark-data*:

　　　　a. For each occurrence of a mark *C in both *loser-marks* and *winner-marks* in the same pair, remove that occurrence of *C from both.

b. If, as a result, no *winner-marks* remain, remove the pair from *mark-data*.

c. If, after the preceding steps, a row of the *mark-data* table contains multiple tokens of the same type of mark, duplicates are eliminated, leaving at most one token of each type.

Step (16c) achieves a further 'purification' of the table by removing multiple tokens of the same mark, which may still occur after cancellation. As stated earlier, all that matters to the learner is which of the candidates in the pair has the largest violation of a constraint; it is therefore irrelevant to know the exact difference in degree of violation.

Table (17) represents the result of the elimination of cancelled marks (steps 16b–c).

(17)   Mark-data Pairs after Mark Cancellation

subopt < opt		loser-marks	winner-marks
b < a	[(pú.ʟiŋ).ka.(là.tʲu)] < [(pú.ʟiŋ).(kà.la).tʲu]	{*ALL-FT-L}	{*ALL-FT-R}
c < a	[(pú.ʟiŋ).ka.la.tʲu] < [(pú.ʟiŋ).(kà.la).tʲu]	{*PARSE-SYL}	{*ALL-FT-L, *ALL-FT-R}
d < a	[pu.ʟiŋ.ka.(lá.tʲu)] < [(pú.ʟiŋ).(kà.la).tʲu]	{*ALL-FT-L, *LEFTMOST, *PARSE-SYL}	{*ALL-FT-R, *RIGHTMOST}
e < a	[(pú.ʟiŋ).(kà.la).(tʲù)] < [(pú.ʟiŋ).(kà.la).tʲu]	{*ALL-FT-L, *FT-BIN}	{*PARSE-SYL}

After this preprocessing by Mark Cancellation, the information generated from the output form [(pú.ʟiŋ).(kà.la).tʲu] is now ready to be fed into the 'core' of the learning algorithm, which deduces the actual constraint hierarchy, and which is called *Recursive Ranking* by Tesar and Smolensky.

Before we look into the actual statement of Recursive Ranking, we must first expand the algorithm's work-slate beyond the *mark-data pairs* table in (17). From now on the algorithm will register rerankings in the *constraint hierarchy*, which will acquire more and more structure until it reaches a point at which no additional rerankings are motivated on the basis of positive evidence available. At that point, the learning process will have terminated, and hopefully we will then find that the algorithm has established a constraint hierarchy which matches the fragment of the grammar of Pintupi. The current state of the constraint hierarchy is still identical to its initial state. Recall that this initial state is not a genuine hierarchy, but includes the entire set of universal constraints without any ranking defined among them. All constraints are lumped together in a single 'stratum'.

(18) H_0 = {ALL-FT-L, ALL-FT-R, FT-BIN, LEFTMOST, PARSE-SYL, RIGHTMOST}

Consecutive states of the hierarchy which result from a demotion of constraints from this initial hierarchy will be notated as $H_1, H_2 \ldots H_n$, etc.

7.3.5 *Recursive Ranking: basic ideas*

The basic ideas underlying Recursive Ranking have already been sketched in section 7.2. Now it is time to discuss these ideas in more detail. The first idea is that only *constraint violations* (not satisfactions) are relevant to constraint ranking. Constraints which are satisfied in the optimal output are less informative since constraint satisfaction need not reflect anything about some constraint's position in the hierarchy. Consider the fact that in all four-syllable words in Pintupi, for example [(má.ḷa).(wà.na)] 'through from behind', PARSE-SYL is satisfied. Yet, we may not conclude from this that PARSE-SYL is undominated. And indeed, output forms with an odd number of syllables ([(pú.ḷiŋ).(kà.la).tʲu]) show that PARSE-SYL is dominated. We may conclude that no solid ranking arguments can be based on constraint satisfaction. However, crucial information on ranking can be deduced from constraint violations. This is because we know for sure that a constraint which is violated in the optimal output *must be dominated* by some other constraint.[4] For if this constraint were not violated in the optimal output, then the optimal output would not be optimal. By definition, the optimal output cannot be improved, under any given constraint hierarchy.

This important idea is captured in the algorithm by constraint demotion, triggered by positive evidence from *mark-data pairs*. Generally speaking, the algorithm demotes constraints assessing *winner-marks* below constraints assessing *loser-marks*. The rationale behind this is the following. The single reason why the optimal output is actually optimal is that its overall evaluation by the constraint hierarchy is superior to any of its suboptimal competitors. Therefore, when the 'winner' fares worse on some constraint than the 'loser', then it must be the case that this constraint C_{winner} is dominated by another constraint C_{loser} on which the 'loser' fares worse than the 'winner'. Given the positive fact that the 'winner' is the 'winner', and the 'loser' is the 'loser', the constraints can only be ranked as below:

---

[4] To be more precise and technical, a top-ranked constraint can be violated by the optimal output as long it is violated at least as many times by every other output. Thanks to Bruce Tesar for pointing this out. (Such a situation may occur, in principle at least, if *Gen* places restrictions on all output candidates.)

(19)

	C_{loser}	C_{winner}
opt ('winner')		*
subopt ('loser')	*!	

If the constraints were ranked reversely, then the 'winner' would become the 'loser', and the 'loser' would become the 'winner'. See tableau (20):

(20)

	C_{winner}	C_{loser}
opt ('no-longer-the-winner')	*!	
subopt ('no-longer-the-loser')		*

Therefore, given mark-data as in (21), in which both cells *loser-marks* and *winner-marks* contain one constraint each (C_{loser} and C_{winner}):

(21)   Mark-data

subopt < *opt*	*loser-marks*	*winner-marks*
'loser' < 'winner'	$\{C_{loser}\}$	$\{C_{winner}\}$

the algorithm can legitimately deduce the ranking in (22):

(22) $\{C_{loser}\}$

        $\gg$

     $\{C_{winner}\}$

The algorithm will achieve this by demoting C_{winner} to a stratum below C_{loser}.

A question promptly arises: what happens when more than one constraint occurs in *loser-marks*? More specifically, to what stratum should a constraint C_{winner} be demoted when the constraints in *loser-marks* occupy different strata in the hierarchy? Should all constraints come to dominate C_{winner}, as depicted in (23a)? Or should one of the constraints in *loser-marks* be selected as dominating C_{winner}, for example the highest-ranked among them, as in (23b)?

(23)   a. $\{C_{loser-1}\}$ b. $\{C_{loser-1}\}$

            $\gg$ $\gg$

            $\{C_{loser-2}, C_{loser-3}\}$ $\{C_{winner}\}$

            $\gg$ $\gg$

            $\{C_{winner}\}$ $\{C_{loser-2}, C_{loser-3}\}$

This issue is not void of empirical content since the rankings in (23a) and (23b) may give rise to different optimal outputs. Is there a hard-and-fast rule which will always produce a correct result? To this issue we will now turn.

The second general idea underlying Recursive Ranking is that all constraints are in the highest possible stratum in the hierarchy which is compatible with the evidence from mark-data (which has been considered so far). In the initial state of the hierarchy, this idea is seen in a most exemplary way: no evidence from mark-data has been considered in that stage, so that all constraints are granted the status of being undominated. Demotions of a constraint are always triggered by positive evidence from mark-data, and even then, no constraint is demoted farther down than can be positively motivated by the marks pattern. This implies that a constraint assessing a *winner-mark* (C_{winner}) is demoted to the highest possible stratum in the hierarchy which is still compatible with mark-data. That is, C_{winner} is demoted to a stratum *immediately below the highest-ranking constraint* C_{loser} in the current hierarchy. Or to state it differently, we opt for demotion strategy (23b), rather than (23a). We safely infer that this constraint cannot be ranked higher in the hierarchy than it should be; for if it were higher-ranked, then it would not be violated in the optimal output. (See again tableaux 19–20.) Each constraint is given the 'benefit of the doubt': the algorithm considers it to be as high in the hierarchy as can be, keeping open the possibility that new evidence may eventually turn up triggering additional demotions of the constraint. This was referred to as a 'conservative' demotion strategy earlier in this section. The full advantages of this strategy become apparent only when we consider alternatives.

Suppose that constraints assessing *winner-marks* (C_{winner}) were instead demoted to a stratum below the lowest-ranked constraint in *loser-marks*. Chances are fair that a demoted constraint falls too deep, so that it must later be 'rehabilitated' by demotions of other constraints which it had passed on its way down. But when these new demotions also occur at random intervals, a never-ending 'jumping over' of constraints may start. Consequently the acquisition process will never converge into the stable state of the target grammar.

This is illustrated schematically in (24), in the form of a cyclic demotion process of three stages. Observe that the result of the final stage (H_{n+3}) is identical to the input to the initial stage (H_n). Demoted constraints appear in bold-face, while '…' indicates a site from which a constraint has been demoted. This loop is *eternal* since the learner will never reach the stable state in which no more demotions can be justified by the data. The alternative strategy of *minimal* demotion, which is part of the Tesar and Smolensky algorithm, serves to guarantee that the learning process *converges* into a stable ranking. We will now see that this indeed works.

(24)

	Stage 1	**Stage 2**	**Stage 3**
	C_{winner}: C_3, C_6	C_{winner}: C_4	C_{winner}: C_5, C_6
	C_{loser}: C_2, C_4, C_5	C_{loser}: C_1, C_5	C_{loser}: C_4

$$H_n \quad \to \quad H_{n+1} \quad \to \quad H_{n+2} \quad \to \quad H_{n+3}\,(=H_n)$$

$$\{C_1, C_2\} \qquad \{C_1, C_2\} \qquad \{C_1, C_2\} \qquad \{C_1, C_2\}$$

$$\gg \qquad\qquad \gg \qquad\qquad \gg \qquad\qquad \gg$$

$$\{C_3, C_4\} \qquad \{\ldots C_4\} \qquad \{\ldots\}$$

$$\gg \qquad\qquad \gg \qquad\qquad \gg$$

$$\{C_5, C_6\} \qquad \{C_5 \ldots\} \qquad \{C_5 \ldots\} \qquad \{\ldots\}$$

$$\gg \qquad\qquad \gg \qquad\qquad \gg$$

$$\{C_6, C_3\} \qquad \{C_6, C_3, C_4\} \qquad \{\ldots C_3, C_4\}$$

$$\gg$$

$$\{C_5, C_6\}$$

Consider the part of Tesar and Smolensky's algorithm which captures this key idea, Constraint Demotion:

(25)   **Constraint Demotion** (repeat this step until no demotions occur)
    For each pair *loser-marks* < *winner-marks* in *mark-data*
        i. find the mark *C_{loser} in *loser-marks* which is highest-ranked in H
        ii. for each *C_{winner} in *winner-marks*
            if C_{loser} does not dominate C_{winner} in H, then demote constraint C_{winner} to the stratum H immediately below that of C_{loser} (creating such a stratum if it does not already exist).

Observe that Constraint Demotion considers the pairs in *mark-data* one by one, extracting information on constraint rankings from their distribution of marks.

Constraint Demotion is *recursive*.[5] That is, it is repeated until no further demotions occur. In our example this stable state of the hierarchy will arise after nine steps, when the complete hierarchy of six metrical constraints of the 'target' grammar of Pintupi will have been deduced. Crucially, the order in which mark-data pairs are examined by Constraint Demotion makes no difference to the final result, although it may be necessary to examine some mark-data pairs more than once. In our test-case below we will actually select the *least efficient* way to reach the target grammar, to emphasize the fact that the correct grammar emerges regardless of the order in which mark-data pairs are examined.

---

[5] We will present the *recursive* version of Tesar and Smolensky's constraint demotion algorithm, entirely for expository reasons. It should be mentioned that there is also a *non-recursive* version of the algorithm, also presented in Tesar and Smolensky (1993), which produces the same results in a somewhat different fashion. This version is actually assumed in most of the literature.

7.3.5.1 *Recursive Ranking in action*

The first mark-data pair in table (17) which Constraint Demotion considers is the one in the top row, that is, $b < a$ or $[(\text{pú.}\lfloor\text{iŋ}).\text{kɑ.}(\text{là.t}^j\text{u})] < [(\text{pú.}\lfloor\text{iŋ}).(\text{kà.lɑ}).\text{t}^j\text{u}]$:

(26)　　　Mark-data (step 1)

subopt < opt		loser-marks	winner-marks
b < a	$[(\text{pú.}\lfloor\text{iŋ}).\text{kɑ.}(\text{là.t}^j\text{u})]$ $< [(\text{pú.}\lfloor\text{iŋ}).(\text{kà.lɑ}).\text{t}^j\text{u}]$	{*ALL-FT-L}	{*ALL-FT-R}

This pair embodies the generalization that Pintupi prefers a *left-oriented* distribution of feet to a right-oriented one. Constraint Demotion is able to deduce the correct ranking:

- The mark *ALL-FT-L is the highest-ranked in *loser-marks* in the current hierarchy, H_0. (This is trivial, since it is the only mark in *loser-marks*.)
- The constraint assessing the *winner-mark* (ALL-FT-R) is not dominated by C_{loser} (ALL-FT-L). (Again this is trivial, since the initial hierarchy H_0 is totally unranked.) Therefore ALL-FT-R is demoted to a position immediately below ALL-FT-L, thereby creating a new stratum in the hierarchy:

(27)　　　State of the constraint hierarchy after step 1

$H_1 = \{\text{ALL-FT-L, FT-BIN, PARSE-SYL, LEFTMOST, RIGHTMOST}\}$

$\gg$

$\{\text{ALL-FT-R}\}$

The second pair which Constraint Demotion considers is $c < a$ in *mark-data*, that is: $[(\text{pú.}\lfloor\text{iŋ}).\text{kɑ.lɑ.t}^j\text{u}] < [(\text{pú.}\lfloor\text{iŋ}).(\text{kà.lɑ}).\text{t}^j\text{u}]$:

(28)　　　Mark-data (step 2)

subopt < opt		loser-marks	winner-marks
c < a	$[(\text{pú.}\lfloor\text{iŋ}).\text{kɑ.lɑ.t}^j\text{u}]$ $< [(\text{pú.}\lfloor\text{iŋ}).(\text{kà.lɑ}).\text{t}^j\text{u}]$	{*PARSE-SYL}	{*ALL-FT-L, *ALL-FT-R}

This pair embodies the generalization about Pintupi that metrification of syllables in feet takes priority over the (left edge and right edge) alignment of feet. Constraint Demotion deduces the corresponding rankings as follows:

- *PARSE-SYL is the highest-ranked *loser-mark* in the current hierarchy, H_1. (Trivially so, since it is the only constraint assessing *loser-marks*.)
- None of the constraints in *winner-marks* (ALL-FT-L, ALL-FT-R) are dominated by C_{loser} (PARSE-SYL). The first, ALL-FT-L, shares a stratum with PARSE-

SYL, while ALL-FT-R is already dominated by PARSE-SYL. Therefore only ALL-FT-L needs to be demoted to the stratum immediately below PARSE-SYL. It comes to share this stratum with ALL-FT-R, which already occupies it:

(29)   State of the constraint hierarchy after step 2

H_2 = {FT-BIN, PARSE-SYL, LEFTMOST, RIGHTMOST}

≫

{ALL-FT-R, **ALL-FT-L**}

Observe that no new stratum is created for ALL-FT-L. This is placed in the stratum already occupied by ALL-FT-R, in accordance with the 'conservative' demotion strategy: no constraint is demoted further down than is justified by the evidence from *mark-data*.

The third mark-data pair to be considered by Constraint Demotion is that of the third row in table (17), $d < a$, or [pu.ʎiŋ.ka.(lá.tʲu)] < [(pú.ʎiŋ).(kà.la).tʲu]:

(30)   Mark-data (step 3)

	subopt < opt	*loser-marks*	*winner-marks*
d < a	[pu.ʎiŋ.ka.(lá.tʲu)] < [(pú.ʎiŋ).(kà.la).tʲu]	{*ALL-FT-L, *LEFTMOST, *PARSE-SYL}	{*ALL-FT-R, *RIGHTMOST}

This mark-data pair embodies the generalization that left-edge primary stress is preferred to right-edge primary stress. Constraint Demotion processes the information as follows:

- *LEFTMOST and *PARSE-SYL are the highest-ranked *loser-marks* (C_{loser}) in the current hierarchy, H_2. Both are in the top stratum. (Observe that the third *loser-mark*, *ALL-FT-L, occupies a dominated stratum in H_1 as a result of its demotion in step 2.)
- Only one constraint assessing *winner-marks* (RIGHTMOST) is not already dominated by C_{loser} (PARSE-SYL, LEFTMOST). Therefore only RIGHTMOST is demoted to the stratum below C_{loser}, which was already occupied by ALL-FT-L and ALL-FT-R:

(31)   State of the constraint hierarchy after step 3

H_3 = {FT-BIN, PARSE-SYL, LEFTMOST}

≫

{ALL-FT-R, ALL-FT-L, **RIGHTMOST**}

The fourth mark-data pair to be considered is the one in the bottom row of table (17), $e < a$ or [(pú.ʆiŋ).(kà.la).(tʲù)] $<$ [(pú.ʆiŋ).(kà.la).tʲu]:

(32)   Mark-data (step 4)

	subopt < opt	loser-marks	winner-marks
e < a	[(pú.ʆiŋ).(kà.la).(tʲù)] < [(pú.ʆiŋ).(kà.la).tʲu]	{*ALL-FT-L, *FT-BIN}	{*PARSE-SYL}

This harmonic ranking reflects the generalization that degenerate feet are no licit strategy to improve exhaustivity of parsing. This information is processed as follows:

- The mark *FT-BIN is the highest-ranked *loser-mark* in the current hierarchy, H_3. (It is in the top stratum, while *ALL-FT-L is in the bottom stratum.)
- The single constraint assessing a *winner-mark* (PARSE-SYL) is not dominated by C_{loser} (FT-BIN). Hence PARSE-SYL is demoted to a stratum immediately below FT-BIN. Again no new stratum needs to be created:

(33)   State of the constraint hierarchy after step 4

$H_4 = \{$FT-BIN, LEFTMOST$\}$

$\gg$

$\{$ALL-FT-R, ALL-FT-L, RIGHTMOST, **PARSE-SYL**$\}$

In four steps, the algorithm has produced a broad division into two strata. The top stratum contains both undominated constraints, while the bottom stratum contains all 'dominated' constraints. However, this hierarchy must be further refined in order to achieve the status of 'target grammar'. In particular, refinements must be achieved in the mutual rankings of the dominated constraints in the bottom stratum.

The algorithm does not 'know' that it has not yet finished its reranking operation, and it steadily goes on considering mark-data pairs. Let us assume that it works through the pairs once more in the same order. The first pair $b < a$ (which we will not fully repeat) contains a *loser-mark* {*ALL-FT-L} and a *winner-mark* {*ALL-FT-R}:

- The mark *ALL-FT-L is the highest-ranked in *loser-marks* in the current hierarchy, H_4. (This is trivial, since it is the only mark in *loser-marks*.)
- The constraint assessing the *winner-mark* (ALL-FT-R) is not dominated by C_{loser} (ALL-FT-L). (Both are in the same bottom stratum of H_4.) Therefore ALL-FT-R is demoted to a position immediately below ALL-FT-L, creating a new stratum in the hierarchy:

(34)   State of the constraint hierarchy after step 5
$$H_5 = \{\text{Ft-Bin, Leftmost}\}$$
$$\gg$$
$$\{\text{All-Ft-L, Rightmost, Parse-Syl}\}$$
$$\gg$$
$$\{\textbf{All-Ft-R}\}$$

Next the algorithm reconsiders the second mark-data pair in (17), $c < a$, which contains the *loser-mark* {*Parse-Syl} and the *winner-marks* {*All-Ft-L, *All-Ft-R}:

- The mark *Parse-Syl is the highest-ranked in *loser-marks* in H_5.
- One constraint in *winner-marks* (All-Ft-L) is not already dominated by C_{loser} (Parse-Syl). Only All-Ft-L is demoted to the stratum immediately below C_{loser}. It comes to share this stratum with All-Ft-R, which already occupied it:

(35)   State of the constraint hierarchy after step 6
$$H_6 = \{\text{Ft-Bin, Leftmost}\}$$
$$\gg$$
$$\{\text{Rightmost, Parse-Syl}\}$$
$$\gg$$
$$\{\text{All-Ft-R}, \textbf{All-Ft-L}\}$$

In two more steps following the first 'round' of four, Constraint Demotion has created the stratum {Rightmost, Parse-Syl} below the topmost stratum, which is in fact part of the target grammar. The only step to take place is a demotion of All-Ft-R below All-Ft-L, which requires a third (and final) 'round' through the mark-data pairs (it will eventually be triggered by the first pair $b < a$). But first we will see two 'vacuous' steps.

Next, Constraint Demotion reconsiders the pair $d < a$, which contains *loser-marks* {*All-Ft-L, *Leftmost, *Parse-Syl} and *winner-marks* {*All-Ft-R, *Rightmost}:

- *Leftmost is the highest-ranked *loser-mark* in H_6,
- while both constraints in *winner-marks* (All-Ft-R, Rightmost) are already dominated by C_{loser} (Leftmost). No demotion takes place, and the hierarchy remains as it is:

(36)   State of the constraint hierarchy after step 7
$$H_7 = H_6$$

A similar story holds for the pair $e < a$, which contains the *loser-marks* {*ALL-FT-L, *FT-BIN}, and the *winner-marks* {*PARSE-SYL}:

- *FT-BIN is the highest-ranked *loser-mark* in H_7 (= H_6),
- while the constraint in *winner-marks* (PARSE-SYL) is already dominated by C_{loser} (FT-BIN). This entails that no demotion takes place.

(37)   State of the constraint hierarchy after step 8
         $H_8 = H_7 = H_6$

What both previous steps have in common is that in both cases, *loser-marks* contain a mark which is assessed by an undominated constraint. In the pair $d < a$ this is *LEFTMOST, and in the pair $e < a$, this is *FT-BIN. These marks are identified as C_{loser}, regardless of the content of *winner-marks* in these pairs. Constraint Demotion says that a constraint can be demoted only *if it is not already dominated by* C_{loser}. But in fact, no *winner-marks* in these pairs are assessed by constraints which are not already dominated by the top stratum of constraints.

Finally, a third round is needed to finish the hierarchy. Once again, the initial pair $b < a$ is considered. It contains a *loser-mark* {*ALL-FT-L} and a *winner-mark* {*ALL-FT-R}:

- The mark *ALL-FT-L is the highest-ranked in *loser-marks* in the current hierarchy, H_8.
- The constraint assessing the *winner-mark* (ALL-FT-R) is not dominated by C_{loser} (ALL-FT-L). (Both are in the same bottom stratum of H_8.) Therefore ALL-FT-R is demoted to a position immediately below ALL-FT-L, creating a new stratum in the hierarchy:

(38)   State of the constraint hierarchy after step 9
         H_9 = {FT-BIN, LEFTMOST}
                 ≫
              {RIGHTMOST, PARSE-SYL}
                 ≫
              {ALL-FT-L}
                 ≫
              {**ALL-FT-R**}

This hierarchy precisely matches the target grammar (6). The learning algorithm has been successful, having accomplished what it should. Interestingly, this hierarchy cannot be changed by any further rounds of reconsiderations of the mark-data pairs in table (17). It is a *stable ranking*, crucially so. Let us see how this conclusion follows. We have already seen that the pairs $d < a$ and $e < a$ cannot lead to further rerankings of the hierarchy. Their *loser-marks* contain a mark which is assessed by an undominated constraint, either FT-BIN or LEFTMOST. But in the final hierarchy, H_9, no constraint occurs which is not already dominated by either of these constraints. Therefore no constraint can undergo a further demotion which is 'triggered' by either FT-BIN or LEFTMOST.

Similar reasoning holds for the two remaining pairs $b < a$ and $c < a$. Evidently the former cannot lead to further demotion, since it was itself the trigger of the final demotion in step 9, which led to the current hierarchy. The latter pair $c < a$ contains the *loser-mark* {*PARSE-SYL} and the *winner-marks* {*ALL-FT-L, *ALL-FT-R}. Again the constraint in *loser-mark* is already dominating both of the constraints in *winner-marks*. Therefore this is insufficient to trigger a demotion.

This result is important, as it shows that the learning algorithm, on the basis of a single output form, *converges* to a state in which all information from this output form has been put to its maximal use. All information has been extracted, and no more can be extracted from the output form under consideration. Regardless of how many times the mark-data pairs are reconsidered by the algorithm, no further changes in the hierarchy will result. The learner is eager, but she knows where to stop.[6]

It may occur (and typically does occur) that a single output form is insufficient to rank completely all constraints. This we have in fact just seen in the Pintupi five-syllable example, from which no mutual rankings of constraints within strata {FT-BIN, LEFTMOST} and {RIGHTMOST, PARSE-SYL} could be deduced. In fact, the language may offer no evidence for a complete ranking. But it is equally possible that when *new output forms* are fed into the algorithm, new rerankings will be motivated. This issue will be taken up in sections 7.4–7.5.

7.3.5.2 *Robustness of Recursive Ranking*

We must now consider what happens when Recursive Ranking processes the mark-data pairs in a different order from the one we assumed in the previous section. Will the algorithm still 'converge' – be able to arrive at the target

---

[6] Bruce Tesar (p.c.) points out that there is a theoretical limit (an upper bound) on the number of 'informative' mark-data pairs necessary to determine a correct constraint hierarchy for a language. An 'informative' mark-data pair is one which contains some information about the ranking that is not contained in the pairs already observed. The upper bound is on the order of the square of the number of constraints. More precisely, if N is the number of constraints, the upper bound on the necessary number of informative mark-data pairs is $N(N-1)/2$. This is just a theoretical limit; in practice, the actual necessary number is much, much lower than this, and in fact it would be quite challenging to construct an optimality theoretic system that actually could require that many pairs.

hierarchy? A positive answer to this question is crucial, since no inherent property of the mark-data pairs would force one order of processing over another. If the learner can get 'stuck' just by considering the data in a 'clumsy' order, something is wrong. In that case the learner will arrive at the target grammar only by chance: by coincidentally picking a 'smart' order. In that case, we can no longer assume that OT grammars are learnable.

But fortunately, the attainment of the target grammar is independent of the order in which mark-data pairs are considered by Constraint Demotion. The only side-effect of selecting one order over another is the number of intermediate stages that must be passed on the way towards the goal. There are efficient and less efficient orders, so to speak. We will not consider a formal proof of this conclusion, but as a way of illustrating the relative length of the trajectory, we will consider another order of processing mark-data pairs.

In fact, the order of mark-data pairs which we considered in the previous section was the *least efficient* of all possible orders. The quickest way to reach the goal considers the mark-data pairs in precisely the reverse order:

(39)   Mark-data pairs considered in reverse order of previous section

subopt < *opt*	*loser-marks*	*winner-marks*
e < **a**	{*ALL-FT-L, *FT-BIN}	{*PARSE-SYL}
d < **a**	{*ALL-FT-L, *LEFTMOST, *PARSE-SYL}	{*ALL-FT-R, *RIGHTMOST}
c < **a**	{*PARSE-SYL}	{*ALL-FT-L, *ALL-FT-R}
b < **a**	{*ALL-FT-L}	{*ALL-FT-R}

Let us go through the essential steps once again, now following the new order. Again, the initial hierarchy has a single stratum only, containing all constraints.

First, consideration of mark-data pair **e** < **a** demotes PARSE-SYL to a new stratum. Second, consideration of mark-data pair **d** < **a** demotes ALL-FT-R and RIGHTMOST into the stratum already occupied by PARSE-SYL. No new stratum is created because demotion is minimal (both of the *highest-ranking* constraints assessing *loser-marks*, ALL-FT-L and LEFTMOST, already dominate this stratum). Third, the mark-data pair **c** < **a** produces a demotion of ALL-FT-L and ALL-FT-R into a new stratum, immediately below that of PARSE-SYL. Fourth, the mark-data pair **b** < **a** leads to a demotion of ALL-FT-R to a new stratum, below that of ALL-FT-L. And that is all! In (40) are the hierarchies which arise after each of these four steps.

(40)   Demotion steps when considering mark-data pairs in reverse order

Steps	Hierarchies after steps 1–4
H_0	{ALL-FT-L, ALL-FT-R, FT-BIN, L-MOST, PARSE-SYL, R-MOST}
H_1 e < a	{ALL-FT-L, ALL-FT-R, FT-BIN, L-MOST, R-MOST} ≫ {**PARSE-SYL**}
H_2 d < a	{ALL-FT-L, FT-BIN, L-MOST} ≫ {PARSE-SYL, **ALL-FT-R**, **R-MOST**}
H_3 c < a	{FT-BIN, L-MOST} ≫ {PARSE-SYL, R-MOST} ≫ {**ALL-FT-L, ALL-FT-R**}
H_4 b < a	{FT-BIN, L-MOST} ≫ {PARSE-SYL, R-MOST} ≫ {**ALL-FT-L**} ≫ {**ALL-FT-R**}

Here it takes *four* steps, rather than *nine*, to arrive at the target grammar. We find a rather large variation in length of the trajectory between the initial state and the target grammar, depending on the order in which mark-data pairs are considered. But this variation does not affect the outcome: in both cases the algorithm converges into the target grammar.[7]

7.3.5.3   *Why demotion must be minimal*

Another question to be addressed is that of why demotion is minimal, rather than maximal. Recall that by *minimal* demotion we understand that a constraint assessing *winner-marks* is demoted to a stratum directly below the *highest-ranking*

---

[7] Yet another issue is that of the generation of informative suboptimal candidates. As mentioned in note 2, an algorithm was developed by Tesar (1995) to accomplish this task. *Error-Driven Constraint Demotion* works by interweaving learning and parsing. The learner uses her current constraint hierarchy, and computes the description for the underlying form which is best. If it matches the correct description (the winner), then learning is done for that winner. If it does not match the winner, then it will make a good loser, so a mark-data pair is made combining the winner (pre-determined) with the currently optimal description as the loser. Constraint demotion can then be applied with that mark-data pair, yielding a new constraint hierarchy. The learner then applies parsing using the new constraint hierarchy, to see if the winner is optimal yet. If not, then the constraint which is best under the new constraint hierarchy becomes the next loser. In this way, learning is stopped for a given winner once a constraint hierarchy is reached which makes that winner actually optimal.

constraint assessing *loser-marks*. We have seen the success of the minimal demotion strategy in the Pintupi case study. But it is useful to understand that minimal demotion is crucial to the success of the algorithm. To understand this, we must consider the alternative strategy of maximal demotion.

By *maximal* demotion we might understand the following: a constraint assessing *winner-marks* is demoted to a stratum below the *lowest-ranking* constraint that assesses *loser-marks*. The failure of maximal demotion can be demonstrated in either of two ways. First, it can be shown that the algorithm continues performing constraint rerankings even when the target grammar has been reached. Of course the algorithm does not 'know' that it has reached the target grammar. Therefore it will continue considering mark-data pairs, and performing rerankings whenever the mark-data pairs motivate these. It is only when rerankings are no longer justified that we say that 'the target grammar has been acquired'. Now suppose that the algorithm would, by chance, arrive at the target grammar. Another demotion would occur if another mark-data pair (say, $e \prec a$) were taken into consideration:

(41)   Target grammar $e \prec a$ Non-target grammar
        {FT-BIN, L-MOST} ≫   →   {FT-BIN, L-MOST} ≫
        {PARSE-SYL, R-MOST} ≫   {R-MOST} ≫
        {ALL-FT-L} ≫   {ALL-FT-L} ≫
        {ALL-FT-R}   {**PARSE-SYL**, ALL-FT-R}

PARSE-SYL is demoted below the lowest-ranking constraint assessing *loser-marks*, which is ALL-FT-L in this case. This means that an algorithm using maximal demotion is *unable to converge* on the target grammar, since it continues changing it once it has reached it.

But in fact, there is even no guarantee that such an algorithm will ever arrive at the target grammar. This is the second argument to the effect that maximal demotion is a non-effective strategy. Table (42) compares sequences of states through which minimal and maximal demotion go when using the order of mark-data pairs in (39).

(42)   Non-convergence of algorithm using maximal demotion

Steps	Minimal demotion	Maximal demotion
H_0	{ALL-FT-L, ALL-FT-R, FT-BIN, L-MOST, PARSE-SYL, R-MOST}	(*identical to minimal demotion*)
H_1 $e \prec a$	{ALL-FT-L, ALL-FT-R, FT-BIN, L-MOST, R-MOST} ≫ {**PARSE-SYL**}	(*identical to minimal demotion*)

Steps	Minimal demotion	Maximal demotion
H_2 d < a	{ALL-FT-L, FT-BIN, L-MOST} ≫ {PARSE-SYL, **ALL-FT-R, R-MOST**}	{ALL-FT-L, FT-BIN, L-MOST} ≫ {PARSE-SYL} ≫ {**ALL-FT-R, R-MOST**}
H_3 c < a	{FT-BIN, L-MOST} ≫ {PARSE-SYL, R-MOST} ≫ {**ALL-FT-L, ALL-FT-R**}	{FT-BIN, L-MOST} ≫ {PARSE-SYL} ≫ {**ALL-FT-L, ALL-FT-R**, R-MOST}
H_4 b < a	{FT-BIN, L-MOST} ≫ {PARSE-SYL, R-MOST} ≫ {ALL-FT-L} ≫ {**ALL-FT-R**}	{FT-BIN, L-MOST} ≫ {PARSE-SYL} ≫ {ALL-FT-L, **R-MOST**} ≫ {**ALL-FT-R**}
H_5 e < a	*(no demotion justified)*	{FT-BIN, L-MOST} ≫ {ALL-FT-L, R-MOST} ≫ {**PARSE-SYL**, ALL-FT-R}
H_6 d < a	*(no demotion justified)*	{FT-BIN, L-MOST} ≫ {ALL-FT-L} ≫ {PARSE-SYL} {**ALL-FT-R, R-MOST**}
H_7 c < a	*(no demotion justified)*	$(=H_3)$
H_8 b < a	*(no demotion justified)*	$(=H_4)$
H_9 e < a	*(no demotion justified)*	$(=H_5)$
H_{10} d < a	*(no demotion justified)*	$(=H_6)$

Minimal demotion arrives at the target grammar in four steps. But maximal demotion has not reached the target grammar even after ten steps, and it has actually started *reiterating* previous stages from H_7 onwards. It has run into an *eternal loop*. Such an oscillation of demotions offers no hope that this algorithm will ever acquire the target grammar. In sum, we have found that constraint demotion must be minimal in order for effective learning to become possible at all.

7.4 The learning algorithm: discussion

Tesar and Smolensky's learning algorithm has been shown to be successful in the complex task of deducing a hierarchy of constraints, that is, an OT grammar. Of course we have only considered a very simple case, involving six constraints whose interactions could be construed from the examination of a single example. But in fact it can be shown that the algorithm will successfully construct a hierarchy of constraints of any complexity, as long as the input data are *consistent*.

Therefore, if the model can learn the constraint hierarchy of an OT grammar, then it means that the problem is logically solvable. Consequently we may assume that the language-learning child is also able to perform the same task. The learnability of constraint rankings is a crucial ingredient of the explanation of learnability of grammars. It is only an ingredient, however, since much more is at stake in learning a grammar than constraint ranking. To this issue we now turn.

Tesar and Smolensky make a number of simplifying assumptions about the nature of the acquisition task, which will (ultimately) have to be reconsidered in order to arrive at a more complete model of the language learner. Let us discuss these assumptions.

First, Tesar and Smolensky's algorithm works on the assumption that output forms are available to the learner in the form of (properly structured) linguistic representations, rather than in a raw phonetic form. Under 'real-life' conditions in which acquisition takes place, we cannot make this assumption, simply because linguistic units such as syllables, feet, and distinctive features are not readily available from the phonetic forms, and must therefore be inferred by the learner. 'Underdetermination' of the linguistic representation in the phonetic form raises the problem of how the learner gets around it. This problem has been addressed recently by Tesar (1996), who has developed an extension of the learning algorithm having the ability to reach progress along two dimensions, by iterative testing of hypotheses about the output's representation and the constraint ranking. Tesar (1996: 1, 7) states the general idea as follows:

> the learner can go back and forth between estimating the hidden structure and estimating the constraint ranking, eventually converging on the correct forms for both... The goal is to find a ranking such that the interpretation of each overt form matches the corresponding optimal description, both of which are determined with respect to the current hypothesis ranking. Changing the hypothesis ranking may change the optimal description assigned to the underlying form of the prior interpretation. But, it may also change the interpretation assigned to the overt form by interpretative parsing.

Tesar demonstrates the feasibility of this approach in an algorithm that is faced with the task of constructing a ranking of metrical constraints on the basis of outputs that have no overt metrical structure, but only 'raw' stress markings.

Second, Tesar and Smolensky's learning algorithm assumes that the learner has already mastered the *lexicon*, including the correct *underlying representations* for each morpheme. Therefore every output form considered by the algorithm will be paired with its correct input form. But in 'real-life' language acquisition, underlying forms are *hypothetical* and have to be inferred from combined analytic assumptions about the output and the constraint hierarchy. Of course this problem is not unique to OT – in fact every theory of phonology which assumes that contextual alternants of a morpheme derive from a single underlying form is faced with it. Note that with the addition of underlying forms to the logical problem of acquisition, in fact *three* variables must be continuously monitored: (a) the underlying form, (b) its output representation, and (c) the constraint hierarchy relating both levels of representation:

(43)   Interdependence of three factors in language acquisition

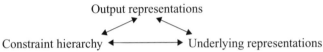

Perhaps a solution to this problem will be possible along the lines of the extended model of Tesar (1996) sketched above, and we will make an attempt at this in section 7.5. This model will have to be extended so as to allow the iterative testing of hypotheses for all three variables.

Third, Tesar and Smolensky assume that the hierarchy of the target language has the property of *total ranking*. The assumption that all constraints are ranked with respect to the others guarantees that each input corresponds with a *single output*. To see this, consider the fact that no two output forms that have distinct violation marks can both be optimal. Hence if two output forms have different violation marks for conflicting constraints, then these forms must have different harmonic values, since both constraints are, by definition, ranked with respect to each other. In close relation to this issue, Prince and Smolensky (1993: 51) remark that the total ranking hypothesis is no a priori assumption of OT, but an empirical matter:

> It is entirely conceivable that the grammar should recognize nonranking of pairs of constraints, but this opens up the possibility of crucial nonranking (neither can dominate the other; both rankings are allowed), for which we have not yet found evidence.

There is potential empirical evidence that bears on this issue. The assumption that an input has *unique output* may be problematic in the sense that languages are known to exhibit widely variability of output forms, even under grammatical control. Some phenomena to display grammar-governed variability in many languages are stress patterns, phonological phrase structure, and syntactic phenomena such as linear order of adjunct phrases (*scrambling*). See chapter 9 (section 9.4) for more discussion of variation in OT.

Finally, it is assumed that among the data presented to the learner no incorrect data (ungrammatical outputs) occur. Again this assumption does not match real-life conditions under which language acquisition takes place. Tesar and Smolensky show that the learning algorithm is capable of signalling such misfits, and make suggestions about the possible role of this 'alarm' function in acquisition.

7.5 Learning alternations and input representations

7.5.1 *The nature of the problem*
The major question arises whether the algorithm can be extended such that it will be able to handle alternations in the shape of morphemes. The key aspect of alternations is that two or more output forms share a single input form – the lexical or underlying representation. Usually the input form is identical to one of the surface alternants, but there is no label on the data to tell the learner which one this is. The learner's task is therefore more complex than was assumed in the previous section, where the input was an unmetrified word. We will consider the question of whether we can generalize the iterative learning strategy to the learning of underlying forms.

The alternation problem will be tackled using a relatively simple set of data from Dutch, involving syllable-final devoicing. As we learned in chapter 1, this language has a voicing contrast in obstruents which is neutralized in syllable-final position, where all obstruents are voiceless. No alternations of voicing in obstruents are apparent in stems such as *pet*, *voet*, and *bloot* (44), in which underlying forms contain voiceless obstruents:

(44)   a.i   pet   /pɛt/   [pɛt]   'cap'
        a.ii petten /pɛt-ən/   [pɛ.tən]   'caps'
        b.i   voet   /vut/   [vut]   'foot'
        b.ii voeten /vut-ən/   [vu.tən]   'feet'
        c.i   bloot   /blot/   [blot]   'naked (predicative)'
        c.ii blote   /blot-ə/   [blo.tə]   'naked (attributive)'

But in stems whose final obstruent is underlyingly voiced, coda devoicing produces voice alternations, as in the singular and plural of *bed*, *hoed*, and *breed* (45):

(45)   a.i   bed   /bɛd/   [bɛt]   'bed'
        a.ii bedden /bɛd-ən/   [bɛ.dən]   'beds'
        b.i   hoed   /hud/   [hut]   'hat'
        b.ii hoeden /hud-ən/   [hu.dən]   'hats'
        c.i   breed   /bred/   [bret]   'wide (predicative)'
        c.ii brede   /bred-ə/   [bre.də]   'wide (attributive)'

The learning algorithm must find the constraint ranking (involving an interaction of well-formedness and faithfulness constraints) on the basis of assumptions about the underlying forms (deducing those of 44–5), and a set of universal constraints. In this set of universal constraints are included the two well-formedness constraints (46a–b) and the faithfulness constraint (46c):

(46)   a. ***VOICED-CODA**
          Coda obstruents are voiceless.
     b. **INTER-V-VOICE**
          Intervocalic consonants are voiced.
     c. **IDENT-IO**(voice)
          Let α be a segment in the input, and β be a correspondent of α in
          the output. If α is [γvoice], then β is [γvoice].

Devoicing of coda consonants and intervocalic voicing of consonants are both processes which are frequently attested in the languages of the world. Also, both are natural states of affairs from an articulatory point of view. Being markedness statements, they are captured by the well-formedness constraints (46a–b).

The grammar of Dutch ranks these constraints in the following way (the notation identifies three strata in the hierarchy):

(47)   A fragment of the grammar of Dutch
          {*VOICED-CODA}
              ≫
          {IDENT-IO(voice)}
              ≫
          {INTER-V-VOICE}

The task facing the language learner is to find the proper constraint hierarchy (47), and also to infer the correct underlying forms which are mapped to the attested outputs. A priori, the learner may state two hypotheses about the alternation [bɛt]~[bɛ.dən] in (45), which involve different markedness constraints. The first (correct) hypothesis is that the stem *bed* has an underlying voiced obstruent /bɛd/, which is devoiced at the end of the syllable in the singular. Syllable-final devoicing involves domination of the markedness constraint *VOICED-CODA over the featural faithfulness constraint IDENT-IO(voice), as we have seen in chapter 1. The alternative hypothesis is that the stem *bed* has an underlying voiceless obstruent /bɛt/, which is voiced in intervocalic position in the plural. Intervocalic voicing involves domination of the markedness constraint INTER-V-VOICE over IDENT-IO(voice). This hypothesis is demonstrably incorrect, as no constraint hierarchy that involves this ranking is consistent with the data. But let us first discuss the mapping of the correct underlying forms to the attested outputs.

Under the correct hypothesis, the underlying forms /pɛt/ and /bɛd/ are mapped onto surface forms by the ranked constraints of (47), as illustrated by the tableaux

(48–9). The evidence for the ranking *VOICED-CODA ≫ IDENT-IO(voice) comes from the singular form [bɛt] in tableau (49), where voiced input /d/ corresponds with voiceless /t/ in the output.

(48)

Input: /pɛt/	*VOICED-CODA	IDENT-IO(voice)	INTER-V-VOICE
a. ☞ pɛt			
b. pɛd	*!	*	

(49)

Input: /bɛd/	*VOICED-CODA	IDENT-IO(voice)	INTER-V-VOICE
a. ☞ bɛt		*	
b. bɛd	*!		

None of these tableaux contain evidence for the ranking of INTER-V-VOICE, since all output candidates which are considered satisfy this constraint. (There is no intervocalic context.)

For evidence for the ranking IDENT-IO(voice) ≫ INTER-V-VOICE we must turn to the tableau of the plural form [pɛ.tən] 'caps', which is faithful to the underlying voiceless /t/ in spite of the pressure to voice this in intervocalic position, due to INTER-V-VOICE:

(50)

Input: /pɛt-ən/	*VOICED-CODA	IDENT-IO(voice)	INTER-V-VOICE
a. ☞ pɛ.tən			*
b. pɛ.dən		*!	

(51)

Input: /bɛd-ən/	*VOICED-CODA	IDENT-IO(voice)	INTER-V-VOICE
a. bɛ.tən		*!	*
b. ☞ bɛ.dən			

Note that tableau (51) of [bɛ.dən] 'beds' gives no information about ranking whatsoever.

Now consider the (incorrect) alternative hypothesis, under which the voiced [d] in [bɛ.dən] derives from an input /t/ in /bɛt-ən/ by intervocalic voicing. The grammar which performs this mapping must crucially rank INTER-V-VOICE above IDENT-IO(voice), since intervocalic voicing violates featural faithfulness to [−voice]. Under this hypothesis there is no reason to demote *VOICED-CODA from its undominated position because it is unviolated in the examples at hand (actually, as it is in all output forms of the language). Therefore we consider the following hypothetical ranking:

(52)   Hypothetical (and incorrect) fragment of the grammar of Dutch
        *VOICED-CODA, INTER-V-VOICE ≫ IDENT-IO(voice)

This ranking actually derives all the forms correctly except one: it predicts *[pɛ.dən] 'caps' rather than [pɛ.tən]. (The incorrect winner is indicated by a ☹ symbol.)

(53)

Input: /pɛt-ən/	*VOICED-CODA	INTER-V-VOICE	IDENT-IO(voice)
a. pɛ.tən		*!	
b. ☹ pɛ.dən			*

The intervocalic voicing contrast has vanished due to the demotion of IDENT-IO(voice).

The argument for the correct grammar (47) over the hypothetical grammar in (52) is based on the voicing alternation in *bed–bedden*, and lack thereof in *pet–petten*. This makes a perfectly straightforward argument. However, we must ask whether the choice in favour of grammar (47) is equally transparent to the learner, who must determine both the underlying forms and the constraint rankings, on the basis of only surface forms and a set of universal constraints. What makes a child learning Dutch eventually select this correct combination of grammar and lexicon, rather than one in which the alternation in *bed–bedden* is due to intervocalic voicing of an underlying /t/? Actually, we will show that the correct grammar and underlying forms are learnable by the Tesar and Smolensky learning algorithm, if only this algorithm is extended by iterative learning in the sense of Tesar (1996). That is, the learner can go back and forth between estimating the underlying forms and estimating the constraint ranking, and eventually converges on the correct forms for both. We will argue that *Lexicon Optimization* plays an important role in this learning procedure.

7.5.2 *Learning the hierarchy on the basis of correct inputs*

We will first prove that the correct constraint ranking is learnable simply on the basis of the correct underlying forms, by the standard Tesar and Smolensky algorithm. That is, we temporarily put aside the problem of how to determine the underlying forms, and return to this in due course. The initial state of the learner is the universal set of unranked constraints contained in a single stratum, of which (54) forms a subset:

(54)   { ... *VOICED-CODA, IDENT-IO(voice), INTER-V-VOICE ... }

Assume that the learner is first confronted with the surface form [bɛt], equipped with the correct underlying form /bɛd/. The mark-data pairs of the optimal candidate [bɛt] and its major competitor [bɛd] are given below:

(55)   Mark-data pairs

subopt < *opt*	*loser-marks*	*winner-marks*
bɛd < bɛt	{**VOICED-CODA}	{*IDENT-IO(voice)}

No cancellation is required. Form here on Constraint Demotion applies as follows. First it is made sure that the constraint which induces the *loser-mark*, *VOICED-CODA, does not dominate the constraint which induces the *winner-mark*, IDENT-IO(voice). This is trivial, since the hierarchy is still in its initial unranked state. Next the constraint which induces the *winner-mark* is demoted to a stratum immediately below that of the constraint which induces the *loser-mark*:

(56)   { ... *VOICED-CODA, INTER-V-VOICE ... } ≫ {IDENT-IO(voice)}

Observe that this happens to be the incorrect hypothetical grammar of (52). What makes the child reject this? It will be clear that no valuable information can be gathered from the surface forms [pɛt] and [bɛ.dən], since these violate none of the three constraints in (56). (See tableaux 48 and 51.) And since there is no interaction of constraints in these cases, no new rankings can be established.

But sooner or later, the Dutch child comes across the crucial surface form [pɛ.tən], which will induce a second round of the constraint demotion algorithm.

(57)   Mark-data pairs

subopt < *opt*	*loser-marks*	*winner-marks*
pɛ.dən < pɛ.tən	{*IDENT-IO(voice)}	{*INTER-V-VOICE}

Again, no cancellation of marks occurs. It is made sure that the constraint which induces the *loser-mark*, IDENT-IO(voice), does not dominate the constraint inducing the *winner-mark*, INTER-V-VOICE. In accordance with the algorithm the latter constraint is demoted to a stratum immediately below that of the former constraint:

(58)   { ... *VOICED-CODA ... } ≫ {IDENT-IO(voice)} ≫ {INTER-V-VOICE}

which is the correct mini-grammar of the voicing alternations in (44–5). We leave
it as an exercise to the reader to establish that the learning algorithm would have
yielded the same result when surface forms were presented in the opposite order,
with [pɛ.tən] preceding [bɛd].

7.5.3 *Learning the hierarchy without given inputs*

Next we provide the child with a severe handicap, which is nevertheless universal
among language learners: no underlying forms are innate, and hence the learner
has to infer them solely on the basis of surface forms. What we do assume is that
the learner is able to do sufficient morphological analysis on surface forms, which
results in a segmentation of the stem and plural suffix /-ən/. (Morphological
analysis is a matter of hypothesis testing itself. In a real-life, full-blown model it
will have to be integrated with the rest of the acquisition, but we will leave this
aspect out of consideration here.)

The same child who has successfully ranked the three constraints in (58) must
now forget all the results of this laborious task, as well as the underlying forms,
and is reinstalled with a constraint ranking in its initial maiden state. The question
is: will this 'naturally handicapped' child still be able to deduce the correct
constraint ranking, as she achieved earlier while knowing all of the underlying
forms? Moreover, will this child be able to deduce the correct underlying forms?
In what follows we will see that the answers to these questions are positive, if we
assume that the child has the innate disposition to go back and forth between
hypotheses about constraint rankings and underlying forms.

A trap which the child must avoid is setting up an analysis of *bed* as /bɛt/,
where the surface form [bɛt] is an exact copy of the input. In connection, a second
trap will have to be avoided, which is to analyse the form [bɛ.dən] as the result
of intervocalic voicing of underlying /t/. When the child falls into such traps, will
she ever be able to proceed on the way to the constraint ranking (47)? Can the
learning algorithm get stuck after making an incorrect assumption about underlying forms? Surprisingly, we will see that the child is a robust learner. Falling
into the first trap – setting up an underlying form /bɛt/ – is not fatal, since this
analysis has no consequences for constraint ranking whatsoever. Perhaps even
more surprisingly, setting up an underlying form /bɛt-ən/ is avoided by the
learner, since an alternative underlying form /bɛd-ən/ is available which will
always be preferred, due to *Lexicon Optimization*.

We will assume that the language learner may cancel out earlier hypotheses
about underlying forms, but *not* hypotheses about ranking. That is, the correct
ranking will be established 'incrementally', as in the Tesar and Smolensky model.
The starting point is a completely flat initial state in which constraints are all part
of a single stratum. Into this initial state more and more hierarchical structure is

introduced, in a succession of stages of stratified hierarchies of increasing complexity. This process terminates in a state in which no further rankings can be established on the basis of any new evidence, which is the target ranking.[8] The property of the learning algorithm that constraint rankings established on the basis of positive evidence need not be undone qualifies it as sufficiently robust for the requirements of 'real-life' language learning.

7.5.3.1 *Setting the trap*

Let us assume that the Dutch child is confronted with the *worst-case scenario*, in which both of the 'poisonous' forms [bɛt] and [bɛ.dən], by accident, are presented to her prior to the forms [pɛt] and [pɛ.tən]. That is, the child will start analysing the voicing alternation on the basis of forms which are fully consistent with both hypotheses, and before having seen the crucial form [pɛ.tən]. Still worse, we will assume that [bɛt] is presented before [bɛ.dən] (this is certainly a realistic scenario, since the singular is likely to be more frequently used than the plural). That is, the trap is set: the child will be lured into setting up an analysis of *bed* as /bɛt/, in which the surface form [bɛt] is an exact copy of the assumed underlying form. Since this analysis involves no violation of any of the three constraints, it is selected by *Lexicon Optimization*.

The mark-data pair in (59) shows that no information about constraint ranking can be extracted, since no constraints interact.

(59)   Mark-data pairs

input	subopt < opt		loser-marks	winner-marks
/bɛt/	bɛd < bɛt		{* *VOICED-CODA, *IDENT-IO(voice)}	

Actually this mark-data pair is never considered by the core algorithm since it is eliminated by provision (16b) of Marks Cancellation even before Constraint Demotion applies. The constraint ranking therefore remains in its initial state.

Let us assume that the learner is now confronted with the plural form [bɛ.dən], and (after judicious morphological analysis) attributes this form to the morpheme /bɛt/ which occurs in the singular [bɛt]. Starting from this – incorrect – lexical form /bɛt/, the following mark-data pairs will be constructed:

---

[8] It is an entirely different question whether the child actually proceeds incrementally on the way to the target constraint ranking. Evidence presently available strongly suggests that children's grammars may have different constraint rankings from adult grammars. See the next section.

(60)   Mark-data pairs

input	subopt $<$ opt	loser-marks	winner-marks
/bɛt-ən/	bɛ.tən $<$ bɛ.dən	{*INTER-V-VOICE}	{*IDENT-IO(voice)}

The *winner-mark* is assessed by IDENT-IO(voice). Therefore Constraint Demotion demotes this constraint directly below the highest-ranking constraint which assesses the *loser-mark*, here INTER-V-VOICE. The result is a new hierarchy:

(61)   { ... *VOICED-CODA, INTER-V-VOICE ... }

         ≫

         {IDENT-IO(voice)}

In fact, this conclusion is *correct*, even though it is based on incorrect premisses. That is, the voicing alternation in the pair [bɛt] ~ [bɛ.dən] necessarily involves *some* violation of faithfulness in either the singular or the plural form. The algorithm incorrectly assumes that this violation occurs in the plural, rather than the singular; but from this it draws a correct conclusion about the hierarchy. The hierarchy (61) encodes precisely this observation: that faithfulness for [voice] is violated. (The learner would have arrived at the same conclusion when she had initially embarked on the correct hypothesis about the input form, /bɛd/.)

Next, the child encounters the singular form [pɛt], which she considers to be on a par with the singular [bɛt], currently attributed to the lexical form /bɛt/. The child simply registers [pɛt] under the lexical form /pɛt/,

(62)   IO-pairings after learner's exposure to output set {[bɛt], [bɛ.dən], [pɛt]}
         a. /pɛt/ [pɛt]
         b. /bɛt/ [bɛt] ~ /bɛt-ən/ [bɛ.dən]

At this stage, the learner is completely unaware of its plural [pɛ.tən], which will induce an important constraint demotion in a later stage of learning. In fact, if the child were asked to produce the plural of [pɛt] in this acquisitional stage, she would have no choice but to reply: '[pɛ.dən]!', since this is literally what the ranking (61) predicts that it should be. The model predicts overgeneralization of phonology in alternations, which is a widely observed characteristic of children's grammars. See section 7.5.4 for Dutch language acquisition data which corroborate this prediction.

The final form which the child is confronted with is [pɛ.tən]. This comes as a shock to the child, as this is the first surface form she encounters in which *INTER-V-VOICE is violated. A mark-data pair is immediately drawn up:

(63)   Mark-data pairs

input subopt < opt	loser-marks	winner-marks
/pɛt-ən/ pɛ.dən < pɛ.tən	{*IDENT-IO(voice)}	{*INTER-V-VOICE}

This presents ranking information which conflicts with that of the form [bɛ.dən] 'beds' in (60). However, since [pɛ.tən] is the 'current' form under analysis, the learner proceeds to track mechanically its consequences for the hierarchy. Let us carefully consider the steps taken by the Constraint Demotion algorithm.

- First, it identifies the mark *IDENT-IO(voice) in *loser-marks* as the highest-ranked in the current hierarchy. (This is trivial, since there is only one mark in *loser-marks*.)
- Second, it establishes that the constraint assessing the *winner-mark* (INTER-V-VOICE) is not dominated by the constraint assessing the *loser-mark* (IDENT-IO(voice)).
- Third, it demotes INTER-V-VOICE to a position immediately below IDENT-IO(voice).

This produces the correct target ranking in (64):

(64)   { ... *VOICED-CODA ... }
              ≫
        {IDENT-IO(voice)}
              ≫
        {INTER-V-VOICE}

The child has actually succeeded in learning the *correct* target ranking. This achievement is remarkable, given the fact that it is based on *incorrect* inferences about underlying forms. But may we also conclude that the child has now successfully acquired the fragment of the grammar which derives the voicing pattern?

Of course we may *not*, since the underlying forms of the pair [bɛt] ~ [bɛdən] are still misrepresented as /bɛt/ ~ /bɛt-ən/. Once the ranking (64) has been established, the child will make the incorrect prediction *[bɛ.tən] for the plural form see tableau (65):

(65)

Input: /bɛt-ən/	*VOICED-CODA	IDENT-IO(voice)	INTER-V-VOICE
a. ☹ bɛ.tən			*
b. bɛ.dən		*!	

In fact, similar types of overgeneralizations are attested in children's language, which is to the credit of the model. But eventually they become extinct, suggesting that underlying forms are subject to restructuring. How this restructuring takes place is what we will consider in the remainder of this section.

7.5.3.2 *Restructuring input forms*

Once the conflict between the acquired ranking (64) and the surface form [bɛdən] has been signalled (the nature of this signal will be discussed below), the child has two options. The first is to *adjust the hierarchy* to the observed output [bɛdən] while preserving its current input /bɛt/. The second option is to *restructure the input* from /bɛt/ into /bɛd/, so that the unchanged hierarchy correctly maps it onto the observed output. We will see that the second strategy, restructuring the input, is the only one leading to success.

The first strategy, going through another constraint demotion, may in fact produce a short-term success with respect to the problematic form, but will not converge into a stable ranking. The mark-data pairs of table (60) reactivate Constraint Demotion in the hierarchy (64). Concretely, IDENT-IO(voice) will be demoted below INTER-V-VOICE:

(66)   {*VOICED-CODA} ≫ {...} ≫ {INTER-V-VOICE} ≫ {IDENT-IO(voice)}

This hierarchy accounts for [bɛdən], but of course we run into a *loop* now, as we have been in this stage before, at a point prior to the introduction of the form [pɛtən]. The learner will go through the entire demotion process once more, exchanging positions between INTER-V-VOICE and IDENT-IO(voice), without ever converging into the target grammar. Note that these stages crucially include the mark-data pairs (60) and the ranking (61). In sum, the first option of repairing the hierarchy by Constraint Demotion produces an eternal loop.

Of all things, eternal loops must be avoided most. Hence the learner must capitalize on any information warning her that she is entering a loop. Actually, a signal is given to the learner right at this point: *a stratum is vacated*. To 'vacate a stratum' means: to demote a constraint from a stratum in which it was the single constraint. An empty stratum has been indicated in (66) by '{...}'.

Stated generally, a loop occurs whenever the learner is presented with *inconsistent* information with respect to the ranking of two constraints.[9] That is, a pair of constraints C_1 and C_2 must be ranked $C_1 \gg C_2$ for one set of forms, and as $C_2 \gg C_1$ for another set of forms. If the learner encounters both sets of forms, an

---

[9] The same idea that vacating of a stratum points to an 'inconsistency' in the underlying forms was used by Broihier (1995) to solve the problem of learning grammars with 'tied' constraints.

eternal process of ranking and reranking starts that never terminates in a stable hierarchy. The diagnostic for inconsistency in the data with respect to ranking is the vacation of a stratum – a consistent target ranking never gives rise to a loop. Since the learner may assume that the target ranking is consistent with the data, any sign of an eternal loop must be due to another cause – an incorrect assumption about *input forms*.

What causes an incorrect assumption about the input? Clearly the error must reside in an *alternating* morpheme, whose alternants are specified as [+F] and [−F], respectively, in different contexts. By Lexicon Optimization, the learner will be led to analyse the first occurring alternant of a morpheme to reflect its input value. Hence, if the learner happens to encounter the alternant [−F] first, she will set up the incorrect input value [−F], even when the correct input value is [+F].

This erroneous assumption on inputs causes the (apparent) inconsistency in ranking, as follows. The value of the feature [F] in a non-alternating morpheme always equals the value of [F] in one of the alternants of an alternating morpheme. This is simply due to the neutralizing nature of the processes causing alternations. (For example, word-final [−voice] occurs in both the alternating form [bɛt] and in the non-alternating form [pɛt].) Alternating and non-alternating morphemes have identical specifications for [F] in a specific context, as is shown schematically below:

(67)

	Neutralization context	Elsewhere context
Alternating morpheme	...[−F]...	...[+F]...
Non-alternating morpheme	...[−F]...	...[−F]...

The problem occurs when the learner attributes both types of morphemes to the same input value, [−F]. This causes an apparent inconsistency in the ranking of faithfulness constraints and markedness constraints in the elsewhere context (here: *bedden* versus *petten*). The loop signals that such a situation occurs.

Signalling an inconsistency in rankings is one thing, but to repair it is another. To avoid eternal loops, we propose that the learning algorithm blocks Constraint Demotion if this would result in an empty stratum. This is stated below as the Anti-Loop Provision:

(68)   **Anti-Loop Provision**

If Constraint Demotion produces an empty stratum:
   a. cancel demotion
   b. adjust the input form in accordance with Lexicon Optimization
   c. adjust the mark-data pairs in accordance with the new input form

Once this alarm bell goes, the learner adjusts her underlying representation of the observed output form in accordance with *Lexicon Optimization*. Restructuring of the current input /bɛt-ən/ into the new input /bɛd-ən/ is forced as the single method of reaching compatibility with the current hierarchy (64). This is achieved by provision (68b):

(69)   Adjustment of underlying form for [bɛ.dən]:
         /bɛt-ən/ → /bɛd-ən/

Moreover, the mark-data pair for [bɛdən] is changed as a consequence of provision (68c). Since *the input now equals the output*, no violation of faithfulness occurs any longer in the optimal form. Hence the mark-data pair becomes uninformative for Constraint Demotion:

(70)   Adjusted mark-data pair for [bɛdən]

input	subopt < opt	loser-marks	winner-marks
/bɛd-ən/	bɛ.tən < bɛ.dən	{*INTER-V-VOICE, *IDENT-IO(voice)}	

Only consideration of new forms might, potentially, lead to additional demotions. Let us see what occurs when the algorithm reconsiders the singular form [bɛt]. Uniqueness of underlying forms implies that the adjustment of the input form of the plural /bɛt-ən/ into /bɛd-ən/ is accompanied by a change of the input of the singular of /bɛt/ into /bɛd/. At the same time, the mark-data pair for [bɛt] is changed as a consequence of provision (68c):

(71)   Adjusted mark-data pairs for [bɛt]

input	subopt < opt	loser-marks	winner-marks
/bɛd/	bɛd < bɛt	{* *VOICED-CODA}	{*IDENT-IO(voice)}

At this point, when the learner is confronted with the output form [bɛt], the hierarchy (64) still holds. The algorithm

- First identifies the mark * *VOICED-CODA in *loser-marks* as the highest-ranked in the current hierarchy, (64).
- Second, it establishes that the constraint assessing the *winner-mark* (IDENT-IO(voice)) is dominated by the constraint assessing the *loser-mark* (*VOICED-CODA). Therefore no demotion is motivated.

Finally, it remains to be demonstrated that no adjustments of the current hierarchy (64) can be triggered by non-alternating forms such as [pɛt]~[pɛ.tən]. Their input forms are unchanged, since the Anti-Loop Provision is only activated by forms which pose the threat of vacating a stratum. It is easy to show that such a threat is not posed by [pɛt] or [pɛ.tən], though. First, mark-data pairs for [pɛt] are trivially uninformative. Second, mark-data pairs of [pɛ.tən] in (63), if anything, might motivate a demotion of INTER-V-VOICE below IDENT-IO(voice). However, this demotion is inapplicable, as IDENT-IO(voice) already dominates INTER-V-VOICE in the current ranking (64). In sum, non-alternating forms are incapable of triggering any demotion, hence the Anti-Loop Provision is never activated, automatically preserving the inputs.

Therefore we may safely conclude that the learning algorithm has converged into the target grammar of Dutch: the hierarchy (64). But even more importantly, the learner has succeeded in establishing the correct set of underlying forms for alternating morphemes. That is, the learner has overcome the handicap that underlying forms are not pre-given, but have to be inferred from output forms on the basis of hypothetical constraint rankings.

It remains to be seen whether the Anti-Loop Provision is sufficiently general to deal with more complex alternations. Alternations involving *multiple features* seem to require a more sophisticated version of input adjustment (provision 68b), limiting adjustment to the feature [F] at stake, while preserving input specifications of other features. The feature [F] must be inferred from the constraints whose ranking is at stake (here, constraints referring to [voice]). Moreover, the problem of how to deal with *dependencies* between alternating features must be solved. We will leave these issues open for future research.

7.5.4 *Intervocalic voicing in child language*
The prediction that Dutch children go through a stage of overgeneralization of intervocalic voicing (discussed in section 7.5.3.1) is corroborated. Actual examples, as produced by Emma, a three-year old, are presented below:[10]

(72) Emma's voicing pattern (3;0–3;3)

	Emma	adult form	
a.i	krij[t] ~ krij[d]en	krij[t]en	'chalks'
a.ii	boo[t] ~ bo[d]en	bo[t]en	'boats'
a.iii	groo[t] ~ gro[d]e	gro[t]e	'big'(infl.)
	(varies with gro[t]e)		

---

[10] I wish to thank Martin Everaert for sharing these data with me.

b.i	kaar[t] ~ kaar[d]en	kaar[t]en	'cards'
b.ii	taar[t] ~ taar[d]en	taar[t]en	'cakes'
c.	olifan[t] ~ olifan[t]en	olifan[t]en	'elephants'
d.	kas[t] ~ kas[t]en	kas[t]en	'cupboards'

During this stage, Emma voices obstruents in intervocalic positions where adult forms have voiceless ones (72a). The context of voicing is actually more general than 'intervocalic'. That is, Emma voices obstruents in between approximants and vowels, as (72b) shows, but not after a nasal (72c) or an obstruent (72d).

Only two months later, the pattern has extended into prevocalic obstruents following nasals (73c), generalizing the process to post-sonorant obstruents:

(73)   Emma's voicing pattern (3;4–3;5)

	Emma	adult form	
a.i	pe[t] ~ pe[d]en	pe[t]en	'caps'
a.ii	poo[t] ~ po[d]en	po[t]en	'paws'
	(varies with po[t]en)		
a.iii	voe[t] ~ voe[d]en	voe[t]en	'feet'
b.i	bul[t] ~ bul[d]en	bul[t]en	'lumps'
b.ii	taar[t] ~ taar[d]ies	taar[t]jes	'small cakes'
c.i	mun[t] ~ mun[d]en	mun[t]en	'coins'
c.ii	achterkan[t] ~ achterkan[d]en	achterkan[t]en	'back sides'

In both acquisitional stages, Emma displays variation in intervocalic voicing, showing that the ranking of INTER-V-VOICE with respect to IDENT-IO(voice) has not yet stabilized. Note also that intervocalic obstruent clusters are never voiced in any acquisitional stage.

7.5.5 *Discussion*

For expository reasons, the alternation problem discussed has been a simple one, involving only a single alternation. Yet our success in solving this problem suggests that the Tesar and Smolensky algorithm is extendable to handle more complex alternations. The central idea that we have explored here is that of building *inertness* of the hierarchy into the learning algorithm, prohibiting the demotion of a constraint which forms a stratum on its own. This presents a 'warning bell' to the learner that current assumptions about input forms may be incorrect, as a result of which lexical restructuring takes place. Such adjustment of input forms by the *Anti-Loop Provision* is always 'concrete', in the sense that it copies phonological structure of the output (here, a feature value for [voice]), in accordance with Lexicon Optimization. In chapter 9 (section 9.6) we will re-evaluate the need for *underlying forms* in OT, sketching an alternative in terms of allomorphs.

SUGGESTIONS FOR FURTHER READING

Parameters

Dresher, Elan and Jonathan Kaye (1990) A computational learning model for metrical phonology. *Cognition* **34**. 137–95.

Connectionist models

Daelemans, Walter, Steven Gillis, and Gert Durieux (1994) The acquisition of stress: a data-oriented approach. *Computational Linguistics* **20**. 421–51.

Gupta, Prahlad and David Touretzky (1994) Connectionist models and linguistic theory: investigations of stress systems in language. *Cognitive Science* **18**. 1–50.

Optimality Theory (see also references to 'OT in computational phonology' in chapter 1)

Hale, Mark and Charles Reiss (1997) Grammar optimization: the simultaneous acquisition of constraint ranking and a lexicon. Ms., Concordia University, Montréal. [ROA-231, http://ruccs.rutgers.edu/roa.html]

Pulleyblank, Douglas and William J. Turkel (1997) Gradient retreat. In Roca. 153–93.

Smolensky, Paul (1996) On the comprehension/production dilemma in child language. *Linguistic Inquiry* **27**. 720–31.

Tesar, Bruce (1996) An iterative strategy for learning metrical stress in Optimality Theory. In E. Hughes, M. Hughes, and A. Greenhill (eds.), *The proceedings of the 21st annual Boston University Conference on Language Development, November 1996.* 615–26. [ROA-177, http://ruccs.rutgers.edu/roa.html]

Tesar, Bruce and Paul Smolensky (1993) *The learnability of Optimality Theory: an algorithm and some basic complexity results.* Technical Report CU-CS-678–93, Computer Science Department, University of Colorado, Boulder. [ROA-2, http://ruccs.rutgers.edu/roa.html]

Tesar, Bruce and Paul Smolensky (1998) Learnability in Optimality Theory. *Linguistic Inquiry* **29**. 229–68.

Constraint ranking software

Hayes, Bruce (1996b) Constraint ranking software. Ms., University of California, Los Angeles. [Manual of computer program ranking OT constraints, on line available from http://www.humnet.ucla.edu/humnet/linguistics/people/hayes/otsoft/otsoft.htm]

Child phonology

Demuth, Katherine (1995) Markedness and the development of phonological structure. In J. Beckman (ed.), *Proceedings of the 25th North East Linguistic Society, II: Papers from the workshops on language acquisitions and language change.* 13–25.

Gnanadesikan, Amalia (1995) Markedness and faithfulness constraints in child phonology. Ms., University of Massachusetts, Amherst. [ROA-67, http://ruccs.rutgers.edu/roa.html]

Goad, Heather (1997) Consonant harmony in child language. In S. J. Hannahs and M. Young-Scholten (eds.), *Focus on phonological acquisition.* Amsterdam: John Benjamins. 113–42.

Syntactic acquisition

Broihier, Kevin (1995) Optimality theoretic rankings with tied constraints: Slavic relatives, resumptive pronouns and learnability. Ms., Department of Brain and Cognitive Sciences, MIT. [ROA-46, http://ruccs.rutgers.edu/roa.html]

EXERCISES

1 Why the learner must use stratified hierarchies

Here we will consider the question of why learning should use stratified hierarchies. Apart from the appeal of beginning with all of the constraints in a single stratum, there is another reason. This is closely related to the argument for minimal demotion made in section 7.3.5.3. The purpose of this problem is to pinpoint the argument for stratified hierarchies.[11] We will assume a hypothetical language which has the following target ranking of three constraints:

(i)   Target ranking (goal): Top ≫ Mid ≫ Low

Suppose we have the example pairs in (ii), **b** < **a** and **c** < **a**.

(ii)

subopt < opt	loser-marks	winner-marks
b < **a**	{*Mid}	{*Low}
c < **a**	{*Top, *Low}	{*Mid}

The goal is to find a ranking of the three constraints such that the winner is more harmonic than the loser, for both pairs. The question is, why not create a new stratum containing the demoted constraint Mid by itself?

---

[11] Thanks to Bruce Tesar (p.c.) for suggestions which have inspired this problem.

    a. First show that constraint demotion with stratified hierarchies produces the correct result from an initial state {TOP, MID, LOW} with all three constraints unranked. (Recall that demotion is minimal.) Construct a table as in (iii) which keeps track of the learner's progress toward the target grammar.

(iii)   Demotion steps using stratified hierarchies, from initial state {LOW, MID, TOP}:

Steps	Hierarchies after steps 1–3
H_0	{LOW, MID, TOP}
H_1 b < a	
H_2 c < a	
H_3 b < a	

    b. Now we change our assumptions, such that demotion can produce stratified hierarchies. Suppose we apply demotion, but *always create a new stratum*. The starting hierarchy is LOW ≫ MID ≫ TOP, the reverse of the target. Construct a new table which keeps track of the learner's progress. Does this strategy always converge on the correct grammar?

2 Learning input forms under positional faithfulness

Read chapter 9, section 9.5 on positional faithfulness. Then propose an analysis of Dutch devoicing using only the following three constraints:

VOP	Obstruents are voiceless.
IDENT-IO(voice)	Output segments preserve values of [voice] for input correspondents.
IDENT-IO(Ons, voice)	Output segments *in onset position* preserve values of [voice] for input correspondents.

Apply the ranking algorithm, including the Anti-Loop Provision, to test the learnability of underlying forms. (Make sure that you present the data to the algorithm in an order that will trigger the incorrect initial input form /bet/, as in the text of section 7.5.3.1.) Do you experience any new difficulties in learning input forms? If so, can you propose a remedy?

8
Extensions to syntax

8.1 Introduction

In this chapter we will look into results of OT in the domain of syntax. It is important to emphasize once again that OT is not a theory of phonology proper, but rather a theory of *grammar*. Therefore the basic idea underlying OT, that of hierarchically ranked constraints which are minimally violated, is, in principle, equally well applicable to non-phonological phenomena. The present chapter should be read as an attempt at such an extension of OT into syntax, an attempt mainly based on a recent paper on English auxiliaries by Grimshaw (1997). We will discuss the syntactic counterparts of constraint types which we have seen active in previous chapters, and will elaborate the OT architecture of faithfulness and well-formedness constraints. Besides defining constraints in the domain of syntax, we will also address the nature of the input in syntax, and the definition of the function of *Gen*. These are non-trivial matters, that merit discussion in their own right. Finally we will develop the factorial typology of the core syntactic constraints of Grimshaw's paper.

8.2 OT and syntax

How could OT contribute to a better understanding of syntactic phenomena? Let us first point out some dimensions along which recent 'Minimalist' syntactic theory and OT-based syntax differ, as well as some aspects in which they are surprisingly similar. (See Radford 1997 for an overview of minimalism in syntax.)

First consider the major notion of *parameter*. In the Principles-and-Parameters Theory of Chomsky (1981b) and much work thereafter, it is assumed that grammatical principles are universal, in the sense of being *inviolable*. On this view, differences between grammars stem from differences in parameter settings. Parameters constitute a subset of the universal and inviolable principles of the theory of grammar, among which they have a special status, offering a (typically binary) choice of options among which languages are free to choose. Parameters serve the descriptive goal of allowing for cross-linguistic diversity ('linguistic typology') without having to give up on universality.[1] Of course, a similar typological goal is on the agenda of OT, but it is elaborated quite differently. Like parametric theory, OT adheres to the notion of a core of universal principles, but shapes these as a set of universal and *violable* constraints. Typologies are obtained by reranking the universal constraints in language-specific hierarchies, rather than 'relativizing' a subset of universal principles to languages, as in parametric theory. Superficially, then, both theories reach the same goal by largely parallel means: languages are free to escape from universal uniformity either by 'switching off' parameters, or by domination of violable constraints. Constraint reranking and parameter setting may thus be thought of as two a priori equivalent ways of reaching linguistic typologies. When a parametric theorist would assert that the absence of some grammatical effect in a language L is due to the 'negative value of parameter P', then an OT-theorist might equally well argue that in this language L the constraint P is 'crucially dominated' by some other constraint, suppressing the effects of constraint P. However, this is an oversimplified and misguided view of the relation between parameters and OT, for the following reasons.

The paramount difference between a parametric approach and OT is that in OT, constraints are not 'switched off', but only 'dominated' by other constraints. Therefore it is predicted that the effects of some constraint may show up *even in a language in which it is dominated*. Given the chance, even a dominated constraint will make its presence felt, and 'break into activity'. The canonical examples of such situations that we have seen in this book are cases of 'the emergence of the unmarked'. In contrast, a parameter, once it has been 'switched off', can never thereafter leave its mark on the grammatical patterns of the language. Consider a language which selects the value 'negative' for the parameter 'onsets are obligatory' (as we may infer from the fact that onset-less syllables occur in the surface patterns of this language). On a parametric view it is predicted that such a language lacks processes avoiding hiatus, or other selectional means to bring about syllables with onsets, rather than onset-less syllables. Yet we know by now, after discussion in previous chapters, that this prediction is simply false. In OT the (correct) prediction is made that the relevant constraint ONSET may continue to be active in a phonology even when the language allows for onset-less syllables. (Onset-less syllables show that ONSET is dominated by faithfulness constraints, obscuring its effects in most contexts.) There is a subtle yet robust difference between parametric theory and OT in this respect. The question then becomes: do similar effects arise in syntax as well? As we will find out in this chapter, there is indeed strong evidence for the activity of dominated constraints.

---

[1] Or as Grimshaw (1997: 405) puts it, parameters serve to 'accommodate language variation in a system of inviolable constraints'.

A stronger kind of parallelism between standard syntax and OT, and one that will also play an important role in the discussion below, is that of *'economy'*. This notion stems from recent work in 'Minimalist' syntactic theory (Chomsky 1993, 1995). At the heart of this theory is the assumption that syntactic derivations and representations must not exceed what is minimally necessary to meet general well-formedness conditions. For example, no movement must take place without some general structural requirement forcing it,[2] and no projection must be present without an overt licensing of this amount of structure.

This notion of economy of derivation and representation is highly similar to the *'do only when necessary'* principle of OT.[3] That is, outputs will be identical to inputs (due to faithfulness constraints) except when divergence between them is forced by a high-ranking well-formedness constraint. But even then, the divergence between input and output will be kept at a bare minimum, that is, to the extent that is required to meet well-formedness constraints. Such 'inertness' follows from interactions of faithfulness and well-formedness constraints, as we have seen on many occasions in earlier chapters of this book, in which we were dealing with phonological phenomena. In fact, inertness eventually follows from the general OT idea that constraints are violable, but that *violation must be minimal*. Minimalism in syntax is based on theoretical assumptions that are sufficiently parallel to OT notions to warrant an attempt at assimilation.[4] The advantage of modelling 'economy' in OT is, of course, that it is a 'soft' system by nature, rather than a 'hard' system such as Minimalist syntax. Recently syntacticians have indeed tried to explain economy using OT assumptions, and we will see some results of this ongoing enterprise below. We will base our discussion on syntactic phenomena of Wh-movement and inversion of subject and auxiliary verb in English, as have been analysed by Grimshaw (1997). We will also sketch some of the typological consequences of an OT analysis of Wh-movement.

From here on, this chapter is organized as follows. Directly below, in section 8.2.1, we will sketch the theoretical assumptions on which OT-based syntax is founded, developing these as variants on more general assumptions underlying OT. Here issues will be taken up such as: 'What defines syntactic inputs?', 'What is the function of *Gen* in syntax?', and 'What is the inventory of syntactic constraints?'. This amount of theoretical background will enable us to outline in

---

[2] Compare the 'ban on unmotivated movement' in pre-minimalist syntax.

[3] This similarity was pointed out by Prince and Smolensky (1993). See chapter 3 (section 3.3.3), for a discussion of 'do only when necessary' in phonology.

[4] One difference between Chomsky's notion of 'economy' and its OT counterpart of 'minimal violation' is the type of evaluation. Chomsky assumes that economy is evaluated locally, rather than globally (as in parallel OT). What are compared are not complete derivations, but only the possibilities arising at specific points in a derivation. Hence a choice made at a particular point in a derivation cannot be influenced by any negative consequences that it may have later on.

section 8.3 an OT-analysis of Wh-movement and inversion of subject and auxiliary verb in English. Typological consequences of this analysis will be outlined in section 8.4, on the basis of a factorial typology. Finally section 8.5 will present conclusions and general perspectives.

8.2.1 *OT-based syntax: general assumptions*

Let us once more state the general assumptions of OT, which will help us to conceive of their implementation in syntactic theory:

- **Universality, violability**: Constraints are universal and can be violated, but violation is minimal.
- **Strict domination**: Constraints are hierarchically ranked in a grammar, such that any higher-ranking constraint takes absolute priority over any lower-ranking constraint.
- **Freedom of analysis**: Any amount of structure may be posited on the input by *Gen*, while keeping within the representational vocabulary of linguistic theory.
- **Harmony**: Candidate outputs are ranked by the grammar according to their relative harmony with the constraint hierarchy. The optimal output candidate is the one that incurs the minimal violation of higher-ranking constraints, possibly at the expense of any number of violations of lower-ranking constraints.

Accordingly, to construct an OT framework for the grammatical domain of syntax, we must at least answer the following questions:

- What is the nature of the input?
- What is the specific representational vocabulary of syntactic theory within which *Gen* must keep?
- What is the constraint inventory of syntactic theory?

8.2.2 *Defining the input of syntax*

Let us first consider the nature of the input of a syntactic component of an OT grammar. Grimshaw's general idea is that syntactic inputs are defined in terms of lexical heads and their argument structure, but are otherwise void of syntactic structure. That is, no syntactic projections are given in the input – the assignment of such structures is the responsibility of *Gen*, to be discussed in section 8.2.3.

Accordingly, Grimshaw defines the input for the type of syntactic constructions that she considers in her paper – verbal extended projections – as follows:

(1)   **Input**
          • a lexical head plus its argument structure
          • an assignment of lexical heads to its arguments

- a specification of the associated tense and semantically meaningful auxiliaries

For example, consider the input of the sentence *What did Mary say?* At the level of the input, this is defined by the lexical head *say*, which is a predicate taking two arguments, plus an assignment of two lexical heads (*Mary, what*) to these arguments.

(2)   *say* (**x, y**)
        x = *Mary*
        y = *what*
        tense = past

Note that no semantically empty auxiliaries (*do, did*) are present in the input. The presence of such elements in the output, and the constraint interactions by which they appear, will be our main concern in this chapter.

Grimshaw makes two further assumptions about the input that are implicitly guided by the principle of *Containment* (Prince and Smolensky 1993),[5] which was briefly discussed in chapter 3 (section 3.3.1). This principle requires that no element be literally removed from the input. This may be stated for the domain of syntax as follows:

(3)   **Containment**
        - competing candidates are evaluated as analyses of the same lexical material
        - competing candidates to be generated for a single input must be semantically equivalent

To state it differently, each analysis of the input competes with other analyses of the same input, and all these analyses must have *non-distinct semantic representations*. In fact, we are already committing ourselves to a definition of *Gen* in syntax, an issue which will be given special attention in the next subsection.

8.2.3 *Defining* Gen *for syntax*

We have already encountered some limitations on candidate analyses generated by *Gen* in the form of the Containment-based principles (3). In this subsection we will consider the residue of structural restrictions on *Gen* as it is defined for syntactic purposes, and also spell out the types of syntactic operations that are allowed to *Gen*.

---

[5] Although Grimshaw does not explicitly mention Containment, her approach is very much similar to that of Prince and Smolensky (1993) in this respect.

Grimshaw defines *Gen* as a function generating all possible analyses of an input within the universal structural requirements of *X' theory*. That is, candidate analyses that are submitted for evaluation by the constraint hierarchy must all be proper X' structures – this may be considered as an inviolable constraint, or alternatively, as a property of *Gen*. Grimshaw in fact assumes the following rather minimal version of X' theory:

(4)   **X' theory** (respected under analysis by *Gen*): each node must be a good projection of a lower one, if a lower one is present.

Note that this X' theory does not require that some *head* be present in every projection: such a requirement will in fact be made by a violable constraint, which is referred to by Grimshaw as OBLIGATORY HEADS. (We will find out why this is a violable constraint later on when we come to discuss patterns of subordinate interrogatives.)

The notion of *extended projection* plays a central role in Grimshaw's paper, as it restricts the nature of the candidate set (only extended projections are fed into *Eval*). It is defined as follows (after Grimshaw 1991):

(5)   **Extended projection**: a unit consisting of a lexical head and its projection plus all functional projections erected over the lexical projection.

By this definition IP and CP are both extended projections of V (the lexical head which has VP as its minimal projection). The schematic structure in (6) contains a verb in its own projection VP, upon which a hierarchy of extended projections are built (here consisting of a Inflectional Phrase and a Complementizer Phrase).

(6)

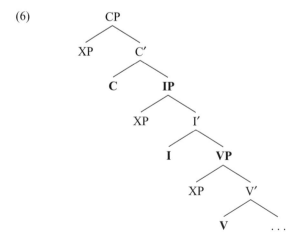

In sum, every candidate analysis of an input must be an extended projection conforming to the minimal X′ theory in (4).

Let us now turn to the types of syntactic operations that *Gen* may perform on the input, while keeping within the previously defined limits. These include the following:

(7)   Operations allowed under analysis by *Gen*
- introducing (extended) projections conforming to X′ theory
- introducing functional heads as they do not appear in the input, due to their lack of semantic content (e.g. the complementizer *that* and *do*-support in English)
- introducing empty elements (traces, etc.), as well as their coindexations with other elements
- moving lexical elements

Note that, in keeping with Containment (3), no elements may be literally removed from the input, and no semantically meaningful elements may be introduced.

Let us now consider a number of candidate analyses of the input of the sentence *What did Mary say?* as it was defined in (2) above:

(8)   Various candidate analyses for {*say* (**x**, **y**), **x** = *Mary*, **y** = *what*, tense = past)
a. [$_{IP}$ Mary [$_{VP}$ said what]]
b. [$_{CP}$ what [$_{IP}$ Mary [$_{VP}$ said t]]]
c. [$_{CP}$ what said$_i$ [$_{IP}$ Mary [$_{VP}$ e$_i$ t]]]
d. [$_{CP}$ what did$_i$ [$_{IP}$ Mary e$_i$ [$_{VP}$ say t]]]

These outputs are all extended projections, conforming to the X′ schema defined in (4–5). Evidently these analyses do not all correspond to grammatical sentences of English: in fact only one does: (8d). This involves Wh-movement, *do*-support, and subject–auxiliary inversion. Yet all of the analyses (8a–c) correspond to grammatical sentences in languages other than English. Analysis (8a), for example, has no movement of any kind, as in Chinese. Analysis (8b) involves Wh-movement, but it lacks both subject–verb inversion and *do*-support (or its analogue), the set of properties found in Czech and Polish. Finally, analysis (8c) has both Wh-movement and subject–lexical verb inversion, but it lacks *do*-support, as in Dutch.

The idea of the OT approach to syntax is that the diversity of syntactic structures across languages reflects differences in the rankings of universal and violable constraints. Each of the analyses in (8) violates one or more constraints, but each can be considered as maximally harmonic (*optimal*) with respect to some ranking of constraints that is specific to some language. But in order to be able to develop such an analysis, we must of course first define the constraints. This will be the topic of the next subsection.

8.2.4 *Defining the syntactic constraint inventory*

The final (and in many respects crucial) component of an OT syntax that we must define is *Eval*, the inventory of universal and violable constraints to evaluate candidate outputs. Grimshaw's paper contains a set of violable constraints, all of which are evaluated at the level of *surface structure*. In this section we will consider a number of constraints that play an important role in Grimshaw's analysis of extended verbal projections.

Exactly as in phonology, *well-formedness* constraints make general requirements of structural well-formedness of the output. Such requirements involve specifiers, heads of projections, government, or other aspects of syntactic structure. An essential function of syntactic well-formedness constraints is to trigger movement of elements. Now consider a first example of a syntactic well-formedness constraint, Op-Spec:

(9)   **OPERATOR IN SPECIFIER** (OP-SPEC)
       Syntactic operators must be in specifier position.

The primary function of this constraint is to force the movement of Wh-elements (which are syntactic operators) into the specifier position of some extended projection, typically the specifier position of a Complementizer Phrase (or Spec-of-CP), as below.[6]

(10)

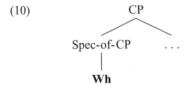

Spec-of-CP will be the single available position for a Wh-element to move into when the specifier position of the next-lower projection, Spec-of-IP, is occupied by the subject. Wh-movement into Spec-of-CP produces a chain of effects in English syntax, which are known as subject–auxiliary inversion and *do*-support.

---

[6] Later we will go into the question of what blocks movement of a Wh-phrase to other specifier positions, such as Spec-of-VP or Spec-of-IP. Furthermore, Grimshaw assumes that the option of base-generating the Wh-phrase in Spec-of-CP is ruled out by the Theta Criterion, which may be interpreted as a part of *Gen*, or as a constraint dominating STAY.

That is, the creation of Spec-of-CP implies the presence of a CP, due to inviolate X′ requirements. This CP, in its turn, is an extended projection subject to structural constraints that, indirectly, trigger the effects mentioned above.

Consider, for example, the following structural constraint, whose function should be clear from its statement:

(11)   **OBLIGATORY HEADS** (OB-HD)
       A projection has a head.

For verbal projections, Verb Phrase and its extended projections Inflectional Phrase and Complementizer Phrase, this implies that each must have a verb as its head. Satisfaction of this constraint may require the movement or insertion of a verb to become the head of an extended verbal projection. For example, OB-HD may trigger *subject–auxiliary inversion*, the movement of an auxiliary to become the head of CP (Den Besten 1983).[7]

The representation below shows the output of subject–auxiliary inversion in the sentence *What will Mary say?*:

(12)

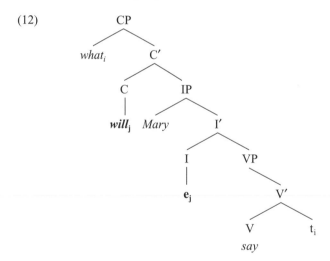

The auxiliary verb *will*ⱼ undergoes head-movement to CP, from its original position in IP, as has been indicated by its trace *e*ⱼ. Crucially, both the auxiliary verb and its trace function as proper heads in their respective extended projections, IP and CP.

---

[7] Of course OB-HD can also be satisfied by a complementizer (*that, whether*, etc.) in the head of CP.

Naturally, *Gen* is allowed to generate competitor candidates to (12). For example consider a schematic candidate (13a) in which the auxiliary *will* is not moved into CP (but remains the head of IP), and yet another candidate (13b) in which *will* is generated as the head of CP, without movement from IP:

(13)   a. CP   b. CP

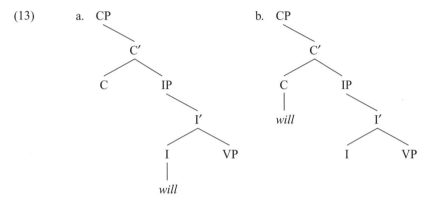

Each of these analyses violates OB-HD, however, since each has one projection that is not headed: CP in (13a) and IP in (13b).

Apart from OP-SPEC and OB-HD, a number of other well-formedness constraints are proposed by Grimshaw (1997). We will not consider these, however, but turn to the question of what are the 'costs', stated in terms of constraint violations, of satisfying OP-SPEC and OB-HD. That is, we now turn to the 'economy', or 'faithfulness', part of the constraint inventory.

To define *faithfulness* constraints in syntax requires some degree of elaboration.[8] The notion of faithfulness, as we have used it throughout this book, involves evaluation of the degree of identity between the input and output. In phonology, the input is defined as a phonological representation itself, hence it is possible literally to compare the input and output as to their degree of identity. This is, of course, the very essence of correspondence constraints: evaluating the degree of similarity between the input and output for various aspects of phonological representation. A priori, it seems entirely logical to conceive of an *anti-movement* constraint as the syntactic counterpart of (phonological) LINEARITY as both militate against differences in the order of elements in the input and the output. Along the same lines, a syntactic constraint 'do not insert' is a plausible counterpart of DEPENDENCE.

---

[8] See Keer and Baković (1997) on syntactic faithfulness. See Bresnan (forthcoming) on syntactic correspondence, as well as a reanalysis of the results of Grimshaw (1997) in the framework of Lexical-Functional Grammar.

However, the input of the syntax as Grimshaw defines it (see again section 8.2.2) is, strictly speaking, not a (hierarchical) syntactic representation itself. It only contains lexical heads and their argument structure, but not extended syntactic projections, nor functional heads. This renders a correspondence approach to 'economy', in principle at least, problematic.

Nevertheless, we may still conceive of syntactic faithfulness constraints in a less 'correspondence-like' fashion. First consider the general *anti-movement* constraint STAY:

(14)   **ECONOMY OF MOVEMENT (STAY)**
         Trace is not allowed.

The function of this constraint is to militate against any movement per se, or in the case of gradient violation, to select the shortest movement, the one that has the minimal number of intermediate steps. What we refer to as a 'movement' is actually construed as a *chain of an element plus its traces* as this occurs at surface structure, the level at which STAY is evaluated. For example, the chain of a Wh-element and its trace t_i in (15a) incurs one violation of STAY, while the chain of an Aux-element and its two traces e_i in (15b) incurs two violations:

(15)   a. $\textbf{\textit{Wh}}_i \ldots \textbf{t}_i$
         b. $\textbf{\textit{Aux}}_i \ldots e_i \ldots e_i$

Next consider the question of why STAY penalizes traces, rather than divergences of word order between the input and output. (A correspondence approach to economy of movement might set up constraints measuring the distance between some element at surface structure and its input correspondent.) One problem, already pointed out above, is that the input is not a syntactic representation, so that the position of input elements cannot be established. Furthermore, under a definition of the input as a lexical head plus its argument structure, it would become impossible to penalize any movement of elements that are not present at the level of the input.[9] A third reason why such a correspondence approach to economy may not be feasible is the following. What matters to economy of movement is the *number of landing sites* of an element between its base position and its position at surface structure, rather than its distance.[10] Since every trace

---

[9] A 'correspondence' approach to economy of movement which would circumvent this problem would involve setting up an intermediate syntactic level of 'deep structure' that is distinct from Grimshaw's input: it is defined as a phrase-marker in which every element occupies its base-generated position. This level would allow the representation of syntactic elements that have no counterparts in the input (or lexical conceptual structure).

[10] Ackema and Neeleman (forthcoming) propose an evaluation of STAY that is based on the number of nodes intervening between positions in a movement chain. It remains an empirical issue which type of evaluation is most adequate.

in a chain incurs a violation of STAY, surface structure chains such as (15) are indispensable in measuring violations.

STAY subsumes all types of movement, including Wh-movement and movement of lexical and functional heads. A more specific ban against movements is made by the next constraint, NO-LEX-MVT:

(16)   **NO MOVEMENT OF A LEXICAL HEAD** (NO-LEX-MVT)
         A lexical head cannot move.

The effect of this constraint is that a lexical head (for example, a lexical verb) must stay in the projection that it heads (e.g. the VP). The configuration (17) presents the typical case of violation of NO-LEX-MVT:

(17) $\dots V_i \dots [_{VP} \dots e_i \dots]$

Note that NO-LEX-MVT is a special case of the general anti-movement constraint STAY. That is, every violation of NO-LEX-MVT implies a violation of STAY, but not conversely. This subset relation means that independent effects of NO-LEX-MVT may occur only in a language which ranks NO-LEX-MVT above STAY (while separating both constraints by some intervening constraint). As we will see below, this is the case in English.

Finally, consider the constraint that militates against the suppression of semantic roles of lexical elements, FULL-INT:

(18)   **FULL INTERPRETATION** (FULL-INT)
         Lexical conceptual structure is parsed.

The key function of this constraint is to ban semantically empty auxiliary verbs, as in *do*-support in English. In a sentence such as *What did Mary say?* the verb *do* is semantically empty, functioning merely as an auxiliary for the lexical verb *say*. It will be assumed that *do* in such sentences is lacking from the input, and inserted from the lexicon into candidate analyses by *Gen*. Since, as was argued above, *Gen* is 'semantically neutral', any insertion of a lexical element must occur at the expense of its lexical conceptual structure. Observe that the lexical verb *do* is a theta-marker (hence, an argument-taker) in a sentence such as *Mary did the vocal parts*. This can be represented as below:

(19)   *do* (**x, y**)

Under *do*-support, this lexical conceptual structure of the verb *do* is not parsed, hence the sentence *What did Mary say?* incurs a violation of FULL-INT. In sum, FULL-INT expresses a faithfulness requirement with respect to lexical elements, which is violated if the output 'suppresses' their theta-marking and argument-taking properties.

Since violation of constraints is minimal, we expect that lexical verbs are used in a semantically empty way only when this is absolutely necessary. This idea is the base of Grimshaw's OT analysis of *do*-support in English, to which we now turn.

8.3   The structure of extended verbal projections in English

Empirically, Grimshaw (1997) focusses on patterns of Wh-movement, subject–verb inversion, and *do*-support in English. All three phenomena strongly interact, and we will see that this interaction centres on 'extended verbal projections': syntactic structures on top of the VP, which include the Inflectional Phrase (IP) and Complementizer Phrase (CP). (See again representations (6), (12), and (13) for illustration.) The specific issue that we will address is this: can 'economy' of derivation and representation, as this is manifest in the domain of extended verbal projections, be reduced to the interaction of syntactic constraints? Our answer will be positive; we will in fact argue that the analysis proposed by Grimshaw (1997) is naturally integrated with general principles of OT, and that it is, point by point, analogous to OT analyses of phonological phenomena involving economy, such as epenthesis.

Directly below (in section 8.3.1) we will discuss Wh-movement and subject–auxiliary inversion, and we will turn to *do*-support in section 8.3.2.

8.3.1   *Wh-movement and subject–auxiliary inversion*

We begin our exploration by considering a declarative sentence containing the auxiliary verb *will* (marking future tense). In declarative sentences such as (20a) the inversion of the subject and auxiliary verb is not allowed (compare the ungrammaticality of 20b):

(20)   a.   Mary will say too much.
          b.   *Will Mary say too much.

In Grimshaw's analysis of a simple declarative sentence such as (20a), the verb phrase (or VP) contains the lexical verb *say* and its object *too much*, while the subject *Mary* and the auxiliary verb *will* occupy positions outside the VP, in the Inflectional Phrase (IP):

(21)   [$_{IP}$ Mary will [$_{VP}$ say too much]]

Each projection, the lexical projection VP and its extended projection IP, is headed by an appropriate head. The VP is headed by the lexical verb (*say*), while the IP is headed by the auxiliary verb (*will*). Since no heads are missing from this structure, there is no need for an additional CP plus inversion of the subject and auxiliary verb, as in (22):

(22)   [$_{CP}$ will$_i$ [$_{IP}$ Mary e$_i$ [$_{VP}$ say too much]]]

Structure (22) has unnecessary complexities in comparison to (21). It has an additional extended projection CP, and it also has an additional movement to fill the head of CP. Such avoidance of unnecessary structure and movement is what Chomsky's Minimalist programme refers to as 'economy'. In OT, 'economy' is subsumed under the '*do only when necessary*' principle. That is, inversion in the absence of any structural necessity leads to a fatal violation of the anti-movement constraint STAY, as in (23b):[11]

(23)

{*say* (**x**, **y**), x = *Mary*, y = *too much*, tense = future, auxiliary = *will*}	OP-SPEC	OB-HD	STAY
a. ☞ [$_{IP}$ Mary will [$_{VP}$ say too much]]			
b. [$_{CP}$ will$_i$ [$_{IP}$ Mary e$_i$ [$_{VP}$ say too much]]]			*!
c. [$_{CP}$ e [$_{IP}$ Mary will [$_{VP}$ say too much]]]		*!	

Candidate (23c) is a failed attempt at improving over candidate (23b). It maintains CP, but leaves the auxiliary *will* in head position in IP. Although avoiding a violation of STAY, this attempt fails by its violation of OB-HD, requiring that every projection must have a head (which is violated by the CP in 23c). In sum, no inversion takes place in declarative sentences because of lack of necessity – both OP-SPEC and OB-HD are satisfied without movement.

We make the additional observation that the economy of the optimal output (23a) is independent of the constraint ranking. It is easy to see that no ranking is possible under which 'less-economical' candidates (23b–c) could ever defeat

---

[11]   Under the hypothesis that the subject is base-generated in the VP (Zagona 1982), an additional candidate merits consideration: [$_{IP}$ will [$_{VP}$ Mary say too much]]. This would even be optimal, since, as compared to (23a), it avoids movement of the subject into Spec-of-IP. Grimshaw rules this candidate out by the constraint SUBJECT '*a clause must have a subject*', in which 'subject' is defined as 'the highest A(rgument) specifier in a clause'. If SUBJECT dominates STAY, the subject is driven out of VP into IP, which would otherwise remain subject-less:

{*say* (**x**, **y**), x = *Mary*, y = *too much*, tense = future, auxiliary = *will*}	OP-SPEC	OB-HD	SUBJECT	STAY
a. ☞ [$_{IP}$ Mary will [$_{VP}$ *t* say too much]]				*
b. [$_{IP}$ will [$_{VP}$ Mary say too much]]			*!	

(23a), which is flawless with respect to all three constraints. A more general prediction is that no language has subject–auxiliary inversion in simple declaratives.

Next consider interrogatives, where Wh-movement is obligatory, in combination with inversion, as in (24a):

(24)   a. What will Mary say?
         b. *What Mary will say?
         c. *Will Mary say what?
         d. *Mary will say what?

Wh-movement without inversion (24b) causes ungrammaticality, and so does lack of Wh-movement (24c–d). Combining this observation on interrogatives with those on declaratives (see 21–2), we arrive at the following generalization:[12]

(25)   Generalization
         Subject–auxiliary inversion occurs *if and only if* Wh-movement applies.

Observe the biconditional nature of (25): subject–auxiliary inversion is obligatory if Wh-movement applies (hence *What Mary will say?*); conversely inversion is impossible elsewhere (hence *Will Mary say too much*). What causes this correlation of Wh-movement and inversion? We can only answer this question by first addressing two related issues. First, what makes Wh-movement obligatory? Second, what functional projections are involved in Wh-movement and inversion?

Wh-movement itself is obligatory due to high-ranking OP-SPEC (9) requiring that syntactic operators occupy a specifier position. Wh-phrases are operators (Rizzi 1991), and hence must move into some specifier position. But to which specifier position can a Wh-phrase in sentences such as (24) move? The subject already occupies the specifier position in IP, hence this position is not available. Therefore an additional extended projection is created outside the IP, which is the CP. At this point, we must consider the following pair of structures, both of which have Wh-movement to CP:

(26)   a. *[$_{CP}$ what [$_{IP}$ Mary will [$_{VP}$ say *t*]]]
         b. [$_{CP}$ what will$_i$ [$_{IP}$ Mary e$_i$ [$_{VP}$ say *t*]]]

In (26a) the Wh-phrase occupies the specifier position of CP, as is required by OP-SPEC. However, the head of CP is missing, which violates OB-HD, the constraint requiring that every projection must be headed. By moving the auxiliary verb into CP, as in (26b), this defect is repaired, since the auxiliary verb provides

---

[12] Inversion is triggered also by yes/no interrogatives, as in *Will Mary say anything?* See Grimshaw (1997) for analysis of this construction.

a proper head for CP. At the same time, its trace 'e_i' in IP still functions as the head of IP. Crucially, both lexical heads and traces can serve as heads of a projection.

We thus arrive at the following scenario: Wh-movement serves to place the Wh-element, an operator, in specifier position of CP (as forced by OP-SPEC); consequently the auxiliary verb must also move into CP to provide a head for this extended projection (due to OB-HD). Both movements naturally take their toll as they occur at the expense of violations of STAY, the general anti-movement constraint. This motivates the following ranking:

(27)   Inversion only under Wh-movement
         OP-SPEC, OB-HD $\gg$ STAY

OP-SPEC must dominate STAY in order for Wh-movement to take place; with the reverse ranking movement would be blocked by STAY. And OB-HD must also dominate STAY in order for head movement of the auxiliary verb to take place. This ranking is shown to be appropriate in the following tableau:

(28)

{*say* (**x**, **y**), **x** = *Mary*, **y** = *what*, tense = future, auxiliary = *will*}	OP-SPEC	OB-HD	STAY
a. [$_{IP}$ Mary will [$_{VP}$ say what]]	*!		
b. [$_{CP}$ **e** [$_{IP}$ Mary will [$_{VP}$ say what]]]	*!	*	
c. [$_{CP}$ what **e** [$_{IP}$ Mary will [$_{VP}$ say *t*]]]		*!	*
d. ☞ [$_{CP}$ what will$_i$ [$_{IP}$ Mary e$_i$ [$_{VP}$ say *t*]]]			**
e. [$_{CP}$ will$_i$ [$_{IP}$ Mary e$_i$ [$_{VP}$ say what]]]	*!		*

The optimal candidate (28d) is the only one which satisfies both OP-SPEC and OB-HD. Its representational perfection is purchased at the expense of two violations of economy of movement (STAY), one for the trace *t* left by Wh-movement, and another for the trace e_i left by head movement. But (28d) is optimal precisely for the reason that it cannot be improved over by other candidates. To improve (28d) could only mean to avoid violations of STAY, hence to reduce movements. This, however, cannot be achieved without violating higher-ranked constraints, OP-SPEC or OB-HD. For example, no improvement is made over (28d) by candidates (28a–b), which totally avoid movements, but consequently run into fatal violations of OP-SPEC (28a), or even worse, of both OP-SPEC and OB-HD (28b). Next, candidate (28c) has the apparent virtue of avoiding head movement to CP.

However, this leaves CP unheaded, fatally violating OB-HD. Finally, candidate (28e) flatly avoids Wh-movement, fatally violating OP-SPEC.[13,14]

Let us now see how the property of 'economy' follows from the OT analysis. For the sake of the argument, we distinguish 'derivational' and 'representational' economy. Derivational economy ('no unnecessary movement') is enforced directly by STAY. Head movement of the auxiliary occurs whenever necessary (that is, in interrogative sentences) to meet the top-ranking structural constraint OB-HD even though movement violates STAY. Naturally any movement of the auxiliary that yields no gains with respect to OB-HD will be blocked by STAY (that is, in declarative sentences). Representational economy ('no empty projections') is achieved without a constraint explicitly militating against 'unnecessary' projections. Instead, exclusion of superfluous extended projections such as CP is achieved *indirectly*, by cooperation of two constraints, OB-HD and STAY. To posit a projection is to accept responsibility for its structural well-formedness. But doing so may cause problems of 'derivational economy': an extended projection left unheaded is ruled out by OB-HD. Alternatively, an extended projection supplied with a proper head by head movement will be ruled out by STAY (except when it yields an improvement with respect to OB-HD).

---

[13] Again it may be interesting to consider the consequences of base-generating the subject in VP. The candidate left out of consideration in tableau (28) is $[_{CP}$ what will $[_{VP}$ Mary say t $]]$, which lacks an IP altogether. The subject *Mary* occupies Spec-of-VP, and the Wh-element is moved to Spec-of-CP. This structure is more economical than optimal (28d = b below) since it has no movement of auxiliary to IP. See the following tableau:

$\{say$ $(\mathbf{x}, \mathbf{y})$, $\mathbf{x} = Mary$, $\mathbf{y} = what$, tense = future, auxiliary = $will\}$	OP-SPEC	OB-HD	STAY
a. ☞ $[_{CP}$ what will $[_{VP}$ Mary say t]]			*
b. $[_{CP}$ what will$_i$ $[_{VP}$ Mary e$_i$ $[_{VP}$ t say t]]]			**!*
c. $[_{CP}$ what e $[_{IP}$ Mary will $[_{VP}$ t say t]]]		*!	**

Grimshaw does not discuss this option, presumably because she assumes that auxiliaries always head the IP, either in situ, or as a trace. Moreover, this additional candidate does not affect the main result that inversion is obligatory in this case, due to the ranking OP-SPEC, OB-HD ≫ STAY. That is, the non-reversing candidate (c) is ruled out in the same way as it is in (28c).

[14] Peter Ackema (p.c.) points out that this analysis requires modifications in order to account for double Wh-constructions. In languages like English, only one Wh-element may move into CP, while all others remain in situ (*Who has given what to whom yesterday?*). Here Grimshaw's analysis, which has undominated OB-HD and OP-SPEC, predicts that every Wh-element will be moved to a new CP, with the auxiliary verb moving upward through the head position of each CP (**Who has what to whom given yesterday?*).

This analysis is unifying in the sense that both types of economy are, either directly or indirectly, reduced to a single economy constraint, STAY. Economy requires no separate constraints for derivation and representation. STAY directly enforces derivational economy, while it indirectly enforces representational economy, assisted by OB-HD.

In sum, given the pair OB-HD and STAY, both movement and extended projections are kept at a bare minimum. No movement will occur, and no extended projection will be constructed, *unless it is necessary.* This warrants the conclusion that economy is enforced by every grammar containing OB-HD and STAY – hence that economy is universal.

8.3.2 *Do-support*

8.3.2.1 *The pattern*

We now turn to the phenomenon of *do*-support as this occurs in interrogative sentences, and to its interaction with Wh-movement and inversion. The generalization to be captured by the analysis is simple: '*do*-support is possible only when it is necessary' (Chomsky 1957, 1991). We will see that OT offers a straightforward explanation of this generalization. Because of space limitations we cannot address the complete distribution of the auxiliary *do* here, and we refer the reader to Grimshaw (1997) for further discussion.

The key observation which we will focus on in this section, and which will serve to highlight Grimshaw's analysis, is that *do* occurs in simple interrogative sentences where it is the single auxiliary verb. Or to state it in negative contexts, *do* cannot occur in positive declarative sentences, nor can it occur in any sentence that has another auxiliary verb. We thus find a complementary distribution of *do* and other auxiliaries.

Firstly, *do* is obligatorily present in simple interrogative sentences:[15]

(29)   a.   What did Mary say?
         b.   *What Mary said?

Observe that *do* occupies a position typical for the auxiliary in interrogatives, immediately after the Wh-element (compare *What **will** Mary say?* in 24a and 30a). This is, of course, a key to the explanation of the complementary distribution of *do* and other auxiliary verbs: *do* functions as obligatory head of the CP, precisely like the auxiliary *will* in (26b). Filling the head position of the CP is

---

[15] A third logical possibility, that of inversion involving the lexical verb (cf. *What said Mary?*), will be discussed in section 8.3.2.2.

what is meant by 'when it is necessary' in the generalization about *do*-support stated above.

Secondly, *do* cannot cooccur with other auxiliary verbs in interrogatives:

(30)   a.   What will Mary say?
         b.   *What does Mary will say?
         c.   *What will Mary do say?

This complementary distribution of *do* and other auxiliary verbs in interrogatives points to the conclusion that *do* functions as a kind of place-holder for the auxiliary (as it appears in sentences such as 30a). When another auxiliary verb is already in place, *do* is no longer necessary, and therefore it will be left out for reasons of economy.

Thirdly, that *do*-support is impossible in positive declarative sentences is shown by (31a) and its ungrammatical counterpart in (31b):

(31)   a.   Mary said much.
         b.   *Mary did say much.

Positive declarative sentences are structured in a way that renders addition of the auxiliary *do* superfluous. As expected under economy, 'superfluity' entails 'prohibition'. (In section 8.3.2.2 we will return to the structure of such sentences.)

Fourthly, as we now expect, the occurrence of auxiliary *do* is ruled out in declarative sentences that already contain another auxiliary verb, such as *will*:

(32)   a.   Mary will say much.
         b.   *Mary does will say much.
         c.   *Mary will do say much.

Again, there is a lack of necessity for *do*-support: (32a) already contains an auxiliary verb in the proper position. Again, this distribution is economical: lack of necessity for *do* goes hand in hand with an actual ban on *do*-support.

Fifthly, auxiliary *do* cannot cooccur with itself, even in interrogatives:

(33)   a.   What did Mary say?
         b.   *What did Mary do say?

A single occurrence of auxiliary *do* suffices, any additional occurrences are ruled out. This is yet another demonstration of economy: no more occurrences of *do*-support take place than are strictly necessary.

The generalization about *do*-support can now be stated in a maximally simple way:

(34)   Generalization about *do*-support (Chomsky 1957, 1991)
        The auxiliary *do* is possible only when it is necessary.

This reminds us of generalizations found earlier in this book, all having the general form 'do only when necessary'. Then 'do' referred to some change imposed on the input, for example an epenthesis or deletion of a segment. Here, 'do' *literally* refers to '*do*-support'.

Grimshaw goes on subsume generalization (34) under the standard OT account for generalizations of the 'do only when necessary' type: a domination of well-formedness over faithfulness.

8.3.2.2   *The analysis*

As argued above, the auxiliary *do* is a *semantically empty* verb, one which only serves the *syntactic* function of head of extended projections which, without it, would be fatally unheaded. The semantic emptiness of auxiliary *do* implies the suppression of the lexical–conceptual properties of its source, the lexical verb *do*, which are roughly similar to that of 'to act'. (Hence the double occurrence of *do* in 'Did you do your homework?': the first *do* is an auxiliary, the second a lexical verb.) The suppression of lexical–conceptual properties of *do* constitutes a violation of FULL-INT (section 8.2.4), requiring that lexical–conceptual structure be parsed. This is the price to be paid for using *do* as an auxiliary verb, which is forced by higher-ranking constraints requiring the presence of some verbal head; specifically OB-HD.

Grimshaw points out that it is not at all a coincidence that English uses *do* as the semantically empty verb: among the lexical verbs of English, *do* is (apparently) the verb which has the smallest lexical conceptual structure of its own. Using *do* as a semantically empty verb causes the minimal suppression of lexical conceptual structure, which explains why other verbs are not used in a semantically empty way. In fact the prediction is broader than English: every language having an equivalent of *do*-support will pick the lexical verb of minimal semantic content. Of course it remains to be seen whether a theory of *semantic lightness* can be developed which picks out the 'minimal' verb for any language.

Note that Grimshaw's analysis of *do*-support bears a resemblance to the analysis of epenthesis presented in chapter 3. Epenthetic segments in phonology are considered to be lacking from the input since they belong to no input morpheme, and lack inherent feature content. In phonology epenthesis follows from interactions of well-formedness constraints (making requirements of syllable structure) and faithfulness constraints (specifically DEP, militating against output elements not present in the input). Again the parallelism extends to the syntactic analysis: *do*-support is triggered by the well-formedness constraint (OB-HD), at the expense of violations of the syntactic 'faithfulness' constraint FULL-INT.

Once we have spotted the main idea behind the analysis, its execution becomes a fairly simple matter. Evidently FULL-INT must be dominated by OB-HD, since violations of FULL-INT (in the form of *do*-support) are tolerated to avoid violations of OB-HD.

(35)   OB-HD ≫ FULL-INT

Turning now to an actual example, this ranking is supported by the comparison of two candidates for an interrogative, one with *do*-support (36a), another without it (36b):

(36)   a.   What did Mary say?
        b.   *What Mary said?

Thus far we have not seen any evidence bearing on the ranking of FULL-INT with respect to STAY. Lacking this evidence, we arrive at a partial hierarchy in (37), which inserts the ranking OB-HD ≫ FULL-INT (35) into the earlier hierarchy OP-SPEC, OB-HD ≫ STAY (27):

(37)   '*do*-support only when necessary'
        OP-SPEC, OB-HD ≫ FULL-INT, STAY

In tableau (38), both candidates (36a–b) are represented as (38a–b). The former candidate is optimal, as it has no violations of either highest-ranking constraint OP-SPEC and OB-HD, while all other candidates violate at least one of these. In (38a) the auxiliary verb *did* heads CP, while its trace e_i properly heads IP. Since all its extended projections are headed, (38a) fully satisfies OB-HD. This happens at the expense of violations of lower-ranked FULL-INT (due to *do*-support) and STAY (due to Wh-movement and head movement of *did* to CP).[16]

---

[16] If subjects are base-generated in VP, a possibility mentioned in notes 11–13, the optimal candidate would be [$_{CP}$ what **did** [$_{VP}$ Mary say t]], leading to the same word order. Movement of *Mary* out of VP is not necessary to provide a subject for the clause (cf. SUBJECT in note 11), hence this would violate STAY without reason. Avoidance of IP brings yet another advantage: the auxiliary need not move to become head-of-CP, but can be simply inserted in that position:

{*say* (**x**, **y**), **x** = *Mary*, **y** = *what*, tense = past}	OP-SPEC	OB-HD	FULL-INT	STAY
a. ☞ [$_{CP}$ what **did** [$_{VP}$ Mary say t]]			*	*
b. [$_{CP}$ what **did**$_i$ [$_{IP}$ Mary e$_i$ [$_{VP}$ t say t]]]			*	***!***

(38)

{say (**x**, **y**), **x** = *Mary*, **y** = *what*, tense = past}	Op-Spec	Ob-Hd	Full-Int	Stay
a. ☞ [$_{CP}$ what **did**$_i$ [$_{IP}$ Mary **e**$_i$ [$_{VP}$ say *t*]]]			*	**
b. [$_{CP}$ what e [$_{VP}$ Mary said *t*]]		*!		*
c. [$_{CP}$ what e [$_{IP}$ Mary **did** [$_{VP}$ say *t*]]]		*!	*	*
d. [$_{CP}$ what e [$_{IP}$ Mary e [$_{VP}$ said *t*]]]		*!*		*
e. [$_{IP}$ Mary [$_{VP}$ said what]]	*!			

Its direct competitor (38b) omits *do*-support, thereby avoiding a violation of
Full-Int, as well as an additional violation of Stay due to head movement of
do. But at a fatal cost: by leaving the CP unheaded, it violates Ob-Hd. Note that
the subject of (38b) occupies Spec-of-VP, a possibility that we did not consider
until here (but see notes 11, 13, and 16). The reason for this previous neglect was
that VP-internal subjects in earlier examples did not affect the result. But from
here on, we will include this option in candidate sets. It will be optimal in some
examples to be discussed below (starting with tableau 42).

Turning to the remaining competitors (38c–e), we find that none can improve
on (38a) by avoiding violations of Full-Int or Stay, without incurring fatal
violations of Op-Spec or Ob-Hd. Candidate (38c) has *do*-support, thus providing
a head for IP, but no head movement, leaving CP unheaded and causing a fatal
violation of Ob-Hd. Next, candidate (38d) not only lacks a head of CP but also
leaves IP unheaded, causing two fatal violations of Ob-Hd. Finally, candidate
(38e) represents an attempt to avoid violations of Ob-Hd by not creating extended
projections, neither IP nor CP. This attempt, of course, runs into Op-Spec, requiring that Wh-elements occupy a specifier position.

The attentive reader may have noticed that one obvious output candidate is
missing from tableau (38). This involves inversion on the lexical verb:

(39)   a. *What said Mary?

b. [$_{CP}$ what said$_i$ [$_{VP}$ Mary **e**$_i$ *t*]]

Apparently the lexical verb is not allowed to move (due to No-Lex-Mvt, introduced in section 8.2.4). We postpone discussion of this construction, including its
typological status, to section 8.4, and now continue our survey of the distribution
of the auxiliary *do* in English.

As noted earlier, the auxiliary *do* stands in complementary distribution with other auxiliaries, such as *will*. *Do*-support causes ungrammaticality in interrogatives containing another auxiliary. See again the set of sentences below, repeated from (30):

(40) a. What will Mary say?
　　　 b. *What does Mary will say?
　　　 c. *What will Mary do say?

This complementary distribution is readily captured by the constraint hierarchy. Recall that the difference between *do* and other auxiliaries (such as *can, will, may*) is that the latter have semantic and functional content, and therefore must occur in the input. In contrast, *do* is semantically empty, hence it is not part of the input. The generalization is that whenever an input auxiliary is available as the head of CP, there is no need for inserted auxiliary *do*. Since epenthesis of an auxiliary amounts to a violation of FULL-INT, *do*-support is avoided whenever the input contains an auxiliary. Similarly, epenthesis in phonology is avoided whenever possible, avoiding unnecessary violation of DEP-IO.

The tableau of *What will Mary say?* contains the three candidates of (40), plus two additional candidates (41d–e), which are ruled out by undominated constraints.

(41)

	{*say* (**x**, **y**), **x** = *Mary*, **y** = *what*, tense = future, auxiliary = *will*}	OP-SPEC	OB-HD	FULL-INT	STAY
a.	☞ [CP what will_i [IP Mary e_i [VP say *t*]]]				**
b.	[CP what **does** [IP Mary will [VP say *t*]]]			*!	*
c.	[CP what will_i [IP Mary e_i [XP **do** [VP say *t*]]]]			*!	**
d.	[CP what e [IP Mary will [VP say *t*]]]		*!		*
e.	[IP Mary will [VP say what]]	*!			

This tableau adduces evidence that FULL-INT dominates STAY.[17] This resides in the fact that candidate (41a) has more violations of STAY than (41b), but is nevertheless optimal as it has no violations of FULL-INT.

The next tableau evaluates candidates for simple declarative sentences that lack an auxiliary (*Mary said little*). Economy ('no *do*-support') follows from the same

---

[17] Grimshaw (1997) does not discuss this ranking.

constraint ranking as before. Interestingly, the ranking now predicts an analysis under which the full clause, including its subject and predicate, is a single VP:

(42)

{*say* (**x, y**), **x** = *Mary*, **y** = *little*, tense = past}	OP-SPEC	OB-HD	FULL-INT	STAY
a. ☞ [$_{VP}$ Mary said little]				
b. [$_{IP}$ Mary **did** [$_{VP}$ say little]]			*!	
c. [$_{IP}$ **e** [$_{VP}$ Mary said little]]		*!		

Consider how this result follows. A matrix clause that lacks auxiliaries in the input is, in a way, *self-supporting*. Specifically it has no need for IP, an extended projection canonically headed by auxiliaries, nor is there any need for CP, due to the lack of Wh-elements. As we have seen often before, when extended projections are unnecessary, syntactic 'faithfulness' rules them out. The economy mechanism is essentially the same as before: introduction of extended projections triggers the well-formedness constraints for projections. Here OB-HD requires that IP be headed, thereby excluding candidate (42c). Moreover, no head of IP can be supplied by movement of an auxiliary as no auxiliary occurs in the input. (The option of moving the lexical verb will be discussed in section 8.4.2.) The single remaining option to provide a head for IP is *do*-support, as in (42b). But this option crashes into FULL-INT. In sum, all attempts at postulating an IP have resulted only in losses, and no gains, as compared to the structurally simpler candidate (42a). Again, representational complexity never wins unless it brings a bonus in terms of lesser violations.

Finally, the observation that *do*-support never cooccurs with itself gives additional evidence that FULL-INT dominates STAY.

(43)

{*say* (**x, y**), **x** = *Mary*, **y** = *what*, tense = past}	OP-SPEC	OB-HD	FULL-INT	STAY
a. ☞ [$_{CP}$ what **did**$_i$ [$_{IP}$ Mary **e**$_i$ [$_{VP}$ say *t*]]]			*	**
b. [$_{CP}$ what **did** [$_{IP}$ Mary **do** [$_{VP}$ say *t*]]]			**!	*
c. [$_{CP}$ what **e** [$_{IP}$ Mary **did** [$_{VP}$ say *t*]]]		*!		
d. [$_{VP}$ Mary said what]	*!			

It is more economical to insert an auxiliary in IP and to move it to CP, than to introduce auxiliaries in both extended projections. (But see note 16.)

All examples of Wh-movement discussed thus far involved Wh-elements which are objects to the lexical verb. In such cases we always find inversion, in combination with *do*-support when the input lacks an auxiliary. Observe that, as compared to Wh-objects, Wh-subjects behave differently, in that *do*-support is no longer required:

(44)   a. Who said that?
        b. *Who did say that?

In fact, this observation readily follows from the analysis as it stands now. The difference between Wh-objects and Wh-subjects is that the latter can satisfy OP-SPEC by staying in Spec-of-VP, a legitimate specifier position for a syntactic operator. In contrast a Wh-object must move out of VP to find a proper specifier position, in particular when Spec-of-VP is already occupied by the subject or its trace.

The following tableau of sentence (44a) shows that without structural necessity for Wh-subjects to move, their movement is blocked:

(45)

{*say* (**x**, **y**), **x** = *who*, **y** = *that*, tense = past}	OP- SPEC	OB- HD	FULL- INT	STAY
a. ☞ [$_{VP}$ who said that]]]				
b. [$_{IP}$ who **did** [$_{VP}$ *t* say that]]]			*!	*
c. [$_{IP}$ who **e** [$_{VP}$ *t* said that]]]		*!		*

This tableau of an interrogative is strikingly similar to that of the simple declarative in (42).[18]

---

[18] The fronted position of the subject Wh-element in *Who will say that?* is due to the constraint SUBJECT, which was previously mentioned in notes 11 and 16. Structure (b) with the auxiliary in I, and the Wh-element in Spec-of-VP, would violate SUBJECT since this constraint requires that the highest A(rgument) specifier in a clause have a subject, in this case Spec-of-IP. Hence Wh-movement becomes obligatory:

{*say* (**x**, **y**), **x** = *who*, **y** = *that*, tense = future, auxiliary = *will*}	OP-SPEC	OB-HD	SUBJECT	FULL-INT	STAY
a. ☞ [$_{IP}$ who will [$_{VP}$ *t* say that]]					*
b. [$_{IP}$ will [$_{VP}$ who say that]]			*!		

This concludes our discussion of Grimshaw's analysis of the interactions of Wh-movement, inversion, and *do*-support. In her paper, Grimshaw discusses a larger array of constructions than we are able to do here, including negative sentences and subordinate clauses. The interested reader is referred to the paper. Before we evaluate the analysis in terms of its adequacy, we will first address its typological consequences, on the basis of constraint reranking, in section 8.4.

8.4   Typological consequences

Below a factorial typology will be sketched of Wh-movement, inversion and *do*-support, as predicted on the basis of Grimshaw's constraint inventory. In chapter 2 we discussed the following assumptions underlying the OT approach to typology. Constraints are universal while their ranking is language-specific. Since language variation stems from reranking the set of universal constraints, the grammatical patterns of languages emerge as variations on universal themes. While typological variation due to constraint reranking is considerable, it is not unlimited: certain grammatical patterns (combinations of properties) are cross-linguistically lacking. Such 'typological gaps' are due to intrinsic properties of constraint interaction, in particular to strict domination and minimal violation. OT predicts that typologies are inherently asymmetrical, as opposed to a theory which assumes a set of logically independent parameters, thereby predicting free combination of their values into symmetrical typologies.

8.4.1   *The general typology*

This reranking approach to language typology will be applied in this section to a small set of syntactic constraints. This set consist of the three constraints which constitute the core of Grimshaw's analysis of Wh-movement and inversion: OP-SPEC, OB-HD, and STAY. Yet this small set is large enough to illustrate the general idea and merits of the reranking approach.

Restricting rerankings to a set of three core constraints {STAY, OP-SPEC, OB-HD}, we find six logically possible rankings:

(46)   Factorial typology of Wh-movement and inversion
      a. STAY ≫ OP-SPEC ≫ OB-HD
      b. STAY ≫ OB-HD ≫ OP-SPEC
      c. OB-HD ≫ STAY ≫ OP-SPEC
      d. OP-SPEC ≫ STAY ≫ OB-HD
      e. OP-SPEC ≫ OB-HD ≫ STAY
      f. OB-HD ≫ OP-SPEC ≫ STAY

Working our way through this typology from top to bottom, we first arrive at the rankings in (46a–b). Here STAY dominates both well-formedness constraints OP-SPEC and OB-HD. When violations of STAY are avoided at the expense of violations of well-formedness, a grammar arises lacking Wh-movement as well as inversion. Languages of this type are attested, for example Chinese (Ackema and Neeleman forthcoming).

Next, ranking (46c), where STAY still dominates OP-SPEC, produces a similar lack of Wh-movement; nor is there movement of auxiliaries into head positions of extended projections due to Wh-movement. Therefore ranking (46c) leads to the same inert picture as both rankings in (46a–b).

We now move on to ranking (46d), which merits some discussion. Here OP-SPEC dominates STAY, hence Wh-movement is forced. But STAY, in its turn, dominates OB-HD, so that inversion cannot be used to fill the head position of extended functional projections which are the result of Wh-movement. In sum, this represents a language that has Wh-movement, but not inversion. Such a language is French (Ackema and Neeleman forthcoming).

Finally, the rankings (46e–f) are apparently equivalent since both have OP-SPEC and OB-HD on top of STAY. As in English, both Wh-movement and inversion occur in violation of STAY, to satisfy both top-ranking constraints. However, as Grimshaw points out, there is a potential empirical difference between the rankings (46e) and (46f) which arises when a fourth constraint comes into play.

8.4.2 *Variations on subject–verb inversion*

We continue our typology discussion by returning to English one more time, to make good on a promise. Recall that we observed a perfectly obvious alternative output candidate for tableau (38) of *What did Mary say?* – the sentence resulting from inversion on the lexical verb *said*:

(47)   a. *What said Mary?

   b. [$_{CP}$ what said$_i$ [$_{VP}$ Mary e$_i$ *t*]]

We must now consider the cause of its ungrammaticality. This structure seems to have a lot in its favour. Wh-movement satisfies OP-SPEC, and the projection thus created (a CP) satisfies OB-HD due to the lexical verb, which has moved out of the VP. On top of all this, structure (47b) avoids *do*-support. Then why should it be ruled out? The answer resides in the undominated constraint NO-LEX-MVT that was introduced in (16) of section 8.2.4, but has been left out of consideration thus far because it was not crucial to any other examples which were previously discussed. NO-LEX-MVT blocks head-movement of a lexical verb out of VP. We may thus extend tableau (38) with the new candidate (47b = 48e) in the following way:

(48)

{*say* (**x**, **y**), **x** = *Mary*, **y** = *what*, tense = past}	No-Lex-Mvt	Op-Spec	Ob-Hd	Full-Int	Stay
a. ☞ [CP what **did**i [IP Mary ei [VP say *t*]]]				*	**
b. [CP what **e** [VP Mary said *t*]]			*!		*
c. [CP what **e** [IP Mary **did** [VP say *t*]]]			*!	*	*
d. [CP what **e** [IP Mary **e** [VP said *t*]]]			*!*		*
e. [CP what said**i** [VP Mary e**i** *t*]]	*!				**

When movement of the lexical verb to the head position of CP is blocked, while this head position must be filled by some verb, then there is nothing better than to insert a form of *do*. English thus prefers violations of FULL-INT to violations of NO-LEX-MVT.

Now we return to the typological aspects of this analysis. Surely one would expect that languages occur in which NO-LEX-MVT takes less priority than it does in English, and even ranks below FULL-INT, so that subject–verb inversion involves the lexical verb. Such a language is Dutch:[19]

(49)   a. Wat ziet Marie?

          b. [CP wat ziet**i** [VP Marie *t* e**i**]]

Wh-movement is supported by the movement of the lexical verb to head position of CP, thus violating NO-LEX-MVT. The following tableau contains the exact Dutch analogues of candidates occurring in the English tableau (48):

(50)

{*say* (**x**, **y**), **x** = *Marie*, **y** = *wat*, tense = past}	Op-Spec	Ob-Hd	Full-Int	Stay	No-Lex-Mvt
a. [CP wat **doet**i [IP Marie ei [VP *t* zien]]]			*!	**	
b. [CP wat **e** [VP Marie *t* zien]]		*!		*	
c. [CP wat **e** [IP Marie **doet** [VP *t* zien]]]		*!	*	*	
d. [CP wat **e** [IP Marie **e** [VP *t* ziet]]]		*!*		*	
e. ☞ [CP wat ziet**i** [VP Marie *t* e**i**]]				**	*

---

[19] The verb moves from a VP-final position, since Dutch has a basic Subject–Object–Verb order.

Grimshaw points out that languages of this type (which allow movement of lexical verbs) are incompatible with a semantically empty auxiliary: there is always a better option than (the analogue of) '*do*'-support, which is moving the lexical verb. This conclusion follows naturally from the analysis developed, in which minimal violation plays a crucial role.

Importantly, the typology does not predict the following situation: *do*-support in a sentence containing a Wh-element, but left unaccompanied by Wh-movement. No possible ranking of constraints will produce this (logically possible) situation, as will be clear from the following argument. First, for Wh-movement to be prohibited, it must be the case that STAY dominates OP-SPEC. Second, for *do*-support to occur, it must be the case that OB-HD dominates FULL-INT. That is, *do*-support is triggered by the requirement that (extended) projections be properly headed. But an extended projection never occurs without structural necessity, in particular Wh-movement. But when Wh-movement is absolutely prohibited, this situation simply cannot arise.

8.5 Conclusions

In this chapter we have demonstrated that OT is a theory of grammar, rather than a theory of phonology proper, since it is applicable to linguistic phenomena outside phonology. The empirical domain was syntactic in nature: we considered interactions between the patterns of Wh-movement, subject–auxiliary inversion, and *do*-support in English. It was demonstrated that inversion and *do*-support have 'economical' distributions: they occur if and only if the construction has properties which make inversion and/or *do*-support necessary. Necessity, stated in terms of independently motivated terms, was then translated into well-formedness constraints (such as OP-SPEC and OB-HD); while syntactic 'effects' (movement, inversion, *do*-support, etc.) were translated into faithfulness constraints (such as STAY, FULL-INT, and NO-LEX-MVT). This set of syntactic constraints, in combination with general principles of constraint interaction (such as strict domination and minimal violation), suffice to explain the observed syntactic patterns, as well as the economy of movements and representations.

The observed 'economy' follows as the natural result of constraint interaction. Movement necessarily involves domination of a syntactic well-formedness constraint over a syntactic faithfulness constraint (STAY). Since any movement incurs a violation of STAY, movement is kept to the bare minimum necessary to obey higher-ranking well-formedness constraints. Any movement in excess of this minimum will serve no purpose in satisfying the higher-ranking constraints, and therefore incurs an unnecessary violation of STAY. This explanation requires no stipulation that movement be 'minimal', but simply follows from general OT principles: that constraints are violable, but violation must be minimal.

Similarly, the explanation for 'economy of representation' is based on the same principle of minimal violation. Any (extended) projection postulated in the analysis of an input is subject to the general well-formedness constraints pertaining to syntactic structure. To satisfy well-formedness constraints, some movement or other 'effect' (for example, *do*-support) may be required. But this, in its turn, incurs violations of (faithfulness) constraints militating against these effects. The explanation for 'economy of representation' is thus reducible to 'economy of movement'.

In the final section we have shown that this OT theory of the interactions of Wh-movement, subject–verb inversion, and *do*-support produces a factorial typology which is adequate in terms of what is currently known about syntactic typology.[20]

SUGGESTIONS FOR FURTHER READING

Minimalist syntax

Chomsky, Noam (1993) A minimalist program for linguistic theory. In K. Hale and S. J. Keyser (eds.), *The view from Building 20*. Cambridge, Mass.: MIT Press. 41–58.

(1995) *The minimalist program*. Cambridge, Mass.: MIT Press.

Radford, Andrew (1997) *Syntax: a minimalist introduction*. Cambridge University Press.

OT syntax

Ackema and Neeleman (forthcoming) Optimal questions. To appear in *Natural Language and Linguistic Theory* **16:3**. [A prefinal version of the paper can be found in ROA-69, http://ruccs.rutgers.edu/roa.html]

Barbosa, Pilar, Danny Fox, Paul Hagstrom, Martha McGinnis, and David Pesetsky (eds.) (1998). *Is the best good enough? Optimality and competition in syntax*. Cambridge, Mass.: MIT Press.

Bresnan, Joan (forthcoming) Optimal syntax. To appear in J. Dekkers, F. van der Leeuw, and J. van de Weijer (eds.), *Optimality Theory: phonology, syntax, and acquisition*. Oxford University Press.

Grimshaw, Jane (1997) Projection, heads, and optimality. *Linguistic Inquiry* **28**. 373–422.

---

[20] Other works pursuing issues of syntactic typology in OT are Ackema and Neeleman (forthcoming) and Legendre, Raymond, and Smolensky (1993).

Keer, Edward and Eric Baković (1997) Have FAITH in syntax. *Proceedings of the West Coast Conference on Formal Linguistics* **16**. [ROA-200, http://ruccs.rutgers.edu/roa.html]

Legendre, Géraldine, William Raymond, and Paul Smolensky (1993) An Optimality-Theoretic typology of case and grammatical voice systems. *Proceedings of the Berkeley Linguistics Society* **19**. 464–78.

Müller, Gereon (1997) Partial Wh-movement and Optimality Theory. *The Linguistic Review* **14**. 249–306.

Pesetsky, David (forthcoming) Some Optimality principles of sentence pronunciation. To appear in Barbosa et al.

Syntax–phonology interaction

Golston, Chris (1995) Syntax outranks phonology: evidence from ancient Greek. *Phonology* **12**. 343–68.

9
Residual issues

9.1 Introduction

The previous eight chapters of this book have offered an overview of Optimality Theory, with an emphasis on areas in which the theory has proved successful. This chapter will add an overview of issues that have not yet been successfully resolved, and developments and modifications in the theory that are currently taking place. The issue that is perhaps most urgently in need of a solution is *opacity*, to be discussed in section 9.2. Remaining sections each deal with a major theme in ongoing research. First, *absolute ungrammaticality* will be addressed in section 9.3. Section 9.4 will evaluate strategies to deal with *optionality* and *free variation*. Next, section 9.5 will discuss *positional faithfulness* in relation to functional approaches to phonology. Finally, section 9.6 will re-evaluate the role of *underlying forms* in OT, linking this issue with phonologically driven *allomorphy*. Conclusions and a perspective on future developments in OT will be presented in section 9.7.

9.2 Opacity

9.2.1 *Introduction*

Opacity refers to the phenomenon that output forms are shaped by generalizations that are not surface-true. Opaque generalizations lurk at a level deeper than the output, which becomes apparent by 'peeling off' effects overlaid by other surface-true generalizations. Opacity is predicted by any theory allowing *non-surface* levels of description (the input, or any level mediating between input and output). However, opacity presents a potential problem for surface-oriented OT, a theory disallowing reference to preoutput levels by well-formedness constraints. (Of course, the fact that a generalization is not surface-true is, by itself, not immediately problematic for OT. Output forms are always in violation of some constraints.) Before we look into strategies for dealing with opacity in OT, we will first discuss its varieties. That is, opaque generalizations are either 'non-surface-apparent' or 'non-surface-true', following McCarthy's (1998) terminology.

We call a generalization *non-surface-apparent* if it takes effect at a level concealed at the surface. A set of forms undergo a process, although they fail to match its structural description at the surface. This kind of interaction occurs in Turkish (Zimmer and Abbott 1978, Kenstowicz and Kisseberth 1979, Sezer 1981, Inkelas and Orgun 1995).

(1)   Opacity of vowel epenthesis in Turkish
        a. Vowel epenthesis
           /baʃ-m/   ba.ʃɨm   'my head'
           /jel-m/   je.lim   'my wind'
        b. Velar deletion
           /ajak-I/ a.ja.ɨ   'his foot'
           /inek-I/ i.ne.i   'his cow'
        c. Interaction
           /ajak-m/ a.ja.ɨm 'my foot'
           /inek-m/ i.ne.im 'my cow'

Vowel epenthesis is motivated by forms such as [ba.ʃɨm], where a consonant cluster at the end of a word is broken up by a vowel (whose quality harmonizes with the stem vowel by a process that is irrelevant here). Next, velar deletion is apparent from [a.ja.ɨ] where /k/ is deleted in intervocalic position. Finally, consider the interaction of both processes in [a.ja.ɨm]. While velar deletion applies transparently (the output contains both vowels that trigger it), epenthesis does not, since only one of the triggering consonants, namely /m/, surfaces. The output is *opaque* with respect to epenthesis, because its context of application is not recoverable at the surface level. The effect is an *overapplication* of epenthesis. (Compare similar overapplications in reduplication and stem-based morphology – chapters 5 and 6.)

    This is not an isolated example: many similar cases have been reported (for a wide variety of other languages), most of which involve well-motivated processes whose application is otherwise completely general. Our second example is from Tunica (Haas 1940, Kenstowicz and Kisseberth 1979).

(2)   Opacity of vowel harmony in Tunica
        a. Vowel harmony
           /pó-ʔaki/   póʔɔki   'she looks'
           /pí-ʔaki/   píʔɛki   'she emerges'
        b. Syncope
           /hípu-ʔuhki/ hípʔuhki 'he dances'
           /náʃi-ʔuhki/ náʃʔuhki 'he leads (someone)'

       c. Interaction
        /hípu-ʔɑki/ hípʔɔki 'she dances'
        /nɑ́ʃi-ʔɑki/ nɑ́ʃʔɛki 'she leads (someone)'

Vowel harmony copies the 'colour' (backness and rounding) of the rightmost stem vowel onto the vowel of the 3 sg. f. suffix /-ʔɑki/.[1] Syncope deletes unstressed vowels standing immediately before /ʔ/. The output form [hípʔɔki] 'she dances' is opaque with respect to vowel harmony, since the stem vowel /u/ that triggers the back and rounded quality of the suffix vowel cannot be recovered from the surface. (It is *indirectly* recoverable, of course, precisely because of the suffix vowel's quality.)

A generalization is *non-surface-true* if it has cases of non-application at the surface that are controlled by a non-surface level. This is the logically opposite situation of the previous case. A set of forms fail to undergo a process even though their surface forms match its structural description. An example comes from Isthmus Nahuat (Law 1958, Kenstowicz and Kisseberth 1979). A process of apocope (optionally) deletes a word-final unstressed vowel. A second process devoices approximants /l, w, j/ at the end of a word:[2]

(3)   Opacity of approximant devoicing in Isthmus Nahuat
        a. Apocope
           támi~tám   'it ends'
        b. Approximant devoicing
           tájoːl̥   'shelled corn'
        c. Interaction
           ʃikɑkíli~ʃikɑkíl 'put it in it'

The effect is an '*underapplication*' of approximant devoicing, in terms of its output form.

It should now be clear that what distinguishes opaque cases from '*exceptions*' is their systematicity. Opaque generalizations become transparent once we take into account a level 'preceding' the output. Usually this level is the input, or *underlying form*. Taking into account the input level, vowel epenthesis in Turkish, vowel harmony in Tunica, and approximant devoicing in Isthmus Nahuat are perfectly transparent. Incidentally, however, opacity involves a level mediating between the input and the output, as we will see later.

---

[1] Glottal stop /ʔ/ is transparent to harmony.
[2] Syllable-final approximants may also be devoiced, under conditions that are irrelevant here.

Opacity has received much attention in rule-based serial phonology since it offers a major argument for this theory. Therefore let us first take a look at opacity from a serial viewpoint. For a rule to apply, all that matters is whether its structural context is satisfied at the point of the derivation at which the rule applies.[3] For this reason serial theory easily captures generalizations that are not surface-true or not surface-apparent, thus predicting *opacity* on principled grounds. The two types of rule interactions that produce opacity are known as 'counterbleeding' and 'counterfeeding', respectively (Kiparsky 1973).

Counterbleeding arises when a rule's structural context is potentially destroyed or removed by the application of a prior rule, but the ordering is such that both rules apply. The second rule, which might have destroyed the context of application for the first rule, applies 'too late' to actually do so. In the Tunica example, harmony first copies rounding and backness of the rightmost stem vowel onto the suffix vowel. This triggering vowel is then deleted by syncope:

(4)   **Counterbleeding** (Tunica and Turkish)
        a. /hípu-ʔaki/   b. /ajak-m/
           hípuʔɔki   Vowel harmony   a.ja.kɨm Vowel epenthesis
           hípʔɔki   Syncope   a.ja.ɨm Intervocalic k-deletion
           [hípʔɔki]   [a.ja.ɨm]

In both examples, a rule (Syncope, Intervocalic k-deletion) deletes the trigger of another rule (Vowel harmony, Vowel epenthesis), but both deletions apply *too late*, missing their chance to 'bleed' the earlier rule. Therefore, in both examples, both rules apply.

Counterfeeding represents the logically opposite situation. The structural context of a rule is potentially satisfied due to the application of a prior rule, but the ordering is such that only one rule applies. The second rule, which might have created the context of application for the first rule, applies 'too early' to actually feed it. Such a counterfeeding order produces opacity of approximant devoicing in Isthmus Nahuat:

(5)   **Counterfeeding** (Isthmus Nahuat)
        /ʃikakíli/
            ---   Devoicing (non-applicable)
        ʃikakíl   Apocope
        [ʃikakíl]

---

[3] At the same time, this 'output-blindness' is a serious disadvantage of serial theory, as we have seen in chapter 2, since it frustrates an account of conspiracies.

Apocope misses its chance to establish the context for devoicing, which does not apply.[4]

Interactions such as those in (4–5) seem to motivate strongly abstract intermediate levels of representation between input and output. OT recognizes no such intermediate levels, in line with standard assumptions stated earlier in this book. In standard OT, the mapping from input ('Lexical Representation') to output ('Phonetic Representation') is *direct*. Moreover, well-formedness constraints state requirements on *output forms* only, ignoring the input. This assumption is another cornerstone of OT, essential to explanation of segment inventories, conspiracies, and the Duplication Problem (see chapters 1–2).

Let us first consider the problem in more detail, focussing on the Turkish case. The two processes involved, both of which can be independently motivated for Turkish, are stated as constraint interactions below:

(6)   a. Intervocalic *k*-deletion
        *VkV ('No intervocalic k') ≫ MAX-IO
    b. Vowel epenthesis
        *COMPLEX, MAX-IO ≫ DEP-IO

*VkV and *COMPLEX never conflict, and cannot be ranked with respect to one another. The rankings (6a) and (6b) are integrated in tableau (7), considering all logically possible combinations of k-deletion and epenthesis, for the input /ɑjɑk-m/:

(7)

Input: /ɑjɑk-m/		*COMPLEX	*VkV	MAX-IO	DEP-IO
a.	ɑ.jɑkm	*!			
b.	ɑ.jɑ.kɨm		*!		*
c.	ɑ.jɑ.ɨm			*	*!
d. ☹	ɑ.jɑm			*	

Candidate [ɑ.jɑ.ɨm] (7c) is the actual output, but it is not the most harmonic candidate. The transparent form [ɑ.jɑm] (7d) has one fewer violation of DEP-IO, obeying the OT adage *do-only-when-necessary*: why epenthesize if there is no

---

[4] Kiparsky (1973) proposes the hypothesis that grammars avoid orderings of rules that produce opacity. That is, the ordering of rules will tend toward a relation that maximizes the transparency of the rules involved. The 'cost' of opaque interactions clearly resides in the abstractness they involve, which increases learnability difficulties. On the other hand, opacity may also be functionally motivated as contributing to learnability since it makes lexical representations recoverable from output representations (Kisseberth 1973, Kaye 1974).

need for it? Note that the case for [ɑ.jɑm] is robust enough to be independent of constraint ranking. A comparison of the violation patterns of both candidates shows that violation marks incurred by (7d) form a proper subset of those incurred by (7c). This finding destroys all hope that the problem is solvable without the help of additional constraints (or even new theoretical machinery).

The 'underapplication' type of opacity, as occurs in Isthmus Nahuat, is equally problematic. Each of the interacting processes, apocope (3a) and devoicing (3b), involves domination of a well-formedness constraint over a faithfulness constraint:

(8)   a. Apocope: FINAL-C ('Stem ends in C') ≫ MAX-IO
        b. Devoicing: *VOICED-CODA ≫ *IDENT-IO(voice)

But no matter how we integrate the subrankings into a total ranking, the opaque candidate (9b) will never become optimal. Instead the transparent candidate (9c) is predicted:

(9)

Input: /ʃikɑkíli/	FINAL-C	MAX-IO	*VOICED-CODA	IDENT-IO (voice)
a. ʃikɑkíli	*!			
b. ʃikɑkíl		*	*!	
c. ☹ ʃikɑkíl̥		*		*

Opaque (9b) and transparent (9c) only differ in their violation marks for *VOICED-CODA and IDENT-IO(voice). However, the mutual ranking of these constraints is forced, since it is independently motivated by approximant devoicing in words such as [tájoːl̥] 'shelled corn' (3b). The incorrect prediction crucially depends on constraint ranking (rather than being independent of it, as in overapplication). This is a clear ranking paradox.

Opacity appears to be a direct empirical refutation of the *surface-based* evaluation of well-formedness constraints in OT. Since opacity is OT's Achilles's heel, researchers have attempted to find solutions for it which maximally preserve the theory's advantages. This section will present an overview of these attempts, reflecting on their relative merits. OT approaches to opacity can be put under various headings, all discussed below:

- Two-level well-formedness (section 9.2.2)
- Intermediate levels (section 9.2.3)
- OO-correspondence (section 9.2.4)

- Sympathy (section 9.2.5)
- Local Conjunction (section 9.2.6)

9.2.2 *Two-level well-formedness*

One approach to opacity allows *reference to the input* by well-formedness constraints, in a more or less direct way. By giving up the assumption that well-
formedness constraints have access to output forms only, this approach preserves
direct mapping of input to output, avoiding intermediate levels. Simultaneous
reference to input and output by well-formedness constraints originates in pre-OT
work by Koskenniemi (1983) and Karttunen (1993). We will refer to this idea as
two-level well-formedness. Note that Correspondence Theory is a 'two-level model'
in a more restricted way, since only faithfulness constraints (and not well-formedness constraints) can refer to the input and output simultaneously.

A conceptually related OT model is the PARSE/FILL theory of Prince and
Smolensky (1993), also known as *Containment Theory*, briefly discussed in chapter 3 as a precursor of Correspondence Theory. This model is named after its key
assumption that no element may be literally removed from the input, which is thus
contained in all candidate outputs. Deletion of an element is represented by leaving it prosodically unparsed, resulting in the lack of phonetic interpretation. Since
deleted input elements are contained in the output representation, they can be
phonologically active.[5] In Correspondence Theory, reference to the input by well-
formedness constraints has been implemented by Cole and Kisseberth (1995),
McCarthy (1995b), Orgun (1995), and Archangeli and Suzuki (1997).

To illustrate the basic idea, let us consider the Tunica example. Opacity of vowel
harmony is accounted for if harmony is *triggered* by input vowels, but *takes effect*
in the output. This can be achieved by a well-formedness constraint that refers to
the input and output simultaneously, for example:[6]

(10)   **HARMONY-IO**

    If input $V_1 \ldots V_2$ *then* V_1 and V_2' agree in backness and rounding.

                   |

    output V_2'

---

[5] In its original form, Containment Theory was never used as a framework for analysing opacity.
Yet the idea that input features are abstractly represented in the output has been elaborated by
Cole and Kisseberth (1995) in 'Optimal Domains Theory'. The innovative aspect of this theory
is its assumption that input features occur in the output in special constituents, or '*F*(eature)-
domains', which largely coincide with (autosegmental) harmony domains. Relations between
F-domains and input features are enforced by violable faithfulness constraints.

[6] A complete analysis should account for the joint reference to backness and rounding ('colour'),
and also explain the directionality of harmony: 'rightward', or more likely, 'stem' to 'affix'.

HARMONY-IO is a two-level well-formedness constraint, stating a requirement of featural agreement between segments at different levels of representation, input and output. It can be read as follows:

(11)   If $V_1 \ldots V_2$ is a sequence of vowels in the input, and V_2' is the correspondent of V_2 in the output, **then** V_1 and V_2' agree in backness and rounding.

Featural harmony between V_1 and V_2' can be said to be *transmitted* by the correspondence relation between V_2 and V_2'. Note that its dependence on correspondence does *not* give HARMONY-IO the status of an IO-faithfulness constraint. The output vowel is required to resemble *another* vowel's input, rather than its own. This is a well-formedness target, not a faithfulness target.[7]

Two-level well-formedness constraints have been extended to express restrictions on the cooccurrence of *different* features. This is exemplified by a constraint proposed by Archangeli and Suzuki (1997):

(12)   **LOWERING-IO**
         Any output correspondent of an input long vowel must be [−high].

LOWERING has the format of a correspondence constraint, but with one crucial difference: correspondents in the input and output are not required to agree with respect to the *same feature* (as in IDENT-IO[F]). Like (12), LOWERING-IO is not an IO-faithfulness constraint, since feature-cooccurrence is required for different features (here, length and height), and for unrelated values. In Archangeli and Suzuki's analysis of Yokuts, LOWERING triggers a featural change from the input value of [high]. Therefore, it functions as a well-formedness constraint, although it has the IO-format of standard correspondence constraints. A theory allowing for constraints such as (10) and (12) essentially gives up the distinction between well-formedness constraints and faithfulness constraints.

Let us now evaluate two-level well-formedness models. The first question to be asked is: 'Do such models account for opacity?', and the second question: 'If so, at what theoretical cost?' We will spot some serious empirical and theoretical problems.

Empirically, two-level well-formedness models fail to account for types of opacity that are not controlled by the input, nor by the output. An opaque generalization may hold at an *intermediate* level, for example with respect to prosodic

---

[7] Nevertheless, HARMONY-IO *interacts* with IO-faithfulness constraints in a 'standard' way – it dominates IDENT-IO(round) and IDENT-IO(back).

structure. (So far we have not seen such cases.) For example, an opaque generalization referring to prosody cannot be analysed by reference to the input, assuming that prosody is not present in input forms.

A well-studied case is compensatory lengthening (CL), a situation where a vowel is lengthened 'to compensate for' the quantity of a deleted consonant (Hayes 1989). An example comes from Oromo (Lloret 1988, Sprouse 1997):

(13)   a.i /feɗ-na/   feena   'we wish'
         a.ii /feɗ-sisa/ feesisa   'I make wish'
         b.i /feɗ-a/   feɗa   'I wish'
         b.ii /feɗ-aɗɗa/ feɗaɗɗa   'wish for self'

A serial derivation shows the origin of the long stem vowel in [feena] 'we wish'. A mora is assigned to the coda consonant closing the first syllable (by Weight-by-Position, chapter 4). This consonant is then deleted before a consonant-initial suffix, but its mora is preserved in the form of an extra element of length on the preceding vowel. Opacity is explained by a counterbleeding rule order (Weight-by-Position → Pre-consonantal deletion):

(14)

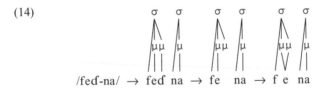

/feɗ-na/ → feɗ na → fe   na → f e   na

As Sprouse (1997) points out, the mora that triggers the lengthening cannot be part of the input. If faithfulness to input moras were to trigger CL, and the consonant /ɗ/ be specified as moraic in the input, then CL should occur in any context in which /ɗ/ cannot hold on to its mora. This is incorrect; see *[feeɗa] (13b), where /ɗ/ surfaces as an onset. Instead CL is restricted to the context of Weight-by-Position. Moreover, if input consonants were contrastively specified as moraic (so that weight of CVC syllables would lexically vary), then certain stems would undergo CL, while other stems would simply undergo deletion. Such contrasts are apparently not found in Oromo. Finally, as McCarthy (1998) points out, input specification of moras runs into a general problem: it is at odds with Richness of the Base, a cornerstone of OT. In sum, the length-triggering mora cannot be part of the input, ruling out a two-level analysis of CL. The best a two-level analysis can achieve is to encode the context of Weight-by-Position into a two-level constraint:

(15)   μ-**Projection**
         Project an output μ for every input C followed by a C.

Of course, this is a bad constraint. Sprouse (1997: 2) notes 'it is more of a rule, combining a well-formedness constraint (how syllables should be organized) with its repair (project a mora) [...] even when the well-formedness constraint can't be evaluated directly since the mora and segment that projects it are never present at the same level'. Finally, μ-PROJECTION loses the generalization that a mora is projected for every coda consonant. It *stipulates* the opaque pattern, rather than explaining it.

The theoretical status of both earlier two-level constraints (10) and (12) is equally problematic. Both function as rules, combining a structural condition (the input structure) and a repair. A theory allowing for two-level well-formedness constraints may stipulate any type of relation between the input and output, being equivalent in this respect to rule-based theory (Lakoff 1993). This power undermines standard OT's solutions to problems inherent to rule-based serialism, in particular *conspiracies* and the *Duplication Problem*. Recall from chapter 2 that standard OT improves over rule-based theory by separating structural conditions (triggers) and structural changes (repairs), thus predicting a range of repair strategies in response to a single well-formedness requirement. However, reference to the input by well-formedness constraints implies a crucial deviation from standard OT. Triggers and repairs become once more entangled, hence the explanation of conspiracies and the Duplication Problem is fatally undermined. As Sprouse (1997) observes, blurring the borderline between well-formedness constraints and faithfulness constraints produces negative consequences for factorial typology as well.

Finally, we may ask to what extent two-level well-formedness constraints can still be considered to be *grounded*. Each of the constraints HARMONY-IO and LOWERING-IO, interpreted as a single-level output constraint, makes a phonetically natural requirement. (Harmony reduces the number of articulatory gestures, and lowering supports the quantity contrast by matching it with the longer intrinsic duration of non-high vowels.) However, phonetic grounding does not carry over to the two-level versions of the constraints since the goals are not manifest in the output. This mismatch is, of course, inherent to opacity. But explanation of opacity will be lost if it is 'hard-wired' into the constraints, rather than reduced to interactions of grounded constraints.

9.2.3 *Intermediate levels*

Yet another approach to opacity is based on *intermediate levels* between input and output. The idea behind this move should be clear: the success of serial theory in accounting for opacity was based precisely on pre-surface levels. Although this gives up the standard OT assumption of *direct mapping*, there is also a potential pay off: preserving the standard *constraint format*. This offers a reverse picture as compared to two-level well-formedness discussed in section 9.2.2, which gave up constraint format while preserving direct mapping.

Let us assume an OT grammar which is internally organized into serially ordered strata (Stratum 1–n, with $n \geq 2$), each containing both functions *Gen* and *Eval*. The input to each stratum is defined by the output of the previous one, except that the input to Stratum 1 is identical to the lexical representation. Within each stratum, the input–output mapping is direct. Each stratum contains its own constraint ranking:

(16)   Multi-stratal evaluation

Multi-stratal models have their origins in derivational Lexical Phonology (Kiparsky 1982b, Mohanan 1982, Booij and Rubach 1987), where they accounted for a range of phenomena, such as word domain effects, affix ordering, structure preservation, and cyclicity. With the emergence of constraint-based theories, direct mapping became the default assumption. Nevertheless, constraint-based multi-stratal models were proposed, by Goldsmith (1993a, *Harmonic Phonology*) and in OT by, among others, McCarthy and Prince (1993b), Inkelas and Orgun (1995), and Sprouse (1997).

In multi-stratal OT the generation of output forms essentially follows a derivation, as in serial theory. This is illustrated below for Turkish, a case of '*overapplying*' opacity, involving counterbleeding in serial theory. This grammar contains two strata. Stratum 1 takes the lexical representation /ɑjɑk-m/ as its input, and produces an intermediate output [ɑ.jɑ.kɨm], where epenthesis has applied but intervocalic /k/ is preserved.

(17)   'Overapplication' in multi-stratal evaluation (Turkish)
        Stratum 1: I_1 /ɑjɑk-m/
                    ↓   *COMPLEX, **MAX-IO** ≫ DEP-IO, *VkV
                   O_1 [ɑ.jɑ.kɨm]

Stratum 2: I$_2$ /a.ja.kɨm/

    ↓   *COMPLEX, *VkV ≫ DEP-IO, **MAX-IO**

O$_2$ [a.ja.ɨm]

The output of S_1, [a.ja.kɨm], is due to the ranking *COMPLEX, MAX-IO ≫ DEP-IO, *VkV:

(18)

Input: /ajak-m/	*COMPLEX	MAX-IO	DEP-IO	*VkV
a. a.jakm	*!			
b. ☞ a.ja.kɨm			*	*
c. a.ja.ɨm		*!	*	
d. a.jam		*!		

This S_1 output is then fed as an input into S_2. Ranking at S_2 is such that intervocalic /k/ is deleted (*VkV ≫ MAX-IO), giving an S_2 output [a.ja.ɨm], which is the surface form.

(19)

Input: /a.ja.kɨm/	*COMPLEX	*VkV	DEP-IO	MAX-IO
a. a.jakm	*!			*
b. a.ja.kɨm		*!		
c. ☞ a.ja.ɨm				*
d. a.jam				**!

In sum, both strata have minimally different rankings, involving only reranking of a well-formedness constraint and a faithfulness constraint.[8]

Let us now briefly discuss a case of '*underapplication*', which is captured in serial theory by counterfeeding. Approximant devoicing in Isthmus Nahuat is opaque, as shown earlier in this chapter. Here intermediate outputs are [ʃikakɪli] and [tajoːl̥], respectively:

(20)   'Underapplication' in multi-stratal evaluation (Isthmus Nahuat)

      Stratum 1: I$_1$ /ʃikakili/ /tajoːl/ MAX-IO ≫ FINAL-C

               ↓   ↓ *VOICED-CODA ≫ IDENT-IO(voice)

           O$_1$ [ʃikakili] [tajoːl̥]

---

[8] It is difficult to establish the ranking of DEP-IO at S_2. We may assume it to be undominated. It marks no violation for 'epenthetic' [ɨ], because this vowel occurs in the input of Stratum 2.

Stratum 2: I_2 /ʃikɑkili/ /tajoːl̥/ FINAL-C ≫ MAX-IO
↓ ↓ IDENT-IO(voice) ≫ *VOICED-CODA
O_2 [ʃikɑkil] [tajoːl̥]

At Stratum 1, apocope is blocked (MAX-IO ≫ FINAL-C), while final approximants become devoiced (*VOICED-CODA ≫ IDENT-IO(voice)). This is shown in two tableaux:

(21)

Input: /ʃikɑkili/	MAX-IO	*VOICED-CODA	FINAL-C	IDENT-IO (voice)
a. ☞ ʃikɑkili			*	
b. ʃikɑkil	*!	*		
c. ʃikɑkil̥	*!			*

(22)

Input: /tajoːl/	MAX-IO	*VOICED-CODA	FINAL-C	IDENT-IO (voice)
a. tajoːl		*!		
b. ☞ tajoːl̥				*

The reverse rankings hold at Stratum 2, where apocope applies (FINAL-C ≫ MAX-IO), but devoicing is blocked (IDENT-IO(voice) ≫ *VOICED-CODA):

(23)

Input: /ʃikɑkili/	FINAL-C	IDENT-IO (voice)	MAX-IO	*VOICED-CODA
a. ʃikɑkili	*!			
b. ☞ ʃikɑkil			*	*
c. ʃikɑkil̥		*!	*	

(24)

Input: /tajoːl̥/	FINAL-C	IDENT-IO (voice)	MAX-IO	*VOICED-CODA
a. tajoːl		*!		*
b. ☞ tajoːl̥				

Consequently each form undergoes only one process, either devoicing or apocope, but not both. (Note that values for [voice] as these occur in the output of Stratum 1 are preserved at Stratum 2, regardless of their values in the 'original' lexical input.)

In contrast to two-level well-formedness theory, an 'intermediate-levels' theory of opacity holds the promise of accounting for types of opacity that are not controlled by the input. Compensatory Lengthening in Oromo (13), for example, may be accounted for by an intermediate level at which Weight-by-Position has applied, but consonant deletion is still blocked. CL becomes an *identity* effect preserving quantity occurring at intermediate levels. In sum, multi-stratal evaluation has the advantage of a broad empirical coverage of opacity effects, being equivalent to serial theory in this respect.

But does it preserve OT's advantages over serial theories, which are largely based on direct mapping and evaluation of output forms? If OT is not to be reduced to a notational variant of serial theory, one major question should be answered: 'Can we have the best of both worlds?' That is, can intermediate levels be restricted in a way that captures opacity, but also preserves OT's advantages? Can the number of strata be restricted to a universal maximum? At present, it is not clear what the ultimate answers to these questions will be, due to a lack of experience with multi-stratal models. We foresee two problems, however.

Firstly, the problem of finding *independent motivation* for strata. Motivation must be independent in the sense that it goes beyond the desire to capture opaque interactions. If such (presumably morphological) evidence cannot be produced, then multi-stratal OT is reduced to a variant of serial theory, differing in having two mechanisms (constraint interaction and derivation) instead of one (derivation). Considerations of generality of explanation would then favour the serial model.

Secondly, multi-stratal evaluation implies that multiple rankings are active within a grammar. This predicts that stratal rankings (hypothetically, at least) can differ as widely as those of different languages. But cases under discussion show that such radically different rankings for strata do not occur. On the contrary, rankings differ only in minimal ways, typically by the reranking of a pair of constraints (a well-formedness constraint and a faithfulness constraint), or perhaps two pairs, but not by massive rerankings.

Thirdly, multi-stratal models are not learnable by Tesar and Smolensky's algorithm, discussed in chapter 8, and it is doubtful whether they are learnable at all, due to the large increase in complexity. However, future research will have to answer this question.

9.2.4 *OO-correspondence*

A third approach to opacity is based on OO-correspondence (McCarthy 1995a; Benua 1995, chapter 6). Opacity involves underapplication and overapplication effects, as noted in section 9.2.1. Hence, it seems logical to extend the apparatus of OO-identity constraints to opacity. If successful, this approach would have the advantage of preserving two core principles of standard OT: direct mapping and strictly output-based well-formedness constraints.

An identity-based approach to opacity requires the following pair of conditions. First, for each opaque output, there must be an output form compositionally related to it. Second, this *base* must be transparent with respect to the generalization. Both conditions hold for the analysis of i-Syncope in Palestinian Arabic (chapter 6, section 6.4).

i-Syncope normally deletes unstressed /i/ in open syllables (25b). It under-applies in (25c), where unstressed /i/ corresponds with a stressed vowel in the base.

(25)   Regular application and underapplication of i-Syncope in Palestinian
        Arabic
        a. /fíhim/   fíhim   'he understood'
        b. /fíhim-na/   fhímna   'we understood'
        c. /[fíhim]-na/ fihímna   *fhímna 'he understood us'

Two-level well-formedness fails here since the abstract stress blocking application of i-Syncope (rendering it opaque in 25c) is not present in the input.

However, an OO-correspondence analysis works, because the 'blocking' stress is recoverable from the base. A BA-identity constraint HEADMAX-BA refers to it:

(26)   **HEADMAX-BA**

        Every segment in the base's *prosodic head* has a correspondent in the
        affixed form.

OO-correspondence reanalyses any cases of opacity accounted for by *cyclic* application in serial theory. Yet it fails wherever opacity is controlled by an *abstract* intermediate level, one that is not recoverable from a morphologically related output form.

For example, vowel epenthesis in Turkish (/ajak-m/ → [a.ja.ɨm], section 9.2.1) cannot be analysed by OO-correspondence. Some form should exist (in the paradigm of /ajak/) that has a 'transparent' epenthetic [ɨ] following the stem. But no such output form can exist, given the phonology of Turkish. If epenthesis applied transparently in any form related to /ajak/, then /k/ would have to resist deletion in an intervocalic context. However, this is precisely what *VkV ≫ MAX-IO excludes. We must conclude that OO-correspondence is insufficiently general to account for all types of opacity.

9.2.5 *Sympathy*

The most recent attack on opacity is due to McCarthy (1998), and it is called *Sympathy*. Its core feature is an extension of the correspondence relation to *pairs of candidate forms*. Faithfulness constraints require the output form to resemble another candidate of *Gen*, the *sympathetic* form, which is analogous to the abstract intermediate representation in serial theory. Sympathy preserves the key features of standard OT: direct mapping of inputs to outputs and the output-based format of well-formedness constraints. However, it implies a vast increase in the correspondence relations involved in selecting the optimal output.

To acquire an intuitive notion of 'Sympathy', we return to tableau (7) of Turkish /ɑjɑk-m/ (repeated below as 27). Recall that the *transparent* candidate (27d) is incorrectly selected as optimal over *opaque* (27c). This result is independent of constraint ranking, as violation marks incurred by the former are a proper subset of those incurred by the latter:

(27)

Input: /ɑjɑk-m/	*COMPLEX	*VkV	MAX-IO	DEP-IO
a.　ɑ.jɑkm	*!			
b.　ɑ.jɑ.kɨm		*!		*
c.　ɑ.jɑ.ɨm			*	*!
d. ☹ ɑ.jɑm			*	

For [ɑ.jɑ.ɨm] to become more harmonic than *[ɑ.jɑm], some constraint *C* must outrank DEP-IO, one which [ɑ.jɑ.ɨm] obeys but *[ɑ.jɑm] violates. The unknown constraint is probably not a well-formedness constraint, since [ɑ.jɑ.ɨm] can boast no advantages over *[ɑ.jɑm] in terms of its featural or syllabic composition. (Its extra [ɨ] only works against it in terms of well-formedness, causing hiatus, and an onset-less syllable.) Therefore constraint *C* must be a *faithfulness constraint*.

To what form can [ɑ.jɑ.ɨm] be faithful which [ɑ.jɑm] is unfaithful to? It cannot be the input /ɑjɑk-m/ for obvious reasons (IO-faithfulness fails, which is precisely the problem). Nor is any transparent output form available for OO-correspondence (as we saw in section 9.2.4). McCarthy opts for a third logical possibility: the opaque candidate output is faithful to a form that is neither an input nor an output, but a *candidate output* itself. That is, he proposes a new type of correspondence relation defined on pairs of output candidates: this relation is called 'Sympathy'.

Let us first consider an intuitive (and informal) way of picking the 'sympathetic' candidate to which [ɑ.jɑ.ɨm] is faithful. Focussing on the candidate pair [ɑ.jɑ.ɨm] and [ɑ.jɑm], we find that whatever advantage of faithfulness the former may have, this must reside in its epenthetic [ɨ]. We deduce that the yet-to-be-identified sympathetic candidate shares this vowel with [ɑ.jɑ.ɨm]. Such a candidate form is [ɑ.jɑ.kɨm] (27b). This happens to be the form in tableau (27) that is otherwise maximally faithful to the input – this observation will be taken up directly below. This sympathetic form will be indicated by the flower '⊛'.

The ⊛-candidate [ɑ.jɑ.kɨm] matches the intermediate form in the serial analysis (4), arising after vowel epenthesis (the input to intervocalic k-deletion). In the OT analysis, [ɑ.jɑ.kɨm] is more faithful to the input /ɑjɑk-m/ than opaque [ɑ.jɑ.ɨm], taking an intermediate position between both. Thus the serial analysis and OT analysis share an insight: both set up an abstract intermediate form 'connecting' the opaque output to the input.[9]

The next step is setting up a correspondence constraint demanding faithfulness to the ⊛-candidate [ɑ.jɑ.kɨm]. We need a constraint militating against 'deletion' of segments, hence a member of the MAXIMALITY family. This constraint, MAX-⊛O, is ranked above DEP-IO, the anti-epenthesis constraint, violation of which would have been fatal to (28c) (as indicated by '¡') if MAX-⊛O had not been there:

(28)

Input: /ɑjɑk-m/ ⊛-Candidate: ɑ.jɑ.kɨm	*COMPLEX	*VkV	MAX-⊛O	MAX-IO	DEP-IO
a. ɑ.jɑkm	*!		*		
b. ⊛ ɑ.jɑ.kɨm		*!			*
c. ☞ ɑ.jɑ.ɨm			*	*	¡*
d. ɑ.jɑm			**!	*	

The *opaque* candidate (28c), which would 'normally' lose to the *transparent* candidate (28d) because of its extra violation of DEP-IO, now becomes optimal due to its maximal faithfulness to the ⊛-candidate. Note that one violation of MAX-⊛O is incurred by each segment of the ⊛-candidate that lacks a correspondent in the output. Therefore, 'opaque' (28c) is unfaithful to the ⊛-candidate by one segment ('deleted' /k/), whereas transparent (28d) is unfaithful by two

---

[9] McCarthy points out that such parallelism is not always exact, particularly in cases involving multiply opaque generalizations.

segments ('deleted' /k/ and /ɨ/), with the additional violation being fatal. Finally, the ⊛-candidate itself fatally violates *VkV.[10]

Next we turn to a case of 'overapplying' opacity that is not controlled by the input (which is problematic to reference-to-the-input models). Again, the ⊛-candidate matches the intermediate representation in a serial analysis, which arises after Weight-by-Position and is the input to consonant deletion. This is [fe$_\mu$d$_\mu$.na] (29b). The opaque output (29c) is faithful to it by satisfying MAX-μ-⊛O, a constraint demanding that each mora of the ⊛-candidate have a correspondent in the output.

(29)

Input: /fe$_\mu$d̪-na$_\mu$/ ⊛-Candidate: fe$_\mu$d̪$_\mu$.na$_\mu$	*WEIGHT-BY-POSITION	CODA-COND	MAX-μ-⊛O	MAX-IO	Dep-μ-IO
a. fe$_\mu$d̪.na$_\mu$	*!	*	*		
b. ⊛ fe$_\mu$d̪$_\mu$.na$_\mu$		*!			*
c. ☞ fee$_{\mu\mu}$.na$_\mu$				*	*
d. fe$_\mu$.na$_\mu$			*!	*	

Finally, consider the case of 'underapplying' opacity in Isthmus Nahuat. In a serial (counterfeeding) derivation (5) of [ʃikɑkil] (from /ʃikɑkili/), an intermediate representation occurs in which devoicing applies, but apocope has not yet applied. Here /ʃikɑkili/ fails to undergo devoicing since its final vowel is still present. Analogously, the ⊛-candidate in tableau (30) happens to be identical to the input:

(30)

Input: /ʃikɑkili/ ⊛-Candidate: ʃikɑkili	FINAL-C	IDENT-⊛O (voice)	MAX-IO	*VOICED-CODA	IDENT-IO (voice)
a. ⊛ ʃikɑkili	*!				
b. ☞ ʃikɑkil			*	*	
c. ʃikɑki̥l		*!	*		*

---

[10] Another plausible output candidate, [ɑj.kɨm], is equally faithful to the sympathetic candidate. The difference is that an input vowel is deleted in [ɑj.kɨm] but an input consonant in [ɑ.ja.ɨm] (the actual output). We assume that this contrast correlates with a distinction between MAX-C and (higher-ranking) MAX-V. (See the analysis of Southeastern Tepehuan in chapter 4.) This assumption is shared by McCarthy (1998), who does not discuss the Turkish case, though.

Candidate (30a), perfectly faithful to the input and to itself (in its quality of ⊛-candidate), is nevertheless rejected for its fatal violation of Final-C. Opaque (30b) is optimal due to Ident-⊛O(voice) ≫ *Voiced-Coda, ruling out transparent (30c).

Observe that this tableau contains *two* faithfulness constraints of the format Ident(voice), a low-ranking one evaluating I–O pairs (Ident-IO(voice)), and a top-ranking one evaluating ⊛-O pairs (Ident-⊛O(voice)). Since the ⊛-candidate happens to be identical to the input, *both faithfulness constraints produce the same evaluation marks*, at different positions in the hierarchy. We will return to this observation shortly below, in connection with the issue of how the choice of the ⊛-candidate is made.

The ⊛-candidate is not a priori given, and it should be determinable on the basis of positive evidence. How can this aim be achieved? In all cases of opacity discussed thus far, the ⊛-candidate *satisfies an IO-faithfulness constraint* that is *violated in the opaque form*. In all three cases, this is Max-IO:

(31)   ⊛-candidate opaque form faithfulness violation
      a. Turkish a.ja.kɨm   a.ja.ɨm   /k/ → Ø (*Max-IO)
      b. Oromo   feₘdₘ.na   feeₘₘ.na   /d/ → Ø (*Max-IO)
      c. Nahuat   ʃikɑkili   ʃikɑkil   /i/ → Ø (*Max-IO)

We noted in section 9.2.1 that opaque generalizations are overlaid by other generalizations of the language. Now we see how the ⊛-candidate is related to the opaque form by 'peeling' off a structural change (here, 'undoing' a segment deletion). The relation between the opaque form and the ⊛-candidate is such that the latter obeys an IO-faithfulness constraint that is violated by the former. This special IO-faithfulness constraint is called the *selector*.

McCarthy claims that the choice of the ⊛-candidate is uniquely determined by the selector, given the (independently motivated) constraint ranking of the language. That is, the ⊛-candidate is the *most harmonic* candidate of all candidates that *satisfy the selector*. For this purpose, we may think of candidate space as divided into two mutually exclusive subsets, one of candidates that satisfy the selector, and another of candidates violating it. Within the former subset, the ⊛-candidate is the optimal candidate, given the constraint hierarchy of the language.

For Turkish this method is successful, given a number of independently motivated observations about constraint ranking. *Complex and Anchoring-IO (militating against final epenthesis) appear to be never violated in Turkish, hence they are undominated. But *VkV is actually violable in paradigms of monosyllabic roots (for example, *ok* 'arrow', *ok-u* 'his arrow', *ok-um* 'my arrow'). That is, no monosyllabic root ending in /k/ loses /k/ in intervocalic contexts. Therefore *VkV must be crucially dominated by some constraint enforcing root-minimality, whose exact nature is irrelevant to our discussion.

The dominated position of *VkV is confirmed by the selection of the ⊛-candidate [ɑ.jɑ.kɨm]. Tableau (32) shows four candidates which obey the selector constraint MAX-IO (omitting candidates that violate this constraint, which do not qualify by definition). The independently motivated constraint ranking indeed selects (32c) as the ⊛-candidate:

(32)   Subtableau for selection of the ⊛-candidate

Input: /ɑjɑk-m/	*COMPLEX ¦ ANCHORING-IO	*VkV	**MAX-IO**	DEP-IO
a. ɑ.jɑkm	*! ¦		✓	
b. ɑ.jɑk.mɨ	¦ *!		✓	*
c. ⊛ ɑ.jɑ.kɨm	¦	*	✓	*
d. ɑ.jɑ.kɨ.mɨ	¦ *!	*	✓	**

This is not the tableau selecting the actual output form but only the part that is relevant to the selection of the ⊛-candidate. In a fully fledged tableau, the choice of the ⊛-candidate is actually made 'in parallel' with the choice of the optimal output form. That is, (32) is a subtableau of (28). Note that tableau (32), unlike (28), does not include MAX-⊛O, the Sympathy constraint. McCarthy argues that the Sympathy constraint must indeed always be invisible to the selection of the ⊛-candidate, to avoid circularity in selection.

The *choice of the selector* is critical, since this determines the ⊛-candidate, hence indirectly the choice of the opaque output. But how is the selector itself being chosen? The selector is always an IO-faithfulness constraint, violable in *actual* output forms of the language (crucially so, in the opaque output itself). Since most faithfulness constraints of a language are undominated, this narrows down its choice. But the bottom line is that any positive evidence regarding the choice of the selector can only reside in the *opaque form itself*. The learner must infer the choice of the selector from the opaque form. This may seem an unsatisfactory conclusion which has a whiff of circularity. However, an analogous conclusion holds for a serial theory of opacity: any evidence pertaining to rule ordering (bleeding or counterbleeding, feeding or counterfeeding) can only come from the opaque form itself.

Let us now briefly discuss this proposal, starting with its virtues. First, Sympathy preserves two cornerstones of standard OT – direct mapping and the output-based format of well-formedness constraints. All interactions are parallel rather than serial, involving ranked constraints rather than ordered levels. Well-formedness constraints never refer to levels other than the output (either inputs or abstract intermediate representations). In its empirical scope, Sympathy surpasses all OT approaches to opacity seen thus far – except Intermediate Levels theory. However, it also has a number of problematic aspects.

First it weakens Correspondence Theory by extending it to candidate-to-candidate faithfulness. Standard correspondence constraints require identity with an independently established, 'concrete', form, either a lexical input (IO-faithfulness), or an actual output form (OO-identity). Increasing the scope of correspondence constraints poses a potential threat to OT's restrictiveness. Faithfulness to abstract forms implies a radical increase in the number of constraint interactions, hence in computational complexity of the theory. A related issue, one which cannot be addressed without additional research, is learnability. Do the results that we discussed in chapter 7 carry over to Sympathy?

Second, it is not clear at all whether the ⊛-candidate is uniquely determinable by the selector on the basis of only the independently motivated hierarchy of the language, as McCarthy suggests. Rankings of undominated constraints, which are not independently motivated by output forms, may become relevant to the selection of the ⊛-candidate. Note that the set of candidates obeying the selector always contains candidates violating one or more undominated constraints. (In the Turkish example, the candidate set includes a candidate [ɑ.jɑkm], violating *COMPLEX.) What happens if, in this set of selector-obeying candidates, no candidates occur obeying all undominated constraints? Such a situation may occur if the selector imposes a requirement that implies the violation of an otherwise undominated constraint in the ⊛-candidate. In such a case, the ranking of undominated constraints is required to break the tie. But the use of 'ranked undominated constraints' contradicts the claim that the independently motivated ranking of the language suffices to choose the ⊛-candidate. By definition, undominated constraints are not rankable on the basis of evidence from transparent outputs, in which they are never violated.

Third, Sympathy does not offer a general theory of opacity, as it cannot deal with 'chain shifts', a kind of counterfeeding opacity that will be discussed in the next subsection.

9.2.6 *Local Conjunction*

A final approach to opacity in OT merits attention, partly because it is complementary to Sympathy, and partly for independent reasons. Under *Local Conjunction*, two constraints are conjoined as a single composite constraint which is violated if and only if both of its components are violated within some domain.

The proposal is due to unpublished work by Smolensky (1993). Consider the schematic tableau (33), which contains four candidates representing all logically possible combinations of violations of constraints C_1 and C_2:

(33)

	C_1	C_2	$[C_1 \text{ \& } C_2]_\delta$
Candidate 1			
Candidate 2		*	
Candidate 3	*		
Candidate 4	*	*	*

The complex constraint $[C_1 \text{ \& } C_2]_\delta$ (the 'conjunction' of constraints C_1 and C_2) is violated if and only if *both of its components* are violated. Moreover, for a violation of $[C_1 \text{ \& } C_2]_\delta$ to occur, both separate violations must arise within a single *domain* δ (a segment, morpheme, etc.). Evidently some domain is needed for conjunction: the severity of output ill-formedness is never increased by combinations of violations in *random* positions in the output. Finally, a conjoined constraint does not replace its components, but it is *separately ranked*. It is generally assumed that a conjoined constraint is universally ranked above the component constraints.

(34)　　　　Universal ranking schema: $[C_1 \text{ \& } C_2]_\delta \gg C_1, C_2$

We will first look at evidence for conjunction from opacity (chain shifts), and then at its wider applications.

The clearest motivation for Local Conjunction of constraints resides in *chain shifts* (Kirchner 1996). A chain shift is a situation in which sounds are promoted (or demoted) stepwise along some scale in some context. Crucially the chain shift does not result in neutralization, since each input takes precisely one step. This is schematized as follows:

(35)　　　$A \rightarrow B$ and $B \rightarrow C$, but **not** $*A \rightarrow C$

That is, 'A' reoccupies the position left vacant by 'B', which itself occupies 'C', etc.

　　A striking example of a chain shift is vowel raising in Western Basque (De Rijk 1970, Kenstowicz and Kisseberth 1979, Kirchner 1996). Mid vowels and high vowels that precede another vowel are raised by one degree (mid to high and high to raised):

(36)   *Indefinite*   *Definite*

			Indefinite	Definite	
a. Mid to high	$e \rightarrow i$		seme bat	semie	'son'
	$o \rightarrow u$		asto bat	astue	'donkey'
b. High to raised	$i \rightarrow i^j$		erri bet	erri^{j}e	'village'
	$u \rightarrow u^w$		buru bet	buru^{w}e	'head'

Kirchner assumes the following specifications for vowels for [low], [high], and [raised]:

(37)   Raised $\{i^j, u^w\}$ [−low, +high, +raised]
              High $\{i, u\}$ [−low, +high, −raised]
              Mid $\{e, o\}$ [−low, −high, −raised]
              Low $\{a\}$ [+low, −high, −raised]

(In the Etxarri dialect, on which Kirchner focusses, low vowels are not raised in hiatus. The raising of clitic vowels /bat/ → [bet] is conditioned by a high vowel in the stem, and we will ignore it.) First we will see that chain shifts are not problematic to serial theory, while they do pose problems to standard OT.

In serial theory the analysis is straightforward: it is a case of counterfeeding *on the focus*. Two counterfeeding rules raise high vowels and mid vowels, respectively:[11]

(38)   Counterfeeding analysis of chain shift

	/seme-a/	/erri-a/
High vowel raising	---	erri^{j}a
Mid vowel raising	semia	---
	[semie]	[erri^{j}e]

Each of the counterfeeding rules applies only once per derivation.

Chain shifts, a kind of underapplying opacity, cannot be analysed under standard OT, as we will now show. Raising in hiatus is triggered by a well-formedness constraint (Kirchner 1996):

(39)   **HIATUS-RAISING**
             In $V_1 V_2$, maximize height of V_1.

Kirchner argues that this constraint is evaluated gradiently, and that different values of V_1 incur the following violations marks: low '***', mid '**', high '*', and raised none. The IO-faithfulness constraints involved are:

---

[11] A third rule raises the suffix vowel from /-a/ to [-e] if it is preceded by a high vowel.

(40)   a. **IDENT-IO**(high)

　　　　If an input segment is [αhigh], then its output correspondent is [αhigh].

　　　 b. **IDENT-IO**(raised)

　　　　If an input segment is [αraised], then its output correspondent is [αraised].

For raising to take place at all, HIATUS-RAISING must be ranked above *both* faithfulness constraints. That is, e → i shows that IDENT-IO(high) is dominated, while i → i^j shows that IDENT-IO(raised) is dominated. This is summarized in the following tableau (which, however, gives only a subset of the output candidates to be finally considered for /e/):

(41)

	HIATUS-RAISING	IDENT-IO (high)	IDENT-IO (raised)
a.i　　e → e	*!*		
a.ii ☞ e → i	*	*	
b.i　　i → i	*!		
b.ii ☞ i → i^j			*

Note, however, what happens if we add a third output candidate, [i^j], to the tableau of /e/. This ranking incorrectly predicts that /e/ is raised to [i^j], going two steps rather than one:

(41)

	HIATUS-RAISING	IDENT-IO (high)	IDENT-IO (raised)
c.i　　e → e	*!*		
c.ii　 e → i	*!	*	
c.iii ☹ e → i^j		*	*

The incorrect prediction is due to undominated HIATUS-RAISING. No possible ranking of these three constraints allows i → i^j, and e → i, while disallowing e → i^j. Mid vowels simply cannot be prevented from going all the way to raised.

The reasoning behind Kirchner's *Local Conjunction* analysis is this: the change e → iʲ involves violation of *two* faithfulness constraints, while each of the individual steps i → iʲ and e → i involves only one violation. Moreover, the faithfulness violations incurred by i → iʲ reoccur separately in the individual steps i → iʲ and e → i. Then what is needed is the conjunction of both faithfulness constraints into a composite constraint. This must be ranked above HIATUS-RAISING in order to restrict raising to a one-step process:

(42) a. High vowel raising: HIATUS-RAISING ≫ IDENT-IO(raised)
   b. Mid vowel raising: HIATUS-RAISING ≫ IDENT-IO(high)
   c. Interaction: [IDENT-IO(raised) & IDENT-IO(high)]$_\delta$ ≫
         HIATUS-RAISING

The composite constraint [IDENT-IO(raised) & IDENT-IO(high)]$_\delta$ is violated if and only if IDENT-IO(high) and IDENT-IO(raised) are violated with respect to a given segment. The domain 'δ' is equal to the segment for which both faithfulness constraints are evaluated.

Tableau (43a) illustrates how the 'fell swoop' candidate e → iʲ is eliminated by the composite constraint:

(43)

	[IDENT-IO(high) & IDENT-IO(raised)]$_\delta$	HIATUS-RAISING	IDENT-IO (high)	IDENT-IO (raised)
a.i e → e		**!		
a.ii ☞ e → i		*	*	
a.iii e → iʲ	*!		*	*
b.i i → e		**!	*	
b.ii i → i		*!		
b.iii ☞ i → iʲ				*

But in tableau (43b), the same output i → iʲ is allowed as it involves only a single step, hence the composite constraint is not violated.

Finally, let us briefly discuss why Sympathy theory cannot deal with chain shifts. To account for opacity of raising in e → i, the output must be maximally faithful to a ⊛-candidate that is [−raised] itself. Therefore IDENT-IO(raised) must be the 'selector', and [i] the ⊛-candidate (which also happens to be the output). Assuming IDENT-⊛O(raised) as the undominated ⊛O-faithfulness constraint, we arrive at tableau (44a):

(44)

	IDENT-⊛O (raised)	HIATUS-RAISING	IDENT-IO (high)	**IDENT-IO (raised)**
a.i e → e		*!*		
a.ii ☞ ⊛ e → i		*	*	
a.iii e → iʲ	*!		*	*
b.i i → e		*!*	*	
b.ii ⊗ ⊛ i → i		*		
b.iii i → iʲ	*!			*

In (44b), however, we see that the same ranking predicts that [i] is the ⊛-candidate, hence the (incorrect) output. Reversing the ranking of IDENT-⊛O(raised) and HIATUS-RAISING may account for i → iʲ, but will spoil the correct outcome for input /e/, predicting e → iʲ. This ranking paradox cannot be resolved.

Local Conjunction has seen wider applications (outside chain shifts) in a range of phenomena, including dissimilation and Obligatory Contour Principle (OCP) effects (Alderete 1997, Itô and Mester 1998) and word stress (Kager 1994, Crowhurst and Hewitt 1997). The shared property of all these phenomena is that multiple violations of 'basic' constraints within some domain are banned, while a single violation of each of the constraints individually is tolerated. A specific case is that where multiple violations of *one* constraint within a domain are banned: *self-conjunction*.

Here we will illustrate this approach for OCP effects. Itô and Mester (1998) discuss various restrictions on the cooccurrence of segments within Japanese morphemes, which ban cooccurring segments sharing the same marked value of some feature. One of these restrictions is known as Lyman's Law:

(45)   Lyman's Law: 'Stems must not contain more than one voiced obstruent.'

Lyman's Law is exemplified by the minimal pairs (46a–c) and systematic gaps (46d):

(46)   a.i   kaki 'persimmon'   a.ii   futa 'lid'
         b.i   kagi 'sign'   b.ii   fuda 'sign'
         c.i   ɡaki 'writing'   c.ii   buta 'pig'
         d.i   *ɡagi (non-existent) d.ii   *buda (non-existent)

This is arguably a case of 'positional neutralization' – voicing is distinctive in obstruents, but up to a certain limit: maximally one voiced obstruent may occur in a stem. Moreover, it can be seen as a static kind of 'dissimilation' – opposite values for voicing are preferred to cooccurrences of [+voice].

Earlier autosegmental analyses of Lyman's Law assumed the tier-adjacency of the feature [voice], excluding adjacent occurrences of [+voice]. Such analyses involved the OCP ('At the melodic level, adjacent identical elements are prohibited').[12] The fact that [+voice] is targeted by the OCP, rather than [−voice], is not an accidental property of Japanese. Cross-linguistically, dissimilations are triggered by adjacent segments specified for *marked* values for a given feature. For this reason, OCP analyses assume the underspecification of unmarked feature values. (See Steriade 1995a for a criticism of such approaches.)

Itô and Mester (1998) take a different view, and argue that the markedness content of Lyman's Law should be captured directly, without underspecification. This involves a constraint banning cooccurrences of marked [+voice] within a morpheme. This constraint is an extension of VOP, the basic markedness constraint banning [+voice] in obstruents (known from chapter 1, section 1.7.5):

(47)   **VOICED OBSTRUENT PROHIBITION** (VOP)
        *[+voice, −son]

Since voicing is distinctive in Japanese obstruents (within the limits imposed by Lyman's Law), VOP must be dominated by IDENT-IO(voice). However, the absolute ban on double occurrences of [+voice] in a stem requires the conjunction of VOP with itself, dominating IDENT-IO(voice). Itô and Mester propose the following schema for self-conjunction:

(48)   *Self-conjunction of constraints:* $[C_1 \,\&\, C_1]_\delta$ with $C_1 = C_1$
        Evaluation of $[C_1 \,\&\, C_1]_\delta$: $[C_1 \,\&\, C_1]_\delta$ is violated in domain δ if there is more than one violation of C_1 in domain δ.

Applying self-conjunction to VOP, this schema produces [VOP & VOP]$_{Stem}$, or VOP^2:

(49)   **VOP^2**
        No cooccurrence of voiced obstruency with itself.

In order to fulfil its function of 'positional neutralizer', VOP^2 must be ranked above the basic sequence IDENT-IO(voice) ≫ VOP. Considering a hypothetical input that has a dual occurrence of [+voice, −son], one of these is erased, while

---

[12] The OCP was originally proposed for tonal systems (Leben 1973, Goldsmith 1976), and later generalized into a wider principle governing dissimilations (McCarthy 1986).

the other is preserved. Which of them is erased cannot be determined here, given the fact that there are no alternations:

(50)

Input: /gagi/	VOP^2	IDENT-IO (voice)	VOP
a. gagi	*!		**
b. ☞ kagi		*	*
c. ☞ gaki		*	*
d. kaki		**!	

Minimal violation of IDENT-IO(voice) guarantees that only one occurrence of [+voice] is erased (rather than both, as in 50d).

Another advantage of Local Conjunction is that it rationalizes existing contextual markedness constraints as conjunctions of two basic constraints (Smolensky 1995, Itô and Mester 1998). For example, *VOICED-CODA ('coda obstruents are voiceless') is construed as the Local Conjunction of the context-free markedness constraint VOP ('obstruents are voiceless') and the prosodic markedness constraint NOCODA ('no codas'). Violation of *VOICED-CODA implies a combined violation of VOP and NOCODA in a single segment. Hence, [NOCODA & VOP]$_{Segment}$ is equivalent to *VOICED-CODA. The example is from Dutch (see chapter 1):

(51)

Input: /bɛd/	[NOCODA & VOP]	MAX-IO	IDENT-IO (voice)	NOCODA	VOP
a. bɛd	*!			*	**
b. ☞ bɛt			*	*	*
c. pɛt			**!	*	
d. bɛ		*!			*

The original constraint is somehow unsatisfactory because it restates two independently needed markedness constraints. In cases such as these, Local Conjunction helps to reduce the set of basic constraints, leading to greater generalization, and decreasing arbitrariness in the statement of individual constraints.

Should Local Conjunction be granted the status of basic theoretical device of OT? It certainly has its positive sides. First, it fills the empirical gap left by Sympathy in the analysis of opacity (chain shifts). Second, in its self-conjunction mode, it offers a highly elegant implementation of the insight that multiple violations of a constraint are worse than a single violation (Mohanan 1993). This extends to OCP effects, as we saw above. However, Local Conjunction also has some negative sides.

Firstly, although banning the *worst-of-the-worst* is undeniably in the spirit of OT, conceptual problems do arise. Local Conjunction seems to stipulate what should come for free in OT, given the architecture of the theory. OT is designed to deal with forms which have more-than-necessary violations, against the principle of minimal violation. However, minimal violation by itself, as a standard property of interactions of basic constraints, should suffice to exclude the worst-of-the-worst, rather than an extra mechanism of constraint conjunction. Accepting it means that the theory has two means to rule out excessive violations of faithfulness: (a) minimal violation of basic constraints, and (b) Local Conjunction.

A second conceptual problem is that Local Conjunction seems to undermine *strict domination*, a core principle of OT. Under strict domination, 'violation of higher-ranked constraints cannot be compensated for by satisfaction of lower-ranked constraints'. (See chapter 1.) But under Local Conjunction, two constraints A and B, each of which is ranked too low to force the violation of C, can nevertheless dominate C by joining forces in a conjoined constraint $[A \& B]_\delta$. Such a situation, in which two constraints 'team up' against a third constraint, conflicts with the intuition behind strict domination (even though Local Conjunction and strict domination are not formally inconsistent).

Finally, questions arise with respect to the huge increase of possible constraints in *Gen* which is implied by Local Conjunction. For example, can any pair of constraints be conjoined? This predicts constraints of a *typologically* doubtful status, such as [ONSET & NOCODA]$_\sigma$ or [*[+round] & PARSE-SYL]$_\sigma$. Can faithfulness constraints be conjoined with markedness constraints?[13] If so, this predicts even more bizarre constraints, such as [*NÇ & IDENT-IO(Place)]. Can any number of constraints be conjoined, or is there a (binary?) upper limit? Without any upper limit, the number of constraints in *Gen* becomes infinite, with fatal effects on *learnability*. But even under maximally restrictive assumptions about Local Conjunction, a vast increase occurs in the amount of constraint interaction.

9.3 Absolute ungrammaticality

The essence of OT is that grammatical outputs are the *best possible* compromise between conflicting needs. This implies that absolute well-formedness of output forms cannot be a criterion for grammaticality. (Some constraints are necessarily violated in every output.) This approach to well-formedness predicts that for every

---

[13] Itô and Mester (1998) exclude this, but see section 9.5 below.

lexical input, some grammatical output exists – the optimal output, which minimally violates the conflicting constraints in a fixed hierarchy. Nevertheless, languages do not strictly conform to this picture, since cases of *absolute ungrammaticality* occur. A specific input has no grammatical output:

(52)   Input → $\boxed{Grammar}$ → Ø

The best-studied examples involve the *blocking* of word formation processes to avoid the violation of some phonological well-formedness constraint. How does OT deal with such cases? Does absolute ungrammaticality motivate a fundamental revision of the model?

We will discuss an example from stress-based conditions on affixation in English, analysed by Raffelsiefen (1996). Raffelsiefen argues that the verbalizing suffix *-ize* may not attach to adjectives ending in a stressed syllable, while it productively attaches to adjectives ending in an unstressed syllable:

(53)   Blocking of *-ize* after bases with final stress in English
         a.i rándom   rándom-ìze   a.ii fóreign   fóreign-ìze
         b.i corrúpt *corrúpt-ìze   b.ii obscéne   *obscéne-ìze

Note that *-ize* is a stressed suffix (it has secondary stress wherever it appears), and that its attachment to a stem with final stress would create a 'stress clash', a situation of adjacent stresses. Intuitively, 'clash avoidance takes priority over affixation'. But how can this be captured in OT, a theory of violable constraints? If word formation were simply blocked if its optimal output violated any phonological constraint, then no word formation would be possible at all. To avoid wholesale nullification of morphology, the lexical input must be *realized* by the grammar, that is, be mapped onto some output. Instead of blocking the input, the grammar selects its optimal output analysis, possibly by a *repair*. In the case in hand, repair may involve violation of accentual faithfulness (MAX-FT-IO 'input stresses occur in the output'), or well-formedness (*CLASH). In sum, absolute ungrammaticality poses a challenge to OT. In contrast, a theory of inviolate constraints has no problems: an output filter (with nullifying power) will reject any outputs violating *CLASH.

Raffelsiefen employs an analytic resource that was originally proposed by Prince and Smolensky (1993). The grammar always produces an output for every input. However, by Freedom of Analysis, *Gen* supplies one special output, which is identical to the input: a set of disjoint morphemes lacking any morphological or phonological cohesion. This *Null Parse* is left unpronounced, due to its lack of morpho-phonological word status. It will be optimal, though, if no other candidate is available that is more harmonic:

(54) Candidates

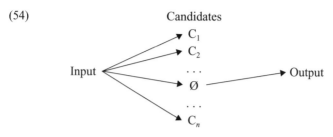

The question then is, how can the Null Parse be optimal? Due to its lack of phonological and morphological word status, it has one substantial advantage over all other candidates: it cannot violate any well-formedness constraints pertaining to the word level. However, the Null Parse violates the following constraint (McCarthy and Prince 1993b):

(55)   **MPARSE**

Morphemes are parsed into morphological constituents.

The ranking of MPARSE in the grammar determines the 'robustness' of word formation. If it is undominated, some (non-null) output will be produced, since anything is better than the null parse. But any constraint that dominates MPARSE has the power of 'annihilating' affixation. This is seen in tableau (56), in which MPARSE is dominated by an OO-identity constraint IDENT ('The stem of the derived word must be identical to the base'), as well as by *CLASH ('Two adjacent stresses are prohibited').

(56)

Input: /kərʌ́pt, -áɪz/	IDENT	*CLASH	MPARSE
a. kɔ́.rəp.tàɪz	*!		
b. kə.rʌ́p.tàɪz		*!	
c. ☞ {kərʌ́pt, -áɪz}			*

The Null Parse (56c) is optimal since all its competitors violate undominated constraints. Hence it is better to have no (tangible) output at all than an ill-formed output.

Orgun and Sprouse (1997: 4) point out empirical problems for MPARSE theory. They argue that '…there are cases of ungrammaticality in which the ungrammatical candidate could be repaired by violating a constraint independently known to be violable in other (grammatical) output forms in the language'. That is, the constraint ranking required to make the Null Parse win is demonstrably inconsistent with the ranking required for non-null forms of the language. If these objections (and the analyses on which they are based) are valid, then they pose serious challenges to MPARSE theory.

Yet another unsatisfactory aspect of the MPARSE model is the assumption that the Null Parse, in spite of its lack of phonetic realization, violates no faithfulness constraints. This assumption is required to prevent the undesired result that the Null Parse is rejected for violating the same constraints that exclude its non-null (ungrammatical) competitors. For example, adding a violation mark for IDENT to the Null Parse (56c), penalizing its lack of phonetically realized stress, would render it less harmonic than all its competitors. Alternatively, it might be stipulated that identity constraints are only activated for outputs that are phonetically interpreted, but that seems equally ad hoc.

Alternatives to MPARSE have been proposed, changing the basic design of the OT grammar, by introducing *inviolate* constraint components. Orgun and Sprouse (1997) argue that a component of inviolate constraints (*Control*) is serially ordered after *Gen* and *Eval* as an output filtering device. As in standard OT, *Eval* selects an optimal candidate, which is submitted to Control. Unlike *Eval*, Control has the power of marking as ungrammatical any outputs violating its constraints. Under this conception the grammar contains two sets of undominated constraints: those whose violation is avoidable by repairs (these are part of *Eval*), and those whose violation is 'beyond repair' (these are part of *Control*). In the case in hand, the output [kə.rʌ́p.tàɪz], optimal under *Eval*, is submitted to *Control*, which filters it out, leaving the input /kərʌ́pt, -áɪz/ without an output.

However, this proposal has its own specific problems. Firstly, it is essential that constraints in *Control*, as output filters blocking affixations, be inviolate in *all* outputs of the language. But for English, most researchers would agree that *CLASH is violable even within a Prosodic Word, as forms like *Chìnése* reveal. Secondly, *Control* is a rather blunt tool, which is principally unable to account for different types of blocking within a single language. For example, a language may have two 'defective' affixations, each of which is blocked in a separate phonological context. Here *Control* would be of no value because it predicts that the affixations share gaps in the same contexts. In contrast, MPARSE theory may deal with such cases by splitting up MPARSE into different affix-specific versions. In sum, 'absolute ungrammaticality' is another challenge which OT has not yet completely mastered.[14]

---

[14] Broekhuis (forthcoming) argues that absolute ungrammaticality can be dealt with by a component of inviolate constraints preceding *Eval*. This proposal is comparable to the assumption that *Gen* contains universally inviolable constraints (Prince and Smolensky 1993), filtering out candidates even before they are submitted to *Eval*. Broekhuis deviates from this idea, however, in his definition of 'input'. In syntax, as we have seen in chapter 8, the input is less clearly defined than in phonology. Broekhuis, for example, defines the input to *Gen* as a complete syntactic representation developed in a component preceding *Gen*, whose requirements ('checking') are inviolable. Whether such a model can deal with absolute ungrammaticality in phonology remains to be seen, however.

9.4 Free variation

Another unresolved issue is *variation*. We will focus on variation of a specific type: the case of a single input being mapped onto two outputs, each of which is grammatical. This is 'free variation', also known as 'optionality':

(57)

Input ⟶ Grammar ⟶ Output₁
                  ⟶ Output₂

By definition, the distribution of both outputs cannot be under grammatical control, since that would restore (ranking-based) determinism in the choice of both variants.

Examples of free variation are abundant in natural languages. Examples below are from English phonology (vowel reduction, 58a) and syntax (complementizer, 58b):

(58)   a. sentim[en]tality   ~ sentim[n]tality
       b. I know that John will leave ~ I know John will leave

The fact that variation is 'free' does not imply that it is totally unpredictable, but only that no *grammatical* principles govern the distribution of variants. Nevertheless, a wide range of extragrammatical factors may affect the choice of one variant over the other, including sociolinguistic variables (such as gender, age, and class), and performance variables (such as speech style and tempo). Perhaps the most important diagnostic of extragrammatical variables is that they affect the choice of occurrence of one output over another in a stochastic way, rather than deterministically. Here we will focus on the consequences of free variation for the grammar.

Why does free variation pose a challenge to OT? An OT grammar is essentially an *input–output* mapping device. The grammar is *deterministic*, in the sense that each input is mapped onto a single output – the most harmonic candidate for a constraint hierarchy. Given a single deterministic competition, how can two candidates ever *both* be optimal? If two output candidates O and O′ are different in grammatical terms, then this difference must be relevant to some constraint(s) in the hierarchy. This implies that O and O′ do not share the same violations marks, hence one is more harmonic than the other with respect to the hierarchy. The question is: how can free variation be reconciled with the deterministic nature of the grammar?[15]

---

[15] It has been argued that some cases of free variation indeed derive from inability on the part of the constraint inventory to distinguish different outputs (Hammond 1994, Smolensky 1996). That is, the constraint inventory simply lacks constraints discriminating between two outputs O₁ and O₂. However, even if this approach is feasible for the particular cases for which it has been proposed, it is clearly not generalizable to all cases of free variation. Most involve presence or absence of grammatical structure which is 'visible' to some constraint (ultimately to *Struc 'no phonological structure').

To be fair, the problem of *non-unique outputs* is not specific to OT. It reoccurs in derivational theory, or in fact any theory of grammar that is faced with the situation (57). A solution at a terminological level is to redefine the 'output of the grammar' for a given input as a set of forms $\{O_1, O_2 \ldots O_n\}$, rather than a unique form. But of course this does not solve the problem of how to generate sets of output forms. In derivational rule-based theory, specific rules may be marked as '*optional*'. In a derivation, an optional rule may be applied (in which case some output results), or be left unapplied (in which case another output results). But what is the counterpart of 'optional rules' in OT? Contrary to rules, constraints are not language-specific devices, but elements of universal grammar that are potentially active in every grammar. Therefore a solution to the 'free variation problem' can only reside in constraint ranking.

A radical method is splitting up the grammar into multiple constraint hierarchies, or *co-phonologies*, each of which selects its own optimal candidate by its own ranking. Such an approach is reminiscent of 'multi-stratal evaluation', discussed in section 9.2.3 in relation to opacity. It is not too difficult to imagine an extension of this stratal idea to free variation. If we assume that strata can be organized *in parallel* (in addition to serially, as in section 9.2.3), an input can be fed into two parallel co-phonologies, giving two outputs:

(59)

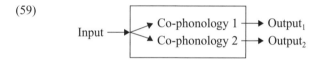

In section 9.2.3 we mentioned weaknesses in models of multi-stratal evaluation, one of which has a direct counterpart in parallel co-phonologies. Splitting a grammar up into subgrammars ('strata' or 'co-phonologies') makes the prediction that each subgrammar is independent, hence that subgrammars can be radically different. This prediction is clearly incorrect for free variation, where both outputs are mostly similar, and differ only in a minor respect. (Co-phonologies are better suited for lexical variation resulting from strata; see Inkelas and Orgun 1995 and Itô and Mester 1995; and exceptionality; see Inkelas, Orgun, and Zoll 1997.)

A less radical alternative is to maintain a single constraint hierarchy, while giving up the idea of a fixed ranking of constraints. Throughout this book we have assumed that constraints are *strictly ranked*. Two conflicting constraints C_1 and C_2 are ranked in either of two ways: C_1 strictly dominates C_2, or C_2 strictly dominates C_1. This assumption was upheld even for cases in which C_1 and C_2 cannot be ranked with respect to each other due to a lack of interaction (so that no empirical evidence can determine the ranking). In such cases we ranked C_1 and C_2 in the same position (called 'stratum' in chapter 7). But we never considered the possibility that constraints were 'crucially unranked'. *Free ranking* was observed as a purely theoretical option by Prince and Smolensky (1993: 51), and has since been argued to be the OT counterpart of optional rule application (Kiparsky 1993b, Kager 1994, 1997b, Reynolds 1994, Anttila 1995). When two constraints C_1 and C_2 are freely ranked, the evaluation procedure branches at that point. In one branch, C_1 is ranked above C_2, while in the other branch the ranking is reversed.

(60)   Interpretation of **free ranking** of constraints C_1, C_2
         Evaluation of the candidate set is split into two subhierarchies, each of which selects an optimal output. One subhierarchy has $C_1 \gg C_2$, and the other $C_2 \gg C_1$.

Note that free ranking preserves strict domination, which holds within each subhierarchy.

A (slightly simplified) example of free ranking is given below for English vowel reduction. The conflict between REDUCE ('vowels lack quality') and IDENT-IO is resolved in favour of either the latter (61a) or the former (61a):

(61)

	IDENT-IO	REDUCE
a.i ☞ sentim[en]tality		*
a.ii sentim[n̩]tality	*!	

	REDUCE	IDENT-IO
b.i sentim[en]tality	*!	
b.ii ☞ sentim[n̩]tality		*

In what way(s) does free ranking differ from parallel co-phonologies? Is what we call 'subhierarchy' just another name for 'co-phonology'? To some extent the answer is 'yes', since free ranking entails evaluation of candidate forms by parallel competitions. There is a substantial difference between the approaches, however. Subhierarchies differ only in constraints whose ranking is not stipulated by the grammar. One may think of a grammar with free rankings as *underdetermined*. Variable ranking remains consistent with the hard rankings stated in the grammar, a limitation explaining the observed similarities between variable outputs. Radical differences between outputs are possible, but this entails a large amount of free ranking, with a corresponding increase in the number of outputs. In a free ranking model, two factors are positively correlated: the *degree of dissimilarity* between variable output forms and the *number* of variable outputs. In contrast, the co-phonologies approach fails to predict such a correlation, since rankings of different co-phonologies are intrinsically unrelated. A grammar with two co-phonologies may select only two variable outputs of radically different shapes. A final point in favour of free ranking is that it offers a fairly accurate estimate of the frequency of occurrence for each output (Anttila 1995).

The free ranking approach to variation looks promising, but a number of potential problems merit attention in future research. First, it is unclear whether OT grammars with free ranking are *learnable* at all. (If so, free ranking is likely to require major adaptions of Tesar and Smolensky's learning algorithm.) Second, not necessarily on a negative note, the notion of free ranking may have consequences for the concept of OT grammar which are sharply at odds with Prince and Smolensky's (1993) principle of strict domination. Fine-tuning of free variation may be achieved by associating a freely ranked constraint with a numerical index indicating its relative strength with respect to all other constraints. This may pave the way to a *probabilistic* view of constraint interaction, replacing the doctrine of strict domination and moving into the direction of connectionism. Such a development is already apparent in functionally oriented OT (Boersma 1997), with precursors in Goldsmith and Larson (1990) and Mohanan (1993).

9.5 Positional faithfulness

Languages exhibit asymmetries with respect to contexts in which phonetic contrasts can be realized. For example, in chapters 1–3, we have seen that, generally speaking, codas display a more restricted set of contrasts than onsets do. We assumed that such positional neutralization is due to *contextual markedness* constraints (militating against a feature value [αF] in specific positions), interacting with 'context-free' faithfulness constraints. But a priori, what we refer to as 'coda neutralization' may equally well be described as 'faithfulness in onsets'. Here we will sketch an alternative view, *positional faithfulness*, which radically revises the roles of markedness and faithfulness constraints. Resistance to neutralization is attributed to constraints that *license* features in specific positions,[16] an interaction with *context-free* markedness constraints.

(62)   Two possible views of positional neutralization:
        a. Context-free faithfulness ⇔ Positional markedness
        b. Positional faithfulness ⇔ Context-free markedness

---

[16] The notion of *licensing* originates in pre-OT phonology (Goldsmith 1990, Kaye, Lowenstamm, and Vergnaud 1990, Steriade 1995a).

In most cases it is simply impossible to find evidence for one view or the other, due to the fact that the contexts of neutralization and faithfulness are both positively characterized by mutually exclusive labels ('onset', 'coda', etc.). In current literature both views have been adopted. Regardless of the issue of whether one or both views are adequate, two general arguments for positional faithfulness can be put forward.

Firstly, positional faithfulness is supported by functional considerations. It is well known that contrasts are best realized in *perceptually salient* positions (Nooteboom 1981, Hawkins and Cutler 1988, Ohala 1990, Ohala and Kawasaki 1984). Salient positions include word-initial consonants, prevocalic (or released) consonants, stressed vowels, and vowels in initial syllables. For example, it may be assumed that all vowels are subject to the same general forces of reduction ('minimize articulatory effort'), regardless of their position or stressing. Yet stressed vowels, by their inherent perceptual salience (tonal and durational) are best equipped to realize featural distinctions, hence to resist general reduction forces.

Recent OT studies have implemented perception-based asymmetries in the notion of *positional faithfulness*. Phonetic grounding renders faithfulness constraints sensitive to perceptually prominent positions. More specifically, a faithfulness constraint for a feature [F] referring to a prominent position dominates the general faithfulness constraint for [F]. This allows a 'sandwiching' of markedness constraints in between positional and general faithfulness constraints, producing positional neutralization:

(63)   Ranking schema for positional neutralization
         IO-Faithfulness (*prominent positions*) ≫ Markedness ≫
         IO-Faithfulness (*general*)

Some researchers (Steriade 1995b, Flemming 1995, Jun 1995, Kirchner 1995, 1997) have argued that perceptual principles should be directly stated in grammars, thus allowing reference to *gradient* and *non-contrastive* phonetic features. Others (Selkirk 1995, Lombardi 1995b, Beckman 1997a, b) maintain a strict separation of phonology and phonetics, in the sense of avoiding reference to gradient features.

The second (empirical) argument for positional faithfulness is that it captures and unifies a number of phonological patterns in different languages. More specifically, there is an overwhelming typological tendency for neutralizing assimilation to preserve feature values of segments in 'salient' positions (onsets, initial syllables, root segments, etc.), at the expense of segments in other positions (codas, medial syllables, affix segments, etc.). In this section we will look into one of these cases – the licensing of the feature [+round] by initial syllables – drawing on non-OT work by Steriade (1995a) and inspired by the OT analysis of Shona vowel harmony by Beckman (1997a).

A typologically common restriction regarding [+round] is that it occurs on vowels in specific positions. For example, several Altaic languages allow rounded vowels only in the initial syllable of the word. This is a case of contextual neutralization: the rounding contrast is suppressed in segments in non-initial syllables. However, an analysis of this pattern by a contextual markedness constraint banning [+round] from non-initial syllables is awkward, as the context of neutralization ('non-initial syllables') is not a natural class. This defect is avoided by a positional faithfulness analysis. A constraint IDENT-IO(round, [σ) militates against the loss of [round] in initial syllables:

(64)   **IDENT-IO**(round, [σ)
         An output segment standing *in the initial syllable* has the same value for [round] as its input correspondent.

This constraint is (nearly) identical to the general faithfulness constraint IDENT-IO(round) (65), the only difference being that the latter fails to refer to initial syllables:

(65)   **IDENT-IO**(round)
         An output segment has the same value for [round] as its input correspondent.

It is assumed that pairs of faithfulness constraints such as (65–6) are universally ranked such that the position-specific constraint is ranked above the general, position-insensitive constraint. (Compare 'harmony scales' discussed in chapter 1, section 1.8.) Hence:

(66)   Harmony scale
         IDENT-IO(round, [σ) ≫ IDENT-IO(round)

This installs the *faithfulness* part of the interaction. Let us now look into the *markedness* part, which is very simple. The faithfulness constraints compete with a general, context-free markedness constraint *[+round], which penalizes round vowels. In Altaic, rounding is lost in all vowels except those that are licensed by an initial syllable. This is expressed in the following ranking:

(67)   Licensing of rounding in initial syllables
         IDENT-IO(round, [σ) ≫ *[+round] ≫ IDENT-IO(round)

Let us assume a hypothetical input with rounding in both of its vowels. Candidate (68c) fatally violates positional faithfulness in its initial syllable. Of the two remaining candidates, (68b) is optimal since it minimally violates *[+round]:

(68)

Input: /u-u/	IDENT-IO (round, [σ])	*[+round]	IDENT-IO (round)
a. u-o		**!	
b. ☞ u-i		*	*
c. i-i	*!		**

This analysis offers an empirical argument for positional faithfulness: it is able to capture contextual neutralization of [round], without reference to a non-natural class 'non-initial syllables' as the context of neutralization.

However, an even better argument can be made for positional faithfulness on the basis of *rounding harmony*. In Yokuts (Newman 1944), [+round] is contrastive in the first syllable only, as in Altaic, but it also spreads beyond its directly licensed position, into affix vowels.[17]

(69)   a.i   dub-hun 'leads by the hand'
                    a.ii dub-mu 'having led by the hand'
                    a.iii dub-nut 'will be led by the hand'
                    b.i   xil-hin 'tangles'
                    b.ii xil-mi 'having tangled'
                    b.iii xil-nit 'will be tangled'

Rounding in non-initial syllables is *indirectly licensed* by the initial syllable. This pattern is a variation on the direct licensing pattern seen in Altaic (67). A markedness constraint HARMONY ('vowels agree in their values of [round]') dominates *[+round]:

(70)   Rounding harmony controlled by initial syllable
                IDENT-IO(round, [σ], HARMONY ≫ *[+round] ≫ IDENT-IO(round)

For a hypothetical input /dub-hin/, this ranking is illustrated by the following tableau:

---

[17] We abstract away from the interaction with vowel height, as well as from opacity (section 9.2).

(71)

Input: /dub-hin/	IDENT-IO (round, [σ])	HARMONY	*[+round]	IDENT-IO (round)
a. ☞ dub-hun			**	*
b. dub-hin		*!	*	
c. dib-hin	*!			*

HARMONY is satisfied in both (71a) and (71c) but only the latter violates positional faithfulness in its initial syllable. This analysis is highly elegant, and it also captures the relation with the *direct* licensing of rounding in the Altaic languages by a simple reranking. (In Altaic, *[+round] dominates HARMONY.) Finally, a positional faithfulness analysis is superior to one based on *contextual markedness*. With only a 'general' faithfulness constraint IDENT-IO(round) to penalize changes of [round], the inertness of the initial syllable must be due to contextual markedness. Even if we assume a constraint militating against [+round] in non-initial syllables (ranking it above *[+round]), its interaction with HARMONY is highly problematic. For example, HARMONY ≫ *[+round] ≫ IDENT-IO(round) predicts a harmony pattern **dib-hin*, regardless of where we rank the contextual markedness constraint. This empirical argument for positional faithfulness complements the typological argument that was discussed earlier.

Steriade (1995a: 162) points out 'extensions of the idea of indirect licensing to the cases of local assimilation in which onsets spread place or laryngeal features onto adjacent coda consonants'. In many languages, codas cannot carry independent values for [voice] (as in Dutch, chapter 1) or place of articulation (recall the discussion of the Coda Condition in chapter 3). In a subset of these languages, coda neutralization is accompanied by coda-to-onset assimilation, resulting in an 'indirect licensing' of features by the onset.

(72)
Coda   Onset

[αF]   [βF]

Steriade's observations on indirect licensing in local assimilation carry over to positional faithfulness in OT, as demonstrated in recent work by Jun (1995), Lombardi (1995b), and Beckman (1997a, b). Similar onset–coda asymmetries have been observed with respect to consonant deletions (see chapter 3, section 3.6). Again, positional faithfulness offers an explanation for such asymmetries (explaining why coda deletion is favoured over onset deletion).

Let us now evaluate the notion *positional faithfulness* by criteria that have played a major role earlier in this chapter. These are constraint format and factorial typology.

First, does positional faithfulness maintain the strict separation between faithfulness constraints and markedness constraints? Recall that in section 9.2.2 we criticized *two-level well-formedness* for blurring this distinction, and giving constraints *rule*-like power. Positional faithfulness constraints resemble two-level well-formedness constraints in their reference to prosodic positions of output segments. Unlike two-level well-formedness constraints, they cannot be violated if the output segment fails to occupy the relevant position, and so can't trigger changes. In this respect, compare (73) and (74) stated in their correspondence formats:

(73)   **Positional faithfulness**
         If an output segment S is [αround] <u>and S stands in an initial syllable,</u>
         then its input correspondent S′ must be [αround].
         (not violated if S is not in an initial syllable)

(74)   **Two-level well-formedness**
         If an input segment S is [αround], then its output correspondent S′
         must be [αround] <u>and stand in an</u> initial syllable.
         (violated if S is not in an initial syllable)

To avoid the problems inherent to two-level well-formedness constraints (including their 'rule'-like nature, mentioned in section 9.2.2), constraints of the type (74) should be disallowed.

A second criterion is *factorial typology*. We have seen that positional faithfulness is promising in several respects, but nonetheless it appears that contextual markedness, as discussed in chapter 1, cannot be simply eliminated. For that would produce the fatally impoverished typology below:

(75)   A factorial typology of markedness and faithfulness
       a.   P-Faithfulness ≫ Markedness ≫ Faithfulness   Positional neutralization
       b.   Faithfulness, P-Faithfulness ≫ Markedness   Full contrast
       c.   Markedness ≫ Faithfulness, P-Faithfulness   Lack of variation

What is lacking from this factorial typology, as compared to the one of chapter 1, is the case of 'allophonic variation'. This arises under a complete domination of faithfulness for a feature [F] by markedness constraints for [F], with contextual markedness dominating context-free markedness. Positional faithfulness fails to reproduce this pattern since total domination of faithfulness obscures any contextual effects of positional faithfulness. The conclusion must be that positional faithfulness cannot replace contextual markedness and that *both* are necessary. This finding implies a more complex factorial typology, which we will not present here, though.

9.6 Underlying Representations versus allomorphy

Classical generative phonology (Chomsky and Halle 1968) is based on three assumptions: (i) all contextual variants of a morpheme derive from a single *Underlying Representation*, (ii) by *rewrite rules* (A → B / X__Y), (iii) applying in a serial *derivation*, based on linear ordering. As we have seen, both the second and third assumptions have been abandoned by OT, but so far we have still assumed that the input of an OT grammar is an Underlying Representation (UR) in the classical sense: a unique lexical form underlying all alternants of a morpheme. The notion of UR may have changed as a result of *Lexicon Optimization*, but it still functions as the input of *Gen*: all candidate outputs evaluated are analyses of a single UR. The standard correspondence model, which includes URs, is given below:

(76)   Standard model (with Underlying Representations)

                              OO-Identity

                   Output   **Base**   ⇔   **Affixed form**

IO-Faithfulness   ⇕   ⇕

                   Input   **UR**   (affixed) **UR**

Base-identity is a priority of language: it enhances the one-to-one relation between lexical items, atoms of meaning, and the sound shapes encoding them. We will call this *uniform exponence*. An overlap in functions exists between base-identity and UR: both maximize uniform exponence. In this sense standard Correspondence Theory, which has two means for a single goal, is conceptually redundant.

   Recently attempts were made to eliminate UR from phonological theory (Burzio 1996, forthcoming, Hayes forthcoming). This development can be seen as yet another extension of the role of output forms in explaining alternations, as well as a logical continuation of ideas on base-identity (Benua 1995, McCarthy 1995a, Kenstowicz 1996).

On the standard view, the input equals an *abstract* UR, which is mapped onto the output, an *actual* surface representation. UR is abstract as it need not surface in its input form, but serves to supply phonotactically unpredictable shape aspects of alternants. If we eliminate UR, ignoring alternations for the moment, then abstractness of the input is no longer necessary, since every input will be identical to its actual output. On this new UR-less view, the input is simply an intended surface form, whose relative harmony is to be determined by *Eval*. If the grammar's optimal output *matches* the input, then the input is 'grammatical'. The role of the grammar as an input–output mapping mechanism changes into a *checking mechanism*.

This checking role of the grammar in fact originates in the standard model, where it forms the cornerstone of the theory of neutralization, allophonic variation, and contrast. Under *Richness of the Base*, any imaginable input may be proposed to *Eval*, but only a subset of inputs actually surface in their original shape. However, if no alternations occur in a morpheme's shape, the learner will never postulate an input deviating from the actual observable output form. Due to *Lexicon Optimization*, the input simply equals the output unless there is reason to deviate (chapter 1, section 1.6).

Let us now extend this checking view to cases in which alternations do exist, that is, cases for which the standard model uses an abstract UR. We start by making the major assumption that each surface alternant of a morpheme has its own input, which is simply identical to its output under Lexicon Optimization. (That is, we temporarily ignore the fact that alternants are systematically related in their shapes.) The assumption of multiple inputs for each morpheme (*allomorphs*) thus allows the grammar to continue to function as a checking device.

In the Dutch example, the input of the singular [bɛt] 'bed' is simply {bɛt}, while that of the plural [bɛdən] is simply {bɛdən}. (We will use the notation {...} for inputs to avoid confusion with the standard UR notation /.../.) Still, under Richness of the Base, an alternative singular input {bɛd} might have been proposed, but this would not have been able to make it to the surface due to a constraint interaction (*VOICEDCODA ≫ IDENT-IO(voice)) neutralizing it into the output [bɛt]. Therefore the optimal lexical input for [bɛt] is {bɛt}, due to Lexicon Optimization. The grammar does not impose such a neutralization on the input {bɛdən}, which makes it to the surface without change:

(77)   Input {bɛt} ⟶ Output [bɛt] Input {bɛdən} ⟶ Output [bɛdən]
         Input {bɛd} ⤏

In this UR-less model, the input (lexical shape) simply equals the output (surface shape). IO-faithfulness maintains its original function of reinforcing parts of the input, protecting it against the neutralizing forces of markedness.

We now have a conceptually simple model, which accounts for neutralization as well as allophonic variation, but which evidently fails to account for *alternations*. On this simple model, shapes of morphologically related outputs ([bɛt] ~ [bɛdən]) are not related in any phonological sense, since they do not share a common input (UR). To deal with alternations, morphologically related output forms must be subjected to constraints which enforce 'uniform exponence', *limiting the phonological dissimilarity between alternants*. This is where OO-correspondence comes into play: it eliminates the function of UR in capturing phonological shape similarities between morphologically related output forms.

As in the standard model, identity between 'base' and affixed forms is enforced by OO-correspondence. However, the key difference from the standard model resides in a new role of the *lexicon*. The lexicon no longer supplies a unique UR for each morpheme, but instead it supplies a set of shape variants of the morpheme, *allomorphs*, chunks ready for insertion in various morphological contexts (base or affixed form). The role of IO-faithfulness is revised accordingly: this checks faithfulness of output allomorphs to their lexical shapes. Finally, well-formedness constraints preserve their function of evaluating output forms. That is, we replace model (76) with model (78).

(78)   Allomorphic model (without Underlying Representations)

		OO-Correspondence		
	Output	**Base**	⇔	**Affixed form**
IO-Faithfulness		⇕		⇕
	Input	{**Base allomorph**,		Contextual
				allomorph}

Such a model has been advocated in Burzio (1996, forthcoming), elaborating ideas on word-based morphology as proposed by Aronoff (1976), Bybee (1988, 1995) and others. Two sets of faithfulness constraints are assumed in this model. OO-correspondence is active in its standard role of checking identity in the network of morphologically related output forms, or the *paradigm*. IO-faithfulness checks identity between *allomorphs* in the lexical input and their *output* counterparts.

Let us come to understand this allomorphic model by an example of an alternation that we have studied before, the case of Dutch final devoicing. In a theory without URs, this alternation depends on allomorphs which have different specifications for the feature [voice]. Here we will abstract away from any other possible shape variation. Furthermore, to avoid complications, we focus on alternations of voice in very simple paradigms which consist of the singular stem and the plural. Therefore we assume that the input is a mini-paradigm, a set of allomorph pairs, each containing one base allomorph (for insertion into the singular stem) and one contextual allomorph (for insertion into the affixed plural). As usual, *Gen* supplies a set of candidate output forms for each input pair, that is, a paradigm consisting of an actual singular stem and an actual affixed plural.

First we will look at the evaluation of an input paradigm {bɛt ~ bɛd-ən}, which the grammar should approve of without changes, producing [bɛt] ~ [bɛd-ən]. *Gen* proposes an infinite set of candidate output paradigms, of which four are shown in (79).

(79)　　　Function of Gen in allomorphic model

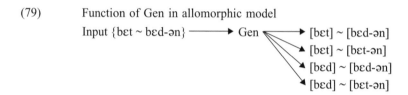

All four are submitted to *Eval*, which selects output paradigm (80a), indeed identical to the input:

(80)

Input: {bɛt ~ bɛd-ən}	*VOICEDCODA	IDENT-IO (voice)	IDENT-OO (voice)
a. ☞ bɛt ~ bɛd-ən			*
b. bɛt ~ bɛt-ən		*!	
c. bɛd ~ bɛd-ən	*!	*	
d. bɛd ~ bɛt-ən	*!	**	*

Note that *faithfulness* IDENT-IO(voice) dominates *uniform exponence* IDENT-OO(voice), a constraint which would have preferred the uniform output paradigm [bɛt] ~ [bɛt-ən] (80b). IO-faithfulness thus assumes its traditional role of penalizing shape differences between inputs (allomorphs) and outputs (candidate paradigms). Here the optimal output paradigm is maximally faithful to both allomorphs in the input. However, complete faithfulness to the input cannot always be maintained, due to high-ranked well-formedness constraints.

For example, *VOICEDCODA must dominate IDENT-IO(voice) so as to filter out the input paradigm {bɛd ~ bɛd-ən}, mapping this input onto [bɛt] ~ [bɛd-ən]:

(81)

Input: {bɛd ~ bɛd-ən}	*VoicedCoda	Ident-IO (voice)	Ident-OO (voice)
a. ☞ bɛt ~ bɛd-ən		*	*
b. bɛt ~ bɛt-ən		**!	
c. bɛd ~ bɛd-ən	*!		
d. bɛd ~ bɛt-ən	*!	*	*

The grammar (actually *Gen*, by Freedom of Analysis) 'produces' an allomorph ([bɛt]) for insertion in the base output if the lexicon fails to supply one. This is the first example of a lexical paradigm being overruled by the grammar: an undersized paradigm is 'inflated' to match the requirements of output well-formedness:

(82)   Inflation of paradigm

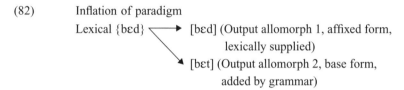

Lexical {bɛd} ⟶ [bɛd] (Output allomorph 1, affixed form, lexically supplied)

[bɛt] (Output allomorph 2, base form, added by grammar)

Simultaneously, we also observe a neutralization of the input paradigms (80) and (81) into a single output paradigm [bɛt] ~ [bɛd-ən].

Up to this point, no activity of *uniform exponence* has been visible. But of course the grammar must allow for such activity, so as to restrict the difference in shape between allomorphs in a paradigm. Without constraints enforcing uniform exponence, *any* pair of input allomorphs would be able to surface (with the only restriction imposed by high-ranked well-formedness constraints).

For example, Dutch allows allomorph pairs such as [bɛt] ~ [bɛd-ən], whereas pairs such as *[bɛt] ~ [pɛt-ən], with voice alternations in *word onset* position, are systematically excluded. Such candidate output paradigms are rejected for violation of an undominated *positional faithfulness* constraint:

(83)   **Ident-OO**(voice, [C)
         Let α be a segment in the base, and β be a correspondent of α in the affixed form.
         If α is in word onset position and [γvoice], then β is [γvoice].
         'Corresponding segments in the word onset of the base and the affixed form must agree in voicing.'

This constraint penalizes any alternations between allomorphs with respect to voicing in the word onset. Any input paradigm is neutralized towards a surface paradigm respecting uniform exponence with respect to word onset voicing. Since this neutralization could occur at the expense of the voicing value of either the base or the affixed form, a 'tie-breaking' constraint is required. In tableau (84), this is the low-ranked constraint VOP:

(84)

Input: {bɛt ~ pɛt-ən}	IDENT-OO (voice, [C])	*VOICED CODA	IDENT-IO (voice)	IDENT-OO (voice)	VOP
a.　　bɛt ~ pɛt-ən	*!			*	*
b.　　bɛt ~ bɛt-ən			*		*!*
c.　☞ pɛt ~ pɛt-ən			*		
d.　　pɛt ~ bɛt-ən	*!		**	*	*

This example demonstrates the interaction of the three major types of constraints in an allomorphy model: OO-identity, IO-faithfulness, and well-formedness.

This is the second example of a lexical paradigm being overruled by the grammar, the case of an 'oversized' paradigm that is 'shrunk' to match the requirements of uniform exponence.

(85)　　Shrinking of paradigm

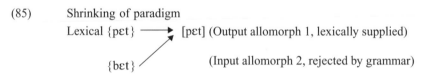

In sum, this allomorphic model captures systematic variation in the shapes of alternants, and it also restricts the variation in shape between alternants. That is, input paradigms are not simply 'copied' to the output, but undergo the filtering function of the grammar. This means that certain input paradigms are 'inflated', adding an allomorph to match the needs of high-ranked well-formedness constraints, while other input paradigms are 'shrunk', removing input variation between allomorphs that exceeds the limits imposed by uniform exponence.

An extension of this model may be considered under which the *distribution of the allomorphs* is also brought under control of the grammar. The Dutch lexicon supplies the set of two allomorphs {bɛt ~ bɛd}, without marking one for insertion into 'stem' and the other for insertion into 'affixed form'. The distribution of allomorphs is fully predictable from well-formedness constraints, primarily *VOICED-CODA but possibly also INTER-V-VOICE, which, in spite of its low ranking in Dutch, may still exert its influence as an 'emergence of the unmarked':

(86)

Input: {bɛt ~ bɛd}	*Voiced Coda	Inter-V-Voice
a. ☞ bɛt ~ bɛd-ən		
b. bɛd ~ bɛt-ən	*!	*

Conceptually, this extension of the allomorph model is quite satisfactory, since it makes the distribution of allomorphs predictable by the same constraints which also check their shape. It remains to be seen, however, whether all types of allomorphy can be subsumed under it. Similar proposals for allomorph distribution governed by well-formedness constraints have been made by Mester (1994) and Kager (1996).

It is simply too early to evaluate the results of a theory that seeks to eliminate URs. However, some major points can be made even on the basis of the simple model outlined above. As usual, the model has pros and cons.

On the positive side, this model reduces the *abstractness* of lexical representation by eliminating the UR. This is a noteworthy result, since reduction of abstractness entails an increase in cognitive plausibility, reducing the role of the learner in inferring patterns that are remote from actual surface patterns. While it has been claimed in the 'classical' generative literature that such abstractness is 'just what it takes to shape an explanatory theory of alternations', any reduction of abstractness that leaves the generalizing power of the theory unaffected is very welcome. (Of course it has to be determined whether such a model indeed matches or even exceeds the explanatory power of UR theory, a point that we will return to below.)

The second point in favour of the allomorphic model is that it presents a *uniform* analysis of all types of alternations, productive and non-productive alike. The lexicon is the place where idiosyncratic properties of a language are listed, so nothing guarantees that every morpheme will indeed exhibit the full range of allomorphs as compared to other morphemes. For example, English is known to have exceptions to a process of trisyllabic laxing (*op*[eː]*que* ~ *op*[æ]*city*, but *ob*[iː]*se* ~ *ob*[iː]*sity*, Kiparsky 1982b). On an allomorphic model the difference between both morphemes is simply this: *opaque* has two allomorphs alternating in vowel length, while *obese* has only one, hence no length alternation. There are no high-ranked well-formedness constraints, nor OO-identity constraints pertaining to vowel length to enforce this allomorphy. Thus complete symmetry is not expected. Or to state it differently, the *grammar* allows space for lexical variation, but the *lexicon* allots this space in the form of allomorphy. The grammar partly controls allomorphy, but does not fully predict it. (Richness of the Base was never intended to fill all the accidental gaps in the lexicon of a language.)

These advantages are counterbalanced by a number of potential problems. First, it may not be wise to lump all kinds of alternations (productive and non-productive) into a single category, given the psycholinguistic evidence. Research in speech production gives evidence for a distinction between two kinds of alternations, which can be summarized as *on line production* versus *lexical look up*. The allomorphy model claims that alternations all depend on look up, even though the grammar defines the notion of possible allomorph (as we saw above). It is unclear how distinctions of productivity between alternations can be captured in this model.

Second, related to the previous point, it may be overly optimistic to assume that a general network of uniform exponence constraints may restrict all types of allomorphy in a language. For example, if the drastic shape variation in allomorphs such as *go ~ went* is indicative of the general position of OO-correspondence constraints for consonant and vowel identity in English, then it is no longer evident that OO-correspondence does any work at all. This poses a difficult dilemma: allomorphic variation must either be radically restricted by high-ranked uniform exponence (losing the *go ~ went* case), or left more or less free (predicting random allomorphic variation all over). A solution may be found in a stratified model, in which different parts of the lexicon set their own specific balance of faithfulness and uniform exponence. However, it is far from clear whether this is feasible.

9.7 Conclusion: future perspectives

At the end of the final chapter of this book, it is time to sketch some future perspectives of OT, partly based on developments sketched in the previous sections.

One development that can be foreseen is that an even greater role will be assigned to *surface forms* in explaining alternations, moving away from abstract underlying forms. This emphasis on surface forms has been a cornerstone of OT in dealing with phenomena as diverse as contrast, neutralization, allophone distribution, conspiracies, overapplication and underapplication (in reduplication and stem-based morphology), and transderivational 'cyclic' dependencies. Extrapolation of this development may lead to the elimination of underlying representations in favour of an 'allomorphic' model, as we have seen in section 9.6. Grammatically adequate and cognitively plausible allomorphic models may be developed which overcome the problems mentioned there. More on a speculative note, allomorphy may also offer an alternative account of opacity, a phenomenon for which current OT has no genuinely surface-based analysis.

A second major development that is likely to continue is a reduction of the role of representations in favour of constraint interaction. Underspecification, once a cornerstone of theories of segment inventories and assimilation, has come under severe pressure from OT analysts (starting with Smolensky 1993, and elaborated by Inkelas 1995, Itô, Mester, and Padgett 1995, and Steriade 1995b) who argue that constraint interactions offer superior accounts. Similar reductionist arguments were made against representational assumptions of feature geometry (Padgett 1995, Ní Chiosáin and Padgett 1997) and syllable structure (Steriade 1995b).

An issue closely related to that of representations concerns the boundary between phonology and phonetics. In work by Steriade, Flemming, Kirchner, Hayes, and others, it is argued that constraints should be able to refer to much more *phonetic detail* (including non-contrastive features and numerical values of acoustic parameters) than is allowed on classical generative assumptions, which maintain a strict separation between phonology and phonetics. (An illustration of this development is the title of Flemming's 1995 UCLA dissertation: 'Auditory representations in phonology'.) This blurring of the phonology–phonetics boundary goes hand in hand with an increased role for *functional* explanations. For example, Jun (1995) and Steriade (1995b), in the footsteps of phoneticians such as Lindblom, Kohler, and Ohala, argue that speakers make more effort to preserve features in contexts where they are most salient. The articulatory and perceptual basis of phonological constraints is emphasized by Archangeli and Pulleyblank (1994), Gafos (1996), Hayes (1996a), Myers (1997b), and others. No doubt, real progress can be made by this approach. An increased role for functional explanations in grammatical theory matches well with a major goal of OT, which is to *encode directly* markedness in the grammar, an enterprise that has been crucial to OT's typological achievements. The merging of the phonetic and phonological components into a single hierarchy of constraints comes tantalizingly close to a *single-step mapping*, another authentic goal of OT.

However, freely mixing phonology and phonetics comes at a certain cost. There is overwhelming support for a level coinciding with the output of phonology and the input to phonetic interpretation. First, while phonological specifications are categorical (that is 'on' or 'off'), phonetic specification of non-distinctive features is gradient and based on interpolation (Keating 1988, Cohn 1993a; see Kirchner 1997 for a theory of contrast in a one-step mapping model). Second, there is surprisingly little evidence that *grammatical* generalizations refer to non-distinctive feature specifications. Third, a relatively abstract (phonetically underspecified) output level of the phonology is confirmed as a cognitive reality by various kinds of independent evidence (language games, speech errors, second language acquisition, etc.: Fromkin 1971, Stemberger 1991). Apart from the evidence for levels, there is yet another potential stumbling block for a direct reductionist approach. A theory reducing phonology to interactions of raw functional (perceptual and articulatory) factors has difficulties in accounting for *symmetry* as a property of phonological systems, since such factors, by definition, interact in a gradient fashion. (But see Hayes 1996a for a theory of learning of symmetrical patterns on the basis of gradient information.) In sum, a theory which gives up the separation of phonology and phonetics holds much explanatory potential, but also faces two fundamental problems in dealing with cognitively plausible levels of representation.

When numerical values (of phonetic parameters) are incorporated into phonology, it seems only logical to take another step into numerical (gradient) types of interaction, so that constraints exert influence according to their relative strength, expressed in an index. In several constraint-based models (for example, *Harmonic Grammar*, Legendre, Miyata, and Smolensky 1990), numerical ranking indeed replaces the principle of strict domination, partly bridging the gap with *connectionism* (Rumelhart and McLelland 1986, Goldsmith and Larson 1990). It is not clear at all whether an OT model based on numerical ranking can preserve the advantages of standard OT. For example, the phenomenon of 'the emergence of the unmarked' depends on strict domination. For discussion see Prince and Smolensky (1993, chapter 10).

In sum, in the foreseeable future phonology may look quite different from what it is today. It has been suggested that there are some striking resemblances between OT and *Structuralism* (with respect to views of allophonic patterns and contrast, surface patterns, functional considerations, and allomorphy), the dominant framework in the pre-generative era. Is history circular? Perhaps, but if so, there are important differences from the earlier days. Due to the generative legacy, there remains a strong emphasis on formal precision in grammatical analysis, combined with the necessity to restrict the descriptive power of linguistic theory. Both theoretical priorities are solidly integrated into OT. Moreover, in-depth phonological analyses of many languages have given us a much better insight into cross-linguistic tendencies and typology than we had half a century ago. The emphasis on formal accuracy and explanatory adequacy, coupled to a still expanding typological basis, provides the background that is necessary to move successfully forward into areas that were previously considered to be 'too surface-oriented' for phonologists to deal with. The concept of grammar is strong enough to survive this continuing enterprise.

SUGGESTIONS FOR FURTHER READING

Opacity and OT

Archangeli, Diana and Keiichiro Suzuki (1997) The Yokuts challenge. In Roca. 197–226.

Idsardi, William J. (1997) Phonological derivations and historical changes in Hebrew spirantization. In Roca. 367–92.

McCarthy, John (1998) Sympathy and phonological opacity. Ms., University of Massachusetts, Amherst. [ROA-252, http://ruccs.rutgers.edu/roa.html]

Orgun, C. Orhan (1995) Correspondence and identity constraints in two-level Optimality Theory. In J. Camacho, L. Choueiri, and M. Watanabe (eds.), *Proceedings of the Fourteenth West Coast Conference on Formal Linguistics.* Stanford: CSLI. 399–413.

Local Conjunction

Alderete, John (1997) Dissimilation as Local Conjunction. In K. Kusumoto (ed.) *Proceedings of the North East Linguistic Society* **27**. 17–31. [ROA-175, http://ruccs.rutgers.edu/roa.html]

Kirchner, Robert (1996) Synchronic chain shifts in Optimality Theory. *Linguistic Inquiry* **27**. 341–50.

Absolute ungrammaticality

Orgun, C. Orhan and Ronald Sprouse (1997) From M-Parse to Control: deriving ungrammaticality. Ms., University of California, Berkeley. [ROA-224, http://ruccs.rutgers.edu/roa.html]

Raffelsiefen, Renate (1996) Gaps in word formation. In U. Kleinhenz (ed.), *Interfaces in phonology.* Studia Grammatica 41. Berlin: Akademie Verlag. 194–209.

Free variation

Anttila, Arto (1995) Deriving variation from grammar: a study of Finnish genitives. Ms., Stanford University. [ROA-63, http://ruccs.rutgers.edu/roa.html]

Kager, René (1997b) Generalized alignment and morphological parsing. *Rivista di Linguistica* **9**. 245–82.

Positional faithfulness

Beckman, Jill (1997a) Positional faithfulness, positional neutralization and Shona vowel harmony. *Phonology* **14**. 1–46.

Lombardi, Linda (1995b) Why Place and Voice are different: constraint interactions and feature faithfulness in Optimality Theory. Ms., University of Maryland, College Park. [ROA-105, http://ruccs.rutgers.edu/roa.html]

Allomorphy

Burzio, Luigi (forthcoming) Cycles, regularization, and correspondence. To appear in J. Dekkers, F. van der Leeuw, and J. van de Weijer (eds.), *Optimality Theory: syntax, phonology, and acquisition.* Oxford University Press.

Hayes, Bruce (forthcoming) Anticorrespondence in Yidiɲ. To appear in B. Hermans and M. van Oostendorp (eds.), *The derivational residue in phonology.* Amsterdam: John Benjamins.

Kager, René (1996) On affix allomorphy and syllable counting. In U. Kleinhenz (ed.), *Interfaces in phonology.* Studia Grammatica 41. Berlin: Akademie Verlag. 155–71.

Functional approaches to phonology

Hayes, Bruce (1996a) Phonetically driven phonology: the role of Optimality Theory and inductive grounding. Ms., University of California, Los Angeles. [ROA-158, http://ruccs.rutgers.edu/roa.html]

Kirchner, Robert (1997) Contrastiveness and faithfulness. *Phonology* **14**. 83–111.

Myers, Scott (1997b) Expressing phonetic naturalness in phonology. In Roca. 125-12.

REFERENCES

Abu-Salim, Issam M. (1980) Epenthesis and geminate consonants in Palestinian Arabic. *Studies in the Linguistic Sciences* **10**. 1–11.

Ackema, Peter and Ad Neeleman (1998) Optimal questions. *Natural Language and Linguistic Theory* **16**. 443–90.

Alber, Birgit (1997) Quantity sensitivity as the result of constraint interaction. In G. E. Booij and J. van de Weijer (eds.), *Phonology in progress: progress in phonology.* HIL phonology papers III. The Hague: Holland Academic Graphics, 1–45.

Alderete, John (1995) Faithfulness to prosodic heads. Ms., University of Massachusetts, Amherst. [ROA-94, http://ruccs.rutgers.edu/roa.html]

(1997) Dissimilation as local conjunction. In K. Kusumoto (ed.), *Proceedings of the North East Linguistic Society* **27**. 17–31.

Alderete, John, Jill Beckman, Laura Benua, Amalia Gnanadesikan, John McCarthy, and Suzanne Urbanczyk (1997) Reduplication with fixed segmentism. Ms., University of Massachusetts, Amherst. [ROA-226, http://ruccs.rutgers.edu/roa.html]

Allison, E. (1979) The phonology of Sibutu Sama: a language of the Southern Philippines. In C. Edrial-Luzares and A. Hale (eds.), *Studies in Philippine Languages* **3:2**. Linguistic Society of the Philippines and Summer Institute of Linguistics.

Anderson, Stephen R. (1974) *The organization of phonology.* New York: Academic Press.

(1975) On the interaction of phonological rules of various types. *Journal of Linguistics* **11**. 39–62.

(1982) Differences in rule type and their structural basis, in H. van der Hulst and N. Smith (eds.), *The structure of phonological representations*, part 2. Dordrecht: Foris. 1–26.

(1985) *Phonology in the twentieth century: theories of rules and theories of representations.* University of Chicago Press.

Anttila, Arto (1995) Deriving variation from grammar: a study of Finnish genitives. Ms., Stanford University. [ROA-63, http://ruccs.rutgers.edu/roa.html]

Archangeli, Diana (1988) Aspects of underspecification theory. *Phonology* **5**. 183–207.

(1997) Optimality Theory: an introduction to linguistics in the 1990s. In D. Archangeli and D. T. Langendoen (eds.), *Optimality Theory: an overview.* Oxford: Blackwell. 1–32.

References

Archangeli, Diana and Douglas Pulleyblank (1994) *Grounded phonology.* Cambridge, Mass.: MIT Press.

Archangeli, Diana and Keiichiro Suzuki (1997) The Yokuts challenge. In Roca. 197–226.

Árnason, Kristján (1980) *Quantity in historical phonology: Icelandic and related cases.* Cambridge University Press.

Aronoff, Mark (1976) *Word formation in generative grammar.* Cambridge, Mass.: MIT Press.

Aronoff, Mark, Azhar Arsyad, Hassan Basri, and Ellen Broselow (1987) Tier conflation in Makassarese reduplication. In A. Bosch, B. Need, and E. Schiller (eds.), *Papers from the Chicago Linguistic Society* **23:2**. 1–15.

Austin, Peter (1981) *A grammar of Diyari, South Australia.* Cambridge University Press.

Bat-El, Outi (1996) Selecting the best of the worst: the grammar of Hebrew blends. *Phonology* **13**. 283–328.

Beckman, Jill (1997a) Positional faithfulness, positional neutralisation and Shona vowel harmony. *Phonology* **14**. 1–46.

(1997b) *Positional faithfulness.* PhD dissertation, University of Massachusetts, Amherst. [ROA-234, http://ruccs.rutgers.edu/roa.html]

Beckman, Jill, Laura Walsh Dickey, and Suzanne Urbanczyk (eds.) (1995) *Papers in Optimality Theory.* University of Massachusetts Occasional Papers in Linguistics 18. Amherst, Mass.: Graduate Linguistic Student Association.

Benton, Richard (1971) *Pangasinan reference grammar.* Honolulu: University of Hawaii Press.

Benua, Laura (1995) Identity effects in morphological truncation. In Beckman, Walsh Dickey, and Urbanczyk. 77–136.

(1997) *Transderivational identity: phonological relations between words.* PhD dissertation, University of Massachusetts, Amherst. [ROA-259, http://ruccs.rutgers.edu/roa.html]

Bird, Steven (1990) *Constraint-based phonology.* PhD dissertation, University of Edinburgh.

Blevins, Juliette (1995) The syllable in phonological theory. In Goldsmith. 206–44.

(1996) Mokilese reduplication. *Linguistic Inquiry* **27**. 523–30.

(1997) Rules in Optimality Theory: two case studies. In Roca. 227–60.

Boersma, Paul (1997) How we learn variation, optionality, and probability. Ms., University of Amsterdam. [ROA-221, http://ruccs.rutgers.edu/roa.html]

Booij, Geert E. (1986) Icelandic vowel lengthening and prosodic phonology. In F. Beukema and A. Hulk (eds.), *Linguistics in the Netherlands 1986.* Dordrecht: Foris. 9–18.

Booij, Geert E. and Jerzy Rubach (1987) Postcyclic versus postlexical rules in lexical phonology. *Linguistic Inquiry* **18**. 1–44.

Borgstrøm, C. Hj. (1937) The dialect of Barra in the Outer Hebrides. *Norsk Tidsskrift for Sprogvidenskap* **8**. 71–242.

Borowsky, Toni (1993) On the word level. In S. Hargus and E. Kaisse (eds.), *Studies in Lexical Phonology.* San Diego: Academic Press. 199–234.

426

Borowsky, Toni and Mark Harvey (1997) Vowel length in Warray and weight identity. *Phonology* **14**. 161–75.

Boxwell, Helen and Maurice Boxwell (1966) Weri phonemes. In S. A. Wurm (ed.), *Papers in New Guinea linguistics*, V. Linguistic Circle of Canberra Publications, Series A, No. 7. Canberra: Australian National University. 77–93.

Brame, Michael (1974) The cycle in phonology: stress in Palestinian, Maltese, and Spanish. *Linguistic Inquiry* **5**. 39–60.

Bresnan, Joan (forthcoming) Optimal syntax. To appear in J. Dekkers, F. van der Leeuw, and J. van de Weijer (eds.), *Optimality Theory: phonology, syntax, and acquisition*. Oxford University Press.

Broekhuis, Hans (forthcoming) Against feature strength. To appear in R. van Bezooijen and R. Kager (eds.), *Linguistics in the Netherlands 1998*. Amsterdam: John Benjamins.

Broihier, Kevin (1995) Optimality theoretic rankings with tied constraints: Slavic relatives, resumptive pronouns and learnability. Ms., Department of Brain and Cognitive Sciences, MIT. [ROA-46, http://ruccs.rutgers.edu/roa.html]

Bromberger, Sylvain and Morris Halle (1989) Why phonology is different. *Linguistic Inquiry* **20**. 51–70.

Broselow, Ellen (1992) Parametric variation in Arabic dialect phonology. In E. Broselow, M. Eid, and J. McCarthy (eds.), *Perspectives on Arabic linguistics* IV: *Papers from the fourth annual symposium on Arabic linguistics*. Amsterdam and Philadelphia: John Benjamins. 7–45.

(1995) Skeletal positions and moras. In Goldsmith. 175–205.

Broselow, Ellen, Su-I Chen, and Marie Huffman (1997) Syllable weight: convergence of phonology and phonetics. *Phonology* **14**. 47–82.

Broselow, Ellen and John McCarthy (1983) A theory of internal reduplication. *The Linguistic Review* **3**. 25–89.

Buckley, Eugene (1995) Cyclicity and correspondence. Handout of paper presented at the Tilburg conference 'The derivational residue in phonology', Fall 1995. [ROA-93c, http://ruccs.rutgers.edu/roa.html]

Burzio, Luigi (1994) *Principles of English stress*. Cambridge University Press.

(1995) The rise of Optimality Theory. *Glot International* **1:6**. 3–7.

(1996) Surface constraints versus Underlying Representation. In J. Durand and B. Laks (eds.), *Current trends in phonology: models and methods*. CNRS, Paris X, and University of Salford. University of Salford Publications. 97–122.

(forthcoming) Cycles, regularization, and correspondence. To appear in J. Dekkers, F. van der Leeuw, and J. van de Weijer (eds.), *Optimality Theory: syntax, phonology, and acquisition*. Oxford University Press.

Bybee, Joan L. (1988) Morphology as lexical organization. In M. Hammond and M. Noonan (eds.), *Theoretical morphology*. San Diego: Academic Press. 119–41.

(1995) Regular morphology and the lexicon. *Language and Cognitive Processes* **10**. 425–55.

References

Bye, Patrik (1996) Correspondence in the prosodic hierarchy and the grid: case studies in overlength and level stress. Cand. Philol. thesis, University of Tromsø.

Chomsky, Noam (1957) *Syntactic structures*. The Hague: Mouton.

(1965) *Aspects of the theory of syntax*. Cambridge, Mass.: MIT Press.

(1981a) Markedness and core grammar. In A. Belletti, L. Brandi, and L. Rizzi (eds.), *Theory of markedness in generative grammar. Proceedings of the 1979 GLOW conference*. Pisa: Scuola Normale Superiore di Pisa. 123–46.

(1981b) *Lectures on government and binding*. Dordrecht: Foris.

(1991) Some notes on economy of derivation and representation. In R. Freidin (ed.), *Principles and parameters in comparative grammar*. Cambridge, Mass.: MIT Press. 41–58.

(1993) A minimalist program for linguistic theory. In K. Hale and S. J. Keyser (eds.), *The view from Building 20*. Cambridge, Mass.: MIT Press. 41–58.

(1995) *The minimalist program*. Cambridge, Mass.: MIT Press.

Chomsky, Noam and Morris Halle (1968) *The sound pattern of English*. New York: Harper and Row.

Churchward, C. Maxwell (1953) *Tongan grammar*. Oxford University Press.

Clements, George N. (1985a) The problem of transfer in nonlinear morphology. *Cornell Working Papers in Linguistics* **7**. 38–73.

(1985b) The geometry of phonological features. In C. Ewen and E. Kaisse (eds.), *Phonology Yearbook* **2**. Cambridge University Press. 225–52.

(1986) Syllabification and epenthesis in the Barra dialect of Gaelic. In K. Bogers, M. Maus, and H. van der Hulst (eds.), *The phonological representation of suprasegmentals*. Dordrecht: Foris. 317–36.

(1990) The role of the sonority cycle in core syllabification. In J. Kingston and M. Beckman (eds.), *Papers in laboratory phonology* I: *Between the grammar and physics of speech*. Cambridge University Press. 283–333.

Clements, George N. and Samuel J. Keyser (1983) *CV phonology: a generative theory of the syllable*. Cambridge, Mass.: MIT Press.

Cohn, Abigail (1989) Stress in Indonesian and bracketing paradoxes. *Natural Language and Linguistic Theory* **7**. 167–216.

(1993a) Nasalisation in English. *Phonology* **10**. 43–81.

(1993b) The status of nasalized continuants. In Huffman and Krakow. 329–68.

Cohn, Abigail and John McCarthy (1994) *Alignment and parallelism in Indonesian phonology*. Ms., Cornell University, Ithaca, N. Y. and University of Massachusetts, Amherst. [ROA-25, http://ruccs.rutgers.edu/roa.html]

Cole, Jennifer and Charles Kisseberth (1995) Restricting multi-level constraint evaluation: opaque rule interactions in Yawelmani vowel harmony. Ms., University of Illinois, Urbana-Champaign. [ROA-98, http://ruccs.rutgers.edu/roa.html]

Colina, Sonia (1996) Spanish truncation processes: the emergence of the unmarked. *Linguistics* **34**. 1199–218.

Crowhurst, Megan and Mark Hewitt (1995) Prosodic overlay and headless feet in Yidiɲ, *Phonology* **12**. 39–84.

(1997) Boolean operations and constraint interaction in Optimality Theory. Ms.,
University of North Carolina, Chapel Hill and Brandeis University. [ROA-229,
http://ruccs.rutgers.edu/roa.html]

Daelemans, Walter, Steven Gillis, and Gert Durieux (1994) The acquisition of stress: a
data-oriented approach. *Computational Linguistics* **20**. 421–51.

Davis, Stuart (1995) Emphasis spread in Arabic and grounded phonology. *Linguistic
Inquiry* **26**. 465–98.

Demuth, Katharine (1995) Markedness and the development of phonological structure.
In J. Beckman (ed.), *Proceedings of the North East Linguistic Society* **25:2**.
13–25.

Derbyshire, Desmond C. (1979) *Hixkaryana*. Lingua Descriptive Studies 1. Amsterdam:
North-Holland.

Dixon, R. M. W. (1977) *A grammar of Yidiɲ*. Cambridge University Press.

(1981) Wargamay. In R. M. W. Dixon and B. J. Blake (eds.), *Handbook of Australian
languages*, II. Amsterdam: John Benjamins. 1–144.

(1988) *A grammar of Boumaa Fijian*. University of Chicago Press.

Downing, Laura J. (forthcoming) Verbal reduplication in three Bantu languages. To appear
in Kager, van der Hulst, and Zonneveld.

Drachman, Gaberell and Angeliki Malikouti-Drachman (1973) Studies in the acquisition
of Greek as a native language, I: Some preliminary findings on phonology. *Ohio State
Working Papers in Linguistics* **15**. 99–114.

Dresher, Elan and Jonathan Kaye (1990) A computational learning model for metrical
phonology. *Cognition* **34**. 137–95.

Dresher, Elan and Aditi Lahiri (1991) The Germanic foot: metrical coherence in Old
English. *Linguistic Inquiry* **22**. 251–86.

Dudas, Karen (1976) *The phonology and morphology of Modern Javanese*. PhD
dissertation, University of Illinois, Urbana-Champaign.

Dunlop, Elaine (1987) English [æ] tensing in Lexical Phonology. Ms., University of
Massachusetts, Amherst.

Eisner, Jason (1997) Efficient generation in primitive Optimality Theory. *Proceedings of
the 35th Annual Meeting of the Association for Computational Linguistics*. [ROA-206,
http://ruccs.rutgers.edu/roa.html]

Elenbaas, Nine (1996) Ternary rhythm in Sentani. In C. Cremers and M. den Dikken (eds.),
Linguistics in the Netherlands 1996. Amsterdam: John Benjamins. 61–72.

(1999) A unified account of binary and ternary stress: considerations from Sentani and
Finnish. PhD dissertation, Utrecht University.

Ellison, Mark T. (1994) Phonological derivation in Optimality Theory. *Proceedings of the
15th International Conference on Computational Linguistics*, II. Kyoto, Japan. 1007–
13. [ROA-75, http://ruccs.rutgers.edu/roa.html]

Ferguson, Charles (1975) 'Short a' in Philadelphia English. In M. E. Smith (ed.), *Studies
in linguistics: in honor of George L. Trager*. The Hague: Mouton. 250–74.

Flemming, Edward (1995) *Auditory representations in phonology*. PhD dissertation,
University of California, Los Angeles.

References

Frank, Robert and Giorgio Satta (1998) Optimality Theory and the generative complexity of constraint violability. *Computational Linguistics* **24**. 307–15. [ROA-228, http://ruccs.rutgers.edu/roa.html]

French, Koleen M. (1988) *Insights into Tagalog: reduplication, infixation, and stress from nonlinear phonology*. Dallas: Summer Institute of Linguistics and University of Texas at Arlington.

Fromkin, Victoria (1971) The non-anomalous nature of anomalous utterances. *Language* **47**. 27–52.

Furby, Christine (1974) *Garawa phonology*. Canberra: Australian National University.

Gafos, Adamantios (1996) *The articulatory basis of locality in phonology*. PhD dissertation, Johns Hopkins University.

Gnanadesikan, Amalia (1995) Markedness and faithfulness constraints in child phonology. Ms., University of Massachusetts, Amherst. [ROA-67, http://ruccs.rutgers.edu/roa.html]

Goad, Heather (1997) Consonant harmony in child language. In S. J. Hannahs and M. Young-Scholten (eds.), *Focus on phonological acquisition*. Amsterdam: John Benjamins. 113–42.

Goldsmith, John (1976) Autosegmental phonology. PhD dissertation, MIT. [Published 1979, New York: Garland.]

(1990) *Autosegmental and metrical phonology*. Oxford: Blackwell.

(1993a) Harmonic phonology. In Goldsmith (1993b). 21–60.

(ed.) (1993b) *The last phonological rule: reflections on constraints and derivations*. University of Chicago Press.

(ed.) (1995) *The handbook of phonological theory*. Oxford: Blackwell.

Goldsmith, John and Gary Larson (1990) Local modeling and syllabification. In M. Ziolkowski, M. Noske, and K. Deaton (eds.), *Papers from the Chicago Linguistic Society* **26:2**. 129–41.

Golston, Chris (1995) Syntax outranks phonology: evidence from ancient Greek. *Phonology* **12**. 343–68.

(1996) Direct Optimality Theory: representation as pure markedness. *Language* **72**. 713–48.

Greenberg, Joseph (1978) Some generalizations concerning initial and final consonant clusters. In J. Greenberg (ed.), *Universals of human language*, II: *Phonology*. Stanford University Press. 243–80.

Grimshaw, Jane (1991) Extended projection. Ms., Brandeis University, Waltham, Mass. (1997) Projection, heads, and optimality. *Linguistic Inquiry* **28**. 373–422.

Gupta, Prahlad and David Touretzky (1994) Connectionist models and linguistic theory: investigations of stress systems in language. *Cognitive Science* **18**. 1–50.

Haas, Mary (1940) *Tunica*. Handbook of American Indian languages, IV. Washington, D.C.: Smithsonian Institute, Bureau of American Ethnography.

Haas, Wim de (1988) *A formal theory of vowel coalescence: a case study of Ancient Greek*. PhD dissertation, University of Nijmegen. Dordrecht: Foris.

Hale, Mark and Charles Reiss (1997) Grammar optimization: the simultaneous acquisition of constraint ranking and a lexicon. Ms., Concordia University, Montreal. [ROA-231, http://ruccs.rutgers.edu/roa.html]

Halle, Morris and George N. Clements (1983) *Problem book in phonology*. Cambridge, Mass.: MIT Press.

Halle, Morris and Jean-Roger Vergnaud (1987) *An essay on stress*. Cambridge, Mass.: MIT Press.

Hammond, Michael (1984) Constraining metrical theory: a modular theory of rhythm and destressing. PhD dissertation, University of California, Los Angeles. [Published 1988, New York: Garland.]

(1994) An OT account of variability in Walmatjarri stress. Ms., University of Arizona. [ROA-20, http://ruccs.rutgers.edu/roa.html]

(1997) Parsing syllables: modeling OT computationally. Ms., University of Arizona. [ROA-222, http://ruccs.rutgers.edu/roa.html]

Hansen, K. C. and L. E. Hansen (1969) Pintupi phonology. *Oceanic Linguistics* **8**. 153–70.

Harris, James (1983) *Syllable structure and stress in Spanish: a nonlinear analysis*. Cambridge, Mass.: MIT Press.

Harris, John (1990) Derived phonological contrasts. In S. Ramsaran (ed.), *Studies in the pronunciation of English: a commemorative volume in honour of A. C. Gimson*. London: Routledge. 87–105.

Hawkins, John and Anne Cutler (1988) Psycholinguistic factors in morphological asymmetry. In J. Hawkins (ed.), *Explaining language universals*. Oxford: Blackwell. 280–317.

Hayes, Bruce (1980) A metrical theory of stress rules. PhD dissertation, MIT. [Published 1985, New York: Garland.]

(1985) Iambic and trochaic rhythm in stress rules. In M. Niepokuj, M. VanClay, V. Nikiforidou, and D. Jeder (eds.), *Proceedings of the Berkeley Linguistics Society* **11**. 429–46.

(1986) Inalterability in CV phonology. *Language* **62**. 321–51.

(1987) A revised parametric metrical theory. In J. McDonough and B. Plunket (eds.), *Proceedings of the North East Linguistic Society* **17**. 274–89.

(1989) Compensatory lengthening in moraic phonology. *Linguistic Inquiry* **20**. 253–306.

(1995) *Metrical stress theory: principles and case studies*. University of Chicago Press.

(1996a) Phonetically driven phonology: the role of Optimality Theory and inductive grounding. Ms., University of California, Los Angeles. [ROA-158, http://ruccs.rutgers.edu/roa.html]

(1996b) Constraint ranking software. Ms., University of California, Los Angeles. [Manual of computer program ranking OT constraints, on line available from http://www.humnet.ucla.edu/humnet/linguistics/people/hayes/otsoft/otsoft.htm]

(forthcoming) Anticorrespondence in Yidiɲ. To appear in B. Hermans and M. van Oostendorp (eds.), *The derivational residue in phonology*. Amsterdam: John Benjamins.

References

Hayes, Bruce and May Abad (1989) Reduplication and syllabification in Ilokano. *Lingua* **77**. 331–74.

Hayes, Bruce and Tanya Stivers (1995) A phonetic account of postnasal voicing. Ms., University of California, Los Angeles.

Healey, Phyllis M. (1960) *An Agta grammar*. Manila: Summer Institute of Linguistics.

Hjelmslev, Louis (1935) La Catégorie des Cas I. *Acta Jutlandica* **7:1**. Aarhus. [Reissued 1972, Copenhagen and Munich.]

Hooper [Bybee], Joan L. (1976) *An introduction to Natural Generative Phonology*. New York: Academic Press.

Hore, Michael (1981) Syllable length and stress in Nunggubuyu. In B. Waters (ed.), *Australian phonologies: collected papers*. Work Papers of SIL-AAB, A5. Darwin: Summer Institute of Linguistics.

Huffman, Marie K. (1993) Phonetic patterns of nasalization and implications for feature specification. In Huffman and Krakow. 303–27.

Huffman, Marie K. and Rena A. Krakow (eds.) (1993) *Phonetics and phonology* V: *Nasals, nasalization, and the velum*. San Diego: Academic Press.

Hulst, Harry van der (1984) *Syllable structure and stress in Dutch*. Dordrecht: Foris.

Hulst, Harry van der and Ellis Visch (1992) Iambic lengthening in Carib. In R. Bok-Bennema and R. van Hout (eds.), *Linguistics in the Netherlands 1992*. Amsterdam: John Benjamins. 113–24.

Hume, Elizabeth (1992) Front vowels, coronal consonants and their interaction in nonlinear phonology. PhD dissertation, Cornell University, Ithaca, N.Y.

(1995) Beyond linear order: prosodic constraints and C/V metathesis. *Proceedings of the Formal Linguistics Society of the Midwest* **6**. Bloomington: Indiana University Linguistics Club.

Hung, Henrietta (1994) *The rhythmic and prosodic organization of edge constituents*. PhD dissertation, Brandeis University, Waltham, Mass. [ROA-24, http://ruccs.rutgers.edu/roa.html]

Hyams, Nina (1986) *Language acquisition and the theory of parameters*. Dordrecht: Reidel.

Hyman, Larry (1985) *A theory of phonological weight*. Dordrecht: Foris.

Idsardi, William J. (1997) Phonological derivations and historical changes in Hebrew spirantization. In Roca. 367–92.

Inkelas, Sharon (1989) *Prosodic constituency in the lexicon*. PhD dissertation, Stanford University.

(1995) The consequences of optimization for underspecification. In J. Beckman (ed.), *Proceedings of the North East Linguistic Society* **25**. 287–302.

(1996) Dominant affixes and the phonology–morphology interface. In U. Kleinhenz (ed.), *Interfaces in phonology*. Studia Grammatica 41. Berlin: Akademie Verlag. 128–54.

(forthcoming) Exceptional stress-attracting suffixes in Turkish: representations vs. the grammar. To appear in Kager, Van der Hulst, and Zonneveld. [ROA-39, http://ruccs.rutgers.edu/roa.html]

432

Inkelas, Sharon and C. Orhan Orgun (1995) Level ordering and economy in the lexical phonology of Turkish. *Language* **71**. 763–93.

Inkelas, Sharon, C. Orhan Orgun, and Cheryl Zoll (1997) The implications of lexical exceptions for the nature of grammar. In Roca. 393–418.

Itô, Junko (1986) Syllable theory in prosodic phonology. PhD dissertation, University of Massachusetts, Amherst. [Published 1988, New York: Garland.]

(1989) A prosodic theory of epenthesis. *Natural Language and Linguistic Theory* **7**. 217–60.

(1990) Prosodic minimality in Japanese. In M. Ziolkowski, M. Noske, and K. Deaton (eds.), *Papers from Chicago Linguistic Society* **26:2**. 213–39.

Itô, Junko, Yoshihisa Kitagawa, and R. Armin Mester (1996) Prosodic faithfulness and correspondence: evidence from a Japanese argot. *Journal of East Asian Linguistics* **5**. 217–94.

Itô, Junko and R. Armin Mester (1992) Weak layering and word binarity. Ms., University of California, Santa Cruz. Linguistics Research Center Report No. 92–09.

(1995) The core-periphery structure of the lexicon and constraints on reranking. In Beckman, Walsh Dickey, and Urbanczyk. 181–210.

(1997) Correspondence and compositionality: the *Ga–gyo* variation in Japanese phonology. In Roca. 419–62.

(1998) Markedness and word structure: OCP effects in Japanese. Ms., University of California, Santa Cruz. [ROA-255, http://ruccs.rutgers.edu/roa.html]

(forthcoming) Realignment. To appear in Kager, Van der Hulst, and Zonneveld.

Itô, Junko, R. Armin Mester, and Jaye Padgett (1995) Licensing and underspecification in Optimality Theory. *Linguistic Inquiry* **26**. 571–614.

Jacobsen, William (1964) A grammar of the Washo language. PhD dissertation, University of California, Berkeley.

Jakobson, Roman (1941) *Kindersprache, Aphasie und allgemeine Lautgesetze*. Uppsala. [Reissued in Jakobson 1962. 328–401.]

(1962) *Selected writings*. The Hague: Mouton.

Jun, Jongho (1995) Perceptual and articulatory factors in place assimilation: an Optimality Theoretic approach. PhD dissertation, University of California, Los Angeles.

Kager, René (1989) *A metrical theory of stress and destressing in English and Dutch*. Dordrecht: Foris.

(1992a) Shapes of the generalized trochee. In J. Mead (ed.), *Proceedings of the West Coast Conference on Formal Linguistics* **11**. 298–311.

(1992b) Are there any truly quantity-insensitive systems? In L. A. Buszard-Welcher, L. Lee, and W. Weigel (eds.), *Proceedings of the Berkeley Linguistics Society* **18**. 123–32.

(1993) Alternatives to the iambic-trochaic law. *Natural Language and Linguistic Theory* **11**. 381–432.

(1994) Ternary rhythm in alignment theory. Ms., Utrecht University. [ROA-35, http://ruccs.rutgers.edu/roa.html]

(1995) Review of Hayes 1995. *Phonology* **12**. 437–64.

References

(1996) On affix allomorphy and syllable counting. In U. Kleinhenz (ed.), *Interfaces in phonology*. Studia Grammatica 41. Berlin: Akademie Verlag. 155–71. [ROA-88, http://ruccs.rutgers.edu/roa.html]

(1997a) Rhythmic vowel deletion in Optimality Theory. In Roca. 463–99.

(1997b) Generalized Alignment and morphological parsing. *Rivista di Linguistica* **9**. 245–82.

(forthcoming) Surface opacity of metrical structure in Optimality Theory. To appear in B. Hermans and M. van Oostendorp (eds.), *The derivational residue in phonology*. Amsterdam: John Benjamins. [ROA-207, http://ruccs.rutgers.edu/roa.html]

Kager, René, Harry van der Hulst, and Wim Zonneveld (eds.) (forthcoming) *The prosody–morphology interface*. Cambridge University Press.

Kahn, Daniel (1976) Syllable-based generalizations in English phonology. PhD dissertation, MIT. [Published 1980, New York: Garland.]

Karttunen, Lauri (1993) Finite-state constraints. In Goldsmith. 173–94.

(1998) The proper treatment of optimality in computational phonology. Ms., Xerox Research Centre Europe, Meylan, France. [ROA-258, http://ruccs.rutgers.edu/roa.html]

Kaye, Jonathan (1974) Opacity and recoverability in phonology. *Canadian Journal of Linguistics* **19**. 134–49.

(1990) *Phonology: a cognitive view*. Hillsdale, N.J.: LEA.

Kaye, Jonathan and Jean Lowenstamm (1981) Syllable structure and markedness theory. In A. Belletti, L. Brandi, and L. Rizzi (eds.), *Theory of markedness in generative grammar: proceedings of the 1979 GLOW conference*. Pisa: Scuola Normale Superiore di Pisa. 287–315.

Kaye, Jonathan, Jean Lowenstamm, and Jean-Roger Vergnaud (1990) Constituent structure and government in phonology. *Phonology* **7**. 193–231.

Kean, Mary-Louise (1975) The theory of markedness in generative grammar. PhD dissertation, MIT.

(1981) On a theory of markedness: some general considerations and a case in point. In A. Belletti, L. Brandi, and L. Rizzi (eds.), *Theory of markedness in generative grammar: proceedings of the 1979 GLOW conference*. Pisa: Scuola Normale Superiore di Pisa. 559–604.

Keating, Patricia (1988) Underspecification in phonetics. *Phonology* **5**. 275–97.

Keer, Edward and Eric Baković (1997) Have FAITH in syntax. *Proceedings of the West Coast Conference on Formal Linguistics* **16**. [ROA-200, http://ruccs.rutgers.edu/roa.html]

Kenstowicz, Michael (1981) Functional explanations in generative phonology. In D. L. Goyvaerts (ed.), *Phonology in the 1980's*. Ghent: E. Story-Scientia. 431–43.

(1994a) *Phonology in generative grammar*. Oxford: Blackwell.

(1994b) Syllabification in Chukchee: a constraints-based analysis. In A. Davison, N. Maier, G. Silva, and W. S. Yan (eds.), *Proceedings of the Formal Linguistics Society of the Midwest* **4**. Iowa City: Department of Linguistics, University of Iowa. 160–81.

(1995) Cyclic vs. non-cyclic constraint evaluation. *Phonology* **12**. 397–436.

(1996) Base-identity and uniform exponence: alternatives to cyclicity. In J. Durand and B. Laks (eds.), *Current trends in phonology: models and methods*. CNRS, Paris X, and University of Salford. University of Salford Publications. 363–93. [ROA-103, http://ruccs.rutgers.edu/roa.html]

Kenstowicz, Michael and Kamal Abdul-Karim (1980) Cyclic stress in Levantine Arabic. *Studies in the Linguistic Sciences* **10**. 55–76.

Kenstowicz, Michael and Charles Kisseberth (1977) *Topics in phonological theory*. New York: Academic Press.

(1979) *Generative phonology: description and theory*. New York: Academic Press.

Kiparsky, Paul (1973) Abstractness, opacity, and global rules. In O. Fujimura (ed.), *Three dimensions of linguistic theory*. Tokyo: Taikusha. 57–86.

(1982a) Analogical change as a problem for linguistic theory. In P. Kiparsky, *Explanation in phonology*. Dordrecht: Foris. 217–36.

(1982b) From cyclic phonology to Lexical Phonology. In H. van der Hulst and N. Smith (eds.), *The structure of phonological representations*, part 2. Dordrecht: Foris. 131–76.

(1984) On the lexical phonology of Icelandic. In C. C. Elert, I. Johansson, and E. Strangert (eds.), *Nordic prosody* III: *Papers from a symposium*. Stockholm: Almqvist and Wiksell. 135–64.

(1985) Some consequences of Lexical Phonology. In C. Ewen and E. Kaisse (eds.), *Phonology Yearbook* **2**. Cambridge University Press. 85–138.

(1986) The phonology of reduplication. Ms., Stanford University.

(1993a) Blocking in nonderived environments. In S. Hargus and E. Kaisse (eds.), *Phonetics and phonology*, IV: *Studies in Lexical Phonology*. San Diego: Academic Press. 277–313.

(1993b) Variable rules. Handout of presentation at the Rutgers Optimality Workshop (ROW1).

(1994) Remarks on markedness. Paper presented at TREND 2.

Kirchner, Robert (1991) Phonological processes without phonological rules: Yidiɲ apocope and penultimate lengthening. In T. Sherer (ed.), *Proceedings of the North East Linguistic Society* **21**. 203–16.

(1995) Contrastiveness is an epiphenomenon of constraint ranking. *Proceedings of the Berkeley Linguistics Society* **21**. 198–208.

(1996) Synchronic chain shifts in Optimality Theory. *Linguistic Inquiry* **27**. 341–50.

(1997) Contrastiveness and faithfulness. *Phonology* **14**. 83–111.

Kisseberth, Charles (1969) On the abstractness of phonology: the evidence from Yawelmani. *Papers in Linguistics* **1**. 248–82.

(1970) On the functional unity of phonological rules. *Linguistic Inquiry* **1**. 291–306.

(1973) Is rule ordering necessary in phonology? In B. Kachru (ed.), *Issues in linguistics: papers in honor of Henry and Renée Kahane*. Urbana: University of Illinois Press. 418–41.

Klein, Thomas B. (1997) Output constraints and prosodic correspondence in Chamorro reduplication. *Linguistic Inquiry* **28**. 707–15.

References

Koskenniemi, Kimmo (1983) *Two-level morphology: a general computational model for word-form recognition and production.* Publication 11, Department of General Linguistics, University of Helsinki.

Kuryłowicz, Jerzy (1949) La nature des procès dits 'analogiques'. *Acta Linguistica* **5**, 15–37. Reprinted in E. Hamp, F. Householder, and R. Austerlitz (eds.) (1966), *Readings in linguistics II.* University of Chicago Press.

Ladefoged, Peter and Ian Maddieson (1996) *The sounds of the world's languages.* Oxford: Blackwell.

Lakoff, George (1993) Cognitive phonology. In Goldsmith. 173–94.

Lamontagne, Greg and Keren Rice (1995) A correspondence account of coalescence. In Beckman, Walsh Dickey, and Urbanczyk. 211–23.

Lapoliwa, Hans (1981) *A generative approach to the phonology of Bahasa Indonesia.* Canberra: Pacific Linguistics D 34.

Law, Howard (1958) Morphological structure of Isthmus Nahuat. *International Journal of American Languages* **24**. 108–29.

Leben, William (1973) Suprasegmental phonology. PhD dissertation, MIT.

Legendre, Géraldine, Y. Miyata, and Paul Smolensky (1990) Harmonic Grammar – a formal multi-level connectionist theory of linguistic well-formedness: theoretical foundations. *Proceedings of the Twelfth Annual Conference of the Cognitive Science Society.* Cambridge, Mass: Lawrence Erlbaum. 388–95.

Legendre, Géraldine, William Raymond, and Paul Smolensky (1993) An optimality-theoretic typology of case and grammatical voice systems. *Proceedings of the Berkeley Linguistics Society* **19**. 464–78.

Leslau, Wolf (1958) *The verb in Harari.* University of California Publications in Semitic Philology 21. Berkeley: University of California Press.

Liberman, Mark (1975) The intonational system of English. PhD dissertation, MIT.

Liberman, Mark and Alan Prince (1977) On stress and linguistic rhythm. *Linguistic Inquiry* **8**. 249–336.

Lichtenberk, Frantisek (1983) *A grammar of Manam.* Honolulu: University of Hawaii Press.

Lloret, Maria-Rosa (1988) Gemination and vowel length in Oromo morphophonology. PhD dissertation, Indiana University.

Lombardi, Linda (1995a) Laryngeal neutralization and alignment. In Beckman, Walsh Dickey, and Urbanczyk. 225–48.

(1995b) Why Place and Voice are different: constraint interactions and feature faithfulness in Optimality Theory. Ms., University of Maryland, College Park. [ROA-105, http://ruccs.rutgers.edu/roa.html]

Lorentz, Ove (1996) Length and correspondence in Scandinavian. In P. Bye, O. Lorentz, and C. Rice (eds.), *Papers from the 2nd Workshop on Comparative Germanic Phonology.* Nordlyd 24. Tromsø: School of Languages and Literature. 111–28.

Lowenstamm, Jean and Jonathan Kaye (1986) Compensatory lengthening in Tiberian Hebrew. In L. Wetzels and E. Sezer (eds.), *Studies in compensatory lengthening.* Dordrecht: Foris. 97–146.

Lynch, John D. (1974) Lenakel phonology. PhD dissertation, University of Hawaii.

Maddieson, Ian (1984) *Patterns of sounds*. Cambridge University Press.

Marantz, Alec (1982) Re reduplication. *Linguistic Inquiry* **13**. 435–83.

Marsack, C. C. (1962) *Teach yourself Samoan*. London: Hodder and Stoughton.

Mascaró, Joan (1976) Catalan phonology and the phonological cycle. PhD dissertation, MIT. [Distributed 1978, Bloomington: Indiana University Linguistics Club.]

Matteson, Esther (1965) *The Piro (Arawakan) language*. University of California Publications in Linguistics 22. Berkeley and Los Angeles: University of California Press.

McCarthy, John (1979) Formal problems in Semitic phonology and morphology. PhD dissertation, MIT. [Published 1985, New York: Garland]

(1981) A prosodic theory of non-concatenative morphology. *Linguistic Inquiry* **12**. 373–418.

(1986) OCP effects: gemination and antigemination. *Linguistic Inquiry* **17**. 207–63.

(1993) A case of surface constraint violation. In C. Paradis and D. LaCharite (eds.), *Constraint-based theories in multilinear phonology*, special issue of *Canadian Journal of Linguistics* **38**. 169–95.

(1995a) Extensions of faithfulness: Rotuman revisited. Ms., University of Massachusetts, Amherst. [ROA-110, http://ruccs.rutgers.edu/roa.html]

(1995b) Remarks on phonological opacity in Optimality Theory. Ms., University of Massachusetts, Amherst. To appear in J. Lecarme, J. Lowenstamm, and U. Shlonsky (eds.), *Proceedings of the Second Colloquium on Afro-Asiatic Linguistics*.

(1997) Process specific constraints in Optimality Theory. *Linguistic Inquiry* **28**. 231–51.

(1998) Sympathy and phonological opacity. Ms., University of Massachusetts, Amherst. [ROA-252, http://ruccs.rutgers.edu/roa.html]

McCarthy, John and Alan Prince (1986) Prosodic morphology. Ms., University of Massachusetts, Amherst and Brandeis University, Waltham, Mass. [Annotated version 1996, issued as Technical report no. 32, Rutgers Center for Cognitive Science.]

(1990) Foot and word in prosodic morphology: the Arabic broken plural. *Natural Language and Linguistic Theory* **8**. 209–83.

(1993a) Generalized Alignment. In G. E. Booij and J. van Marle (eds.), *Yearbook of Morphology 1993*. Dordrecht: Kluwer. 79–153.

(1993b) Prosodic Morphology I: constraint interaction and satisfaction. Ms., University of Massachusetts, Amherst and Rutgers University. [To appear as Technical report no. 3, Rutgers University Center for Cognitive Science. Cambridge, Mass.: MIT Press.]

(1994a) The emergence of the unmarked: optimality in prosodic morphology. In M. Gonzàlez (ed.), *Proceedings of the North East Linguistic Society* **24**. 333–79.

(1994b) Two lectures on prosodic morphology. Handouts of two lectures at OTS/HIL Workshop on Prosodic Morphology, Utrecht University, July 1994. [ROA-59, http://ruccs.rutgers.edu/roa.html]

(1995a) Faithfulness and reduplicative identity. In Beckman, Walsh Dickey, and Urbanczyk. 249–384.

(1995b) Prosodic morphology. In Goldsmith (1995). 318–66.

(forthcoming) Faithfulness and identity in prosodic morphology. To appear in Kager, van der Hulst, and Zonneveld.

Merchant, Jason (1996) Alignment and fricative assimilation in German. *Linguistic Inquiry* **27**. 709–19.

Merlan, Francesca (1982) *Mangarayi*. Lingua Descriptive Series 4. Amsterdam: North Holland.

Mester, R. Armin (1990) Patterns of truncation. *Linguistic Inquiry* **21**. 478–85.

(1991) Some remarks on Tongan stress. Ms., University of California, Santa Cruz.

(1994) The quantitative trochee in Latin. *Natural Language and Linguistic Theory* **12**. 1–61.

Mester, R. Armin and Junko Itô (1989) Feature predictability and underspecification: palatal prosody in Japanese mimetics. *Language* **65**. 258–93.

Mills, Roger F. (1975) Proto South Sulawesi and Proto Austronesian phonology. PhD dissertation, University of Michigan.

Mohanan, Karuvannur P. (1982) Lexical phonology. PhD dissertation, MIT.

(1993) Fields of attraction in phonology. In Goldsmith. 61–116.

Moravcsik, Edith (1978) Reduplicative constructions. In J. Greenberg, C. Ferguson, and E. Moravcsik (eds.), *Universals of human language* III: *Word structure*. Stanford University Press. 297–334.

Müller, Gereon (1997) Partial Wh-movement and Optimality Theory. *Linguistic Review* **14**. 249–306.

Mutaka, Ngessimo and Larry Hyman (1990) Syllable and morpheme integrity in Kinande reduplication. *Phonology* **7**. 73–120.

Myers, Scott (1987) Vowel shortening in English, *Natural Language and Linguistic Theory* **5**. 485–518.

(1991) Persistent rules. *Linguistic Inquiry* **22**. 315–44.

(1997a) OCP effects in Optimality Theory. *Natural Language and Linguistic Theory* **15**. 847–92.

(1997b) Expressing phonetic naturalness in phonology. In Roca. 125–52.

Myers, Scott and Troi Carleton (1996) Tonal transfer in Chichewa. *Phonology* **13**. 39–72.

Nash, David (1980) Topics in Warlpiri grammar. PhD dissertation, MIT. [Published 1986, New York: Garland.]

Newman, Stanley (1944) *Yokuts language of California*. Viking Fund Publications in Anthropology 2. New York.

Newton, Brian. 1972 *The generative interpretation of dialect: a study of Modern Greek phonology*. Cambridge University Press.

Ní Chiosáin, Máire and Jaye Padgett (1997) Markedness, segment realisation, and locality in spreading. Report LRC-97-01, Linguistic Research Center, University of California, Santa Cruz. [ROA-188, http://ruccs.rutgers.edu/roa.html]

Nooteboom, Sieb G. (1981) Lexical retrieval from fragments of spoken words: beginnings vs. endings. *Journal of Phonetics* **9**. 407–24.

Nouveau, Dominique (1994) Language acquisition, metrical theory, and optimality. PhD dissertation, Utrecht University.

Odden, David (1986) On the role of the Obligatory Contour Principle in phonological theory. *Language* **62**. 353–83.

Ohala, John J. (1983) The origin of sound patterns in vocal tract constraints. In P. F. MacNeilage (ed.), *The production of speech*. New York: Springer. 189–216.

(1990) The phonetics and phonology of aspects of assimilation. In J. Kingston and M. Beckman (eds.), *Papers in laboratory phonology* I: *Between the grammar and physics of speech*. Cambridge University Press. 258–75.

Ohala, John J. and H. Kawasaki (1984) Phonetics and prosodic phonology. In C. Ewen and E. Kaisse (eds.), *Phonology Yearbook* **1**. Cambridge University Press. 113–27.

Ohala, John J. and Manjari Ohala (1993) The phonetics of nasal phonology: theorems and data. In Huffman and Krakow. 225–49.

Onn, Farid M. (1976) Aspects of Malay phonology and morphology: a generative approach. PhD dissertation, University of Illinois, Urbana-Champaign.

Orgun, C. Orhan (1994) Monotonic Cyclicity and Optimality Theory. In M. Gonzàlez (ed.), *Proceedings of the North East Linguistic Society* **24**. 461–74.

(1995) Correspondence and identity constraints in two-level Optimality Theory. In J. Camacho, L. Choueiri, and M. Watanabe (eds.), *Proceedings of the West Coast Conference on Formal Linguistics* **14**. 399–413.

(1996) Sign-Based Morphology and Phonology: with special attention to Optimality Theory. PhD dissertation, University of California, Berkeley. [ROA-171, http://ruccs.rutgers.edu/roa.html]

Orgun, C. Orhan and Ronald Sprouse (1997) From M-Parse to Control: deriving ungrammaticality. Ms., University of California, Berkeley. [ROA-224, http://ruccs.rutgers.edu/roa.html]

Orr, Carolyn (1962) Ecuador Quichua phonology. In B. Elson (ed.), *Studies in Ecuadorian Indian languages*. Norman, Okla.: Summer Institute of Linguistics. 60–77.

Osborn, Henry (1966) Warao I: phonology and morphophonemics. *International Journal of American Linguistics* **32**. 108–23.

Padgett, Jaye (1995) Feature classes. In Beckman, Walsh Dickey, and Urbanczyk. 385–420.

Paradis, Carole (1988) On constraints and repair strategies. *Linguistic Review* **6**. 71–97.

Paradis, Carole and François Prunet (eds.) (1991) *The special status of coronals: internal and external evidence*. San Diego: Academic Press.

Pater, Joe (1995) On the nonuniformity of weight-to-stress and stress preservation effects in English. Ms., McGill University. [ROA-107, http://ruccs.rutgers.edu/roa.html]

(1996) *NÇ̊. In K. Kusumoto (ed.), *Proceedings of the North East Linguistic Society* **26**. 227–39.

(forthcoming) Austronesian nasal substitution and other NÇ̊ effects. To appear in Kager, Van der Hulst, and Zonneveld. [ROA-160, http://ruccs.rutgers.edu/roa.html]

Payne, David L. (1981) *The phonology and morphology of Axininca Campa*. Arlington: Summer Institute of Linguistics Publications in Linguistics.

Pesetsky, David (1998) Some optimality principles of sentence pronunciation. In P. Barbosa, D. Fox, P. Hagstrom, M. McGinnis, and D. Pesetsky (eds.), *Is the best good enough? Optimality and competition in syntax*. Cambridge, Mass.: MIT Press. 337–83.

References

Piggott, Glyne L. (1993) The geometry of sonorant features. Ms., McGill University, Montreal.

(1995) Epenthesis and syllable weight. *Natural Language and Linguistic Theory* **13**. 283–326.

Popjes, Jack and Jo Popjes (1986) Canela-Krahô. In D. C. Derbyshire and G. K. Pullum (eds.), *Handbook of Amazonian languages*, I. Berlin: Mouton De Gruyter. 128–99.

Poser, William (1989) The metrical foot in Diyari. *Phonology* **6**. 117–48.

Prentice, D. J. (1971) *The Murut languages of Sabah.* Pacific Linguistics, series C, no. 18. Canberra: Australian National University.

Prince, Alan (1980) A metrical theory for Estonian quantity. *Linguistic Inquiry* **11**. 511–62.

(1983) Relating to the grid. *Linguistic Inquiry* **14**. 19–100.

(1984) Phonology with tiers. In M. Aronoff and R. Oehrle (eds.), *Language sound structure.* Cambridge, Mass.: MIT Press. 234–44.

(1990) Quantitative consequences of rhythmic organization. In M. Ziolkowski, M. Noske, and K. Deaton (eds.), *Papers from the Chicago Linguistic Society* **26:2**. 355–98.

(1994) Optimality: constraint interaction in generative grammar. Handout of lectures at Utrecht University, January 1994.

Prince, Alan and Paul Smolensky (1993) Optimality Theory: constraint interaction in generative grammar. Ms., Rutgers University, New Brunswick and University of Colorado, Boulder. [To appear as Technical report no. 2, Rutgers University Center for Cognitive Science. Cambridge, Mass.: MIT Press.]

(1997) Optimality: from neural networks to universal grammar. *Science* **275**. 1604–10.

Radford, Andrew (1997) *Syntax: a minimalist introduction.* Cambridge University Press.

Raffelsiefen, Renate (1996) Gaps in word formation. In U. Kleinhenz (ed.), *Interfaces in phonology.* Studia Grammatica 41. Berlin: Akademie Verlag. 194–209.

Rehg, Kenneth L. and Damien G. Sohl (1981) *Ponapean reference grammar.* Honolulu: University of Hawaii Press.

Reynolds, William T. (1994) Variation and phonological theory. PhD dissertation, University of Pennsylvania, Philadelphia.

Riad, Tomas (1992) Structures in Germanic prosody: a diachronic study with special reference to Nordic languages. PhD dissertation, Stockholm University.

Rice, Curtis (1992) *Binarity and ternarity in metrical theory: parametric extensions.* PhD dissertation, University of Texas, Austin.

Rice, Keren (1993) A reexamination of the feature [sonorant]: the status of 'sonorant obstruents'. *Language* **69**. 308–44.

Rizzi, Luigi (1991) Residual verb second and the Wh Criterion. Technical Reports in Formal and Computational Linguistics 2. Faculté des Lettres, University of Geneva.

Roca, Iggy (1994) *Generative phonology.* London and New York: Routledge.

(ed.) (1997) *Constraints and derivations in phonology.* Oxford University Press.

Rosenthall, Sam (1994) Vowel/glide alternation in a theory of constraint interaction. PhD dissertation, University of Massachusetts, Amherst. [ROA-126, http://ruccs.rutgers.edu/roa.html]

(1997) The distribution of prevocalic vowels. *Natural Language and Linguistic Theory* **15**. 139–80.

Rumelhart, D. E. and J. L. McLelland (1986) On learning the past tenses of English. In D. E. Rumelhart and J. L. McLelland (eds.), *Parallel Distributed Processing: explorations in the microstructure of cognition.* Cambridge, Mass.: MIT Press. 216–71.

Russell, Kevin (1993) Morphemes as constraints: the case of 'copy-back' reduplication. In K. Beals, G. Cooke, D. Kathman, S. Kita, K.-E. McCullough, and D. Testen (eds.), *Papers from the Chicago Linguistic Society* **29**. 375–89.

Sapir, Edward (1930) Southern Paiute, a Shoshonean language. *Proceedings of the American Academy of Arts and Sciences* **65:1–3**.

(1965) *A grammar of Diola-Fogny.* Cambridge University Press.

Schachter, Paul and Victoria Fromkin (1968) *A phonology of Akan: Akuapem, Asante, and Fante.* Los Angeles: University of California.

Scobbie, James (1991) Attribute-value phonology. PhD dissertation, University of Edinburgh.

Selkirk, Elisabeth O. (1980) The role of prosodic categories in English word stress. *Linguistic Inquiry* **11**. 563–605.

(1981) Epenthesis and degenerate syllables in Cairene Arabic. In H. Borer and J. Aoun (eds.), *Theoretical issues in the grammar of Semitic languages.* Cambridge, Mass.: Department of Linguistics and Philosophy, MIT.

(1984) *Phonology and syntax: the relation between sound and structure.* Cambridge, Mass.: MIT Press.

(1986) On derived domains in sentence phonology. *Phonology* **3**. 371–405.

(1995) The prosodic structure of function words. In Beckman, Walsh Dickey, and Urbanczyk (eds.). 439–69.

Selkirk, Elisabeth and Tong Shen (1990) Prosodic domains in Shanghai Chinese. In S. Inkelas and D. Zec (eds.), *The phonology–syntax connection.* University of Chicago Press. 313–38.

Sezer, Engin (1981) The k/Ø alternation in Turkish. In G. N. Clements (ed.), *Harvard studies in phonology.* Bloomington: Indiana University Linguistics Club. 354–82.

Shaw, Patricia (1987) Non-conservation of melodic structure in reduplication. In A. Bosch, B. Need, and E. Schiller (eds.), *Papers from the Chicago Linguistic Society* **23:2**. 291–306.

(1991) Ling 253: morphology. Handout of LSA Linguistic Institute 1991.

Sherer, Tim (1994) Prosodic phonotactics. PhD dissertation, University of Massachusetts, Amherst. [ROA-54, http://ruccs.rutgers.edu/roa.html]

Sherrard, Nicholas (1997) Questions of priorities: an introductory overview of Optimality Theory in phonology. In Roca. 43–89.

Siegel, Dorothy (1974) Topics in English morphology. PhD dissertation, MIT.

Smith, Neilson V. (1973) *The acquisition of phonology: a case study.* Cambridge University Press.

References

Smolensky, Paul (1993) Harmony, markedness, and phonological activity. Handout to talk presented at Rutgers Optimality Workshop 1, 23 October 1993, New Brunswick, N. J. [ROA-87, http://ruccs.rutgers.edu/roa.html]

(1995) On the internal structure of the constraint component *Con* of UG. Handout to talk presented at University of California, Los Angeles, 7 April 1995. [ROA-86, http://ruccs.rutgers.edu/roa.html]

(1996) On the comprehension/production dilemma in child language. *Linguistic Inquiry* **27**. 720–31.

Sommer, Bruce (1981) The shape of Kunjen syllables. In D. L. Goyvaerts (ed.), *Phonology in the 1980's*. Ghent: E. Story-Scientia.

Spaelti, Philip (1994) Weak edges and final geminates in Swiss German. In M. Gonzàlez (ed.), *Proceedings of the North East Linguistic Society* **24**. 573–88.

Spencer, Andrew J. (1994) Syllabification in Chukchee. In R. Wiese (ed.), *Recent developments in Lexical Phonology*. Theorie des Lexikons. Arbeiten des Sonderforschungsbereichs 282, No. 56. Düsseldorf: Heinrich Heine University. 205–26.

Spring, Cari (1990) Implications of Axininca Campa for prosodic morphology and reduplication. PhD dissertation, University of Arizona, Tucson.

Sprouse, Ronald (1997) A case for Enriched Inputs. Handout of a presentation at TREND, 3 May 1997. [ROA-193, http://ruccs.rutgers.edu/roa.html]

Stahlke, Herbert (1976) Segment sequences and segmental fusion. *Studies in African Linguistics* **7**. 44–63.

Stampe, David (1972) How I spent my summer vacation (a dissertation on Natural Phonology). PhD dissertation, University of Chicago. [Published 1979, New York: Garland.]

Steinbergs, Aleksandra (1985) The role of MSC's in OshiKwanyama loan phonology. *Studies in African Linguistics* **16**. 89–101.

Stemberger, Joseph P. (1991) Radical underspecification in language production. *Phonology* **8**. 73–112.

Steriade, Donca (1982) Greek prosodies and the nature of syllabification. PhD dissertation, MIT.

(1987) Redundant values. In A. Bosch, B. Need, and E. Schiller (eds.), *Papers from the Chicago Linguistic Society* **23:2**. 339–62.

(1988a) Reduplication and syllable transfer in Sanskrit and elsewhere. *Phonology* **5**. 73–155.

(1988b) Review of G. N. Clements and S. J. Keyser (1983). *Language* **64**. 118–29.

(1993) Closure, release, and nasal contours. In Huffman and Krakow. 401–70.

(1995a) Underspecification and markedness. In Goldsmith (1995). 114–74.

(1995b) Positional neutralization. Ms., University of California, Los Angeles.

(1996) Paradigm uniformity and the phonetics–phonology boundary. Paper presented at the 5th Conference in Laboratory Phonology, Evanston, Illinois, July 1996.

Stonham, John (1990) Current issues in morphological theory. PhD dissertation, Stanford University.

Street, Chester S. and Gregory Panpawa Mollinjin (1981) The phonology of Murinbata. In B. Waters (ed.), *Australian phonologies: collected papers.* Work Papers of SIL-AAB, A5. Darwin: Summer Institute of Linguistics.

Tesar, Bruce (1995) *Computational Optimality Theory.* PhD dissertation, University of Colorado, Boulder.

(1996) An iterative strategy for learning metrical stress in Optimality Theory. In E. Hughes, M. Hughes, and A. Greenhill (eds.), *The proceedings of the 21st annual Boston University Conference on Language Development, November 1996.* 615–26. [ROA-177, http://ruccs.rutgers.edu/roa.html]

Tesar, Bruce and Paul Smolensky (1993) *The learnability of Optimality Theory: an algorithm and some basic complexity results.* Technical Report CU-CS-678-93, Computer Science Department, University of Colorado, Boulder. [ROA-2, http://ruccs.rutgers.edu/roa.html]

(1998) Learnability in Optimality Theory. *Linguistic Inquiry* **29**. 229–68.

Trigo, R. Lorenza (1993) The inherent structure of nasal segments. In Huffman and Krakow. 369–400.

Trommelen, Mieke and Wim Zonneveld (1979) *Inleiding in de Generatieve Fonologie.* Muiderberg: Coutinho.

Trubetzkoy, Nicolai S. (1939) *Grundzüge der Phonologie.* Travaux du Cercle Linguistique de Prague **7**. [English translation: *Principles of phonology.* Berkeley and Los Angeles: University of California Press, 1969.]

Uhrbach, Amy (1987) A formal analysis of reduplication and its interaction with phonological and morphological processes. PhD dissertation, University of Texas, Austin.

Urbanczyk, Suzanne (1996) Morphological templates in reduplication. In K. Kusumoto (ed.), *Proceedings of the North East Linguistic Society* **26**. 425–40.

(forthcoming) Double reduplications in parallel. To appear in Kager, van der Hulst, and Zonneveld. [ROA-73, http://ruccs.rutgers.edu/roa.html]

Vance, Timothy J. (1987) *An introduction to Japanese phonology.* Albany, N.Y.: SUNY Press.

Vijver, Ruben van de (1998) *The iambic issue: iambs as a result of constraint interaction.* HIL dissertations 37. Leiden: Holland Institute of Generative Linguistics.

Vogel, Irene (1976) Nasals and nasal assimilation patterns, in the acquisition of Chicano Spanish. *Papers and Reports on Child Language Development* **15**. 201–14.

Walther, Markus (1996) OT SIMPLE: a construction-kit approach to Optimality Theory implementation. Ms., Heinrich Heine University, Dusseldorf. [ROA-152, http://ruccs.rutgers.edu/roa.html]

Wexler, Kenneth and Peter W. Culicover (1980) *Formal principles of language acquisition.* Cambridge, Mass.: MIT Press.

Whitney, William D. (1889) *Sanskrit grammar.* Cambridge, Mass.: Harvard University Press.

Wilbur, Ronnie (1973) The phonology of reduplication. PhD dissertation, University of Illinois, Urbana-Champaign.

References

Willett, Elizabeth (1982) Reduplication and accent in Southeastern Tepehuan. *International Journal of American Linguistics* **48**. 164–84.

Willett, Thomas L. (1991) *A reference grammar of Southeastern Tepehuan.* Summer Institute of Linguistics and University of Texas at Arlington Publications in Linguistics 100. Arlington: University of Texas.

Yip, Moira (1988) The Obligatory Contour Principle and phonological rules: a loss of identity. *Linguistic Inquiry* **19**. 65–100.

(1993) Cantonese loanword phonology and Optimality Theory. *Journal of East Asian Linguistics* **2**. 261–91.

Zagona, Karen (1982) Government and proper government of verbal projections. PhD dissertation, University of Washington, Seattle.

Zimmer, Karl and Barbara Abbott (1978) The k/Ø alternation in Turkish: some experimental evidence for its productivity. *Journal of Psycholinguistic Research* **7**. 35–46.

Zoll, Cheryl (1996) Parsing below the segment in a constraint based framework. PhD dissertation, University of California, Berkeley. [ROA-143, http://ruccs.rutgers.edu/roa.html]

INDEX OF LANGUAGES

Index of languages

INDEX OF SUBJECTS

(**bold**-face numbers refer to definitions and special discussions)

447

Index of subjects

INDEX OF CONSTRAINTS

Index of constraints

$*V_{ORAL}N$ 28
$*VwV$ 245
$*ær]_\sigma$ 260
*[ŋ] 241
$*[ŋ]^W$ 245
æ-Tensing 275
Coda-Cond 131
Cor-high 128
Harmony 410
Hiatus-raising 394
Inter-V-Voice 325
No [a] 283
No [i] 284
OCP 56
PostVcls 241
Reduce 406
VOP (Voiced Obstruent Prohibition) 40, 340, 398
VOP^2 398

Prosodic markedness constraints
*Clash 165
*Complex (cover constraint) 288
$*Complex^{Cod}$ 97
$*Complex^{Ons}$ 97
$*Final-C-\mu$ 268
$*3\mu$ 268
$*\sigma_\mu$ 283
Final-C 377
Ft-Bin 156, 161, 184, 300
Ft-Form (cover constraint) 184
HNuc 215
No-Coda 94, 112
[NoCoda & VOP]_{Segment} 399
NonFinality 151, 165
Onset 93, 110
Parse-Syl 153, 162, 300
Quant-Form (cover constraint) 271
Rh-Contour 174, 184
RhType=I 172, 184
RhType=T 172
Son-Seq 267, 288
Stress-to-Weight 268
Syll-Form (cover constraint) 288

Uneven-Iamb 151
Weight-by-Position 147, 269
WSP 155, 172
  WSP-Ft 184

Various phonological constraints
*Struc 404
Harmony-IO 378
Fill 99
Lowering-IO 379
MParse 402
Parse 100
μ-Projection 380

Alignment constraints
Align-L 111
Align-Morph-L 115, 136
Align-R 113, 290
Align-Red-L 226
Align-Stem-R 119
Align-Syllable-R 119
Align-um-L 122
Align-Wd-Left 169
Align-Wd-Right 169
All-Ft-Left 157, 163, 300
All-Ft-Right 163, 300
Edgemost 122, 167
GrWd=PrWd 152, 166
Leftmost 167, 300
Red=Stem 220
Red=σ 227
Red=$\sigma_{\mu\mu}$ 182, 217
Rightmost 167, 300
Stem=PrWd 220, 264
Trunc=σ 265, 271

Syntactic constraints
Economy of Movement (Stay) 351
Full-Interpretation (Full-Int) 352
No Movement of a Lexical Head (No-Lex-Mvt) 352
ObligatoryHeads (Ob-Hd) 349
Operator in Specifier (Op-Spec) 354
Subject 354

452